A. L. Comunian, U. Gielen (Eds.)

International Perspectives on Human Development

Foreword: Pittu Laungani

WITHDRAWI

PABST SCIENCE PUBLISHERS
Lengerich, Berlin, Riga,
Rom, Wien, Zagreb

Library of Congress Cataloging-in-Publication Data

International Perspectives on Human Development /
Anna Laura Comunian, Uwe Gielen (Eds.). - Lengerich ;
Berlin ; Rom ; Riga ; Wien ; Zagreb : Pabst Science Publ., 2000
ISBN 3-934252-87-7

© 2000 Pabst Science Publishers, D-49525 Lengerich

Printing: KM Druck, D-64823 Groß Umstadt

ISBN 3-934252-87-7

CONTENTS

PREFACE

During the editors' graduate school days in the late sixties and early seventies, the systematic cross-cultural study of human development received minimal attention. To be sure, there were the much-discussed works of Margaret Mead on adolescence in Samoa, gender roles in New Guinea, and the supposed absence of animistic thinking among certain Melanesian children. American psychologists had just "discovered" Vygotsky and Piaget and were now beginning to ask whether Piaget's stages were actually universal as postulated by him. Beatrice and John Whiting and their students were involved in comparative observational studies of children and mothers across a variety of mostly nonwestern cultures. David C. McClelland was tracing achievement needs as depicted in elementary school readers published around the world and showed that they were systematically related to the economic growth of nations. However, these and similar studies had only a very limited impact on mainstream developmental psychology in the United States and Europe. Cross-cultural psychology in general, and developmental studies across cultures in particular, remained tangential to the interests of the overwhelming majority of psychologists who instead were attempting to describe and analyze supposedly universal mechanisms of learning and information processing.

This dismal situation began to change in the 1980s and 1990s when public opinion in the United States and Western Europe came under the sway of multiculturalism, and globalization became a generally accepted fact of life. For the first time ever, cross-cultural psychology assumed a definite identity and began to be taught at a variety of universities around the world. Multicultural boxes and inserts began to invade developmental textbooks and more contextual, culture-sensitive, and culture-inclusive theories were proposed. Cross-cultural psychology, which had been quite marginal to the concerns of mainstream developmental psychology, finally began to have an impact. At the same time, it remains true even today that much theoretical, methodological, and empirical work must be completed before cross-cultural considerations can be said to have assumed their rightful place in the enterprise of developmental psychology. One example may illustrate this. At present, some 85% of all children and adolescents live in the so-called developing world. More children and adolescents, for instance, live in India than in all western countries combined. Yet, in most textbooks, references to studies investigating the lives of these children remain small in number. Consequently, the children and their lives assume a kind of "exotic" appearance, and their development is implicitly or explicitly compared to that of more "representative" Euro-American children who remain the yardstick of comparison. Similarly, no mainstream developmental textbook known to us contains a chapter outlining on the basis of readily available global statistics data where most children, adolescents, and adults spend their lives and how these lives develop over time. This is a pretty sad state of affairs!

We developed this volume in order to support the internationalization of developmental psychology and to make readers aware of the increasingly sophisticated cross-cultural theories, methods, and findings now changing the face of the field. Consequently, the volume includes a broad variety of cross-culturally oriented chapters on the human life cycle by a distinguished group of international contributors. The chapters provide an overview of historical and international perspectives in developmental psychology, introduce a broad variety of theoretical perspectives, review pertinent methodological issues, trace issues related to socialization and socioemotional development during various phases of the life cycle, delineate various aspects of moral development, discuss collaborative action research focused on reflective practice, and introduce a variety of cross-cultural views and findings on aging.

This volume is intended to be read by psychologists, cultural and psychological anthropologists, and graduate students interested in international and cross-cultural contributions to the study of the human life cycle. The book should be of interest to both teachers and researchers.

The idea of developing such a broadly conceived book arose in connection with the Regional Conference of the International Council of Psychologists held in Padua University, Italy between July 21-23, 1997. The theme of the conference was *Cross-cultural Perspectives on Human Development.* This highly successful venture brought together 105 participants from 28 countries who for three days discussed their cross-cultural research in an atmosphere of warmth and enthusiasm. The conference had been organized by a Scientific Committee consisting of Anna Laura Comunian, Uwe P. Gielen, George De Vos, and Gustav Jahoda. They took care of countless organizational details and made memorable the stay of the conference participants at the "Bo," one of Europe's oldest universities. The university has two of Europe's largest psychology departments and provided an ideal setting for both formal and informal scientific exchange.

After the conference, we asked our contributors to expand their conference presentations in light of the discussions that had taken place at the meeting. In addition, we solicited further contributions from scholars who are well known for their creative work in cross-cultural developmental psychology.

We organized the Padua conference in part because we believed that the cross-cultural study of human development has taken off during the last two decades. In our opinion, the broad array of ideas, methodological approaches, and research findings discussed first at the conference and now in this volume has proven us right. We only have to compare the vague theories, dubious (and often racist) assumptions, and sketchy observations on "savage" children described by Jahoda in his chapter on "The Prehistory of Cross-cultural Development Research" with the complex interdisciplinary and biopsychosocial theorizing, concern for avoiding bias in cross-cultural testing, and detailed observations of infants, children, adolescents, and the aged reported in the chapters to follow in order to realize that recent progress in the area of cross-cultural development research has been dramatic. For both researchers and theorists of human development, the various chapters contained in this volume present the most current advances and consider as well the complex issues revolving around the international study of human development.

These include fundamental development questions such as: How did the cross-cultural perspective on human development studies evolve and come to the fore? How does human development change over time and across cultures? How does culture influence human development research? What does human development throughout the life span look like in different cultures? Our contributors address these and other issues and they especially consider the overall guiding theme for the book: development in sociocultural context. For instance, one of the ways in which current research has moved beyond former perspectives is by providing new approaches for studying how to arrive at integrated interdisciplinary research efforts, programs, and ways of thinking. Issues related to child care and sociocultural change, unbiased multicultural assessment, adult development, the abuse of children and adolescents in different societies, adolescence in cross-cultural perspective, mental health and interventions, East Asian and German studies of moral development and prosocial behavior, the importance of role-taking and reflection in teacher training, applied cross-cultural research, and problems of aging are among those that guide the research in this volume. They make the current research significant.

Moreover, theories and research in disciplines such as anthropology, biology, demography, and sociology have influenced much of the most innovative psychological work on human development. Thus, although the focus of this book is on psychological investigations, most of the authors make reference to theorists and researchers in other disciplines; this is part of what makes the topic of cross-cultural human development so compelling. A good example in this regard is provided by George De Vos' chapter entitled "Toward an Integrated Social Science" that is based, in turn, on his keynote address at the Padua conference.

Modern developmental psychology is characterized by four broad trends that are gradually transforming the field. The first trend has led the field away from its former rather single-minded emphasis on childhood and adolescence toward a much broader and extended focus on the overall human life cycle.   This shift derives in part from rapidly changing demographic constellations in all industrialized countries, which point to a steady increase of aged persons in the population pyramid.   Even in the less industrialized countries, the average number of children per family has been declining for decades, and the world's population is becoming older.

A second shift has led the field to question the general validity and usefulness of unitary stage theories such as those originally proposed by Freud, Gesell, and Piaget.   Instead, we find now an increasing interest in contextual theories that attempt to locate the developing person in a complex array of ecological and sociocultural forces.   Bronfenbrenner and Vygotsky are two prominent representatives of this "new" theoretical outlook.   It is interesting to note that the newer evolutionary theories have also followed this trend since they increasingly tend to downplay the importance of biologically fixed action patterns and instincts in favor of intricate interactions between organismic predispositions, ecological settings, and evolutionary facilitating conditions and constraints.   Other theorists and researchers, however, remain convinced that at least some of the older stage theories should be expanded and revised rather than abandoned.

A third trend reflects the recent rise of cross-cultural and multicultural psychology.   While earlier developmental theories were almost always created and tested in Euro-American settings, modern developmental psychology demands that no developmental theory can be said to possess general validity unless it has been tested in a broad variety of sociocultural settings.   At the same time, the number of developmental psychologists in nonwestern countries has been rising steadily, a trend that is gradually leading to more culturally varied and culturally sensitive theories, methodologies, and investigations.   This shift is also reducing the field's inherent ethnocentrism since it confronts western developmental psychologists with the fact that their theories contain numerous implicit and explicit value judgments.   These emphasize, for instance, individualistic conceptions of maturity, autonomy, and self-reliance at the expense of more collectively oriented ideals of interpersonal sensitivity, self-sacrifice, dignity, and honor.

A fourth trend has led to an increased awareness that no single and sovereign master theory is likely to be able to account for the highly varied developmental trajectories that can be found both within and across various societies.   Instead, we need a broad variety of competing theories and methodologies whose strengths add up while their weaknesses may more or less cancel each other out.   At the same time, interdisciplinary problem-centered research has come to the fore in which ecological considerations, shifting demographic constellations, cultural belief systems, and societal institutions are all taken into account together with the more traditional concerns for childrearing practices, family systems, and developmental stages and sequences.

This volume contains many contributions that faithfully reflect the four trends just outlined. The initial chapters provide a historical and international perspective on the evolution of developmental psychology with a special emphasis on cross-cultural contributions. The subsequent chapters in Sections II and III outline a variety of theoretical positions that emphasize the integration of ideas derived from separate fields such as evolutionary biology and psychology, psychological anthropology, psychoanalysis, cultural psychology, cross-cultural psychology, demography, and even Buddhism. The papers included in Section IV contain some detailed discussions of methodological issues that arise when human development is studied across cultural divides both within a given society as well as across national and cultural boundaries. The four contributions contained in Section V share a common concern for socialization practices in a broad variety of cultures and their interaction with the psychological growth of infants and children.

The three chapters included in Section VI focus on the nature of adolescence and adolescent identity around the world. One important question raised here is whether adolescence constitutes a universal stage or whether spreading industrialization and modern schooling systems mostly create it. The cognitive-developmental approach as conceived by Dewey, Mead, Piaget, Kohlberg, and their successors informs the contributions contained in Sections VII and VIII. The focus here is on specific research studies as well as the application of cognitive-developmental approaches to the training of teachers, school counselors, psychologists, and social workers. The contributions contained in Section IX consider a broad array of biological, psychological, demographic, and sociocultural aspects of aging from a cross-cultural perspective.

This book could only come into existence because of the continued help and support given us by many colleagues, coworkers, and students. First of all, we would like to thank the many contributors to this book who not only submitted their chapters, but also agreed to revise them in light of our suggestions. We would also sincerely like to thank Petra Bernard, Hazel Davis, Natasha Carty, and Monica Michalski who not only endlessly typed and retyped much of what is contained in this book, but also made numerous suggestions for improving the manuscript and the various chapters contained therein.

The editors express appreciation to the University Seminars at

Columbia University for assistance in the preparation of the manuscript for publication. Material drawn from this work was presented to the University Seminar on Moral Education. We would also like to thank St. Francis College for the support it provided to the whole project.

We dedicate this book to the international community of cross-cultural researchers and life-span psychologists.

Anna Laura Comunian
Laboratory for International
Cross-Cultural Psychology,
Padua University, Padua, Italy

Uwe P. Gielen
Institute for International and
Cross-Cultural Psychology,
St. Francis College, New York, U.S.A.

April, 2000

FOREWORD

Pittu Laungani, South Bank University, England

About eighteen months ago, I received a letter from Professor Uwe P. Gielen (the co-editor of this volume) in which he outlined details of a book which he was planning to edit in collaboration with Professor Anna L. Comunian. In the letter, he asked me if I would be willing to contribute what he referred to as the "end-chapter" to the volume. Given my research interests — and dare I say, personal too? — in the area of Death and Bereavement Across Cultures, I wondered if he meant I should write a chapter on some aspect of death, dying, grieving, mourning, or whatever. I felt privileged that he had singled me out for such an honor. I looked forward to producing a chapter, which would be in keeping with the general tenor of the book, and also in keeping with the major theme being pursued in the book. I wrote back to Professor Gielen, accepting his generous offer to contribute the "end-chapter."

And then, a few days later, he phoned me at home, asking me if I would consider writing a Foreword for this volume. In my reply, I told him how deeply I was gratified to be asked to introduce such an internationally oriented and broadly conceived volume, which includes the contributions of numerous prominent developmentalists living in different parts of the globe.

That is how it started. And now let us turn to the book that is in your hands. As you can see from the title, the book is concerned with the theme of human development, which is examined from diverse international perspectives. Human development has always been an extremely popular area within psychology; it has also attracted anthropologists, psychiatrists, psychoanalysts, sociologists, educators, and even poets, playwrights, and novelists. So much has been written by so many with such wisdom and distinction that one might be led to believe that one had reached the "end of knowledge" in this area — and there would be little need ever again to write another word, let alone another book, in this over ploughed and over cultivated field.

Why then, one might ask, produce yet another book on human development?

The answer is simple. For a start, Karl Popper, in his brilliant exposition of the notion of falsification in science, has pointed out quite clearly that our knowledge of the external world (which of course, includes books, documents, monographs, theoretical formulations, scientific propositions, etc.) can never be certain. Certainty involves making predictions of events as yet unencountered. And this, as David Hume pointed out in the 18th century, leads to an *inductive fallacy*. And so far, no philosopher of science has found a way of successfully rebutting the inductive fallacy dilemma. The search for certainty in objective knowledge is like the Quest for the unattainable Holy Grail. Knowledge therefore tends to be tentative. And since knowledge is tentative, humility demands that we open ourselves to the possibility of having our most cherished theories, our most beloved ideas, falsified. A stubborn, tenacious, and even universal defense of a falsified theory is not a virtue; Popper sees it as a crime against scholarship and learning. Since we can never be sure that we have learnt all there is to be learnt in the field of human development, there is a strong need—even a moral imperative—to pursue the field with increasing zeal and vigor. Therein lies the first justification for producing this book.

There are other equally compelling reasons too, which justify its publication. An area or a field of study which attracts academics, practitioners, therapists, and consultants of different persuasions—which indeed is the case in the field of human development—is likely to generate a broad variety of theoretical perspectives. Given that each perspective offers its own concepts, terminologies, meanings, nuances, configurations, diagnostic nomenclature, research methodologies, therapeutic strategies, and outcome measures, commensurability becomes a serious problem. Although the problems of commensurability are referred to in some of the chapters, the main focus of most chapters is on elucidating and clarifying the major historical, conceptual, methodological, and ethical problems related to the cross-cultural study of human development.

The editors have shown great sagacity and wisdom in producing a book that examines the multifarious themes of human development as seen from a variety of international perspectives. In so doing, the editors have acknowledged the importance of understanding human development from a variety of culturally informed perspectives, and not just from a mononational perspective, viz., American, as has largely been the case in the past.

To a large extent, the history of world psychology during the post-World War II era has been the history of American psychology. American psychology has continued to exercise a powerful, if not overpowering, influence over world psychology. Such was the awesome power of American psychology that even during my own undergraduate days in India, we were fed and nourished on (but never weaned off) American psychology. This occurred despite the fact that many of the findings of American research lacked *ecological validity*, not just in their own culture but even more significantly, in non-Western cultures. Admittedly, there were several powerful and vibrant European influences on the growth and development of psychology, which emerged from Germany, Austria, France, Switzerland, Britain, and the Soviet Union. The spectacular contributions of the psychophysicists and the physiologists, the gestaltists and the genetic epistemologists, the neurologists and the biologists, the statisticians and the psychometricians, the evolutionists and the Social Darwinists, the Freudians and the post-Freudians, instilled some doubts concerning the unchallenged superiority of American psychology. But the doubts remained unvoiced and did not in any way create serious cognitive dissonance in our Americanized attitude toward psychology. No doubt, European psychology caused some minor twinges of conscience, but in our self-delusional naïveté, psychology to us was how the Americans defined it, described it, studied it, and above all, proselytized it. Despite our doubts and reservations, despite the fact that many of the problems and issues to which most Americans paid great attention were of little or no concern to our own cultural needs, we still retained a trusting belief in the all-pervading power of American psychology and its ability to solve most, if not all, human problems. Like the three wise men waiting to see the Star of Bethlehem, we waited to see the peaceful solution of world human problems—thanks to the miracle of American psychology.

But unlike the wise men, we waited in vain. The expected miracle never occurred. Human problems of the world remained unresolved. To a large extent they still are mental illness, schizophrenia, depression, child maltreatment, drug abuse, international violence and aggression, prejudice, and xenophobia, to name but a few. Doubts concerning the power of American psychology turned to disenchantment. Psychologists all around the world in the late sixties and early seventies began to question the usefulness and the value of American mainstream psychology as a means of understanding their own unique cultural problems. They realized, a trifle belatedly, that their own cultural concerns were frequently not shared by American psychology. They also realized that the Americans themselves had not been able to put their own house in order, so to speak. American psychology, like a false prophet, had failed them.

In dribs and drabs, they began to turn away from American psychology. *Their salvation, as they saw it, lay in pursuing psychology from their own cultural standpoint.* What had started as a trickle, turned into a stream, and it will not be long before the tide will turn and when taken at its flood, hopefully lead on to a new era in psychology. One can already see the mushrooming of several culturally diverse psychologies, cultural psychology, indigenous psychologies, and of course, cross-cultural psychology, which enjoyed a head start over the fledglings. Whether the birth and the development of such diverse psychologies will in any way diminish the stronghold (or as many psychologists see it, the stranglehold) which American psychology exercises over world psychology remains a futuristic issue. It looks as though its undisputed hegemony is now beginning to be seriously questioned.

The above book therefore, could not be more timely. One of its many charms lies in the fact that it has chosen to adopt diverse international and cross-cultural approaches to the problem of human development. The editors need to be applauded for having collected between the covers of the book, numerous highly distinguished academics, research scholars, and therapists from all around the world, who have with great simplicity and clarity expounded the problems which, to them, are of great concern.

One cannot but admire the way in which the book has been structured. It has been divided into nine sections. Great care has been taken to ensure that the sections are interrelated. Each chapter has been written with great clarity, making it eminently readable, informative, and even enjoyable. The transition from one chapter to another is smooth and undisturbed. The sections have been planned with great care. Each section contains several chapters. Let us examine each section briefly.

Section I presents historical and international perspectives on human development. In his opening chapter, Gustav Jahoda, with the patience of an archeologist, takes us on a guided tour of the prehistory of cross-cultural development research; he digs up old stereotypes which, when examined carefully, turn out *not* to be significantly different from current stereotypes concerning people, nationalities, and races. Human behavior appears not to have undergone cataclysmic changes. Strange as this may sound, you will find that Hogan and Sussner in their subsequent chapter have examined the work of those European psychologists who have had a significant influence on U.S. developmental psychology. Their exposé gives fresh life to many forgotten names and their excellent contributions to the growth of developmental psychology. Deborah L.Best in her chapter examines the current trends in cross-cultural studies of human development thereby connecting the past to many current and exciting trends in cross-cultural psychology.

Section II is concerned mainly with describing and examining some of the major theoretical approaches to cross-cultural developmental psychology. George De Vos's chapter, based on his keynote paper which he presented at the International Council of Psychologists' Regional Conference in Padua in 1997, argues for an integrated social science development. The chapter is extremely well written and very carefully argued. Harry C. Triandis, in his chapter, starts by examining the differences between cross-cultural and cultural psychology, and then offers a synthesis between the two. Çigdem Kagitçibasi in her lucidly written chapter argues that the study of human development must include detailed examination of the context in which developmental processes occur. Failure to take note explicitly of the social and cultural context will not permit a detailed understanding of the cultural variations in the process of development. Heidi Keller's chapter examines the major evolutionary approaches to the study of the life cycle that have gained prominence in recent years. Evolutionary psychology has become much more sophisticated in character, and it is especially suited to explain the effects of those distal causes on the long-term evolution of behavior that are neglected by most other approaches.

Section III starts with the chapter written by Daniel G. Freedman and his associates. The chapter is concerned with offering a holistic approach to the problem of human development. It posits an internal working model, and in keeping with psychoanalytic theory, argues that early experiences are the major determinants of individual differences in social attitudes and behaviors. Studies and case studies conducted in Iceland and mainland China are cited to substantiate the validity of their approach. The next chapter by Antonella Delle Fave and Fausto Massimini examines from a biocultural perspective subjective experiences and the building of parental roles; the chapter also offers a succinct review of the different approaches to the study of parenthood. The chapter is tightly argued, and it is supplemented by an in-depth study of five Italian women and their husbands. The chapter by Eric De Vos pursues a similar theme, viz., the process by which cultural patterns are transmitted from one generation to the next. He presents a biocultural perspective. Several interesting research studies undertaken in different parts of the world are quoted to substantiate the role of biocultural factors in the transmission of cultural values. Dinesh Sharma, in his chapter on children's sociocultural and familial worlds, argues that the children's worlds in the developing and the developed world are constructed differently. He examines the impact of culture, demographic factors, and within-culture variabilities that lead to such differentiations.

The emphasis of **Section IV** is on considering the use of appropriate research methods and strategies in the area of human development. David E. Cournoyer in his chapter concentrates on a variety of research strategies employed in universalist research, which he analyzes by drawing on examples from research based on Rohner's Parental Acceptance-Rejection Theory. In his chapter on *Multicultural Assessment of Child and Adolescent Personality and Psychopathology*, Richard H. Dana examines the role of psychodynamic and psychometric testing in cross-cultural settings. He touches upon some of the inherent methodological problems that are involved in the use of psychometric instruments in multicultural situations. Esther Helpern, in her fascinating chapter on *Cross-cultural Methodological Issues in Developmental Research*, describes her unique pictorial scale which was used to investigate a variety of development related issues in several countries.

Section V examines the major issues related to child-parent relationships in cross-cultural settings. Alice S. Honig, in her chapter on infants and toddlers, adopts a historical approach and traces the major theoretical models to test the increasing range of variables which have been used in this type of research, including parental values, child-rearing techniques, health, nutrition, and language development. In their chapter on family structure and parent-child involvement, Jaipaul Roopnarine and his team bring their joint research interests to focus on Caribbean families. Given the fact that the Caribbean is a vast region, inhabited by diverse ethnic groups, with several languages, including English, French, French Creole, Patois, Spanish, Hindi, and Chinese, spoken there, they have made an excellent attempt in providing an overall synopsis of parent-child relationships in the English-speaking Caribbean, mainly Guyana, Trinidad and Tobago, Antigua, Jamaica, and other countries. They have examined patterns of socialization, parental involvements with their children, and have offered practical and workable recommendations for future research and family policies. In the chapter written by Xinyin Chen, we move from the Caribbean to China, are exposed to problems of growing up in a collectivist culture, and get an insight into the processes underlying the socialization and emotional development of Chinese children. Chen reports on the longitudinal studies, which he and his colleagues have conducted on children's social relationships and socioemotional adjustment. Similarities and differences in behaviors, attitudes, parenting processes, and other behavioral manifestations, such as temperament and adjustment problems, between the Chinese and the North American children, have been very clearly encapsulated in the studies reported. George Domino's comparison of the social values of the Chinese and U.S.- American children dovetails nicely with Chen's research and shows considerable continuity in the respective value patterns in the two countries. Edith Grotberg's fascinating research on resilience in children is concerned with the kinds of actions which parents undertake to promote resilience in their children up to the age of twelve. Other related questions that she attempts to answer are concerned with interactions between age, gender, and resilience and with cross-cultural similarities and differences in resilience in children.

Section VI is concerned with the problems of adolescence. The first paper by Judith H. Gibbons provides an overview of a considerable amount of cross-cultural research comparing adolescents in preindustrial and in industrialized countries with respect to personal and social development. India's leading developmental psychologist T. S. Saraswathi examines the problems of adolescence in India and considers the intriguing question whether adolescence in India is a myth or an emerging reality. She examines gender and class differences in adolescence and argues that the process of child-adult continuity is more evident in females than in males in India and more evident in the upper social classes than in the lower two social classes. The third chapter by Pedro R. Portes and his team attempts to test the validity of Eriksonian conceptions of identity formation in different cultural settings. The authors report the findings of an empirical study undertaken in three cultural groups, the U.S., Haiti, and Colombia, and come to the conclusion that the cultural context is predictive of variations in identity formation.

Section VII concerns itself with examining moral development in different cultures. The first chapter written by Georg Lind poses an intriguing question which forms the title of his chapter: *Are Helpers Always Moral?* In an attempt to answer the question, he describes and analyzes the findings from a longitudinal empirical study that was undertaken on medical students in Germany. In his chapter, he questions and tests the assumed and unchallenged relationship between moral development and helping behavior. On the basis of his research findings, he comes to the conclusion that the assumed relationship between moral development and altruism or helping behavior does not hold in all cases. The second chapter by Uwe P. Gielen and Emily S. C. Y. Miao describes a study which looks at parental behavior and the development of moral reasoning in students from Taiwan, where the Confucian and neo-Confucian heritage still plays a major role in the development of moral reasoning. They set out to test three research hypotheses, using a variety of empirical strategies, including questionnaires translated into Mandarin Chinese and adapted to Taiwanese circumstances.

The chapters in **Section VIII** attempt to unite theory with practice. The first chapter, entitled: *Promoting Reflective Practice within a Cognitive-Structural Framework: Theory, Research, and Practice*, is written by Alan J. Reiman. He is of the opinion that the value of reflective practice in teaching needs to be elucidated from both theoretical and empirical points of view. In the chapter, he summarizes the important aspects of Vygotsky's theory and Piaget's theory as they relate to reflection and praxis and offers a cognitive-structural framework for understanding and researching the role of guided reflection. The chapter also considers the wider cross-cultural implications of adopting a reflective approach. Pursuing a similar theme, Sharon N. Oja describes an empirical study, which examines the unique place of *Role-taking and Reflection in Collaborative Action Research*. She considers the advantages of collaborative action research in universities and the improvement and understanding it engenders in the teacher-researcher. The final chapter in this section is written by Sandra D. Peace. In this chapter she argues that in a diverse, multicultural society, there is an increasing need for school counselors, psychologists, and social workers to develop reflective skills, higher levels of thinking, and empathy and other social skills, which could then be used to promote greater equality, justice, and humane conditions in schools and society. She describes an empirical study, which was carefully designed and executed to bring about the desired changes.

Section IX raises the problem of aging and dying, thus bringing about a neat completion of the life-cycle approach adopted in the book. The first chapter by Ursula Lehr, Elisabeth Seiler, and Hans Thomae sets the scene, by surveying research on the process of aging in numerous cross-cultural settings. They examine a variety of fascinating concepts in their chapter: distinguishing the different notions of aging in industrialized and non-industrialized societies, demographic changes that influence one's understanding of aging across cultures, and the influence of cultural factors on psychophysical and psychosocial correlates of longevity. They argue that notwithstanding the popularity of the disengagement theory of aging, it is the perceived life satisfaction that appears to be the decisive yardstick of successful aging. Findings from a large-scale cross-national study confirm their hypothesis. Eva Sandis, in her chapter, *The Aging and Their Families: A Cross-National Review*, pursues a similar line of enquiry by examining world population trends among the elderly, as well as their impact on family structures and functions. She provides an excellent survey of the related problems of aging across the world in her clearly written chapter. The third chapter written by Margot Nadien is entitled *Gender, Health, and Behavior Among Aging North Americans*. The chapter focuses on the physical and psychosocial functioning of aging females and males in the U.S.A. and Canada and the genetic influences that influence the aging person. Several interesting questions related to health, illness, behavioral, and gender are raised in the chapter, and tentative answers, based on carefully reviewed research in the area, are offered. The Italian psychologist Guido Amoretti has constructed a manageable test battery to access cognitive abilities in old age. In his chapter, he reports the results of a combined longitudinal-cross-sectional study conducted among several cohorts of normal and pathological Italian respondents. His results emphasize the importance of cognitive rehabilitation based on training in metacognitive and other techniques. The next chapter is a collaborative effort. Leonore Loeb Adler and her international team report the findings of a *Cross-Cultural Investigation Comparing Attitudes Toward Living and Dying*. After reviewing the salient literature on attitudes of people toward death across cultures, they describe their cross-cultural investigation which was carried out in four countries: Kuwait, South Korea, Sri Lanka, and the U.S.A. on three age groups: young adult, middle age, and old age. A questionnaire was used to obtain the data. Interesting and revealing findings have been reported in their study. The end-chapter of the section and indeed of the book, by Pittu Laungani, concerns itself with examining the beliefs, attitudes, and values which people have toward death and dying. The chapter, after comparing Eastern and Western attitudes to death and dying in general, focuses more specifically on India and England. The chapter argues that the strongly ingrained religious beliefs of Hindus concerning *Karma* and its inexorable effects on birth, life, death, and rebirth tend to protect an individual from the fears and terrors associated with dying and extinction. Their Western counterparts, for a variety of reasons that are articulated in the chapter, have been denied the benefits of such psychologically and spiritually protective devices.

    The book closes with Marshall H. Segall's "Epilogue." Professor Segall, a former president of the International Association for Cross-Cultural Psychology, urges us to adopt more frequently a policy-relevant stance on real world problems: We now know enough about human development, he says, to assist policy makers in their search for a better world. They need all the help they can get!

My sincere congratulations to Professors Anna L. Comunian and Uwe P. Gielen for assembling such a remarkable book!

Pittu Laungani, Ph.D.
London, England
21st October, 1999

ABOUT THE EDITORS

Anna Laura Comunian, Ph.D., is Professor of Theories and Techniques of Personality Tests as well as Director of the Laboratory for International and Cross-Cultural Psychology at the University of Padua. She also teaches Group Dynamics. A former member of the Board of Directors of the International Council of Psychologists, she is the author or co-editor of *La Dinamica dei Gruppi Ottimali* (1993), *Ricerche con la Matrice dei Processi Intra ed Inter Personali nel Gruppo in Italia* (1994), *Advancing Psychology and its Applications: International Perspectives* (1994), *The Family and Family Therapy in International Perspective* (1998), *International Approaches to the Family and Family Therapy* (1999) and numerous book chapters and articles. Together with Uwe P. Gielen, she has published a series of studies on moral development in Italian culture. Most recently, her academic and clinical interests have focused on cross-cultural aspects of rehabilitation, health, and education. She has been Visiting Professor at Boston University.

Uwe P. Gielen received his Ph.D. in social psychology from Harvard University where he was a student of the late Lawrence Kohlberg. He is now Professor of Psychology and Director of the Institute for International and Cross Cultural Psychology at St. Francis College (USA), after serving as chairman of its Psychology Department from 1980-1990. He co-editor of *Psychology in International Perspective: 50 Years of the International Council of Psychologists* (1992); *Cross-cultural Topics in Psychology* (1994); *Advancing Psychology and its Applications: International Perspectives* (1994); *The Family and Family Therapy in International Perspective* (1998); *International Approaches to the Family and Family Therapy* (1999); *Psychology in the Arab Countries (1998)*; and co-author of *The Kohlberg Legacy for the Helping Professions* (1991). Dr. Gielen is a past president of both the International Council of Psychologists and the Society for Cross-Cultural Research, the former editor of *World Psychology*, and the present editor of the *International Journal of Group Tensions*. Dr. Gielen and Dr. Comunian are also editing the Italian Series on International and Cross-Cultural Psychology that is being published by UNIPRESS.

SECTION I: HISTORICAL AND INTERNATIONAL PERSPECTIVES

Cross-cultural studies are a relatively new field in which research on human development plays a central role. Today the field of cross-cultural psychology is remarkably diverse, consisting of a variety of viewpoints and different definitions of the field itself. In Berry, Poortinga, and Pandey's (1997) newly revised *Handbook of Cross-cultural Psychology*, Cross-cultural Psychology is defined as "the systematic study of relationships between the cultural context of human development and the behaviors that become established in the repertoire of individuals growing up in a particular culture" (p. x).

The chapters in this section discuss a variety of historical and international perspectives to illustrate linkages between cultural, historical, and cross-cultural psychological processes. The historical perspective represented in the chapters permits the investigation of the social psychology of cultural dynamics as applied to the cross-cultural study of human development.

In his chapter *On the Prehistory of Cross-cultural Development Research*, the British psychologist Gustav Jahoda discusses some early cross-cultural conceptions and studies in child development that were attempting to delineate differences between European and "savage" children. Ideas, "theories," and observations concerning what was for a long time called "savage" and later "primitive" childhood are surveyed. During most of the earlier period, the theory of "arrested development" held sway, to be superseded later by the "biogenetic law" that is also incorporated into many psychoanalytic renderings. An alternative biological theory was "neoteny" theory; however, it led to the same conclusions about the alleged intellectual inferiority especially of people of African origin. Throughout the centuries of European expansion, the intelligence and psychological development of "savage" children was of little interest to Europeans although there existed a whole cluster of negative stereotypes.

In the 19th century, the children of the so-called savages were found to be quite intelligent and really not that different from European children. Later, an extensive debate arose about African infants' precocity or "arrested development," and this debate has persisted in various forms well into the 20th century. Jahoda examines theories of the second half of the 19th century designed to account for the supposed failure of "lower races," as exemplified by the so-called "biogenetic law," also known in psychology as the "recapitulation theory." The theory postulates that the cultural stages of the progress of humanity are functionally related to biologically fixed phases and that the progress of individuals representing the "lower races" is arrested once they reach their biological limit. G. Stanley Hall's theory is an example of such a theory, and it claims to account for "arrested development" on the basis of social-evolutionary theory.

As exceptions, Jahoda cites anthropological studies by Margaret Mead and Meyer Fortes as well as Abram Kardiner's neopsychoanalytic theory, which between the 1920s-1940s led to the expansion of empirical studies conducted with children from a wide range of cultures. For Gustav Jahoda these developments represent the end of the prehistory of cross-cultural psychology. However, he suggests that one should not underestimate the power and persistence of old ideas and beliefs in more recent theoretical formulations such as those advanced by Eysenck and Hallpike.

In their chapter *European Influences on U.S. Developmental Psychology: A Historical Perspective*, the American psychologists John D. Hogan and Bradley D. Sussner discuss some historical links between American and European developmental psychology. Developmental psychology in the United States in the earliest years was a normative and descriptive science, with a primary focus on the child. In recent years, the field has focused on process and theory, and it has increased its range to cover the entire life span. Hogan and Sussner observe that historical accounts of the evolution of developmental psychology have been scarce in American textbooks and consequently the valuable contributions of many European pioneers of developmental psychology have been overlooked in these books. Hogan and Sussner emphasize that apart from Freud, Piaget, and Vygotsky, references to non-U.S. contributions to developmental psychology tend to be meager. Hogan and Sussner's chapter should serve as a reminder that American psychology, including developmental psychology, has important roots in Europe, and that a better understanding of these links is essential to grasp not only historical but also modern trends in the field.

The authors introduce some American pioneers emphasizing the value of evolutionary theory in developmental psychology (G. Stanley Hall and James Mark Baldwin) and some of the European pioneers (Wilhelm Preyer, George Romanes, and Francis Galton). The implications of the ethological school (e.g., Konrad Lorenz and Niko Tinbergen) on human development researches are outlined and John Bowlby and Mary Ainsworth's theories are examined for the development of attachment theory and research on young children. The early foundations of life-span developmental psychology are also introduced through the 18th-19th century work of Johann Tetens, Friedrich Carus, and Adolph Quetelet. Two European "educator-psychologists," Alfred Binet and Maria Montessori, are presented as largely uncredited developmentalists. The works of other European psychologists such as Seguin, Stern, Wallon, and Basov are highlighted since they are poorly known in the U.S. but bring important and original contributions to developmental psychology.

Recent Trends in Cross-cultural Studies of Human Development: The Role of Current Research Traditions is the topic developed by Deborah Best, the President-Elect of the International Association for Cross-Cultural Psychology (IACCP). She introduces a short text, *Cross-cultural Human Development* by Lee and Ruth Munroe (1979), as the first comprehensive attempt to survey in a more comprehensive fashion cross-cultural developmental research. Twenty years later, numerous researchers are involved in cross-cultural developmental psychology and with cross-cultural and cultural themes. Cross cultural psychology is in demand but the nagging question remains whether mainstream developmental psychology has begun to take culture seriously.

Following the 1994 edition of the reissued book by the Munroes, Deborah Best identifies four current research traditions and notes recent studies that serve to exemplify modern developments in the four traditions. In this context, sociobehavioral approaches, context-specific studies, bioevolutionary approaches, cognitive approaches, universalistic approaches, studies conceived within various cultural-context frameworks, the cultural-practice perspective, and cultural-historical activity theories are discussed. After briefly reviewing the main ideas and current research conceived within each of these approaches, Deborah Best concludes that understanding variability both within and across cultural settings must be one of the primary goals of developmental psychology.

In the 1960s and 1970s, sociobehavioral research emphasized children's natural environment, and bioevolutionary studies addressed the possible adaptedness of behavior development within a variety of culturally constructed niches. In the 1980s, more universalistic and cognitively oriented approaches focused on the effects of schooling and other experiences that influence the acquisition of more effective information-processing strategies. In the 1990s, theories emphasizing the crucial role of cultural regulation and examining a variety of cultural practices have demonstrated that biologically-driven universal stages of development can nevertheless be altered by different cultural contexts. Understanding intracultural variation and the consistency-inconsistency and continuity-discontinuity dimensions of behavior in the framework of specific developmental contexts continue to pose new challenges for developmental psychology.

The three chapters contained in this section provide valuable historical background for the later contributions in this volume. Jahoda reviews some ideas on the nature of "savage" children prevailing in the 19th and early 20th century and finds that a racist Zeitgeist held sway over them.

Hogan and Sussner show that in the area of developmental psychology, intellectual traffic across the Atlantic has frequently been spotty. This has sometimes led American psychologists to neglect the contributions of various European pioneers as well as those of the more recently active European developmentalists. Best's contribution brings the story up to date by delineating four broad trends prevailing in the cross-cultural study of human development. Taken together, the three chapters suggest that the evolution of the cross-cultural study of human development has itself been governed by the developmental master principles of increasing differentiation and integration: While in earlier times there were only a few impressionistic studies of children and adolescents in nonwestern societies, we now have access to a considerable variety of more fine-grained studies of human development around the globe. In addition, we can now draw a much more comprehensive and realistic picture of the various biological, demographic, sociocultural, historical, and economic factors that appear to drive this development. The articles in the remainder of this volume provide considerable evidence for this contention.

ON THE PREHISTORY OF CROSS-CULTURAL
DEVELOPMENT RESEARCH

Gustav Jahoda
University of Strathclyde, United Kingdom

Systematic studies of child development are a relatively new field, and cross-cultural studies of child development arc of even more recent origin. The reason for such a long prevailing lack of interest was probably the fact that in the past development was not regarded as problematic. As the poet Wordsworth put it succinctly, even though politically incorrectly, "the child is father of the man;" in other words, children naturally grow up to become adults, and that was all there was to it. Hence it is hardly surprising that over the centuries of European expansion overseas there was little concern with the children of "savages." So-called "Histories of childhood" like those of Philippe Ariès (1973) or Lloyd de Mause (1976) deal exclusively with European children. It was not until the 19th century with its dogmatic race theories that questions began to be more widely asked about the differences between European and "savage" children. The reasons for this were also connected with the growth of missionary efforts; and later, when colonial expansion was under way, colonial administrators were concerned with the need to train low-level cadres.

It is also necessary to understand that over the centuries Europeans held a whole cluster of negative stereotypes about what were originally called "savages" and later "primitives." They were seen as devoid of morals, especially sexual, often viewed as cannibals, and nearly always believed to be stupid, even if not altogether lacking reason. During earlier periods, from about the Renaissance to the 18th century, accounts of savages related almost invariably to adults; but there were some very occasional references to children which foreshadow later ideas. For instance, the 16th-century Dominican Tomas Ortiz commented with regard to the newly discovered South American Indians:

> The higher the age reached by these people, the nastier they become. While they are still 10 or 12 years old, one can still believe that they possess some civility and virtue, but later they truly degenerate into brute animals (Cited in Todorov, 1985, pp. 182-183).

Some two hundred years later De Pauw, writing about North American Indians, expressed closely similar notions:

> One has to admit that the children...display some glimmer of intelligence up to the ages of 16 or 17...but towards the 20th year stupidity suddenly develops (De Pauw, 1770, Vol.2, p. 156).

As exploration went apace with what Herder called "philosophical fury," more extended contacts with "savages" multiplied from mid-18th century onwards. Explorers, travelers, and missionaries were expected to say something about the "character" of the peoples they encountered, or as we would say their psychology.

From these sources reports multiplied from early 19th century onwards to the effect that the children of savages, in contrast to their elders, were quite intelligent and really no different from European children; sometimes they were even believed to be in advance of them. This came to be accepted as an established fact even by extreme biological race theorists such as James Hunt:

> With the Negro, as with some other races of man, it has been found that children are precocious; but that no advance in education can be made after they arrive at the age of maturity; they still continue, mentally, children .... (Hunt, 1863, p. 27).

Let me mention in passing that about a century later, during the late 1950s, a similar claim was made about alleged African *infant* precocity. This led to an extensive debate, and it was eventually shown that the precocity was illusory (Super, 1981).

Returning to the 19th century, it will be obvious that the brightness of "savage" children presented an awkward puzzle for race theorists. Accordingly, they came up with the notion of "arrested development." But why should there be such an arrest? Some, like Carl Vogt who proclaimed the simian character of blacks, saw it as a simple biological law: "It is undeniable that the sudden metamorphosis which at the time of puberty takes place in the Negro...is a repetition of the phenomena occurring in the anthropoid apes" (1864, p. 191). Apes, according to Vogt, are "intelligent and very apt to learn and become civilized," but afterwards they become "obstinate savage beasts, incapable of any improvement. And so it is with the Negro."

What happens, it was claimed, is that the bones of the skull fuse earlier at the sutures in the "lower races," thereby preventing further expansion of the brain. This notion of "arrested development" persisted in various forms until the early 20th century. Thus, in 1896 the ethnologist Keane proposed that the more intense mental activity of Europeans cause the brain to throb, thereby preventing the closure of the sutures until later in life (Keane, 1896, p. 45).

While this was the highpoint of the "sutures" theory, another explanation for arrested development had been gaining ground. It was vividly expressed by Dudley Kidd in the introduction to his *Savage Childhood* (1906/1969). This is noteworthy as having been the first systematic empirical study of "primitive" children, carried out in South Africa. Kidd was generally very warm and sympathetic in writing about the children, whom he obviously liked. And yet, he believed in the doctrine of arrested development, as indicated by his introduction:

> ....the savage is at his best, intellectually, emotionally, and morally, at the

dawn of puberty. When puberty is drawing to a close, a degenerative process seems to set in, and the previous efflorescence of the faculties leads to no adequate fruitage in later life.

....in nothing is this more marked than in the case of the imagination. Not a few observers have pointed out that the imagination in the Kaffirs runs to seed after puberty: it would be truer to say that it runs to sex (pp. VIII-IX).

What is only surprising is that this explanation did not come up earlier, given the age-old European belief that savages are characterized by unbridled sexuality.

There were few who did not take the reality and universality of "arrested development" for granted. One exception was Francis Galton, who in connection with his chapter on "Ethnological Inquiries on the Innate Character and Intelligence of Different Races" (Galton 1883), sought to investigate some of the issues empirically. After his death a questionnaire was found among his papers intended for travellers, missionaries, and people residing in the colonies (Pearson, 1924, Vol.2, pp. 352-353). The following was obviously designed to verify the then common beliefs:

Children of many races are fully as quick, and even more precocious than European children, but they mostly cease to make progress after the season of manhood. Their moral character changes for the worse at the same time. State if this has been observed in the present instance.

Another question relates to numerous stories of children reverting to "barbarism:"

Children of savages, who have been reared in missionary families, have been known to throw off their clothes, and quit the house in a momentary rage, and go back to their people, among whom they were afterwards found in apparently contented barbarism. State authentic instances of this, if you know of any, with full particulars.

Unfortunately no examples of responses were among Galton's papers. Perhaps it might be useful at this stage to comment briefly on how, with hindsight, these 19th-century ideas are to be interpreted. The potential of "savage" children could be recognized by the Victorians, but as soon as they had become full members of their culture they were seen as having degenerated. This was because for educated Victorians intelligence was manifest in the technological and scientific achievements of Europe, and those who failed to live up to this standard were, for them, obviously deficient of rationality. As one writer put it:

In proportion as modern knowledge has made us penetrate more deeply into the minds of races—since we are no longer content to study them superficially *in the ordinary manifestations of life* [my emphasis], which we may call "commonplace," and which belong to nearly all countries—we perceive that insuperable limits separate one set of men from another (Pouchet, 1864, p. 65).

This implies that superb native skills in various spheres of life, close knowledge of nature, and often highly ingenious adaptations to hostile environments, counted for nothing.

Furthermore, it was inconceivable for the Victorian public that individuals who had enjoyed the benefits of education provided by missionaries might yet prefer to live the life of their own culture; hence they tended to attribute what they saw as retrogression to biological urges.

Let me now turn to the emergence during the second half of the 19th century of another theory designed to account for the supposed failure of the "lower races" to reach the same level of development as Europeans. This was the so-called "biogenetic law," better known in psychology as "recapitulation theory." Propounded by Ernst Haeckel initially in 1866, it stated that "The history of the foetus is a recapitulation of the history of the race" (Haeckel, 1905, Vol.1, p. 5). Haeckel's formulation was confined to embryology, but the general idea came to be extrapolated to *postnatal* human development in order to account for race differences. It was postulated that the cultural stages of the progress of humanity were functionally related to the biologically fixed phases of the psychological maturation of individuals. These phases recapitulate, in miniature as it were, the mental capacities and dispositions corresponding to the hierarchy of cultural stages; and the progress of individuals in the lower races is arrested when they reach their biological limit.

The most extreme version of this theory was expounded by George Romanes, a follower of Darwin who wanted to show that organic is paralleled by mental evolution. He produced a remarkable table of equivalents of mental development, and some of the key features of it are reproduced in Table 1 (abridged from Romanes, 1880, Lecture 9).

A baby of three weeks, as far as mental development is concerned, is said to be at the same level as a worm! He admits having had quarrels with mothers about this, and evidently they had more sense than the distinguished scientist.

Freud read Romanes' *Mental Evolution in Man* and wrote in his *General Introduction to Psychoanalysis* (1938, p. 177) ".... each individual repeats in some abbreviated fashion during childhood the whole course of the development of the human race;" Jung was also a recapitulationist.

The American guru of child and educational psychology, Stanley Hall, claimed that each stage of child development corresponds to some primitive ancestral one, and that it is only during adolescence that the latest advances of the race become dominant. Non-white children go through the same stages until adolescence, when in most cases (and at least he granted some exceptions) they go no further. It will be evident that Stanley Hall's theory was only another version of "arrested development" based on social-evolutionary theory. When it came to the question as to why development stops, the answer was the same: an excessive preoccupation with sex.

Hall's own efforts to provide evidence for his views were very unconvincing, but the work of one of his students is of considerable interest.

Table 1
Romanes' Scale of Developmental Periods

The Psychological Scale	Human Age Equivalent	"Idiots"
Existing man	adult	
Highly civilized	15 yrs	
Civilized	10 yrs	
Savages and partly civilized	5 yrs	feeble-minded
Low savages	3 yrs	imbeciles
Lowest savages	30 mths	high idiots
Primitive man	28 mths	"counting" idiots
Almost human ape	20 mths	"talking" idiots
Anthropoid apes	9 mths	"babbling" idiots
Horses, pigs, etc.	5 mths	
Birds	18 wks	
Spiders & crabs	14 wks	
Worms	3 wks	
Jellyfish	birth	

This was a Ph.D. dissertation by Appleton (1910/1976) concerned with the educational implications of what she called the "culture-epoch theory," characterized by the author as:

"The theory that the child recapitulates the psychical as well as the physical evolution of his race, and hence that his mental growth is best promoted by assimilation of the cultural products belonging to that stage of *race* development, which corresponds to his own" (p. 1).

Although this was not spelled out, it implies a parallel series of stages of development in the individual "civilized" child that corresponds to mental dispositions present at successively higher cultural levels. Appleton's aim was to test this theory, at least in a preliminary way. Doing it comprehensively would have entailed covering the whole range of then existing cultures, taking these as reflecting a linear evolutionary progression. In practice that was not feasible, and the project was confined to:

> "...an attempt to make a beginning of an unprejudiced study of the actual mental characteristics of some of the lowest of savage tribes with a view to finding whether their mental life does or does not reveal any definite types similar to those found in ontogenetic development" (p. 1).

In much of the later discussions this limitation was lost sight of, and conclusions were drawn as though the whole of the supposed "phylogenetic series" had been examined. The method of investigation consisted of using existing studies of children's play, of the kind favored by Stanley Hall, and ethnographic data about tribes "low in savagery," one from each continent. For the classification of play some broad and rather vague categories were used.

While ample information was provided on the five tribes, that about "civilized children" remained rather scanty. The analysis consisted of a comparison of the two sets of samples according to types of play. Given the looseness of the categories, such comparisons must have involved a great deal of arbitrary judgement. The general conclusion reached was one of at least partial support for recapitulation theory:

> "So far as somatic characteristics of play activities are concerned, very close though not perfect correspondence is found between the savage and the child. In the matter of organization of play activities, wide differences appear, while in the psychological characteristics of their play those qualities, such as, for example, rhythm, dramatization, and competition, which, with civilized children, are very strong in very early life, are also very strong with the savages.... On the other hand, the more purely abstract and intellectual phases of children's play are almost absolutely lacking" (p. 4).

The actual text indicates that the last of these claims was, even within the given framework, far too extreme. In the conclusions at the end of the monograph it is conceded that the tribes do have some "purely intellectual play," but this resembles that of "civilized children" between the ages of six and eleven. The lesson to be learnt from all this for educational practice was said to be that:

> "....it is necessary to bring the specific products of the culture epochs corresponding most closely to [the child's] own, into the realm of formal instruction. But to do this intelligently, it is necessary that the teacher add to his knowledge of genetic pedagogy a genetic anthropology" (p. 83).

I have described this in some detail, since it was one of the earliest attempts to apply what has since become known as the "hologeistic" method used in conjunction with the Human Relations Area Files.

The famous French psychologist Henri Piéron addressed a meeting of the

Ecole d'Anthropologie de Paris, published under the title *Psychological Anthropology*, over half a century before this term came to denote a specialized field (Piéron, 1909). His main message was to stress the relevance of psychology to anthropology, which in France at that period was almost entirely physical. In the course of his address he alluded to recapitulationism in a rather skeptical manner, suggesting the need to undertake "researches on the development of primitive children, less affected by the heavy and indeterminate heredity of civilized generations" (p. 125).

At about the same time Lévy-Bruhl published his famous thesis about the "pre-logicality" of primitives. Far from equating the mentalities of European children and adult primitives, as was then commonly done, he warned explicitly against this. Yet in spite of that, and no doubt under the influence of the old theories, Pierre Janet and Henri Wallon in the 1920s compared the mentality of savages and even of the mentally ill to that of European children. Similar comparisons were later sometimes made by Vygotsky.

Particularly interesting is the case of Piaget, who discussed the implications of Lévy-Bruhl's thesis in considerable depth (Piaget, 1928). It is not possible here to discuss his lengthy and complex arguments in detail. Let me just say that, accepting the similarity between the thought processes of primitives and European children, he proposed that they stem from different causes: in the case of European children it is *egocentrism*, while in that of primitives it results from *cultural constraints*. Generally, the influence of Lévy-Bruhl is very evident in Piaget's early writings such as *Language and Thought of the Child* (1932), where he made frequent references to Lévy-Bruhl.

All these were theoretical speculations informed by the survival of 19th-century ideas, and in the absence of direct empirical studies of children in non-European cultures. In fact, as will appear shortly, there were hardly any such studies during the inter-war period. But before going on to this I wish to give one further example illustrating the power of preconceived ideas.

Already in Stanley Hall's time the star of recapitulation theory was on the wane, though it lingered on for a considerable period. But an alternative biological theory was put forward, namely "neoteny." It refers to the retention after sexual maturity of some juvenile characters, produced by a relative slowing down of bodily development. This is much more pronounced in humans than in animals, and it was argued by some that it also accounts for the inferiority of non-European races who continue developing for a longer time period. Thus it is almost the exact opposite of recapitulation theory, yet for racists led to the same conclusion: heads Europeans win, tails non-Europeans lose! Neoteny is not just of historical interest: the argument from neotony was resurrected not long ago by Eysenck (1971), who referred to the previously mentioned notion of African precocity. This led him to propose that such precocity explained the alleged intellectual inferiority of blacks.

The period between the two world wars saw the rise of the intelligence test movement, which was soon extended to a range of cultures outside Europe and America. Its history is too well known to be rehearsed here, except perhaps for one particular episode. In South Africa Fick (1939) published a monograph in which he stated on the basis of IQ test results that "around the ages of 13 and 17 Native children are from 4 to 5 years inferior to European children" (p. 54). From this he concluded that there are few ".... Natives who can benefit by education of the ordinary type beyond the rudimentary" (p. 56). These claims stimulated Simon Biesheuvel (1943) to write a book in refutation, in which he for the first time examined in detail cultural and other influences on test performance.

Otherwise the inter-war period was a fallow one as regards empirical studies of child development, with two important exceptions, both by anthropologists. One was the versatile Margaret Mead, who had a special interest in psychological issues and went into the field equipped with psychological test material. She undertook an intensive study of Melanesian children's modes of thought, partly inspired by Piaget's writing on animism. Her method was mainly observational, though she also collected spontaneous drawings and obtained responses to inkblots. The results were published in an article with the title *An Investigation of the Thought of Primitive Children, with Special Reference to Animism* (Mead, 1932). Her somewhat controversial conclusion was that among the Manus it is the adults rather than the children whose thought is animistic.

The other study, that has become a classic, was described by Jerome Bruner et al. (1966, p. 60) as "by far the most detailed field study of the learning process of children in an indigenous society." It was done by Meyer Fortes (1938), in Taleland (now Northern Ghana). He had originally been trained as an educational psychologist, which accounts for his clear awareness of methodological problems and his apologetic statement that "It is impossible...to follow up a special psychological problem in a manner commensurate with the criteria of experimental research in England" (p. 7). However, he spent a whole year in careful observation; and his description of phases of development from infancy onwards is still a model of its kind. Fortes is most illuminating on social development, the ways in which Tale children become integrated into their culture. For instance, each person and clan has prohibitions against eating certain animals, and "a 5-year-old knows his or her personal or clan taboo, and can state it emphatically" (p. 39). Adults never constrain their conversations because of the presence of a child, which results in "comprehensive and accurate sexual knowledge of a 6-year-old, though direct instruction in these matters is never given" (p. 27). Tale parents have an expectation of "natural development" which means that explicit teaching is rare: "Everybody takes it for granted that any person participating either already knows, or wants to know, how to behave in a manner appropriate to the situation and in accordance with his level of maturity" (p. 26). So, for instance, there is no deliberate toilet training, and mothers are content to wait until the child independently attains control. It is an approach that has come into fashion only recently in Euramerican culture!

Fortes also showed in detail how children spontaneously enact in play the survival skills and ritual practices of their society. Two extracts will illustrate this, the first relating to a group consisting of three children of about 6 or 7 and one, Ton, aged about ten (exact ages cannot usually be ascertained) whose task was to scare birds away:

"Gomna had wandered off a few yards and now came running up with three locusts. "These are our cows" said Gomna, "let's build a yard for them." Zoo and the little girl foraged around and produced a few pieces of decayed bark. The children, Gomna dominant...set about building a "cattle yard" of the pieces of bark. Ton...squatted down to help. He and Gomna constructed an irregular rectangle with one side open...The little girl stood looking on. Gomna carefully pushed the locusts in...and declared "We must make a gateway." Rummaging about, the boys found two pebbles which they set up as gate posts...suddenly the whole structure collapsed and Ton started putting it up again. The little girl meanwhile had found a pair of stones and a potsherd and was on her knees "grinding grain." Suddenly the two boys dashed off into the growing grain, shouting to scare the birds" (p. 50).

The relevance of such play rehearsal of what will become their adult tasks is clear; moreover, they do it without prompting and find evident enjoyment in it. Similarly, young boys build shrines for themselves in the cattle yard, and if they construct play houses, "shrines" are added as in a real house. If they catch a mouse, they "sacrifice" it to their miniature shrine. Thus the ritual duties of adults are enacted in play. Let me mention in passing that close involvement of children with the beliefs and practices of their elders can have its darker side. In Ashanti I have come across a child of about ten who believed herself to be a witch, and many such cases are well documented (Field, 1960).

The next development occurred across the Atlantic where the neo-Freudian, Abram Kardiner, began to lay the foundations of the "Culture and Personality" school (Kardiner, 1939). His anthropological colleagues collected, among other data, selective (in accordance with neo-psychoanalytic theory) information about children. Kardiner then interpreted the findings, deriving therefrom the material for building a grandiose theoretical edifice. Although it has rightly been called "a magnificent failure," it was the starting point of an expansion of empirical studies of children in a wide range of cultures.

This, in my estimation, was the end of pre-history. However, at this stage, I would like to answer a question that may be in the minds of at least some readers. Namely, what is the point for modern researchers to stir around in the dustheap of history, regurgitating old theories which today strike us as utterly absurd? In answer I would suggest that one should not underestimate the power and persistence of old ideas and beliefs. They are apt to spread first among specialists, as I have shown; but they also filter down to wider circles and can have important practical consequences. I shall conclude by giving some examples of this. A psychiatrist working during the late 1940s in what was then Northern Rhodesia claimed:

"....the typical African is somewhat arrested in mental development. An observation which I myself have made also arises from the weaning situation, from which the ambivalent attitude of the African develops. This is that up to puberty there is in my opinion very little difference in the intelligence and learning ability between Bemba and European children. After that a marked difference occurs, the European far outstripping the African child. This, I think, is due to the early release and gratification of the genital sexual impulse in the average African child" (Davidson, 1949, p. 77).

A few years later another psychiatrist published a monograph on *The African Mind* sponsored, it should be noted, by the World Health Organization. In it he wrote:

"...the whole-hearted concentration on sex which characterizes the African adolescent...is merely one symptom of a general condition—one more example of the all-or-none attention which is part and parcel of the lack of personal integration which has now become the clearest feature of African mentality" (Carothers, 1953, pp. 106-107).

It must not be thought that such thinking was confined to psychiatrists. For instance Werner's "Comparative organismic theory" used to be likened to Piaget's theoretical edifice. A revised edition of his *magnum opus* appeared in 1948 and was reprinted several times, my copy dating to 1957. It contains the following passage:

"Development among primitive people is characterized on the one hand by precocity and, on the other, by a relatively early arrest of the process of intellectual growth" (Werner 1957, p. 27).

This could have been penned in mid-19th century! In fact, if one checks up on his references as I have done, it turns out that nearly three-quarters of them were to works prior to 1920. Even more recently an anthropologist, Hallpike (1979), claimed that the cognitive functioning of "primitives" remains stuck at Piaget's "pre-operative" stage, which corresponds to that of European children of about seven. Admittedly, he attributed this to environmental rather than biological causes, but it is still as absurd as it sounds. Let me add that practically all his colleagues dismissed his ideas.

One might be tempted to dismiss the whole business as fanciful and outdated aberrations of no great consequence. While this may be the case today, though I doubt it, such doctrines certainly had significant practical implications. While the tracing of detailed causal chains is not feasible, even a limited perusal of sources suggested that the idea of arrested development was initially put forward by explorers and travellers and then taken over and in turn reinforced by European teachers in colonial territories. It was certainly not confined to writers in ivory towers. This was shown by the now largely, and undeservedly forgotten psychologist Ombredane (1952), who was a pioneer of research in the Belgian Congo during the years after World War II. He interviewed people in responsible positions in the then colony about the idea of "arrested development" of blacks. While it was of course rejected by black Africans themselves, he found that many of the whites firmly believed it to be true:

"A senior magistrate: The black, when he is young, can be more alert than the white, but when he reaches puberty he becomes mindless."

"A senior administrator: The arrest of intelligence at puberty is *a reality*. This can be seen in the infantile behavior of the adult, in his exhibitionism. Up to 8 or 9 years, the black kid is at least as smart as the white kid. Towards puberty a sclerosis sets in due to sexual excesses" (pp. 522-523, emphasis in the original).

There is little doubt that such beliefs are likely to have influenced the behavior of colonial officials towards the people over whom they exercised authority. Perhaps even more serious would have been the educational effects, since low expectations on the part of the teachers are likely to have resulted in correspondingly low performance.

All the ghosts have not been laid, and they still occasionally emerge in scientific guise. Thus Rushton (1995) links precocious sexuality and lower intelligence in what he calls "Negroids;" and to that extent prehistory is still with us.

BIBLIOGRAPHY

Appleton, L.E. (1910/1976). *A comparative study of the play activities of adult savages and civilized children*. Chicago, IL: University of Chicago Press. Reprint by Arno Press.

Ariès, P. (1973). *Centuries of childhood*. Harmondsworth: Penguin.

Appleton, L.E. (1910/1976). *A comparative study of the play activities of adult savages and civilized children*. Chicago, IL: University of Chicago Press.

Biesheuvel, S. (1943). *African intelligence*. Johannesburg: South African Institute of Race Relations.

Bruner, J.S., Olver, R.R., Greenfield, P.M., et al. (1966). *Studies in cognitive growth*. New York: Wiley.

Carothers, J.C. (1953). *The African mind in health and disease*. Geneva: World Health Organization.

Davidson, S. (1949). Psychiatric work among the Bemba. *Rhodes-Livingston Journal 7*, 75-86.

De Mause, L. (Ed.). (1976). *The history of childhood*. London: Souvenir Press.

De Pauw, C. (1770). *Recherches philosophiques sur les Américains*, 3 vols. Berlin: Decker.

Eysenck, H.J. (1971). *Race, intelligence and education*. London: Temple Smith.

Fick, M.L. (1939). *The educability of the South African native*. Pretoria: South African Council for Educational and Social Research, Res. Ser. No. 8.

Fortes, M. (1938). Social and psychological aspects of education in Taleland. Supplement to *Africa*, *2* (4).

Field, M.J. (1960). *Search for security*. London: Faber.

Freud, S. (1938). *A general introduction to psychoanalysis*. London: Hogarth.

Galton, F. (1883). *Inquiries into human faculty and its development*. London: Macmillan.

Haeckel, E. (1870/1905). *The evolution of man*, 2 vols. London: Watts.

Hallpike, C.R. (1979). *The foundations of primitive thought*. Oxford: Clarendon Press.

Hunt, J. (1863). On the physical and mental characters of the Negro. *Anthropological Review*, *1*, 386-391.

Kardiner, A. (1939). *The individual and his society*. New York: Columbia University Press.

Keane, A.H. (1896). *Ethnology*. Cambridge: Cambridge University Press.

Kidd, D. (1906/1969). *Savage childhood*. New York: Negro Universities Press.

Mead, M. (1932). An investigation of the thought of primitive children, with special reference to animism. *Journal of the Royal Anthropological Institute*, *62*, 173-190.

Ombredane, A. (1952). Principes pour une étude psychologique des noirs du

Congo Belge. In H. Piéron, A. Fessard, & P. Fraisse (Eds.), *L'Année Psychologique*, *50*, 521-547. Paris: Presses Universitaires de France.

Pearson, K. (1924). *The life, letters and labour of Francis Galton*, 2 vols. Cambridge: Cambridge University Press.

Piaget, J. (1928). Logique génétique et sociologie. *Revue Philosophique*, *105*, 165-205.

Piaget, J. (1932). *The language and thought of the child*. London: Routledge & Kegan Paul.

Piéron, H. (1909). L'anthropologie psychologique. *Revue de l'Ecole d'Anthropologie de Paris*, *19*, 113-127.

Pouchet, G. (1864). *The plurality of human races*. London: Longman.

Romanes, G.J. (1880). Mental evolution. *Glasgow Science Lectures 1878-80*; Lecture 9. Glasgow: Menzies.

Rushton, J.P. (1995). *Race, evolution and behavior*. New Brunswick, NJ: Transaction Publishers.

Super, C.M. (1981). Behavioral development in infancy. In R.H. Munroe, R.L. Munroe, & B.B. Whiting (Eds.), *Handbook of cross-cultural human development* (pp. 181-270). New York: Garland.

Todorov, T. (1985). *Die Eroberung Amerikas*. Frankfurt: Suhrkamp.

Vogt, C. (1864). *Lectures on man*. London: Longman.

Werner, H. (1957). *Comparative psychology of mental development*. New York: International Universities Press.

EUROPEAN INFLUENCES ON U.S. DEVELOPMENTAL PSYCHOLOGY: A HISTORICAL PERSPECTIVE

John D. Hogan and Bradley D. Sussner
St. John's University, U.S.A.

Developmental psychology has always had a close alliance with cross-cultural psychology. Although the two areas are distinct, they share common problems and ask related questions. While cross-cultural psychology looks at differences between cultures, developmental psychology looks at differences across the age range, resulting in a host of methodological similarities. Both are intensely interested in the universality of psychological phenomena or the lack of it. While developmental psychology is sometimes viewed as largely of American origin, it has been strongly influenced by other cultures, particularly European culture.

Developmental psychology in the United States has gone through some remarkable changes. In its earliest years, it was primarily a normative and descriptive science, principally focused on the child. As a result, for many years the field was simply called "child psychology." In recent years, the field has become more concerned with process and theory, and it has increased its range to cover the entire lifespan, hence its designation as "developmental psychology."

Along with a change in focus has come a shift away from the so-called "experimental child" movement, which was largely dominated by learning theory. Instead, some developmental psychologists have begun to return to the questions and approaches first proposed in the earliest years of the field's existence. These approaches, often referred to as "classical" developmental psychology, typically involve a greater concentration on maturational or biological aspects of development. At the same time, other developmental psychologists have placed a great emphasis on the role of context, resulting in a vibrant and ongoing debate in the field.

This reemphasis on some of its roots has provoked a renewed interest in the history of the discipline. Several articles and monographs have appeared and, recently, an entire book was devoted to an historical overview (Parke, Ornstein, Rieser, & Zahn-Waxler, 1994). Even the great handbooks of the discipline which, for several editions, contained no historical material, have included such material in the last two editions (Cairns, 1997).

With few exceptions, however, the history of developmental psychology has been absent from textbooks in the history of psychology. (It should be noted that while the two histories, overlap to some degree, they are far from identical.) As one example of the unequal treatment, G. Stanley Hall, America's first great developmental psychologist, usually receives little coverage in history of psychology textbooks. When he appears, he is likely to be identified as the founder of the American Psychological Association or as the man who engineered Freud's only visit to the U.S. Even when his landmark two-volume work on *Adolescence* is mentioned, its importance is rarely discussed. James M. Baldwin, America's other pioneer developmental psychologist, is typically missing from textbooks entirely.

European influences on developmental psychology receive uneven coverage, if they are covered at all. Of course, the texts acknowledge psychology's debt to Sigmund Freud and Jean Piaget. It would be difficult to ignore the towering contributions of the two most important developmentalists of the twentieth century. But Freud is frequently introduced as a representative of clinical psychology, and Piaget is often depicted as a precursor of the cognitive movement. Their contributions to developmental psychology, as such, are often shifted to the background.

In recent years, with the emergence of the "contextualist" movement, the work of Lev S. Vygotsky (1896-1934), the Russian developmentalist, has attained a substantial degree of visibility. In fact, he may be the most important contemporary developmentalist in America, even though he died in Russia more than sixty years ago. But the references to him do not indicate a general sensitivity to influences outside of the U.S. Other Russian developmentalists, such as Basov or Blonsky, are rarely mentioned.

The fact is that beyond Freud, Piaget, and now Vygotsky, any reference of non-U.S. contributors to developmental psychology is likely to be meager. This is consistent with a general xenophobic trend in U.S. psychology (Gielen, 1994). Certainly a reader would have to search long and hard through American textbooks to find a mention of such European contributors as Tetens, Preyer, Spranger, Claparède or the Bühlers. And these names represent only a few of the people who were important to the history of developmental psychology.

This chapter discusses a few of the links between American and European developmental psychology. Some of the people mentioned may be familiar, others less so. The list is not meant to be exhaustive, and the reader may know of other names more worthy of inclusion. The chapter does not include Freud, Piaget, or Vygotsky directly, or their immediate followers (e.g., Anna Freud, Bärbel Inhelder), since each has received substantial coverage elsewhere. (The psychoanalytic connections alone would require a chapter at least twice as long as the current one.) More than anything, the chapter should serve as a reminder that, in a very real sense, American psychology, including developmental psychology, has important roots in Europe. If the specialty is to be fully understood and appreciated, a greater understanding of these connections is essential.

EVOLUTIONARY THEORY AND TWO AMERICAN PIONEERS IN DEVELOPMENT

Among scholars, the publication of Charles Darwin's *The Origin of Species* in 1859 is considered one of the most important events of the last century and a half. It is difficult to overestimate the impact of the book on developmental psychology, both in Europe and the United States. While evolutionary ideas had been popular for many years—Charles Darwin's grandfather Erasmus Darwin was a highly visible spokesman for evolutionary theory—the earlier ideas were not supported by data. Charles Darwin's book changed all that, and the impact was enormous.

G. Stanley Hall (1844-1924), the father of developmental psychology in America pronounced himself hypnotized by the word "evolution" (Hall, 1923, p. 357). During much of his life, he promoted a type of evolutionary theory derived from Darwin but based, more directly, on the ideas of Ernst Haeckel of the University of Jena in Germany. The central developmental principle of Haeckel was recapitulation, the belief that individuals, in their development, repeat the history of the development of their species.

Hall's belief in the principle of recapitulation informed much of his work in development, from the publication of his landmark book *Adolescence* (1904), to his use of the questionnaire method. The use of questionnaires eventually came to define much of psychology at Clark University where Hall was president. Hall first published an empirical study using the questionnaire method in 1883. The study was titled "The Contents of Children's Minds" and was inspired by work conducted in Germany, beginning in 1869. The study played a major role in establishing Hall as a leader of the child-study movement in America.

James Mark Baldwin (1861-1934), the other pioneer of American developmental psychology, was also influenced by evolutionary theory but his approach took a different direction from that of Hall. His work constituted one of the first attempts to build a systematic theory of development within the "new" psychology.

Although his thinking was greatly affected by Europeans, notably George Romanes, Herbert Spencer, and Wilhelm Preyer, he, in turn, had an important effect on the field in Europe. Many of his thoughts about child development are seen as precursors to the more detailed, and empirically grounded, work of Jean Piaget. Others find evidence of his work in the developmental theory of Lev Vygotsky. Finally, even Piaget noted Baldwin's impact on the work of Pierre Janet (cited in Cairns, 1992).

EVOLUTIONARY THEORY AND EUROPEAN PIONEERS IN DEVELOPMENT

Wilhelm Preyer (1841-1897), an Englishman who lived and taught in Germany, was another staunch Darwinist. His publication, in 1882, of *Die Seele des Kindes* [The Mind of the Child] is frequently identified as the beginning of the modern child psychology movement (e.g., Hardesty, 1976). Preyer's work was inspired by the publication in 1877 of Darwin's study of his son, William. Preyer's biographical sketch, in turn, stimulated the developmental work of many others, including James M. Baldwin, Karl and Charlotte Bühler, and William Stern (Vidal, Buscaglia, & Vonèche, 1983).

George Romanes (1848-1894), the British biologist, was not only a strong believer in Darwinism, he was also a friend of Charles Darwin himself. Although his earliest work was concerned with sea creatures, he was an early convert to Darwinism and soon became interested in the continuity in cognitive functions between man and animal. He outlined and described a series of increasingly complex cognitive tasks leading to human reasoning. The series could be seen, in contemporary terms, as "resting upon information-processing complexity" (White, 1983, p. 60). This focus on development through species, though now uncommon, was a part of developmental psychology for many years. (See Jahoda, this volume, for a further discussion of Romanes' scale of developmental periods.)

Francis Galton (1822-1911) was a half-cousin to Charles Darwin (they shared a grandfather, Erasmus Darwin) and, although he is not usually thought of as a developmental psychologist, some of his contributions to the specialty were profound. With his role in the formation of statistical correlation, he provided one of the basic tools for psychological research, including research on development. In his quest to find a measure of intelligence to support his work in eugenics, he not only defined the nature/nurture controversy, he also created the co-twin method and collected lifespan data on physical and psychological characteristics. These data were, in their originality, second only to those of Quetelet.

His work on intelligence, though largely unsuccessful, paved the way for the centrality of that concept in later developmental research. Even his emphasis on individual differences helped psychology turn in a new direction. Although it is not generally known, he identified some important influences on development, including the role of parents and birth order. It has even been argued that he "was the first to introduce family structure as a key environmental context affecting the course of human development" (Bronfenbrenner, 1983, p. 152).

THE ETHOLOGICAL SCHOOL

The ethological approach to behavior studies animals and man within an evolutionary context. As such, Darwin may be considered the first ethologist. However, *Konrad Lorenz* (1903-1989) and *Niko Tinbergen* (1907-1988) are usually identified as the first of the modern ethologists. Lorenz, an Austrian, earned a medical degree, then later a Ph.D. in zoology from the University of Vienna. Tinbergen, born in the Netherlands, held a Ph.D. in biology from the University of Leiden. For their ethological work, they were honored in 1973 with the Nobel Prize in medicine and physiology.

Many of the doctrines of the ethological school have found their way into modern developmental psychology. For instance, the belief of ethologists that animals can be understood only in their natural settings can be seen as one of the important beginnings for ecological approaches to human development. Of all their research, however, probably nothing in ethology had more of an impact on developmental research than the depiction by Lorenz of the process of imprinting. Although Lorenz was not the first to study imprinting, his writing on the subject developed an appreciative audience. The implications of his work for human development, particularly for children, were enormous.

Later, the ethologists saw their work extended far beyond their interest in animals. The British psychoanalyst, *John Bowlby* (1907-1990), had observed attachment problems among children who had been raised in institutions or who had experienced significant separations from parents. Such children were frequently unable to form intimate relationships with others. He saw in ethology an explanation for these problems, and he proposed his own critical periods for the development of attachment.

Mary Ainsworth (1913-1999), a Canadian, completed a dissertation titled *Adjustment and the Concept of Security* at the University of Toronto just prior to World War II. She then worked with Bowlby for several years in London, and later conducted research in Uganda and in Baltimore, MD, which helped to modify Bowlby's theory (Bretherton, 1992). Her emphasis was on the range of normal parenting behaviors and the quality of attachment that follows. Ainsworth's "strange situation," which she used to study attachment, has been employed with great frequency in developmental research with young children.

LIFESPAN DEVELOPMENTAL PSYCHOLOGY

Increasingly, more and more developmental writers refer to their approach as a "lifespan" approach. By definition, this approach does not confine itself to age-based or age-limited conceptions of development. Rather it attempts to describe developmental principles that apply to a broader age range.

Although the approach has many adherents in the U.S., its history can be most easily traced to three early European contributors (Baltes, 1983). One of those contributors was *Johann N. Tetens* (1736-1807), a German physicist and philosopher, who not only foresaw the founding of experimental psychology but he is said to have inspired Wundt (Muller-Brettel & Dixon, 1990). He is also thought to have anticipated many of the questions of contemporary developmental psychology. Among other areas, he wrote of nature/nurture issues, language development, and individual differences. His ideas frequently spoke of development as plastic and contextual, with individuals playing an active role in their own development (Baltes, 1983). All of these thoughts are consistent with, even central to, modern ideas of lifespan development.

The two other contributors identified by Baltes as early contributors to the lifespan developmental approach are *Friedrich A. Carus* (1770-1808) and *Adolphe Quetelet* (1796-1874) (Baltes, 1983). Carus, who died young and whose major work was published posthumously, had a view of development that was similar in many ways to Tetens. For Carus, aging was not to be viewed simply in terms of loss and decline, but as an occasion for perfectibility and growth. In that view, he was in the mainstream of lifespan development.

Adolphe Quetelet, a Belgian statistician, was probably the first to collect data on a range of physical and psychological variables across the lifespan. In addition, he highlighted several methodological issues of concern to research in lifespan development. He served as an inspiration to later researchers, including Galton.

Unfortunately, the work of these pioneers in lifespan development was largely ignored both in Europe and the U.S. In both places, the focus of development was on children. It was not until the 1920s and 1930s, with the publication of several textbooks on development (e.g., Hollingworth, 1927; Bühler, 1933; Pressey, Janney, & Kuhlen, 1939), that lifespan approaches began to assume some of their earlier importance (Baltes, 1983).

TWO UNCREDITED DEVELOPMENTALISTS

Two European educator/ psychologists do not usually receive recognition as developmental psychologists, although they are renowned for other work. Yet each made important contributions to the understanding of development. They are *Alfred Binet* (1857-1911) and *Maria Montessori* (1870-1952).

Alfred Binet is best known to students of psychology for his research in the development of the Binet-Simon scales of intelligence which led to the modern era of intelligence testing. What is forgotten is that his work was much more comprehensive, and that it included important contributions to other aspects of cognitive development. At about the same time that G. Stanley Hall was establishing the child study movement in the U.S., Binet was establishing a foundation for modern experimental child psychology at the Sorbonne (Cairns, 1997). It was this work, not Binet's work with testing, which made up the bulk of his research Siegler, 1992).

Binet, who was born in Nice, France, first studied law, and then medicine, but did not complete his studies in the latter. He had no formal university training in psychology, but schooled himself by reading at the national library. He conducted research on hysteria while at La Salpêtriere with Charcot, but his methodology was attacked as flawed. Mortified, he never returned to La Salpêtriere, but he did not make the same methodological errors again.

He became a member of the staff of the Laboratory of Physiological Psychology at the Sorbonne, and later its Director, a position he held until his death. During his 21 years there, he produced more than 200 books, articles, and reviews, in experimental, developmental, educational, social, and differential psychology (Siegler, 1992). Significant among his publications was his work on prose memory, cognitive styles, children's suggestibility, and, of course, the nature of intelligence. His views on cognitive development, particularly its constructivist nature, have been compared to those of Piaget. He is even thought to have made an important contribution to the psychoanalytic movement (Cairns, 1997) Among his other accomplishments, Binet founded an experimental laboratory school, apparently the first such school in Europe (Wolf, 1973).

Maria Montessori is perhaps even better known than Binet, but her contributions are usually thought to be strictly pedagogical. In fact, she developed an extensive theory of development that supported the specifics of her educational system.

Montessori was born in Ancona, Italy, and was trained as a physician, the first woman in modern Italy with such training. Early in her career, she worked with mentally retarded children, and in her attempts to serve them more effectively, she studied the work of Jean-Marc Itard and Edouard Seguin, among others. Later, she took over the leadership of a school for poor children, which she called the *Casa dei Bambini* (Children's House). This school became her laboratory for the study of children.

Her approach to developmental theory owed much to Rousseau and was consistent with others of the European enlightenment. For Montessori, acquisition of knowledge stems from the child's own maturational promptings. The greatest hindrance to a child's spontaneous development is direct intervention by an adult. The primary role of the adult—and the teacher—is to allow the child to mature and become independent and responsible (Hainstock, 1986).

The Montessori approach focused heavily on the use of sensitive periods, which were somewhat similar to the critical periods later used by the ethologists. Such periods were developmental "windows of opportunity" during which children had the chance to master a variety of tasks. If the "window" was not exercised, the opportunity for growth and mastery in this area would be more difficult or, perhaps, impossible. Montessori's sensitive periods were far ranging and included periods for order, motor behavior, and language.

Montessori was ahead of her time in her thoughts on critical periods in intellectual development. Her beliefs about the development of language are consistent with those of the modern theorist, Noam Chomsky (Crain, 1992). Her work has gone through alternate periods of visibility and decline in the U.S. Although she became well known throughout the world early in the century, her work was largely forgotten in the U.S. for several decades. Then, in the 1960s, there was renewed interest in her approach. Although she is not often identified as an important theorist by U.S. developmental psychologists, many of those who were influenced by her are considered very important. They include Anna Freud, Erik Erikson, Alfred Adler, and Jean Piaget.

FOUR NAMES FOR FURTHER STUDY

There are a number of contributors whose work should be better known among U.S. developmental psychologists. From that list, we have chosen four who are of particular interest to us. In our view, the contributions of each have been substantial and unusual, yet each has been largely ignored by mainstream psychology.

Edouard Seguin (1812-1880). Although he had no formal university training, the impact of Edouard Seguin on the education and care of the mentally retarded was profound. Curiously, he is not well known among psychologists in the U.S. even though much of his later work was actually conducted in the U.S. Part of this lack of recognition can be attributed to the focus of his work, the intellectually disabled, a concentration that has not always been considered a part of mainstream developmental psychology.

Some consider Seguin to be more of a teacher than a psychologist, and his credentials as an innovative teacher are strong. However, he conducted studies on the long-term adjustment of the retarded. He promoted the use of meticulous record keeping of behavior over time and mother-interviews in an effort to correlate these data with postmortem information. Taken in its entirety, his approach can be considered to be a broad, almost dynamic, theory of human behavior (Talbot, 1967-1968).

Seguin is probably best known for his association with Jean-Marc Itard, the French physician, who was himself known for his connection with Victor, the Wild Boy of Aveyron. Itard's sense-training techniques formed the core of Seguin's method of teaching the mentally handicapped. Seguin first began an experimental class in 1839 at La Salpêtriere in Paris where he worked with mentally handicapped children. In 1841, he organized a program for exceptional children at the Bicêtre. During this period, Seguin continued to modify Itard's original training methods and supplement them with techniques of his own.

Seguin's effect on theory and practice in America was hastened with his emigration to the U.S. in 1848 as a voluntary political refugee (Kanner, 1960). Seguin was keenly aware of the process of development and used this as a teaching guide for socialization. He was a firm believer in the orderly and predictable sequence of human development. He attempted to produce development in the mentally deficient that was in the "ordinary sequence," with the quality of response expected from that of a normal child.

To advance the understanding of the developmental process, Seguin advocated the comparative study of normal and abnormal development. The need for developmental norms is evident in his work and alluded to in his writing. His desire to extend the use of the physiological method to the teaching of normal children was later realized through the work of Maria Montessori who translated his writing and applied his philosophy to the education of normal children.

William Stern (1871-1938). It is not surprising that the contributions of William Stern are so little known in the United States. Much of his work remains untranslated and many of his papers were destroyed by the Nazis before he left Germany and came to the U.S. in the 1930s. Those who do know his name are likely to identify him as the one who gave psychology the concept of the intelligence quotient.

William Stern was born in Berlin and entered the University of Berlin in 1888 to study philosophy and psychology. He completed his dissertation in 1893 under Hermann Ebbinghaus, and followed Ebbinghaus to the University of Breslau where he remained for 19 years. It was during this period that he produced twelve books and numerous articles on personalistic perspectives in psychology, the role of biological and environmental factors in human development, the psychology of testimony, and differential psychology (Hardesty, 1976; Kreppner, 1992). It was also during this period that he developed the concept of the IQ.

Like many psychologists who were to follow, Stern and his wife observed their own children to learn more about early human development. After analyzing the activities and language use of their children, William and Clara Stern published their findings in a book entitled *Die Kindersprache* [The Language of Children] in 1907. Their investigation of language also included an analysis of the autobiography of Helen Keller, some elements of which were later confirmed during a meeting with her.

In 1915, Stern applied for a professorship in philosophy at the Institute for Colonial Studies in Hamburg that became vacant following the death of Ernst Meumann. The institute quickly evolved into the University of Hamburg and Stern became known as the "most influential psychologist in Germany at that time" (Misiak & Sexton, 1966, p. 108).

Two of Stern's assistants—Heinz Werner and Martha Muchow—helped Stern to establish the Psychological Institute in Hamburg. Later, they each became well-known psychologists in their own right. Werner, who eventually taught at Clark University in the U.S., became recognized for his organismic and comparative theories of development. Muchow became known for her work in the field of environmental psychology.

Much of Stern's work focused on what he considered the "personalistic perspective" of human development (Eyferth, 1976). Unlike many of his colleagues, Stern did not believe that human beings could be viewed as a set of individual functions. Rather, he felt that one must understand the whole person, including the individual's intentions and motivation. Stern argued that one must recognize and understand the roles played by the environment, the person, and the interaction between the two (Kreppner, 1992). Along with many scholars who had been banned from German institutions, Stern emigrated to the United States where, in 1934, he accepted a professorship at Duke University, but he died only a few years later.

Henri Wallon (1879-1962). Although he is considered one of the founding fathers of French child psychology, the work of Henri Wallon is almost entirely unknown in the U.S., as it is in most English-speaking countries. The reasons for his obscurity are not clear although several possibilities have been suggested (Birns, 1973; Van der Veer, 1996). Among them, he wrote only in French and his style was complex. In addition, he was an avowed Marxist and his work overlapped considerably with that of Piaget.

Wallon was born in Paris to a politically active family, and he grew up sensitive to what he believed to be his societal responsibilities. He began to teach at the Sorbonne in 1919, and in 1937 was named the first professor of child psychology at the prestigious Collège de France. Early in his career he was a member of the Socialist Party. Later, during the German occupation of France in the 1940s, he joined the Communist Party. He founded the Laboratoire de Psycho-Biologie de l'Enfant in 1922, at which he worked until his death (Netchine-Grynberg, 1991). Among his influences were Pierre Janet, whom he succeeded at the Collège de France, and his teacher and close personal friend, L. Lévy-Bruhl.

Wallon is frequently compared to Piaget and Vygotsky, and the comparisons are appropriate. Vygotsky is believed to have been influenced by Wallon's work (Van der Veer, 1996), and all three agreed on many important items. However, they also differed in substantial ways. Trained as a physician, Wallon was interested in abnormal as well as normal development. Committed to Marxism, he had a deep interest in the power of the environment to shape lives, an interest he shared with Vygotsky. Another interest they shared was the role of cultural tools, and the way in which the child "is part of a world already organized at the material and the symbolic levels" (Netchine-Grynberg, 1991, p. 364).

Typically, Wallon drew on cross-cultural data to understand development. While Piaget was interested in the way the child manipulated the environment, he appeared less interested in the effect of the environment on the child (Birns, 1973). In this sense, Wallon might be considered more of an interactionist than Piaget.

Among the other differences between Wallon and Piaget were their approaches to the role of language and the development of imitation (Birns, 1973). More fundamentally, Wallon was interested not only in the cognitive development of the child, which Piaget had studied so completely, but also in emotional development. In Wallon's view, the two interacted and should not be considered separately. Such a difference has great importance when considering practical issues such as compensatory education. For Wallon, a compensatory educational program would be useless, and show no cognitive progress, without also focusing on the emotional support behind it.

For Wallon, a child's affective states are expressed in certain motor behaviors that are then subject to social interpretation. These interpretations lead to the specific expression of the affective states themselves. It is this social aspect which so distinguishes Wallon from Piaget. In the area of child care, Wallon wrote of the shared emotions which link children and their caregivers. This work was apparently the inspiration for some of the contributions of René Spitz regarding attachment (Van der Veer, 1996)

Mikhail Basov (1892-1931) is probably the most obscure name of all those mentioned here. Nonetheless, his innovations in developmental psychology in Russia were highly valued by Vygotsky and others, and he was given a prominent role in Russian developmental psychology in an early overview by Luria (Valsiner, 1988). Today, he is all but unknown, even in Russia.

Basov, born to a peasant family, entered the St. Petersburg Psychoneurology Institute in 1909 where he was exposed to research in both personality-oriented and behavioristic explanations of behavior. Although he later worked under Bekterev, he never became a complete behaviorist. He was always attempting to bridge the gap between the subjective world and the behavioral one (Valsiner, 1988). His "pedology" was more than simply data collection; it was an attempt to build a science of development (Valsiner, 1991b). In fact, Basov made it clear that his principles of development had equal applicability for adults (Basov, 1991).

In 1923, Basov published a manual for the observation of children in naturalistic settings. In its detail, it is said to contain many lessons for the contemporary developmentalist. "The emphasis on the richness of empirical observational detail together with theoretically thoughtful and careful analysis...remains unsurpassed up to the present time in all of Soviet psychology, and in most international research that uses observational methods to study child development" (Valsiner, 1988, p. 169).

From the early 1920s until his death, Basov worked with a small but active research group that he had established. They investigated such topics as perceptual processes in preschoolers, the structure of free play in young children, and methodological issues of observational research (Valsiner & Van der Veer, 1991a). During this period he also initiated a large scale investigation of children's conceptions of social issues.

Like Vygotsky, Basov drew ideas from many different sources. Within psychology, his approach had elements of Gestalt theory, including that of Kurt Lewin, as well as the thinking of Claparède and Piaget (Valsiner, 1988). Above all, he seemed to be a synthesizer.

Central to his concept of development was his emphasis on the "active organism," which he considered the very essence of development (Basov, 1991). Such thinking is, of course, consistent with that of Piaget and much of contemporary interactionist writing. At the time, it also fit in well with Marxism, although he did receive some criticism in this regard toward the end of his life.

Some have argued that Basov's contributions are comparable in value to that of Vygotsky (Valsiner, 1988) or, perhaps, even surpass them. In any case, most agree that he has remained unnoticed for too long. Mikhail Basov died suddenly of a work-related accident at the age of 38 (Valsiner & Van der Veer, 1991b).

SUMMARY AND CONCLUSIONS

This chapter has touched on only a few historical connections between European and U.S. developmental psychology. The entire history is richer and, sadly, not often told. It should be. Psychologists in the U.S. need to be reminded that many of their achievements found their beginnings in Europe. Besides, European psychology regularly reimported American ideas when it was useful to do so.

In the early years of developmental psychology, European and U.S. relationships were clearer. Most students of history know that America's first great developmentalist, G. Stanley Hall, brought Sigmund Freud to America where psychoanalysis flourished as it did nowhere else. How many know that

Hall also brought Preyer's *Die Seele des Kindes* to the U.S., providing the introduction to the American publication of the volume (Cairns, 1997)? Or, that at the same ceremony at Clark University in which Sigmund Freud received an honorary degree (the only one he would ever receive), an honorary degree was also conferred upon William Stern?

An understanding of these connections enriches our psychology. It helps us to appreciate many of the ideas and the people who have preceded us. More than that, it reminds us of the mutual enhancement of U.S. and European psychology which resulted from the sharing of ideas. Perhaps, most of all, it reminds us of the need to continue to share our ideas.

BIBLIOGRAPHY

Baltes, P. B. (1983). Life-span developmental psychology: Observations on history and theory revisited. In R. M. Lerner (Ed.), *Developmental philosophical psychology: Historical and perspectives* (pp. 79-111). Hillsdale, NJ: Erlbaum

Basov, M. I. (1991). The problem of development in psychology. *Soviet Psychology*, *29*(5), 41-43.

Birns, B. (1973). Piaget and Wallon: Two giants of unequal visibility. *International Journal of Mental Health*, *1*(4), 24-28.

Boring, E. G. (1950). *A history of experimental psychology* (2nd ed.). New York: Appleton Century.

Bretherton, I. (1992). The origins of attachment theory: John Bowlby and Mary Ainsworth. *Developmental Psychology*, *28*, 759-775.

Bronfenbrenner, U. (1983). Context of development and development of context. In R. M. Lerner (Ed.), *Developmental psychology: Historical and philosophical perspectives* (pp. 147-184). Hillsdale, NJ: Erlbaum

Bühler, C. (1933). *Der menschliche Lebenslauf als psychologisches Problem.* [The human life cycle as a psychological problem]. Leipzig: Hirzel.

Cairns, R. B. (1992). The making of a developmental science: The contributions and intellectual heritage of James Mark Baldwin. *Developmental Psychology*, *28*, 17-24.

Cairns, R. B. (1997). The making of developmental psychology. In W. Damon (Ed.), *The handbook of child psychology* (5th ed.) (pp. 25-105). New York: Wiley.

Crain, W. (1992). *Theories of development: Concepts and applications* (3rd ed.). Englewood Cliffs, NJ: Prentice Hall.

Eyferth, K. (1976). The contribution of William and Clara Stern to the onset of developmental psychology. In K. Riegel & J. A. Meacham (Eds.), *The developing individual in a changing world, Vol. 1: Historical and cultural issues* (pp. 9-15). The Hague: Mouton.

Gielen, U. P. (1994). American mainstream psychology and its relationship to international and cross-cultural psychology. In A. L. Comunian & U. P. Gielen (Eds.), *Advancing psychology and its applications: International perspectives* (pp. 26-40). Milan: FrancoAngeli.

Hainstock, E. (1986). Montessori's views of her work. In E. Hainstock (Ed.), *The essential Montessori: Introduction to the woman, the writings, the method, and the movement* (pp. 46-90). New York: Plume.

Hall, G. S. (1904). *Adolescence: Its psychology and its relations to physiology, anthropology, sociology, sex, crime, religion and education.* New York: Appleton.

Hall, G. S. (1923). *Life and confessions of a psychologist.* New York: Appleton.

Hardesty, F. P. (1976). Early European contributions to developmental psychology. In K. Riegel & J. A. Meacham (Eds.) *The developing individual in a changing world, Vol. I: Historical and cultural issues* (pp. 3-8). The Hague: Mouton.

Hollingworth, H. L. (1927). *Mental growth and decline: A survey of developmental psychology.* New York: Appleton.

Kanner, L. (1960). Itard, Seguin, Howe—Three pioneers in the education of retarded children. *American Journal of Mental Deficiency, 65,* 2-10.

Kreppner, K. (1992). William L. Stern (1871-1938): A neglected founder of developmental psychology. *Developmental Psychology, 28,* 539-547.

Lerner, R. M. (Ed.). (1983). *Developmental psychology: Historical and philosophical perspectives.* Hillsdale, NJ: Erlbaum

Misiak, H., & Sexton, V. S. (1966). *History of psychology: An overview.* New York: Grune & Stratton.

Muller-Brettel, M., & Dixon, R. A. (1990). Johann Nicolas Tetens: A forgotten father of developmental psychology? *International Journal of Behavioral Development, 13,* 215-230.

Netchine-Grynberg, G. (1991). The theories of Henri Wallon: From act to thought. *Human Development, 34,* 363-379.

Parke, R., Ornstein, P. A., Rieser, J. J., & Zahn-Waxler, C. (Eds.). (1994). *A century of developmental psychology.* Washington, DC: American Psychological Association.

Pressey, S. L., Janney, J. E., & Kuhlen, R. G. (1939). *Life: A psychological survey.* New York: Harper.

Riegel, K., & Meacham, J. A. (Eds.). (1976). *The developing individual in a changing world, Vol. 1: Historical and cultural issues.* The Hague: Mouton.

Ross, D. (1972). *G. Stanley Hall: The psychologist as prophet.* Chicago, IL: University of Chicago Press.

Siegler, R. S. (1992). The other Alfred Binet. *Developmental Psychology, 28,*

179-190.

Talbot, M. (1964). *Edouard Seguin: A study of an educational approach to the treatment of mentally defective children.* New York: Teachers College Press.

Talbot, M. (1967-1968). Edouard Seguin. *American Journal of Mental Deficiency, 72,* 184-189.

Valsiner, J. (1988). *Developmental psychology in the Soviet Union.* Bloomington, IN: Indiana University Press.

Valsiner, J., & Van der Veer, R. (1991a). Mikhail Basov: An intellectual biography. *Soviet Psychology, 29*(5), 6-13.

Valsiner, J., & Van der Veer, R. (1991b). Introduction. *Soviet Psychology, 29*(6), 3-7.

Van der Veer, R. (1996). Henri Wallon's theory of early child development: The role of emotions. *Developmental Review, 16,* 364-390.

Vidal, F., Buscaglia, M., & Vonèche, J. J. (1983). Darwinism and developmental psychology. *Journal of the History of the Behavioral Sciences, 19,* 81-94.

White, S. (1983). The idea of development in developmental psychology. In R. M. Lerner (Ed.), *Developmental psychology: Historical and philosophical perspectives* (pp. 55-77). Hillsdale, NJ: Erlbaum

Wolf, T. H. (1973). *Alfred Binet.* Chicago, IL: University of Chicago Press.

RECENT TRENDS IN CROSS-CULTURAL STUDIES OF HUMAN DEVELOPMENT: THE ROLE OF CURRENT RESEARCH TRADITIONS

Deborah L. Best
Wake Forest University, U.S.A.

In 1975, Lee and Ruth Munroe wrote *Cross-Cultural Human Development*, a short text designed as a supplement to the current developmental textbooks available, none of which did more than mention some behavior or practice in a culture or two that was "different" from those in Western cultures, such as the Hopi's use of cradle boards or Margaret Mead's research in New Guinea (Best & Ruther, 1994). One could assume that the authors of these texts included these pithy views of other cultures to make the reading more interesting for the typical undergraduate. None of these cultural entries made comparisons with other cultures nor did they even attempt to examine possible causal factors involved. Culture was seen as neither an independent variable nor an organizing variable, simply as an anomalous variable.

The Munroes' book was the first comprehensive attempt to gather cross-cultural developmental research into a textbook format that cast human development in a broad perspective. The first chapter of the book examined life stages in three traditional cultures (the Ainu of Japan, the Trobrianders of Melanesia, and the Gusii of East Africa) and the next seven chapters covered standard developmental topics—physical growth and motor skills; affect; language and perception; cognition; dependence, aggression and sex; sex roles; and social motives. These topics continue today to be fundamental research areas in both mainstream and cross-cultural developmental psychology.

The Munroes' small text began the trickle in the 1980s and early 1990s of books, most not in textbook format, devoted to cross-cultural developmental issues: The *Handbook of Cross-Cultural Human Development* in 1981, and books by Bornstein (1980), Stevenson and Wagner (1982), Fishbein (1984), Dasen and Jahoda (1986), Super (1987), Lamb and his colleagues (Lamb, Sternberg, Hwang, & Broberg, 1992), to name a few. As one might expect, mainstream developmental textbooks incorporated cross-cultural issues at a slower pace than did the literature directed toward the professional audiences, a trend reported in a paper several years ago that examined developmental textbooks, handbooks, and book series for the *Journal of Cross-Cultural Psychology* (Best & Ruther, 1994). Today, most researchers involved with cross-cultural developmental psychology are besieged with requests to add cross-cultural and cultural themes to texts being published, or to review what another author has already written to see if the cross-cultural and cultural information is appropriate. Suddenly, cross-cultural psychology is in demand, particularly in the textbook world where marketing is of the essence.

Yet, after all this attention, the question remains: "Has mainstream developmental psychology begun to take culture seriously?" In their introduction to Volume 2 of the *Handbook of Cross-Cultural Psychology* (1997) which was just published, Volume Editors Saraswathi and Dasen answer this question with "Not really." They lament the fact that there is little evidence that new developmental theories are systematically put to the cross-cultural test, even such approaches as life-span development, neo-Piagetian theories, or co-constructivism that include sociocultural dimensions from the beginning. As with the more traditional theories, there is an enormous time lag between the emergence of a theory, usually in the context of a single culture, and its application to other cultural settings. Non-cross-cultural psychologists are cautious these days not to claim universality for their theories without explicit testing, but the assumption is often implicit.

In 1994 almost 20 years after its first publication, the Munroes were asked to reissue their 1975 book, and in the Preface to the 1994 edition, they expressed the feeling that they should justify its reissue. The Munroes suggested that their book continued to offer something to the field of human development because it has a comparative orientation and because it is thoroughly cross-cultural, permitting the evaluation of the robustness of Western-based findings for various developmental topics (Munroe & Munroe, 1994). Truly cross-cultural books are conspicuously absent even today, with only a few exceptions (e.g., Cole & Cole, 1996; Gardiner, Mutter, & Kosmitzki, 1998).

In the foreword to the reissued book, the Munroes identified four current research traditions that differ markedly in approach and their categorization is similar to those identified by other researchers (Cole, 1992; Laboratory of Comparative and Human Cognition [LCHC], 1983; Super & Harkness, 1994). These theoretical approaches to research often become the lenses through which behavior is examined, focusing broadly when searching cross-culturally for developmental universals, or more narrowly when seeking to understand an individual's behavior in its historical-cultural context (e.g., Cole, 1996). As a way of reviewing cross-cultural psychology's recent achievements, these research traditions will be described along with one or two of the most recent studies that have used each approach in addressing developmental questions.

SOCIOBEHAVIORAL APPROACHES (MUNROE & MUNROE, 1994)/CONTEXT-SPECIFIC APPROACHES (LCHC, 1983)

This approach has close ties with the anthropological emphasis on the naturalistic observation of children's behavior in everyday settings. The sociobehavioral tradition was initiated by the Whitings' Six Culture Study (Minturn & Lambert, 1964; Whiting, 1963; Whiting, Child, Lambert, Fischer, Fischer, Nydegger, Nydegger, Maretzki, Maretzik, Minturn,

Romney, & Romney, 1966; Whiting & Whiting, 1975) and the addition of six new societies from sub-Saharan Africa and India (Whiting & Edwards, 1988). This context-specific framework treats culture and aspects of development as parts of a single, interactive system of coordination between individuals and the contexts of their everyday lives (LCHC, 1983). The traditional environmental view, which can be traced back to Locke, shares many similarities with this position, as do American learning theories.

The Whitings' studies demonstrated impressive cross-cultural commonalties in interpersonal behavior that were predicted by the company that children keep. In the societies studied, a child's behavior was shown to be dependent with its mother, dominant with younger peers, and nurturing with infants. Patterns of aggressive behaviors were also found, with boys showing more aggression than girls in eight societies, equal levels of aggression in two, and lower aggression in none (Munroe & Munroe, 1994). Gay and Cole's (Gay, 1973; Gay & Cole, 1967) descriptions of Kpelle (Liberian) children's difficulties in learning mathematics in Western-style schools and Super's (Super, 1981a, 1981b) examination of Kipsigi (Kenya) infants' precocious motor development describe the context-specific viewpoint, as does Munroe and Munroe's (1992) four-culture observational study examining the development of aggression in father-absent versus father-present 3- to 9-year-old boys. While the Munroes' findings demonstrated that socialization resulted in context specific sex roles, other research demonstrates the strong cross-cultural consensus in stereotypes about the characteristics that both children and adults attribute to males and females (Williams & Best, 1982, 1990). These somewhat contradictory findings point to the differences that can be found with dissimilar methodologies even when looking at related behaviors.

Two sociobehavioral studies (Arrowood & Best, 1997; Best & Arrowood, 1997), resulting from questions generated by Williams and Best's (1982, 1990) previous stereotype research, using this methodology have just been completed in five European countries (England, Finland, France, Germany, Turkey) and the U.S.A. The first is an observational study of public interpersonal interactions and the second is a questionnaire study exploring attitudes toward touching and physical displays of affection. The convenience of small video cameras has simplified naturalistic observations, making this very time-consuming approach less onerous. While this approach may have changed with technological innovations, it continues to be a valuable context-specific cross-cultural approach for studying behavior.

The remarkable stability in relationships between the biophysical makeup and the socioecological setting are clearly seen with the context-specific, sociobehavioral approach. Indeed, limits on the generalizations of behaviors are demonstrated in these studies, calling attention to the value of cross-cultural research in providing a potentially broad range of behavioral variation.

Antecedent and consequent events in a child's culture determine what behaviors will develop.

Current Research

One of the most fascinating yet abhorrent problems societies face today concerns children growing up in difficult circumstances, an area of literature reviewed by Aptekar and Stöcklin in the new *Handbook of Cross-Cultural Psychology* (1997). They point out that "difficult circumstances" can be a culturally misleading category since cultural factors determine how circumstances and situations are interpreted. For example, in the recent war between Iraq and Iran, Iranian children willingly marched at the head of the front lines to trip land mines, protecting the following adults who could fight the infidels. These children were given the religious status of martyrs and their behaviors were condoned by the state (Boothby, 1986). Was this behavior abusive? Is it abusive for parents who are suffering famine and cannot feed all their children sufficiently to concentrate their resources on only a few? These situations illustrate how different cultural values and circumstances can lead to different interpretations.

Aptekar and Stöcklin review the extensive literature on the lives of street children and of children exposed to severe stress, some of whom develop post-traumatic stress disorder. Observations of these children demonstrate that it is not just the type or degree of violence that a child experiences that determines his or her psychological response. Cultural context and values mediate the sometimes horrendous events that children in particularly difficult circumstances experience.

BIO-EVOLUTIONARY APPROACHES (MUNROE & MUNROE, 1994)

An extension of the neo-Darwinian and ecological traditions, this approach uses concepts such as "variation selection" and "adaptation" (LeVine, 1982), "developmental niche" (Super & Harkness, 1986, 1994), and "reproductive strategy" (Draper & Harpending, 1982) to examine the cultural-evolutionary adaptedness of child-rearing, the culturally constructed microenvironment of the child, and differences between fathers who invest in parenting and those who invest in frequent but unstable sexual relationships (Munroe & Munroe, 1994; see also the chapter by Keller in this book). As with the first approach, the emphasis has been on studying children in their natural environments.

Current Research

Super, Harkness, and their colleagues (Super, Harkness, van Tijen, van der

Vlugt, Dykstra, & Fintelman, 1996) have recently reported on a study concerning parents' socialization of infant arousal states in Dutch and American families. While there has been occasional cross-cultural scrutiny of related topics, such as bedtime routines (Wolf, Lozoff, Latz, & Paludetto, 1996) and co-sleeping (Abott, 1992; Morelli, Rogoff, Oppenheim, & Goldsmith, 1992), there are virtually no previous studies of the larger patterns of engagement and respite (the one exception is Super & Harkness, 1982). In their study, data were collected on the basis of parental interviews, diaries of infant experiences, and behavioral observations in the home. They found that parents in the two communities studied held different ethnothcories of sleep and arousal that reflected the organization of daily life, and these beliefs were related to the environmentally induced patterns of arousal found in their infants. Although these two cultures are Western and somewhat similar, parents in the two communities had divergent cultural histories that led to the creation of different culturally integrated developmental niches in which infant arousal patterns developed.

It is interesting to note that Super and Harkness are grappling with some of the same questions dealt with 40 years earlier by Sears, Maccoby, and Levin in their *Patterns of Child Rearing* (1957). Sears and his colleagues identified three kinds of questions that can be asked about child-rearing practices and values. First, and the simplest, is "How do parents rear children?" This wants a purely descriptive answer. The second goes deeper and asks what effects different kinds of training have on children. The third relates to the mothers themselves, asking what leads a mother to use one method rather than another. These three questions parallel Super and Harkness' (1997) conceptualizations of the cultural environment as a social setting for daily life, as a collection of customary practices that convey messages to the child, and as a reality fashioned by the caretakers' shared beliefs about children and child care. Each of these sheds light on the larger problem of culture and individual development but each neglects important insights, failing to integrate various elements of the child's cultural environment and ignoring the endogenous aspects of development that necessarily interact with the environment.

It is interesting to note that Sears and colleagues lamented that "in spite of its proverbial importance as a determinant of adult character, [child-rearing] has not been much investigated by scientific procedures....If personality is partly a product of childhood experiences, then there seems some likelihood, too, that the forms of behavior which characterize a whole society may be partly explicable on the same basis" (p. 2, p. 4). They saw child-rearing practices as a process that could help explain both the development of personality and the transmission of culture.

COGNITIVE APPROACHES (MUNROE & MUNROE, 1994)/
UNIVERSALISTIC APPROACHES (LCHC, 1983)

This orientation stretches back to the early 19th century when researchers wanted to see how traditional peoples would perform on standardized psychological tests and instruments (Haddon, 1901; Péron, 1807-1816; Porteus, 1931, 1937). Generally a standard task was used, and it was assumed to be universally valid and culturally neutral. The inherent assumption in these studies was that there were no important cultural variations, with development following a universal course. Whatever differences were found between cultural groups were only superficial and inconsequential.

With the increased interest in Piaget's stage theory in the late 1960s, cross-cultural research on children's cognitive development became prevalent (Berry & Dasen, 1974). Questions focused on whether Piaget's cognitive stages were universal and whether individuals in all cultural groups would proceed through these stages in a fixed order, as his theory suggested. Cross-cultural findings indicate that the concrete operational stage is general and coherent, but its emergence varies considerably across both individuals and across cultures. On the other hand, the stage of formal operations is closely tied to culture, even in Western societies, and it only appears under certain conditions (Segall, Dasen, Berry, & Poortinga, 1990). Similarly, cross-cultural tests of Kohlberg's cognitive-developmental theory of moral reasoning have shown stage-like, perhaps universal patterns at the lower levels but limited consistencies at the higher levels, particularly with more traditional cultural groups (Eckensberger, 1994; Eckensberger & Zimba, 1997; Edwards, 1981; Harkness, Edwards, & Super, 1981; Snarey, 1985; see the chapters by Lind and by Gielen & Miao in this volume).

Evaluations of formal education also have followed this approach and have shown that children's performance improves with the acquisition of effective information-processing strategies (Rogoff, 1981). Schooling experiences that may appear to be similar, e.g., USA vs. Japanese and Taiwanese children (Stevenson & Stigler, 1992), often lead to different levels of performance, prompting researchers to seek more subtle explanations.

Although stage-theory-based research that finds cultural differences may lead to conceptions of inferiority and superiority, such as deficit models of cultural variation, most researchers have zealously avoided such comparisons and have focused on cognitive processes and structures (Dasen, 1977; Dasen & Heron, 1981).

Current Research

Since the emergence of psychology around the beginning of the century, the parent-child relationship has been given central status in the development of personality and socialization, perhaps largely due to Freud's early conceptualization of personality (Lamb, Ketterlinus, & Fracasso, 1992). The most popular conception of the process of parent-child attachment is that of Bowlby (1969) and Ainsworth (1979). According to this model, individual differences in attachment behavior are generally assessed using the Strange Situation (Ainsworth & Wittig, 1969; Ainsworth, Blehar, Waters, & Wall, 1978), designed to subject 10- to 24-month-old infants to increasing stress induced by brief separation from the parent and the entrance of an unfamiliar person. The infant's Strange Situation behavior is assumed to reflect the quality of the parent-child relationship and to predict future social behavior.

When American infants and parents are observed in the Strange Situation, around 70% demonstrate secure attachment behaviors (pattern B; proximity seeking, fear of strangers, separation anxiety, joy at reunion), about 20% behave in an avoiding manner (pattern A; turning away from parent at reunion), and around 10% show resistant behaviors (pattern C; ambivalent and rejecting of reunion, no parent-as-safe-base exploration). In a recent chapter, Lamb, Ketterlinus, and Fracasso (1992) reviewed findings from a number of studies conducted in other countries using the Strange Situation and found that even though the procedure is structurally the same, it appears to have different psychological meaning for infants in other cultures. Higher proportions of Japanese and Israeli kibbutz infants were classified as resistant (C), and a very high number of German infants were avoidant (A). Research with Hispanic mothers and infants in the USA revealed different maternal behaviors than those found with European-Americans and also dramatic sex differences: 2/3 of the boys were securely attached, but 2/3 of the girls were insecurely attached, a pattern not generally found in other cultures studied. Culture-specific rearing practices and/or temperamental differences accounted for at least some of the variation found across cultures, but the findings also challenge the validity of the Strange Situation when used in different sociocultural contexts. (For additional research related to this approach, see the chapter by Freedman, Olafsdottir, Guoan, Park, and Gorman in this volume.)

CULTURAL-CONTEXT FRAMEWORK (MUNROE & MUNROE, 1994)/CULTURAL PRACTICES PERSPECTIVE (LCHC, 1983)/ CULTURAL-HISTORICAL ACTIVITY THEORY (COLE, 1996)

This perspective is commonly associated with the Russian psychologists Leontiev, Luria, and Vygotsky (Leontiev, 1981; Luria, 1976, 1979, 1981; cf. van der Veer & Valsiner, 1991; Vygotsky, 1978; Wertsch, 1985) who recognized the importance of the cultural-historical context in which the child grows up (Cole, 1996; Cole & Cole, 1993; Gauvain, 1993). Universal stages of development could be altered by sufficiently different contextual frameworks. For example, Brazilian street vendor children have been shown to solve rather complicated math problems 98% of the time using their informal "street arithmetic" but solved equivalent problems only 37% of the time when using standard algorithms in school (Carraher, Carraher, & Schielmann, 1985). Indeed, learning to read and write, independent of schooling, appears to produce very limited consequences instead of more pervasive cognitive enrichment (Cole, 1978; Scribner & Cole, 1981).

Rogoff's (1990) studies of guided participation have shown a mechanism by which Vygotsky's zone of proximal development can impact cognitive development. Variations in everyday cognitive skills (reading, weaving) and values (speed in performance, harmonious interaction) which reflect the role of culture are learned and practiced in very different situations (Lave, 1988; Rogoff & Lave, 1984; Segall et al., 1990). Specific developmental situations and the activities of daily life shape the course of cognitive development. However, by focusing on specific pieces of behavior, it becomes difficult to discern global characteristics of mental life that generalize broadly across contexts (Cole, 1990; Jahoda, 1980). The physical features of the environment, the social sharing of knowledge, and the presence of cultural resources, such as language and literacy, help provide a bridge between contexts (LCHC, 1983).

Current Research

One of the most challenging questions on the horizon for developmental psychologists today concerns the formidable controversies that have arisen regarding formal school education. In Volume 2 of the new *Handbook of Cross-Cultural Psychology*, Serpell and Hatano (1997) discuss some of the current debates and the social histories of schooling in three different sociocultural traditions: The Western tradition of Europe and the USA, the Sino-Japanese tradition linking China with Japan, and the Islamic tradition. For these three traditions, the central culturally derived themes of child development differ: Individual self-expression, cognitive detachment, and technical expertise are stressed in Western culture; moral perfectibility and emulation in the Sino-Japanese tradition; and definitive authority of sacred texts in the Islamic tradition. Western models of schooling have become a part of the accepted model of modernization adopted by international development agencies. Serpell's (1993) longitudinal study of how schooling impacted the everyday lives and careers of young people in rural Zambia found many who were disillusioned, with few who were adequately skilled enough to enter technical occupations. The basic curriculum was essentially alien in form and content from the indigenous culture of the students' homes. Serpell and Hatano suggest that because there are many ways of learning literacy, or mathematics, science, etc., there must be many different ways of teaching. A culturally sensitive method of assessing cognitive development must go beyond the pre-established models and attend to the sociocultural goals of education.

CONCLUSIONS

As is evident from this brief review of methodologies and recent research, understanding variability both within and across cultural settings is one of the ultimate goals of developmental psychology. Developmental psychologists are just beginning to understand the role of cross-cultural variation and the impact of culture on the developmental process.

In the 1960s and 1970s, comparative research illuminated the existence of behavioral and developmental variations outside the American and European middle-class tradition which had dominated developmental research until that time. Early *sociobehavioral* research, pioneered by the Whitings and their colleagues, highlighted naturalistic observation of children's behavior in everyday situations and demonstrated the coordination between biophysical maturation and the socioecological context in which development takes place. By conceptualizing development as a unitary, interactive nature-nurture system, these context-specific studies revealed the limits of behavioral generalization. While sharing the sociobehavioral emphasis on children's natural environment, *bio-evolutionary* studies addressed the adaptedness of the behaviors that developed within culturally constructed niches. In the 1980s, researchers began examining causality, or independent variables, looking at broad aspects of cultural variation and their relationship to different patterns of development (Super & Harkness, 1997). *Cognitive, universalistic* approaches, which had prompted widespread cross-cultural comparisons as early as the beginning of the 19th century, shifted toward the examination of factors that mediated differences in cognitive performance. The effects of schooling and other experiences that influence the acquisition of more effective information-processing strategies became the focus.

The 1990s have seen the acceptance of the crucial role that cultural regulation plays in development and the emphasis has shifted to investigating how such regulation occurs. Examination of *cultural practices* has demonstrated that biologically driven universal stages of development can be altered or negated by sufficiently different *cultural contexts*.

It is evident that transitions in the general theoretical and methodological perspectives in cross-cultural and cultural psychology over the past few decades have helped to reframe questions concerning the process of development. However, understanding intracultural variation, for example how children move between cultural settings such as between home and school, has not yet been achieved. Understanding consistency/inconsistency and continuity/discontinuity of behaviors across specific developmental situations continues to pose an immense challenge for developmental psychology.

In our pursuit of Wundt's "second psychology" (Farr, 1983), the one in which the task is to understand how culture enters into the psychological process, our research lenses must clearly focus upon variability both between and within cultures in order to achieve a clear understanding human development.

BIBLIOGRAPHY

Abbott, S. (1992). Holding on and pushing away: Comparative perspectives on an Eastern Kentucky child-rearing practice. *Ethos*, *20*, 33-65.

Ainsworth, M.D.S. (1979). Attachment as related to mother-infant attachment. In J.G. Rosenblatt, R.A. Hinde, C. Beer, & M. Busnel (Eds.), *Advances in the study of behavior* (Vol. 9, pp. 1-51). New York: Academic Press.

Ainsworth, M.D., Blehar, M.C., Waters, E., & Wall, S. (1978). *Patterns of attachment*. Hillsdale, NJ: Erlbaum.

Ainsworth, M.D.S., & Wittig, B.A. (1969). Attachment and exploratory behavior of one-year-olds in a strange situation. In B.M. Foss (Ed.), *Determinants of infant behavior* (Vol. 4, pp. 111-136). London: Methuen.

Aptekar, L., & Stöcklin, D. (1997). Children in particularly difficult circumstances. In J.W. Berry, P.R. Dasen, & T.S. Saraswathi (Eds.), *Handbook of cross-cultural psychology: Vol. 2. Basic processes and human development* (pp. 377-412). Boston, MA: Allyn and Bacon.

Arrowood, K.N., & Best, D.L. (1997). *Touch me, touch me not: Across-cultural study of attitudes toward haptic behavior*. Unpublished manuscript. Wake Forest University.

Berry, J.W., & Dasen, P.R. (Eds.). (1974). *Culture and cognition: Readings in cross-cultural psychology*. London: Methuen.

Best, D.L., & Arrowood, K.N. (1997). *Social interactions: Across-cultural look at distance, eye contact, and body orientation*. Unpublished manuscript. Wake Forest University.

Best, D.L., & Ruther, N. (1994). Cross-cultural themes in developmental psychology: An examination of texts, handbooks, and reviews. *Journal of Cross-Cultural Psychology*, *25*, 54-77.

Boothby, N. (1986). Children and war. *Cultural Survival Quarterly*, *10*, 28-30.

Bornstein, M. (1980). Cross-cultural developmental psychology. In M.H.

Bornstein (Ed.), *Comparative methods in psychology* (pp. 231-281). Hillsdale, NJ: Erlbaum.

Bowlby, J. (1969). *Attachment and loss: Vol. 1. Attachment.* New York: Basic.

Carraher, T.N., Carraher, D.W., & Schliemann, A.D. (1985). Mathematics in the streets and in schools. *British Journal of Developmental Psychology, 3,* 21-29.

Cole, M. (1978). Literacy without schooling: Testing for intellectual effects. *Harvard Educational Review, 48,* 448-460.

Cole, M. (1990). Cultural psychology: A once and future discipline? In J.J. Berman (Ed.), *Nebraska symposium on motivation, 1989* (Vol. 37, pp. 279-335). Lincoln, NE: University of Nebraska Press.

Cole, M. (1992). Culture in development. In M.H. Bornstein & M.E. Lamb (Eds.), *Developmental psychology: An advanced textbook* (3rd ed., pp. 731-789). Hillsdale, NJ: Erlbaum.

Cole, M. (1996). *Cultural psychology: A once and future discipline.* Cambridge, MA: Harvard University Press.

Cole, M., & Cole, S.R. (1993). *The development of children* (2nd ed.). New York: Scientific American Books.

Cole, M., & Cole, S.R. (1996). *The development of children* (3rd ed.). New York: Scientific American Books.

Dasen, P.R. (Ed.). (1977). *Piagetian psychology.* New York: Gardner Press.

Dasen, P.R., & Heron, A. (1981). Cross-cultural tests of Piaget's theory. In H.C. Triandis & A. Heron (Eds.), *Handbook of cross-cultural psychology* (Vol. 4, pp. 295-341). Boston, MA: Allyn and Bacon.

Dasen, P.R., & Jahoda, G. (Eds.). (1986). Cross-cultural human development: Special issue. *International Journal of Behavioral Development, 9,* 417-437.

Draper, P., & Harpending, H. (1982). Father absence and reproductive strategy. *Journal of Anthropological Research, 38,* 255-273.

Eckensberger, L.H. (1994). Moral development and its measurement across cultures. In W.J. Lonner & R. Malpass (Eds.), *Psychology and culture* (pp. 71-78). Boston, MA: Allyn and Bacon.

Eckensberger, L., & Zimba, R. (1997). Education, schooling, and literacy. In J.W. Berry, P.R. Dasen, & T.S. Saraswathi (Eds.), *Handbook of cross-cultural psychology: Vol. 2. Basic processes and human development* (pp. 299-338). Boston, MA: Allyn and Bacon.

Edwards, C.P. (1981). The comparative study of the development of moral judgment and reasoning. In R.H. Munroe, R.L. Munroe, & B.B. Whiting (Eds.), *Handbook of cross-cultural human development* (pp. 501-528). New York: Garland.

Farr, R.M. (1983). Wilhelm Wundt (1832-1920) and the origins of psychology as an experimental and social science. *British Journal of Social Psychology*, 22, 289-301.

Fishbein, H. (1984). *The psychology of infancy and childhood: Evolutionary and cross-cultural perspectives*. Hillsdale, NJ: Erlbaum.

Gardiner, H.W., Mutter, J.D., & Kosmitzki, C. (1998). *Lives across cultures: Cross-cultural human development*. Boston, MA: Allyn and Bacon.

Gauvain, M. (1993). Sociocultural processes in the development of thinking. In J. Altarriba (Ed.), *Cognition and culture* (pp. 299-316). Amsterdam: Elsevier Science.

Gay, J. (1973). *Red dust on green leaves*. East Glastenburg, CN: Inter-Culture Associates.

Gay, J.H., & Cole, M. (1967). *The new mathematics and an oldculture: A study of learning among the Kpelle*. New York: Holt, Rinehart & Winston.

Haddon, A.C. (1901). *Reports of the Cambridge anthropological expedition to Torres Strait: Vol 2. Physiology and psychology*. Cambridge, England: The University Press.

Harkness, S., Edwards, C.P., & Super, C.M. (1981). Social roles and moral reasoning: A case study in a rural African community. *Developmental Psychology*, 17, 593-603.

Jahoda, G. (1980). Theoretical and systematic approaches in cross-cultural psychology. In H.C. Triandis & W.W. Lambert (Eds.), *Handbook of cross-cultural psychology* (Vol. 1, pp. 69-142). Boston, MA: Allyn and Bacon.

Laboratory of Comparative and Human Cognition (LCHC). (1983). Culture and development. In P.H. Mussen (Series Ed.) & W. Kessen (Vol. Ed.), *Handbook of child psychology: Vol. 1. History, theory, and methods* (pp. 295-356). New York: Wiley.

Lamb, M.E., Ketterlinus, R.D., & Fracasso, M.P. (1992). Parent-child relationships. In M.H. Bornstein & M.E. Lamb (Eds.), *Developmental psychology: An advanced textbook* (3rd ed., pp. 465-518). Hillsdale, NJ: Erlbaum.

Lamb, M.E., Sternberg, K.J., Hwang, C.P., & Broberg, A.G. (Eds.). (1992). *Child care in context: Cross-cultural perspectives*. Hillsdale, NJ: Erlbaum.

Lave, J. (1988). *Cognition in practice: Mind, mathematics and culture in everyday life*. Cambridge, MA: Cambridge University Press.

Leontiev, A.N. (1981). *Problems of the development of the mind*. Moscow: Progress Publishers.

LeVine, R.A. (1982). *Culture, behavior, and personality* (2nd ed.). New York: Aldine.

Luria, A.R. (1976). *Cognitive development: Its cultural and social foundations*. Cambridge, MA: Harvard University Press.

Luria, A.R. (1979). *The making of mind*. Cambridge, MA: Harvard

University Press.

Luria, A.R. (1981). *Language and cognition*. Washington: V.H. Winston; New York: Wiley.

Minturn, L., & Lambert, W.W. (1964). *Mothers of six cultures*. New York: Wiley.

Morelli, G.A., Rogoff, B., Oppenheim, D., & Goldsmith, D. (1992). Cultural variation in infants' sleeping arrangements: Questions of independence. *Developmental Psychology, 28*, 604-613.

Munroe, R.H., Munroe, R.L., & Whiting, B.B. (Eds.). (1981). *Handbook of cross-cultural human development*. New York: Garland.

Munroe, R.L., & Munroe, R.H. (1975, 1994). *Cross-cultural human development*. Prospect Heights, IL: Waveland Press.

Munroe, R.L., & Munroe, R.H. (1992). Fathers in children's environments. In B.S. Hewlett (Ed.), *Father-child relations* (pp. 213-229). New York: Aldine de Gruyter.

Péron, F. (1807-1816). *Voyages de découvertes aux Terres Australes exécuté sur les corvetttes "le Géographe," "le Naturaliste," et la goélette "le Casuarina" pendant les années 1800, 1801, 1802, 1803, et 1804* (2 vols.). Paris: de l'Imprimérie.

Porteus, S.D. (1931). *The psychology of a primitive people*. London: Edwards Arnold.

Porteus, S.D. (1937). *Primitive intelligence and environment*. New York: Macmillan.

Rogoff, B. (1981). Schooling and the development of cognitive skills. In H.C. Triandis & A. Heron (Eds.), *Handbook of cross-cultural psychology* (Vol. 4, pp. 233-294). Boston, MA: Allyn and Bacon.

Rogoff, B. (1990). *Apprenticeship in thinking*. New York: Oxford University Press.

Rogoff, B., & Lave, J. (Eds.). (1984). *Everyday cognition: Its development in social context*. Cambridge, MA: Harvard University Press.

Saraswathi, T.S., & Dasen, P. (1997). Introduction to volume 2. In J.W. Berry, P.R. Dasen, & T.S. Saraswathi (Eds.), *Handbook of cross-cultural psychology: Vol. 2. Basic processes and human development* (pp. xxv-xxxvii). Boston, MA: Allyn and Bacon.

Scribner, S., & Cole, M. (1981). *The psychology of literacy*. Cambridge, MA: Harvard University Press.

Sears, R.R., Maccoby, E.E., & Levin, H. (1957). *Patterns of child rearing*. Evanston, IL: Row, Peterson and Company.

Segall, M.H., Dasen, P.R., Berry, J.W., & Poortinga, Y. (1990). *Human behavior in global perspective*. New York: Pergamon.

Serpell, R. (1993). *The significance of schooling: Life-journeys in an African society*. Cambridge, MA: Cambridge University Press.

Serpell, R., & Hatano, G. (1997). Education, schooling, and literacy. In H.C. Triandis & A. Heron (Eds.), *Handbook of cross-cultural psychology* (Vol. 4, pp. 339-376). Boston, MA: Allyn and Bacon.

Snarey, J.R. (1985). Cross-cultural universality of social-moral development: A critical review of Kohlbergian research. *Psychological Bulletin, 97*, 202-232.

Stevenson, H.W., & Stigler, J.W. (1992). *The learning gap.* New York: Summit Books.

Stevenson, H., & Wagner, D. (Eds.). (1982). *Cultural perspectives on child development.* San Francisco, CA: W. Freeman.

Super, C.M. (1981a). Behavioral development in infancy. In R.H. Munroe, R.L. Munroe, & B.B. Whiting (Eds.), *Handbook of cross-cultural human development* (pp. 181-270). New York: Garland.

Super, C.M. (1981b). Cross-cultural research on infancy. In H.C. Triandis & A. Heron (Eds.), *Handbook of cross-cultural psychology: Developmental psychology* (Vol. 4, pp. 17-53). Boston, MA: Allyn and Bacon.

Super, C. (1987). The role of culture in developmental disorder. In C. Super (Ed.), *The role of culture in developmental disorder* (pp. 1-8). New York: Academic Press.

Super, C.M., & Harkness, S. (1982). The infants' niche in rural Kenya and metropolitan America. In L.L. Adler (Ed.), *Cross-cultural research at issue* (pp. 47-55). New York: Academic Press.

Super, C.M., & Harkness, S. (1986). The developmental niche: A conceptualization at the interface of child and culture. *International Journal of Behavioral Development, 9*, 545-569.

Super, C.M., & Harkness, S. (1994). The developmental niche. In W.J. Lonner & R. Malpass (Eds.), *Psychology and culture* (pp. 95-99). Boston, MA: Allyn and Bacon.

Super, C.M., & Harkness, S. (1997). The cultural structuring of child development. In J.W. Berry, P.R. Dasen, & T.S. Saraswathi (Eds.), *Handbook of cross-cultural psychology: Vol. 2. Basic processes and human development* (pp. 1-39). Boston, MA: Allyn and Bacon.

Super, C.M., Harkness, S., van Tijen, N., van der Vlugt, E., Dykstra, J., & Fintelman, M. (1996). The three R's of Dutch childrearing and the socialization of infant arousal. In S. Harkness & C.M. Super (Eds.), *Parents' cultural belief systems: Their origins, expressions, and consequences* (pp. 447-466). New York: Guilford Press.

van der Veer, R., & Valsiner, J. (1991). *Understanding Vygotsky.* Cambridge, MA: Blackwell.

Vygotsky, L.S. (1978). *Mind in society: The development of higher psychological processes* (M. Cole, V. John-Steiner, S. Scribner, & E. Souberman, Eds. & Trans.). Cambridge, MA: Harvard University Press.

Wertsch, J. (1985). *Vygotsky and the social formation of mind.* Cambridge, MA: Harvard University Press.

Whiting, B.B. (Ed.). (1963). *Six cultures: Studies of child rearing.* New York: Wiley.

Whiting, B.B., & Edwards, C.P. (1988). *Children of different worlds: The formation of social behavior.* Cambridge, MA: Harvard University Press.

Whiting, J.W.M., Child, I.L., Lambert, W.W., Fischer, A.M., Fischer, J.L., Nydegger, C., Nydegger, W., Maretzki, H., Maretzki, T., Minturn, L., Romney, A.K., & Romney, R. (1966). *Field guide for a study of socialization.* New York: Wiley.

Whiting, B.B., & Whiting, J.W.M. (1975). *Children of six cultures: A psychocultural analysis.* Cambridge, MA: Harvard University Press.

Williams, J.E., & Best, D.L. (1982). *Measuring sex stereotypes: A thirty nation study.* Beverly Hills, CA: Sage.

Williams, J.E., & Best, D.L. (1990). *Measuring sex stereotypes: A multination study* (rev. ed.). Newbury Park, CA: Sage.

Wolf, A.W., Lozoff, B., Latz, S., & Paludetto, R. (1996). Parental theories in the management of young children's sleep in Japan, Italy, and the United States. In S. Harkness & C.M. Super (Eds.), *Parents' cultural belief systems: Their origins, expressions, and consequences* (pp. 364-384). New York: Guilford Press.

SECTION II: THEORETICAL APPROACHES TO CROSS-CULTURAL DEVELOPMENTAL PSYCHOLOGY

Today the possibility that theories about culture can be developed and that they may account for psychological phenomena has become so important that earlier atheoretical views are being abandoned. In this context, the reader might have his or her own explanations why some topics prove popular during one era, but are of little interest in another era. The modern recognition of the relevance of context has important implications for theory and research in human development. An interdisciplinary, cross-cultural approach can lead to new theoretical insights when studying linkages between child development, cultural patterns, and social organization. More integrative, interdisciplinary knowledge centering around a variety of topics derived from theories of the social construction of knowledge is not only important for the study of childhood socialization and various changes during the adolescent years, but also for studies of the life span on a cross-cultural basis.

In his chapter *Toward an Integrated Social Science*, the psychological anthropologist George De Vos asks, What are the impediments to improved integrative knowledge about human behavior? In his view, attention to social institutions, economic and political structures, and cultural patterns cannot be separated from studies of psychological motivation and the biological mechanisms underlying human behavior. Scientific inquiry in the natural sciences is in itself an attempt to raise consciousness of the mechanical causal patterns which can be better manipulated by intentional human intervention. De Vos observes that many of the social sciences fail to consider the integration of disciplines needed to study consciousness itself in its role of innovative intentionality in the structuring of societies. The author explores the impediments to better integrative efforts including political rivalries that separate disciplines and historical traditions from each other as well as deeply felt values that reject certain lines of inquiry. For instance, psychologists are especially prone to consider forms of individual social pathology from a developmental and somewhat universalistic point of view. In contrast, most anthropological and sociological viewpoints remain entrenched in environmental relativism and are not easily reconciled with opposing beliefs in human psychological universals. In his wide-ranging essay, De Vos uses examples from his own research to explore the positivistic reluctance to study human consciousness, the relationship between minority status and classroom competence, defensive self-identity, selective permeability and "non-learning," and the competing influences of peer group versus family in their role as reference groups. De Vos' cross-cultural research has emphasized the continued usefulness of projective tests such as the TAT for the study of underlying motivational dynamics including patterns of achievement motivation in various cultural groups.

In various studies conducted among minority groups in the U.S. and Japan, the author has found that structural psychological problems can remain severe as they are passed on from one generation to the next. To understand relative adaptation in relationship to ethnic background, one has to look back to specific cultural traditions within the family. Characteristic patterns of parental discipline contribute to subcultural patterns of peer group interaction and influence the patterns of learning. These interactive processes contribute not only to the development of social self-identity, but also affect sociocultural patterns of learning.

One of the key debates in recent psychological theorizing on the role of culture has been between the proponents of "cross-cultural psychology" and those of "cultural psychology." In his chapter, *Cross-cultural versus Cultural Psychology: A Synthesis?* Harry Triandis, the dean of cross-cultural psychologists, proposes a synthesis among these competing points of view since he considers both approaches valuable. Cross-cultural psychologists and cultural psychologists deal with different topics, focus on different degrees of cultural differences, and use different units of analysis. Triandis discusses the problem in terms of thesis, antithesis, and synthesis. In his view, cross-cultural psychologists are studying topics of social psychology and their unit of analysis is the person in context (thesis), while cultural psychologists are studying child development, their unit of analysis being the child's activity in culture (antithesis). Each of these approaches has a place in our attempt to relate culture and psychological processes (synthesis).

Culture acts as an additional independent variable specifying how people will respond in different situations, but the basic processes underlying learning and information processing may be the same. Methodologically, cross-cultural psychologists look for culture-specific (emic) ways to measure universal (etic) theoretical constructs. In contrast, cultural psychologists argue that culture shapes all psychological processes. They argue that psychological processes are not internal to the individual, but instead are inextricably linked to cultural contexts. According to cultural psychologists, cultural meanings pose no barriers for research but rather constitute the central topic of investigation. In the same vein, the emphasis is not on the meaning of the concepts but on meaningful actions. This approach is distinct from a cross-cultural psychology approach because the latter examines aspects of persons as members of cultures.

An important methodological difference between cross-cultural psychology and cultural psychology is that cross-cultural psychologists attempt to develop equivalence in the scales used across different cultures. Cultural psychologists, however, focus on the meaning of the theoretical constructs and these meanings are expected to differ by culture. The unit of analysis used by cultural psychologists is the human activity or event, and the universal processes are revealed more by noncomparative methods. According to cross-cultural psychologists, the unit of analysis is the individual and the reactions of the individual to specific stimuli and comparable methods and quantitative comparisons between cultures can reveal universal processes. There are elements of culture that are stable while other elements are constantly changing. If one is working with the former, the methods of cross-cultural psychology are appropriate, but if one is working with the latter, the methods of cultural psychology are appropriate. Harry Triandis stresses that future work on the relationship between culture and psychology must include more investigations that simultaneously use the methods of cultural and cross-cultural psychology. Collaboration between cultural psychologists who can provide the data from one culture, and cross-cultural psychologists who attempt to utilize the data of cultural psychology coming from various cultures, would help us understand better both the universal and the specific roles of culture in psychological processes.

In her chapter *Cultural Contextualism Without Complete Relativism in the Study of Human Development*, the Turkish psychologist Çigdem Kagitçibasi argues that context is the most important clue to an adequate understanding of human development, both in terms of the development of competence skills and the development of the self. The historical roots of a sustained contextual emphasis and related theoretical precursors within psychology emerged in mid-century in diverse areas ranging from social psychology to perception: the number and the diversity of the theoretical perspectives and research programs focusing on context is impressive. In cross-cultural psychology, contextual perspectives on human development attempt to reach out to the more encompassing culture.

The author suggests that two different though related meaning dimensions are confounded in the widely employed individualistic construct of "autonomy": interpersonal distance (relatedness-separateness) and agency (autonomy-heteronomy). These two dimensions are "unconfounded" in her model of family change which utilizes a contextual-developmental-functional approach to the examination of family functioning and the development of the self. The model outlines three family interaction patterns: 1) the traditional family (based on the interdependence between generations), 2) the individualistic model (based on independence), and 3) a dialectical synthesis of these two (based on independence, but emotional interdependence between generations). In the third model there is recognition of the possible coexistence of relatedness and autonomy. Three different types of selves are said to emerge in the three different family models: the related self, the separated self, and the autonomous-related self. The first develops in the family model of total dependence; the second develops in the family model of independence; and the third in the family model of emotional interdependence.

Contextual variations have significant and predictable implications for the family and for the development of the self. Contextual diversity and changes in the context have also implications for the development of competence. Using a functional perspective, Kagitçibasi shows that the effect of context is systematic and predictable. This type of conceptualization is quite different from a relativistic orientation. A contextual and functional approach to human development has to take into account the changes in context. A universalistic perspective appears to better predict the common patterns of changes than a relativistic perspective and also leads to policy-relevant applied implications. Combining cultural contextualism with universal standards and a focus on functional links is a strategy well suited to address sociopsychological change. To improve the existing situation, standards of culturally sensitive research which entails cultural contextualism are required. By developing an integrative synthesis of context and universal standards (as seen in the constructs of "autonomous-related self" and "social-cognitive definition of intelligence"), one can understand how behavior changes in a predictable way with changes in context. Cultural contextualism without complete relativism provides a model for the study of human development across cultures that at the same time is sensitive to cultural factors.

In her chapter *Evolutionary Approaches to the Life Cycle*, the German psychologist Heidi Keller, applying evolutionary thinking to human functioning, demonstrates the decisive role of cultural contextual variables for defining behavioral adaptation. The author emphasizes that evolutionary theory is based on the equal acceptance of the validity of laws of selection and adaptation for humans as any other species. It means that in addition to morphology, physiology, and anatomy, the patterns of social and nonsocial behavior as well as the architecture of the human psyche are shaped in the direction of optimizing reproductive success. This approach also links behavior patterns between generations, since the early socialization environment of one generation is defined by the investment efforts of the previous parental generation. Each individual phase can be conceived as contributing to the ultimate goal of optimal reproductive success. For instance, cultures differ substantially with respect to the time span between the possible and the actual onset of reproduction. The segmentation of the life cycle can be understood as an adaptation toward contextual-cultural demands. In order to understand better intercultural as well as intracultural differences, we need to keep in mind that general ecocontextual conditions and intracultural variability seem to be influenced by socioemotional factors. If the human life cycle can be regarded as an evolved reproductive strategy, where a nonconscious rationality directs the generative behavior, cultures might evolve so that they mediate the prescriptions and rules necessary to support various reproductive strategies. In this context, Keller proposes that mating efforts and parental investments must both be analyzed in more detail, combining population-related variables with aspects of psychological functioning.

The chapters contained in this section stress the complimentarity of various perspectives. For instance, evolutionary psychology proposes that culture may have a direct causal effect on behavior and that those effects are typically moderated by individual variations. Evolutionary theory poses various challenges because it offers a broad scope for the integration of different and separate fields such as biology, psychology, anthropology, sociology, philosophy, and other disciplines. At the same time, it has moved far away from the kind of Social Darwinism that disfigured some of its early history. Whether, however, evolutionary theory can adequately account for the historical contingencies that shape the cultural contexts within which human development takes place remains to be seen.

The four chapters included in Section II include trenchant comparisons of many of the theoretical approaches that have dominated recent discussions in cross-cultural psychology and its sister discipline, psychological anthropology. The theoretical ferment in these disciplines is all to the good although the theoretical discussions must sometimes compete with the dustbowl empiricism to be found in some of the leading cross-cultural journals. In this context, theories simultaneously attempting to take into account processes occurring at the biological, psychological, societal, and cultural levels are of special importance. The influence of such theories also makes itself felt in many of the contributions to be found in the remainder of the book.

TOWARD AN INTEGRATED SOCIAL SCIENCE

George A. De Vos
University of California at Berkeley, U.S.A.

TO DATE: A FAILED REALIZATION

As I am soon to embark upon my 75th year of life, I beg your indulgence in allowing me to present a retrospective overview of 55 years of study of our yet fragmented investigations of human behavior. The social sciences remind me of the European continent now still struggling to become a single interactive entity, uniting its historical social-ethnic diversity into some form of better-functioning whole. Being of Frankish-European origin, I am well aware of the centuries of failed reunification that followed the fall of a Christianized imperial Rome. The Holy Roman Empire never succeeded despite the efforts of Charlemagne, Charles V, or Napoleon. And as a social scientist working in academia, I have personally witnessed from the 1940s on some planned unification of human disciplines, even involving dynastic intellectual marriages of leading members of departments. But it has been obvious that serious integration within the social sciences is as yet far off. Yet, today, at the end of my personal career, I find myself still laboring at what has been termed an interdisciplinary approach.

From my days as a graduate student at the University of Chicago in the 1940s, I have witnessed a number of attempts within several universities to bring about some better theoretical and methodological cooperation, if not integration in the study of what was then termed culture and personality. For my theoretical master's thesis in anthropology, written in 1948, under the guidance of Robert Redfield and Lloyd Warner, I had attempted to integrate some central concepts used by the sociologist, Emile Durkheim with those forwarded by the psychoanalyst, Abram Kardiner who was then, together with anthropologist Ralph Linton, at Columbia University, attempting to bring psychodynamic insights into the study of child development, culture patterns, and social organization. In other Ivy League American universities, principally at Harvard and Yale, some psychologists, sociologists, and anthropologists were attempting to merge into new departments such as the Department of Social Relations at Harvard. Most of these efforts have faded away. However, there are as yet extant at Chicago and some American faculties elsewhere, for example, at Harvard and at the University of California at Davis and at Santa Cruz, some pre-doctoral interdisciplinary, university-oriented programs, usually called "Human Development" which attempt to bring about more integrative, interdisciplinary training centering around a variety of topics taken from the social construction of knowledge, childhood socialization, or changes in the adult years. Although these attempts have remained peripheral, at best, there is again an increasing acknowledgment especially in psychology, that cultural differences are perpetuated not only through childhood socialization patterns but throughout the life span.

There is also an increasing interest in studying what is termed the "self." As witnessed by those attending this conference there is a continuously felt need that something more should be done toward better integrating new research efforts aimed at improving our scientific understanding of the forms of causality governing self-conscious humans as personally reflective social animals.   Through the purposeful direction of consciousness we are attempting to change not only the material environment but the societies we live in.   We have well demonstrated our capacity to materially alter our physical environment on a planetary scale, with negative as well as positive results.   Yet many in the social sciences are still attempting to reduce the understanding of human behavior itself to inescapable organizational patterns arising out of technology.   They fail to consider the integration of disciplines needed to study consciousness itself or the role of innovative intentionality in the structuring of societies.

What we are witnessing here at this conference is some voluntary recognition among specialists, especially in psychology, that the determinants of human behavior cannot be isolated or conceived of theoretically in any single discipline, specialized theory, or research methodology. We must pursue our knowledge about human behavior beyond the arbitrary historical boundaries into which academic departments have become divided. Attention to the social institutions, economic and political structures or culture patterns that are determinative of human behavior cannot be separated from studies of psychological motivation and/or the biological mechanisms underlying human behavior. There needs to be one overarching social science which explains human behavior, not many too-separated, ill-communicating disciplines.

What are the actual impediments to better integrative efforts? This is a topic I would like to explore briefly with you. Some of these difficulties relate both to the enormity of the task and to the human intellectual and emotional limitations necessitating specialization.

Some difficulties obviously relate to political rivalries and quasi-religious adherences that separate historical traditions from each other as they seek one hegemonic theoretical dominance favoring particular values and methods.

Some difficulties relate to deeply-felt political and social values that reject certain lines of inquiry since they threaten favored social policies of amelioration, or religiously held views of how human society should be organized.

Some difficulties are emotional. They relate to our various insensitivities or to personal repression that make it difficult for some of us to penetrate inward into .our own selves. To be truly dispassionate about human psychology leads us to consider the discomforting causal patterns underlying human thought as they are intertwined with patterned emotions from which we, remaining human, cannot be completely freed.

THE POSITIVISTIC RELUCTANCE TO
STUDY HUMAN CONSCIOUSNESS

A basic historical difficulty in the human sciences, especially psychology has been the felt need to attain an objectivity which allows us to separate dispassionate investigation from established belief. The threat posed by Galileo to religious orthodoxy, and the spirited independence of thought seeking more freedom from political and religious interference which marked the founding of the University of Padua, both exemplify the difficulties encountered by the attempts of generations of scholars to separate science from institutionally established political or religious thought. A truly scientific psychology, as other social sciences, has had to establish a framework of external objectivity by first freeing itself from such hampering religious concepts as soul or free will.

In declaring scientific independence from a religious ordering of the universe, the physical and biological sciences have by now been able to create the visions of a mechanically functioning universe with predictable patterns of interactive causality, and they are thus now freed from any interfering intentionality such as the idea of an observing creator who is capable of changing events at will by miraculous acts.

By the 19th century the laws of physics were becoming freed of intentionality, not to be measurably bent by any change of mind or will. In the 19th century, this struggle for intellectual objectivity developed into attempts to charter objective, religion-free if not entirely culture-free forms of human science. In the earlier part of that century, sociology as a science of human society was born. In seeking scientific objectivity, Auguste Comte and others such as Karl Marx, began to conceptualize the operation of social systems whose patterns could be understood without any imprecise concerns with regard to individual intentional causality, or without the quasi-religious preoccupations of questions regarding the individual free will versus social determinism debate. Behaviorist psychologists have been the inheritors of the most extreme form of this positivist tradition in the social sciences.

But today, we are turning again to the study of consciousness in what may be considered a post-positivist period. Today, we are increasingly aware of how emergent consciousness in life forms, when approaching the level of human thought has created a non-reducible, non-reductionist set of intentional causal determinants governing human behavior and human history. Human intentionality has penetrated into atomic physics, and the very ecological destiny of planet Earth itself. We cannot reduce it so that it would become part of a mechanical universe.

We are not totally, either genetically or socially, programmed. While motivational or structuring social forces, to some degree, exist outside of the ordinary conscious awareness of most members of any social group, awareness of individual and social causality, albeit imperfectly experienced subjectively, becomes part of a shared conscious social awareness. Scientific inquiry into the natural sciences itself has been an attempt to raise general conscious awareness of non-vital mechanical causal patterns which themselves can be better manipulated by the living intentionality of human intervention.

In the social or human sciences, in which a psychological dimension is central, there has arisen this further complication. Transcending positivism, a social scientist must now attempt to better objectify intentionality itself. Because consciousness is transcendent from mechanism and cannot be simply reduced to mechanistic explanations, it is determinative in influencing the social systems in which individuals are embedded. When self-reflective intentionality becomes involved, empirical exploration cannot be reduced to underlying mechanical positivist explanations, since various levels of consciousness become instigators of not easily predictable changes in subsequently patterned, motivated individual and collective human behavior.

The facts which prompt a concern with human consciousness as a determinant in all the social sciences are hard to accept by those who wish to remain scientific by reductive mechanistic explanations, because by accepting intentional casualty there seems to be a possible dangerous reintroduction of past religiously based concerns with supernatural forces that interfere with a well-ordered predictable mechanical universe.

Scientists are not different from religious adherents who seek the assurance of a controlled universe. The Uncertainty Principle or Chaos theory are now challenging any capacity for complete predictability and suggest inevitable loss of scientific control. Loss of control inescapably results from any necessary consideration of individual units, especially in the social sciences, studying motivated life forms that themselves have become self-reflective.

PREVIOUS INTERTWINING OF INTEREST IN THE DEVELOPMENT OF THOUGHT IN A CULTURAL CONTEXT

Despite a past lack of integration, at various times there have been some overarching concerns that have brought together some of the social sciences as they were motivated by a common preoccupation. One example of such a focal concern during the 19th century was the concept of evolution as a process governing all forms of life, including man. The physical universe may be governed by mechanical laws, but what has governed the evolution of intelligence in life forms?

Biological explorations of evolutionary sequences inspired the developing interpenetrating interests of psychologists and anthropologists as they sought to explore the implications of evolutionary processes of man as a survivor. As suggested by Vygotsky and others, human survival has been brought about by forms of social life involving signals of communication eventuating in a capacity for language that could be internalized as human thought. As Durkheim elucidated it, societies are constructed of members who have internalized communicative collective representations.

Anthropology in the late 19th century became a multifaceted evolutionary discipline with several highly divergent research methods. It began as an archeological exploration of the evolutionary sequence of past societies through examining material remains of artifacts and architectural structures. Remaining wood can now be carbon-dated. Biological Anthropology has increasingly moved away from a simple search for bones as physical evidence of our simian ancestry to a search for genetic markers. DNA evidence is now available from primatology as well as from human remains. Alas, we now find that Neanderthals were probably not part of our ancestry. Anthropologists working less with material evidence but with human thought have found it harder to reduce their science to mechanism or artifact. Nevertheless, there is a search for developmental sequences in language structure that might suggest an evolutionary progression.

Finding some evolutionary sequences in human thought from the concrete to the abstract or from signs to metaphors, was a favored ordering topic when what is now called cultural anthropology was born. It was presumed for example, that earlier forms of human thought were to be found embedded in religious representations. By the end of the 19th century, English, French, and German schools diverged as they attempted to trace the earliest forms of magical or religious thought, especially in terms of conceptualizing god or the supernatural.

Edward Tylor (1871) has been considered by most as the first to use the word "culture" in its modern sense and the first to apply a cultural approach to studying more primitive human society. Tylor contended that religious concepts such as that of the soul evolved through the experiencing of human dreams in which one seemed to travel free of the sleeping body. The dead also return to us in our dreams.

Durkheim, in his own evolutionary reconstruction of religion, *The Elementary Forms of the Religious Life* argued against these contentions of

Tylor. As a sociologist, he would have us focus rather on the internalized and highly aroused collective experience of participating ritualistically in social groups. The ecstatic sense of group participation as part of a collective consciousness empowered the individual beyond any personal limitations. The excitement of ritual could give rise to an inner experience of the awesome power of society. This raised sense of power beyond the ordinary could also become blended with power as observed in nature to result in the experience of god.

Freud, in his volume, *Totem and Taboo* composed his own evolutionary myth on the origin of religious thought and embellished his theories about the return of the repressed in dreams as part of a collective unconscious. Religious ritual commemorated the first collective patricide which was the cause of a sense of internalized guilt transmitted across generations as part of human evolution. This mythic first transgression related to incestuous wishes became collectively represented in various taboos inhibiting sexual and aggressive behavior.

During this intellectual period at the turn of the century, an evolutionary analogy had also been developed by Lévy-Bruhl and others which equated the minds of supposedly less evolved primitive people with a developmental sequence to be noted in the thoughts of children. Psychoanalytically oriented psychologists used a more extended general concept of regression to characterize a return to more primitive thinking in evolutionary patterns, and found such regressions among the mentally disturbed.

Piaget, in his earlier formulations of stages (1930, 1932) preceding logical thought, was guided somewhat by such evolutionary analogies. His earlier work reveals both the influence of such psychoanalytic thought and the formulations about the discrete forms of primitive thought discussed by Lévy-Bruhl (1923). In his own research he demonstrated how in Swiss children prelogical forms of thought sequentially developed toward more self-reflective forms. Given proper social stimulation children eventually manifested in their causal thought a capacity to separate mechanical from intentional sequences which they had confused in earlier precausal forms. He suggested how a self-reflective and more conscious objectivity increasingly comes to govern the sequential stages of moral reasoning.

From the 1920s onward, there has been a radical shift in contemporary social science away from diachronic evolutionary thought toward the synchronic study of presently operative social systems. In a gestalt sense, as Kurt Lewin and others have contended, human psychology and social behavior can be made explicable without any historical reference to previous stages. Although varying from the materialist emphasis of Marxist theory to the more ideational explanations of thought and practice found in Max Weber and Emile Durkheim, operative social organizational patterns and the dynamics of group participation have been the key explanations found in present day sociological theory.

Anthropological theory in the United States, in breaking with the evolutionary approach of the 1920s has followed three diverging traditions. The first approach through organizational theory, exemplified by the functionalist school of Radcliffe-Brown in British social anthropology, borrowed heavily from Durkheim. This dominant approach in European anthropology was not appreciably different from that found in sociology, although both in Europe and the United States anthropologists were emphasizing research in non-Western settings and therefore were more interested than sociologists in pursuing what they termed a *comparative* approach. Most such empirical studies focused on the appreciable differences apparent among supposedly more simple isolated societies with supposedly separate autonomous traditions. Sociologists generalized on the basis of having studied the christianized, but politically divided Western cultural tradition. Marxism, however, never gave up an evolutionary concern borrowed by Engels from the American 19th century anthropologist, Lewis Morgan who had posited an organizational sequence from what was termed "savagery," through barbarism into feudalism. Engels added the capitalist social forms which were to evolve into an eventual realization of socialist society. This conception remains an operative belief system among the remaining Communist adherents.

The second approach in American anthropology remained evolutionary in focus, but has moved back toward forms of biological determinism and the genetic continuities in the human species. The physical anthropologist has become a biologist. He or she has moved into the laboratory to do genetic research, and a thin stream of what is now called sociobiology has reasserted itself as providing the best explanations of human behavior. One might note a parallel in modern psychiatry which has become heavily dependent on ameliorative drugs and now leans more toward biological rather than psychological or social explanations of deviant and dysfunctional behavior. In anthropology, we have not returned to trying to find a correlation between cranial configurations and social behavior as espoused by Lombroso. Parenthetically, the University of Rome still honors this tradition. During the time of my activities with delinquency at the United Nations in Rome in 1972-1973, my colleague in delinquency investigation was the late Professor Franco Ferracuti who was then occupying the Lombroso Chair of Criminal Anthropology. Fortunately for my interests and his, he was a gifted, dynamic psychiatrist who was far more interested in psychological dynamics than physiological determinants.

The third approach taken by American anthropology in the 1920s was potentially a more integrative one reaching out especially toward dynamic psychological theory to be used in the comparative context of cross-cultural studies. It was first fostered by Franz Boas at Columbia University. It was his disciples, Margaret Mead, Ruth Benedict, Edward Sapir, and Otto Klineberg in psychology who became the forerunners of the Personality and Culture movement which was to search for a more unified approach to human behavior. The popularity of these interests crested from the World War II period into the 1960s. The heart of this movement has been an interest in comparative childhood developmental studies tracing out how culture configurations experienced from infancy on, pattern humans from one generation to the next. Thirty-two years ago, in 1967, I began preparing a chapter, called "Cultural Psychology, Comparative Studies of Human Behavior" which was published in 1969, in the *Handbook of Social Psychology*, edited by Lindzey and Aronson. In this chapter I pulled together the publications to that date. I find that the topics I discussed then are still the operative concerns of those seeking to bring together, in one way or another, the developmental and the social aspects of study. The chapter also gave consideration to the biological functions of the thinking human animal.

STUDY OF THE DEVIANT, CONFLICTIVE, OR PATHOLOGICAL INHERENT IN THE HUMAN SCIENCES

I found, then as now, that in each of these approaches, the organizational, the biological, and the developmental approaches, there is some division between those interested in what is normative or capable of being actualized in contrast to what is deficient, conflictive, or deviant. We tend to remain Aristotelian in our analytic processes describing a normative ideal. But a Galilean form of observation of an interactive society or operative individuals is necessary. Any theoretical approach, in order to remain true to observed behavior, must explain irregularity, social and individual change, internal conflict or dysfunction, and what is usually termed "deviant" or "pathological behavior" which occurs with some characteristic incidence within the particular system or society being studied. Such systematically reoccurring irregularities of behavior, as those brought out in the comparative study of European suicide conducted by Durkheim, or the seasonal statistics on the use of prostitutes in Paris as reported by an early social scientist in the 1830s are examples of investigations guided by theories that study the deviant as well as the socially acceptable as part of social life within a city.

Observation of real behavior may allow us to theorize about a potential or ideal developmental or normative social pattern, but the continual appearance of deviancy necessitates better explanations that include what is inevitably malfunctioning or what can be considered pathological as an inherent component present in all human social and personal functioning.

The study of evolution suggests that most species of life have become extinct. Cultures and civilizations have disappeared, or become so transformed that their previous patterning can no longer be recognized. During my career in psychology and anthropology I have, however, noted a definite reluctance by most social scientists to responsibly incorporate the deviant in their theoretical expositions. For example, in Marxist theory, or in developmental psychology there is an unwillingness to address irrational behavior—whether collective or individual—as part of the inevitable human condition. There is the persistent optimism that rational human thought will triumph in the end and the forces driven by more primitive emotional considerations will be overcome. Freud, in his mythological theory at least, was not so sanguine. He gave Thanatos equal power with Eros in an eternal struggle that continues, whatever the technological advances found in human civilization.

Let me illustrate the difficulty of incorporating the deviant, drawing upon two abiding strands of my own work. First, I have been trying to understand some forms of deviant behavior as they appear among members of the Japanese culture. Second, I have explored how minority status in society is related to the appearance of deviancy, especially in youth. In the course of such endeavors I have encountered many of the difficulties inherent in pursuing some integration of the social sciences. First, much of developmental or so-called cognitive psychology is not concerned with the deviant. Cognitive theorists can create purified theories of cognitive development in which humans theoretically resemble computers. There is no interweaving of the errant effects of ever-present emotional processes. Kasparov, in losing to IBM's Big Blue in the recent chess battle matching of Man against Computer, was defeated, in his own judgment, by interfering emotional failings. Many cognitive theorists admit to no such weakness in their idealized theoretical structures of human development.

Crime and delinquency involve social attitudes. There is frequently a political dimension to what the police authorities consider criminal. There are situations of ethnic, caste, or class dominance where a state lacks an overall moral authority over its subjects. However, let us not deal with this topic, but, rather keep to certain perimeters of general social consensus on what is considered deviant behavior. There is a fairly universal agreement that there are three categories of acts considered criminal which involve transgressions related respectively to the person, the property, or the social status of others. Within modern societies these may vary a bit but there are universal definitions of stealing, assault, rebellions against proper authority, and forbidden forms of sexual activity. Sociologists stress the organizational over the developmental in explaining such behavior. Psychologists are more prone to consider forms of individual social pathology whether of a developmental or physiological basis.

In the course of my research work started in 1947, I have noted that psychology must develop not only a more dynamic learning theory, but also a more dynamic *non-learning* theory to understand the specifics of persistent ethnic differences in groups, as well as relative indices of deviant behavior to be noted in these different groups. Socialization as well as heredity are both selective, in terms of the relative realization or lack of realization of what is considered desirable in the human potential.

Trained in clinical psychology as well as anthropology, I moved from a study of pathological thought processes in schizophrenia to a comparative study of juvenile delinquency. With a large grant from the National Institute of Mental Health I spent several years in this pursuit. In 1963, I also received a grant to visit the French Ministry of Justice research unit at Vaucresson. Then in 1972, I became involved with the research unit of the United Nations in Rome. This unit studied problems in juveniles and was called The Social Defense Research Institute. It was so named euphemistically, because the Soviet Union at that time refused to participate in any United Nations unit set up with any word suggesting "juvenile delinquency" in its title. According to the Marxist thought of the time, no socialist state harbored delinquent youth, as this was a characteristic problem only to be found in capitalist states. They admitted to having youthful hooligans, but these were a sad leftover from pre-Communist times and would in due time simply disappear.

While not so directly political, I have still found much other research in delinquency governed by theoretical ideologies that selectively focus on what is to be studied. The most irksome to me has been the inability of American sociologists to consider the obvious psychological level of debilitation found in many of our African-American youth. Simply doing away with discrimination will not solve abiding psychological problems engendered in dysfunctional families in youth regardless of their ethnic origin.

Explanations for the overall indices of crime and delinquency now tend to be organizational and developmental rather than of a hereditary organic nature.   This is not to ignore the occasional forms of individual psychopathology related to a physiologically based lack of control over sexual or aggressive behavior. It is generally agreed that comparative differential rates of crime and delinquency or deviancy are directly related to social patterns. However, in my own direct exploration with Japanese colleagues based on the extensive delinquency literature written by various specialists in English or in Japanese, for example, I have found very few works in which the biological, the organizational, *and* the developmental have been integrated to any extent. In most present-day explanations of delinquent behavior in youth as a social problem, or the relative adaptive social functioning of different ethnic groups, there tends to be either psychological *or* sociological explanations.

In the sociology classes at the University of Chicago which I attended in the 1940s I was well exposed to theories of how social discrimination against ethnic and racial minorities was directly related to both poor school performance and various forms of deviant and delinquent behavior in youth. In the late 1940s, the Japanese were moving into the high delinquency areas of the city whose various areas were being so well studied in the 1930s and 1940s. Sociologists at the Chicago Institute for Juvenile Research had documented the patterns of juvenile crime among ethnic minorities in the inner city of Chicago with its special "zone of transition." Psychologists as well as sociologists were predicting numerous patterns of personal and family breakdown for the Japanese being released from the internment camps where they had been transported by the American government during World War II. However, when several of us began to study the Japanese-Americans moving into the city we found that they were not performing as negatively as would be expected of members of a minority facing strong social and economic discrimination. Here was a group of people who had been subject, not only to the usual forms of racially directed prejudice, but to the additional ordeal of being wrenched from their homes on the American West Coast and put into special camps for several years. They were not behaving according to negative predictions, especially with respect to school performance (Caudill & De Vos, 1956; Darsie, 1926; De Vos, 1954; Strong, 1934).

My special doctoral project involved using the Rorschach test as well as interviews with a sample of 160 individuals, including both the immigrant generation (Issei) and their American-born children (Nisei). These results demonstrated that on the level of personality structure a strong drive to accomplish was a characteristic trait to be found in many American-born Japanese as well as in their immigrant parents (De Vos, 1952, 1954, 1966b; De Vos & Boyer, 1989). How were we to explain that unlike the other minorities residing in Chicago's zone of transition with its very high rates of delinquency and crime the Japanese children were doing so well in school, and afterwards, despite prejudice, were finding jobs and advancing quickly in their occupations?

As a result of our collaborative work with Japanese in Chicago, Caudill, who used the Thematic Apperception Test (TAT), and I postulated some psychocultural contentions about internalized achievement motivation as related to a continuing cultural pattern based on primary family socialization practices and the nature of family cohesion (Caudill & De Vos, 1956). Our findings contradicted a straight sociological approach to discrimination. We advanced the then still novel idea that cultural patterning was more determining of minority adaptive behavior than sociological conditions of severe discrimination. This theme has been pursued by me in my subsequent work with normative samples of Japanese in Japan starting in 1953 (De Vos, 1973; De Vos & Boyer, 1989). This contention has been reinforced more recently with findings about the adaptive occupational, educational, and psychological patterns of immigrant Koreans, whose family and community interaction patterns bear striking resemblance to Japanese immigrants two generations removed (De Vos, 1983b; De Vos & Kim, 1993; De Vos & Lee, 1981).

Examining patterns of minority adaptation both in the U.S. and Japan I have come to decry sociological theories considering delinquency or deviancy solely in terms of the situational social factors such as those operative in American city ghettoes. These theories do not explain why different minority groups viewed longitudinally over several generations develop different patterns of adaptation in response to discrimination and economic hardship in different situations of migration. Conversely, sociological forces cumulatively act over several generations, and unfortunately, in reverse, cannot be easily ameliorated by legal acts once a debased social status has been internalized as part of childhood socialization.

Anthropologists also can overlook the psychological factors involved. When anthropologists attempt to examine persistent culture patterns they have been too prone to dismiss negative psychological patterns and advocate a non-judgmental cultural relativism that ignores the fact that some forms of culturally persistent socialization are more problematical than others, either from the standpoint of mental health or from the standpoint of socially adaptive functioning in situations of change. There are panhuman forms of psychopathology. Their incidence can vary widely with culture. Working with Rorschach records comparatively has convinced me, for example, that there are within-group variances in paranoid thinking patterns that occur with overall higher frequency in some cultural groups, (e.g., Algerians), than in others.

As yet, "anthropological" or "sociological" beliefs in environmental relativism have not been well reconciled with opposing beliefs in human "psychological" universals. We now suffer from ideological strictures in anthropology departments that are part of academic "political correctness" stressing cultural relativity rather than panhuman proneness to psychological malaise.

American society emphasizes optimistic quick solutions. We like to be optimistic about the plasticity of human learning. We have become uneasy about the social implications of finding any genetic differences in intelligence. Concerns with direct negative social conditions far overshadow any attention to psychophysiological differences or cognitive measures of intellectual functioning (see the chapter by Freedman, Olafsdottir, Guoan, Park, and

Gorman in this volume). Relativistic disbelief in psychopathology decries any attempt to develop a more universal use of psychodiagnostic testing, or clinical diagnosis. Similarly, emphases on the cultural patterning found in gender-role behavior too quickly rule out any gender linked cognitive or emotional biological propensities in males or females.

Relativistic anthropological theories tend to see adaptive differences in groups simply as a result of cultural considerations which rule out any possible judgment as to the relative adequacy or inadequacy of their attempts at adaptation. Those espousing cultural relativism do not recognize that differences may be due to potentials for internal maladjustment related to persistently inadequate socialization practices that hinder rather than facilitate optimal psychosocial development. Social behavior found prevalent in some groups are often symptomatic of underlying psychological rigidities induced in childhood which make it difficult to adapt to change. There are psychological consequences that become evident in the behavior of members of some groups related to the deprivation and neglect as well as abuse experienced during their socialization. Achieving adequate mental and emotional balance is a common problem in all societies. There are panhuman criteria of what are more or less adequate forms of psychological adjustment. Not to recognize that we humans are psychophysiologically alike despite the different socialization experiences common to different cultures is to ignore the fact that the socialization of cognition and emotion in some of the youth of particular ethnic minorities is negatively influenced by disrupted family life as well as by continuously derogated status across generations within such complex societies as the United States, Japan, or in present-day European societies (De Vos, 1980; Wagatsuma & De Vos, 1984).

The converse is also true. There is a danger that psychological studies do not sufficiently avoid ethnocentrism in their generalizations. For example, as I first began working with Japanese-Americans I have become increasingly critical of some overarching psychological theories of achievement motivation.(1) Particular forms of psychological adaptation cannot be seen independent of a total social pattern. From this standpoint I have argued in the past against the psychological approach to achievement motivation taken by McClelland, Atkinson, Clark, and Lowell (1953) and others. In their approach there is an implicit overemphasis on ethnocentrically perceived *individualistic* modes of achievement. I have found the Japanese to be much more dependent and less individualistic than Americans, but intensely achievement motivated for family rather than individualistic motives.

In other studies, looking at the relative adaptation of children of different minorities in both the U.S. and Japan, it should be very evident that cultural, psychological, and sociological factors all play a role in the behavior of minorities. Unfortunately, research is not equally attentive, since many social scientists would like to give most weight to one or another favorite pattern of causality. Both the unexpectedly better adaptation in the face of discrimination of the Japanese and Koreans as minorities in the U.S., and the continuing problems manifest in some minorities, both in the U.S. and Japan bear continual examination and explanation in a comparative context on all levels of analysis. Structural psychological problems can remain severe as they are passed on from one generation to the next by the inadequate parenting more common to some historically debased minorities. Psychological problems of a maladaptive nature are not simply to be quickly ameliorated by a diminution of outer social discrimination.

MINORITY STATUS AND CLASSROOM COMPETENCE

The field of cross-cultural psychological assessment has been a difficult one to pursue since socially evaluative judgments are often connected to results that indicate the fact that socialization experiences can negatively affect the optimal utilization of those cognitive patterns which are considered "intellectual" in nature. Intelligence tests, when used comparatively, are considered to be "unfair" to some groups, since the items have first been standardized on a dominant class segment of a Western society. This sense of unfairness is aggravated by the fact that some genetic component is assumed to be operative in the inheritance of intellectual capacities. Dominant groups are socially advantaged, therefore the fact that they are apt to do better on these tests suggests genetic superiority to an unwarranted degree. Another well-considered criticism is that the administration of tests often fails to consider appropriately not only the general social circumstances, but also the testing situation itself. Any sort of testing can be unfair to those having less experience with test taking. Moreover, test taking for some individuals evoke inhibitory patterns of affective arousal that negatively influence test performance.

Criticism of cross-cultural testing is a very complex topic, and it is not my purpose to enter into it here. Given past inadequacies of judgment on the part of some examiners, or the readiness to make direct inferences about optimal biological functioning of others, there has been much to criticize. However, the systematic patterns found in the testing of groups when testing has been attempted cannot be too easily dismissed. Normative results on tests *are* relevant to an understanding of social functioning, even when they show some differences between groups. Of course, these differences can be interpreted by the bigoted or prejudiced in a socially derogatory manner as hopeless inferiority rather than as indications of debilitating or inhibiting social experiences affecting some groups compared with others.

Not only has there been serious questioning about the possibility of using existent psychological tests cross-culturally, but many question the advisability if not the validity of using seemingly culturally biased psychological test measurements in the classroom in a multiethnic society. IQ tests, and particularly as they were used in the past, demonstrated relatively poor scores for certain ethnic minorities. Were the tests simply wrong? Or do they not indicate an existing competitive weakness in meeting the expectations of vocational functioning in a complex modern society demanding long-term formal education of youth to prepare them for skilled vocations rather than for unskilled forms of manual labor.

I shall not enter into the ongoing controversy about test results related to adequate school functioning. It is a fact, however painful or disconcerting it may be, that early testing of children does predict later school performance to a highly significant degree. In my judgment, this does not argue for a biological or physiological constancy as much as for the deeply formative effects of early preschool experience on the facilitation or inhibition of given cognitive and affective structural patterns observable in effective social learning.

In the case of the poor school performance of Japanese minorities, I have written about interrelated problems of negative self-esteem that appear very early in the preschool period among the Burakumin (De Vos & Wagatsuma, 1966). The Burakumin are the close to three million descendants of a social caste in Japan that resembled the Untouchables of India in being considered inherently polluted individuals. In a related context, I have also considered the constrictive psychological defenses found in Native American Apache (Day, Boyer, & De Vos, 1975; De Vos, 1978b).

In my own experience, tests when used systematically can be used as valid instruments if one is thoroughly aware of cultural factors governing the selection of certain items. Given care, test results can be adequately compared *between* groups as well as *within* groups. What is sought is not whether an item is technically answered in a "correct" or incorrect way. What can be fruitfully examined is *how* an item is answered. What is the cognitive pattern revealed by how a problem is approached? *How* does one attempt to solve a problem? *How* persistent is the attempt at mastery? What amount of energy is mobilized or invested when the individual is engaged with the task, as well as how well is one motivated? What is the reaction to perceived success or failure? What interferes with problem solving? How rigid or flexible is the approach taken to problem solving?

Moreover, I have argued that, regardless of possible cultural biases, or if you will, characteristic modes of coping found in between-group testing among members of specific groups, the validity of assuming panhuman coping patterns is documented by the fact that *within-group* differentiation is highly predictive of the relative performance of specific individuals in whatever group is tested. This applies to IQ tests, projective tests, and such seemingly culture-bound tests as the California Psychological Inventory (CPI).(2)

Comparative analyses of test results demonstrate that the tests are valid predictors of comparative performance within the cultures examined, whether they are American, European, Japanese, or Chinese. In Japan we have noted that there are quite apparent relationships between minority status, poor IQ scores, poor school performance, lack of family cohesion, and high rates of delinquency.(3) These interrelationships are complex. For example, school performance is related to IQ. It is also related to delinquency. However, delinquency and IQ have no significant relationship. In Japan, as in the United States, delinquency is significantly higher in broken families. We also have demonstrated in both Japan and Italy with Tulio Bandini of the University of Genoa that male delinquency occurs in families with little internal cohesion, poor supervision, inconsistent discipline, and lack of affection afforded a particular son (De Vos, 1980a; Wagatsuma & De Vos, 1984). Truancy and poor performance in school are significantly higher among some minorities and not others, as is delinquency, and yet, in no minority group we have dealt with intensively can we report any lack of parental respect for schooling or any devaluing of formal education. I would contend that social values about education are not that different among American minority groups. What differs is the priority of other psychologically and socially disruptive social concerns prevalent in some groups and the appearance of negative patterns of neglect and maternal deprivation, lack of a father during particular childhood years, and the faulty methods of discipline used by parents to encourage internalization of social expectations on the part of their children.

In the United States, not only is there a relatively poor showing of some ethnic minorities in the schools, but delinquency and other manifestations of personal alienation are now almost overwhelming since they are appearing with greater frequency among youth generally. On a sociological level, I would consider American society to be characterized by increasing anomie. This anomic condition is most intensively experienced in the increasing breakdown of family cohesion and the resultant more widespread experience of alienation on the part of children experiencing family breakdown.

We have examined the appearance of poor school performance related to delinquency in the majority group, in Japan (De Vos & Wagatsuma, 1973), and in minorities in both Italy (De Vos, 1980, 1981b) and Japan (De Vos & Wagatsuma, 1966; Lee & De Vos, 1981). In each instance there is strong evidence of dysfunctional families. Among the Japanese majority, whom we studied in great depth by a case-history approach, it was family disruption that was the most telling factor in the social history of delinquent youth. In brief, poor school performance combined with the appearance of delinquent behavior are related to poor family cohesion.

On a cognitive level, poor school performance is related to the predominance of field dependency in thought processes. It is my contention, now being at least indirectly substantiated in the research of Curtis Vaughn (1988), that both are related to a difficulty in internalization or identification in the psychoanalytic sense. As witnessed in the work of Witkin and others, what is called a field-dependent cognitive pattern appears in individuals who have not as yet sufficiently internalized and who therefore are not yet as psychologically sure of themselves to make an independent judgment from internal perceptual cues. They remain dependent on outside cues to interpret what they perceive (Witkin).

DEFENSIVE SELF-IDENTITY, SELECTIVE PERMEABILITY, AND NON-LEARNING

As a son of immigrant Flemings from Belgium I spoke Flemish with my parents until I entered the American school system. I have no memory of this process, but after entering school I refused to speak any Flemish at home and spoke henceforth only in English. Unconsciously, I had become American. Later, when I visited my relatives in Belgium at age 14 I began again to speak some Flemish. When I now visit, I am greeted with some amusement by younger people because I speak a dialect that is fast disappearing as everyone is now speaking standard Nederlands. Older people, however, can immediately recognize that my family came from East Flanders immediately south of Gent. The same processes of standardization are now happening in Italy. This experience caused me to think of how people in Europe could live so closely by one another for hundreds of years, yet keep their separate dialects. I then thought of how we all continue to perceive selectively no matter where we travel or even migrate.

These thoughts I have related to a basic psychological mechanism I term "exclusion." This mechanism has been explored extensively in the clinical psychoanalytic literature, most primitively considered as "denial," and later in neurotic symptoms, as "repression." In considering the general formation of the social self one must examine the defensive selectivity of both experience and perception as it influences the interpretation of a social reality that distinguishes members of given social groups one from another.

In my comparative research, I have used the concept of *selective permeability* to relate certain structural components of personality to how reference groups influence social behavior (De Vos, 1992, chapter 7). I have formed a structural conception of how repression works defensively in maintaining separation between proximate social groups. The concept of "selective permeability," as I use it, is an analogy, borrowed from biology, comparing the functioning of the ego to the functioning of a living cell. The continuity of the living cell depends on the adequate operation of a permeable membrane that is both actively and passively selective in what is allowed to come into the organism. In an analogous sense, the functioning ego depends on a working membrane that selectively allows only certain stimuli to penetrate as "experiences" that may or may not become an integral part of one's conscious self. Such a concept is helpful to me in considering how social distance is maintained individually as well as collectively between different cultural and subcultural groups. Selective permeability is involved defensively in what is, or is not, "internalized."

Experiences are of relative saliency of influence in different reference groups with their different role expectations and special inducements or sanctions to adopt a particular line of thought or behavior. The most important reference group is the one that can cause the most ready selective penetration of experience in line with the "meaning" the group attributes to the experience either consciously or unconsciously.

Usually, in a relatively well functioning culturally conditioned ego, those ideas dangerous or contradictory to one's primary group membership will not be allowed to come into consciousness. They may either be totally "denied" or unconsciously "repressed." This concept of selective permeability is related to how some degree of consistency is maintained within the social self. Dangerously inconsistent or potentially disruptive discordant elements are protectively kept out so that they do not upset the homeostasis necessary for the continuity of the living structure.

In discussing group differences between classes or ethnic groups there is a prevalent misconception that the different cultural modes of living or language lead to a lack of understanding between individuals from different groups. On the contrary, for purposes of argument one could say that it is not the differences in behavior themselves that cause misunderstanding, but a self-protective need to preserve distinguishing barriers between individuals and groups. Distancing operations which cause individuals to experience events differently are particularly noticeable where caste or caste distinctions are being used by one segment of the population against the other (De Vos & Suárez-Orozco, 1990, chapter 5). Differences are maintained as a barrier to any possible assimilation process, or they are used in a selectively defensive manner by those subordinated so that they can maintain their integrity when they meet with lack of acceptance in situations of possible social assimilation. Despite common schooling, the English lower class maintains it own variant of English as do American Blacks in the inner American city. If one changes one's accent, one is changing one's group affiliation. In American schools, there is a selective minority "non-learning" which persists and maintains patterns of social segmentation.(4)   I cannot help but extend this line of thought about non-learning to the intellectual discourse found in the university. We are selectively receptive to whatever fits into our own line of inquiry but easily exclude what is potentially disruptive.

PEER GROUP VERSUS FAMILY AS A REFERENCE GROUP

Let me extend this line of thought to the generational conflict one notes among youth in modern societies everywhere. Same-age reference groups are becoming stronger than family ties or other forms of age-graded community structures for many youth in contemporary society. The same-age peer group takes on an increasingly salient social reference value governing the adolescent's thought and behavior.

An important question in discussing the subcultural modes of adaptation of minority youth in Europe or the United States is, under what conditions do youth become antagonistic not only to the majority society but more specifically to their own parental generation? In contrast to the frequent conflicts between the peer group, the parents, and the school found among African-American and Mexican-American children, one could see until recently in contemporary Japan and among many Japanese-American children in the U.S a peer-group orientation which mutually reinforced an intense emotional commitment to the formal learning processes of the school (Lewis, 1989).

However, harmony of peer-group and family directives does not prevail under all circumstances among the Japanese-Americans. This is well illustrated when comparing the strikingly positive record of the American-born Nisei within the regular American school system with the very poor results obtained in teaching Japanese in the Japanese-language schools established by Japanese parents in the 1920s and 1930s. While the parents wanted their children to preserve the language and culture of their homeland, the special Japanese language schools to which children were sent after regular school hours did not work. There was great implicit as well as explicit resistance to learning the Japanese language among the American born. In this instance, the peer group reinforced the more general social attitudes found among the children of other American immigrant groups who resisted learning the parental language. Such resistance had been a characteristic of the social self-identity of American immigrants rather generally, and it was also adopted by the American-born Japanese.

In regular schools, however, the social attitudes shared by the Japanese community and by Japanese families were reinforced by the collective activity of the Nisei peer group. In this respect, the behavior of the Japanese in the ordinary public schools resembled that of middle-class rather than lower-class American children. The automatic American social self-identity taken on by the Nisei child resembled, therefore, the assimilative patterns taken on by waves of European immigrants in the American cities. That is to say, the language of the Japanese child, as happened with European children in Chicago and New York schools at the turn of the century, became the lingua franca—English. Any attempt to maintain at least a bilingual heritage, as in most immigrant ethnic minorities, was defeated by peer group resistance. Spontaneously, English became the "natural language" of most American-born children of immigrants.(5) Japanese youth did not become alienated. This pattern differs from what has happened with other minorities in Europe or the United States. In Belgium and France, I have been informally observing how the Italian, Spanish, and Portuguese are disappearing into the ordinary population. The Turks and Moroccans and Algerians are not. Their youth are more alienated, do poorer in school, and are more prone to delinquent activities.

In the United States, alienated patterns are especially common among African-Americans and Mexican-Americans as well as Puerto Ricans and Hawaiians. This is not simply racial. Adaptation is not completely linked to perceived color differences. In the U.S., Haitians and Jamaicans are adapting more positively than American Blacks from the south. Symbolically, separate modes of speech—"Ebonics," "Black English," "Latino," "Pidgin,"—are reinforced in dissident peer groups as part of the continuity of a separate peer identity. In these extreme cases, the peer group also opposes any socially assimilative type of school interaction. It is noticeable now that Mexican-American and Black peers tend to create a separating interaction with the other groups in any school population. They are equally alienated from their own parental generation who, in good part, hope that their children will do well in school to guarantee them an adequate future.

In response to school contacts in earlier European immigrant situations the general language of the peer group usually became English regardless of other ethnic differences. Depending on cultural and class background, the American school was variously used as an adaptive instrument by the children of immigrants for social and educational advancement.

To understand relative adaptation related to ethnic background, one has to look back to specific cultural traditions in the use of cognitive styles within the family, including verbal communication between parents and children beginning in early childhood. Moreover, it is very important to consider differences in the methods of childhood discipline used to foster internalization of modes of cognitive functioning. The matter is further complicated by the fact that characteristic patterns of parental discipline contribute to subcultural patterns of peer group interaction that aid or hinder learning in the schools. Also, there exist subcultural variations in the type of interaction established between the family and the peer group as primary reference groups. These interactive processes continually contribute not only to the development of social self-identity in the children of migrants or minorities, but these processes also affect the patterns of learning used by the child in the school.

Examined on a cognitive psychological level, a crucial issue is how parents' discipline, whether deliberately or inadvertently, causes forms of internalization that emphasize particular cognitive coping mechanisms. The development of field independent thought is not only related to *how* a child internalizes the standards and values of the adult society, but it equally affects the availability of adaptive patterns allowing for the utilization of abstract thought.

One must then ask, how do characteristic forms of internalization originally fostered in the family relate to the complementary use of the peer group as a further formative influence in the final development of an identity that defines satisfactory adult economic and social roles? To my knowledge, these important questions have not as yet been subjected to sufficient systematic research inquiry either in the U.S. or in Europe.

I could go on, but I think I have illustrated my points. In the real world there are no ideal developmental patterns. There are imperfectly operative human patterns. Just as Galileo had to consider air pressure when studying gravity, we must study the emotions when studying human cognitive and social behavior. There are patterns that imperfectly socialize us, one generation to the next. In the academic community there are imperfect disciplines that socialize us one generation to the next. Though we seek unity our languages and customs tend to keep us apart.

BIBLIOGRAPHY

Abbott, K.A. (1975). Culture change and the persistence of the Chinese personality. In G.A. De Vos (Ed.), *Responses to change, society, culture and personality* (pp. 74-104). New York: D. Van Nostrand.

Caudill, W., & De Vos, G.A. (1956). Achievement, culture and personality: The case of the Japanese Americans. *American Anthropologist, 58*(6), 1102-1126 (reprinted: 1961, 1966, 1967, 1971).

Darsie, M.L. (1926). The mental capacity of American-born Japanese children. *Comparative Psychological Monographs, 3,* 15.

Day, R., Boyer, B.B., & De Vos, G.A. (1975). Two styles of ego development: A cross-cultural longitudinal comparison of Apache and Anglo school children. *Ethos, 3* (3).

De Vos, G.A. (1952). A quantitative approach to affective symbolism in Rorschach responses. *Journal of Projective Techniques, 16*(2), 133-150.

De Vos, G.A. (1954). A comparison of the personality differences in two generations of Japanese Americans by means of the Rorschach Test. *Nagoya Journal of Medical Science, 17*(3), 153-265 (reprinted: No. 34, 1966).

De Vos, G.A. (1966). *A comparison of the personality differences in two generations of Japanese Americans by means of the Rorschach Test.* Honolulu: University of Hawaii Press.

De Vos, G.A. (1973). *Socialization for achievement: Essays on the cultural psychology of the Japanese.*   Berkeley, CA: University of California Press.

De Vos, G.A. (1980). Delinquency and minority status: A psychocultural perspective. In G. Newman (Ed.), *Crime and deviancy: A comparative perspective* (pp. 130-180). Beverly Hills, CA: Sage.

De Vos, G.A. (1980b). L'identité ethnique et le statut de minorité. In P. Tap (Ed.), *Identités Collectives et Changements Sociaux.* Private Text.

De Vos, G.A. (Ed.). (1986). Insight and symbol: Dimensions of analysis in psychoanalytic anthropology. *Journal of Psychoanalytic Anthropology, 9* (3), 199-233.

De Vos, G.A. (1992). *Social cohesion and alienation: Minorities in the United States and Japan.* Boulder, CO: Westview Press.

De Vos, G., & Boyer, L.B. (1989). *Symbolic analysis cross-culturally: The Rorschach test.* Berkeley, CA: University of California Press.

De Vos, G., & Hippler, A.E. (1969). Cultural psychology: Comparative studies of human behavior. In G. Lindzey & E. Aronson (Eds.), *The handbook of social psychology*, Vol. 4 (2nd ed.) (pp. 323-417). Reading, MA: Addison-Wesley.

De Vos, G., & Kim, E.-Y. (1993). Koreans in Japan: Problems with achievement, alienation, authority.   In I. Light & P. Bhachu (Eds.), *California immigrants in world perspective.* NJ: Transaction Books.

De Vos, G., & Takao, S. (Eds.). (1986). *Religion and the family in East Asia* (rev. ed.). Berkeley, CA: University of California Press.

De Vos, G., & Suárez-Orozco, M.M. (1990). *Status inequality: The self in culture.* Newbury Park, CA: Sage.

De Vos, G., & Wagatsuma, H. (1966). *Japan's invisible race: Caste in culture and personality* Berkeley, CA: University of California Press.

De Vos, G. A., & Wetherall, W.O. (1983). Japan's minorities: Burakumin, Koreans, Ainus and Okinawans. Updated by Kate Stearman. *Minority Rights Group,* Report No. 3, London.

Durkheim, E. (1915). *The elementary forms of the religious life.* London: Allen and Unwin.

Durkheim, E. (1951). *Suicide.* Chicago, IL: The Free Press.

Freud, S. (1913/1950). *Totem and taboo.* London: Routledge & Kegan Paul.

Freud, S. (1930). *Civilization and its discontents*. London: The Hogarth Press.

Gough, H., De Vos, G., & Mizushima, K. (1968). A Japanese validation of the CPI Social Maturity Index. *Psychological Reports*, *22*, 143-146.

Kardiner, A. (1939). *The individual and his society: The psychodynamics of primitive social organization*. New York: Columbia University Press.

Changsoo L., & De Vos, G. (1981). *Koreans in Japan: Ethnic conflict and accommodation*. Berkeley, CA: University of California Press.

Lévy-Bruhl, L. (1923). *Les fonctions mentales dans les sociétés inférieures* [*Primitive mentality*]. Boston, MA: Beacon Press.

Linton, R. *The study of man*. New York: Appleton-Century.

McClelland, D.C., Atkinson, R.H., Clark, & Lowell, E.L. (1953). *The achievement motive*. New York: Appleton-Century-Crofts.

Marsella, A., De Vos, G.A., & Hsu, F. (Eds.). (1985). *Culture and self: Asian and Western perspectives*. London: Methuen.

Mizushima, K., & De Vos, G.A. (1967). An application of the California Psychological Inventory in a study of Japanese delinquency. *Journal of Social Psychology*, *71*, 45-51.

Piaget, J. (1930). *The child's conception of physical causality*. London: Kegan Paul, Trench, Trubner.

Piaget, J. (1932). *The moral judgment of the child*. London: Kegan Paul, Trench, Trubner.

Redfield, R. (1953). *The primitive world and its transformations*, Ithaca, NY: Cornell University Press.

Robertson-Smith. W. (1889). *Lectures on the religion of the Semites*. Edinburgh: Black.

Romanucci-Ross, L., & De Vos, G.A. (Eds.). (1995). *Ethnic identity: Creation, conflict, and accommodation*. Walnut Creek, London, New Delhi: Altamira Press.

Strong, E.K. (1934). *Second generation Japanese problems*. Palo Alto, CA: Stanford University Press.

Tylor, E.B. (1871). *Primitive culture*. London: Allen & Unwin.

Vaughn, C. (1988). *Cognitive independence, social independence, and achievement orientation: A comparison of Japanese and U.S. students*. Unpublished doctoral dissertation, University of California, Berkeley.

Vygotsky, L.S. (1978). *Mind in society*. Cambridge, MA: Harvard University Press.

Warner, L. (1963). *Yankee City*. New Haven, CT: Yale University Press.

Warner, L., Havighurst, W.R.J., & Loeb, M.B. (1944). *Who shall be educated?* New York: Harper.

Witkin, H.A. (1967). Cognitive styles across cultures. *International Journal of Psychology*, *2*, 233-250.

Witkin, H.A. (1969). Social influences in the development of cognitive style. In D.A. Goslin (Ed.), *Handbook of socialization theory and research.* New York: Rand McNally.

Witkin, H.A., & Berry, J.W. (1975). Psychological differentiation in cross-cultural perspective. *Journal of Cross-Cultural Psychology, 6,* 4-87.

ENDNOTES

1. See especially my criticism of McClelland (1965), in De Vos (1965), and again in De Vos and Suárez-Orozco (1990).
2. In our research comparing delinquents with non-delinquents in Japan and in Taiwan, we found that the CPI differentiated not only between delinquent and non-delinquent subjects, but also between the parents of delinquents and those of non-delinquents (Abbott, 1976; Gough, De Vos, & Mizushima, 1968; Mizushima & De Vos, 1967).
3. See De Vos and Wagatsuma (1966). There we spell out these relationships in the statistics then available for the *Burakumin* compared with majority Japanese. (These comparative statistics for the *Burakumin* are no longer publicly available since 1969.) The statistics on the relationship between broken homes and delinquency are still similar to those reported in the 1960s.
4. Note that *exclusion* and its manifestation in repression are basically different from *expulsion* as manifest in projection.
5. Again, one must note the difference generally cited in the sociological literature between *cultural* or *behavioral* assimilation, and *structural* or *social* assimilation. Some groups can assimilate the dominant culture, but be excluded from the dominant group, or *choose* to remain socially separate. There was a division among Japanese American Nisei in the 1930s between those who readily interacted with majority peers and those who kept to themselves, but maintained the same social patterns as the majority in the high schools they were attending. They remained socially separate by deliberate choice.

CROSS-CULTURAL VERSUS CULTURAL
PSYCHOLOGY: A SYNTHESIS?

Harry C. Triandis
University of Illinois, U.S.A.

The relationship of culture and psychology is conceived rather differently by different kinds of psychologists. In this paper, I propose to explore some of these conceptions and propose a possible synthesis among the various points of view.

Stated very simply, most psychologists who deal with culture think of culture as an independent variable that may influence psychological processes. There are three ways this conception is used, and they are shown on the top of Figure 1:

1. The Situation (S) and Culture (C) jointly activate Psychological Processes (P) which cause Behavior (B).
2. The Culture (C) changes the probabilities of Situations (S) and the Situations activate the Behavior (B).
3. The Situation (S) is perceived differently in different cultures, depending on Culture (C). This perception activates the Psychological Process (P), which causes the Behavior (B).

Figure 1A
Cross-Cultural Psychology Conceptions

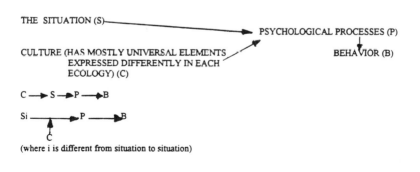

THE SITUATION (S)⟶ PSYCHOLOGICAL PROCESSES (P)

CULTURE (HAS MOSTLY UNIVERSAL ELEMENTS
EXPRESSED DIFFERENTLY IN EACH
ECOLOGY) (C)   BEHAVIOR (B)

$C \longrightarrow S \longrightarrow P \longrightarrow B$

$S_i \longrightarrow P \longrightarrow B$
$\uparrow$
C

(where i is different from situation to situation)

Note that in the top of Figure 1 the process can be handled with a regression analysis, with S and C determining P, which determines B. The second conception is $B=f(P)$, $P=f(S)$, and $S=f(C)$. The third one is $B=f(P)$, $P=f(\text{different kinds of } S)$, where the kind of S is dependent on culture.

82 TRIANDIS

Figure 1B
Indigenous Psychologies

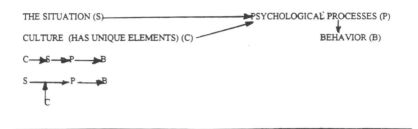

In dialectical terms we can state the position of cross-cultural psychologists as the thesis. The antithesis, to which cultural psychologists subscribe, argues that culture and psychology "make each other up" so that there is no psychological process that does not reflect culture, and culture is constantly shaped by human behaviors.

A somewhat intermediate position is taken by indigenous psychologists (e.g., Kim & Berry, 1993), and it is shown on the bottom of Figure 1. Here culture is operationalized as consisting of both universal and unique cultural elements, and each of the latter is labeled in a unique way.

Much of the work of indigenous psychologists concerns reactions to particular concepts or to particular situations (e.g., scenarios); thus, the work focuses on the *meaning* of particular concepts or situations. For example, they write about the meaning of *amae* in Japan (Doi, 1986), or *philotimo* in Greece (Triandis, 1972), and the role of these concepts in modifying psychosocial processes in unique ways. Indigenous psychologies (Sinha, 1997) are especially rich with such emic concepts. Indigenous psychologists explore the antecedents and consequences of these unique concepts and often want to know how the construct changes meaning across time (e.g., Vassiliou & Vassiliou, 1966) or in various segments of a culture. The argument is that these unique features of the culture are so pervasive that one cannot understand important segments of the psychological processes that occur in those cultures without taking these emic concepts into account.

The antithesis, that is cultural psychology, is shown in Figure 2. It argues that all psychological processes are cultural; behavior changes culture so that culture and psychology make each other up.

Figure 2
Cultural Psychologies

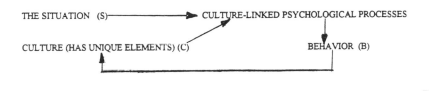

The synthesis that I will outline below is that cross-cultural psychologists and cultural psychologists deal with different topics, focus on different degrees of cultural differences, and use quite different units of analysis. Thus, each of them is correct for the kinds of situations and topics being investigated.

I will now describe in more detail the thesis, the antithesis, and the synthesis.

THE THESIS

Culture is often defined as the human-made part of the environment (Herskovits, 1955). It has both objective (e.g., tools, roads) and subjective (categories, associations, beliefs, attitudes, role and self definitions, norms, values) aspects (Triandis, 1972). Humans have much in common. In fact, human and chimpanzee genetic structures are 99 percent the same (King & Wilson, 1975) so that by contrast with chimpanzees humans everywhere are genetically almost identical. Whatever differences we observe among humans can be traced to the different environments to which humans adapted during the last 3.5 million years.

Different environments provide different opportunities to learn how to perceive, deal with information, and behave. Consequently, there are cultural influences on perception (Segall, Campbell, & Herskovits, 1966), the content of categories (Landar, Ervin, & Horowitz, 1960), the frequency of associations (Szalay & Deese, 1978), beliefs, attitudes, self-definitions (Markus & Kitayama, 1991; Triandis, 1989), role definitions (Triandis, Vassiliou, & Nassiakou, 1968), and norms and values (Schwartz, 1992, 1994).

In all these cases the basic process is the same, but the environment changes the level of adaptation (Helson, 1964). That means that the neutral point for perceiving and making judgments is different because it reflects the experiences obtained in a particular ecology. When data from one culture are compared with data from another culture we get differences that reflect the differences in the levels of adaptation. In short, culture acts as an additional independent variable specifying how people will respond in different kinds of situations, but the basic processes are the same.

Methodologically, cross-cultural psychologists look for culture-specific (emic) ways to measure universal (etic) theoretical constructs. Thus, for instance, if they are studying the ideal ways for a leader to act in different cultures, they might interview subordinates and leaders in different cultures, and ask them how the leaders should behave in different kinds of situations. Some of the behaviors obtained from such interviews may emerge in only one culture, thus they are emics. For example, Smith and Bond (1994) reported that in Japan the ideal leader does not criticize a subordinate directly, but conveys a criticism indirectly, by asking a fellow-worker of the subordinate to inform him of the supervisor's displeasure. This indirect way avoids loss of face, but does convey the necessary information, so that the subordinate may change his or her behavior. The etic theoretical constructs here are "maintenance of good relationships," and "group effectiveness." These etics can be accomplished in different ways in each culture, and the emic Japanese way can be related to this more abstract etic way of describing leadership behavior. The emic American way may well be that the supervisor calls the subordinate to her office and presents the criticism, in a way that does not reduce self-efficacy. Both the Japanese and American behaviors are consistent with maintaining the relationship and being effective, but the behaviors are different.

Note that in this example, culture functions as a *setting* for making observations. It has the same status as an experimental treatment, or an independent variable.

Another example comes from the study of values. Schwartz (1992, 1994) asked participants in some 50 countries to rate the importance of 56 values (e.g., EQUALITY, FREEDOM) on 9-point scales, indicating the extent to which each value is a guiding principle in their life. The importance of particular patterns of values was the outcome of this study. In the West people endorsed more strongly self-direction values, while in the East people endorsed more strongly tradition and conformity values. The method assumes that the 9-point scale has the *same* meaning in every culture. The basic psychological process of seeing a stimulus, such as the word "equality," and responding on the scale is assumed to be *identical* in every culture. The context of the process, such as, for instance, whether the respondent is in a hierarchical or egalitarian relationship with a supervisor at the time that the responses are given is considered irrelevant, because the respondent is responding only to the widely shared meaning of "equality." The only difference is that in some cultures the experiences that people have had when dealing with "equality" might have been different, and these experiences might have shifted their levels of adaptation for judging the importance of the stimulus. Similarly, if people had child-rearing experiences that emphasized self-discovery, exploration, and creativity their ratings will show self-direction, and when the child-rearing patterns emphasized obedience, conformity, and doing one's duty the ratings will emphasize conformity.

Note that the ideal way of data collections of cross-cultural psychologists is to use a large number of cultures, with psychometrically equivalent measurements. For example, if respondents from collectivist cultures are more willing to deceive an antagonist in a negotiation (Triandis et al., submitted) and this phenomenon is seen in four collectivist cultures while it is not seen so clearly in four individualist cultures, rival hypotheses (e.g., explaining the obtained cultural differences on the basis of differences in the understanding of the task, or differences in the social class of the particular samples) become less plausible, allowing the researcher to argue that it is the *cultural* variable (in this example collectivism) that influences the phenomenon. That means that cross-cultural psychologists rely on colleagues from different cultures for data collection. They do not learn all the relevant languages, since that would be impractical. By contrast, cultural psychologists argue that the researcher must learn the local language and act like an anthropologist, which makes data collection in many cultures for comparative purposes completely impractical.

ANTITHESIS

Cultural psychologists argue that culture has pervasive ways of modifying all psychological processes. They argue that psychological processes are not just internal to individuals, but include the cultural context. Many psychological processes include cognitive structures that existed in the culture prior to their being acquired by specific individuals. For example, Kitayama (personal communication, 1996) sees "each person's adaptation ... reflecting his or her ecological, cultural, and social environment."

For cultural psychologists, cultural meanings are not barriers for research but the central topics of investigation (Greenfield, 1997a). Cultural psychologists usually work in one culture, and contrast it with their own culture. They evaluate work done in many cultures as "superficial" and "useless" (E. E. Boesch, personal communication, July 1992). The emphasis is on the unique, emic aspects of one culture and how it contrasts with the culture of the researcher. For example, how do Indians and Americans respond to situations involving social responsibilities (e.g., Miller, 1997; Miller, Bersoff, & Harwood, 1990). The typical methodology is ethnographic—interviews and the like, sometimes supplemented with surveys.

In some cases the emphasis is not on the meaning of *concepts*, but on the meaning of *action*. Rogoff (1992) presents three ways of relating person and culture. (1) *Fusion* is the conception where the individual and the social processes are one and the same. The interpersonal processes have been absorbed in the intrapersonal. (2) *Separation* is the view that person and culture are distinct, though interdependent. (3) *Mutual definition* is the conception that the person's activity and culture "mutually define each other" (p. 318). The unit of analysis is the person's *activity*, which occurs within the traditions, practices, institutions, and values of the culture. One can study the person or the culture separately, without losing sight of the fact that the other entity exists, just as one can study the heart without losing sight that it belongs to the body. Focusing on one aspect does not erase the other aspect. Rogoff argues, however, that focusing on the person is less revealing than focusing on the *person's activities*. This makes her approach distinct from cross-cultural psychology approaches because the latter usually examine aspects of the *persons* who are members of cultures.

In some cases the work of cultural psychologists is not too different from the work of cross-cultural psychologists, as the following illustration will reveal. Tobin, Wu, and Davidson (1989) video-taped 20 minutes of activity in preschools in China, Japan, and the USA. In each preschool they attempted to get shots of free play, structured learning activities, lunch, snack, bathroom, and nap time behaviors. Then they showed the tapes to participants in each of those cultures, and asked them to make a large number of judgments such as "Is this a good preschool?" The stimulus was translation equivalent but the responses clearly reflected the cultural framework of the respondents.

This method allows the participants to provide a "text" as an answer. This approach almost guarantees that cultural elements will enter the responses. The psychological process is perceiving a video tape by bringing each person's own cultural experiences into the act of perception and judgment of each of the qualities that the researchers ask one to use (e.g., is this preschool emphasizing *group activities*?).

These judgments are multidimensional. They reflect all the salient stimuli that have relevance at the moment of judgment. When comparing these texts the researchers found major opportunities to detect the influence of culture on the responses.

The researchers also showed the tapes and interviewed the people who were in the tape (e.g., "Why did you take so long to break up that argument?"). Thus, they obtained the attributions of the actors concerning their behavior, as it was presented in the tape. Here the respondent brings in a complex set of possible attributions (e.g., I always do that, or the school principal expects me to do that, or the parents pressure me to do that, or I like to do that, or if I do that there will be several desirable consequences). Many of these attributions were shaped by culture. So, the responses were culturally loaded.

Furthermore, the researchers showed the tape to 300 or so parents, teachers, administrators, child development specialists, and university students in *each* culture. Thus, the Chinese tape was seen by Chinese and also Japanese and Americans; the American tape was similarly seen by the three cultural groups.

Each group had a somewhat different perspective. For example, the Japanese preschool was perceived as much too "groupie" by the Americans, and even the Chinese found it too "groupie." But the definition of what it is to be "groupie" was different. The Japanese teachers taught different things to each group, and expected the children in each group to learn a lot from each other; the Chinese asked all the children to do things together as a group (even to go to the bathroom at the same time). The Japanese emphasized student-student interactions within each group, while the Chinese emphasized teacher-to-student group interactions. The Japanese rated the Chinese classroom as having "too few group activities," because according to their way of thinking when everyone does the *same* thing that is *not* a "group activity." In short, there is a divergent, implicit cultural definition of what is a "group activity"—the Japanese see each group doing something different; the Chinese see the whole class doing something together as a group. The American view is that both are group activities, and both are to be avoided (!), because each *child* is unique and should learn on her own, to reach her unique potential.

The Japanese classroom emphasizes fusion and unity with something larger than the self, which is the essence of horizontal collectivism (Triandis & Gelfand, 1998). The Chinese classroom emphasizes subjugating the self to the group, which is the essence of vertical collectivism (Triandis & Gelfand, 1998).

The Chinese raters were proud of the regularity and good order that came across from the tape—e.g., all children going to the bathroom at the same time. Teachers in that preschool require the children to go to the bathroom four times per day. They saw the purpose of the school to instill self-control, discipline, social harmony, and responsibility. The word used most frequently by the Chinese was *guan* (governing). This word has positive connotations, such as "to care" and "to love" as well as "to govern."

The Americans assume that there are individual differences among the children, and never question that assumption (culture IS unstated assumptions!); the Japanese assume that the children are fundamentally alike, and never question that assumption.

Only 7% of the Americans listed "good health, hygiene, and grooming habits" among the top three important things the children were supposed to learn, while 49% of the Japanese and 60% of the Chinese did so. On the other hand, child abduction and child abuse were concerns *only* among the Americans!

The important things children are supposed to learn included, among the top three choices, *perseverance* in China (20%) and Japan (16%), but this quality was mentioned by only 5% of the raters in the USA. Sympathy and empathy were listed by 80% of the Japanese and only 39% of the Americans. "Begin reading and math" was listed by only 1% of the Japanese (because children learn that at home) and 22% of the Americans. Self-reliance was listed by 73% of the Americans, and only 29% of the Chinese.

Note now an important methodological difference between cross-cultural and cultural psychologists. Cross-cultural psychologists attempt to develop equivalence in the scales used across cultures (e.g., Triandis, 1992). In some cases they seek equivalence even for the items, as is the case when they use item response theory to reject items that do not have the same meaning in the different cultures (Hulin, Drasgow, & Parsons, 1983). However, in the Tobin et al. (1989) study there is no concern for such equivalence. The focus is on the meaning of the theoretical constructs (e.g., "what is a group activity?") and these meanings are expected to be different.

What emerges very clearly in the results of this method is that the cultural assumptions of each culture, such as vertical collectivism in China, individualism in the USA, come through in numerous ways, and are totally embedded in the results.

The Tobin et al. method focuses on the *context*: when the Chinese teacher views the American video tape she uses her Chinese framework, with all its cultural standard operating procedures and unstated assumptions. Thus the responses she gives reflect Chinese culture (the culture of the rater), as well as American culture (the culture depicted by the videotape). Similarly, when the Americans find the Chinese way of requiring the children to go to the bathroom together "quite horrible" they reflect their individualism, which assumes that individual differences are extremely important.

Greenfield (1997a), while advocating the methods of cultural psychologists states: "The paradox is that universal processes are revealed more by *noncomparable methods* and *theoretical comparison* than by *comparable methods* and *quantitative comparison* across cultures." (italics in original, p. 335)

However, the paradox may be due to the fact that the unit of analysis used by many cultural psychologists is not the *individual*, and the reactions of individuals to specific stimuli, as is the case for cross-cultural psychologists, but the *human activity* or event. For instance, Rogoff argues that sociocultural activities, involving people in shared endeavors with cultural history and organizations should be used as the units of analysis (Rogoff & Chavajay, 1995). Barbara Rogoff (personal communication, 1996) put it this way: "If activity is used as the unit of analysis, a researcher must attend to the contributions made by individuals, groups, and cultural communities. I argue that different researchers and research traditions may study the roles of individuals, groups, and cultural communities as their primary focus, but must give attention to the other *planes of analysis* in order to interpret what is happening within their primary focus. This is because the roles of individuals, groups, and communities are not independent but mutually constituting. I use the term "planes of analysis" rather than levels, because I see the varying focus taken in particular studies as an analytic tool rather than a reflection of the actual existence of independent entities (or levels) of individual, group, and community. I argue that the division of individual and culture into dependent and independent variables is a way for researchers to get a handle on things, and not the state of the world. I think that if our methods of analysis are treated as veridical windows on the world, through force of habit we blind ourselves to the possibilities of other ways of understanding the world. Our methods may be serving as unquestioned cultural assumptions in the research community. I use the term *community* rather than culture to emphasize that people participate in multiple communities which themselves change, as do the individuals. Using *activity* as the unit of analysis inherently focuses greater attention on development and process (or communities and groups as well as individuals) than has been the case when individuals have served as the unit of analysis."

This view results in the use of real life contexts for research settings. For example, it requires studying people's "everyday cognition" as they make complicated woven patterns or narrate complicated historical accounts (Rogoff & Chavajay, 1995, p. 863) or decide about sleeping arrangements (Shweder, Jensen, & Goldstein, 1995). Examining the numerical abilities of children must include information about cultural tools available to them, such as the existence of the Chinese or Japanese abacus.

SYNTHESIS

Examination of the kinds of people who are studied by cross-cultural psychologists suggests that they are not members of extremely exotic cultures. In fact, if we consider the construct of "cultural distance" (see elaboration in Triandis, 1994) as reflecting differences in language (e.g., the languages of researcher and the population studied are either from the same or from a different language family), social structure (e.g., monogamy versus polygyny), religion (e.g., specific Christian versus specific Buddhist sect), socioeconomic condition (e.g., Gross National Product per capita of, say, US $30,000 versus $300), political system, level of literacy, etc. we see that cross-cultural psychologists frequently study samples where the cultural distance is small (e.g., managers from relatively economically advanced countries). By contrast, cultural psychologists frequently study children in cultures where the cultural distance is large (e.g., non-literate societies versus information societies).

Greenfield (1997b) presents a strong case for the difference between schooled and unschooled populations. Schooled populations have learned to deal with abstract reality. Most of the events that take place in schools are in books, lectures, and visual aids that represent the events, but the student is not in direct contact with the entities under discussion, but simply with symbols of these entities. That is very different from the life of a child that is only in direct contact with objects. Most of the methods employed by psychologists require abstract thinking. One does not see a lion, but rather the word "lion" on a test item. The subjective cultures of the researcher and the child are not the same, so there is no adequate communication between the two, and thus the usual methods of psychologists cannot be used with unschooled populations. Unschooled children are not used to communicating in impersonal manners, without context, as is required when answering a questionnaire or test. In many collectivist cultures one is not supposed to have or state an individual belief, but one must rather express a group belief or attitude. The very act of asking a question of a child is incompatible with established cultural patterns where children are supposed to listen to adults and not speak. The very act of communicating with strangers is rare in many cultures, so that a researcher may have to spend much time establishing friendly relationships before any "psychological measurement" can take place.

Thus, the methods that can be used when the cultural distance between researcher and respondents is large are more restricted than the methods that can be used when the respondents are university students. It follows that cultural psychologists cannot use sophisticated scales, tests, structured questionnaires, experiments, and the like, and thus they use ethnographic methods. Such methods are likely to impress them with the extent to which culture is intertwined with the psychological processes they are investigating.

Boesch (1996) makes similar points in an article discussing the "seven flaws of cross-cultural psychology." He does not see the possibility of (1) using culture as an independent variable, (2) getting representative samples in each culture, (3) equivalent measurement across cultures, (4) avoiding biases due to the interaction between the presence of a specific researcher and particular participants, (5) studying topics that are not totally culturally specific, (6) dealing with participants as sources of information, instead of (7) objects of friendly interaction and observation. In sum, he argues that valid data can be obtained from members of a culture only through ethnographic methods.

This position is probably correct when the cultural distance is large, and especially when the participants are not literate, but it is not necessarily correct when the cultural distance is small and the participants are university students.

In addition, the topic under investigation often pushes developmental psychologists toward the cultural psychology conception and methodology, while it pushes social psychologists toward the cross-cultural psychology position. In fact, Cole defines culture as whatever helps things to grow (Cole, 1992). This is a meaning of culture found in microbiology, where organisms are placed in cultures in order to grow. When that perspective is used, the way culture interacts with development becomes naturally the focus of conceptualization and investigation and the organism is conceived of as being "in the making." Rogoff's mutual definition of the person's activity and culture is indeed a very useful conception.

On the other hand, when social or industrial psychologists are trying to understand why social behavior is different in different cultures, they are not examining the person "developing in culture." The person *encounters* a culture, as is the case when an American manager has the job of managing several Thai subordinates. In this case, it is more useful to examine some aspects of American and Thai subjective cultures and how their consequences are reflected in behavior.

Thus, the unit of analysis of cultural psychologists is often *behavior*, such as how does a child do something, while the unit of analysis of cross-cultural psychologists is the *person* in the cultural context. In order to study, for instance, why Thais may leave their jobs without telling their employers that they are leaving, cross-cultural psychologists need to examine cognitive processes that might be reflected in ratings of stimulus words on several scales.

In addition, as Kashima has pointed out (lecture at University of Illinois, October 16, 1997), one can conceptualize culture as something relatively static that changes only when generations of individuals change alternatively or as something dynamic that involves meanings that change from moment to moment. There are elements of culture that are stable and other elements that are changing from moment to moment. If one is working with the former elements, and with populations of individuals responding to those elements, the methods of cross-cultural psychology are appropriate. If one is working with the latter elements, and with populations of individuals that are responding to those elements, the methods of cultural psychology are appropriate.

In short, each of the approaches has a place in our attempt to relate culture and psychological processes. The methods of cultural psychologists are appropriate for developmental psychology and are often the only ones that can be used with non-literate participants. They allow for wide exploration. For instance, the researcher may note some relationship at one point during the research process and develop a partial test of the hypothesis at a subsequent point. Curvilinear hypotheses might emerge during such explorations. The methods are especially appropriate when the researcher is not familiar with the culture, is not testing specific hypotheses but rather is exploring, and is attempting to provide the best description of the culture.

On the other hand, because ethnographic methods are not quantitative, it is difficult to obtain precise measures of their reliability and validity. The methods are to some extent subjective and the researcher's preconceptions have a greater chance to be reflected in the outcomes than is the case in the work of cross-cultural psychologists.

Nevertheless, the methods used by cross-cultural psychologists also have limitations: they can create reactivity (e.g., the respondents may try to make a good impression, may show their apprehension about how they will be evaluated, may try to support or spoil the test of some hypothesis that they believe is being tested, and so on). To balance this disadvantage, however, the methods of cross-cultural psychologists are more easily subjected to exact replications and to multimethod construct validation than the methods of cultural psychologists. It is easier to do parametric studies in order to examine whether a phenomenon no longer appears once a parameter is high or low. It is easier to control for rival hypotheses, by using a large number of cultures having some cultural elements in common and all other cultural elements different.

The future of the relationship of culture and psychology may include more investigations like those of Tobin et al. (1989), which used methods of both cultural and cross-cultural psychology, and collaborations between cultural psychologists providing the data from one culture, and cross-cultural psychologists utilizing the data of cultural psychologists from many cultures to understand both universals and culture-specific influences of culture on psychological processes.

BIBLIOGRAPHY

Boesch, E. (1996). The seven flaws of cross-cultural psychology: The story of a conversion. *Mind, Culture and Activity*, *3*, 2-10.

Cole, M. (1992). Culture and cognitive development: From cross-cultural comparison to model systems of cultural mediation. In A.F. Healey, S.M. Kosslyn, & R. M. Shiffrin (Eds.), *From learning processes to cognitive processes: Essays in honor of William K. Estes* (pp. 279-305). Hillsdale, NJ: Erlbaum.

Doi, T. (1986). *The anatomy of conformity: The individual versus society.* Tokyo: Kadansha.

Greenfield, P.M. (1997a). Culture as process: Empirical methods for cultural psychology. In J.W. Berry, Y. H. Poortinga, & J. Pandey (Eds.), *Handbook of cross-cultural psychology* (2nd ed.) (pp. 301-346). Boston, MA: Allyn and Bacon.

Greenfield, P M (1997b). You can't take it with you: Why ability assessments don't cross cultures. *American Psychologist*, *52*, 1115-1124.

Helson, H. (1964). *Adaptation level theory.* New York: Harper & Row.

Herskovits, M.J. (1955). *Cultural anthropology.* New York: Knopf.

Hulin, C.L., Drasgow, F., & Parsons, C.K. (1983). *Item response theory: Applications to psychological measurement.* Homewood, IL: Irwin.

Kim, U., & Berry, J. W. (1993). *Indigenous psychologies.* Thousand Oaks, CA: Sage.

King, M.C., & Wilson, A.C. (1975). Evolution at two levels of humans and chimpanzees. *Science*, *188*, 107-116.

Landar, H. J., Ervin, S. M., & Horowitz, A. E. (1960). Navaho color categories. *Language*, *36*, 368-382.

Markus, H., & Kitayama, S. (1991). Culture and self: Implications for cognition, emotion and motivation. *Psychological Review*, *98*, 224-253.

Miller, J.G. (1997). Theoretical issues in cultural psychology. In J.W. Berry, Y. H. Poortinga, & J. Pandey, (Eds.), *Handbook of cross-cultural psychology* (2nd ed.) (pp. 85-128). Boston, MA: Allyn and Bacon.

Miller, J.G., Bersoff, D.M., & Hartwood, R.L. (1990). Perceptions of social responsibilities in India and the United States: Moral imperatives or personal decisions? *Journal of Personality and Social Psychology*, *58*, 33-47.

Rogoff, B. (1992). Three ways to relate person and culture: Thoughts sparked by Valsiner's review of *Apprenticeship in thinking*. *Human Development*, *35*, 316-320.

Rogoff, B., & Chavajay, P. (1995). What's become of research on the cultural basis of cognitive development? *American Psychologist*, *50*, 859-877.

Segall, M., Campbell, D.T., & Herskovits, M.J. (1966). *The influence of culture on visual perception*. Indianapolis, IN: Bobbs-Merrill.

Shweder, R., Jensen, L., & Goldstein, W. (1995). Who sleeps by whom revised: A method for extracting the moral goods implicit in practice. In J.J. Goodnow, P. Miller, & F. Kessler (Eds.), *Cultural practices as contexts for development* (pp. 21-39). San Francisco, CA: Jossey-Bass.

Sinha, D. (1997) Indigenizing psychology. In J.W. Berry, Y.H. Poortinga, & J. Pandey (Eds.), *Handbook of cross-cultural psychology* (2nd ed.) (pp. 129-170). Boston, MA: Allyn and Bacon.

Szalay, L., & Deese, J. (1978). *Subjective meaning and culture: An assessment through word associations*. Hillsdale, NJ: Erlbaum.

Schwartz, S.H. (1992). Universals in the content and structure of values: Theoretical advances and empirical tests in 20 countries. In M. Zanna (Ed.), *Advances in experimental social psychology* (Vol. 25, pp. 1-66). New York: Academic Press.

Schwartz, S.H. (1994). Beyond individualism and collectivism: New cultural dimensions of values. In U. Kim, H.C. Triandis, C. Kagitcibasi, S-C. Choi, & G. Yoon (Eds.), *Individualism and collectivism: Theory, method and applications* (pp. 85-122). Newbury Park, CA: Sage.

Smith, P.B., & Bond, M.H. (1994). *Social psychology across cultures*. Boston, MA: Allyn and Bacon.

Szalay, L.R., & Deese, J. (1978). *Subjective meaning and culture: An assessment through word associations*. Hillsdale, NJ: Erlbaum.

Tobin, J.J., Wu, D.Y.H., & Davidson, D.H. (1989). *Preschool in three cultures: Japan, China and the United States*. New Haven, CT: Yale University Press.

Triandis, H.C. (1972). *The analysis of subjective culture*. New York: Wiley.

Triandis, H.C. (1989). Self and social behavior in different cultural contexts. *Psychological Review*, *96*, 269-289.

Triandis, H.C. (1992). Cross-cultural research in social psychology. In D. Granberg & G. Sarup (Eds.), *Social judgment and intergroup relations:*

Essays in honor of Muzafer Sherif (pp. 229-244). New York: Springer Verlag.

Triandis, H.C. (1994). *Culture and social behavior.* New York: McGraw-Hill.

Triandis, H.C., & Gelfand, M. (1998). Converging measurement of horizontal and vertical individualism and collectivism. *Journal of Personality and Social Psychology, 74,* 118-128.

Triandis, H.C., Vassiliou, V., & Nassiakou, M. (1968). Three cross-cultural studies of subjective culture. *Journal of Personality and Social Psychology Monograph Supplement, 8*(4), 1-42.

Triandis, H.C., Carnevale, P., Gelfand, M., Probst, T.M., Radhakrishnan, P., Robert, C., Kashima, E.S., Dragonas, T., Chan, D., Chen, X.P., Kim, U., Kim, K., de Dreu, C., van de Vliert, E., Iwao, S., & Schmitz, P. (submitted). *Culture and the use of deception in negotiations.*

Vassiliou, G., & Vassiliou, V. (1966). Social values as a psychodynamic variable: Preliminary explorations of the semantics of philotimo. *Acta Neurologica et Psychiatrica Hellenika, 5,* 121-135.

CULTURAL CONTEXTUALISM WITHOUT COMPLETE RELATIVISM IN THE STUDY OF HUMAN DEVELOPMENT

Çigdem Kagitçibasi, Koç University, Turkey

CONTEXT

Context is the most important clue to an understanding of human development, both in terms of the development of competence and also the development of the self. As such, any theory of human development must incorporate context. There is a growing recognition of the importance of context today; however, this is a rather recent trend. For a long time, the psychological study of human development entailed examining more specifically "child development" from "organismic" and "mechanistic" perspectives. The organismic perspective, as seen for example in Gesell's approach and the widely accepted Piagetian thinking, focused on maturational unfolding. Piaget's stages depend on the interaction between universal features of the environment, maturation, plus other factors. The mechanistic perspective, as exemplified by the behavioristic tradition, reduced context to the proximal environment of the "stimulus" (see Kagitçibasi, 1990 for a discussion of these models).

The noncontextual orientation of mainstream developmental psychology has also meant the neglect of culture. Thus, it has been claimed that "developmental psychology has largely missed the opportunity to consider the child in the cultural milieu, which is the *sine qua non* of the developmental completion of human nature" (Schwartz, 1981, p. 4). Since the goal was set as reaching universal laws of development, uniformities and generalities were targeted. Any contextual variation was therefore seen as "noise"—a source of error. The longstanding dominance of the organismic paradigm has more recently been strengthened further by the advances in biological psychology, behavior genetics, and neuroscience.

Nevertheless, contextual or environmental orientations to human development have also a long history, constituting the main competing perspective to the biological orientation. The historical roots of the contextual emphasis can be traced back to the philosophy of the enlightenment. Theoretical precursors within psychology emerged in mid-twentieth century in diverse areas ranging from social psychology to perception.

Table 1 presents the main threads of influence, recent developments, and current directions in which context figures in an important way. It reflects the main lines of theory/research, with some overlap among them. The researchers and references comprise only a few examples, and not at all a representative sample of the work involved. There is also overlap, and a particular person may be seen as belonging to another entry or to more than one entry. The number and the diversity of theoretical perspectives and research programs focusing on context are impressive. They each arise from

Table 1
The Increasing Relevance of Context

HISTORICAL ANTECEDENTS:
Enlightenment (J. Locke and J. J. Rousseau)
John Dewey
Early developmental and comparative psychology (Baldwin, 1895, 1909; Novikoff, 1945; von Bertalanffy, 1933)
THEORETICAL PRECURSORS:
Lewin's (1951) topological psychology and field theory
Brunswik's (1955) "environment-organism-environment arc"
Barker's (1968) ecological psychology
Berger & Luckman's (1967) social constructivism
J.W. Whiting & Child (1953); B.B. Whiting (1963): Cross-cultural anthropology
MORE RECENT IMPETUS AND CURRENT DIRECTIONS:
Ecological perspectives
Ecological theory (Bronfenbrenner, 1979)
Ecocultural theory (Berry, 1976, 1980)
Systemic models of person—environment interaction (von Bertalanffy, 1968)
Sociohistorical theory
Vygotsky (1962, 1978) (direct effects on "Culture and cognition" below)
Life-span development theory and developmental contextualism
Baltes & Brim (1979); Baltes (1987); Baltes et al. (1980); Lerner & Busch-Rossnagel (1981); Lerner et al. (1983); Valsiner (1994)
Interpretive anthropology (symbols and meanings approach)
Marsella & White (1984); Marsella, DeVos, & Hsu (1985); Shweder & LeVine (1984); Shweder & Bourne (1984)
Culture and cognition (everyday cognition, cultural psychology)
Cole, Sharp, & Lave (1976); Cole (1992), Serpell (1976); Greenfield & Lave (1982), Rogoff (1981, 1990); Scribner (1990); Nunes et al. (1993)
Culture and human development
Munroe, Munroe, & Whiting (1981), Super & Harkness (1981); Dasen (1984); Sigel et al. (1992); Goodnow et al. (1995); Kagitçibasi (1996)
Problem- and policy-oriented research
Family and disadvantage:
Bronfenbrenner & Weiss (1983); Laosa & Sigel (1982); Dym (1988); Patterson & Dishion (1988); Sameroff & Fiese (1992); Huston (1991)
Ethnic minority research (U.S.A.):
Laosa (1980, 1984); Coll (1990); McLoyd (1990); Harrison et al. (1990);

Table 1 Continued

Szapocznik & Kurtines (1993)
Intervention research
  Slaughter (1988); Zigler & Weiss (1985); Meisels & Shonkoff (1990);
  Kagitçibasi (1995, 1996)

---

different traditions but share a common recognition of the significance of context. With so many current perspectives involved, the table reflects an *increasing* relevance of context.

The recognition of the relevance of context has important implications for theory and research in human development. Starting in the 1980s, following the seminal work of Bronfenbrenner on the *Ecology of Human Development* (1979), much contextual emphasis is seen in theory and in research in the field (e.g., Bornstein, 1991; Bronfenbrenner, 1986; Dasen, 1984; Greenfield & Cocking, 1994; Jahoda, 1986; Kagitçibasi, 1984, 1992, 1996a; Rogoff et al., 1984; Rogoff & Morelli, 1989; Valsiner, 1989).

In cross-cultural psychology, contextual perspectives on human development reach out to the more encompassing culture. Culture is incorporated in terms of its influence on the more circumscribed home environment, in particular parental values and behaviors, childrearing patterns, and shared meaning systems. A great deal of research has examined cultural influences on the development of the self and of competence. I will first deal with the former by analyzing "autonomy" as a case in point.

AUTONOMY

Cross-cultural research points to variations in cultural meaning systems. It is not sufficiently recognized, however, that not just people's everyday meaning systems but also construals of the self within the discipline of psychology are subject to cultural influence. For example, there is ample evidence showing how a culturally defined meaning is attributed to "self" in psychology (for reviews see Kagitçibasi, 1990, 1996a; Markus & Kitayama, 1991; Shweder & Bourne, 1984). More specifically, autonomy, as an important self-attribute is understood in a particular way in Western psychology which has every sign of being a Western emic or Western indigenous social construction.

Psychology, reflecting the individualistic ethos of the Western world, construes autonomy as separateness from others. Even though autonomy does not necessarily imply distancing oneself from others, such a meaning is commonly attributed to it. This is because it is assumed that being independent requires being separate. Independence and separateness are seen as prerequisites for autonomy, as it is seen to be an outcome of the "separation-individuation" process (Mahler et al., 1975). Therefore, from such a perspective, an interdependent self-construal would be assumed to exclude autonomy (for reviews see Kagitçibasi, 1990, 1996a; Markus & Kitayama, 1991).

Two different, though related, meaning dimensions appear to be confounded in an individualistic construal of autonomy. One of these is the interpersonal distance dimension, reflecting different degrees of interpersonal separateness and relatedness. The other has to do with agency, ranging from an agent-like to a pawn-like (dependent) functioning. The terms "autonomous" versus "heteronomous" morality, as used by Piaget (1948) reflect this second meaning dimension (Table 2).

Table 2
Two Underlying Dimensions

Interpersonal Distance:	Separateness	....	Relatedness
Agency:	Autonomy	....	Heteronomy (Dependency)

The two dimensions of interpersonal distance (relatedness-separateness) and agency (autonomy-heteronomy) are based on two basic human needs recognized by conflict theories of personality (e.g., Angyal, 1951; Bakan, 1966, 1968). They are different from one another both logically and psychologically. Thus, a person's standing on the interpersonal distance dimension may or may not affect his/her standing on the agency dimension. In other words the two dimensions are orthogonal, and to what degree they relate to one another is an empirical question. Yet, these two dimensions are often confounded and used interchangeably.

It is quite possible, for example, for a person to be high in both agency and relatedness. However, given the psychological constructions which influence our thinking, agency and relatedness appear as if they were mutually exclusive constructs, and their combination is seen as a contradiction in terms (see Kagitçibasi, 1996b for a more thorough discussion of this issue).

Such confounding of these two basic dimensions and seeing agency and relatedness as opposites has rather interesting cross-cultural implications. It leads to the assumption that highly interrelated interconnected selves lack autonomy. This type of a view is particularly common in descriptions of interpersonal relations regarding the so-called collectivist societies and is based on confusing relatedness with heteronomy (dependence) (Hofstede, 1980,

1991; Triandis, 1987, 1988).

There is a parallel here between the confounding of the agency and the interpersonal distance dimensions and that of what I have called "normative" and "relational" individualism/collectivism (I/C) (Kagitçibasi, 1997). Normative I/C refers to socially accepted norms upholding the primacy of the group (family) or the individual, with normative collectivism prescribing the subservient role of the individual toward the group and thus a low level of individual agency (heteronomy). Relational I/C, however, has to do with the level of interpersonal connectedness, with collectivism referring to a greater degree of relatedness. Frequently, the closer interpersonal distance (connectedness) in collectivism is interpreted as lack of autonomy because the distinction between these two different aspects of I/C is not recognized.

There is quite a bit of current theorizing regarding the different types of selves and their behavioral correlates (e.g., Markus & Kitayama, 1991; see Kagitçibasi 1996a for a review). These views are helpful in pointing to cross-cultural diversity. Context figures in these conceptualizations in a general way, for example in terms of collectivist or individualistic culture.

However, an emphasis on diversity in contexts and self-construals can easily lead to a merely descriptive anthropological approach that stresses the uniqueness of each culture/context. Yet, contexts are not necessarily unique; they can be compared. What is needed is to go beyond mere description and to search for the underlying causes of the observed diversity. Such a search also promises to bring out possible similarities, as well as differences, among contexts and human phenomena.

There is much work, carried out by sociologists and anthropologists, which examines childrearing patterns in different sociocultural contexts. However, there is not enough linking of the research results in different disciplines. In particular, sociological and anthropological conceptual tools would be valuable when examining why certain kinds of childrearing and socialization patterns occur in different sociocultural contexts and when a change in the process of self-development may be expected.

What is the relevance of the above conceptualization for understanding diversity and change in childrearing patterns and the self?

FAMILY AS A DEVELOPMENTAL CONTEXT

I have developed a model of family change that utilizes a contextual-developmental-functional approach to the examination of family functioning and the development of the self (Kagitçibasi, 1990, 1996a). Three family interaction patterns are differentiated: 1) the traditional family characterized by total interdependence between generations in both material and emotional realms; 2) the individualistic model based on independence; and 3) a dialectical synthesis of these two, involving material independence but emotional interdependence between generations.

The model of total interdependence is prevalent in rural agrarian societies where intergenerational interdependence is necessary for family livelihood. Children contribute to the family economy while young and especially when they grow up, as they have "old-age security value" for their parents (Kagitçibasi, 1982). In this context the independence of the child is not functional, thus not valued, because an independent child may leave the family and look after his own self interest. Thus, obedience orientation is dominant in childrearing.

The contrasting pattern of independence is characteristic of the prototypical Western, particularly American middle-class nuclear family, at least in its professed ideals. Affluence and sources of support render dependence on adult offspring unnecessary and even unacceptable; thus, children are brought up to be independent and self-sufficient. Autonomy is highly valued and is often misconstrued as separateness.

The third model reflects the changing family in much of the "Majority World" with "cultures of relatedness." These are the contexts where closely-knit family/human ties prevail, but where economic and social structural transformations are seen with increasing education, urbanization, and industrialization. What appears to happen is that with increased affluence, *material* interdependence between generations decreases because elderly parents do not need any longer to depend on the economic support of their adult offspring. Nevertheless, *emotional* or psychological interdependence continues, since it is ingrained in the collectivist culture and is not incompatible with the changing lifestyles.

In the third model, emotional interdependence, we see the type of childrearing that instills both relatedness and autonomy. Both are functional. With decreasing material interdependencies, there is room for an autonomy orientation to emerge in childrearing. This is because when the economic contribution of the offspring is no longer necessary for family survival, the child's autonomy is no longer seen as a threat. However, even though autonomy is now valued, there is still firm control in childrearing because separation is not the goal. Relatedness or interconnectedness is still valued.

The model of emotional interdependence is relevant to the previous discussion concerning the distinctiveness of the two dimensions of relatedness-separateness (interpersonal distance) and autonomy-heteronomy (agency). This is because there is a recognition here of the possible coexistence of relatedness and autonomy. What we see here is a synthetic (dialectic) model integrating two attributes that are often assumed to be contradictory.

WHY SHOULD AUTONOMY COME IN?

We have seen above that autonomy *can* emerge in the family model of emotional interdependence because it is no longer seen as a threat to family livelihood, given the decreased material intergenerational interdependence. However, why *should* it emerge? The answer to this question rests in the changing lifestyles that accompany urbanization and socioeconomic development.

An obedience orientation in childrearing is functional in sociocultural economic contexts where mere compliance is sufficient for success. This is true, for example, for simple agriculture in traditional agrarian societies and for menial labor. However, with urbanization, an increasing specialization in the work place, and greater prevalence of schooling, simple compliance is no longer sufficient for success and especially for social mobility. The experience and wisdom coming down from the older generation become less valuable; capacity for individual decision making emerges as a new asset. Autonomy, therefore, becomes functional in urban contexts.

Childrearing that emphasizes relatedness thus also allows for the development of the child's autonomy, in response to the changing life styles. Kohn (1969) made a similar functional analysis earlier in an examination of childrearing patterns in middle and working classes in England. What is different in the present analysis is a recognition of the coexistence of autonomy with relatedness, given the basic collectivist culture (culture of relatedness).

Putting everything together, one can see the development of three different types of selves in the three different family models as indicated in Table 3. The first one is the related self, which is high in relatedness but low in autonomy; it develops in the family model of total interdependence. The second one is the separated self, which is high in autonomy but low in relatedness; it develops in the family model of independence. The third one is the autonomous-related self, which is high in both relatedness and autonomy; it develops in the family model of emotional interdependence. Thus, contextual variations have significant and predictable implications for the family and for the development of the self.

The autonomous-related self is an "integrative synthesis." It is based on a reconceptualization of autonomy, evoking its meaning as agency and untangling it from the interpersonal distance dimension (relatedness). Differentiating agency and interpersonal distance dimensions renders this conceptualization possible.

Quite a bit of research supports the synthetic model of emotional interdependence (for a review, see Kagitçibasi, 1996a). The other two models, independence and total interdependence are also commonly known. The fourth model in Table 3 is at this point rather hypothetical. It is possible to observe it

Table 3
Agency, Interpersonal Distance, and the
Types of Selves in Context

| | AGENCY | |
	AUTONOMY	HETERONOMY
RELATEDNESS	Family model of emotional interdependence	Family model of interdependence
INTERPERSONAL DISTANCE	Control and autonomy orientation	Obedience-orientation
SEPARATION	Autonomous-related self Family model of independence	Related self Hierarchical rejecting family
	Self-reliance orientation	Rejecting, obedience-orientation
	Separate self	Separate-heteronomous self

in hierarchical families with rejecting and obedience-oriented childrearing, instilling in the child a separated but heteronomous self (Fisek, 1991).

COMPETENCE

Contextual diversity and in particular changes in lifestyles accompanying socioeconomic development also have implications for the development of competence.

Much research carried out in the traditional society with closely knit human relations and the culture of relatedness, especially in Africa, points to a so-called social definition of intelligence (for a review, see Kagitçibasi, 1996a). In other words, parents' definitions of an "intelligent" child involve social responsibility, positive social behavior, obedience, etc. As discussed above, obedience orientation, rather than autonomy, in childrearing is common in such contexts, because a child's conformity is functional for occupational requirements (Kohn, 1969) or for old-age security of the parents and family livelihood (Kagitçibasi, 1982). Compliance of children may be valuable even for survival in hazardous environments (LeVine, 1974, 1988). Such expectations from the child affect definitions of competence, also.

Learning is functional; it is adaptive to environmental demands. Therefore, children's competence is promoted in culturally valued domains, whereas development in other domains lags behind. If parents define competence mainly in social terms, then social skills and self-help skills will develop, while cognitive (school-like) skills may lag behind. This is in fact what is found in research in traditional contexts with closely-knit human relations where children perform important social functions. For example, Harkness and Super (1992) found children in Africa to be highly skilled in household chores, taking care of younger siblings, animals, etc., but to be poor in simple cognitive tasks such as retelling a story. And Dasen (1984) noted that the Baoule of Africa value social skills and manual dexterity in their childrearing because intelligence is primarily defined in terms of these skills.

Cognitive or school-like skills are functional for survival and success in school and in urban jobs. Social skills are also functional for adapting to the school environment (Okagaki & Sternberg, 1993). However, they need to be accompanied by cognitive skills that are adaptive to school and to more specialized functions in modern society.

A social definition of intelligence and inculcating conformity in childrearing may be quite functional in the context of rural agrarian lifestyles, paralleling the lack of autonomy, discussed above. However, with changing lifestyles, and especially with urbanization and the introduction of schooling, modifications in these childrearing patterns are bound to happen. Analogous to the emergence of autonomy in childrearing, a cognitive definition of intelligence is also called for. However, it needs to be noted here that autonomy does *not replace* relatedness, but is rather *added to it* because both are compatible with urban lifestyles and satisfy basic human needs. Similarly, a cognitive definition of intelligence does not have to replace a social definition, but can be added to it.

The implications of this for childrearing are important, especially regarding early language development. Usually, learning of social skills and manual skills occurs through observation and imitation and not much verbal explanation is involved in this "teaching by doing" (Gay & Cole, 1967; Helling, 1966; LeVine & LeVine, 1966; Teasdale & Teasdale, 1992). However, early cognitive development depends heavily on verbal communication with the child that supports his/her language skills. A child development-oriented childrearing involves verbal responsiveness and elaborated verbal reasoning with the child. This is found to be much less common in the rural and low socioeconomic contexts, compared with urban middle-class homes (Coll, 1990; Goodnow, 1988; Laosa, 1980).

Similarly, parents with traditional rural backgrounds and low socioeconomic status may have childrearing values that do not quite fit those of the school culture. For example, Nunes (1993) noted that immigrant Mexican parents in the United States believed, erroneously, that if their children are quiet, obedient, and listen to the teacher, then they will do well in school. Okagaki and Sternberg (1993) found that immigrant Cambodian, Filipino, Mexican, and Vietnamese parents valued social and practical skills more than cognitive skills, unlike Anglo-Americans, and that parents' belief about the importance of conformity correlated negatively with children's school performance.

IMPLICATIONS FOR CONCEPTUALIZATION

I have discussed how diverse cultural contexts influence the development of the self and of competence, particularly regarding the impact of the changes in context. I have tried to show, using a functional perspective, that the effect of context is systematic and predictable. In other words, we can understand why there is a certain type of family functioning in a particular sociocultural-economic context. The resultant type of self and type of competence also fit the picture. More importantly, we can predict in which direction changes will take place with socioeconomic development. In other words, there is a contextual analysis here which points to the systematic interface between different types of contexts and children's developmental trajectories. This interface has universal validity.

This type of conceptualization is quite different from a relativistic orientation to the same cultural diversity. A relativistic perspective also focuses on the context, utilizes a functional approach and stresses, in particular, the role of the context in defining reality. The adaptive nature of "everyday learning" is emphasized. For example, the "everyday cognition" tradition, informed by the Vygotskyan sociohistorical school of thought, considers all learning as "goal directed action" and thus functional in adapting to contextual requirements (e.g., Childs & Greenfield, 1980; LCHC, 1983; Rogoff, 1990; Rogoff et al., 1984). Up to this point the "everyday cognition" perspective and the analysis I have pursued in this paper are very similar, indeed. In the next step, however, there is a significant divergence in orientation. The cultural relativist position of the "everyday cognition" school stresses the specificity of each learning context and avoids generalization. When this view of context-specific learning is seen to define all learning (Shweder, 1990), then we are left with no shared attributes, no common standards, and no possibility of comparison. Then any learning is as good as any other, be it traditional weaving skills or school learning. For example, there is research into the everyday learning of child street vendors who gain mathematical skills (Carraher, Schliemann, & Carraher, 1988; Nunes, Schliemann, & Carraher,

1993) or learning different skills through apprenticeship (Lave, 1977; Rogoff, 1990). The everyday learning perspective claims that since all learning is functional and context dependent, school learning is not superior to or even different from any other type of learning; "its apparent superiority...is to some extent an artifact of cross-cultural experimental design" (Greenfield & Lave, 1982, p. 185).

However, traditional everyday learning may not pay off in changing contexts. For example, research in Nigeria (Oloko, 1994) found that despite the popular belief that street trading facilitates greater arithmetical skills, nonworking school children outperformed working ones most in arithmetic. In literacy tests, also, nonworking students did better than working ones. The researcher points to "street work representing maladaptation to a modernizing economic, social and political environment" (p. 220).

Quite a bit of traditional learning, though not all, involves learning specific procedural skills (*how* to do something), rather than conceptualization. This is especially the case where there is limited verbal explanation, as I discussed before. This type of procedural learning does not easily transfer to new situations (Hatano, 1982). If most learning experience of children is procedural or based on imitation and "learning by doing," it presents a problem when new types of school-like cognitive capacities are required. This is especially the case when people move from rural areas to urban centers or when there are changes in economic activities and job markets involving more specialized cognitive skills.

Schooling is the prime route to upward mobility in most societies. With increased public education in developing countries, children's school performance becomes a crucial factor in obtaining higher-status employment and full participation in a changing society. In a changing environment, then, the criteria for social competence also change. A contextual and functional approach to human development has to take into account the changes in context. What may be functional at one place and time may no longer be functional at another place and time. Given the *similarities* in environmental changes accompanying urbanization and socioeconomic development, a universalistic perspective appears to better predict the common patterns of change than a relativistic perspective. This is because, with increased similarities, the use of comparative standards for human development gains validity.

Coming back to parents' conceptualization of intelligence, then, a new cognitive definition of intelligence *added* to a social definition of intelligence is functional with socioeconomic development. It has direct implications for childrearing orientations. This is parallel to an autonomy orientation becoming functional with the same process of socioeconomic change. In both cases, whether we are looking into the development of the self or of competence, parental definitions and values are reflected in childrearing, as summarized in Table 4.

POLICY IMPLICATIONS

There are policy-relevant applied implications of this view. For example, if parental values and conceptualizations persist while more macro environmental requirements for success are changing, a universalistic approach prescribes intervention while a relativist position does not. This is because with a universalistic approach comparison among similar contexts becomes possible, and if there is a substandard level of performance in one context, it can be improved. Thus, misfits between environmental requirements and children's developmental trajectories can be addressed.

Such comparative standards are not used by a relativist approach. The specificity of contexts is stressed, and the functional as well as interpretive links with the context are seen to preclude comparison. This has the implication that comparative standards cannot be used. An unacceptable result of such relativism is a double standard of using comparative cognitive (school-like) standards for children in urban middle-class western contexts, but not in non-western traditional societies or among ethnic groups in western countries. Using comparative cognitive standards for all from a universalistic perspective avoids such double standards. It has the additional advantage that while a contextual approach is used and functional links are examined, by focusing on the common patterns of socioeconomic societal development, it can better address change.

To improve the existing situation, to instigate change, one needs standards with which to compare the case in hand. If psychologists are able and willing to develop such standards, their work could be more socially relevant. There is a great need for culturally sensitive research that entails cultural contextualism. However, such research need not succumb to cultural relativism. By developing integrative syntheses, such as the constructs of "autonomous-related self" or "social/cognitive definition of intelligence," one can both understand behavior in context and also how it changes in a predictable way with changes in context. Social change is not haphazard; it shows systematic and common patterns. Cultural contextualism without complete relativism promises to detect the corresponding patterns of change in human development.

Table 4
Contextual Change and its Outcome
(An Integrative/Functional Perspective)

Context	Rural/traditional	→	Urban
	Less specialized tasks	→	More specialized tasks
	Low levels of schooling	→	Increasing schooling

Family	Family model of total	→	Family model of emotional
	interdependence		interdependence
	Old-age security VOC	→	Material interdependence
	important; material		decreasing
	interdependence		

Child-	Obedience-orientation	→	Autonomy becomes
rearing	functional		functional
and the	The related self	→	The autonomous-related
Self			self

Teaching	Teaching through	→	Verbal explanation;
and	demonstration and		School-like learning;
Learning	modeling; apprenticeship		cognitive and language
	in everyday learning		skills become functional

Com-	Social intelligence	→	Social & cognitive
petence	competence		

BIBLIOGRAPHY

Angyal, A. (1951). A theoretical model for personality studies. *Journal of Personality, 20*, 131-142.

Bakan, D. (1966). *The duality of human existence.*   Chicago, IL: Rand McNally.

Bakan, D. (1968). *Disease, pain and sacrifice.* Chicago, IL: University of Chicago Press.

Baldwin, J.M. (1895). *Mental development in the child and the race.* New

York: Macmillan.

Baldwin, J.M. (1909). *Darwin and the humanities*. Baltimore, MD: Review Publishing.

Baltes, P.B. (1987). Theoretical propositions of life-span developmental psychology: On the dynamics between growth and decline. *Developmental Psychology, 23*, 611-626.

Baltes, P.B., & Brim, O. (Eds.). (1979). *Life-span development and behavior* (Vol. 2). New York: Academic Press.

Baltes, P.B., Reese, H.W., & Lipsitt, L.P. (1980). Life-span developmental psychology. *Annual Review of Psychology, 31*, 65-110.

Barker, R.G. (1968). *Ecological psychology*. Stanford, CA: Stanford University Press.

Berger, P.L., & Luckmann, T. (1967). *The social construction of reality*. New York: Doubleday.

Berry, J.W. (1976). *Human ecology and cognitive style: Comparative studies in cultural and psychological adaptation*. New York: Sage/Halsted.

Berry, J.W. (1980). Ecological analyses for cross-cultural psychology. In N. Warren (Ed.), *Studies in cross-cultural psychology* (Vol. 2, pp. 157-189). New York: Academic Press.

Bertalanffy, L. von (1933). *Modern theories of development*. London Oxford University Press.

Bertalanffy, L. von (1968). *General systems theory*. New York: Brazilier.

Bornstein, M.H. (1991). *Cultural approaches to parenting*. Hillsdale, NJ: Erlbaum.

Bronfenbrenner, U. (1979). *The ecology of human development:Experiments by nature and design*. Cambridge, MA: Harvard University Press.

Bronfenbrenner, U. (1986). Ecology of the family as a context for human development: Research perspectives. *Developmental Psychology, 22*(6), 723-742.

Bronfenbrenner, U., & Weiss, H.B. (1983). Beyond policies without people: An ecological perspective on child and family policy. In E.F. Zigler, S.L. Kagan, & E. Klugman (Eds.), *Children, families and government: Perspectives on American social policy* (pp. 393-414). New York: Cambridge University Press.

Brunswik, R. (1955). Representative design and probabilistic theory. *Psychological Review, 62*, 236-242.

Carraher, T.N., Schliemann, A.D., & Carraher, D.W. (1988). Mathematical concepts in everyday life. In G.B. Saxe & M. Gearhart (Eds.), Children's mathematics: *New directions in child development* (pp. 71-87). San Francisco, CA: Jossey-Bass.

Childs, C.P., & Greenfield, P.M. (1980). Informal modes of learning and teaching: The case of Zinacantoco weaving. In N. Warren (Ed.), *Studies in cross-cultural psychology* (Vol. 2, pp. 269-316). London: Academic Press.

Coll, C.T.G. (1990). Developmental outcome of minority infants: A process-oriented look into our beginnings. *Child Development, 61*, 270-289.

Cole, M. (1992). Culture and cognitive development: From cross-cultural comparisons to model systems of cultural mediation. In A.F. Healy, S.M. Kosslyn, & R.M. Shiffrin (Eds.), *Essays in honor of William K. Estes* (pp. 279-305). Hillsdale, NJ: Erlbaum.

Cole, M., Sharp, D., & Lave, C. (1976). The cognitive consequences of education: Some empirical evidence and theoretical misgivings. *Urban Review, 9*, 218-233.

Dasen, P.R. (1984). The cross-cultural study of intelligence: Piaget and the Baoule. *International Journal of Psychology, 19*, 407-434.

Dym, B. (1988). Ecological perspectives on change in families. In H.B. Weiss & F.H. Jacobs (Eds.), *Evaluating family programs* (pp. 477-496). New York: Aldine.

Fisek, G.O. (1991). A cross-cultural examination of proximity and hierarchy as dimensions of family structure. *Family Process, 30*, 121-133.

Gay, J., & Cole, M. (1967). *The new mathematics and an old culture.* New York: Holt, Rinehart & Winston.

Greenfield, P.M., & Cocking, R.R. (Eds.). (1994). *Cross-cultural roots of minority child development.* Hillsdale, NJ: Erlbaum.

Greenfield, P.M., & Lave, J. (1982). Cognitive aspects of informal education. In D. Wagner & H. Stevenson (Eds.), *Cultural perspectives on child development* (pp. 181-207). San Francisco, CA: Freeman.

Goodnow, J.J. (1988). Parents' ideas, actions, and feeling: Models and methods from developmental and social psychology. *Child Development, 59*, 286-320.

Goodnow, J.J., Miller, P., & Kessel, F. (1995). (Eds.). *Cultural practices as contexts for development.* San Francisco, CA: Jossey-Bass.

Harkness, S., & Super, C.M. (1992). Parental ethnotheories in action. In I.E. Sigel, A.V. McGillicuddy-DeLisi, & J.J. Goodnow (Eds.), *Parental belief systems* (2nd ed., pp. 373-391). Hillsdale, NJ: Erlbaum.

Harrison, A.D., Wilson, M.N., Pine, C.J., Chan, S.R., & Buriel, R. (1990). Family ecologies of ethnic minority children. *Child Development, 61*, 347-362.

Hatano, G. (1982). Cognitive consequences of practice in culture specific procedural skills. *Quarterly Newsletter of the Laboratory of Comparative Human Cognition, 4*(1), 15-18.

Helling, G.A. (1966). *The Turkish village as a social system.* Los Angeles, CA: Occidental College.

Hofstede, G. (1980). *Culture's consequences.* Beverly Hills, CA: Sage.

Hofstede, G. (1991). *Cultures and organizations: Software of the mind.*

London: McGraw-Hill.

Huston, A.C. (1991). Antecedents, consequences, and possible solutions for poverty among children. In A.C. Huston (Ed.), *Children in poverty: Child development and public policy* (pp. 282-315). Cambridge, England: Cambridge University Press.

Jahoda, G., & Dasen, P.R. (Eds.). (1986). *International Journal of Behavioral Development, 9*(4), 413-416.

Kagitçibasi, Ç. (1982). *The changing value of children in Turkey.* Honolulu, HI: East-West Center, Publ. No. 60-E.

Kagitçibasi, Ç. (1984). Socialization in traditional society: A challenge to psychology. *International Journal of Psychology, 19,* 145-157.

Kagitçibasi, Ç. (1990). Family and socialization in cross-cultural perspective: A model of change. In J. Berman (Ed.), *Cross-cultural perspectives: Nebraska symposium on motivation,* 1989 (pp. 135-200). Lincoln, NE: Nebraska University Press.

Kagitçibasi, Ç. (1992). Linking the indigenous and universalist orientations. In S. Iwawaki, Y. Kashima, & K. Leung (Eds.), *Innovations in cross-cultural psychology* (pp. 29-37). Lisse, The Netherlands: Swets & Zeitlinger.

Kagitçibasi, Ç. (1995). Is psychology relevant to global human development issues? Experience from Turkey. *American Psychologist, 50,* 293-300.

Kagitçibasi, Ç. (1996a). *Family and human development across cultures: A view from the other side.* Mahwah, NJ: Erlbaum.

Kagitçibasi, Ç. (1996b). The autonomous-relational self: A new synthesis. *European Psychologist, 1* (3), 180-186.

Kagitçibasi, Ç. (1997). Individualism and collectivism. In J.W. Berry, M.H. Segall, & Ç. Kagitçibasi (Eds.), *Handbook of cross-cultural psychology* (2nd. ed., Vol. 3, pp. 1-50). Boston, MA: Allyn and Bacon.

Kohn, M.L. (1969). *Class and conformity: A study in values.* New York: Dorsey.

Laboratory of Comparative Human Cognition (LCHC) (1983). Culture and cognitive development. In W. Kessen (Ed.), *Handbook of child psychology* (4th. ed., Vol. 1, pp. 295-356). New York: Wiley.

Laosa, L.M. (1980). Maternal teaching strategies in Chicano and Anglo-American families: The influence of culture and education on maternal behaviour. *Child Development, 51,* 759-765.

Laosa, L.M., & Sigel, I.E. (1982). *Families as learning environments for children.* New York: Plenum.

Laosa, L.M. (1984). Ethnic, socioeconomic, and home language influences upon early performance on measures of abilities. *Journal of Educational Psychology, 76,* 1178-1198.

Lave, J. (1977). Tailor-made experiments and evaluating the intellectual consequences of apprenticeship training. *Quarterly Newsletter of the*

Institute for Comparative Human Development, 1, 1-3.

Lerner, R.M., & Busch-Rossnagel, N.A. (1981). *Individuals as producers of their development: A life span perspective.* New York: Academic Press.

Lerner, R.M., Hultsch, D.F., & Dixon, R.A. (1983). Contextualism and the character of developmental psychology in the 1970s. *Annals of the New York Academy of Sciences, 412,* 101-128.

LeVine, R.A. (1974). Parental goals: A cross-cultural view. *Teachers' College Record, 76,* 226-239.

LeVine, R.A. (1988). Human parental care: Universal goals, cultural strategies, individual behavior. *New Directions in Child Development, 40,* 37-50.

LeVine, R.A., & LeVine, B. (1966). *Nyansongo: A Gusii community in Kenya.* New York: Wiley.

Lewin, K. (1951). *Field theory in social science.* New York: Harper.

Mahler, M., Pine, F., & Bergman, A. (1975). *The psychological birth of the human infant.* New York: Basic Books.

Marcus, H.R., & Kitayama, S. (1991). Culture and the self: Implications for cognition, emotion, and motivation. *Psychological Review, 98*(2), 224-253.

Marsella, A.J., DeVos, G., & Hsu, F.L.K. (Eds.). (1985). *Culture and self: Asian and Western perspectives.* New York: Tavistock.

Marsella, A.J., & White, G.M. (Eds.). (1984). *Cultural conceptions of mental health and therapy.* Boston, MA: Reider.

McLoyd, V.C. (1990). The impact of economic hardship on black families and children: Psychological distress, parenting, and socioemotional development. *Child Development, 61,* 311-346.

Meisels, S.J., & Shonkoff, J.P. (Eds.). (1990). *Handbook of early childhood intervention.* Cambridge, UK: Cambridge University Press.

Munroe, R.L., Munroe, R.H., & Whiting, B.B. (Eds.). (1981). *Handbook of cross-cultural human development.* New York: Garland.

Novikoff, A.B. (1945). The concept of integrative levels of biology. *Science, 62,* 209-215.

Nunes, T. (1993). Psychology in Latin America: The case of Brazil. *Psychology and Developing Societies, 5,* 123-134.

Nunes, T., Schliemann, A.D., & Carraher, D.W. (1993). *Street mathematics and school mathematics.* New York: Cambridge University Press.

Okagaki, L., & Sternberg, R.J. (1993). Parental beliefs and children's school performance. *Child Development, 64,* 36-56.

Oloko, A.B. (1994). Children's street work in urban Nigeria: Dilemma of modernizing tradition. In M.P. Greenfield & R.R. Cocking (Eds.), *Cross-cultural roots of minority child development* (pp. 197-224). Hillsdale, NJ: Erlbaum.

Patterson, G.R., & Dishion, T.J. (1988). Multilevel family process models:

Traits, interactions, and relationships. In R.A. Hinde & J. Hinde (Eds.), *Relationships within families* (pp. 283-310). Oxford: Clarendon Press.

Piaget, J. (1948). *The moral judgment of the child.* Glencoe, IL: Free Press.

Rogoff, B. (1981). Schooling and the development of cognitive skills. In H.C. Triandis & A. Heron (Eds.), *Handbook of cross-cultural psychology:* Vol. 4. *Developmental psychology* (pp. 233-294). Boston, MA: Allyn & Bacon.

Rogoff, B. (1990). *Apprenticeship in thinking.* New York: Oxford University Press.

Rogoff, B., Gauvain, M., & Ellis, S. (1984). Development viewed in its cultural context. In M.H. Bornstein & M.E. Lamb (Eds.), *Developmental psychology: An advanced textbook* (pp. 533-571). London: Erlbaum.

Rogoff, B., & Morelli, G. (1989). Perspectives on children's development from cultural psychology. *American Psychologist, 44*(2), 343-348.

Sameroff, A.J., & Fiese, B.H. (1992). Family representations of development. In I.E. Sigel, A.V. McGillicuddy-DeLisi, & J.J. Goodnow (Eds.), *Parental belief systems* (pp. 347-369). Hillsdale, NJ: Erlbaum.

Schwartz, T. (1981). The acquisition of culture. *Ethos, 9,* 4-17.

Scribner, S. (1990). A sociocultural approach to the study of mind. In G. Greenberg & E. Tobach (Eds.), *Theories of the evolution of knowing: The T.C. Schneirla Conference series* (Vol.4, pp. 107-120). Hillsdale, NJ: Erlbaum.

Serpell, R. (1976). *Culture's influence on behaviour.* London: Methuen.

Sigel, I.E., McGillicuddy-Delisi, A., & Goodnow, J. (1992). *Parental belief systems.* Hillsdale, NJ: Erlbaum.

Shweder, R.A. (1990). Cultural Psychology—What is it? In W. Stigler, R.A. Shweder, & G. Herdt (Eds.), *Cultural psychology: Essays on comparative human development* (pp. 1-43). Cambridge, UK: Cambridge University Press.

Shweder, R.A., & Bourne, E.J. (1984). Does the concept of the person vary cross-culturally? In R.A. Shweder & R.A. LeVine (Eds.), *Culture theory: Essays on mind, self and emotion* (pp. 158-199). Cambridge, UK: Cambridge University Press.

Shweder, R.A., & LeVine, R. (1984). *Culture theory.* New York: Cambridge University Press.

Slaughter, D.T. (1988). Black children, schooling, and educational interventions. In D.T. Slaughter (Ed.), *Black children and poverty: A developmental perspective* (pp. 109-116). San Francisco, CA: Jossey-Bass.

Super, C.M., & Harkness, S. (1986). The development niche: A conceptualization at the interface of child and culture. *International Journal of Behavioral Development, 9,* 545-570.

Szapocznik, J., & Kurtines, W.M. (1993). Family psychology and cultural diversity. *American Psychologist, 48,* 400-407.

Teasdale, G.R., & Teasdale, J.I. (1992). Culture and curriculum: Dilemmas in the schooling of Australian Aboriginal children. In S. Iwawaki, Y. Kashima, & K. Leung (Eds.), *Innovations in cross-cultural psychology* (pp. 442-457). Lisse, The Netherlands: Swets & Zeitlinger.

Triandis, H.C. (1987). Individualism and social psychological theory. In Ç. Kagitçibasi (Ed.), *Growth and progress in cross-cultural psychology* (pp. 78-83). Lisse, Netherlands: Swets & Zeitlinger.

Triandis, H.C. (1988). Collectivism and individualism: A reconceptualization of a basic concept in cross-cultural psychology. In G.K. Verma & C. Bagley (Eds.), *Personality, attitudes and cognitions* (pp. 60-95). London: MacMillan.

Valsiner, J. (1989). *Child development in cultural context.* Toronto: Hogrefe.

Valsiner, J. (1994). *Comparative-cultural and constructivist perspectives.* Norwood, NJ: Ablex.

Vygotsky, L.S. (1962). *Thought and language.* Cambridge, MA: MIT Press.

Vygotsky, L.S. (1978). *Mind in society: The development of higher psychological processes.* Cambridge, MA: Harvard University Press.

Whiting, B.B. (Ed.). (1963). *Six cultures: Studies in child rearing.* New York: Wiley.

Whiting, J.W., & Child, I. (1953). *Child training and personality.* New Haven, CT: Yale University Press.

Zigler, E., & Weiss, H. (1985). Family support systems: An ecological approach to child development. In R. Rapaport (Ed.), *Children, youth, and families: The action-research relationship* (pp. 166-205). Cambridge, UK: Cambridge University Press.

Evolutionary Approaches to the Life Cycle

Heidi Keller
University of Osnabrück, Germany

INTRODUCTION

Applying evolutionary thinking to the study of human psychology implies the equal acceptance of the validity of the laws of selection and adaptation than for the study of any other species. This implies that in addition to morphology, physiology, and anatomy, the patterns of social and nonsocial behavior as well as the architecture of the human psyche in general are also shaped by selective forces aimed at optimizing reproductive success. Since Maynard Smith (1964) introduced the principle of kin selection, reproductive success has been evaluated in terms of inclusive fitness (Hamilton, 1964), this being the combined effects of one's own reproduction (Darwinian or direct fitness) as well as the reproductive success of genetic relatives (indirect fitness).

It is assumed that the complex nature of the reproductive interests of humans (as well as that of other species) is not represented on a conscious level or pursued intentionally (Alexander, 1988), but that they instead represent specific ways of responding to the environment on the basis of genetically coded predispositions. Given this, the following two categories of causes are important: *ultimate causes* which relate directly to reproductive success and *proximate causes* which concern the interplay of motivational and behavioral forces and enable the individual to pursue his or her reproductive interests. The goal of an evolutionary psychology, then, consists of analyzing the behavior of humans and their minds *as if* they would try to optimize their reproductive success.

Once genetic defects are excluded, the decisive variable for determining reproductive success is the accessibility and availability of resources. Resources are constituted through ecological, demographic, social, and psychological factors.

Evolutionary biology distinguishes between two basic categories of environmental conditions that are considered the endpoints of an environmental continuum. These two categories are r-selection and K-selection and they are depicted in Tables 1 and 2.

These strategies can only be defined in relational terms (if one compares a fish who produces 6,000 eggs per year with an oyster producing 500,000,000 eggs per year, the fish is a K-strategist, but compared to mammals, the fish is a r-strategist [example by Voland, 1993]). Although the formulation of these strategies is aimed at differentiating species, an intra-species application in terms of interindividual differences has also been proposed. This is especially evident for the K-strategists per se, namely human beings who, in the

Table 1
Ecological and Demographic Characteristics of r- and K-selection
(as per Voland, 1993, p. 204)

r-selection	K-selection
• Climate variable • Low environmental predictability	• climate constant • environment predictable
• Variable mortality • Catastrophes • Extreme infant mortality • Mortality independent from population density (e.g., winter cold, dryness, flooding)	• mortality dependent on population density • stable mortality rates • low infant mortality
• Population extremely variable • Frequent possibilities of new or re-settlement through spatial expansion (opportunistic habitat use)	• population relatively constant • satiated habitat • no spatial expansion (consistent habitat use)
• Variable environment • Low and variable intra-species competition	• stable environment • high intra-species competition

Note: K concerns the capacity of a biotype in terms of population statistics (Pianke, 1970). Two reproductive strategies can be formulated accordingly.

Table 2
r- and K-strategies (as per Voland, 1993, p. 203)

r-strategy	K-strategy
I. faster development	IX. slower Delopment
II. shorter height	X. taller height
III. shorter life-span	XI. longer life-span
IV. earlier onset of reproduction	XII. later onset of reproduction
V. shorter spacing intervals	XIII. longer spacing intervals
VI. more offspring	XIV. less offspring
VII. less parental investment	XV. more parental investment
VIII. smaller brain size	XVI. larger brain size

individual case, might therefore be oriented more quantitatively or more qualitatively.

It is evident that most strategic parameters concern the course and patterning of the lifespan and the life cycle, since primate development has led to an increase in the duration of the individual lifespan (see Figure 1).

Figure 1
The Development of the Life Span in Primates (as per Jolly, 1975)

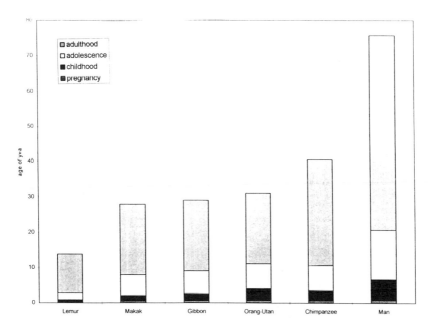

Because the human lifespan has reached an extreme length, a substantial parental (=maternal as well as paternal) investment is needed in order to prepare the offspring for being better adapted adults (better adult hypothesis; Alexander, 1988). Interindividual variation is guaranteed since selection focuses not on the group level, but rather on the individual, or more precisely, gene level. However, as Mayr (1984) has argued, it is not the "naked gene" which is exposed to selection pressures, but the gene as part of the system constituted by the specific genotype. Accordingly, individuals have to solve a variety of problems in "designing" their lifespan: most prominent are reproductive decisions, like the onset of reproduction, the inter-birth intervals (spacing), the number of offspring, and the allocation of investment. Reproductive decisions have to be matched against the (constraining) environmental factors that contribute further to interindividual differences, since external forces are different for different individuals within a population. Life histories represent individual solutions. Thus, intragroup as well as intergroup variability is to be expected (Voland & Engel, in press).

ONSET OF REPRODUCTION

The onset of reproduction constitutes the first decision in the reproductive cycle. Especially, the onset has to match investment with somatic growth or survival and sexual maturation, e.g., reproduction. It therefore constitutes a crucial variable in determining the individual life history as a "genetically organized set of general strategies and specific tactics for allocating energy to survival, growth and reproduction" (Kenrick, Sadalla, Groth, & Trost, 1990, p. 1500).

In traditional and historical societies, the onset of reproduction usually comes immediately after menarche (Urdy & Cliquet, 1982). If reproductive strategies are developed in response to environmental demands, the beginning of menarche should be a context-sensitive parameter. In concordance with this expectation, the beginning of menarche has been uniformly qualified as a highly variable factor. The most obvious influence can be attributed to the nutritional condition in terms of body fat or weight/height relation. Historically, the age frame for menarche has declined in most Western countries from roughly 14 years at 1900 to about 12 years in present times (Tanner, 1962). The age frame for menarche in traditional societies is substantially higher than in industrialized societies (see Table 3).

Conditions of malnutrition and resource scarcity, thus, delay reproduction. In such situations, persons allocate their investment instead to their own growth and development. Even within societies, however, substantial variability is found with respect to the onset of menarche (see Table 4).

The following factors have been discussed as contributing to this variability (Graber, Brooks-Gun, & Warren, 1995; Surbey, 1990; Belsky, Steinberg, & Draper, 1991; Chasiotis, Riemenschneider, Cappenberg, Völker, Keller, & Lohaus, 1997):

1. Developmental status, mainly weight and percentage of body fat: In line with the cross-cultural evidence, a good nutritional condition lowers the onset of the menarche, whereas deficiency symptoms such as anorexia nervosa, delay the onset (Voland & Voland, 1989).

2. A high level of physical exercise (dancing, athletics) delays the onset

Table 3
Age of Menarche in Traditional Societies

Society	Mean Age at Menarche	Source
Cameroon: (1997)		Dzeaye (in prep.)
Bakweri	± 14	
Bamoun	± 14	
Banyangie	± 14	
Bassa	± 14	
Beti	± 14	
Douala	± 14	
Fulani	± 14	
Yambah	± 14	
Bamelike	± 15	
Nso	± 15	
Kalahari: (1963-1973)		
!Kung	16.6 ± 1.3	Howell (1979)*
New Guinea:		
Bundi (1967)	18.0	Malcolm (1970)*
Ganj (1978)	20.9 ± 0.9	Wood et al. (1985)*

(* cited as per Voland & Engel, in press).

Table 4
Variability of Onset of Menarche within Societies

	n	Mini-mum	Maxi-mum	X	STD	Source
San José, Costa Rica (1996)	34	9	16	13.04	1.6	Chasiotis & Keller
Germany (1992-1994)	329	8	17	13.15	1.4	(in prep.); Riemen-
Athens (1994)	88	10	15.8	12.9	1.3	schneider
Aberdeen (1994)	42	10	16	12.7	1.2	(1995)

(Calabrese et al., 1983; Warren et al., 1991).
3. Psychosocial factors, such as father absence, marital discord, and negative family climate during childhood (i.e., prior to the onset of puberty), also lower the onset (Belsky et al., 1991; Chasiotis, Keller, & Restemeier, 1992;

Chisholm, 1996; Moffit, Caspi, Belsky, & Silva, 1992; Surbey, 1990). The experience of early social stressors appears to have a delaying effect. Flinn and England (1995), for instance, report an association between chronic stress and delayed sexual maturity (see also Tanner, 1970). However, after reviewing the literature, Chasiotis (in press) suggests an inverted U-shaped function in the sense that environmental stress can initiate both early and late onset of menarche: psychosocial stress tends to lead to early onset, and ecological stress to late onset.

Especially in industrialized societies with more or less stable ecological factors, the emotional context of early development becomes a major factor in explaining reproductive variance. Specifically, the attachment quality between small children and their caregivers is considered a switching mechanism for developmental trajectories with respect to reproductive history (Belsky et al., 1991; Chisholm, 1996). Insecurely attached individuals, having experienced non-rewarding early communicative environments, are younger at the beginning of their menarche than securely attached individuals who grew up in contexts of rewarding early social environments. In a study of German women, the difference was 7 months (12.29 vs. 12.9 years; Chasiotis & Keller, in prep.). This difference may be connected to a greater emphasis on mating (mating effort) in early maturers rather than on parenting (parental effort), leading to an earlier beginning of sexual activity and reproduction. A study of 327 women from the three European countries, Greece, Germany, and Scotland, showed that early maturers who had experienced socioemotional stress during their childhood (e.g., divorce of parents), had their first sexual intercourse 13 months earlier than late maturers, and they gave birth to their first child 3 years earlier (Chasiotis et al., 1997).

POSSIBLE AND ACTUAL ONSET OF REPRODUCTION

Cultures differ substantially with respect to the time-span between possible and actual onset of reproduction. In a study involving a subsample of the Standard Cross-cultural Sample, Whiting, Burbaye, and Ratner (1986) introduced the term "maidenhood" for the length of time intervening between a girl's menarche and her marriage (e.g., onset of reproduction). In evolutionary terms, it concerns "... the most important or pervasive trade-off ... between current and future reproduction" (Chisholm, 1996, p. 10).

One of the major forces determining that trade-off appears to be extrinsic mortality rates (Draper & Harpending, 1988). Chisholm (1996, p. 11) refers to Stearns (1992, p. 208) when stressing the importance of understanding both how habitat affects mortality and then how mortality affects life histories. In societies characterized by early adult mortality, individuals start reproduction earlier than individuals living in societies with later adult mortality; in societies with high infant mortality rates, individuals tend to have more offspring than individuals in societies with lower rates of infant mortality.

The economic structure of a society also plays an important role. In societies with a resource- and capital-oriented economic base, delayed reproduction might be more favorable, since time is needed to develop a competitive psyche to be able to get access to the restricted resources (Voland & Engel, in press). For instance, in Germany, the average woman's age when her first child is born is about 28 years. Traditional societies existing at an economic subsistence level favor both early marriage and early onset of reproduction, i.e., soon after the beginning of menarche (cf. Table 5; see also Schlegel & Barry, 1991).

Table 5
Possible and Actual Onset of Reproduction

Ethnic Group	Begin of Menarche	Age of Marriage	Age at Birth of First Child	Source
Germany	± 12	27.3	28.1	Statistical Federal Office of Germany
Cameroon:				Dzeaye (in prep.)
Bakweri	± 14	± 19	± 20	
Bamoun	± 14	± 16	± 17	
Banyangie	± 14	± 19	± 20	
Bassa	± 14	+ 19	+ 20	
Beti	± 14	± 17	± 19	
Douala	± 14	± 19	± 20	
Fulani	± 14	± 12	± 15	
Yambah	± 14	± 15	± 16	
Bamelike	± 15	± 18	± 19	
Nso	± 15	± 18	± 19	
India: Urban slum		16		Saraswathi (1997)
Japan: Ainu		16/17		Munroe & Munroe (1995)

Note: According to the Census of India 1981, 43.47% of girls in the age group 15-19 years were married (Sharma, 1996).

Obviously, there exist substantial differences in the average number of children in different societies that are linked to the onset of reproduction (see Table 6).

Table 6
Mean Number of Offspring in Different Societies

Ethnic Group	Mean Number of Children	Mean Life Expectancy In Years	Source
Italy	1.17	80.3	
Spain	1.18	80.5	
Germany	1.25	79.3	*Demographic*
Denmark	1.8	77.7	*Yearbook of the*
Ireland	1.81	77.9	*United Nations*
USA	2.1	78.8	(1995)
Developed countries	1.7	74.4	Birg (1996)
Cameroon:			Dzeaye (in prep.)
Yambah	± 7	40	
Banyangie	± 4	45	
Bassa	± 5	48	
Bamelike	± 5	50	
Beti	± 6	50	
Nso	± 5	50	
Bakweri	± 5	51	
Bamoun	± 6	51	
Douala	± 5	52	
Fulani	± 4	65	
Developing countries	± 3.5	62.3	Birg (1996)

These differences might reflect evolutionary based pathways that channel life histories in human societies. Selection parameters for two types of environmental conditions can be broadly identified (see Table 7):

Consequently, we can identify components of the r-/K-continuum and also arrive at better quantitative and qualitative parameters in the case of reproductive strategies for human societies (Keller, 1997).

Two important aspects from the interspecies discussion, however, have not yet been mentioned: the role of brain size and intelligence and the role of differential parental investment. While there are efforts stressing intelligence as one component of human reproductive histories (Rushton, 1985, 1987), we certainly do not wish to contribute to that literature. This is so because there exist substantial cultural differences in the conception of intelligence as well as the role of formal schooling in shaping specific components of intelligence (Lonner & Adamapoulos, 1996; Keller & Eckensberger, in press).

Table 7
Selection Parameters in Two Environmental Conditions

Type A: • Environmental conditions of limited or unpredictable resources	• higher mortality rate • shorter life-span • direct transfer from childhood to adulthood (adult-child continuity; Saraswathi, 1997) • onset of reproduction contingent upon entry into puberty • high fecundity/fertility • short life-span
Type B: • Environmental conditions of industrialized societies	• lower mortality rate • prolonged life-span • increased height • adolescence moratorium • extremely delayed onset of reproduction • few offspring • prolonged life-span

The concept of parental investment, on the other hand, probably plays an important role for humans. Parental investment concerns any investment by a parent in his or her descendents which increases the survival of a particular descendent and his or her reproductive value to the parent while simultaneously decreasing the parent's possibility to invest in other descendents (Trivers, 1972, p. 139). The evolutionary prediction would be that Type A is correlated with low parental investment, whereas Type B reflects increased parental investment. This conclusion, however, seems to be premature. If we compare different early socialization environments, we find traces of different forms of investment, but not necessarily on a scale ranging from less to more. Table 8 depicts different categories of parental care.

It can be speculated that these different socialization experiences result in different construals of the self in relation to the respective environment. Type B socialization might lead to a relatively independent and highly competitive individual who is able to secure access to limited resources, and to raise descendents who are even better adapted to the competitive environment, thereby investing more in direct than indirect fitness. In contrast, Type A socialization might result in a self-conception, which is mainly built on the individual's relationships with significant others with

Table 8
Two Types of Parental Investment

	Type A	Type B
Physical care: • breast-feeding	• 2-4 years	• 1-3 months
• carrying	• more than 50% of the day during the first years (e.g., Aka Pygmy: Hewlett, 1991; Efe: Tronick et al., 1992)	• mostly as a short response to crying
• body contact	• day and night (co-sleeping)	• low: "packaged" babies(Whiting, 1990) ("crib and cradle cultures"; Whiting, 1981)
• extra maternal care	• other relatives • siblings	• paid baby sitter
Emotional care	• long periods of co-occurring care • prolonged body contact and body communication • supporting long dependency	• short periods of exclusive care • short face-to-face episodes • fostering early independence
Education	• concurrent, observational learning • early economic independence	• formal and institutional education • long economic dependency

whom he or she cooperates to collectively exploit the available resources. This allows for a considerable investment in relatives as well, which should increase the indirect aspects of inclusive fitness.

Although many questions remain open, it seems as if the human life cycle can be regarded as an evolved reproductive strategy where an unconscious or nonconscious rationality directs the generative behavior accordingly. Cultures might evolve so that they mediate prescriptions and rules to support the respective strategies (Keller, 1997; Keller & Eckensberger, in press). In human societies, however, the unitary character of an r- or K-strategy has to be replaced by a more flexible arrangement of individual components. There are, however, switchboards during ontogeny, where specific associations become manifest. Onset of reproduction constitutes such a biological marker, which substantially influences later reproductive decisions.

It appears that general ecocontextual conditions modify the onset of menarche across cultures. In addition, the intracultural variability of the menarche seems to be influenced by socioemotional factors. Early and late maturers within various cultural groups seem to differ with respect to their reproductive behavior in ways that can also be found across cultures. Evidence for this interpretation does not only come from studies in Western societies (Chasiotis et al., 1997), but also from those conducted in traditional societies. Borgerhoff Mulder (1990) reports that early maturing Kipsigis women from Kenia have three more surviving children than late maturing women (Voland & Engel, in press). In order to understand better intracultural as well as intercultural differences, mating effort and parental investment must both be analyzed in more detail, combining population-related variables with aspects of psychological functioning.

BIBLIOGRAPHY

Alexander, R.D. (1988). Über die Interessen der Menschen und die Evolution von Lebensläufen. In H. Meier (Ed.), *Die Herausforderung der Evolutionsbiologie* (pp. 129-171). Munich: Piper.

Belsky, J., Steinberg, L., & Draper, P. (1991). Childhood experience, interpersonal development, and reproductive strategy: An evolutionary theory of socialization. *Child Development, 62*, 647-670.

Birg, H. (1996b). *Die Weltbevölkerung. Dynamik und Gefahren.* München: Beck.

Borgerhoff Mulder, M. (1990). Kipsigis women's preference for wealthy men: Evidence for female choice in mammals? *Behavioral Ecology and Sociobiology, 27*, 255-264.

Calabrese, L.H., Kirkendall, D.T., Flayd, M., Rapoport, S., Williams, G.W., Weiker, G.F., & Bergfeld, J.A. (1983). Menstrual abnormalities, nutritional patterns, and body composition in female classical ballet dancers. *Physician and Sports Medicine, 11*, 86-98.

Chasiotis, A., Keller, H., & Restemeier, R. (1992). *Childhood experience, parental attitudes and family development: A longitudinal test of evolutionary assumptions.* Paper read at the Conference of the "European Sociobiological Society (ESS)," Augsburg, Germany.

Chasiotis, A. (in press). Natürliche Selektion und Individualentwicklung. In H. Keller (Ed.), *Lehrbuch Entwicklungspsychologie.* Bern: Huber.

Chasiotis, A., & Keller, H. (in prep.). *Cross-cultural perspectives on the evolutionary theory of socialization.*

Chasiotis, A., Riemenschneider, U., Restemeier, R., Cappenberg, M., Völker, S., Keller, H., & Lohaus, A. (1997). Early infancy and the evolutionary theory of socialization. In W. Koops, J.B. Hoeksma, & D.C. van den Boom (Eds.), *Development of interaction and attachment: Traditional and non-traditional approaches* (pp. 305-312). Amsterdam: Royal Netherlands Academy of Sciences.

Chisholm, J. (1996). The evolutionary ecology of attachment organization. *Human Nature, 7*(1), 1-38.

Draper, P., & Harpending, H. (1982). Father absence and reproductive strategy: An evolutionary perspective. *Journal of Anthroplogical Research, 38*, 255-273.

Dzeaye, R.J. (in prep.). *An investigation of breastfeeding and mother-infant interactions in the face of cultural taboos and belief systems. The case of Nso and Fulani mothers and their infants of 3-5 months of age in Mbvem, Subdivision of the Northwest province of Cameroon.* Unpublished manuscript, University of Osnabrück.

Flinn, M., & England, B. (1995). Childhood stress and family environment. *Current Anthropology, 36*(5), 854-866.

Graber, J., Brooks-Gunn, J., & Warren, M. (1995). The antecedents of menarcheal age: Heredity, family environment, and stressful life events. *Child Development, 66*, 346-359.

Hamilton, W. (1964). The genetic evolution of social behaviour (I + II). *Journal of Theoretical Biology, 7*, 1-52.

Hewlett, B.S. (1991). *Intimate fathers: The nature and context of Aka Pygmy paternal infant care.* Ann Arbor: University of Michigan Press.

Keller, H., & Eckensberger, L.H. (in press). Kultur und Entwicklung. In H. Keller (Ed.), *Lehrbuch Entwicklungspsychologie.* Bern: Huber.

Keller, H. (1997). Evolutionary approaches. In J.W. Berry, Y.H. Poortinga, & J. Pandey (Eds.), *Handbook of cross-cultural psychology, Vol. 1: Theory and method* (2nd ed., pp. 215-255). Boston, MA: Allyn & Bacon.

Kenrick, D.T., Sadalla, E.K., Groth, G., & Trost, M.R. (1990). Evolution, traits, and the stages of human courtship: Qualifying the parental investment model. *Journal of Personality, 58*(1), 97-116.

Lonner, W.J., & Adamapoulos, J. (1996). Culture as antecedent to behavior. In J.B. Berry, Y.H. Poortinga, & J. Pandey (Eds.), *Handbook of cross-cultural psychology, Vol. 1: Theory and method* (2nd ed., pp. 43-83). Needham Heights, MA: Allyn & Bacon.

Maynard Smith, J. (1964). Group selection and kin selection. *Nature, 201*, 1145-1147.

Mayr, E. (1984). *Die Entwicklung der biologischen Gedankenwelt.* New York: Springer.

Moffit, T.E., Caspi, A., Belsky, J., & Silva, P.A. (1992). Childhood experience and the onset of menarche: A test of a sociobiological model. *Child Development, 63*, 47-58.

Munroe, R.L., & Munroe, R.H. (1995). *Cross-cultural human development.* Monterey: Brooks/Cole.

Pianka, E.R. (1970). On r- and K-selection. *American Naturalist, 104*, 592-597.

Riemenschneider, U. (1995). *Geschlechtsunterschiede in der Sozialisation junger Erwachsener aus der BRD, Griechenland und Großbritannien.* Unpublished master's thesis, University of Osnabrück.

Rushton, J.P. (1985). Differential K-theory: The sociobiology of individual and group differences. *Personality and Individual Differences, 6*, 441-452.

Rushton, J.P. (1987). Differential K-theory of human multiple birthing: Sociobiology and r-/K-reproductive strategies. *Acta Geneticae Medicae et Genellologiae, 36*, 289-296.

Saraswathi, T.S. (1997). *Adolescence in India.* Paper read at the 1997 Regional Conference of the International Council of Psychologists, Padua, July.

Schlegel, A., & Barry, III, H. (1991). *Adolescence.* New York: Maxwell Macmillan International.

Sharma, N. (1996). *Identity of the adolescent girl.* New Dehli: Discovery Publishing House.

Stearns, S. (1992). The role of development in the evolution of life histories. In J. Bonner (Ed.), *Evolution and development* (pp. 237-258). New York: Springer-Verlag.

Surbey, M. (1990). Family composition, stress, and human menarche. In F. Bercovitch & T. Ziegler (Eds.), *The socioendocrinology of primate reproduction* (pp. 71-97). New York: Liss.

Tanner, J.M. (1962). *Wachstum und Reifung des Menschen.* Stuttgart: Thieme.

Tanner, J.M. (1970). Physical growth. In P.H. Mussen (Ed.), *Carmichael's manual of child psychology* (Vol. 1, pp. 77-155). New York: Wiley.

Trivers, R.L. (1972). Parental investment and sexual selection. In B.

Campbell (Ed.), *Sexual selection and the descent of man 1871 - 1971* (pp. 135-179). Chicago, IL: Aldine.

Tronick, E.Z., Morelli, G.A., & Ivey, P.K. (1992). The Efe forager infant and toddler's pattern of social relationships: Multiple and simultaneous. *Developmental Psychology, 28*(4), 568-577.

Urdy, J.R., & Cliquet, R.L. (1982). A cross-cultural examination of the relationship between ages at menarche, marriage, and first birth. *Demographie, 19*, 53-63.

Voland, E. (1993). *Grundriß der Soziobiologie*. Stuttgart: Fischer.

Voland, E., & Engel, C. (in press). Menschliche Reproduktion aus verhaltensökologischer Perspektive. In A. Dieckmann, U. Mueller, & B. Nauck (Eds.), *Handbuch der Bevölkerungswissenschaften*. Berlin: de Gruyter.

Voland, E., & Voland, R. (1989). Evolutionary biology and psychiatry: The case of anorexia nervosa. *Ethology and Sociobiology, 10*, 223-240.

Warren, M. P., Brooks-Gunn, J., Fox, R., Lancelot, C., Newman, D., & Hamilton, W.G. (1991). Lack of bone accretion and amenorrhea in young dancers: Evidence for a relative osteopenia in weight bearing bones. *Journal of Clinical Endocrinology and Metabolism, 72*, 847-853.

Whiting, J.W.M. (1981). Environmental constraints on infant care practices. In R.H. Munroe, R.L. Munroe, & B.B. Whiting (Eds.), *Handbook of cross-cultural human development* (pp. 155-179). New York: Garland.

Whiting, J.W.M. (1990). Adolescent rituals and identity conflicts. In J.W. Stigler, R.A. Shweder, & G. Herdt (Eds.), *Cultural psychology. Essays on comparative human development* (pp. 357-365). New York: Cambridge University Press.

Whiting, J.W.M., Burbank, V.K., & Ratner, M.S. (1986). The duration of maidenhood across cultures. In J.B. Lancaster & B.A. Hamburg (Eds.), *School-age pregnancy and parenthood: Biosocial dimensions* (pp. 273-302). New York: DeGruyter.

ENDNOTES

1. Manuscript read at the Regional Conference of the International Council of Psychologists in Padua, July 1997.
2. r is the symbol for the growth rate of a biotype.
3. Since life-history trajectories differ for males and females, we restrict our considerations to females, since their reproductive decisions can be more easily assessed.
4. Extrinsic morality refers to death from predation, disease, accidents, etc. In contrast, intrinsic morality refers to death from the costs of the trade-offs involved in reproductive effort (Chisholm, 1996, p.11).

SECTION III: BIOCULTURAL AND SOCIOCULTURAL APPROACHES

The theoretical debates outlined in the various contributions contained in Section II find a ready echo in the papers included in Section III. Of special interest here is the question of how the relationship between the biological basis of behavior and its expression on the cultural level can be formulated and investigated in an optimal way. Thus, human behavior can be studied as the product of gene-environment interactions, but it can also be seen as the outcome of creative and historical processes. Recent perspectives on the interrelationship between cultural and biological aspects of human behavior have challenged the traditional contrast between nature and nurture. In the newer view, genes and environment are seen as having become attuned to each other in the development of the human species, but their interaction is difficult to trace in either cultural or cross-cultural psychology. Social, cultural, and biological dimensions of the processes, which together make up experience, become incorporated in future behavior.

The chapters in this section present distinct theoretical and empirical perspectives on caregiving settings as a medium for cultural continuity and change. The various authors illustrate the self's interpersonal construction as a relational entity that transmits a biocultural legacy. This legacy is carried through physiological, psychological, and ideational structures that interact dynamically during ontogenetic processes. The ontogenetic complexity must be addressed empirically.

The international team of Daniel Freedman, Valgerdur Olafsdottir, Yue Guoan, Larry Park, and Jane Gorman, in their chapter titled *The Internal Working Model in Biological and Cultural Perspective*, strive for a unified approach to the "mystery" of human behavior. The internal working model is a hypothetical construct intended to help explore the idea that early attachment experiences leave permanent traces in one's personality. The authors extend this concept beyond individual differences to cross-cultural differences as seen in an evolutionary perspective. Two samples of 13 mother-toddler pairs each, one from Iceland and the other from Tianjin, China, were examined through videotaped interviews and these were evaluated with the help of a Q-sort procedure. The results were interpreted within a framework incorporating both biological and sociohistorical perspectives. In this context, the authors use and would like to encourage a more poetic approach to the study of the interaction between culture and biology.

In *Subjective Experience and the Building of Parental Roles in a Biocultural Perspective*, the Italian theorists Antonella Della Fave and Fausto Massimini analyze the relationship between cultural context, gender, and the subjective experience of adopting the parental role. Five primiparous Italian couples were examined during and after pregnancy. Results gave insight into biological, cultural, and individual factors influencing the development of parental roles. Gender differences emerged in quality of experience, and on issues concerning parenthood and the newborn, in terms of motivation and involvement. The findings are discussed from the theoretical perspective of the biocultural inheritance system. Both biological traits (sex) and the cultural context appear to influence strongly the individual behavior and development while, at the same time, individuals actively interact with the environment, selecting information according to the related quality of experience. A factor of psychological selection also needs to be taken into account in order to understand individual differences. However, human reproduction and childrearing are given complex and additional meanings, and are not reducible to biological explanations in evolutionary terms.

The development of cultures has led to a variety of parenting practices. A holistic approach cannot fail to emphasize the individual's role as an active and selective contributor to the transmission of both biological and cultural instructions by means of his or her self-awareness and psychological selection. In the authors' opinion, the quality of daily experience is the ultimate criterion on which the replication or extinction of such biocultural information depends. The dominance of specific cultural norms concerning parenthood in a given social context is insufficient to predict an individual's parental behavior. Individuals are both primary carriers of biocultural information and the agents of its selective transmission.

In *Biocultural and Experiential Bases of Cultural Continuity and Change*, Eric De Vos examines the processes by which cultural patterns are transmitted from one generation to the next. His principal focus is on how culturally constituted mental representations, belief systems, and patterns of behavior are developed. He suggests that transgenerational continuities in "states of being" and the human experience of the self constitute the essence of cultural transmission. Here a biocultural perspective is underlined because the capacity to transmit states of being is "inexplicably built upon the available neurological and psychological hardware." De Vos stresses that the incorporation of early experiences into states of being may be the most important basis of the self and suggests that this process has not been sufficiently explored in developmental psychology. The subjective and objective aspects of bioculturally-constituted beings and the self are conceptualized as neither being absolutes, nor permanent, nor singular—a theoretical position that finds some striking parallels in traditional Buddhist conceptions of a noncontinuous, "nonsubstantial," but always interrelated self.

De Vos integrates individual and social analysis in a biocultural framework. In this context, he considers the family a dynamic social and biocultural system, and as a convergent manifestation of evolutionary, biological, psychological, social, and historical forces. The author discusses biological continuity manifesting itself ontogenetically as a neurological organization of behavioral patterns forming the bases of human experience.

In his chapter entitled *Children's Sociocultural and Familial Worlds: Pathways and Risks through the Demographic Transition*, the Indian-American psychologist Dinesh Sharma raises questions about the nature of childhood and its relation to social change. Adopting the lens of psychoanalysis, he addresses the question of how rapid modernization processes generate fundamental changes in the contexts of child care which, in turn, determine the prevalence of interpersonal, social, and mental "dysfunctions" in a society or cultural group. The author proposes a broadly comparative and historical approach to childcare, drawing on the existing demographic, anthropological, and psychological literature on cross-cultural differences. The nature of the family and of childcare in the traditional world and in the postindustrial societies is compared, and the author argues that psychoanalytic controversies about psychosexual development, object relations, the nature of oedipal feelings, and the development of self need not only consider sociocultural differences but also the historical and economic conditions of nonwestern societies. Child and human development are determined by multiple contextual and endogenous factors. The dominant western model emphasizing autonomy, separation, and dyadic interaction is seen as only one possible framework that can be further diversified when attending to variation within and across societies. The author stresses that the notions of child and human development, and of developmental risks, are influenced by cultural beliefs and practices that are socially and economically mediated. This means that processes of human development cannot be completely understood through the lens of psychological perspectives.

The contributions included in Section III are characterized by their broad theoretical sweep and their sophistication. Freedman et al. use their unique Chinese and Icelandic data to arrive at an evolutionary overview simultaneously encompassing the transmission of culture-specific attachment styles via "internal working models," cultural diversity, and gene-pool differences. Della Fave and Massimini interpret their Italian data from a viewpoint combining an evolutionary emphasis regarding the selective nature of biological pressures on mate selection, pair bonding, and parental behavior with cultural models of gender and parenting roles, and an appreciation of the importance of subjective experience and individual life histories. De Vos arrives at a unique conceptualization of the genesis and nature of the self by integrating the unique perspective of Tibetan Buddhism with modern approaches to the study of transgenerational continuities in "states of being." Finally, Sharma takes a bird's-eye view of the families and numerous children now being a part of the demographic transition between traditional societies shaped by agriculture and modern societies shaped by radically new structures of global industrialization and information transmission. Taken together, the four contributions allow us to arrive at a much more holistic and global understanding of child-parent interactions than is commonly found in mainstream developmental textbooks.

THE INTERNAL WORKING MODEL IN BIOLOGICAL
AND CULTURAL PERSPECTIVE[1]

Daniel G. Freedman, University of Chicago, U.S.A.
Valgerdur Olafsdottir, Iceland
Yue Guoan, Nankai University, Tianjin, P.R. China
Larry Park, University of Chicago, U.S.A.
and
Jane Gorman, New Mexico Highlands University, U.S.A.

In this paper we shall strive for a unified approach to the mystery of human behavior, one that travels beyond the old heredity vs. environment roadblock. In our view, one may look at an organism from one place of parallax (say, as an ethnologist), and tend to see the environment at play; but with the head at another angle, say as a sociobiologist, we may well see the instincts and genes in the lead. The parallel with quantum mechanics is striking, where different realities take over under different viewing conditions. We have become habituated to believe we really can split and dissect heredity from environment, innate from acquired, and that we can then put them together again if we wish. But experience and the wisdom of the East ("the inseparability principle") have brought us to a new point. The social science reality, at this point in our intellectual history, is metamorphosing, and the one and only anchor is the great singularity we call life. Descartes' coordinates indeed led to great scientific advances, but it would appear that the time for artifice and dissection has passed. It seems that we are entering an age of integration and holism—including perhaps a revisitation with sanctity and deism (Bloom, 1994).

With regard to the specific concept, the "internal working model," it would appear clear to those of our century, building on the legacy of Freud in particular, that our earliest social experiences enter our fabric and help shape our character. This is a truism not only for mankind, but also for great classes of beasts, for example, the Anatidae among birds (i.e., ducks and geese), as well as those mammals that enter the world infantilized and dependent upon parental rearing. That is, the more learning that is involved in a creature's adaptation, the greater the individuality, hence idiosyncrasy, of each animal. The imprinting phenomenon in ducks and geese that has been reported by Lorenz (1935/1957) has captured our imaginations because intense early attachments, and the terror of being abandoned by the parent, are behaviors that we share with these birds. But in ducks the major learning (imprinting) occurs over a few days so that, for the most part, they are creatures of instinct. Entering mammalia, domestic dogs can illustrate the unique complexities which may grow out of an extended babyhood (e.g., Freedman & Gorman, 1993), and people, of course, are the best example of "obtained character" given their extreme infantilization, the reliance on a learned reality, and lengthy dependency. This phylogenetic perspective, then, enables us to see the commonalties between imprinting and the psychodynamic notion of the "internal working model," and enables us to put forward a tentative hypothesis that the two are homologous phenomena.

It follows that one of our concerns will be the biological *function* of the ontogenetic persistence of these early social acquisitions. We hope to demonstrate that there is a species advantage to such "conservative" behavioral patterns, in that early imprinting to a natal group facilitates the production of genetic diversity. This argument will be taken up below.

The usual way the attachment literature deals with internal working models is to try to measure the individual differences that result from different attachment experiences. The literature suggests that secure attachment experiences with mother lends the child optimistic expectations when in other social encounters, whereas tense and ambivalent relations with her predict comparably troubled relations with others. (We present some case histories below that appear to bear this out.) On the face of it, this theory seems little more than common sense, so why are the academy and the clinical world embracing it? Partly it is a cohort effect—many of the people now in charge were in psychoanalytic treatment in their earlier years. Partly, it is the accrued evidence supporting the idea that early experiences indeed are major determinants of individual differences in social attitude, thus maintaining the main claim of dynamic psychology and psychiatry in the face of continuous onslaught from many sources (e.g., Hillman & Ventura, 1992; Masson, 1988).

This is not to say that therapeutic healing follows naturally from the insight that one's early experiences were crucial in shaping habitual patterns of behavior. The fact is that it is difficult to reshape the attitudes and appetites formed in the early years, particularly when there has been great emotional arousal as in early sex abuse. Sexual offenders who were themselves abused as children, for example, are notoriously resistant to re-socialization (van der Kolk, McFarlane, & Weisdeth, 1996). Thus, it is the resistance of this early character formation to change, even when it is attended by continuous social pain, as in re-arrested sexual offenders, that provides us with evidence for it's biological and evolutionary importance.

In this regard, recent neuroendocrine evidence strongly suggests that if something is learned by a child in an emotionally charged situation, the lesson may become permanently fixed at a biological level (van der Kolk, 1989). "Trauma can be repeated on behavioral, emotional, physiologic and neuroendocrinological levels. Repetition on these different levels causes a large variety of individual and social suffering. Anger directed against the self or others is always a central problem in the lives of people who have been violated, and this is itself a repetitive re-enactment of real events from the past" (p. 404). Given the totality of evidence, it is quite probable that we are all fixated to some degree, and even those raised by loving, doting parents tend to be repetitively compulsive in some aspects of their social behavior. Why is this so, and can an evolutionary approach help us understand this resistance to change in our social patterns?

Our evolutionary argument, in brief, goes as follows: A living group operates best if all individuals are attuned to one another, and "know" what to expect of each other. A beehive is such an example. In the Anatidae (ducks, geese, swans), both flexibility and assurance of continuity coexist via the imprinting process; wherein the model of a conspecific is relearned each generation, usually vis-à-vis parents. However, once assimilated neurologically (Johnson & Morton, 1991), it cannot be retrained during that bird's lifetime. The flexibility permits some genetic movement, as in Canadian geese, which flock in two basic colors, white and blue. Generally, white mates with white, blue with blue, and they are thus incipient species. They can as yet mate with each other, but with the passage of time these may become true species, and if so the imprinting process will have been crucial (Cooke & Davies, 1983). We are, of course, accepting as a given in this argument that speciation and the attendant process of genetic differentiation lends the line an ultimate evolutionary advantage. Currently, many biologists insist on keeping evolutionary theory reduced to the level of individual advantage, thereby solving some issues, but blinding themselves to many more (Wilson & Sober, 1994).

With these ideas in mind, let us examine our own species more closely. We clearly learn our own ethnic group via our families: their activities, languages, attitudes, and other behaviors including what we could call group-wide neuroses. As Neel and Ward (1970) have demonstrated via the fissioning of South American Indian groups, after a village splits (and they all do over time), each group retains a substantial degree of homozygosity (tribal members are usually at the second-cousin level), and since the split is always agonistic, friendly sexuality between the two groups is now unlikely. Thus, the two daughter groups are "well on the way towards the formation of a new tribe." One hundred years of such continual fissioning seems all that is necessary for new, mutually non-understandable languages to evolve. In other words, human diversity is no accident: it is the result of evolutionary processes that mimic (or are mimicked by) the Old Testament's injunction to be fruitful and multiply, at both the individual and group levels. If evolution may be said to have a goal, it is this one— diversify in the face of opposing homozygous (e.g., ethnocentric) valences; and like all other creatures we exhibit inter- as well as intra-group differences in a wide array of behavioral traits (Freedman, 1974; Rushton 1995; Stern, 1973).[2]

To take but one example of an intergroup difference, ethnologist after ethnologist has described the North American tribe he/she was working with as stoical, (interpretation: "they are not as tempestuous as me or my people") without considering (in print) the possibility that this *difference* (between the Indians and themselves) may be an issue of temperament, and thus biosocial and possibly inherited. In this spirit, my wife and I studied Navajo newborns and found them to exhibit traits that might well be described as "stoical" soon after birth: At two days of age, we found them to be less excitable and more adaptable to various testing procedures (including a cloth held over the nose, the Moro drop, a flashing light on the eyes) than a comparable group of Caucasians (Freedman, 1974a, 1974b). We can surmise that some of the sinuous explanations of the origins of stoicism by earlier ethnologists came about simply because it was then improper to speculate about inbred differences. And this brings us to the nub of the paper: a demonstration of how group differences in early rearing styles are (minimally) the result of cultural, sociopolitical, geographic, genetic, and evolutionary forces—and the accompanying argument that trying to separate out any of these elements (the Cartesian tradition) involves misplaced rationality.

In this paper we focus on two sets of data from Iceland and Tianjin, China, obtained from two- and three-year-olds and their mothers. The main data came from a thirty-minute videotape of the mother and toddler, engaged in three activities. These were 1) a shape-sorter, with the direction "Help the child finish as many times as she can in ten minutes," 2) A Stanford-Binet test kit—"Play any way you wish with these materials," and 3) We filmed whatever the child happened to do in the last ten minutes.

Mothers also completed an extensive interview called the Adult Attachment Inventory (George, Kaplan, & Main, 1985), a probe of early attachments to the key adult figures of their childhood. This made possible a rating of the mother's attachments as a child, as well as her attachment to her own child. In the Tianjin study we also made use of Rohner's (1984) Parental Acceptance/Rejection Questionnaire.

The videotapes were subjected to a Q-sort (Brown & Brenner, 1972), consisting of 100 items. About a third of the items described mother-child interactions, a third child characteristics, and a third maternal characteristics. Each item was typed on one card, and all 100 were forced into a normal distribution by a "scorer," a procedure that made statistical comparisons possible. The placement of a card depended on whether it was "most like what I saw on the video" to "least like what I saw."

The present article, comparing Iceland and Tianjin, is part of a larger study in which ten cultural groupings were compared. Table 1 depicts correlations between the average Q-sorts on mothers and toddlers of Kibbutz respondents and the corresponding Q-sorts of nine other cultural groupings. The Kibbutz group was the most child-oriented group in our study. Consequently, high correlations with the Kibbutz group reflect other child-centered cultures, whereas low correlations point to adult-centered (authoritarian) or ambivalent cultures. Thus, Tianjin ($r=.70$) rates as child-centered, while we are prone to place the Chicago Cantonese ($r=.44$) and Israeli Arab ($r=.53$) samples under an authoritarian rubric.[3] Iceland, a total outlier at $r=.24$, we believe is best described as *ambivalent* about their children and about each other, a theme we develop below.

Table 1
Correlations Between Kibbutz Group and Nine Other Cultural Groups Based on Averaged Q-sorts on Mothers and Toddlers

Korean adopted	$r= 0.85$
Japanese	$r= 0.77$
Milan, Italy	$r= 0.76$
American (middle class)	$r= 0.74$
Mainland Chinese (Tianjin–middle class)	$r= 0.70$
American (working class)	$r= 0.68$
Arabic	$r= 0.53$
Chinese (Cantonese-Chicago)	$r= 0.44$
Icelandic	$r= 0.24$

Since results of the Q-sort must be reported as comparisons between groups, we are somewhat arbitrarily comparing Icelandic scoring with middle-class white America and middle-class Japanese temporarily in the United States. While all societies have class systems, Iceland, as a small relatively inbred society, is not meaningfully divisible into upper, lower, and middle, and so we have omitted social class.

American middle-class toddlers were judged more assertive, less dependent, more distractible, more energetic, and more emotionally in touch with their mothers than the Icelandic. American mothers were assessed as more verbal, less directive, more emotionally present, while Icelandic mothers were seen as discouraging independence, more uncertain,and more distant. In the Icelandic-Japanese comparison, Japanese

Figure 1
Summary of Main Differences between Samples from Two
Child-oriented Cultures, Middle-class America and Japan, and Iceland

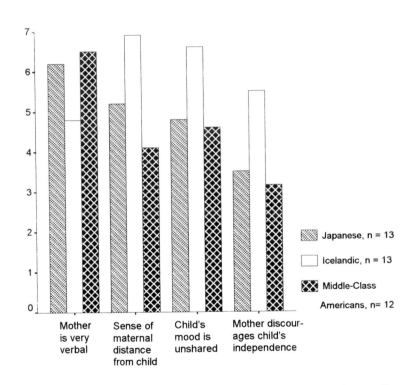

mothers were seen as more verbal, warmer, and more understanding, whereas Icelandic mothers were seen as more distant, less emotionally sharing, more annoyed with the child, and more discouraging of independence and exploration. In Figure 1, the combined comparison shows us that, compared to both the Japanese and middle-class Americans, Icelandic mothers discouraged their child's independence, were relatively silent, distant, and did not wish to share their emotions.

It thus appeared clear that Icelandic mothers and toddlers were uniquely out of touch with each other, and we may ask, what predisposed the mothers to be this way? What was the mothers' own childhood like? Let us look to two representative Adult Attachment Interviews, and then discuss the entire set of thirteen. The first interview was chosen for its typicality:

H is a 22-year-old unmarried mother of one. She remembers a nonsupportive, insecure environment and instability in the home. "You never knew how the day was going to end—there was no discipline, no guidance." Her parents divorced when she was one year old and she had to spend a lot of time in daycare, which she resented. She describes feelings of isolation and rejection. Her mother worked a lot and "was never home;" their relationship was "strong but very difficult." She feels drawn to her mother and describes dependence on her, which she also resents. She feels that her mother was unavailable, distant, unpredictable, unstable, and not supportive. "She never listened, somehow didn't care enough. I needed Mom when I was little but she was never there for me. She had to work. She expected a lot from me—I tried, but never enough. I didn't go to mother with my problems, not to anybody. I used to think about why my parents had me in the first place since they were getting a divorce. I tried, but it just didn't work." H had no relationship with her father and describes him as unavailable and distant. She had a good relationship with her grandparents who were supportive of her. Currently, she is more accepting of her parents, especially her father: "I have given up trying to know him, but I'm determined to keep in contact with him—without trying too hard." She describes her relationship with her parents as quite good now, although "I would choose not to see too much of them."

Even the more positive protocols have an air of interpersonal distance, as in M, a 31-year-old mother of three children: She describes her parents as reliable and states there was discipline along with high expectations in her childhood home. Her father "worked a lot, but when he was home he was with us and we did something fun." M feels that many moves as a child had adverse affects on her, and retrospectively feels she wanted much more affection. She wishes she could have been closer to her mother, "that my mother could have been more of a friend and that I could have talked to her more." M remembers wanting to please her parents and not wanting to bother them too much—but nevertheless finding her home environment predominantly supportive. Now she wants to provide her children with stability and show them more open affection than she herself experienced.

We developed a rating system for the full protocols based on van IJzendoorn's (1992) descriptions of attachment styles:

Autonomous. Attachment relationships are valued and regarded as influential on personality. Subjects give coherent descriptions of attachment relationships, whether those experiences are negative or positive. There is no idealization of parents and subjects do not feel anger about their experiences. This category may either result from secure rearing or exceptional self-discovery and transcendence over one's history.

Dismissive. There is a tendency to devalue the importance and impact of attachment relationships for subjects' own lives and/or to idealize the parents without concrete examples of secure interactions. This style is deemed continuous with avoiding behavior in infancy.

Preoccupied or Enmeshed. Subjects are unable to describe their attachment history in a coherent way, still being very much involved and preoccupied with the past. Some anger may be present. This category is deemed continuous with ambivalent or resistant behavior in young children.

Disoriented. Responses reflect unresolved, conflicted feelings about attachment relationships and a lack of completion of mourning processes. It is surmised that as young children these subjects would have been rated as "disorganized."

It may not be surprising that we found, without exception, all subjects were mixed types, and in fact much more complex than the rating system (and most probably any rating system) could account for. Nevertheless, in an attempt at minimal objectivity, *the respondents were rated on a 0 to 4 scale in each of the four categories* by a panel of graduate student judges. The low end meant there was little or no evidence of this category in the transcript, the high end the opposite. Of the thirteen interviewees, only three were judged as predominantly autonomous. The remaining ten were assessed as predominantly preoccupied/enmeshed, or else disoriented. As will be noted below, there was little evidence of "dismissiveness." (Please see the Appendix for short abstracts of the remaining 11 cases and ratings of all 13 cases.)

Of the thirteen, eight described little or no relationship with their fathers, while two described the relationship in an unrealistic and idealized fashion. For the most part, however, the respondents showed openness to and awareness of the past—that is, there was little dismissiveness of what were frequently fractious histories. Finally, most exhibited doubts about the trustworthiness of their parents and confusion about the relationship, which is rather strikingly concordant with the Q-sorts based on the videotapes and described above.

What are we to conclude? That entire cultures can exhibit pathology? But that's trivial, or at least old hat, in that it was perhaps the major theme of the culture and personality literature of the 1930s and 1940s. Of more interest is the fact that we now know something of the mechanisms whereby this behavior is faithfully reproduced. An Icelandic child may well want to contact its Mom, but Mom's ambivalence about affection and love subtly prevent it. On the tapes we often see nonplused children who, at two years, may still have the potential for warm encounters. We assume that this confusion shifts towards acceptance of the reality of a mother frightened about warmth and contact, and that this becomes the child's internal model of relationship; for he too is now uncertain about his desires for closeness. At the national level, this is Iceland.

While there is great pain in such ambivalent attachments, the ideal of painless, joyous, secure attachments fostered by the attachment literature we believe to be a culture-specific (American) imposition on the field. It is a tribute to American power in the world that its social science has become the yardstick throughout academia, even as German universities were once the models. Because our middle class raises its kids for autonomy, and has done so at least since de Toqueville described our astonishing children in 1848, normality has taken an American turn: a child's needs come first, and normal punishment, say in Canton (Wang, 1993), is child abuse here.

As far as we can tell, the Icelanders' pride in their land is as great as that of any other nationality in the world, and the nation is certainly in no danger of disintegration over these painful relationships. To the contrary, it is clear to us that the distancing we see between the parent and child is part of what Icelandic culture is, and that it helps maintain the nation's sense of unity. Through the commonly experienced emotional pain people identify with each other, and feel the mutuality that comes out of such sharing. For example, in Iceland obituaries are prominently featured in newspapers, and many Icelanders have the insight that for them this interest taps into their disposition to participate in one another's suffering.

How would it affect the culture if the parenting habits could be changed and we could have a picture closer to what the attachment theorists call "secure" relationships? Would this prepare the people for the darkness, hardship, and short to non-existent summers? Would the feeling of solidarity in the struggle with the forces of nature still be there? Can the battle be fought without this kind of painful preparation? And finally, would there be any reason left to remain on this godforsaken, treeless island of ice, fire, and pain? Icelandic authors, in one way or another, repeatedly deal with these questions (e.g., Laxness, 1946/1997). There is also the logic, developed above, that once such rearing (ambivalent attachment) becomes the norm, a deep biosocial conservatism arises that discourages change. We will leave the final words in this section to Iceland's Nobel Prize winning author, Haldor Kiljan Laxness, musing about his own childhood:

"A wise man once said that next to losing their mother, few things were better for young children than to lose their father. Although I am far from agreeing with all aspects of this statement, I am not one to oppose it completely. I would probably have worded this statement without the bitterness or rather without the sting that is inherent in the words themselves."

"Irrespective of what you may think about this statement, it became my lot in life to be without parents in this world. I do not claim that to be my fortune, it would be an exaggeration. I would not call this a misfortune either, at least not my misfortune, because the consequence was that I acquired grandparents. However, it could be argued that this was my parents' misfortune, not because I would have been such an exemplary son, quite the contrary, but simply because children are more useful to their parents than their parents are to them" (Laxness, 1957, p. 7, our translation).

We all belong to groups, which are variations on the human theme, and to the extent that we belong to different inbred lines, we may speak of contrasting gene pools. At a gross level, then, we can say that Chinese and Europeans have been, to a considerable extent, genetically isolated from one another for millennia, and thus are probably represented by some degree of gene-pool difference. (Certainly this would be the case with comparable isolation in two related groups of, say, frogs.) With this in mind, my wife, who is Chinese, and I tested 24 Chinese-American and 24 European-American newborns (Freedman & Freedman, 1969), and found a number of clear-cut behavioral differences:

While all infants cried at some point in the procedure, Chinese infants were often dramatically immediate in their cessation of crying when picked up and spoken to, and they also stopped crying sooner without soothing. In general, Chinese neonates adapted more quickly to an array of stimuli: A light shone on an infant's eye results in its blinking, and Caucasian infants continued to blink with seven or eight retrials, whereas Chinese infants tended to stop blinking after about four; a cloth placed over the nose of Caucasian infants caused them to swipe at it and turn away, whereas Chinese infants tended to impassively accept it; similarly, when placed in the pram, Caucasian infants tended to immediately turn their heads to one side, whereas Chinese infants lay with face in the bedding, easing their heads to one side after some time. We concluded that the major differentiating items were temperamental, that the Chinese infants were simply less excitable and perturbable, and that this was, given comparable data from Navajo and Korean infants, a demonstration of differences in East-West gene pools.

No one has publicly claimed we were wrong, but the findings are rarely mentioned, and so it behooves us to resurrect them in the present context of patterns of developmental uniqueness between cultural groups. Part of that uniqueness, logic would have it, is biological, particularly when it is as clearly demonstrable as in our studies. Once again, within an overarching evolutionary context the biological is always a contributing factor—and the challenge is in demonstrating that.

One way into this challenge is to see if Oriental toddlers of greatly different social and economic backgrounds nevertheless demonstrate commonality in behavior relative to Europeans or European-Americans. With this in mind we have tested newborns in Japan and on the Navajo reservation (Callaghan, 1980), a group of Korean toddlers adopted into middle-class, white American homes (Brooks, 1990), Korean toddlers in Korean homes, both in Korea and America (Kim, 1994), Japanese toddlers, Chinese working-class toddlers of Cantonese descent in Chicago's Chinatown (Smith & Freedman, 1982), and most recently a group of highly educated mothers associated with Nankai University and their toddlers, in Tianjin, China (the focus of this second half of our paper). But first, given all these studies, what can we say about the "biosocial?" I think it fair to summarize that Korean, Cantonese, and Tianjin toddlers concentrate on tasks with extraordinary persistence and interest relative to any other group we have researched. It is also fair to say that the Korean children adopted into the Caucasian middle class are not locked into tasks in the same way, but that they nevertheless concentrate more on tasks than their Caucasian middle-class counterparts (Brooks, 1990). Thus, reports from California schools regarding higher levels of academic achievement by Oriental students may well relate to this predisposition to concentrate on and master tasks as well as a deeply embedded desire to please (see especially Pye, 1992), in addition to the usual environmentalist standby, highly demanding parents. Once again, give these kids a middle-class Caucasian rearing (the adoption study) and they will slack off a bit; but put them in their natural setting, with parents whose temperament acts as catalyst to their similarly constituted children—and the yield is extraordinary achievement.

The Cantonese working class of Chicago provided an interesting contrast to Tianjin. When examined, the differences were in the mothers, not the children. Cantonese mothers were very demanding and rarely exhibited affection, and their children did not protest this extreme task orientation. By contrast, Tianjin mothers openly enjoyed their kids, and were more willing than the Cantonese to depart from the presumed agenda. For the most part Tianjin mothers were overtly proud of their toddlers and often quietly affectionate, whereas the Cantonese seemed to eschew any open affection. The children of both groups were largely fixed on the tasks presented, and curiously in both settings, as a result of the concentration, almost no eye contact was made with the attending mother, even during conversations. Tianjin mothers often had their children recite little poems, or count in English, in order to show them off, something that the Cantonese did not do.

The Adult Attachment Interviews given the Tianjin mothers were most revealing. Scored on the same system as the Icelandic protocols, ten of the fifteen mothers were judged as predominantly autonomous, exhibiting a mild enmeshment with their families of origin. Only one respondent was judged disorganized. (In Iceland, only two of the thirteen were judged predominantly autonomous, and every respondent had some score in the disorganized column.) With a few exceptions, the group was articulate, optimistic, highly accomplished, and very ambitious for their only children. They were quite open about difficulties in their own childhood and their parents were often perceived as having been too busy and away a lot (for the most part, both had worked). In this cohort reverberations from the Cultural Revolution were frequent (e.g., "father had to go away for a year"). Affection and love were often shown via sweets, food treats, and presents, particularly during illnesses. Unlike Iceland, all fifteen families had remained intact and, for the most part, sibs and parents lived nearby. Filial piety often overrode conflict, and it is a frequent theme in these Chinese protocols. As in Iceland, relationships with parents often improved when the women themselves became mothers. On average, fathers were seen as more distant than mothers, but unlike Icelanders, they were concerned, available, and frequently are major influences on career choice and in encouraging and enforcing hard study. Finally, when asked about separation from their own toddlers, the Tianjin mothers shivered at the thought. Clearly the bonds are very tight in this new Chinese generation of the one child. (We urge the reader to read the Adult Attachment Interview abstracts and attachment rating in the Appendix; only then will the flavor of difference between the two cultures become palpable.)

We now present abstracts of two interviews, both ranking high in "autonomy" and as somewhat "enmeshed;" they are good representations of the elite families in our sample.

"I was born in Tianjin. My parents were government workers, and I remember my life conditions were quite good. As a child I went to see my mother's father in Shaanxi province when he was ill, but my only feeling was that he was poor and a strange old person. I have two elder sisters, both of whom are married and live near us.... When I was young my parents loved me very much. They have never beaten me. I often spoke aloud my opinion on family matters, and my parents often used my ideas. My parents and sisters all thought me beautiful and clever, and I was very self confident when young. In high school my parents were concerned about my studies, and my father hired a tutor for me. They were very, very glad I was able to enroll in a famous university.

"I view my parents as friends, and I tell them almost everything. My father often told me how to become a real person—it was very useful to me. My mother was always very busy in her work and taking care of the whole family, and this is my only regret—that because she was so busy my intelligence was not as enriched as it might have been. She often went abroad, but bought nothing for herself, bringing back presents for her daughters and husband. Her attitude toward life, family, and social matters is rational. I am proud of my parents. Sometimes my father's temper is short, but overall he is a kind person. After marriage, my husband and I still live together with my parents."

The videotapes of this respondent and her 33-month-old son are a tribute to having herself been a beloved child—to the passing on of love and affection. She is seen hovering gently over her efficient son as he typically sticks to the task, eschewing eye contact. In the second sequence with the Stanford-Binet kit, the toys are prepared for him, and the impression is that she is a nice human to grow up with, organized in an easy way. He too appears gentle, and plays in an unscattered manner.

Our second case is another highly accomplished young mother. Her own mother had been her gymnastics teacher in childhood, and a strict disciplinarian who sometimes used corporal punishment. Her father, also a gymnast, was kinder, more humorous, and played the role of mother in the early years because mother was away organizing national gymnastic events. "I talked about many things with my father, because he was a very kind, very nice man. He knew Chinese medicine, Chinese massage, acupuncture, all these things." She had a younger brother but says confidently, "Some families pay more attention to boys than to girls—but in my family they paid much attention to me." Her statement about illnesses in childhood is remarkably common throughout all the protocols. Illness is remembered as a time when busy parents became suddenly very concerned, gave you good things to eat, and bought you presents: "I liked to be ill because they would give me good things to eat."

At fourteen, "I joined the army...in order to escape Mao's policies. My parents were very sad, but I was happy. I went up to the mountains and to the countryside...When I got to the army base I missed my family very much...and I often came home to visit. When I left my mother often cried." During this period her mother would also travel to meet with her— clearly a very close relationship despite the daughter's ambivalence. She valued her army experience in that it "can teach you about interacting with others." Her going off had been foreshadowed by comparable parental experiences: "When (my parents) graduated from college they both worked far away from their homes..., and they knew the difficulties."

In college she graduated from the philosophy department and then studied Chinese literature for four years. However, she wants her son to be a MD because "the arts are empty." Both grandparents (father's side) were doctors, mother's father a scholar (a persistent influence: he has exposed her toddler to classic poetry). Her younger brother and his wife are both postgraduate students, and her parents were both with the university as are she and her husband, clearly an elite family line. Like her father, her husband is "a tender, kind, nice man" who does "a lot of housework." She describes herself as more like her mother, as "neurotically neat" and wants her son to acquire comparable good habits. She wants him "to learn more...to get a good job...(and hopes) he can find a good, kind wife from a good family."

In the videotape, she acts the teacher, while her son is relatively uncommunicative, but sticks to his task. One viewer summarizes, "Seems a good relationship, but really humorless."

To summarize the Tianjin material, we have here a group of talented, high achieving women; many of them married to similarly accomplished husbands. The families are all intact, but not without internal difficulties, some chronic. Nevertheless, the great majority of the families have remained close, and sibs and parents frequently live near one another. Daughters who had difficulties with an overly strict parent were usually reconciled after the birth of their own child. Younger daughters in this cohort often felt especially beloved, and it is difficult to resist the speculation that their personal success owes much to that resource. The videotapes indicate that those who felt beloved are passing some of that sense of well-being on to their children. In general, ambition for children is rampant, both in the respondents' histories and in the expectations for their own children. In the past poverty was a hindrance to personal accomplishment in areas such as music and arts. Now, with a booming economy and only one child, we can envision after-school lessons of all kinds.

The most frequent retort to, What do you want for your child? is the laissez-faire, "it will be up to him/her." In most cases, this is then modified with various ambitious dreams. Idealism seems limited to wanting the kids to be "good citizens." All in all, this is an optimistic elite, and this first only child cohort may well be even more self confident, given the loving concentration on them of parents, parental sibs, and grandparents. Intelligent, perfectionistic, hard working, and durable describes this group of mothers—as well as their children.

Finally, there are hints of temperamental differences here and there in the data, with the most recurrent being the intense concentration over tasks shown by most of the three-year-olds, at the "expense" of eye contact with their mothers. Since we also saw this in our Cantonese data in Chicago but in none of the non-Oriental groups, this difference is too remarkable to dismiss.

What have we learned from these comparisons of child-rearing in a number of cultures, especially Iceland and the Nankai University group in

Tianjin? We have tried to make the case for a true holism—in which an evolutionary overview encompasses the facts of (a) cultural diversity, (b) gene-pool differences between relatively isolated populations, and (c) the transmission of culture-specific attachment styles via "internal working models." These are admittedly tentative beginnings towards a unified biosocial approach for the social sciences. We have eschewed determinism, and refuse to join E.O. Wilson, for example, in granting biology a supremacy in his *consilience* of academic specialties (Wilson, 1998). Further, we have barely mentioned geographic and sociopolitical factors affecting child-rearing, which must be added to the mix. All Icelanders are aware that their lives are affected by the unique geography of their nation, as well as the inbred nature of their gene pool (Stefansson, 1997). Sociopolitical factors are perhaps more glaring in the Tianjin material, with the Cultural Revolution and the one-child policy so central to our case histories. Certainly the one-child policy is a rare instance in the history of mankind wherein family dynamics and population dynamics, hence evolution (which never ceases), have been affected by a single government edict—one which the urban population appears to support. For us, such factors are as pertinent as our findings on differences between European and Chinese temperament; and perhaps we are pointing a way in which a true unity of the social and the biological can be achieved—wherein, for example, the contextual reality of culture need not take a secondary position to some "underlying" genetic explanation.[4]

Most importantly, we are here calling for an end to doing science by opposition. *Heredity vs. environment, innate vs. learned, mind vs. body* we now know to be worse than useless oppositions, since they lead only to stasis—to the headache of the insoluble (e.g., Freedman, 1997). In our view, these polarities are aspects of a singular (non-dual) process, a conception that, once adhered to by enough workers in both the social and biological sciences, will yield new insight and perhaps a unification of these two arenas of knowledge.   In the meantime we would like to encourage a more poetic approach to the issues of culture and biology, one basking in love for the subjects and avoiding mere "disinterested objectivity"—a point Lorenz (1970) made many years ago concerning the proper observation of animals. In the present comparison of Iceland and Tianjin we can only recommend the same: view the data with intelligence, critical acumen, respect for complexity and, above all, with love for the varying human condition.

BIBLIOGRAPHY

Bloom, H. (1994). *The Western canon*. New York: Riverhead Books.

Brooks, L.K. (1990). *Temperament in 5- and 6-year-old Anglo-American, Korean-American, and adopted Korean children.* Unpublished doctoral dissertation, University of Chicago.

Brown, S.R., & Brenner, D.J. (Eds.).(1972). *Science, psychology and communication: Essays honoring William Stephenson.* New York: Teachers College Press.

Callaghan, J.W. (1980). *Anglo, Hopi and Navajo infants and mothers: Newborn behaviors, interaction styles, and child-rearing beliefs and practices.* Unpublished doctoral dissertation, University of Chicago.

Chagnon, N. (1979). Male competition, forming close kin, and village fissioning among the Yanomamo Indians. In N. Chagnon, & W. Irons (Eds.), *Evolutionary biology and social behavior.* No. Scituate, MA: Duxbury.

Cooke, F., & Davies, J.C. (1983). Assortative mating, mate choice and reproductive fitness in snow geese. In P. Bateson (Ed.), *Mate choice* (pp. 279-309). New York: Cambridge University Press.

Freedman, D.G. (1974a). *Human infancy: An evolutionary perspective.* Hillsdale, NJ: Erlbaum.

Freedman, D.G. (1974b). *Cross-cultural differences in newborn behavior* [Film]. (Available from Pennsylvania State Audio-Visual Services, University Park, PA, No. 22605).

Freedman, D.G. (1979). *Human sociobiology: A holistic approach.* New York: Free Press.

Freedman, D.G. (1997). Is non-duality possible in the social and biological sciences? Small essays on holism and related issues. In N.L. Segal, G.E. Weisfeld, & C.C. Weisfeld (Eds.), *Uniting psychology and biology* (pp. 47-80). Washington, DC: American Psychological Association.

Freedman, D.G., & Freedman, N.A. (1969). Behavioral differences between Chinese-American and European-American newborns. *Nature, 224*, p.1227 only.

Freedman, D.G., & Gorman, J. (1993). Attachment and the transmission of culture—an evolutionary perspective. *Journal of Social and Evolutionary Systems, 19,* 297-329.

Freedman, D.G., Cox, S., & Berg, L. (1988). *Affective attunement and intersubjectivity in cross- cultural perspective: Methodological issues.* Paper presented to International Conference on Infant Studies, Washington, DC, April.

George, C., Kaplan, N., & Main, M. (1985). *The Berkeley Adult Attachment Interview. Unpublished protocol,* Department of Psychology, University of California, Berkeley.

Hillman, J., & Ventura, M. (1992). *We've had a hundred years of psychotherapy and the world's getting worse.* New York: Harper Collins.

Johnson, M.H., & Morton, J. (1991). *Biology and cognitive development.* Oxford: Blackwell.

Kim, L.M. (1994). *Mother-child attachment: A Korean sample.* Unpublished master's thesis, University of Chicago.

Laxness, H.K. (1946/1997). *Independent people.* New York: Vintage Books.

Laxness, H.K. (1957). *Brekkukotsannáll.* Reykjavik: Helgafell.

Lorenz, K. (1935/1957). Companionship in bird life. In C. Schiller (Ed.), *Instinctive behavior* (pp. 83-128). New York: International Universities Press.

Lorenz, K. (1970). *Studies in animal and human behavior,* Vol. 1. Cambridge, MA: Harvard University Press.

Masson, J.M. (1988). *Against therapy.* New York: Atheneum.

Neel, J.V., & Ward, J.H. (1970). Village and tribal genetic distances among American Indians: The possible implications for human evolution. *Proceedings of the American Academy of Sciences, 65,* 323-330.

Pye, L. (1992). *The spirit of Chinese politics.* Cambridge, MA: Harvard University Press.

Rohner, R.P. (1984). *Handbook for the study of parental acceptance and rejection.* Storrs, CT: Center for the Study of Parental Acceptance and Rejection.

Rushton, J.P. (1995). *Race, evolution, and behavior.* New Brunswick, NJ: Transaction Press.

Smith, S., & Freedman, D.G. (1982). *Mother-toddler interaction and maternal perception of child temperament in two ethnic groups.* Unpublished paper presented to biannual meeting of the Society for Research in Child Development. Detroit, MI.

Stefansson, K. (1997). Personal communication.

Stern, C. (1973). *Principles of human genetics* (3rd ed.). San Francisco, CA: Freeman.

van der Kolk, B.A. (1989). The compulsion to repeat trauma: Revictimization, attachment and masochism. *Psychiatric Clinics of North America, 12,* 389-411.

van der Kolk, B.A., McFarlane, A.C., & Weisdeth, L. (1996). *Traumatic stress.* New York: Guilford.

van IJzendoorn, M.H. (1992). Intergenerational transmission of parenting: A review of studies in nonclinical populations. *Developmental Review, 12,* 76-99.

Wang, N. (1993). Personal communication.

Wilson, D.S., & Sober, E. (1994). Reintroducing group selection to the human behavioral sciences. *Behavioral and Brain Sciences, 17*, 585-654.

Wilson, E.O. (1998). *Consilience.* New York: Knopf.

Wynne-Edwards, V.C. (1962). *Animal dispersion in relation to social behavior.* Edinburgh: Oliver & Boyd.

ENDNOTES

[1]Where the pronoun "I" is used in the text it refers to the first author.

[2]The genetic aspects of such diversity, as far as American psychology is concerned, is limited to differences between individuals, whereas group differences, say, in intelligence, invite a hornet's nest of conflicting opinions. This is largely due to the hominid tendency, particularly well developed in males, to rank-order valued traits and to compete for the top rungs of any chosen hierarchy: athletic ability, mathematical ability, wealth, intelligence (in this century often measured by IQ scores), and so forth. Ethnocentrism seems little more than an extension of this tendency to the ranking of groups, and the ranking of groups by intelligence is particularly incendiary.

[3]The Israeli Arab and Kibbutz contrast is also of interest along this line, and has been discussed in a previous paper by Freedman, Cox, and Berg (1988).

[4]A major hurdle in achieving this unity will be the continuous acrimony aroused by the memory of theories of racial superiority, but the present view does not run from this debate, and seeks rather to understand it by placing the debate itself in an encompassing biosocial perspective (Freedman, 1997).

APPENDIX

Appendix 1: Icelandic Interview Summaries

In attempting to categorize our subjects according the van IJzendoorn criteria of attachment styles (see text) we found that without exception they were mixed types. We thus developed a 0-4 rating scale, rating each interview on all four categories. A=autonomous, D=dismissive, E=enmeshed/preoccupied with the past, U=disoriented. The actual Adult Attachment Interviews took well over an hour each, and these must be considered skeletal summaries. The scores are the averages of 3-5 raters.

A is a 28-year-old mother of two. She describes an unsupportive environment in her childhood home where she felt insecure and untrustworthy. Since her parents' divorce when she was five, she has had no relationship with her father. Currently, relationship with mother is better; "I can trust her more now." Ratings: A=1.3, D=2.0, E=2.5, U=2.7.

B is an unmarried 26-year-old mother of one child. She describes distance from parents who never held her, a lack of understanding, intense dependency on mother, and a father who was very strict, angry, and unavailable. Regarding mother, "I depended on her—but maybe it was she who depended on me. I don't know now." B feels isolated and is still resentful; "Somehow, there is something missing." A=0.7, D=1.0, E=3.0, U=2.5.

C, a 35-year-old mother of three, reports supportive environment, balance, and warmth in her childhood home. Describes self as shy, withdrawn, and not needing other people. "I had my own agenda and my parents trusted me and for that I'm grateful." A=2.7, D=1, E=1, U=1.

D, a twin, is an unmarried 27-year-old mother of one child. With the loss of her father at age 8 she lost stability in her life. Sexually abused from 9-11 years, describes mother as cold, controlling, threatening, and unavailable. "You don't talk to my mother about emotional issues...she is too emotionally handicapped." And, "I am emotionally handicapped myself, but I try to do things differently with my child." A=0.5, D=0.7, E=3.5, U=2.3.

E, a 32-year-old unmarried mother of one child. Parents divorced when she was two, mother remarried when she was five. Order and many rules in house, with stepfather distant, strict, and critical, mother controlling, demanding, but warm. "I didn't go to mother with problems, but she felt it when something was wrong. The trouble was they were solved her way. I could never win." Currently little relationship with mother, better with stepfather. Hopes son will not be as shy and withdrawn as she has been. A=1.8, D=0.5, E=1.8, U=2.5.

F, a 38-year-old mother of three reports supportive environment in childhood home. Mother was available, affectionate, warm, and strict. "There were lots of rules, but there was trust." Father was "maybe a little cold, distant, not affectionate, uninvolved." Relationship with parents "still good." There is some denial and distance from her own feelings. A=2.8, D=1.5, E=1.0, U=1.7.

G, a 24-year-old mother of one, was raised by mother and grandparents after a divorce when she was one. Saw her father regularly and reports supportive environment and many supportive attachment figures, although mother was controlling, "and played me like a piano." Describes good relationship with mother now, but sees little of father. A=2.2, D=0.5, E=2.3, U=0.5.

H reported in text. A=0.7, D=0.8, E=2.5, U=3.2.

I is a 38-year-old mother of three. She remembers a "wonderful" relationship with both parents, especially father, who died when she was 14. Idealizes mother who, however, "was rather cold, not loving, but giving...She was everything to me, mother, father, best friend...but she controlled me...lived through me." Feels insecure. Having a delinquent son and being twice divorced, she wonders, "why is everything going wrong for me?" A=1.5, D=1.3, E=2.2, U=2.0.

J, a 38-year-old mother of three, grew up with a twin brother in an unsupportive environment with an alcoholic mother, no father, but a good, reliable grandfather who took care of the twins in the first years. After he was ill, they were in foster care. Mother was unavailable, unreliable, but easy to love. The main theme of her story, however, is "I still did OK." A=2.5, D=0.5, E=1.3, U=1.5.

K is a 31-year-old mother of one child, who had a very close, intense relationship with her mother who "was loving, caring, and provided stability" in the early years. "But the crash came when I went to high school. That's when I discovered my mother couldn't do anything for me." Father "was unfamiliar, threatening. I never went to him for anything." Currently still feels enmeshed with mother, and a little closer to father. "I understand him better now." A=1.6, D=0.0, E=3.2, U=2.5.

L is a 32-year-old mother of two girls. Her relationship with mother was "lacking in intimacy, nor was she a support in any way during childhood." Her father was alcoholic, whose drinking dominated the household, and at age ten L moved out to live with her older brothers. "From the age of eight or nine I just took care of myself." The relationship with her parents has improved since she became a parent. "I got to know them in a very different way." A=4.0, D=3.0, E=0.5, U=2.0.

M reported in text. A=3.0, D=0.5, E=2.0, U=1.5.

Appendix 2: Tianjin Interview Summaries

Each of these women is a mother of a two- or three-year-old, which will be their only child because of the one-child policy in the Peoples Republic. All were recruited through Nankai University. In some cases ages or work position is missing.

S1 is 31 as is her husband. She was an older sister to two brothers. "Mother liked me very much and often bought me food and toys." "When I felt sad, I would take it out on my younger brothers." "My parents lives were very hard, (but) every Chinese New Year my parents bought new clothes and toys for the three of us. That's why the relationship between my parents and myself was very good (sic)." Between two and four years she was sent to grandparents and "I couldn't stop crying. My parents often saw me and brought some good food for me during this time." I now respect my parents (show filial piety) and see them at least once a week." Hopes her child learns frugality, respect for elders, and understands the hard life of his parents (both office workers). A=2.0, D=1.0, E=3.0, U=0.

S2 reported in text, case 1. A=3.5, D=O, E=1.0, U=0.

S3, 27-years-old, is a teacher at the University, and her husband, 29, is an office worker. She is the second of three daughters. Has a more prestigious job than husband has, even as mother was the more salient, and maternal grandmother more of a presence than grandfather was. "My mother wanted to be best at everything, (and) I had to try my best because I didn't want to make her angry." Very ambitious for own daughter (a toddler) and wants her to study abroad. She was a frightened child and frightens own daughter to prevent "dangerous things." Proud of her own independence, but "sometimes I don't know how to ask others to help me." A=3.0, D=1.5, E=2.5, U=0.

S4, 32-years-old, is a translator at the CAAC (airline) College, and her husband, 38, a teacher at Nankai University. She has an older and younger brother and an older sister all of whom live nearby. "I had a kind mother and a serious father." "As a child I often thought of how I could make my parents happy...If we had good things to eat, I wanted them to eat it." Likewise, "When I was ill, my parents bought me many, many good things to eat and also some toys." Because my parents loved me very much, I am strong willed (although) strongly dependent." Her mother died suddenly when she was 16, and she finds herself attracted to helping elderly ladies. She hopes her child "will have a higher position than others." A=3.5, D=0, E=1.5, U=0.

S5, 28-years-old, lectures in mathematics at the University, and her husband, also 28, is an office worker in the Graduate School. Beloved baby of the family, has two sisters, 14 and 16 years older, and a brother 10 years older. Older sister, who is like a mother, named her. "Middle-class" family in which music plays a big role: brother played guitar (Chinese), sister sang, father played an instrument and could dance. "I was quiet and smart...parents very proud of this." Mother a nursery school teacher, and "I attended her class..., and I was with her day and night until two years." Because of the Cultural Revolution brother and sisters didn't go to school, "so they could stay home and take care of me." Father was the educator and model of integrity for the children. "I don't know why, but he made my mother angry." "I was a good listener...and revered authority" "From my childhood I know I must be strict and obey norms. I hope my child learns to be self confident and creative...he is a boy...growing up in new times." A=3.0, D=0, E=2.0, U=0.

S6, 29-years-old, is an assistant professor of biology married to 31-year-old MD-surgeon. A beloved youngest child of working-class parents. Talented, but with no opportunities to play an instrument because of poverty (a common theme). She was a very bright child, admired by father and mother. Equally close to both (unusual), but the two of them got on "so-so." When ill, "my parents bought candy and sweets for me." Ambitions for child are interpersonal—hopes she "will become open-minded, kind hearted, and full of love, have many close friends, and be an outstanding person." She herself felt confident and independent and "always wanted to be number one." Also, "My parents' love has made me a person full of love...in school I loved my teachers, classmates...and after graduation, I loved my students, friends, my husband, and my child." A=3.5, D=1.5, E=2.5, U=0.

S7's occupation and age omitted, but she speaks English and she is probably about 28 (child is about 28 months). Respondent's father an engineer and "famous intellectual," her mother a medical worker. Has an older sister. "Mother took care of my life, father of my studies." During the Cultural Revolution mother went to the countryside for a year. When she came home, "I put my arms around her leg, and never let go." Her words for mother are "close, friendly, love each other, attachment" and for father "respect, reverence, fear, obedience." "When I got ill, mother didn't work, so sometimes I would hope to get ill." "My self confidence is weak, so now I ...pay attention to my child's training..., and I hope she will be independent and self-confident...." A=2, D=1, E=2.5, U=0.

S8's occupation and age omitted; has an elder sister. Family life was "so-so.... The relationship between my father and me is closer than the relationship between my mother and me. This is because my father didn't often criticize me." "During my childhood, when I felt sad, I hoped I could eat some snacks or sweets. When ill, my parents bought some wonderful food, and would fulfill any request." "The knowledge I obtained in my childhood was naive. I think I am not special, and I have no special hopes for my child." A=0.5, D=3.5, E=2.5, U=2.5.

S9's occupation and age omitted. Older sister to brother, by six years. "Because my parents were busy working, I had to look after my brother. When I was in elementary school and he in nursery school, I took him and waited for him to come home...At times I went to the market...and before long I could cook...so I matured early." Very independent and accomplished in school; also calm under crisis, as when diagnosed with TB. Close to both parents, but turns to Dad for serious matters. "I speak to mother about trivial things, such as eating and dressing." Visited grandmother in Chang Chun by herself when seven—sees self as strong character, never homesick. Not excessively attached to own child, and if separated "I would miss my child as a mother." Also, "I wouldn't plan his future according to my will [although wants him] to be self reliant." A=4.0, D=0, E=0, U=0.

S10, a 30-year-old factory worker, is married to a 30-year-old factory printer worker. "I had two older sisters but my second sister died of encephalitis when she was six and I was four. This was very upsetting for my parents, who blamed themselves, and for me—for I deeply regretted having fought with her...Because I am the youngest daughter, and my younger brother is much younger than I am, my parents loved me very much when I was young." However, "after my younger brother was born, my parents reduced their love for me—relatively speaking—and transferred it to him." Her mother, is "concerned about everything, oil and water (the parental relation), constantly chattering, pleasantly surprised, and very angry." Her father is "kind, relaxed, one can say anything to him, lets me do anything." She described an oedipal situation: "When I was young my father was very kind, and we would play together. My mother, on the other hand, often got angry and stopped us from playing!" She summarizes, "In my childhood there was happiness as well as sorrow. I hope my child has more happiness and less sorrow." A=2, D=1.0, E=3.0, U=0.

S11 is 35-years-old, her husband 37, and both are lecturers in English at the University. She is an older sib and became responsible early. "I began to do washing, cleaning, knitting and shopping when I was seven. But when I had questions or met with frustration I went to my father, for I couldn't get satisfactory answers from my mother.... My father, owing to his own miserable childhood, was determined to raise his children scientifically.... quite different from the traditional way. My grandma's death...when I was 13...made me begin to understand life..., and I took up almost all the housework as well as caring for my sister and brother." If separated from her child, "I think I will not be too sad about it, but I am sure I will worry...." Wants him "to be tall—at least 180 cm— industrious..., and to get his bachelor's degree." A=3.5, D=0.5, E=1.0, U=0.

S12 is a 35-year-old lecturer at the university married to a lecturer (subject not provided). She is an older sib. The Cultural Revolution had a number of repercussions: A family baby-sitter had to leave, the parents were sent to Cadre School ("I took care of my brothers"), and she herself went off at 12 "to live independently." My mother "adapts well to new situations. She encourages us to try new, creative things. My father is more serious...hopes we obey his orders. I'm closer to my mother...she is kinder." Both   "like   me   and   hope   I   accomplish   outstanding things...Studying hard has many rewards...(but) I have no great demands on my own child." A=3.0, D=0, E=0.5, U=0.

S13 is 31 years old and works at the University. Hers is case 2 in the text. A=4.0, D=0, E=1.0, U=0.

S14 is a 34-year-old housewife/elementary schoolteacher, married to 33-year-old college administrator. She was the fourth of six brothers and sisters, and speaks of "a tedious childhood... father was away working and mother hardly paid attention to any of us." "Mother intimidated us— once threatening to jump in the river—but she was kind hearted and had a reputation for generosity." Father was stern and all the children tried to avoid him. Fond memories of illnesses, "It was better to be sick." Two brothers are farmers. "When I went to the university both my mother and I cried...and when I got married I felt I did not belong to my parents anymore." Her wishes for child are tepid, and seem to follow from a life of not being specially regarded. A=2.0, D=2.0, E=1.0, U=0.

S15 is a 32-year-old professor at T.C.M. College married to a 30-year-old MD. She had a very supportive childhood, with an especially supportive mother and a father who was also there for her and the other two children. Father had been the sole breadwinner, and the stricter disciplinarian. Her Rohner test score of 0 bespeaks a childhood of non-deprivation and an exceptionally good self-image, and her studiousness and success in academia seem to flow from that. Her first separation, a tearful one, was at age 18 when she went to college. She sees her parents often, as do the other sibs. She wants her child to study hard—as she had, and she is one of the few mothers who admits to frightening her child into obedience, with a tale of a tiger at the door. She doesn't recall her parents doing so with her. A=3.0, D=0, E=1.5, U=0.

SUBJECTIVE EXPERINCE AND THE BUILDING OF PARENTAL ROLES IN A BIOCULTURAL PERSPECTIVE

Antonella Delle Fave
Università IULM, Milano, Italy
Fausto Massimini
Università degli Studi di Milano, Italy

In virtually all cultures parenting has traditionally been considered one of the most significant life expericnces for the individual, the family, and the social system. Childbirth and childrearing are the fundamental activities ensuring the transmission and reproduction of biological and cultural information. Since reproduction and parenting have momentous implications for the evolution of the human species, various theoretical approaches have been developed, each of them shedding new light on the complexity of the phenomenon. In this paper we will focus on three different but interrelated approaches to the study of parenting: the biological, the cultural, and the experiential ones.

THE INFLUENCE OF BIOLOGY

Research work concerned with parenting obviously has to take into account the biological aspects of the phenomenon, in that pair bonding, reproductive behavior, and childrearing are intluenced by selective biological pressures. The evolutionary psychology approach, based on a great number of theoretical works and field studies on mammals, maintains that mate selection, pair bonding, and parental behavior represent strategies that evolved in ordcr to ensure the species' survival and reproduction in our ancestors' EEA (Environment of Evolutionary Adaptedness, Symons, 1990). Hence, every component of parenting behavior which enhances the probability of the offspring to survive and to reproduce is expected to be differentially selected and transmitted to the next generation. This also includes the gender-specific differences in mate selection preferences and in parenting behavior (Buss, 1989; Daly, 1990; Lampert, 1997; Trivers, 1972).

Gender-specific constraints on parenting roles are unquestionable: pregnancy, delivery, and breast-feeding are the domains of women. However, the actual influence of biological factors on parents' behavior as caretakers is far from being demonstrated. Experimental studies on the role of hormones in determining appropriate parental behavior have analyzed gender differences in terms of hormonal profile both during pregnancy and after childbirth.

Recently, attention has been devoted to prolactin, the hormone stimulating lactogenesis, whose levels in women rise during pregnancy and fall within a few weeks after childbirth. While prolactin seems to facilitate maternal behavior in rats (Bridges, DiBiase, Loundes, & Doherty, 1985), its influence on humans is not yet clearly understood (Warren & Shortle, 1990; Fleming, 1990). Clinical findings suggest that adaptive maternal behavior is associated with female hormonal "readiness." For instance, teenage girls run higher medical risks during pregnancy and in addition, statistics indicate their poor performance in being mothers (Montagu, 1981; Warren & Shortle, 1990).

As concerns fathers, current knowledge on the physiological changes associated with childbirth is still incomplete. An increasing number of studies have focused on hormonal fluctuations, especially of prolactin. Again, there is evidence of higher prolactin levels in nurturing males among gerbils (Brown, Moger, & Murphy, 1989) and marmosets (Dixson & George, 1982), but no clear results have so far been obtained from human samples. More attention is also being paid to the couvade syndrome, a complex set of physical and psychosomatic symptoms reported by a significant proportion of men in industrialized societies during their partner's pregnancy and delivery (Lipkin & Lamb, 1982; Teichman & Lahav, 1987; Trethowan & Conlon, 1965). The term "couvade" comes from the anthropological literature, and it originally referred to rituals performed by fathers in some preindustrial cultures shortly before and after childbirth (Malinowski, 1927; Munroe, Munroe, & Whiting, 1981). Its meaning in humans has been investigated from different perspectives: evolutionary psychologists interpret it as a pattern of physiological changes mediating paternal responsiveness (Elwood & Mason, 1994), while other scholars emphasize the influence of psychological involvement and of social and cultural factors on its onset (Bogren, 1983; Clinton, 1985; Yogman, 1990).

The study of biological modifications associated with pregnancy and parenthood can explain cross-culturally common reproductive and parental behaviors by means of genetic inheritance rules. Differential time and energy allocation by mothers and fathers in regard to their offspring has been interpreted as the consequence of gender differences in reproductive strategies: females have a limited amount of opportunities in their life to transmit their genes, and they are consequently very careful parents; on the contrary, the most adaptive strategy for males is to inseminate as many females as possible, thus obtaining a high number of descendants (Hrdy, 1981; Towsend, Kline, & Wasserman, 1995).

The biological origins and meaning of specific behavioral habits have also been studied: for example, left-side cradling preference in most human cultures and great apes has been related to the soothing effects of heartbeat on the infant (Salk, 1960) and to the neural transmission of left-side visual stimuli to the right hemisphere of the mother, thus allowing her to adequately perceive the emotional state of the child (Manning & Chamberlain, 1991). Genetically transmitted traits constantly interact with the natural environment, which places survival and reproduction constraints on individual behavior (Kaplan & Hill, 1992). Nevertheless, one of the peculiar features of homo sapiens is its almost ubiquitous presence in the various ecological niches. Differences in natural environment frequently determine striking variations in survival and reproduction strategies adopted by human groups in terms of eating habits, family structures, production and use of artifacts, and economical and social organization (Peterson & Somit, 1981; Super & Harkness, 1986). As far as social structure is concerned, the ecological constraints also determine labor and role divisions between men and women; as a consequence, childrearing practices and fertility rates have to adjust to the environmental niche (Low, 1989). For example, Werner (1979) in her broadly conceived cross-cultural study noticed that childrearing practices in stratified agricultural societies tend to be based on strict authoritarian rules: this would lead to cooperative, non-self-assertive adults, well adapted to an environment requiring cooperation and interdependence in subsistence activities.

THE ROLE OF CULTURE

Several studies on both gender roles and parenting highlight the role of cultural habits and rules in human behavior. The system of socially learned and transmitted information which peculiarly characterizes the history of homo sapiens deeply influences the way human groups cope with their environmental challenges. As several researchers have pointed out, culture undergoes an evolutionary process (Richerson & Boyd, 1978; Sahlins & Service, 1960): in time, cultural systems show changes both in the set of socially transmitted intrasomatic rules and in the set of artifacts—the extrasomatic vehicle of cultural information (Cloak, 1975; Massimini & Calegari, 1979). Such changes are often related to modifications of the ecological niche, but sometimes they take part in the differentiation process between human groups sharing the same natural environment. This process can be traced back to the differential replication of cultural units, or memes (Dawkins, 1976), which compete for their own survival and transmission against other memes in the cultural system to which they belong. The competition of memes engenders an evolutionary trend whose outcomes can be very different from, and in some cases even opposite to, the trends natural selection would produce (Boyd & Richerson, 1985; Massimini, Inghilleri, & Toscano, 1996). The differential reproduction of memes is determined by the level of cultural fitness, that is, the adaptiveness of memes to the cultural environment. Cultural and biological fitness may be compatible but not always: the differential replication of memes can also imply the suppression of genes. For instance, religious and political martyrs, monks, and nuns choose to give up their genes' transmission in order to reproduce memes.

Altman and Chemers (1980) pointed out that biological, environmental, and cultural contributions cannot be independently inferred from phenotypic behavior, and consequently they proposed to consider the triad individual-environment-culture as a whole. Subsequent studies adopted the model of the Living Systems Theory (Miller, 1970). They called for a circular causal relationship between the three elements, each of them being influenced by the others, and in turn, each influencing the others (Massimini, 1982; Richerson & Boyd, 1978). The recent biocultural approach (Boyd & Richerson, 1985; Durham, 1982; Ruyle, 1973) emphasizes the intermingling of genetic and cultural inheritance in phenotypic behavior. A dual inheritance system can be recognized for humans, in which culture turns out to be a set of instructions transmitted across generations which gradually gain autonomy. Moreover, in the deeply modified environment of most industrialized countries, cultural artifacts rule and frequently subvert the original ecosystem. They can change and develop at a very fast rate, as happened in most Western countries in this century. Therefore, the enculturation process has a strikingly evident influence on daily human behavior, and it persists as a life-long learning process. A comprehensive and reasonably detailed ecocultural model of the interaction among biological and cultural factors influencing human behavior has been proposed by Berry et al. (1992).

Current cross-cultural studies make valuable contributions to the analysis of the differences in reproductive behavior and childrearing patterns in human groups, which in many cases can only be partially explained by the different natural environments in which groups must survive. Some examples out of the enormous number of existing studies can illustrate this approach. As far as reproductive behavior is concerned, the negative growth curve of the Italian population (Volpi, 1996) is just one of the numerous cases of divergent genetic and cultural fitnesses that have been reported for industrialized countries in recent years. Even if the amount of family resources could ensure the survival and reproduction of several descendants, higher parental investment is devoted to only one or two children, who will have both better opportunities to learn and to exploit cultural resources. Moreover, parents—especially mothers—will save time as caretakers, diverting part of their attention to work and hobbies.

The study of gender-specific habits has also highlighted the relation of sexual behavior to cultural more than biological fitness. An example is the highly debated question concerning female infibulation and/or circumcision in several African countries (Caldwell, Orubuloye, & Caldwell, 1997; Leonard, 1996). Some scholars argue that the main reason for such a practice is a biological one. For instance, Hrdy (1981) claims that infibulation preserves wives' chastity, making males certain of their paternity. Grassivaro, Gallo, and Viviani (1992) suggest a relation between infibulation and women's role as shepherds: the practice reduces the production of female sexual odors, which negatively affect herbivores, while also attracting predators.   In our opinion, however, this devastating mutilation of female's outer genitalia can find a satisfying explanation in cultural norms concerning sexual stratification, women's social roles, and expected behavior within a patrilineal society (McCormack & Strathern, 1980). Recurrent urinary tract infections, high-risk pregnancies, difficulties at delivery, transmission of infectious diseases to the newborn, and last but not least, impairment in sexual pleasure and orgasm are only a few of the problems infibulated women have to face (Cook, 1976). These are serious constraints for biological fitness, and paternity certainty can hardly counterbalance such maladaptive outcomes. We suggest instead that memes concerning infibulation are selectively reproduced and transmitted because they fit into the cultural environment, despite the biological disadvantages this mutilation engenders.

The same general explanation can also be applied to the widespread practice of artificially modifying the sex ratio of children in favor of males. In preindustrial societies this goal is usually pursued after birth, through female infanticide and/or reduced levels of care and nutrition (Cleland, Verrall, & Vassen, 1983; Mealey & Mackey, 1990; Williamson, 1976). In more recent times, technology advancements have made the practice possible already during pregnancy: ultrasound scanning is frequently used in China and in various other Asian urban areas to carry out abortion if the fetus is female (Park & Cho, 1995). In the People's Republic of China, the selective suppression of females is also justified in the name of the recent one-child family policy, adopted to cope with excessive population growth. These customs are mostly connected to the high costs of raising a girl in a patrilineal culture, where a dowry is needed to find a husband, and where a married daughter is of no help to her parents, because she lives with her husband's family. The artificial sex-ratio modifications stem mostly from cultural rules, but they can also influence natural selection since within a population, an excessively low number of females can lead to biological maladaptation regarding the survival and reproduction of the whole group.

The fathers' level of involvement in childcare has also to be related to cultural habits. Recent studies have emphasized the importance of gender role divisions within various social contexts, economic constraints, and employment policies. Together these determine the male's active engagement as nurturer (Yogman, 1990). Over the last decades a deep change in the general attitude toward fathers' performance as caretakers has occurred in the industrialized countries which have been promoted by the high percentage of full-time working women and the spreading of the nuclear family model. Nowadays, most fathers actively participate in childcare. Specific studies have highlighted the increasing amount of time men spend with their children (Cooksey & Fondell, 1996), and the growing number of single-father families (Meyer & Garaski, 1993).

There is an additional consideration when considering the role of culture in parenting behavior. Each human being is a transmitter of a fragment of the information contained in the cross-generational cultural pools developed by our species during its history, in whatever ecological niche it may have settled. Parents pass on to their offspring half of their genes, but also a set of behavioral instructions inherited by their culture. In this perspective, the contents of childrearing practices and the educational styles adopted by parents are selectively replicated memes, which will influence the children's behavior as members of the cultural context and again later when they become parents.

THE IMPORTANCE OF SUBJECTIVITY

Alongside biological features and cultural norms, there is a third factor to be taken into account in order to understand common traits and differences in parental behavior: the role of mothers, fathers, and children as active subjects. As frequently underlined in current psychology research, individuals are not only the carriers of biological and cultural information, they also actively interact with the environment. Subjective experience and individual life history play an important role in parental behavior. Studies on imprinting, attachment, and "internal working models" (Freedman, this volume) show that missing or poor caretaking generates highly maladaptive consequences for the offspring, both during adolescence and adulthood, in terms of self-identity, social behavior, and parenting (Bowlby, 1969, 1988; Freedman, 1994; Freedman & Gorman, 1993; Main & Goldwin, 1984). This implies that life events, in particular individuals' peculiar experiences as infants, play a central role in the transmission of parental behavioral patterns. Early relationships have evolutionary consequences, both in biological and cultural terms. Children who are not adequately taken care of by their parents are less likely to survive and reproduce in adulthood. If they do survive and reproduce, they run the risk of becoming poor parents in their turn, lowering the biological fitness of their own children and often providing them with insufficient or inadequate cultural models and behavioral norms. (For a different emphasis, see Keller's essay in this volume.) This has been clearly highlighted among non-human primates in the classical experiments of Harlow and Harlow (1965); as concerns humans, a clear example may be seen in the non-organic "failure to thrive" syndrome of those infants whose mothers suffered deprivation of reliable relationships during childhood (Benoit, Zeanah, & Berton, 1989; Gorman, 1988). In several studies, the quality of the home environment and the care the infant received proved to be related to its emotional states and temperament (Luster, Boger, & Hannan, 1993; Seifer, Schiller, Sameroff, Resnick, & Riordan, 1996).

As Simons, Beanman, Conger, and Chao (1993) point out, a parent's personal enjoyment and satisfaction in the relationship with the child—and with the spouse—play a crucial role in the quality of parental care. However, to date few studies have focused on the global quality of the experience fathers and mothers report in their daily interactions with their children. Research studies most frequently analyze the relationships between child behavior and development, on one hand, and parents' educational, social, economic, and familial background, on the other. When psychological variables are taken into account in parents' behavior, data usually come from *una tantum* questionnaires and scales assessing general aspects, such as self-esteem, level of involvement, and problems perceived in childrearing. Too little attention has been paid to the quality of parents' interactions with their children in terms of day-by-day experience.

Yet, within the constraints biology and culture place on humans, daily behavior is directed step-by-step by subjective evaluations of the environmental demands and challenges. Thanks to their neurological equipment, human beings spend their life selecting the opportunities available in the environment, in compliance with their perceived needs. These needs can be biologically or culturally driven, but they can also have a psychological origin. The actual guide of daily behavior is the quality of experience that a person associates with activities, situations, social contexts, and this quality directs a process defined as *psychological selection* (Csikszentmihalyi & Massimini, 1985; Massimini, Inghilleri, & Delle Fave, 1996). The result of this unceasing, life-long selection process is the individual behavior, considered as a set of peculiar activities and preferences, such as study and work interests, hobbies, and social relations. From a theoretical point of view, individuals tend to selectively reproduce activities associated with challenging, enjoyable, and rewarding experiences (Optimal Experiences) and to avoid situations perceived as negative in character (Csikszentmihalyi, 1975, 1978, 1990). Considerable cross-cultural experimental data have been gathered over the last two decades in favor of this assumption (Csikszentmihalyi & Csikszentmihalyi,

1988; Delle Fave & Massimini, 1991, 1992; Kubey & Csikszentmihalyi, 1990; Massimini, Csikszentmihalyi, & Carli, 1987).

In order to study the quality of daily experience, a specific procedure has been developed, the Experience Sampling Method (ESM). It is based on self-report forms filled out by respondents in their real life context, upon reception of a pager's random signal (Csikszentmihalyi & Larson, 1987). Each ESM form includes 50 questions, providing on-line information about subjects' activity, location, social context, and content of thoughts at the signal's reception (open-ended questions), and about their quality of experience (as measured by Likert scales assessing affective, cognitive, and motivational variables). ESM session units are usually one week long, with 6-8 signals a day.

Psychological selection molds a subject's lifestyle, goals, and attitudes toward environmental opportunities and events; in other words, it influences the selective cultivation of those activities and relationships which become part of an individual's exclusive "Life Theme" (Csikszentmihalyi & Beattie, 1979). In this perspective, major events like childbirth and parenting can be analyzed in experiential terms by means of the Experience Sampling Method. On one hand, we can obtain a detailed description of everyday parenting behavior and experience; on the other, longitudinal studies can provide insights into the cultivation of parental roles and relationships with the child.

OVERVIEW OF AN ITALIAN SAMPLE

In order to get some information about the daily experience of new parents, we studied five primiparous Italian women and their husbands during and after pregnancy. The respondents were from 23 to 31 years old. Nine of the ten respondents were full-time workers, all lived in Piedmont (northwest Italy), and all had attained at least a high school degree. The five mothers experienced healthy pregnancies and full-term deliveries, all children but one were breast-fed, all of them were healthy at birth, and during the whole sampling period they showed normal rates of physical and psychological development.

The couples were examined by means of the above described ESM procedure. Each sampling unit was 7-12 days long, with 6-8 signals a day, and husbands' and wives' pagers were synchronized. Eight sessions of ESM sampling were performed: four before delivery (10th, 20th, 30th, and 35th week of pregnancy) and four after childbirth (3rd and 7th week, 3rd and 6th month). The respondents filled out 4,033 valid forms.

Our results provide interesting insights into various biological, cultural, and individual factors influencing the development of the parental role. Gender differences emerged in the allocation of daily attention to matters concerning parenthood and the newborn, and with respect to the quality of related experiences. In line with the aim of this paper, we will briefly discuss a small amount of the data we gathered. Figures 1 and 2 summarize data regarding the quality of experience parents reported in two different contexts: during infant-care activities, and in every other daily situation.

Several dimensions of the experience were taken into account. Three of them (Challenges, Skills, Goals) are directly measured in the ESM forms, and the others represent general factors, each loading on four ESM variables: Mood (Happy, Cheerful, Sociable, Friendly), Engagement (Concentration, Alert, Active, Involved), Confidence (Control of the situation, Clear ideas, Strong, Ease of concentration), and Intrinsic Reward (Wish doing the activity, Free, Satisfied, Relaxed). The data were standardized, with the mean of each respondent's mean ratings corresponding to the zero point, as is appropriate for repeated measurement analysis.

As the data highlight, both parents perceived child-related activities as significantly more engaging, challenging, and relevant for their life goals, in comparison with the rest of the daily situations. As respect to gender differences, the fathers reported significantly higher values of positive mood and intrinsic reward when interacting with the child while the mothers reported significantly lower levels of confidence and personal skills.

These results, however synthetic, enable us to detect some experiential features of the new parents. Parenthood is perceived as a complex and demanding situation where the respondents have to cope with new and highly significant challenges. The perceived importance of childbirth is a prerequisite for adequate investment of attention regarding childcare and education. From a biocultural perspective, it will ultimately facilitate the cross-generational transmission of those behavioral instructions needed by the child to fit smoothly into the biocultural environment.

The mothers reported some difficulties in coping with their new role. This can be related to at least three major factors: they are primiparous, thus inexperienced mothers; they spend much more time with the child than their husbands do (see Figures 1 and 2) and consequently face most of the daily childcare challenges, and they are expected to be the person in charge of the newborn, as is still common in both pre-industrial and industrialized countries. In contrast, the fathers' interactions with their children are highly enjoyable and rewarding *per se*. This finding is consistent with other studies on parent-child interaction. For example, Yogman (1990) describes fathers' child-related behavior as more playful, stimulating, and arousing

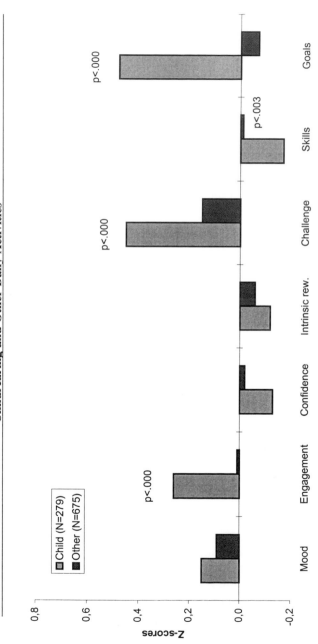

Figure 1
Mothers' Quality of Experience: Comparison Between
Childrearing and Other Daily Activities

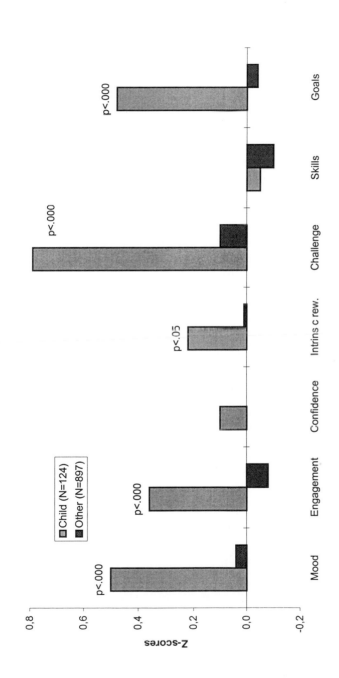

Figure 2
Fathers' Quality of Experience: Comparison Between
Childrearing and Other Daily Activities

than the mothers' behavior. Because males are not traditionally socialized to become caretakers, their wives' constant presence and prominent role enable them to perceive the exciting and motivating aspects of childcare. In contrast, the mothers seem to be more aware of the psychological burdens and responsibilities entailed in their daily parenting activities.

CONCLUSIONS

Conclusions can be drawn from this brief review of different approaches to the study of parenthood. Offspring's procreation is the basic means of Homo Sapiens' propagation. Given the fundamental role childbirth plays in adaptation, specific evolutionary traits have developed in order to ensure its occurrence and effectiveness. However, human reproduction and child-rearing are often given complex and additional meanings, which are not always reducible to biological explanations in evolutionary terms. On one hand, the development of cultures sometimes led to highly varied parenting practices. On the other hand, a holistic approach cannot fail to emphasize the individual's role as an active and selective contributor to the transmission of both biological and cultural instructions by means of his/her self-awareness and psychological selection. As Fleming states (1990, p.185), "in the absence of a positive psychological predisposition to be a mother or respond nurturantly to infants, the hormonal events will not create nurturant feelings or behavior in the new mother." Similarly, the dominance of specific cultural norms concerning parenthood in a given social context is insufficient to predict an individual's parental behavior. Individuals are the primary carriers of biocultural information, but they are also the agents of its selective transmission. In our opinion, the quality of daily experience is the ultimate criterion on which the replication or extinction of such information depends. Whatever the behavior investigated, more attention should be paid to these issues.

BIBLIOGRAPHY

Altman, I., & Chemers, M.M. (1980). *Culture and environment.* Monterey, CA: Brooks/Cole.
Benoit, D., Zeanah, C.H., & Barton, M.L. (1989). Maternal attachment disturbances in failure to thrive. *Mental Health Journal, 10,* 185-202.
Berry, J.W., Poortinga, Y.H., Segall, M.H., & Dasen, P.R. (1992). *Cross-cultural psychology: Research and applications.* Cambridge: Cambridge University Press.

Bogren, L.Y. (1983). Couvade. *Acta Psychiatrica Scandinavica, 68,* 55-65.

Bowlby, J. (1969). *Attachment and loss. Vol. 1. Attachment.* New York: Basic Books.

Bowlby, J. (Ed.). (1988). *A secure base.* New York: Basic Books.

Boyd, R., & Richerson, P.J. (1985). *Culture and the evolutionary process.* Chicago, IL: Chicago University Press.

Bridges, R.S., DiBiase, R., Loundes, D.D., & Doherty, P.C. (1985). Prolactin stimulation of maternal behavior in female rats. *Science, 227,* 782-784.

Brown, R.E., Moger, W.H., & Murphy, P.B. (1989). *Prolactin and parental behaviour in the male monglian gerbil.* Hormones & Behaviour Conference, Belgium, 1989.

Buss, D. (1989). Sex differences in human mate preferences: Evolutionary hypotheses tested in 37 cultures. *Behavioral and Brain Sciences, 12,* 1-49.

Caldwell, J.C., Orubuloye, I.O., & Caldwell, P. (1997). Male and female circumcision in Africa from a regional to a specific Nigerian examination. *Social Science & Medicine, 44,* 1181-1193.

Cleland, J., Verrall, J., & Vassen, M. (1983). Preference for the sex of children and their influence on reproductive behavior. *Comparative Studies, 27,* International Statistical Institute, Voorborg.

Clinton, J.F. (1985). Couvade: Patterns, predictors, and nursing management. *Western Journal of Nursing Research, 7,* 221-243.

Cloak, F.T. (1975). Is a cultural ethology possible? *Human Ecology, 3,* 161-182.

Cook, R. (1976). *Damage to physical health from Pharonic circumcision (infibulation) of females: A review of the medical literature.* Report from regional advisor of World Health Organization to Division of Family Health. WHO, Geneva.

Cooksey, E.C., & Fondell, M.M. (1996). Spending time with his kids: Effects of family structure on fathers' and children's lives. *Journal of Marriage and the Family, 58,* 693-707.

Csikszentmihalyi, M. (1975). *Beyond boredom and anxiety,* San Francisco, CA: Jossey Bass.

Csikszentmihalyi, M. (1978). Attention and the holistic approach to behavior. In K.S. Pope & J.L. Singer (Eds.), *The stream of consciousness* (pp. 335-358). New York: Plenum.

Csikszentmihalyi, M. (1990). *Flow: The psychology of optimal experience.* New York: Harper and Row.

Csikszentmihalyi, M., & Beattie, O. (1979). Life themes: A theoretical and empirical exploration of their origins and effects. *Journal of*

Humanistic Psychology, 19, 677-693.

Csikszentmihalyi, M., & Csikszentmihalyi, I. (Eds.). (1988), *Optimal experience: Psychological studies of flow in consciousness*, New York: Cambridge University Press.

Csikszentmihalyi, M., & Larson, R.W. (1987). Validity and reliability of the Experience Sampling Method. *Journal of Nervous and Mental Disease, 175*, 526-536.

Csikszentmihalyi, M., & Massimini, F. (1985). On the psychological selection of bio-cultural information. *New Ideas in Psychology, 3*, 115-138.

Csikszentmihalyi, M., Rathunde, K., & Whalen, S. (1993). *Talented teenagers*. New York: Cambridge University Press.

Daly, M. (1990). Evolutionary theory and parental motives. In N.A. Krasnegor & R.S. Bridges (Eds.), *Mammalian parenting* (pp. 25-39). Oxford: Oxford University Press.

Dawkins, R. (1976). *The selfish gene*. Oxford: Oxford University Press.

Delle Fave, A., Massimini, F. (1991). Modernization and the quality of daily experience in a Southern Italy village. In N. Bleichrodt & P.J.D. Drenth (Eds.), *Contemporary issues in cross-cultural psychology* (pp. 110-119). Amsterdam: Swets & Zeitlinger.

Delle Fave, A., & Massimini, F. (1992). Experience Sampling Method and the measuring of clinical change: A case of anxiety syndrome. In M.W. deVries (Ed.), *The experience of psychopathology* (pp. 280-289). Cambridge: Cambridge University Press.

Dixson, A.F., & George, L. (1982). Prolactin and parental behaviour in a male New World primate. *Nature, 295*, 551-553.

Durham, W.H. (1982). Interactions of genetic and cultural evolution: Models and examples. *Human Ecology, 10*, 289-323.

Elwood, R.W., & Mason, C. (1994). The couvade and the onset of paternal care: A biological perspective. *Ethology and Sociobiology, 15*, 145-156.

Fleming, A. (1990). Hormonal and experiential correlates of maternal responsiveness in human mothers. In N.A. Krasnegor & R.S. Bridges (Eds.), *Mammalian parenting* (pp. 184-208). Oxford: Oxford University Press.

Freedman, D.G. (1994). *Ethological studies of subjectivity: The Internal Working Model*. Special Address to the 12th Annual Congress of the International Society for Human Ethology, Toronto, Canada.

Freedman, D.G., & Gorman, J. (1993). Attachment and the transmission of culture. An evolutionary perspective. *Journal of Social and Evolutionary Systems, 16*, 297-329.

Gorman, J. (1988). *Maternal attachment legacies in non-organic failure to thrive.* Unpublished doctoral thesis, University of Chicago.

Grassivaro Gallo, P., & Viviani, F. (1992). The origin of infibulation in Somalia: An ethological hypothesis. *Ethology and Sociobiology, 13,* 253-265.

Harlow, H.F., & Harlow, M.K. (1965). The affectional systems. In A.M. Schrier, H.F. Harlow, & F. Stollnitz (Eds.), *Behavior of non-human primates* (pp. 287-334). New York: Academic Press.

Hrdy, S.B. (1981). *The woman that never evolved.* Cambridge, MA: Harvard University Press.

Kaplan, H., & Hill, K. (1992). The evolutionary ecology of food acquisition. In E.A. Smith & B. Winterhalder (Eds.), *Evolutionary ecology* (pp. 167-201). Hawthorne, NY: Aldine de Gruyter.

Kubey, R., & Csikszentmihalyi, M. (1990). *Television and the quality of life,* Hillsdale, NJ: Erlbaum.

Lampert, A. (1997). *The evolution of love.* Westport, CT: Praeger.

Leonard, L. (1996). Female circumcision in Southern Chad: Origins, meaning, and current practice. *Social Science & Medicine, 43,* 255-263.

Lipkin, M., Jr., & Lamb, G.S. (1982). The couvade syndrome: An epidemiological study. *Annals of Internal Medicine, 96,* 509-511.

Low, B.S. (1989). Cross-cultural patterns in the training of children: An evolutionary perspective. *Journal of Comparative Psychology, 103,* 311-319.

Luster, T., Boger, R., & Hannan, K. (1993). Infant affect and home environment. *Journal of Marriage and the Family, 55,* 651-661.

MacCormack, C., & Strathern, M. (Eds.). (1980). *Nature, culture and gender.* Cambridge: Cambridge University Press.

Main, M., & Goldwyn, R. (1984). Predicting rejection of her infants from mother's representation of her own experience: Implications for the abused-abusing intergenerational cycle. *International Journal of Child Abuse and Neglect, 8,* 203-217.

Malinowski, B. (1927). *Sex and repression in savage society.* London: Routledge.

Manning, J.T., & Chamberlain, A.T. (1991). Left-side cradling and brain lateralization, *Ethology and Sociobiology, 12,* 237-244.

Massimini, F. (1982). Individuo, cultura, ambiente: i Papua Kapauku della Nuova Guinea Occidentale. *Ricerche di Psicologia, 22-23,* 27-154.

Massimini, F., & Calegari, P. (1979). *Il Contesto Normativo Sociale.* Milano: FrancoAngeli.

Massimini, F., Csikszentmihalyi, M., & Carli, M. (1987). Optimal experience: A tool for psychiatric rehabilitation. *Journal of Nervous and Mental Disease, 175,* 545-549.

Massimini, F., Inghilleri, P., & Delle Fave, A. (Eds.). (1996). *La Selezione Psicologica Umana*. Milano: Cooperativa Libraria IULM.

Massimini, F., Inghilleri, P., & Toscano, M. (1996). La selezione culturale umana. In F. Massimini, P. Inghilleri, & A. Delle Fave (Eds.), *La Selezione Psicologica Umana* (pp. 301-348). Milano: Cooperativa Libraria IULM.

Mealey, L., & Mackey, W. (1990). Variation in offspring sex ratio in women of differing social status. *Ethology and Sociobiology, 11*, 83-95.

Meyer, D.R., & Garasky, S. (1993). Custodial fathers: Myths, realities, and child support policy. *Journal of Marriage and the Family, 55*, 73-89.

Miller, J.G. (1970). *Living systems*. New York: McGraw-Hill.

Montagu, A. (1981). The adolescent's unreadiness for pregnancy and motherhood. *Pediatric Annals, 10*, 497-511.

Munroe, R.L., Munroe, R.H., & Whiting, J.W.M. (1981). Male sex role resolutions. In R.H. Munroe, R.L. Munroe, & B.B. Whiting (Eds.), *Handbook of cross-cultural human development* (pp. 611-632). New York: Garland.

Park, C.B., & Cho, N. (1995). Consequences of son preference in a low fertility society: Imbalance of the sex ratio at birth in Korea. *Population Development Review, 21*, 59-84.

Peterson, S.A., & Somit, A. (1978). Methodological problems associated with a biologically-oriented social science. *Journal of Social and Biological Structures, 1*, 1-26.

Richerson, P.J., & Boyd, R. (1978). A dual inheritance model of human evolutionary process: Basic postulates and a simple model, I. *Journal of Social and Biological Structure*, 127-154.

Ruyle, E.E. (1973). Genetic and cultural pools: Some suggestions for a unified theory of biocultural evolution. *Human Ecology, 1*, 201-215.

Sahlins, M.D., & Service, E.R. (Eds.). (1960). *Evolution and culture*. Ann Arbor, MI: University of Michigan Press.

Salk, L. (1960). The effects of the normal heartbeat sound on the behavior of the newborn infant: Implications for mental health, *World Mental Health, 12*, 168-175.

Scifer, R., Schiller, M., Sameroff, A.J., Resnick, S., & Riordan, K. (1996). Attachment, maternal sensitivity, and infant temperament during the first year of life. *Developmental Psychology, 32*, 12-25.

Simons, R.L., Beanman, J., Conger, R.D., & Chao, W. (1993). Childhood experience, conceptions of parenting, and attitudes of spouse as determinants of parental behavior. *Journal of Marriage and the Family, 55*, 91-106.

Super, C.M., & Harkness, S. (1986). The developmental niche: A conceptualization at the interface of child and culture. *International Journal of Behavioral Development, 9*, 545-569.

Symons, D. (1990). Adaptiveness and adaptation. *Ethology and Sociobiology, 11*, 427-444.

Teichman, Y., & Lahav, Y. (1987). Expectant fathers: Emotional reactions, physical symptoms and coping styles. *British Journal of Medical Psychology, 60*, 225-232.

Tooby, J., & Cosmides, L. (1992). The psychological foundations of culture. In J. Barkow, L. Cosmides, & J. Tooby (Eds.), *The adapted mind: Evolutionary psychology and the generation of culture* (pp. 19-136). New York: Oxford University Press.

Towsends, J.M., Kline, J., & Wasserman, T.H. (1995). Low-investment copulation: Sex differences in motivations and emotional reactions. *Ethology and Sociobiology, 16*, 25-51.

Trethowan, W., & Conlon, M.F. (1965). The couvade syndrome. *Journal of British Psychiatry, 111*, 57-66.

Trivers, R.L. (1972). Parental investment and sexual selection. In B. Campbell (Ed.), *Sexual selection and the descent of man 1871-1971* (pp. 136-179). Chicago, IL: Aldine.

Volpi, R. (1996). *I figli d'Italia* Firenze: La Nuova Italia.

Warren, M.P., & Shortle, B. (1990). Endocrine correlates of human parenting: A clinical perspective. In N.A. Krasnegor & R.S. Bridges (Eds.), *Mammalian parenting* (pp. 209-226). Oxford: Oxford University Press.

Werner, E.E. (1979). *Cross-cultural child development: A view from the planet Earth*. Monterey, CA: Brooks/Cole.

Williamson, N.E. (1976). *Sons or daughters: A cross-cultural survey of parental preferences*. Beverly Hills, CA: Sage.

Yogman, M.W. (1990). Male parental behavior in humans and nonhuman primates. In N.A. Krasnegor & R.S. Bridges (Eds.), *Mammalian parenting* (pp. 461-481). Oxford: Oxford University Press.

BIOCULTURAL AND EXPERIENTIAL BASES
OF CULTURAL CONTINUITY AND CHANGE

Eric S. De Vos
Saginaw Valley State University, U.S.A.

INTRODUCTION

Social scientists have long been interested in the processes by which cultural patterns are transmitted from one generation to the next. Much of this interest has focused on how culturally constituted mental representations, belief systems, patterns of behavior, etc. are developed as a result of persons' participation in a social environment, whether through interpersonal interactions or through the use of socially provided mental and physical artifacts. We recently have seen discussions of the development of knowledge systems and their related goal structures, self-representations, or the person's dialogic participation in social discourse (D'Andrade & Strauss, 1992; Markus & Kitayama, 1991; Tedlock & Mannheim, 1995). Socialization is commonly seen as an intentional or purposive transmission (or mutual negotiation) of intellectual artifacts or behavioral patterns, such as mental tools, value systems, ideological systems, linguistic systems, social forms, etc. The neo-Vygotskian perspective, in particular, sees the issue from this angle (Rogoff, 1990). Yet approaches that emphasize knowing and doing may be missing an essential element of cultural continuity, i.e., the development of our subjective experience of being.

In the present paper I suggest the alternative perspective that transgenerational continuities in "states of being" and in the human experience of the self are the essence of cultural transmission. I will frame the discussion from a biocultural perspective, because the capacity to transmit states of being is inescapably built upon the available neurological and physiological hardware as it develops dynamically during ontogenesis. Through developmental changes that occur in this hardware, our interpersonal experiences are incorporated into our selves, into the very core of our being, into what I shall call the "flavor" of our subjective experience. These flavors of experience are so much a part of our being that they are "transparent" to us, even as we see the world through them (Hutchins, 1980).

I will suggest that this incorporation of early experiences into transparent constituents of our being is perhaps the most important basis for and consequence of cultural transmission. They flavor our subjective experience, predispose us to accept or resist socialization or acculturation, and influence our self-concepts, gender-related identities, role enactments, parenting behavior, and so on. I will describe how this is an underexplored area in developmental psychology, partly because of a tradition in the West that reifies our selfhood in a dualistic objectification of our being.

SOCIAL, PSYCHOLOGICAL, AND IDEOLOGICAL DIMENSIONS OF CULTURAL CONTINUITY: AN INTERDISCIPLINARY TASK

At the heart of the socialization process are the most proximate social interactions, i.e., the relationships of the child with parents and other family members, or their surrogates, who enact socioculturally constituted caregiving or peer roles. These interpersonal relationships serve as the context for the development of the child's internal self-regulatory mechanisms and the child's capacity for socially appropriate behavior, while at the same time providing the child some degree of satisfaction of human nurturance needs. Caregivers may be aware that they are personally implementing a socially constructed agenda as they enact their roles, but the specific characteristics of these enactments, as they manifest in relationships between caregiver and child, are determined by far more than any intentional agenda. They are determined also by the biological make-up of the individual child and by the enduring effects of the caregiver's own developmental experiences.

There are social, ethnological, psychological, and biological dimensions of the processes by which culturally constituted experiences become incorporated into future behavior. Using an interdisciplinary social sciences approach (De Vos, 1997), one could discuss these from a variety of theoretical and empirical perspectives, ranging from evolutionary to phenomenological and from socio-historical analysis to hormone assay. For example, the socio-historical construction of social roles and the conditions of their enactment become a legitimate subject of sociological inquiry. The culturally constituted content of transmitted knowledge, culturally patterned exposure to behavioral interactions, etc., are all legitimate subjects for anthropological inquiry (De Vos, 1997; Spindler, 1978). The psychological mechanisms by which culturally constituted patterns become represented internally in each person and thereby direct action, are legitimate subjects for psychological inquiry. The neurological and physiological hardware that serves as the substrate for cognitive and behavioral functions are legitimate subjects for developmental-biological inquiry. However, as discussed by Chodorow (1995), many theorists emphasize social or cultural construction without adequate attention to psychological and biological ontogenetic continuities.

What is of concern here is a tendency in the social sciences towards upward reductionism, wherein the social level is granted an ontological status that supersedes the individual human beings that comprise the system.   Obviously, in some instances there are emergent properties of social systems that are properly analyzed at the social level.   However, upward reductionism in the discussion of cultural continuity reminds me of the question asked by Schwartz: "Where is the culture?" (Schwartz, 1978).   I am convinced that our search for continuities in culture must not overlook its intrapersonal developmental bases, i.e., the dynamic structures that are the biological and mental media upon and in which any social construction must reside.   We must not ignore the internal functional characteristics of individual human beings, and the developmental processes that produce them.

Although there is an essential role for psychology in our effort to understand cultural continuity, mainstream psychologists have historically neglected to set up research in field settings to work with culturally distinct groups.   Some exceptions are found in efforts to test developmental theories cross-culturally, yet this has not been a mainstream effort in psychology.   Paradoxically, this inattention to the developing and socially-embedded neuro-psyche as a medium for cultural continuity may be based in mainstream psychology's tendency towards a narrow and proximate focus on the behavior of the individual human being, and a failure to see behavior as what it really is: only a brief moment in an ancient biocultural continuity that manifests ontogenetically as neurological organizations and behavioral patterns forming the bases for our human experience.

I am not arguing that we should abandon either individual or social analysis, only that they be integrated within a biocultural framework.   For example, the family as a dynamic system is identifiable at the social level of analysis (Cox & Paley, 1997) and that has obvious relevance to the transmission of culture.   Yet, the family is not only a social system.   As a biocultural entity, it is a convergent manifestation of evolutionary, biological, psychological, social, and historical forces.

Social and historical forces certainly have substantially altered family structures and the conditions under which family systems function.   New (1997, 1998) has discussed how social and historical changes, including public policies, have influenced continuities in the Italian family.   Changes in family systems can in turn influence the personal developmental patterns that derive from the child's participation in socially structured interactions that constitute the family system (or that occur in the context of other social institutions providing basic care).   Historical changes in family systems (see Sharma, this volume) can alter essential patterns, such as attachment relationships, child-caregiver co-regulations, and disciplinary patterns, as well as motivational characteristics.

An interesting example of the potentially dramatic impact of public policy changes comes from the experience of China following the implementation of the one-child rule. Given demographic trends, resource issues, and China's historical experience with mass starvation, one can see a very real pragmatic rationale for the implementation of serious population control methods such as the one-child rule. Yet the leadership that drafted it may not have foreseen the social, psychological, and ultimately the political consequences of the rule. Some reported changes in the Chinese family system include parental overprotectiveness, indulgent and inconsistent discipline from multiple adult caregivers, as well as an increase in one-on-one interactions between child and caregivers. The new family structures appear to be producing a more selfish, yet also intellectually gifted, physically healthy, and creative individual, with personality characteristics not unlike those found in only-children in the West (Rosenberg & Jing, 1996).

It is interesting to note that while the large-scale production of individualists may undermine the continuity of the Confucianist family system, it may paradoxically also undermine current Chinese Communist political structures, for those may depend on Confucianist cultural patterns to an extent not adequately understood by cultural revolutionaries who use ideological rather than materialist-empirical social science methods. I would argue that social-historical, ethnographic, and psychological analyses alike must be plausibly integrated within a biocultural developmental framework, and the full complexity of human ontogenesis must be considered when social activists or policy makers plan to change social or public policies that affect family systems and childcare patterns. Insufficiently informed policies can either fail to override a biocultural legacy (where such change might be desirable), or fail to preserve important elements of the legacy when the policies cut at the culture's ontogenetic roots.

Effects of historical changes in family structures are informative. But we can also look at varieties of family systems within any given society and historical period. We now have substantial work documenting varieties of infant-caregiver interactions and styles of attachment within the modern family. Developmental psychology has seen provocative findings from research by Ainsworth (1985), Reite and Field (1985), Stern (1985), Trevarthen (1993), and many others. Research on the coordination of behavior and arousal between the infant and caregiver, through processes of "attunement" or "mutual regulation" or "co-regulation" provides evidence that early infant-caregiver interactions are of central importance. This type of research has provided research data that support what were initially clinically-derived formulations from the object-relations schools of psychoanalysis about the importance of internalized infant-caregiver relationships in the formation of behavioral and experiential patterns that persist through life.[1]

As Chodorow (1978) and others have already noted, the psychoanalytic account of object-relational development has generally assumed that infant-caregiver interactions are dyadic, involving one infant and one female primary caregiver. Yet, not all cultures are limited to the nuclear family structure that is typical of the modern, Western, urban, industrialized society. The relatively isolated monogamous nuclear family is not universal throughout the world. Children in many cultural groups are raised by multiple caregivers, including adults as well as siblings. Sharma and Levine (1998) have discussed the early family context of infant development in India, where one finds multiple caregivers in an extended family setting. Freedman (this volume) has described evidence for biocultural processes whereby group differences in parental behavior are related to group differences in infant behavior and in the development of internal working models. As previously noted by Levine (1990), the examination of patterns of development in a variety of family structural settings puts universalist psychodynamic explanations to the test, and should ultimately strengthen psychodynamic theory, as well as other developmental theories.

The character of both parent and child is being formed through these early interactions. It is in the context of these interactions, and in the anticipation of these interactions, that the parent comes into actual being. Working from a biocultural perspective, Delle Fave and Massimini (this volume) have described the subjective experiences of new Italian parents as they anticipate and then become involved in the experience of parenting. Yet, when I say that both the parent and the child are created in the family system, I am not talking only about changes in role behavior that develop in these interactions. Nor am I talking only about changes in psychological function. Social interactions go deeper than that; they involve the mammalian nervous system and neuroendocrine-physiological systems (Krasnegor & Bridges, 1990). In his landmark volume on Affect Regulation and the Origin of the Self, Schore (1994) has presented broadly based and convincing evidence that early interpersonal experiences become embodied as patterns of neurological and physiological organization, and that these patterns serve as an enduring basis for later emotional regulation and interpersonal interaction, including those that become the next generation's parental behavior. Personal characteristics that are developed in this manner are not merely socially constructed conceptual frameworks in a cognitive system, nor merely socially reinforced behavior patterns. They represent a direct and enduring social regulation of biological systems at the level of neurological and physiological organization.

We can see clear biocultural continuities as social coordinations produce these neurologically-based behavioral and experiential patterns that persist through life. It is upon the resulting organized biological structures and processes that the social construction of the person is built. By influencing these patterns of early organization, family systems and caregiving patterns determine the child's capacity to later engage in socially acceptable behavior, or to participate or fail to participate consensually in the larger set of agreements that constitute society.

The outcomes of these developmental-biological processes are constrained within the individual's reaction range, i.e., the range of viable biological possibilities. This range of adaptations, at the levels of neurological and physiological organization as well as behavioral consequences, sets limits to biocultural continuity. Infant-caregiver interactions that fall outside the viable range may produce marginally functional human beings, or survivors whose long-range fecundity is in danger, if they survive long enough to become either destructive of the social community that sustains them or destructive of their own children.

In North America we presently see evidence of this type of problem in a generation of extremely dangerous human beings, sometimes called superpredators. While overall crime is declining, we are seeing an increase in very violent crimes by the very young, some of whom are not yet even ten years old, and who often show little if any remorse nor concern for their own lives or futures. Such individuals increasingly populate North American prisons. The type of human experience that is involved in this behavioral pattern can be understood, from an object-relations perspective, as unregulated rage that develops in the absence of adequate self-objects (Seinfeld, 1996). Such a psychological explanation must not be neglected or supplanted by sociological or ideological explanations that try to account for the individual human experience on the basis of social-historical, class-based or race-based discrimination. Those distal forces are very real, but if such social forces are to have any impact on a person's behavior, they can do so only as mediated by way of the more proximate family systems, and ultimately by way of the most proximate neuropsychological systems that either regulate or fail to regulate specific behavior.

THE "SELF": SUBJECTIVE AND OBJECTIFIED
ASPECTS OF BIOCULTURALLY-CONSTITUTED BEING

I am not here advocating that one should place all emphasis on the neurological developmental patterns. When social interactions alter the development of the biological organism, they obviously also produce a range of behavioral and cognitive possibilities for the individual. From the perspective of subjective being, among the most important of these are the conceptual structures we sometimes call the "self." By some accounts, this self is primarily a socially-constructed, self-reflective, self-objectifying conceptualization that also serves to help regulate behavior. However, it is important to remember that social interactions also produce states of subjectivity itself and an experiential repertoire with which we flavor this subjective experience. This is also an important aspect of our selfhood. If there is anything interesting to me about human culture, it is the variety of human subjective experiences made possible through biocultural transmission. That is not to say that material artifacts or normative cognitive and behavioral patterns are irrelevant. For me, they are interesting only inasmuch as they contribute to lived states of being (Low, 1994).

States of being are an under-explored terrain in Western developmental psychology. Yet, the relationship between infant and caregiver can be seen as primarily a mutual coordination of states of being. Indeed it is this mutual creation of a non-conceptual self-regulatory system that may form the core of our experience of a self. The object relations schools have emphasized this important aspect of the child's being, that originates in relational experiences, and becomes an "inner physical experience of body integrity and a more internal 'core of the self' that derives from inner sensations and emotions, and which remains a 'feeling self' around which a 'sense of identity' is established" (Chodorow, 1978, p. 67).

Outside the psychoanalytic and clinical camps, the Western conception of the self has not generally emphasized this feeling self, and has failed to recognize the states of "being" that may be at the core of an individual's identity. It has instead emphasized the primacy of a "knowing" self that knows selves as objects, and also knows its own self as an object, in what can be seen both as a reification and an objectification of the person's identity. Additionally, as Paranjpe (1995) has noted, even where some branches of Western psychology (e.g., behaviorism) have abandoned this kind of reification of the self, they have often paid for this by refusing to recognize subjectivity itself. This is in contrast to Eastern psychology's emphasis on the "technology of the self" (Paranjpe, 1995, p. 9). Yet, despite the variety of scholarly positions we might take, we remain troubled by the inner awareness that we experience our being as a continuous subjective identity, and we wonder where this continuous experience of being resides. To resolve this problem, we often distinguish between the "I" and the "Me."

The "Me" is a relatively easy move. "Me" is an objectifiable set of characteristics, much as a box or a table would be. I can imagine "Me" standing in front of you, caught in your gaze. Help! I'm a box! We can develop a lexicon of adjectives to describe our selves and others. Today, I am a tall box, deep but not as wide as I once have been. To be satisfied with this kind of description, however, is an instance of the nominalist fallacy that plagues theories of human personality; it does not constitute an understanding of how the "I" experiences its states of being.

This other aspect of our selves, the "I," may be a richer field for discovery. Most of us experience our subjective being as a fundamental perceptual reality. We remain convinced that there is an "I," an identity that actually exists at the center of our world, even though, as Descartes, Hume, and many others have found, you cannot apprehend this "I" anywhere. In the words of Daniel Dennett (as quoted in Neisser, 1993), "Searching for the self can be somewhat like [this]. You enter the brain through the eye, march up the optic nerve, round and round in the cortex, looking behind every neuron, and then, before you know it, you emerge into daylight on the spike of a motor nerve impulse, scratching your head and wondering where the self is" (Neisser, 1993, p. 4).

Personally, in keeping with Schore, I am not as pessimistic as Dennett about identifying a neurological basis for the experiences we call the self. As the neurologist Damasio (1994) has argued, it is very clear that the mind cannot be disembodied. He believes that Descartes' essential error was to conclude that the mind, whose principal purported activity is to think, requires no material substrate. The depth of Descartes' mystification is clearly illustrated by Robert Thurman, of Columbia University, when he rephrases Descartes' cogito ergo sum as something like this: "I have looked and looked everywhere I could, yet I could find my self nowhere. Therefore I conclude that I must exist" (paraphrase of Thurman, 1993).

Yet, unlike Descartes or Dennett or others, I am not mystified by our inability to find the "I" as an entity for objectification. I do not think it is necessary to resort to mystified dualistic fabrications of a distinction between subjective and objective universes. I am satisfied to find the self as a variety of integrated and organized states of experiential being. Rather than trying to reify the self through external objectification or through absolutist imputations of divine origination, I prefer to see the self as an emergent property of complex self-regulating, self-stabilizing, and enduring neurological and physiological organizations that integrate our social, interpersonal, intrapersonal, and other experiences.

Modern psychologists may no longer be trying to disembody the mind through reference to a dualistic universe of distinct material and mental substantialities. Yet, for many, the self continues to be disembodied analytically. The relational or dialogic or ecological self has taken on a transpersonal character, removed from the body or even from the person.

The self is now seen as a relational being, that does not reside entirely within an individual skin, and whose very existence is interpersonal or dialogic.   Whether working from cognitive, social-constructivist, ecological, or psychoanalytic perspectives, we now posit a relational model of the self, while on the other hand we posit its actual existence, and on a virtual third hand, we act as if it is disembodied.

Neisser's comments on the "self perceived" represent a good example of this (Neisser, 1993). He does admit that the developmental evidence indicates that the child first has experiences of being that predate the experience of knowing the self. And he grants that we can perceive the feelings of others in a direct way, because "as Soloman Asch (1952) noted many years ago, there is a natural congruence between feelings and their expressions" (p. 11). Yet in his analysis, Neisser makes too little of this. In his description of what he calls the "interpersonal self," Neisser minimizes the importance of the internal experiences that are engendered within the person-in-relationship.   He explicitly states that "The interpersonal self is not an inner state to be communicated, or chiefly a detector of such states in others; it is simply a person engaged in a social exchange" (p. 11). Apparently, empathic interpersonal experience is not relevant to the interpersonal selfhood of the infant, because, being inferred, it is not reliable perception. For Neisser, the infant's interpersonal self has no relevant experiencing of the inner states of others prior to four years of age, when the child can first "think of others as having specific mental states," that is, in other words, when the child has developed an objectifying concept of mind.   It appears that the inner experience of interpersonal "being" then becomes irrelevant.

That analysis neglects the enduring consequences of powerful, preconceptual experiences that derive from mutual coregulation. For such experiences to have developmental effects, the child need not have objectively accurate empathic awareness of the inner states of others.   In fact, I doubt very much that the infant cares about the objective reliability of its perceptions of others; it is more probably embedded entirely within the subjective reality of its own state of being. I would argue that it is precisely Psychology's failure to adequately attend to nonconceptual states of being, and its emphasis on the cognizing mind, that leads us to undervalue this key dimension of biocultural transmission: the transmission of states of being, which are often states of being-in-relationship-with (with a generalized other, with specific others, with objects or places, and with our cosmos).

THE CONTINUOUS SELF: NOT ABSOLUTE,
NOT PERMANENT, NOT SINGULAR

The general assumption in our Western discourse about the self is that all human beings actually have the experience of a continuous identity, even though there must certainly be cultural variations in this. This is an error similar to the one made in psychoanalytic accounts that erroneously assume all infant-caregiver interactions to be dyadic, involving one infant and one primary caregiver. Much as there is a diversity of object relational forms in diverse cultures, there are also diverse experiences of selfhood that can be felt directly. Many of us can remember feeling a sense of unfamiliarity or unease or special pleasure when we have interacted with people from cultures different from our own. This is not just a cognized awareness of differences in body movement, posture, proximity, etc. It is the evocation of an unfamiliar state of being within our own being as we attempt to engage relationally with the other.

The diversity of possible states of being also includes the possibility of experiencing the absence of a continuous self. The clinical evidence in fact indicates that this is not at all fantastic. Some human beings do have an actual experience of annihilation, or a terror of annihilation, and some individuals who have experienced inadequate empathic relationships in infancy report the experience of not actually having a solid sense of self. Clinical patients will sometimes use terms like "empty" or "in a void" to describe their state of selfhood (Balint, 1963; Chodorow, 1978; Seinfeld, 1996). It is generally assumed that such experiences are pathological, yet it may not be correct to assume that our Western preoccupation with the certainty of our individual selfhood is the optimal experiential form for all occasions. For example, the serious Buddhist practitioner will actively seek experiences of no-self (Wilson, 1980). As the Buddhist meditator works diligently (by means of analytical meditation) to cease "clinging" to a falsely imputed self, there can ensue a sense of terror or vertigo on approaching self-annihilation. This effort to cease being attached (to cease clinging) to the self, to cease what is known as "self-cherishing," is the most central task for the Buddhist practitioner. For self-cherishing is considered to be a root delusion, from which arise many other subsidiary delusions or afflicted emotional states that produce suffering for sentient beings. Yet there is a risk that the development of reduced attachment to what are seen as falsely imputed delusional fabrications, such as the self, can also lead to a condition known as the pitfall of nihilism. This pitfall involves confusing the desired non-attached state of being (which is substantially imperturbable) on the one hand, with conditions such as not caring about others, feeling that nothing really matters, a condition of anomie or a lack of normative grounding, and so on, on the other hand. Not surprisingly, the Buddhist curriculum for spiritual development (e.g., Pabongka, 1991; Tsongkapa, 1988) has cures for this dangerous pitfall of nihilism. In the Tibetan system, trained meditators receive detailed instructions and guidance on how to implement these cures in practice, and the no-self that is experienced intentionally is presumably not the same as the non-self that is experienced psychopathologically. One of the cures is an emphasis on compassion, on feeling from the heart, a generalized empathy towards all sentient beings. A second cure is an emphasis on finding emptiness/selflessness/impermanence/conectedness in the careful examination of phenomena, not in the annihilation of phenomena. This is a key point in the Tibetan metaphysics, and serious examination of this particular philosophical point is a good cure for the traditional Western misconception that the Buddhist philosophy is nihilistic. In the Tibetan system, it is advised that the elimination of personal grasping after selfhood is best accompanied by the deepest activation of empathic feeling, as well as an almost Cartesian insistence on the discovery of patterns of causation in an empirically knowable though relativistic world.[2] Thus the Tibetan practical psychology has recognized the essential human need for empathic relating, and also our need for a firm though relativistic ground, even while it refuses to acknowledge the self as having inherent existence.

As Varela, Thompson, and Rosch (1991) have so well described, the implications of our discovery that we can only find the self relationally have not been fully recognized by Western psychology. In terms that bridge a cognitive systems-theory approach and the Buddhist Madhyamika philosophical tradition, they suggest that the self is not to be discovered in dualistic terms as either object or subject. Rather than trying to reify the self through external objectification or through absolutist imputations of subjective existence or divine origination, they suggest that we see the self as an embodied being that has emergent properties that exist only as it enacts a reciprocally creative relationship with the world in which it is enmeshed. I would suggest that among the necessary causes and conditions for the emergence of this type of self is the biocultural transmission of states of being through human relationship in infancy. This produces the enduring neurological and physiological organizations that integrate our experiences into the being that most of us experience as a continuous identity, a continuous experience of self.

Metaphysical insights are taken very seriously by many Buddhists, and have concrete consequences in the intentional transformation of states of being. For the most part, the Tibetan developmental psychology is concerned with intentional transformations of states of subjective experience, that are accomplished by means of a variety of meditative practices (e.g., Gyatso, 1995; Klein, 1995). These practices emphasize detailed introspective examination and manipulation of both the contents of the mind and the workings of the mind. They also involve the practice-based fostering of attentional skills that enable stable concentration and undistracted attainment of a variety of definably and describably distinct states of subjective experience. They do not, however, emphasize the ontogenesis of these experiences during childhood.

The emphasis on intentional transformation of subjective experience is in contrast to the central focus on behavioral observation in Western developmental psychology, whether in naturalistic settings or in laboratory exploration of cognitive development, whether during childhood or over the life span. Nevertheless, despite the fact that this emphasis is prevalent in the research-oriented developmental sciences, clinically-oriented psychologists and even social psychologists have been concerned with the ontogenesis of subjective experiences of selfhood. Some psychologists have taken the position that experiences related to our selfhood can be changed through conscious activity. For example, one can manipulate the objectified "me" through changes in self-attributions (e.g., Bandura, 1982). Object-relations theorists further point to experiential states of being that originate in early relationships. Although these are subject to change, they may be difficult to change outside the context of direct relational experience (Seinfeld, 1993).[3]

The self may be changed in the face of changing circumstances, or through the power of conscious effort, but the self also resists change. To counter any remaining doubt that there is an embodied self whose existence does not depend on ecological continuities, one need only observe our efforts to preserve our selves in the face of disagreement, to deny guilt when subject to false accusation, or to preserve our unique identity in the midst of others who do not share our beliefs, attitudes, styles of interaction, and so on. In the Tibetan system, it is precisely the self that resists false accusation that is the object of analytical negation (Thurman, 1993; Wilson, 1980).[4]

There are certainly individual differences in the rigidity or flexibility with which people accept or resist change, or acquiesce to social expectations. Social psychologists have aptly demonstrated not only the power of peer pressure but also that individuals resist peer pressure (Smith & Bond, 1994). There is within many of us a force that does not easily submit. For many from Western cultures, losing the self interactionally while enacting social roles is seen as not desirable, it is seen as inauthentic. For many people, the authentic self is experienced as a continuous inner self that is distinct from the self that changes in relationship. For others, however, loss of self into social roles is not a problem, and may comprise a substantial portion of social life (Geertz, 1972; Goffman, 1959). For still others, loss of self in social roles may be desirable but not manageable intrapsychically, and may require the private maintenance of an inner self (Lebra, 1992).

There is clear evidence that there is a self that persists despite contingencies in the immediate environment, despite obvious advantages of consensual participation. For example, to account for aspects of ethnic identity and minority status, De Vos has proposed the concepts of "selective permeability" and "non-learning" (G.A. De Vos, this volume), which he illustrates with examples of circumstances in which individuals refuse to incorporate information, learn a new language, pass examinations, participate in mainstream society, and so on. If selfhood is actually embodied as patterns of neurological and physiological organization, then it may be that asking an inner-city youth, raised on the streets, to hold down a job and agree to become a mainstream social participant may be as naive as asking a heterosexual person to become homosexual. No matter how desirable it might be, change at this level may not be readily accomplished simply by edict. It is naive to expect changes in motivated behavior, and certainly naive to expect changes in experienced states of being without first producing transformations of underlying constitutional patterns, such as the changes obtained through practice (whether musical, muscular, meditative, or martial), through exposure to new personal relationships or experiences (whether in psychotherapy or in everyday life), or through transforming ritual.

In contrast to the resistance to acculturation that is found on the part of ethnic youth from oppressed groups, one finds an eagerness to acculturate in immigrant populations that have voluntarily migrated (Gibson & Ogbu, 1991; Suarez-Orosco & Suarez-Orosco, 1995). Although political exile cannot necessarily be equated with voluntary migration, many Tibetans are doing well in exile (Mahmoudi, 1992), acculturating rapidly and intermarrying with Westerners. It is possible that the emphasis on the non-absolute nature of the self in Tibetan religious culture has translated into cultural patterns that produce people who are highly adaptive in the face of many kinds of stress and change. Perhaps the self-as-a-box is not so constraining if the objectified self is not culturally favored over the experiential self. Perhaps this cultural pattern will also be found manifest in family interaction patterns. If, as many developmental psychologists believe, early caregiver-infant interactions are important determiners of later adaptive capacities, it could be interesting to explore the possibility that the Tibetan family system includes some style of infant-caregiver interaction that serves as the ontogenetic root of the Tibetans' unique and successful alternative variety of adaptive subjective experience in adulthood.

Yet the downside to ready acculturation in a modern world is that this may actually threaten the continuity of the Tibetan family system as a biocultural entity. Unlike the Japanese self, which has been extensively studied as representative of Eastern selfhood, the ontogenetic origins of the Tibetan experience of self have not been studied by developmental psychologists. It might be wise for us to study the biocultural patterns that produce the Tibetan form of experiential being, lest they fade with acculturation and modernization.

I will end with a brief poem:

Your self,
an echo of my echo,
Ripples
Fading into you.
Both of us an empty core
Grasping at reflections.

Light from our hearts radiates
Giving color to those around us.
And then we grasp for its reflection
Like children chasing rainbows.

BIBLIOGRAPHY

Ainsworth, M.D.S. (1985).   Patterns of infant-mother attachments: Antecedents and effects on development. *Bulletin of the New York Academy of Medicine*, *61*, 771-791.

Asch, S. (1952). *Social psychology*. New York: Prentice Hall.

Bandura, A. (1982). Self-efficacy mechanism in human agency. *American Psychologist*, *37*, 122-147.

Balint, E. (1963). On being empty of oneself. *International Journal of Psycho-Analysis*, *44*, 470-480.

Chodorow, N. (1978). *The reproduction of mothering: Psychoanalysis and the sociology of gender*. Berkeley, CA: University of California Press.

Chodorow, N. (1995). Gender as a personal and social construction. *Signs*, *20*, 516-544.

Cox, M.J., & Paley, B. (1997).   Families as systems. *Annual Review of Psychology*, *48*, 243-267.

D'Andrade, R.G., & Strauss, C. (Eds.). (1992).   *Human motives and cultural models*. New York: Cambridge University Press.

Damasio, A. (1994). *Descartes' error: Emotion, reason, and the human brain*. New York: Putnam.

Geertz, C. (1972). Deep play: Notes on the Balinese cockfight. *Daedalus,* *101*, 1-37.

Gibson, M., & Ogbu, J. (Eds.). (1991). *Minority status and schooling: A comparative study of immigrant and involuntary minorities.* New York: Garland.

Goffman, E. (1959). *The presentation of self in everyday life.* New York: Doubleday.

Gyatso, G.K. (1995). *The meditation handbook.* London: Tharpa.

Hutchins, E. (1980). *Culture and inference: A Trobriand case study.* Cambridge, MA: Harvard University Press.

Klein, A.C. (1995). *Meeting the Great Bliss Queen: Buddhists, feminists, and the art of the self.* Boston, MA: Beacon Press.

Krasnegor, N.A., & Bridges, R.S. (Eds.). (1990). *Mammalian parenting: Biochemical, neurobiological, and behavioral determinants.* New York: Oxford University Press.

Lebra, T.S. (1992). Self in Japanese culture. In N. Rosenberger (Ed.), *The Japanese sense of self* (pp. 105-120). New York: Cambridge University Press.

Levine, R.A. (1990). Infant environments in psychoanalysis: A cross-cultural view. In J.W. Stigler, R. A. Shweder, & G. Herdt (Eds.), *Cultural psychology: Essays on comparative human development* (pp. 454-474). New York: Cambridge University Press.

Low, S.M. (1994). Embodied metaphors: Nerves as lived experience. In T.J. Csordas (Ed.), *Embodiment and experience: The existential ground of culture and self* (pp. 139-162). New York: Cambridge University Press.

Macy, J. (1991). *Mutual causality in Buddhism and general systems theory: The Dharma of natural systems.* Albany, NY: State University of New York Press.

Mahmoudi, K.M. (1992). Refugee cross-cultural adjustment: Tibetans in India. *International Journal of Intercultural Relations, 16*, 17-32.

Markus, H., & Kitayama, S. (1991). Culture and self. *Psychological Review, 98*, 224-253.

Neisser, U. (1993). The self perceived. In U. Neisser (Ed.), *The perceived self: Ecological and interpersonal sources of self-knowledge. Emory Symposia in Cognition, 5*, 3-21. New York: Cambridge University Press.

New, R. (in press/1998). *Social competence in early childhood education in Italy. Socioemotional development across cultures—New directions in child development*, Vol. 81. San Francisco, CA: Jossey Bass Press.

New, R. (1997). Cultural values and child care in contemporary Italy. In

E.S. De Vos & D. Sharma (Co-chairs), Child Care and Sociocultural Change: Interdisciplinary Perspectives. *Symposium conducted at the ICP Regional Conference on "Cross-Cultural Perspectives on Human Development,"* Padua, Italy.

Pabongka Rinpoche (1991). *Liberation in the palm of your hand: A concise discourse on the path to enlightenment.* Boston, MA: Wisdom Publications.

Paranjpe, A.C. (1995). The denial and affirmation of self: The complementary legacies of East and West. *World Psychology, 1*(3), 9-46.

Reite, M., & Field, T. (Eds.). (1985). *The psychobiology of attachment and separation.* Orlando, FL: Academic Press.

Rogoff, B. (1990). *Apprenticeship in thinking: Cognitive development in social context.* New York: Oxford University Press.

Rosenberg, B.G., & Jing, Q. (1996). A revolution in family life: The political and social structural impact of China's one-child policy. *Journal of Social Issues, 52,* 51-69.

Schore, A.N. (1994). *Affect regulation and the origin of the self: The neurobiology of emotional development.* Hillsdale, NJ: Erlbaum.

Schwartz, T. (1978). Where is the culture? Personality as the distributive locus of culture. In G.D. Spindler (Ed.), *The making of psychological anthropology* (pp. 417-441). Berkeley, CA: University of California Press.

Seinfeld, J. (1993). *Interpreting and holding: The paternal and maternal functions of the psychotherapist.* Northvale, NJ: Jason Aronson.

Seinfeld, J. (1996). *Containing rage, terror, and despair: An object relations approach to psychotherapy.* Northvale, NJ: Jason Aronson.

Sharma, D., & LeVine, R.A. (in press/1998). *Child care in India: A comparative view of infant social environments. Socioemotional development across cultures—New directions in child development,* Vol. 81. San Francisco, CA: Jossey Bass Press.

Smith, P.B., & Bond, M.H. (1994). *Social psychology across cultures: Analysis and perspectives.* Boston, MA: Allyn and Bacon.

Spindler, G.D. (Ed.). (1978). The making of psychological anthropology. Berkeley, CA: University of California Press.

Stern, D. (1985). *The interpersonal world of the infant.* New York: Basic Books.

Suarez-Orosco, M., & Suarez-Orosco, C. (1995). *Transformations: Immigration, family life and achievement motivation among Latino adolescents.* Stanford, CA: Stanford University Press.

Tedlock, D., & Mannheim, B. (Eds.). (1995). *The dialogic emergence of culture.* Chicago, IL: University of Illinois Press.

Thurman, R.A.F. (1984). *The central philosophy of Tibet: A study and translation of Jey Tsong Khapa's "Essence of True Eloquence."* Princeton, NJ: Princeton University Press.

Thurman, R.A.F. (1993). *From a commentary on Chandrakirti's sevenfold reasoning.* Paper presented at the Jewel Heart Summer Retreat, Yankee Springs Recreation Area, MI.

Trevarthen, C. (1993). The self born in intersubjectivity: The psychology of an infant communicating. In U. Neisser (Ed.), *The perceived self: Ecological and interpersonal sources of self-knowledge. Emory Symposia in Cognition, 5,* 121-173. New York: Cambridge University Press.

Tsongkapa (1988). *The principle teachings of Buddhism.* Howell, NJ: Mahayana Sutra and Tantra Press

Varela, F.J., Thompson, E., & Rosch, E. (1991). *The embodied mind: Cognitive science and human experience.* Cambridge, MA: The MIT Press.

Wilson, J.B. (1980). *Chandrakirti's sevenfold reasoning: Meditations on the selflessness of persons.* Dharamsala, India: Library of Tibetan Works and Archives.

ENDNOTES

[1]Some psychologists prefer a term like "coordination" rather than "regulation," because the latter implies coercion or compliance with regulations, whereas the former addresses the mutual and relational infant-caregiver system. However, the term "regulation" is also quite appropriate as it is used in physiology to refer to homeostatic physiological regulation within a dynamically self-stabilizing organismic system.

[2]"Appearance dispels absolutist extremism and emptiness dispels nihilism; when emptiness dawns as cause and effect, you will not be deprived by any extremist views" (Tsongkapa, as translated by Thurman, 1984, p. 170). The Tibetan term that is translated into English here as "emptiness" has also been translated as "voidness." Yet these English terms often bring confusion. When properly used, the concept includes the idea that "emptiness" is one among many characteristics of phenomena, much as height and weight are characteristics of objects. The concept of "emptiness" or "voidness" seen this way is NOT well served by reference to a "vacuum of empty space" analogy. Instead, one must realize that the term applies to an absence of some falsely imputed characteristic of real things. So one uses the terms "empty of self" or "lacking inherent existence" to describe one of the qualities of real phenomena. As Tsongkapa has clearly stated, the correct (i.e., non-extremist)

understanding of emptiness requires an understanding of a corollary concept that has sometimes been phrased in English as "dependent arising." From this view, correct understanding or even direct perception of any given phenomenon's "emptiness of inherent existence" can be developed on the basis of careful observation of patterns of causality, where the existence of all phenomena is seen to be completely dependent on causes and conditions. See Macy (1991) for an excellent presentation of how this Eastern philosophical perspective is similar to what is known as "general systems theory" in modern Western science.

[3]The Tibetan system also recognizes this with its emphasis on "guru yoga" as a means for spiritual development. This involves a set of practices that focus on the development of a profound discipleship relationship with the spiritual mentor wherein the mentee has the explicit task of internalizing the mentor's characteristics.

[4]In the Gelukpa tradition, which derives historically from the teachings of Tsongkapa, blind faith in various points of philosophy or belief is discouraged; indeed it is sometimes known otherwise as "idiot faith." Instead, the individual is encouraged to obtain the evidence for himself or herself. Instructors will provide curricular guidelines for thought exercises and other types of meditative practices that should serve to convince a rational mind that various points of the philosophy are indeed correct. Facts are thereby established as profound realizations based on rational thought as well as by the alteration of psychological states of being. Among the most important of these facts is the notion that the self (as normally construed) is empty of inherent existence. One example of this type of curricular instruction can be found in the textbook known as Chandrakirti's Sevenfold Reasoning: Meditations on the Selflessness of Persons (translated by Wilson, 1990). This text provides guidelines for a series of mental exercises that help the practitioner identify the object of logical negation, which in this particular case would be the falsely imputed "inherently existent self."

CHILDREN'S SOCIOCULTURAL AND FAMILIAL WORLDS: PATHWAYS AND RISKS THROUGH THE DEMOGRAPHIC TRANSITION

Dinesh Sharma, Columbia University, U.S.A.

"Parents seek to promote the survival and success of their offspring, but their behavior is adapted to the socioeconomic and demographic conditions of agrarian and urban-industrial (and emerging post-industrial) societies and further differentiated by local cultural traditions" (LeVine, 1988, p. 3).

According to the "demographic transition" theory human populations are divided into two very different kinds of worlds: 1) the "developed" or rapidly growing post-industrial world, including Europe, America, and Far East Asia, and 2) the "underdeveloped" and "developing" or slowly growing world, which includes South Asia, Africa, China, and parts of Latin America (Brown & Jacobson, 1986; Goldthorpe, 1996). In the context of world population, the economically more viable developed world consists of a small minority of people, mostly although not exclusively Western populations, while the economically challenged developing world is in the majority, mostly although not exclusively non-Western populations (Kagitçibasi, 1996).[1]   Infant mortality, fertility, morbidity, and other human development indices are relatively higher in developing countries when compared to the developed world (UNDP, 1996). Consequently, children's worlds in the underdeveloped and the developing world are constructed differently and children face greater challenges to their well-being when compared to children in the developed world. While the discourse of "lost" or "stolen" childhoods is prevalent in many parts of the world today, the antecedents and consequences of such sociocultural and familial conditions are not well understood. Thus, an analysis of children's worlds across the sociodemographic divide which separates the developed from the developing world, is highly relevant for psychologists, mental health practitioners, and policy makers.

CHILDHOOD IS SOCIALLY AND HISTORICALLY CONSTRUCTED

Beginning with Ariès's *Centuries of Childhood* (1962), there has been a growing consensus among social scientists that childhood is socially and historically constructed. Even those who doubt childhood determinism admit that as a critical stage of the life cycle a "good enough" childhood is crucial for later adult development (Konner, 1991).

Tremendous variation exists in childhood environments between "traditional" societies, where a large percentage of people live in rural settings, and those of contemporary, "developed" countries, where urban living standards are more common, underscoring the need for a comparative and historical study of children and childhoods:

"Children in developed countries today are more likely to be aborted before birth and less likely to be killed or die after birth, to become orphans, to experience the death of a sibling, or to suffer the effects of fatal or debilitating illness or accident. They are also more likely to have surviving grandparents and divorced parents, and to live in a single-parent household than were children in the premodern world. "Modern" children have fewer siblings and are physically larger, healthier, better housed than were most children in traditional societies. After the age of five they are more likely to spend time in schools and engage in supervised play with children of their own age than were children in the past, who were more likely to be in the presence of adults working and learning a craft, trade, or occupation. The parents of "modern" children are more likely to consult "experts" about child rearing than were their premodern counterparts. At home, children today are more likely to have access to their own "private" space than were children in premodern societies, where living space was at a premium. Also, the electronic media, especially television, have created a special world for children that was unimaginable in premodern times. Finally, children in developed countries are more likely to have a clearly defined status than were children in traditional societies, where kin and parental rights tended to be predominant" (Hiner, 1991, p. 7).

The population perspective as seen through sociodemographic trends represents an ideal framework for the analysis of children at risk and of difficult childhoods. It is at once cultural and historical, because it studies both synchronic structures and practices of a group of people and diachronic change related to demographic shifts in the human population. Child and adult development experts concern themselves mostly with species-specific and person-specific characteristics. Most psychological theories advance claims about the human species in terms of individual differences that have emerged in studies of Euro-American populations. However, a population level analysis that is broadly cross-cultural and historical is central to understanding variation in human adaptation.

Population level differences exist in social organization, cultural meaning systems, and individual and group behavior that can be seen through demographic trends. Basic adaptive patterns, such as subsistence, reproduction, communication, and social hierarchy are highly variable across human populations (LeVine, 1990). Population units themselves tend to be highly variable and not as easy to define as organisms and species. Different in scale, complexity, and stability of boundaries, all population units are interactional networks, consisting of mating and other communicative processes. Such networks exist in the contemporary world at the local, national, and transnational levels. A population generally shares an environment, a symbolic and communicative framework for encoding it, and a sociocultural organization for adapting to it. Its features are recognizable in local beliefs and practices, "reinforcing its centripetal tendencies in reproduction and communicative processes and propagating a population specific code of conduct that reduces random variation in the ways members live their lives" (LeVine, 1990, p. 101).

From a population perspective, the following lessons are evident: 1) Sociodemographic changes related to families in the West (e.g., smaller households, maternal employment, changes in reproductive technologies) are culture-specific features that impact the domestic sphere when compared with families in many non-Western and non-industrialized societies. 2) Sociocultural variations in children's environments, recognizably a major research interest among developmentalists, can suggest valuable ontogenetic insights regarding predispositions to various behavioral and social risks by highlighting the value of social groups in children's development. 3) Finally, the constructivists' notions about normative development modified to reflect the developmental pathways in different cultures must alter our notions of deviance in both at-risk and general populations.

The conditions of children and childhoods in the West, when compared with the patterns of childcare in India, Japan, China, and many other non-Western societies demonstrate the relative "separateness" of children from the adult world of family and community. This separateness can be traced to the rise of modern ideas about childhood in sixteenth and seventeenth century Europe and America (Ariès, 1963; DeMause, 1988), which in recent times may have been moderated somewhat due to an increase in early daycare (Belle, 1989; Hareven, 1989). Recent global transformations edging towards rapid modernization in the developing countries and towards post-industrial changes in the developed countries are introducing new risk conditions to children's well-being (Stephens, 1995). For example, the recent changes in family, technology, and society in the West may have pushed the conditions of many children to extreme forms of psychosocial risk (Lerner, 1995), while in the majority of the non-Western world the high risks children encounter are to their physical health and survival (LeVine et al., 1994). An analysis of children's lives needs to consider these population level differences across the developing and developed world in order to fully understand the social and cultural construction of childhood.

FAMILIES IN CONTEXT

"Happy families are all alike; every unhappy family is unhappy in its own way" (Tolstoy, 1950) is a particularly apt description for contemporary family contexts. The news of the decline of the Euro-American family, beginning most clearly in the 1960s, is not exaggerated. Part and parcel of the "second demographic transition," the statistics on women's employment, an increase in divorce rates, single-parent homes, premarital cohabitation patterns, and teenage pregnancies are well documented (Becker, 1981; Mason & Jensen, 1995; Melon, 1995). The basis of human development depends on "good enough" parenting in "an average expectable environment." Many anthropologists and sociologists of the family claim that the nuclear family, consisting of a mother, a father, and a child is a biological universal. "The last man will spend his last hours searching for his wife and child" (Linton, 1949, p. 21). Nuclear families are present in societies even where a Western type of social organization is absent. The human family is at the base of all human institutions, an archetypal pattern inherited through human evolution that has indelibly shaped the natural history of the self, although the forms and structures families assume in particular cultures, historical periods, and institutional frameworks can be multiplex and diverse. Similarly, the representations of motherhood across cultures reveal broad archetypal similarities as well as culture-specific variations.[3]   In modern Western societies, the nuclear family unit itself has been under attack. "Most of the writing on the modern family takes for granted the 'isolation' of the nuclear family not only from the kinship system but from the world of work. It assumes that this isolation makes the family impervious to the outside influences. In reality, the modern world intrudes at every point and obliterates its privacy" (Lasch, 1976, p. 113).

Generally, in most of South Asia and India, the preferred family pattern is some form of extended household unit even in the midst of modernization. The association between modernization, urbanization, and the frequently discussed increase in nuclear families is specific primarily to Euro-American societies. Sociodemographic and family change can take multiple pathways depending upon the societal context, economic conditions, and governmental policies. The evidence from India on this issue is unequivocal (Madan, 1993). While the signs of change in the family due to social transformations are evident, they are neither uniform nor predictable by Western standards. In Japan, recent technological and economic advancement has not been achieved at the erosion of the Japanese family and collective values, where modified stem families continue to be the alternative to Western style nuclear families (Quale, 1992). In Latin America, the family and household composition shares much in common with its Southern European roots, without a nuclearization of families and couples along northwestern European lines, displaying an extended structure that is different from the Asian patterns (DeVos & Soufe, 1987). With attacks in the academy on everything traditional and patriarchal, it is unpredictable which form of family organization will cohere in the post-industrial era (Goldschnieder & Waite, 1991; Lasch, 1976; Lerner, 1995). The evidence from India, Japan, and many other parts of the world on extended families serves to highlight the dramatic changes that have reshaped the domestic sphere in the West during the last two to three decades.

The changes afflicting the modern family are associated with the social ills in at-risk populations. Family contexts have become increasingly diverse in the U.S. (Lerner, 1995), where foster care has risen by 50% and infants less than 12 months are most likely to be placed in such care when compared to children from other age groups. By the age of 6 years, developmental contexts as measured by social class differences have shifted at least twice for about 54% of the children. While at the turn of the century 40% of all American children lived in two-parent farm families, another 40% in two-parent non-farm families, and only 10% in one-parent or no-parent families, today fewer than 5% live in two-parent farm families, less than 30% in intact non-farm families, and about 70% in either dual earner non-farm families or in one-parent families. Indeed, more than 25% of the children live in one-parent families, where 80% of them never experience living with a grandparent. These dramatic changes have accompanied an unprecedented decline in the structure, composition, and functions of the American family, so that parents must now rely heavily on professional childcare workers for the care of their young.

When fully applied, the population perspective reflects the sociodemographic influences on the shaping of risk conditions. The majority of children in high-income, low-fertility, low-mortality societies, such as the U.S. confront risks not to their basic physical survival, but to their psychosocial health from such ills as substance abuse, unsafe sex, lack of preparation in entering an industrial economy, delinquency, crime, and violence. All of these factors are associated with the decline of the family and interact with child outcomes from a young age in creating vulnerabilities in maternal and infant health. A majority of children in low-income, rural societies face different risks, primarily to the survival of the young, due to malnutrition, poor health, unsafe living conditions, and low maternal education, not unlike the risk conditions in low-income zones of industrialized societies.

The changes in life styles and reproductive technologies may change parenting, childcare, and the domestic sphere in developed countries even further, with a potential to affect those developing societies which can afford these changes. Resulting declines in fertility will accompany changes in household composition and socioeconomic patterns in the workplace. Attention to children's needs and welfare emerged in Europe and America during a general economic expansion during 1860-1910, which marked a break with the welfare of the lineage to the welfare of the household (Quale, 1992), representing the "first demographic transition." Ariès and Ranum (1980) have described this as the era of the "child-king" and Lesthaeghe (1987) as the "embourgeoisement." Individual-centeredness came to the fore in the general economic expansion during 1945-1970 in most developed societies as large numbers of children became unnecessary for industrial growth, representing "the second demographic transition" (van de Kaa, 1987; Quale, 1992), and the end of the "child-king" era. The current changes in the Western nuclear family, along with transformations in parent-child relations is potentially exposing large segments of the Euro-American populations to extreme psychosocial risks (Lerner, 1995; Jenks, 1996). In this context, the role of developmentalists is to rethink the idea of child and human development in a comparative and historical perspective. Psychologists and mental health practitioners need to modify the narrow individualistic notions about human development, taking into account the value of children's social networks and changes in the family and other social groups.

CULTURAL PATHWAYS TO HUMAN DEVELOPMENT

Lifespan and life-history perspectives have been around for decades, but their impact on cultural research with children has been very limited (Chisolm, 1992; Keller & Ecksenberger, 1994). A cursory examination of children's worlds in different societies makes apparent that the influence of domestic and social groups on the lives of children is pervasive. For example, Gusii infants in Kenya are cared for by their siblings beginning in the first year of life (LeVine et al., 1994). The Efe, a foraging society in Zaire rely not only on siblings, but also on surrogate mothers and fathers to care for their young (Tronick et al., 1987). The Japanese approach to childcare draws on the mother as the most important caregiver but the Japanese family is a highly interdependent unit (Peak, 1995). The Javanese approach to childcare relies heavily on respect as the basis for socializing children to relate to family and community members from a very young age (Geertz, 1959). The Kaluli mothers of Papua New Guinea begin teaching their children reciprocity and exchange through child and adult talk with members of the social group beginning in the first few weeks of life (Schieffelin, 1990). Hindu children in India and much of South Asia are brought up in extended households with multiple caregivers (Sharma, 1996; Sharma & LeVine, in press). Even in much of the Western world, children are increasingly placed in extended networks of peer and adult caregivers from a young age (Belle, 1989; Hareven, 1989). Thus, much of what is considered "normative" in developmental psychology reflects various modernist discourses (Burman, 1994), which promote individualistic parental childrearing practices that may not be reflective of the everyday interactions even of Western children.

The evidence from India on childcare where multiple caregiving is prevalent reveals the modernist bias (Sharma, 1996; Sharma & Levine, in press). While the mother clearly emerges as a significant caregiver, the extended family group collectively takes care of young children 59% of the time. The context of early care in North India provides a vivid example of the embeddedness of social life. Children growing up in these families are constantly in the presence of adults and children alike who are not their biological parents and siblings. The ecological conditions, conducive to the acquisition of open and permeable social and ego boundaries, provide opportunities for reciprocity with every village member in direct face-to-face communications, giving children a sense of immediate connection with others around them. They receive physical care, affection, direction, and monitoring from a cadre of caregivers. Cultural ideas reinforce practices which foster a greater sense of interdependency, reliance on others, and belongingness. The socializing agents for these children, while located in individual persons, are distributed among a variety of caregivers. The multiplicity of social relationships in Western day-care or residential care settings resemble somewhat the interpersonal environments in those cultures, where familial and social groups are accorded greater importance than individualized relationships and the maintenance of a network of significant and close relationships is customary practice.

The stability of the group at the onset of children's lives may provide these children with alternative developmental pathways. The assumption that development is driven by greater autonomy and separation within the framework of a small number of individualized relationships may be one-sided and misleading. Instead, development may be seen as proceeding within circles of social embeddedness, creating more or less intense connections and reflecting different ranges of social experience. In this view, development is not so much a ladder, but more a tree with multiple branches representing various individual capacities (Fischer, 1993; Fischer & Ayoub, 1994). Level of individual development is thus judged not only by the ability to function independently, but even more so by interpersonal integration and by the connections a person is able to maintain with others.

The Japanese model of development provides a vivid example of an alternative pathway to human growth (Peak, 1995). The Japanese mother-child bond is based on bodily contact and communication between infant and caregiver. Consisting of co-sleeping, prolonged breastfeeding, and shared bathing, "skinship" emphasizes a harmonious and natural connection between mother and child. Children are taught from a young age to be empathic and responsive to the needs of others, that is, "to feel what others are feeling, to vicariously experience the pleasure or pain that they are undergoing, and to help them satisfy their wishes" (Peak, 1995, p. 15). The Japanese form of empathy is, as Lebra (1993) puts it, at the opposite pole from egocentricity. The Japanese family can be seen as an organic unit which, although hierarchical, is based on the concept of mutual indulgence and reciprocity. Carrying these values to their preschool, together with personal as well as role modifications, Japanese children reenact them in relation to their peers and to their teachers. The resultant group process compounds upon feelings of interdependency, belongingness, and *amae* (a special kind of mutuality). In this context, children resolve their own disputes under the watchful guidance of their teachers.

Similarly, in India the group of maternal caregivers is a principal socializing agent in the lives of children during the preschool years. While the mother is a key figure in the lives of children, childcare activities are distributed among extended family members. With regard to attachment behaviors in the first three years of life, these children seek proximity to, follow directions from, and are responded to when in distress by a group of caregivers. It is plausible that this may lead to different "internal working models" of security and trust and to culture-specific pathways of human growth and development, phenomena relatively unexplored by developmental and cross-cultural psychologists.

CULTURALLY CONSTITUTED "RISKS"

Aberrant behavior in one context can easily be seen as normative in another context and vice versa. Modern and post-modern societies have interesting notions of risk, not necessarily generalizable to pre-modern or traditional societies. Terms such as "disability," "developmentally delayed," "maladjusted," and "vulnerable," which are suggestive of at-risk populations, have often been associated with the "culture of poverty." Thus, the usage of the term "risk" becomes problematic when applied across cultures and ethnic groups. Categories such as "abnormal," "deviant," and "at-risk" are most useful when applied within a well-defined context.

Linguistic categories organize thought, communication, and social reality. Constructed in local worlds, social categories often carry specific meanings that can be misused when transferred to other domains. Historical trends make this clear. New categories and trends adhere to deep structural divisions in the socio-political order, and they are hard to change and frequently resorted to during social transformations. The category of the "abnormal" is one such term that now has a slightly benign or neutral cast in what are known as populations "at risk." In Western cosmologies, the term "abnormal" has been associated with other connotations such as, "sinful," "irrational," "less developed," "uncivilized," "primitive," and with "disparaged groups" or "the other" (Foucault, 1977). Children have been the target of most of these attributes within Western societies and continue to be in many parts of the world (DeMause, 1988), yet who and what is seen as being at risk varies according to the strengths and weaknesses of social systems embedded in a particular of culture.[4] All risk conditions, whether they are universal (i.e., biologically determined) or particular (i.e., socioculturally determined) are constructed in local historical and political contexts.

Approximately one hundred years ago, children in Europe and America were defined by the absence of adulthood, and seen as incomplete though worthy objects of study (Mead & Wolfenstein, 1955). "Just as most children's lives do not reflect the enormous importance we accord childhood today, the child of history stands paradoxically at the center of human priority and at its margin" (Safford & Safford, 1996, p. 1). The conditions of children's nurture continue to be determined by adult reasons, whether cultural, economic, and political, which may explain why children are easily marginalized. While historical change may have introduced new parenting, educational, socioeconomic, and health conditions, children's nurture remains a conditional and problematic subject. Today, exogenous influences on children's bodies, selves, and minds are unprecedented in their age of onset and their content (Stephens, 1995). Yet, old themes persist although oriented toward different ends, means, and targets (Safford & Safford, 1996). Groups of children continue to be at "exceptional risk" or having various "disorders," as defined by the cultural utilitarian standards specific to industrialized societies. While child-killing (especially by a parent) has been seen as a horrific crime in all times and places, the abandonment of children and the murder of newborn infants is practiced even in the most advanced societies. Although relatively uncommon in industrialized societies, folk and religious practices and beliefs frequently attribute childhood physical and psychological dysfunctions to supernatural agents and forces. These may include the aftereffects of actions in previous lives or evil spells coming from the social environment.

The marked change in the perception of children as separate beings, and the rise of childhood as a stage preceding adulthood, followed by movements to eradicate child abuse, neglect, and servitude crystallized in Europe and America in the eighteenth and nineteenth centuries. Childhood as a stage has existed in many non-western cultures since antiquity, yet oftentimes without an explicit understanding of children's separateness and rights; alternative histories of children and childhood in other parts of the world have yet to be fully explored. By the middle of the nineteenth century, an ideology of childhood had become a powerful force in middle-class Europe and North America, consisting of a firm commitment to bringing up children in families, an acknowledgment of childhood determinism, and an awareness of children's rights and privileges (Archad, 1993; Cunningham, 1995). Almost a century later, the conditions of children are undergoing yet another major shift, related to the unprecedented global spread of modern-Western notions of the child and reflecting structural changes impacting the family, work, and women's roles. In both the industrialized and the developing societies, there is a growing recognition of the "disappearance of childhood," leading to a proliferation of the discourse of child abuse, victimization, exploitation, and abandonment

(Lerner, 1995; Stephens, 1995; Weissbourd, 1996).

Contemporary concerns with "at-risk" populations suggest that psychologically, socially, and politically marginalized groups are especially likely to be seen as predisposed to risk. Examples include ethnic children in the U.S. or children of migrant laborers in the developing countries. While borrowed from the preventive medical model, the term "prevention," when carried over to the sociocultural domain may similarly classify groups of people as congenitally violent, promiscuous, and poor. Mary Douglas (1992) has accurately noted, "The theme well known to anthropologists is that in all places at all times the universe is moralized and politicized. Disasters that befoul the air and soil and poison the water are generally turned to political account: someone already unpopular is going to be blamed for it" (p. 5). In other words, every risk needs someone to blame. This "forensic theory of danger" explains misfortune in at least three ways: in the form of self-criticism as self-blame; in the form of in-group criticism where some already disparaged group is scapegoated; and by projecting criticism on an out-group. The three types of blame lead to different forms of justice. While communities tend to be strongly aligned along one of these systems, most societies employ all three forms of blaming simultaneously.

Unlike hierarchical cultures, individualistic cultures value a market orientation to social goods (Douglas, 1990). All ideas, practices, and people are valued in relation to what they are worth in the marketplace. Since children cost more than they produce, they often receive a lower priority. Furthermore, whereas in hierarchical societies the differences between the high and the low social strata are not masked, in modern individualistic societies such differences are easily obscured because theoretically they do not exist. Whereas in a hierarchical society discrimination is practiced openly and a well organized minority consciousness is frequently evident, in an individualistic democratic society where "all men are created equal" and everyone ought to succeed on merit, minority consciousness tends to be fragmented and vulnerable to collective denial and blame. For instance, the African-American infant mortality rate is emblematic of the structural impediments and risks that certain minority populations confront in American society. These differences have been consistently shown for the last 20 years; for example, the black infant mortality rate as well as the black maternal and neonatal rates of death have been twice as high as those of the majority white populations (Thomas, 1995). No single cause can explain this trend; rather, the differences reflect a structural impediment that is caste-like and almost immutable. Similar impediments in traditionally hierarchical societies are often traceable to explicit cultural biases against one group or another.

On the issue of risk, the term "culture" has been appropriated by social scientists to suggest a whole range of differences related to race, ethnicity, power relations, and social class. Currently, there is a proliferation of the culture concept. Writers use the term "culture" interchangeably with societal, racial, and ethnic differences or merely to denote and "explain" some difference.[5] The view presented in this chapter has conceptualized "culture" as a system of meanings, in context, in practice, and in history. However, even within anthropology there has been little discussion about the politicization of culture and its impact on children (Stephens, 1995). Everyone agrees that "childhood" is not an entirely natural category, but social scientists seem less than eager to demonstrate how childhood is socially and culturally constructed. At the center, there is confusion about "what is a child?" Just like the term "risk," the term "child" now travels throughout the world ("The Year of the Child," "the rights of the child," "in the interest of the child"), yet there is an uncertainty as to the definition of "the child." More profoundly, what is the nature of childhood risks given the rise of child-labor in Asian societies and the alleged prevalence of sexual abuse in Euro-American families? The steady dissemination of Western ideas about children's development, imported by non-Western societies together with modernization, industrialization, Americanization, and exported through immigration from non-European cultures to Western societies has diversified the demographics of childhood. When conditions of children are considered world-wide, the concept of risk must include the impact of sociodemographic and structural forces that vary significantly across societies and groups. It is essential to grasp both the local as well as the global influences on children's lives in order to better understand the contemporary conditions of childhood.

CONCLUSION

Child and human development is determined by multiple contextual and endogenous factors. The dominant Western model of development emphasizing autonomy, separation, and dyadic interaction is only one possible framework that can be further diversified when attending to variations within and across societies. The developmental sciences can learn a lesson from the biological sciences, where the theories of unilinear evolution have been discredited. The population perspective offers an account of the variation in sociocultural and socioeconomic conditions present in different regions of the world, where the clearest differences can be found between the developing and the developed world (see Table 1). Developmental goals, processes, and pathways in agrarian, developing societies with both high fertility and high mortality rates are concerned principally with human survival and later participation in subsistence farming and in some service-related professions. In more urban and developed societies, where a large majority of the newborn population survives past the first five years, human development is shaped within the context of training for participation in an industrialized society. The emerging post-industrial societies are further confronted with unprecedented challenges to the psychosocial health of children and families, which have yet to be fully documented and understood. Significant population level differences concerning a whole range of risk conditions and behaviors can also be found within the U.S. or within other developed societies across ethnic, racial, and socioeconomic lines. Thus, the notions of child and human development and of developmental risks must be seen as influenced by cultural beliefs and practices that tend to be socially, economically, and historically mediated. Essentially, processes of human development cannot be understood completely through the lens of psychological perspectives.

Table 1
Sociocultural Worlds Through the Demographic Transition

Index	Developing World	Developed World
Demographic Transition	First Transition	Second Transition
Social Organization	Rural/Semi-urban	Urban/Post-industrial
Economics	Familial/Labor (farming, manual services)	Labor/Information (goods, information services)
Family Type	Extended/Nuclear	Nuclear/Alternative
Socialization Pathways	Kin-oriented	Individual-oriented
Risk Conditions	Physical Survival (e.g., High IMR)	Psychosocial Adaptation (e.g., school dropout)

BIBLIOGRAPHY

Archad, D. (1993). *Children-rights and childhood*. New York: Routledge.
Ariès, P. (1962). *Centuries of childhood*. New York: Vintage Books.

Ariès, P., & Ranum, P. (1980). Two successive motivations for the declining birth rate in the West. *Population and Development Review, 6* (4), 645-650.

Becker, G.S. (1981). *A treatise on the family.* Cambridge, MA: Harvard University Press.

Belle, D. (1989). *Children's social networks and social support.* New York: Wiley.

Bourdieu, P. (1980). *Outline of a theory of practice.* Palo Alto, CA: Stanford University Press.

Brown, L.R., & Jacobson, J.L. (1986). *Our demographically divided world.* Washington, DC: Worldwatch Institute.

Burman, E. (1994). *Deconstructing developmental psychology.* New York: Routledge.

Chisholm, J. (1992). Putting people in biology. In T. Schwartz, G. White, & C. Lutz (Eds.), *New directions in psychological anthropology* (pp.125-149). New York: Cambridge University Press.

Cunningham, H. (1995). *Children and childhood in Western society since 1500.* London: Longman.

DeMause (1988). *The history of childhood.* New York: Atcom Press.

DeVos, G., & Soufe, T. (1987). *Religion and the family in East Asia.* Berkeley, CA: University of California Press.

Douglas, M. (1992). *Risk and blame.* New York: Routledge.

Douglas, M. (1990). Risk as a forensic resource. *Daedalus, 119* (4), 1-16.

Fischer, K.W. (1993). Analyzing diversity in developmental pathways. In R. Case & W. Edelstein (Eds.), *The new structuralism in cognitive development* (pp. 33-56). Basel: Karger.

Fischer, K.W., & Ayoub, C. (1994). Affective splitting and dissociation in normal and maltreated children. In D. Cicchetti & S. Toth (Eds.), *Disorders and dysfunctions of the self* (pp.149-221). Hilldale, NJ: Erlbaum.

Foucault, M. (1977). *Madness and civilization.* London: Tavistock.

Geertz, H. (1959). The vocabulary of emotions. *Psychiatry, 22,* 225-237.

Goldscheider, F., & Waite, L. (1991). *New families, no families?* Berkeley, CA: University of California Press.

Goldthorpe, J.E. (1996). *The sociology of post-colonial societies.* New York: Cambridge University Press.

Haraven, T. (1989). Historical changes in children's networks in the family and community. In D. Belle (Ed.), *Children's social networks and social supports* (pp. 15-36). New York: Wiley.

Hiner, R. (1991). Introduction. In J. Hawes and R. Hiner (Eds.), *Children in historical and comparative perspective* (pp. 1-12). New York: Greenwood Press.

Jenks, C. (1996). *Childhood*. New York: Routledge.

Kagitçibasi, Ç. (1996). *Family and human development across cultures*. Hillside, NJ: Erlbaum.

Keller, H., & Eckensberger, L. (1994). *Lehrbuch der Entwicklungspsychologie* [Textbook of developmental psychology]. Bern: Huber Verlag.

Konner, M. (1991). *Childhood*. New York: Little Brown.

Lasch, C. (1976). *Haven in a heartless world*. New York: Basic Books.

Lebra, T.S. (1976). *Japanese patterns of behavior*. Honolulu, HI: University of Hawaii Press.

Lebra, T.S. (1993). Mother and child Japanese socialization. In P. Greenfield and R. Cocking (Eds.), *Cross-cultural roots of minority child development* (pp. 259-274). Hillside, NJ: Lawrence Erlbaum.

Leiderman, P.H., Tulkin, S.R., & Rosenfeld, A. (1977). *Culture and infancy*. New York: Academic Press.

Lerner, R.M. (1995). *America's youth in crisis*. New York: Sage.

Lesthaeghe, R. (1987). Family formation and dissolution—the two transitions. *Tijdschrift voor Sociologie, 8* (2-3), 9-33, 279.

LeVine, R.A. (1988). Human parental care. In R. LeVine, P. Miller, & M. West (Eds.), *Parental behaviors in diverse societies* (pp. 3-12). San Francisco, CA: Jossey-Bass.

LeVine, R.A. (1990). Enculturation. In D. Chechetti & M. Beeghly (Eds.), *The self in transition* (pp. 99-117). Chicago, IL: University of Chicago Press.

LeVine, R.A., Dixon, S., LeVine, S., Richman, A., Leiderman, H., Keefer, C., & Brazelton, B. (1994). *Child care and culture*. New York: Cambridge University Press.

Link, B., & Phelan, J. (1996). Understanding sociodemographic differences in health—the role of fundamental social causes. *American Journal of Public Health, 86*, (4), 471-473.

Linton, R. (1949). The natural history of the family. In R.N. Anshem (Ed.), *The family: Its function and destiny* (pp.18-38). New York: Harper.

Madan, T.N. (1993). The Hindu family and development. In P. Uberoi (Ed.), *Family, kinship and marriage in India* (pp.416-434). New Delhi: Oxford University Press.

Marcus, G., & Fischer, M. (1989). *Anthropology as cultural critique*. Chicago, IL: University of Chicago Press.

Mason, K.O., & Jensen, A. (1995). *Gender and family change in industrialized countries*. New York: Oxford University Press.

Mead, M., & Wolfenstein, M. (1955). *Childhood in contemporary cultures*. Chicago, IL: University of Chicago Press.

Melon, G. (1995). *The individual, the family, and social good*. Lincoln, NB:

University of Nebraska Press.

Peak, L. (1995). *Learning to go to school in Japan.* Berkeley, CA: University of California Press.

Quale, G.R. (1992). *Families in context.* New York: Greenwood Press.

Safford, P.L., & Safford, E.J. (1996). *A history of childhood and disability.* New York: Teacher's College Press.

Schieffelin, B. (1990). *The give and take of everyday life.* New York: Cambridge University Press.

Sharma, D. (1996). *Child care, family and culture: Lessons from India.* Unpublished doctoral dissertation. Harvard University, Cambridge, MA.

Sharma, D., & LeVine, R. (in press). Child care in India: A comparative view of the infant social environment. In D. Sharma & K. Fischer (Eds.), *Socioemotional development across cultures.* San Francisco, CA: Jossey Bass.

Stephens, S. (1995). *Children and the politics of culture.* Princeton, NJ: Princeton University Press.

Stevens, A. (1982). *Archetypes, a natural history of the self.* New York: Morrow Books.

Susser, M., & Susser, E. (1996a). Choosing a future for epidemiology I—eras and paradigms. *American Journal of Public Health, 86* (5), 668-673.

Susser, M., & Susser, E. (1996b). Choosing a future for epidemiology II—from black box to Chinese boxes and eco-epidemiology. *American Journal of Public Health, 86* (5), 668-673.

Thomas, G. (1995). *Race and ethnicity in America.* Washington, DC: Taylor & Francis.

Tolstoy, L. (1950). *Anna Karenina.* New York: Modern Library.

Tronick, E.Z., Winn, S., & Morelli, G.A. (1987). Multiple caretaking of Efe (Pygmy) infants. *American Anthropologist, 89* (1), 96-106.

UNDP (1996). *Human development report.* New York: Oxford University Press.

van de Kaa, D. (1987). Europe's second demographic transition. *Population Bulletin, 42* (1), 1-59.

Weisbourd, R. (1996). *The vulnerable child.* New York: Addison Wesley.

ENDNOTES

1. The term "developing" includes "underdeveloped" societies as well; they are clustered together for the sake of parsimony. Such terminology glosses over sociocultural variation in different societies, but approximates certain broad socioeconomic similarities. Most developed societies have till recently been Western although this is beginning to change.

2. The population perspective is informed by epidemiological ideas and methods about "fundamental social causes" (Link & Phelan, 1996), with an attempt to combine them with the broadly anthropological approaches to studying culture.

3. This idea cannot be explored in greater detail here; suffice it to say that there are similarities between Jung's ideas about the "archetypes" and what ethologists call "innate action tendencies" (Stevens, 1982).

4. Epidemiologists, who generally tend to be positivistic in orientation, have been calling for a broadly "ecological epidemiology" that goes beyond "risk factor analysis" and takes into account environmental, institutional, and sociocultural factors (Susser & Susser, 1996a; Susser & Susser, 1996b).

5. The positivistic concepts of "culture" (e.g., Radcliffe-Brownian structural-functionalism, Levi-Straussian structuralism) have been highly debated among anthropologists, giving way to a more "reflexive" view of culture that encompasses history, power relations, and social class (Bourdieu, 1980; Marcus & Fischer, 1989).

SECTION IV: METHODS AND TECHNIQUES

Cross-cultural research is difficult to conduct given the numerous methodological problems that consistently crop up when researchers attempt to compare respondents from different cultures on psychological measures. The distinction between culture-specific (emic) and universal (etic) categories for the conceptualization of behavior poses a major challenge for the development of cross-cultural instruments. When cultures are distant from each other in terms of history, worldviews, level of economic development, literacy rates, etc., cross-cultural comparisons may be seemingly impossible— or that is what some cultural psychologists have concluded (Boesch, 1996; see also Triandis' chapter in this volume). In contrast, universalists such as Ronald Rohner and his student David E. Cournoyer assert that a multimethod strategy based simultaneously on observational techniques, questionnaires, interviews, and the holocultural approach is most likely to overcome the methodological problems posed by cross-cultural comparison.

In his chapter, *Universalist Research: Examples Drawn from the Methods and Findings of Parental Acceptance/Rejection Theory*, David E. Cournoyer introduces us to Rohner's Parental Acceptance/Rejection Theory (PAR Theory) and methodology which together represent one of the most sustained and coherent attempts to overcome the hurdles posed by cross-cultural comparison. PAR Theory postulates that children everywhere experience their parents' attitudes toward them according to an implicit dimension ranging from warmth and acceptance to rejection and neglect. Children's experiences of warmth tend to be associated with positive personality characteristics such as perceived self-adequacy, high self-esteem, emotional stability, emotional responsiveness, a lack of hostility, a positive worldview, and so on. To test this theory on a worldwide basis, Rohner and his students have developed questionnaires, conducted observational and interview studies in communities, and employed the holocultural method based on ethnographic reports about a wide range of predominantly nonwestern societies. It is the consistency of their results obtained across many different societies, using quite varied methodologies, and reported in more than 200 studies by numerous investigators that lends a special credibility to PAR Theory.

With the increasing importance of multiculturalism in the United States of America and elsewhere, psychologists have become increasingly concerned about the feasibility and validity of personality assessment of children and adults across ethnic and other cultural boundaries. One of the leaders in this movement is Richard H. Dana, whose chapter on *Multicultural Assessment of Children and Adolescent Personality and Psychopathology* provides us with a state-of-the-art overview of the issues raised by multicultural assessment specialists. Uppermost in their minds is the desire to avoid bias—something not easily accomplished when respondents come from a wide variety of ethnic, linguistic, religious, and social class backgrounds. The author suggests that reduction of bias can be accomplished as part of a professional education program for assessors that focuses on "cultural competence" as an important requirement for assessment practice with a multicultural population. He emphasizes the adaptation of standard tests, as well as the design and standardization of new tests for particular cultures. Both etic and emic sources of information are pertinent to the application of standardized tests and for making informed recommendations for multicultural assessment practice.

In her chapter *Cross-cultural Methodological Issues in Development Research,* the Israeli psychologist Esther Halpern takes a micro-look at some methodological issues that arose when the Pictorial Experimental Paradigm (PEP)—a pictorial and verbal test designed to assess death and separation anxiety—was administered to young children from five cultures. Her chapter highlights some of the methodological problems that came to the fore during the research process involving a "guest" researcher and her "host" partners. These problems were by no means obvious in the initial phases of the research project, but helped the researchers gradually to see and experience the cultural distance that separated some of the groups under investigation. As so often in cross-cultural research, various methodological devils could be found hiding among the details of the research procedures.

The three chapters contained in this section share a common concern for problems related to possible bias regarding the adaptation of standard tests (the importance of moderator variables, establishing varying norms for cultural ethnic groups, intricate problems of cross-cultural and cultural-specific interpretation), the development of etic tests and questionnaires designed for multicultural application, and the importance of emic tests and questionnaires developed for a particular population. More generally, our personality theories, psychiatric classification procedures, and service delivery systems need constant revision in order to be more suitable for the members of both minority and nonwestern cultures. Test translators need to employ systematic procedures to get closer to the ideal of linguistic equivalence across cultural divides. Theoretical constructs must be examined for cross-cultural validity by using a variety of methodologies which may be based on either low- or high-inference strategies. Such considerations play a crucial role in cross-cultural psychology because the field may be said to have a double identity: It represents as much a methodological strategy of theory testing as it is a substantive field.

UNIVERSALIST RESEARCH: EXAMPLES DRAWN FROM THE METHODS AND FINDINGS OF PARENTAL ACCEPTANCE-REJECTION THEORY

David E. Cournoyer, University of Connecticut, U.S.A.

INTRODUCTION

One of the challenges facing modern cross-cultural psychology is the development of principles of human behavior that are species wide in their applicability, and at the same time useful for predicting and explaining human behavior within particular sociocultural contexts. This is a difficult challenge, since meeting it requires that we adopt two very different perspectives on theory development and testing. Developing theory that is useful in formulating interventions within a particular sociocultural context requires attention to the symbols and belief systems unique to those specific groups. However, the development of theory that is species wide in applicability requires a focus on concepts that are relevant across the range of human diversity, with the potential loss of precision when theories are applied within a particular sociocultural context. While it seems logically possible to construct theories applicable to both small and large scale contexts, in practice we often rely on one set of concepts to explain behavior in large heterogeneous collections of cultures, and others to account for individual variation within smaller, more homogeneous populations.

It is difficult to develop theory that is useful both locally and species wide because both conceptualizations of variables and choice of research methods depend on where on the continuum from very small populations to very large ones we focus. Conceptualization of variables is influenced by the population studied because of language, our empiricism, and the manner in which we traditionally resolve issues of measurement validity and reliability. That is, given a set of potential indicators of a particular concept, those included in our operational definitions of that concept will be those that empirical studies tell us are valid and reliable across the widest range of units. Changing the diversity within the population studied will almost certainly reveal changes in the status of indicators, and corresponding changes in operational definitions. Since our empiricism binds us to synchronize conceptualization with observation, changes in operational definitions are likely to change our conceptualizations of variables as well. In fact, one of the attractions of cross-cultural and comparative research is that the researcher's view of her or his own culture is often substantially altered by the experience.

Likewise, the choice of a population in which to generate theory also constrains our choice of research methods. Research designs may be based on the requirements of pure logic, but the designs actually employed reflect constraints rooted in the social systems as much as the logical demands of theory testing. Access to viable roles as observer and scientist, access to resources, political reactions to the values that underlie theories, and ethical sensibilities all place constraints on how one may approach a given research question. While within our own culture we may have access to social roles needed to implement research designs, such as experiments, that can provide strong tests of theory, these designs require that the scientist have sufficient power to control variables and settings at levels that are unavailable outside of our primary reference group.

Before we become too lost in a jungle of methodological abstractions, let us return to the original concern: How are we to develop theories that are applicable at both the individual level and species wide? How can we develop conceptualizations and operationalizations of variables that reflect the particular, but are applicable across the species? How can we develop tests of theories when the strongest designs may be difficult or impossible to mount?

Fortunately, reasonable answers to these questions have been around for a while. Research methods are techniques designed to improve the quality of inference by minimizing the influence of logical errors and mistakes (Cournoyer & Klein, 1999). There appears to be consensus (Campbell & Fiske, 1959; Maccoby & Martin, 1983; Rohner, 1986; Webb, Campbell, Schwartz, & Sechrest, 1966) that all available methodologies and research procedures have certain strengths, weakness, deficiencies, and potential forms of bias. Strong inference is not the result of ritual application of research designs, but careful attention to the important threats to internal and external validity operating in a particular inquiry. Since it appears unlikely that any one design will handle all the plausible threats to inference, research that uses multiple methods is our only recourse. To paraphrase Rohner (1986), only a convergence of methodologies seems likely to provide tests of theories that reasonably skeptical people can believe.

The purpose of this chapter is to describe a particular research program that incorporates a multimethod approach to the testing of psychological theory both within particular sociocultural systems and cross-culturally. This research program has been labeled "Parental Acceptance-Rejection Theory" (commonly referred to as PAR Theory) by its founder and principal proponent, Ronald P. Rohner (Rohner, 1986). This area of inquiry is worthy of note as a contributor to a substantive theory of socialization capable of accounting for both species-wide regularities and intracultural variation. PAR Theory is also an example of a truly multimethod research program.

This chapter will discuss and present examples of the broad spectrum of research paradigms and methods used to test both universalistic and culture specific principles related to the antecedents and consequences of parental acceptance and rejection. The reader who is interested in a more exhaustive review of PAR Theory, including theory, research methods, and findings of empirical tests, should consult the following four sources. Rohner (1986) provides a detailed description of PAR Theory, including epistemology, methods, and the results of empirical tests of the theory. Rohner (1990) presents a research handbook describing in detail how to conduct research using the major research paradigms and measurement techniques he recommends. The Center for the Study of Parental Acceptance and Rejection (CSPAR) at the University of Connecticut publishes an annotated bibliography of empirical tests of PAR Theory that is updated yearly (Rohner, 1999a). Finally, a summary of the major findings of PAR Theory is summarized by Rohner (1996b).

PARENTAL ACCEPTANCE-REJECTION THEORY

PAR Theory arose from the interest of Western psychologists in parent-child interaction (Rohner, 1975, 1986). Rohner notes that by the turn of the 20th century, interest in the importance of parent-child interaction, especially parental acceptance had grown steadily among American psychologists. Early interest in parent-child interaction was kindled by psychoanalytic theory (e.g., Bowlby, 1940, 1944; Burlingham & Freud, 1944; Ferenczi, 1929). Later, social learning theorists continued the interest including important works concerning measurement of parental behaviors (e.g., Champney, 1941; Schaefer, 1965; Schluderman & Schluderman, 1970, 1971; Siegelman, 1965a, 1965b, 1966, 1973; Symonds, 1939, 1949).

Rohner's own research into the universal importance of parental warmth first appeared in his M.A. thesis, a cross-cultural comparative study of parental acceptance (Rohner, 1960). PAR Theory was first described in detail by Rohner (1975) and expanded and clarified in Rohner (1986). Trained in both psychology and anthropology, Rohner brought a strong universalist interest to the study of child socialization as well as an understanding of the range and importance of sociocultural variation. Dozens of social scientists worldwide have participated in testing PAR Theory related research questions. A bibliography compiled by CSPAR lists more than two hundred studies and articles on the topic (Rohner, 1999).

PAR Theory is a theory of socialization that attempts to identify the sociocultural antecedents and consequences of certain parental behaviors and the mental representations of those behaviors by children and adults. PAR Theory focuses primarily on an aspect of parent-child interaction labeled the warmth dimension. The warmth dimension is the component of the parent-child relationship that carries messages about love, or the lack of love. Rohner (1986) sees the warmth dimension as a continuum. At one end of the continuum is acceptance (warmth and affection). At the other pole lies rejection (aggression, hostility, indifference, neglect, undifferentiated rejection). PAR Theory proposes that all individuals experience the warmth dimension as a salient aspect of parent-child relationships and can place their experience with parents and other important caregivers somewhere on a continuum between the extremes of complete acceptance or complete rejection.

The warmth dimension refers to both an attribute of social interaction, particularly between caregivers and children, and also the mental representation of that social interaction. As a social phenomenon, the warmth dimension consists of words, gestures, and actions that are used to convey either acceptance, or its opposite, rejection. As a mental event, the warmth dimension refers to individuals' subjective perceptions of the degree to which they are loved and accepted, or disliked and rejected by persons who are important to them, such as parents and other caregivers. PAR Theory predicts that the specific words, gestures, and actions used to convey acceptance-rejection will be culturally determined, but that subjective feelings of rejection will produce similar consequences for self-concepts across the species (Rohner, 1986).

PAR Theory provides explanation and prediction at both the individual and sociocultural system levels. At the individual level, the explanation and predictions are contained in what has been labeled PAR Theory's Personality Theory. This group of ideas is used to explain and predict relationships between perceived acceptance-rejection, personality dispositions, and behaviors at the individual level. At the large systems level, a sociocultural systems model is used to explain and predict how system wide patterns of acceptance and rejection will be reflected in the maintenance and expressive subsystems of the system.

PAR Theory's Personality Theory predicts that children who feel more rejected than accepted, when compared to children who feel accepted more than rejected, will demonstrate greater frequency of certain negative self-concepts and adjustment problems expressed in culturally determined ways. The expected negative self-concepts include self-perceived hostility and aggression, low self-esteem, low self-adequacy, emotional instability, emotional unresponsiveness, negative worldview, and either extreme dependency or defensive independence.   PAR Theory predicts that these dispositions will be reflected in culturally specific behavior problems.   In many cultures these are likely to include delinquency and criminal behavior, substance abuse, poor school performance, and other culturally defined indicators of maladjustment.   PAR Theory also postulates that the effects of rejection in childhood are likely to persist into adulthood when adult personality, marital relationships, occupational choices, and parenting styles will all reflect the degree of acceptance-rejection that persons perceived from their caregivers.

PAR Theory also focuses on parental acceptance-rejection at the sociocultural system level.   A sociocultural systems model proposed by Rohner (1986) postulates a feedback arrangement where maintenance and expressive subsystems of the sociocultural system synchronize with dominant socialization patterns.   For example, in sociocultural systems characterized by higher levels of parental rejection, socialization of future generations of children is likely to be characterized by rejection as rejected children become parents.   Likewise, occupational preferences are likely to reflect the negative self-concepts produced in part by rejection.   In addition to expression in art and music (Rohner & Frampton, 1982), societies with higher levels of perceived rejection by children are likely to include a harsh punishing deity in their cosmology (Rohner, 1975, pp. 107-108).

THE UNIVERSALIST APPROACH

As psychology struggles to be a science of human behavior, skepticism persists that many psychological theories are not on strong grounds concerning claims that they reflect a science of humanity (Matsumoto, 1994; Munroe, Munroe, & Whiting, 1981; Rohner, 1986).   These concerns are rooted in two separate issues.   One concern is the possibility that the very questions researchers tend to study reflect Western culture and thus only a partial accounting of what is important to know about human behavior.   A second concern is that scientific study of psychological theory is methodologically flawed.   These flaws include measurement problems and threats to internal and external validity.   Measurement problems concern the validity of measures expressed in the language and values of one cultural group being applied to another group.   Misattribution of causality due to weak, nonexperimental designs and poor control of plausible rival explanations is a prime concern with field studies and quasi experiments.   The overdependence on Western samples, or on sociocultural groups that are convenient, allow history and culture diffusion (Galton's problem) to stand as rivals to the research hypotheses. Weak measurement strategies, such as failure to separate out cultural knowledge from other concepts under study, limit reliability and validity in cultural contexts other than those in which the procedures were developed.

From its earliest years, research inspired by PAR Theory demonstrated concern with methodology in addition to substantive matters related to child socialization. In the preface to his 1975 book, Rohner noted that the first 15 years of research into what would be later labeled PAR Theory were guided by the intention "(a) to introduce a conceptual and methodological perspective called the 'universalist approach,' and (b) to use this approach in exploring the pan cultural antecedents and effects of parental acceptance-rejection."

Rohner's (1975, 1986) universalist approach arose primarily in response to concerns related to methodological weakness in psychological research. Rohner reasoned that if psychology is to achieve the objective to be a science of human behavior (not simply Western behavior), research methods for testing psychological theories that could eliminate cultural bias as a plausible rival to the research hypotheses need to be applied.

Like Campbell and Fiske (1959), Rohner's (1986) idea of a research program included multiple methods of measurement to overcome the limitations of each particular method. The experimental method, a powerful mainstay of psychological research, is of limited value in the study of child socialization. In particular, the subject matter of PAR Theory (parental acceptance and rejection) does not lend itself well to experimental manipulation and laboratory research on both practical and ethical grounds. Therefore, tests of PAR Theory must rely on nonexperimental methods. Although arguably stronger in external validity than laboratory research, nonexperimental methods fail to protect from one or more threats to internal validity. This situation suggests that a combination of methods might be needed to provide rigorous theory testing. Rohner (1975, 1986) urged the use of three general methodologies: holocultural studies involving worldwide sampling of ethnography to resolve questions of sampling bias (Rohner, Naroll, Barry, Divale, Erickson, Schaefer, & Sipes, 1978), ethnographic community studies to provide grounded knowledge, and quantitative-descriptive studies (labeled the psychological research approach by Rohner, 1986), to provide precise measures of individual variation. Concerning measurement, researchers are encouraged to employ participant observation, interviews, questionnaires, and secondary analysis of narratives such as ethnography. Application of proper checks for validity such as translation and back-translation (Brislin, 1970) and factor analyses (Rummell, 1970) of translations are also emphasized. Reliability is to be assessed in each new sociocultural group using conventional methods such as, Cronbach's Alpha, and/or test-retest measures. Behavior observations and coding of secondary data should employ multiple raters and estimates of inter-rater reliability (Rohner, 1986; Rohner & Ness, 1975). As will be seen below, these methods were all employed in a remarkable effort to understand how children's socialization experiences influence individual behavior and sociocultural systems.

EMPIRICAL TESTS OF PAR THEORY

The range of methodologies used in empirical tests of PAR Theory includes eight holocultural studies (Rohner, 1960, 1975; Rohner, Dewalt, & Ness, 1973; Rohner & Frampton, 1982; Rohner & Ness, 1975; Rohner & Rohner, 1981, 1982); one major ethnographic study (Rohner & Chaki-Sircar, 1988), dozens of smaller scale community studies combining ethnographic field methods and quantitative descriptive methods (e.g., Rohner, Kean, & Cournoyer, 1991), and hundreds of quantitative descriptive studies worldwide (Rohner, 1999).

Quantitative-descriptive studies have made extensive use of the Parental Acceptance-Rejection Questionnaire (PARQ) (Rohner, 1990). This commonly used measurement instrument has been translated into 24 different languages (Rohner, 1990). A comparison of the factor structure of the PARQ showed the same strong two-factor structure (a rejection factor and an acceptance factor) across eight sociocultural groups scattered widely around the world (Rohner & Cournoyer, 1994). The PARQ and other research instruments including a measure of self-concepts (the Personality Assessment Questionnaire—PAQ), interview schedules, and techniques for conducting observations are summarized in a field research manual published by the CSPAR at the University of Connecticut (Rohner, 1990).

Let us now examine examples of the different research strategies and the evidence each provides with regard to the basic questions raised by PAR Theory.

Holocultural Studies

Research using holocultural methods are best suited for addressing questions of the worldwide distribution of phenomena that are general enough to have been reported by ethnographers. Holocultural research starts with all the known and well-described cultural groups in the world as a sampling frame. These groups (perhaps as many as 4000 groups both contemporary and historical) are organized into clusters called culture areas on the basis of shared history, customs, culture contact, and culture diffusion. Within each of these culture areas, a limited number of groups are selected to be included in the sample, thus providing a representative sample of the species with regard to culture.

PAR Theory researchers have made use of a standard cross-cultural sample originally described in Murdock and White (1969) and a 101-society sample reported by Rohner (1975). Both samples were designed to include representation of the full range of cultural and linguistic groups worldwide.

Once a representative sample of sociocultural groups has been selected, ethnographic descriptions of these groups are collected and examined for descriptions of the phenomenon of interest. In the case of PAR Theory, the phenomenon of interest included parent-child interaction and related behaviors. A scoring key is developed and multiple raters read each passage, develop independent ratings of the phenomenon, compare results, and resolve disputes. The result is a database of ratings of the characteristics of cultural groups. Standards for holocultural studies were proposed by Rohner, Naroll, Barry, Divale, Erickson, Schaefer, and Sipes (1978). The Human Resource Area Files (HRAF) is a major repository of holocultural codes in print and computer readable form.

Holocultural research was utilized to examine the range of parental acceptance-rejection across the species. One study employing a sample of 101 societies, the "Love sample" was originally reported in Rohner (1975). A second (Rohner, 1986) employed the standard cross-cultural sample described by Murdock and White (1969). In both cases, the samples were stratified by culture area to alleviate sampling bias introduced by culture diffusion, migration, and historical contact (Galton's problem). In both studies, two independent raters read passages describing parent-child interaction and child behavior contained in the ethnographies of the sample societies. The raters' codes were taken as reflecting typical patterns of behavior in those groups at the time the ethnographies were written (Rohner, 1975; Rohner & Rohner, 1981). Analyses of the codes from these two holocultural studies reveal the diversity of parental acceptance-rejection. Using a scale that ranged from 2 (rejection) to 10 (acceptance) ethnographers' reports were coded for the amount of acceptance-rejection observed. Analysis of the communities in the 101-society sample (Rohner, 1975) revealed that the modal treatment of children in these communities was seen as accepting, as indicated by average ratings at eight or above on a ten-point scale. Considerable variability was also found. For example, communities included in the

North American sample received ratings ranging from ten to four, with French Canadians at ten being highest, Tepoztecans at four the lowest, and Americans at seven being midrange. Similar diversity was also found in Africa, East Eurasia, Insular Pacific, and South America. Rohner (1975) lists the entire collection of ratings of parental acceptance-rejection and personality characteristics for the 101 societies in Table A10 of that work (also available in computer readable form from HRAF).

Examination of the correlations between ratings of parental acceptance and personality characteristics within the sample of 101 societies confirmed the expectation that the more rejection ethnographers reported, the more likely the ethnographers were to also report a constellation of negative personality characteristics in both children and adults. These characteristics included virtually all those predicted by PAR Theory, including hostility and aggression, self-evaluation, dependence, emotional responsiveness, worldview, and emotional instability. Rohner (1986) reports Pearson correlations between ratings of parental acceptance-rejection based on ethnographic descriptions and ratings of personality characteristics within the 101-society samples between .39 and .73 (all significant beyond the .01 level). That is, across these diverse cultural groups, and across multiple ethnographers and multiple raters, the more rejecting behaviors the ethnographers saw, the more likely they also were to report evidence of negative self-concepts as predicted by theory. Similar findings are reported in Rohner and Rohner (1981) concerning the standard cross-cultural sample of 186 societies.

At a sociocultural systems level, Rohner (1975) also reports a test indicating that the view of gods as malevolent was positively associated with the amount of child rejection observed, and that gods tended to be viewed as benevolent in communities where parents were reported as accepting.

Holocultural tests inspired by PAR Theory have also resulted in the coding of such features of parent-child interaction as the extent of care-giving roles by parents and other kin, and continuity/discontinuity in socialization of children to adult roles (Rohner & Rohner, 1982). The presence of these codes allows for the testing of large system questions concerning the relationships between social structure, socialization techniques, and individual and collective behavior patterns.

These holocultural studies are an important source of data regarding the species wide generalizability of PAR Theory. Although holocultural studies are susceptible to several forms of bias, the inclusion of multiple observers (the ethnographers), diverse subject populations (the groups studied), and multiple methods of data collection tend to alleviate the measurement and sampling bias that limit the external validity of generalizations derived from monocultural studies. In particular, concern that the connection between acceptance-rejection and measures of psychological adjustment may reflect response set or social desirability bias are rendered less plausible by these studies. Also, ethnographic methods are more likely than one-shot descriptive studies to generate observations that are grounded in the cultural systems in which the behavior occurred. Thus, these holocultural tests provide strong support for the idea that the association between parental rejection and personality dispositions is widespread, transcending cultural boundaries.

Quantitative-descriptive Studies

The confirmation through holocultural studies that, worldwide, observers' reports of parental rejection correlate with reports of a particular constellation of personality dispositions provides support for the theory not readily available from other research strategies. However, holocultural studies provide very coarse measures of societal trends and little information about behavioral variations within a sociocultural system. Quantitative-descriptive studies are superior methods for examining individual differences and relationships between variables at the intracultural level. With appropriate attention to measurement problems cross-culturally, high degrees of reliability, validity, and precision are possible through the use of questionnaires, surveys, and behavior observations (Brislin, 1970).

An important instrument in quantitative-descriptive studies has been the PARQ, a 60-item questionnaire designed to elicit respondents' perceptions of parental acceptance and rejection (Rohner, 1990). The PARQ consists of four scales corresponding to the four principal forms in which the warmth dimension is believed to exist in all sociocultural groups: warmth/affection (20 items), hostility/aggression (15 items), indifference/neglect (15 items), and undifferentiated rejection (10 items).

Examples of items include "My (parent) makes me feel wanted and needed." (warmth/affection); "My (parent) goes out of her/his way to hurt my feelings." (hostility/aggression); "My (parent) ignores me as long as I do nothing to bother her/him." (indifference/neglect); "My (parent) does not really love me." (undifferentiated rejection). Individuals respond to statements such as these on a four-point, Likert-like scale ranging from "almost always true" to "almost never true." An overall rejection score is obtained by reverse coding the warmth/affection scale and summing all scale scores. To date the PARQ and its companion, the PAQ (Rohner,

1990) that measures seven self-concepts, have been translated and back-translated into 24 languages.

It is important to note that the PARQ solicits the individual's subjective interpretations of a cluster of nonspecific parental behaviors. That is, the PARQ assumes that all sociocultural groups will have some way of using behaviors and words to communicate warmth and affection, hostility and aggression, or neglect and indifference, and that these concepts, not particular behaviors, are likely to constitute the universal dimension of parental acceptance and rejection. Therefore, each respondent is left to interpret actual parental behavior through his/her own cultural lenses. This is one feature of the PARQ that makes it so useful in cross-cultural research. The researcher is freed from making false interpretations of the meanings of superficial parental behaviors. However, employing questions indicating common meaning categories (i.e., warmth/affection, aggression/hostility, neglect/indifference, and undifferentiated rejection) helps to preserve the validity of the measure cross-culturally.

This subjective, phenomenological approach to the study of human development is not without its critics. Psychology has a long history of skepticism and debate about the reliability and validity of self-reports, summary judgments, and recall (e.g., Schwarz, Barton-Henry, & Prozinsky, 1985; Schweder & D'Andrade, 1980). Two common concerns are that (1) self-reports and reports of outside observers will differ in important ways (interpreted as low inter-rater reliability), and (2) retrospective self-reports and summary judgments will be distorted to reflect current beliefs (suggesting a lack of validity). However, as Cournoyer and Rohner (1996) note, when the item of interest is the internal representation of experience by individuals, the lack of agreement between outside observers and self-reports is not necessarily an indication of poor reliability. PAR Theory is interested in how individuals' subjective experiences of parental acceptance and rejection influence their behavior and self-concepts. Therefore, lack of agreement between ratings of parental behavior by siblings, parents, and other observers and children's self-reports of perceived rejection, should these disagreements occur, do not necessarily invalidate self-reports of subjective perception. Rather, these differences reflect the likelihood that individuals extract meaning concerning objective experiences through the use of cultural and individual lenses.

While the lack of external validation of subjective perceptions is less important when the perceptions are the subject of the inquiry, rejection of the systematic distortion hypothesis is important to the establishment of the validity of such self-reports. One may thus ask, do self-reports of acceptance-rejection reflect the actual feelings and experiences of the respondents during childhood, or are these self-reports distorted to reflect individual's present circumstances? Cournoyer and Rohner (1996) provided a limited test of this possibility by comparing PARQ self-reports of acceptance-rejection by children when they were 7-11 years old, with retrospective PARQ reports by the same children taken seven years later when they were adolescents aged 14-18. Modest correlations ($r = .62$, $p <$ .0001, $n = 49$) between the two sets of scores suggest that adolescents' retrospective recollections of childhood perceptions were in moderately substantial agreement with their self-reports during childhood.

A more general concern related to validity is whether the concept acceptance-rejection has enough shared meaning cross-culturally. Although the use of subjective interpretations allows the PARQ to be meaningful to persons from diverse cultural and linguistic groups, the subjective approach at least potentially may lead to problems with cross-cultural compatibility. That is, do PARQ scores map to the same constructs across cultural contexts? While it is probably true that children experience acceptance and rejection in ways that are unique to their own culture, the evidence of the cross-cultural validity of the PARQ is illustrated in a factor comparison study conducted by Rohner and Cournoyer (1994) in eight sociocultural groups. Raw responses to the PARQ from Egypt, India (Bengali speakers and Telugu speakers), Korea, Puerto Rico, St. Kitts, and the United States (separate samples of Blacks and Whites) were entered into a common factor analysis. The analysis showed a similar factor structure, with a strong acceptance factor and a strong rejection factor in all groups. Furthermore, the items on the PARQ scales loaded reasonably on the two factors, suggesting acceptable validity for the scale in several of its translations. While it seems likely that each cultural group has unique ways to express acceptance or rejection the evidence from factor comparison suggests that a common set of behavior domains reflected in the PARQ define that experience.

Quantitative-descriptive studies using the PARQ and PAQ have strongly supported two of the major findings of the holocultural studies, that most children are accepted, and that rejected children tend to display a series of negative self-concepts and behaviors. Analysis of scores on the PARQ in 15 communities (Rohner, 1986, Tables 4 & 5) around the world revealed a mean acceptance score that corresponds very closely to the median value found in the holocultural studies described above. That is, in general, children within most cultural groups report that their caregivers are basically accepting. Furthermore, the correlations between perceptions of acceptance-rejection and the predicted seven personality dispositions are also high intraculturally (Rohner, 1986). That is, within any given society, the children and adults who see themselves as having been accepted tend to be the better adjusted individuals (Rohner, 1986). A partial listing of the sociocultural groups where this finding has been replicated includes: the United States with Caucasian, Black, Puerto Rican (Rohner, 1986), and Korean samples (Rohner, Kahn, & Rohner, 1980), and in Puerto Rico (Saavedra, 1980), India (Rohner & Chaki-Sircar, 1987, 1988), Egypt (Salama, 1987), Turkey (Erkman, 1992), Nigeria (Haque, 1985), Pakistan (Haque, 1987), Czechoslovakia (Matejeck & Kadubcova, 1984), St. Kitts, W.I. (Rohner, Kean, & Cournoyer, 1991), Japan (Morishita, 1988), Korea (Rohner & Pettingill, 1985), Mexico (Rohner, Roll, & Rohner, 1980), Bahrain (Al-Falaij, 1991), and Peru (Gavilano, 1988).

These findings indicate that PAR Theory works well as a theory of intracultural differences in personality and behavior in addition to its usefulness in accounting for large-scale differences between sociocultural systems (as indicated by the holocultural studies).

Ethnographic Community Studies

A limitation of research strategies that use fixed response measurement strategies such as questionnaires and assessment scales is that these may represent translatable, but culture bound concepts. Although the factor comparison studies mentioned earlier establish the existence of some shared meaning, such studies do not necessarily reveal what portion of the concept may have been left out. Ethnographic community studies supplement questionnaires and scales by providing rich descriptions of the cultural context in which the observations were conducted, allowing a more complete picture of human relations, including acceptance-rejection. By allowing the unanticipated anomalies that do not fit the preconceived notions of the researcher to be detected, ethnographic studies provide some protection from employing unreasonably narrow operationalizations of variables.

The clearest example of ethnographic methods applied to PAR Theory is contained in Rohner and Chaki-Sircar (1988). In their work *Women and Children in a Bengali Village*, a Western social scientist teamed up with an indigenous social scientist to profile family life, in particular parental acceptance-rejection, in a village of about 1,275 persons in West Bengal, India. The fieldwork that underlies this study consisted of traditional ethnographic methods and quantitative descriptive methods including questionnaires and interviews. The resulting description presents the reader with not only statistical information concerning parent-child relationships, but also with rich detail concerning the context in which children and parents live and love in a contemporary Indian village.

One example of the usefulness of combining questionnaires, ethnographic research, and a focus on subjective interpretations of the respondents is found in an apparent discrepancy between the perceptions of Indian parenting contained in the literature and what Rohner and Chaki-Sircar (1988) found. Ethnographers tend to report Indian mothers as ranking below the pan-cultural average in ratings of warmth to children (Rohner, 1986). Western social scientists who had previously observed Indian communities concluded that Indian mothers were low in warmth toward children based on behavior observations (for example, Minturn & Lambert, 1964; Seymour, 1976). However, Rohner and Chaki-Sircar (1988) examined maternal warmth as perceived by children and found a different pattern. In their work, only about 2% of the children perceived any significant rejection as measured by the PARQ. Although not necessarily expected, interviews with parents and children revealed that children's views of the mothers were generally shared by the mothers, as were the children's self-concepts. There are two potential explanations for the disagreement. First, unpublished reports discussed in Rohner and Chaki-Sircar (1988) reveal a broad range of perceived acceptance-rejection in parent-child relationships in Indian communities. In other words, India is a complex society about which it is difficult to make generalizations. Also, it seems possible that even the most astute of outside observers may have trouble determining the extent to which children feel accepted or rejected.

Without attempting to replicate the abundant detail of ethnography here, it is easy to see how the richness of these observations enhances our understanding of the statistical findings. Profiles of families and children show how children and adults manage their interpersonal relationships, including those characterized by discord. For example, one of the most rejected children in Rohner and Chaki-Sircar's (1988) study had access to loving alternate caretakers and showed some positive self-concepts, in addition to the expected negative ones. The ability to observe as well as ask about perceptions is a major resource for examining the validity of survey data in cross-cultural studies.

COMMENTARY

The multimethod approach of PAR Theory provides convincing evidence that perceived parental acceptance-rejection is a salient dimension in the mental life of humans worldwide. In addition to demonstrating the meaningfulness of the notion of parental acceptance-rejection, the evidence clearly indicates that perceptions of acceptance and rejection are correlates of a group of negative self-concepts, and behavioral indicators of maladjustment-adjustment. Regardless of sociocultural context, high levels of rejection are associated statistically with negative self-concepts and poorer adjustment. Clearly, parental warmth is not the sole cause of children's adjustment problems, nor will warm parents necessarily assure their children's positive adjustment. Nonetheless, substantial correlations between measures of perceived rejection, self-concepts, and behavior are consistent with the idea that perceived acceptance-rejection may be one important cause of differences in personality and behavior.

The causal forces that underlie the correlations between acceptance-rejection, personality, and behavior are less well demonstrated from existing research. PAR Theory suggests that rejection is probably a contributor to both the development of negative self-concepts and a source of their resistance to change. Research methods used to date have not conclusively established the direction of causality. It seems just as reasonable to assume that children's negative self-concepts and feelings of rejection might both originate in some third variable, perhaps physiological differences in temperament or mental functioning. For example, literature concerning the physiological causes of some conduct disorders is consistent with this method of drawing the causal arrow (Caspi, Elder, & Bem, 1987; Shoda & Mischel, 1990). Establishment of the direction of causality will require application of a different research design. For example, experimental manipulation of the behavior of parents identified by their children as rejecting would seem to be both ethically feasible and informative in this regard.

Perhaps the most exciting aspect of PAR Theory is its contribution to the challenge mentioned at the beginning of this chapter. From one perspective PAR Theory is a modest collection of empirical studies and scholarly writings about child socialization. However, in casting his gaze at this seemingly narrow aspect of the human condition, Rohner has shown us a powerful approach to theory testing. That method, his universalism, does more than increase our understanding of child socialization. In constructing and applying his methodology Rohner presents a reasonable case, as a small group of others has, that species wide theories that are useful within particular cultural contexts are possible. Spanning more than two decades of postmodern and social constructionist nihilism, this is no small accomplishment.

It is a triumph of PAR Theory in that it encompasses both the individual and the collective, the particular and the universal. PAR Theory gives us clues concerning why a particular child is adjusting poorly, and how that adjustment may be related not merely to the behavior of a particular set of parents, but also to the fabric of the sociocultural system, and to human nature, enhancing our understanding of what we are as a species. It is only by using a combination of methodologies, and looking both broadly across the species, and narrowly within specific sociocultural systems that this sweeping panorama is possible.

BIBLIOGRAPHY

Al-Falaij, A. (1991). *Family conditions ego development, and sociomoral development in juvenile delinquency: A study of Bahraini adolescents.* Unpublished doctoral dissertation. University of Pittsburgh.

Brislin, R. (1970). Back-translation for cross-cultural research. *Journal of Cross-Cultural Psychology, 1,* 185-216.

Bowlby, J. (1940). The influence of early environment in the development of neurosis and neurotic character. *International Journal of Psychoanalysis, 21,* 154-178.

Bowlby, J. (1944). Forty-four juvenile thieves: Their characters and home life. *International Journal of Psychoanalysis, 25,* 107-128.

Burlingham, D. T., & Freud, A. (1944). *Infants without families.* New York: International University Press.

Campbell, D. T., & Fiske, D. W. (1959). Convergent and discriminant validation by the multitrait-multimethod matrix. *Psychological Bulletin, 56,* 81-105.

Caspi, A., Elder, G. H., & Bem, D. J. (1987). Moving against the world: Life-course patterns of explosive children. *Developmental Psychology, 23* (2), 308-313.

Champney, H. (1941). The measurement of parent behavior. *Child Development, 12,* 131-166.

Cournoyer, D. E., & Klein, W. C. (2000). *Research methods for social work.* Boston, MA: Allyn & Bacon.

Cournoyer, D. E., & Rohner, R. P. (1996). Reliability of retrospective reports of perceived maternal acceptance-rejection in childhood. *Psychological Reports, 78,* 147-150.

Erkman, F. (1992). Support for Rohner's parental acceptance-rejection theory as a psychological abuse theory in Turkey. In S. Iwawaki, Y. Kashima, & K. Leung (Eds.), *Innovations in cross-cultural psychology: Selected papers from the tenth international conference of the*

International Association for Cross-Cultural Psychology (pp. 384-395). Lisse: Swets & Zeitlinger.

Ferenczi, S. (1929). The unwelcome child and his death instinct. *International Journal of Psychoanalysis, 10*, 125-129.

Gavilano, G. (1988). *Maternal acceptance-rejection and personality characteristics among adolescents in different socioeconomic sectors* [in Lima Peru]. Unpublished thesis, Catholic University of Peru, Lima, Peru. (in Spanish)

Haque, A. (1985). Relationship between perceived maternal acceptance-rejection and self-esteem among young adults in Nigeria. *Journal of African Psychology, 1*, 15-24.

Haque, A. (1987). Social class differences in perceived maternal acceptance-rejection and personality dispositions among Pakistani children. In Ç. Kagitçibasi (Ed.), *Growth and progress in cross-cultural psychology* (pp. 189 -195). Lisse: Swets & Zeitlinger.

Maccoby, E. E., & Martin, J. A. (1983). Socialization in the context of the family: Parent-child interaction. In P. H. Mussen (Series Ed.) & E. M. Hetherington (Vol. Ed.), *Handbook of child psychology:* Vol. 4. *Socialization personality and social development* (4th ed., pp. 1-101). New York: Wiley.

Matejcek, Z., & Kadubcova, D. (1984). Self-perception in Czech children from the point of view of Rohner's parental acceptance-rejection theory. *Ceskoslovenska Psychologie, 28*, 87-96.

Matsumoto, D. (1994). *People: Psychology from a cultural perspective.* Pacific Grove, CA: Brooks/Cole.

Minturn, L., & Lambert, W.W. (1964). *Mothers of six cultures.* New York: Wiley.

Morishita, M. (1988). Mother-child relations and personality development in school age children. *Japanese Psychological Review, 31* (1), 60-75.

Munroe, R. H., Munroe, R. L., & Whiting, B. B. (1981). *Handbook of cross-cultural human development.* New York: Garland.

Murdock, G. P., & White, D. (1969). Standard cross-cultural sample. *Ethnology, 8*, 329-369.

Rohner, R. P. (1960). *Child acceptance-rejection and modal personality in three Pacific societies.* Unpublished masters thesis, Stanford University.

Rohner, R. P. (1975). *They love me, they love me not.* New Haven, CT: Human Relations Area Files.

Rohner, R. P. (1986). *The warmth dimension.* Beverly Hills, CA: Sage.

Rohner, R. P. (1990). *Handbook for the study of parental acceptance and rejection*. (Available from the Center for the Study of Parental Acceptance and Rejection, University of Connecticut, Storrs, CT 06269)

Rohner, R. P. (1999a). *Parental acceptance-rejection bibliography*. (Available from the Center for the Study of Parental Acceptance and Rejection, University of Connecticut, Storrs, CT 06269).

Rohner, R. P. (1999b). Acceptance and rejection. In D. Levinson, J. Ponzetti, & P. Jorgensen (Eds.), *Encyclopedia of human emotions*. New York: Macmillan Reference.

Rohner, R. P., & Chaki-Sircar, M. (1987). Caste differences in perceived maternal acceptance in West Bengal, India. *Ethos, 15*, 406-425.

Rohner, R. P., & Chaki-Sircar, M. (1988). *Women and children in a Bengali village*. Hanover, NH: University Press of New England.

Rohner, R. P., & Cournoyer, D. E. (1994). Universals in youths' perceptions of parental acceptance and rejection: Evidence from factor analyses within eight sociocultural groups worldwide. *Cross-Cultural Research, 28* (4), 371-383.

Rohner, R. P., Dewalt, B. R., & Ness, R. C. (1973). Ethnographer bias in cross-cultural research: An empirical study. *Behavior Science Notes, 8*, 278-317.

Rohner, R. P., & Frampton, S. (1982). Perceived parental acceptance-rejection and artistic preference: An unexplained contradiction. *Journal of Cross-Cultural Psychology, 13*, 250-259.

Rohner, R. P., Kahn, B. C., & Rohner, E. C. (1980). Social class differences in perceived parental acceptance-rejection and self-evaluation among Korean-American children. *Behavior Science Research, 15*, 55-66.

Rohner, R. P., Kean, K. J., & Cournoyer, D. E. (1991). Effects of corporal punishment, perceived caretaker warmth, and cultural beliefs on the psychological adjustment of children in St. Kitts, West Indies. *Journal of Marriage and the Family, 53*, 681-693.

Rohner, R.P., Naroll, R., Barry, H.B.III, Divale, W.T., Erickson, E.E., Schaefer, J.M., & Sipes, R.G. (1978). Guidelines for holocultural research. *Current Anthropology, 19* (1), 128-129.

Rohner, R. P., & Ness, R. C. (1975). Procedures for assessing the validity and reliability of data in cross-cultural research. *JAS catalog of selected documents in psychology, 5*, 190 (MS. 865), 40 pp.

Rohner, R. P., & Pettingill, S. M. (1985). Perceived parental acceptance-rejection and parental control among Korean adolescents. *Child Development, 56*, 524-528.

Rohner, R. P., & Rohner, E. C. (1981). Parental acceptance-rejection and parental control: Cross-cultural codes. *Ethnology, 20*, 2245-260.

Rohner, R. P., & Rohner, E. C. (1982). Enculturative continuity and the importance of caretakers: Cross-cultural codes. *Behavior Science Research, 17*, 91-114.

Rohner, R. P., Roll, S., & Rohner, E. C. (1980). Perceived parental acceptance-rejection and personality organization among Mexican and American elementary school children. *Behavior Science Research, 15*, 23-39.

Rummel, R. R. (1970). *Applied factor analysis.* Evanston, IL: Western University Press.

Saavedra, J. M. (1980). Effects of perceived parental warmth and control on the self-evaluation of Puerto Rican adolescent males. *Behavior Science Research, 15*, 41-54.

Salama, M. (1987). Children's fears and their perception of parental acceptance-rejection. *The Egyptian Journal of Psychology, 2*, 54-59.

Schaefer, E. S. (1965). Children's reports of parental behavior: An inventory. *Child Development, 36*, 413-424.

Schluderman, E., & Schluderman, S. (1970). Replicability of factors in children's report of parental behavior (CRPBI). *Journal of Psychology, 76*, 29-39.

Schluderman, S., & Schluderman, E. (1971). Adolescent report of parental behavior (CRPBI) in a Hutterite communal society. *Journal of Psychology, 79*, 29-39.

Schwarz, J. C., Barton-Henry, M. L., & Prozinsky, T. (1985). Assessing child-rearing behaviors: A comparison made by mother, father, child and sibling on the CRPBI. *Child Development, 56*, 462-479.

Schweder, R. A., & D'Andrade, R. G. (1980). The systematic distortion hypothesis. In R.A. Schweder (Ed.), *New directions for methodology of behavioral science,* Vol. 4, *Fallible judgment in behavioral research* (pp. 37-58). San Francisco, CA: Jossey-Bass.

Seymour, S. (1976). Caste/class and child rearing in a changing Indian town. *American Ethnologist, 3*, 783-796.

Shoda, Y., & Mischel, W. (1990). Predicting adolescent cognitive and self-regulatory competencies from preschool delay of gratification: Identifying diagnostic conditions. *Developmental Psychology, 26*(6), 978-986.

Siegelman, M. (1965a). Evaluation of Bronfenbrenner's questionnaire for children concerning parental behavior. *Child Development, 36*, 164-174.

Siegelman, M. (1965b). College student personality correlates of early parent-child relationships. *Journal of Consulting Psychology*, *29*, 558-564.

Siegelman, M. (1966). Loving and punishing parental behavior and introversion tendencies in sons. *Child Development, 37*, 985-992.

Siegelman, M. (1973). Parent behavior correlates of personality traits related to creativity in sons and daughters. *Journal of Consulting and Clinical Psychology, 40*, 43-47.

Symonds, P. M. (1939). *The psychology of parent-child relationships*. New York: Appleton-Century.

Symonds, P. M. (1949). *The dynamics of parent-child relations*. New York: Teachers' College, Columbia University Bureau of Publications.

Webb, E. J., Campbell, D. T., Schwartz, R. D., & Sechrest, L. (1966). *Unobtrusive measures*. Chicago, IL: Rand McNally.

MULTICULTURAL ASSESSMENT OF CHILD AND ADOLESCENT PERSONALITY AND PSYCHOPATHOLOGY

Richard H. Dana
Portland State University, U.S.A.

INTRODUCTION

Personality assessment of children and adolescents in the United States is informed by four major paradigms (Tuma & Ebert, 1990). A medical approach seeks to identify organic conditions. Internal psychological processes and behaviors are examined with projective tests using high-inference interpretation referenced by psychodynamic theory. Psychometric tests provide single and multidimensional measurement of traits or symptoms using low-inference interpretation. Behavioral assessment uses objective rating scales with parents or teachers. In practice there is some overlap of these approaches together with strong assessor preferences for either high- or low-inference interpretation as well as particular paradigms depending upon their training and the purposes of assessment.

This chapter will focus on tests of psychodynamic and psychometric origins for describing personality and psychopathology. Both test-oriented approaches now enjoy renewed popularity among clinical assessors because comparable reliability and validity have been demonstrated for them. Nonetheless, these paradigms were designed primarily for assessment of Anglo-Americans although they have been used with all children and adolescents in the United States. Such applications to multicultural populations expose a variety of sources of bias attributable to assessors, the service delivery process, the use of standard tests based on Euro-American personality theories, and the current system of diagnostic classifications. This chapter suggests that reduction of bias can be accomplished as part of a professional education for assessors that focuses on cultural competence as an important requirement for assessment practice with multicultural assessment populations. Of particular emphasis here are adaptations of standard tests for multicultural populations as well as the design and standardization of new tests for particular cultural/racial populations. Recommendations are made for multicultural assessment practice in the United States as well as suggestions pertinent to the application of standard tests that have been exported to other countries.

BIAS

Bias can affect the entire assessment process as well as the outcomes of assessment, particularly as associated with the treatment planning and implementation of any of these subsequent interventions. Assessment bias is contributed by the assessor, often inadvertently, and occurs whenever the service delivery style interferes with task-orientation and rapport. Bias may be inherent in the instruments used for personality study or associated with the clinical diagnostic process. Bias may also occur in the sources of information on personality used to inform the interpretation of test data. Finally, the psychiatric classification systems, particularly the DSM-IV, often confound culturally normative behaviors with psychopathology. This section will examine the sources of bias and avenues for remediation that are summarized in Table 1.

Assessor

Ethnocentrism is exposed by the assumptions that similarities are greater than differences among persons of various cultural backgrounds and that assimilation is an anticipated consequence of residence over time and across generations in the United States. However, many persons remain ensconced in traditional cultures with English as a second language (e.g., 65% of Asians and 70% of Hispanics). Others become bicultural and even larger numbers remain marginal with an admixture of values and behaviors from two or more ethnic/racial heritages (for estimates of percentages in cultural orientation groups, see Dana, 1998d). Professional psychologists, however, have minimized cultural differences for the purposes of assessment and intervention and their clients are typically regarded as amenable to mainstream services or as assimilated. The result of this degree of ethnocentrism among assessors is that these populations underutilize mental health services. During the assessment process cultural differences are overlooked or ignored in the selection and subsequent interpretation of instruments. Another consequence of ethnocentrism is that group differences may be labeled as deficits, for example, when Anglo assessors examine African-Americans (Wyatt, Powell, & Bass, 1982) or similar symptoms may be regarded as equivalent in diagnostic significance when, in fact, they are not indicators of psychopathology and the person may not even be diagnosable (Neighbors, Jackson, Campbell, & Williams, 1989). By the same token, an incorrect assumption of difference can lead to ignoring bona fide symptoms of psychopathology.

Stereotypy in the form of unwarranted expectations for particular behaviors typically occurs without awareness, intent, or malice as a consequence of false beliefs and overgeneralizations that each group entertains concerning other groups. For example, Anglo-American clinicians tend to misperceive the behaviors of their Chinese clients as anxious, confused, and reserved while Chinese-American clinicians do not discern these behaviors in the same clients (Li-Repac, 1980). Similarly, African-American clients are

Table 1
Sources of Bias in Assessment Services for Children from
Multicultural Populations in the United States

Source	Bias	Remediation
Assessor	Ethnocentrism	Examine own cultural/racial identity
	Stereotypy	Living experience in another cultural setting
	Insufficient knowledge	Immersion in culturally relevant materials
		Training/supervision
Service Delivery	Anglo-style social etiquette: task-oriented, formal, impersonal	Culture-specific styles
Test	Anglo tests used as etics or pseudo-etics	Cross-cultural validity: equivalence in language (translation), (metric), and constructs
Personality theory	Anglo-European male theories and constructs used as standard for personality description	Development of culture-specific theories and research-generated constructs
		Description of cultural self
		Description of cultural/racial identity
Psychiatric classification	Culture-psycho-pathology confound in DSM-IV	Use cultural formulations and glossary of culture bound disorders
	Limited range of presented problems included in DSM-IV	Recognize acculturative stress, cultural identity issues, problems-in-living, and oppression-induced conditions
	Many existing tests of psychopathology have poor concordance with DSM-IV	Continued development of tests congruent with DSM-IV classifications

perceived to have inappropriate sexuality (Wyatt et al., 1982), and even their grossly disturbed behaviors may be accepted as culturally appropriate by Anglo-clinicians (Lewis, Shanok, Cohen, Kligfield, & Frisone, 1980).

Remediations for assessor bias may be found in training, supervised assessment experience with multicultural populations, immersion in culturally relevant materials, examination of one's own cultural/racial identity, and living experience in another cultural setting. However, the training resources now available in doctoral psychology programs have not been sufficient to instill feelings of competence among Anglo-graduates who service their diverse clients. Survey studies document that a majority of these clinicians do not feel competent to provide services for persons whose cultural/racial identities differ from their own in spite of having received some training (Allison, Crawford, Echemendia, Robinson, & Kemp, 1994; Allison, Echemendia, Crawford, & Robinson, 1996). Clearly, the available training in professional psychology programs at the present time is deficient in amount and quality. Immersion in culturally relevant descriptions of personality and psychopathology research has been difficult because adequately designed and conducted research studies are infrequent in the literature and have not been widely used as resources for competence training. For this reason, it is necessary to pay close attention to literary and artistic works produced by members of a particular cultural/racial group to become acquainted with their everyday lives, including common problems, quality of experiences, and how stress is encountered and handled. This self-study may necessitate fluency in Spanish, for example, to encompass Latin-American examples, which suggest the extent of cultural differences by country of origin. Only one review of these materials including both the personality/psychopathology psychological literature and research-based materials is available for cultural competence training of assessors (Dana, 1998b). A discussion of various approaches to the cultural/racial identities of service providers has been recommended as a training resource for Anglo-American psychologists (see chapter 4, Dana, 1998d). Careful examination of an Anglo assessor's cultural identity can include preparation of a genogram (e.g., Hardy & Laszloffy, 1995) during assessment training, although to my knowledge this occurs only infrequently.

Finally, and probably of greatest importance, is an opportunity for sustained living experience in another cultural setting. This can occur during summers or in connection with living accommodations during an internship. Such an experience provides opportunity for acquiring skill in a language other than English, developing social relationships, sharing daily events, and learning how the world may be construed from another perspective in which reality can assume dimensions that differ radically from one's own culturally conditioned beliefs.

Service Delivery

Professional mental health service providers from many countries come to the United States and are impressed by the quality and availability of services but are appalled by the service delivery style. In the United States, professional psychological services have long been associated with the medical services tradition, that is, they have a history of rendering services that are often relatively impersonal and task-oriented with the power vested in the provider and expectations for unquestioning compliance by clients. Nonetheless, each culture has an expected and comfortable style of service delivery with a special social etiquette required for credibility of the service provider and acceptance of the particular service. In general terms, clients expect the service delivery to be credible and "gift-giving" or providing something of value as part of an assessment or intervention session (Sue & Zane, 1987). If the style of service delivery does not conform to expectations, sufficient task orientation will fail to occur leading to inadequate test data in terms of numbers, quality, and representativeness of response. The assessor is often unaware that his or her data are too meager for purposes of personality conceptualization or to provide a cultural formulation leading to a valid clinical diagnosis. Clients may be diminished as persons and the frequent result is an increased risk of pathologization.

Tests

The tests used by psychologists to examine and evaluate children and adolescents in the United States are of Euro-American origins and, therefore, culture-specific or oriented toward the emic perspective. Few reviews of tests for applications with various cultural/racial groups in the United States are available (e.g., Dauphinais & King, 1992). Surveys of assessment practitioners do not inquire about test usage with particular cultural/racial populations or perceived assessor cultural competence (Archer, Maruish, Imhof, & Piotrowski, 1991; Pinkerman, Haynes, & Keiser, 1993). Nonetheless, these instruments are applied to other cultural/racial populations in the United States and worldwide as if they were universal or etic measures.

However, at best these instruments are pseudo-etics. Their applicability must be demonstrated by research for each non-Anglo-American cultural/racial population, and for each new country in which a test is introduced. While some genuine etic tests are now available (Díaz-Guerrero & Díaz-Loving, 1990), these tests have been used primarily in research. In this context Dana (1997, 1998c, 1998d) has discussed an assessment-intervention model in which the potential usefulness of etics is included.

The cross-cultural validity of standard tests is demonstrated by equivalence in language, construct, and metric. Translations are designed to yield linguistic equivalence in another language, but adequate test adaptation by translation can only be accomplished using systematic procedures incorporating explicit rules (e.g., Brislin, 1976). Tests in English cannot be translated into some languages if the language structure is too dissimilar from that of English. Draguns (1984) has demonstrated that translations frequently fail to document the intensity, communality, and range of usage for a construct. English language tests can be translated into most European languages with considerable fidelity using systematic procedures because of a shared Indo-European language family.

Only a small fraction of exported tests have been translated using systematic procedures even in European countries. Adequate and uncompromising translations are necessary because the cross-cultural use of these tests is ultimately dependent upon subsequent validation using culture-syntonic measures of the same construct in each country of application (Irvine & Carroll, 1980). Another way of expressing this truism is that personality constructs and psychopathological symptoms are intrinsic to a particular culture and competent examination can only occur within an indigenous perspective (Marsella & Kameoke, 1989).

Construct validation is difficult to accomplish. Although a variety of other validation methods are available, including the convergent-discriminant, multitrait-multimethod matrix developed by Campbell and Fiske (1959), factor analysis has been frequently chosen for this purpose. The quest for stability of replicated factors poses technical problems of interpretation, and no consensus exists on how these issues may best be resolved (Ben-Porath, 1990). Nonetheless, there are examples of tests for personality and psychopathology with demonstrated cross-cultural construct validity including the Holtzman Inkblot Test (Holtzman, 1988; Holtzman, Thorpe, Swartz, & Herron, 1961) that embodies Extraversion and Intraversion, the Eysenck Personality Questionnaire (Eysenck & Eysenck, 1975) measuring Introversion-Extraversion, Neuroticism, and Psychoticism, and the Individualism-Collectivism Scale (Hui, 1988) that may be genuine etics. These tests are not generally used in clinical assessment of children and adolescents in the United States.

Metric validity entails the adequacy of the formats used to present test content. Metric equivalence can be important for assessees who are inexperienced in taking paper-and-pencil tests due to age, reading ability, educational level, social class, or origins in cultures without a written language or where tests have been infrequently used in mental health examinations. Tests constructed in the United States have often been standardized with unrepresentative samples that failed to include some or many of these variables. Greater recognition of metric validity issues is required particularly for persons entering this country without a history of practice in taking tests and who lack the developed skills needed for this purpose. In addition, formal tests, especially for adolescents and children should include stimulus materials of intrinsic interest, use pictures and/or require interactions with the materials rather than answers, or offer a choice of alternative answers to printed questions.

Personality Theory

All major personality theories taught in professional psychology programs are of European or North American derivation and many are also of psychoanalytic origins. Psychoanalytic theory has been preoccupied with internalization processes linked to a technology for therapeutic practice that has not been demonstrated to possess cross-cultural validity, but rather represents an Euro-American emic. However, psychoanalysis as transmogrified by Doi (1971) became a culture-specific emergent in Japan rather than an application of supposedly universal personality theory. In spite of an early interest by Henry Murray (1938) and Carson (1969) in external influences on personality, such theories have had only limited impact on the development of tests. The inner-directedness of psychoanalysis and the ensuing focus on only a limited range of behaviors and cognitive processes prevented redirection to external sources of influence on individual personality. Moreover and with only a few exceptions men developed the personality theories required in graduate education. Jane Loevinger's (1976) ego development theory is a recent exception to this trend and is now presented in some graduate courses. Her theory is relevant for both genders in the United States and may be an etic. This theory and technique, as embodied in systematic translations of the Washington University Sentence Completion Test, has been used in six European countries, Japan, Vietnam, and India (Hy & Loevinger, 1996).

Psychologists apply their Euro-American personality theories in high-inference assessment practice almost exclusively because they have not been exposed in their professional training to theories with origins in other cultural/racial populations. In fact, there are only a few non-Euro-American emic personality theories, although there are many literary sources of informal information (Dana, 1998b). Personality theories relevant to these populations would focus much more directly on external, environmental, and social factors that influence psychological functioning in addition to the internal systems that compose the person (Cuéllar & González, 1998, in press). Some theories do embody these principles for other cultural/racial groups, notably most Asians (e.g., Hsu, 1971) and Mestizos in the United States (e.g., Ramirez, 1983). Nonetheless, it is difficult for assessors to conceptualize persons from other cultural/racial groups without the benefit of emic personality theories as guides for the interpretation of personality tests or for understanding what are the appropriate or dysfunctional behaviors in a particular culture. To date, only a small number of personality constructs have received support from cross-cultural validation (Dana, 1996b; Lonner, 1980). As indicated earlier, these constructs include Introversion, Extraversion, Neuroticism, Psychoticism, Individualism, and Collectivism. Not only are there few candidates for genuine emic constructs but there are also few genuine emic theories of personality available to assessors (e.g., Etzioni, 1968).

Psychiatric Classification

There has been discord among psychologists concerning the appropriateness of using the Diagnostic and Statistical Manuals published by the American Psychiatric Association (DSM-I, II, III, IV) for children and adolescents. The discord reflects a history of inability to diagnose 70% of children with the DSM-I (Rosen, Badn, & Kramer, 1964) that has continued through subsequent DSM editions in spite of a gradual incorporation of additional categories. This history has raised the problem of whether labeling children's behavior as psychopathological is either desirable or useful as a precursor to interventions (Goldman, Stein, & Guerry, 1983). An earlier review of classification of child psychopathology has provided alternatives that include descriptions of problems, assets, and behaviors (Achenbach & Edelbrock, 1978). The American Psychological Association is currently engaged in helping the World Health Organization (WHO) revise its international diagnostic system. Revision of the International Classification of Impairments, Activities, and Participation (ICIDH) will be completed by the year 2000 to permit comparisons across countries (Mjoseth, 1998).

ADAPTATION OF STANDARD TESTS

The standard tests examined in this chapter include objective tests, particularly the Minnesota Multiphasic Personality Inventory for adolescents (MMPI-A) (Butcher, Williams, Graham, Archer, Tellegen & Ben-Porath, 1992) and the Personality Inventory for Children (PIC) as well as representative projective tests used frequently with children and adolescents; these include the Rorschach, Thematic Apperception Test, Projective Drawings, and Sentence Completion tests. Readers are referred to appropriate chapters in Knoff (1986) for reviews of both projective tests and the PIC for children and adolescents, and to Dana (1993) for critiques of all these standard tests as applied to multicultural populations in the United States. Adaptations of standard tests include (a) moderator variables applied as corrections, (b) special norms, and (c) cross-cultural and culture-specific interpretive procedures in addition to the translations described earlier in this chapter. Readers are also referred to guidelines for translations as adaptations (Geisinger, 1994).

Moderator Variables

A variety of moderator variables are now available which can act as "corrections" for standard tests. These include (a) measures of cultural orientation and acculturation, (b) instruments to assess worldview components, (c) response sets, and (d) demographic information such as socioeconomic status and educational level. Cultural orientation status instruments generally provide bimodal measures of acculturation to the host culture as well as measures assessing the strength of an original cultural identification. These measures may be group-specific or be useful across several cultural/racial groups. These measures can provide categorical information (e.g., the cultural orientation statuses of assimilated, bicultural, marginal, traditional) for research purposes or selection of subsequent tests within an assessment process, as well as multidimensional content relevant to cultural identity description and the development of cultural formulations for use with the DSM-IV.

The most widely researched group-specific measure, the Acculturation Rating Scale for Mexican Americans (ARSMA and ARSMA-II) (Cuéllar, Arnold, & Maldonado, 1995), has become an emic prototype in the development of measures for other cultural groups. This instrument not only provides basic categorical information on cultural orientation status but in its ARSMA-II version it also contains the necessary information for the development of cultural formulations. Acculturation measures for immigrant groups such as Vietnamese and Southeast Asians are also being developed in addition to measures for culturally different populations in the United States, including African-Americans (Landrine & Klonoff, 1994), American-Indians/Alaska Natives (Allen & French, 1996), and Asian-Americans (Suinn, Rickard-Figueroa, Lew, & Vigil, 1987). Instruments to assess worldview also provide information on cultural identity. Some examples include the Scale to Assess World Views (Ibrahim & Kahn, 1987), the Self-Construal Scale (Singelis, 1994), and the Individualism-Collectivism Interpersonal Assessment Inventory (Matsumoto, Weissman, Preston, Brown, & Kupperbusch, 1997). These tests also provide content for a cultural description of personality and add important information for use in the preparation of cultural formulations to increase the reliability of clinical diagnoses.

The use of objective tests with multicultural adolescent populations requires an awareness of the influence of response sets including randomness, positivity or agreement, negativity or disagreement, and individual profile variation or lack of item differentiation (Watkins & Cheung, 1995). Response sets are often culture-specific. For Asians, dimensions of shame or stigma, symptom tolerance or bothersomeness, and cultural familiarity or common presence of symptoms have been proposed (Okazaki, 1998). For Hispanics, the use of response sets for acquiescence and positivity among traditional people diminishes with acculturation (Marín, Gamba, & Marín, 1992). While it may be impossible to expunge response sets from objective tests (Helmes & Reddon, 1993), it is of particular importance to be aware that different response sets characterize the test performance of each cultural/racial group. These response sets contribute to the elevation or depression of test scores and thereby facilitate misinterpretation.

Persons of color in the United States have repeated encounters with racism in their daily lives and these experiences may adversely affect the quality of assessments conducted by Anglo examiners. Some of this distrust may be alleviated by the use of culture-specific social behavior during assessment to provide a relationship conducive to task-orientation. It is also important to have documentation based on measures such as the Schedule of Racist Events (Landrine & Klonoff, 1996) and the Perceived Racism Scale (McNeilly, Anderson, Armstead, Clark, Corbett, Robinson, Pieper, & Lepisto, 1996) because scores on standard tests may be affected by these experiences.

Special Norms

Objective tests and some projective tests are interpreted on the basis of normative data. These norms become guides for low-inference interpretation and serve to define the limits of normal behavior in statistical terms. The available norms for standard tests are intended to be adequate for all cultural/racial populations and a need for special norms has been denied by many testing authorities in the United States (e.g., Greene, 1987). These available norms, however, typically include only very small numbers of persons in cultural/racial groups. There is often underrepresentation or distorted representation of census data because of inadequate inclusion of persons with lower socioeconomic and educational status or sampling on too few relevant demographic variables.

Although general norms may be inadequate, special norms for these groups would mask the extent of diversity and lead to an unwarranted minimization of within-group cultural differences. For example, although Mexican-Americans, Cuban-Americans, and Puerto Ricans are all Hispanics, the use of the same norms for these subpopulations would be unacceptable and misleading. Nonetheless, a criterion percentage of misclassifications using conventional norms could be used to suggest when special norms are desirable or mandatory. A suggestion has been made that MMPI profiles based on special norms and general norms be compared for assessees in multicultural groups (Dahlstrom, Lachar, & Dahlstrom, 1986, p. 85). Extraordinary misclassification rates on the MMPI may justify the use of special norms. For example, special norms have been recommended for Native American Indian tribes from isolated areas such as Northern Ontario in Canada where language and traditional culture are relatively more intact than in other tribal settings (Charles, 1988).

The ARSMA was developed originally to reduce an overinterpretation of psychopathology in the MMPI records of college students, which tended to reflect the confounding influences of culture (Montgomery & Orozco, 1985). One possible solution to the dilemmas posed by use of available general norms and the limited utility of special norms for particular cultural/racial groups is the development of the ARSMA cultural orientation status norms for standard tests. For example, the ARSMA was used to select Mexicans, Mexican-Americans, and Anglo-Americans for comparison of their performances on selected Halstead-Reitan neuropsychological tests (Arnold, Montgomery, Castaneda, & Longoria, 1994). In the study different degrees of traditionality affected some measures while other measures were unaffected. Acculturation status is thus related to neuropsychological test performance. The subsequent interpretation of these tests is facilitated by an explicit recognition of traditional cultures not only for Hispanics but, as these authors emphasize, for African-Americans, Jewish-Americans, and Chinese-Americans as well. One way of making these adjustments in interpretation is to include norms for traditional persons from various cultural/racial groups on standard tests (Dana, 1998a).

Norms developed in the United States may create similar dilemmas when used for test interpretation in other countries to which standard tests have been exported in spite of adequate linguistic equivalence. An example of this presumed generalizability is provided by the Rorschach Comprehensive System (RCS) in Iberoamerican countries and elsewhere. Although it has been argued that the norms for children have wide cross-cultural applicability (Exner & Weiner, 1995), there is strong evidence from samples in many countries that the constructs represented by test scores and ratios may have different meanings than in the United States leading to an unwarranted pathologization of children and adolescents. Large and significant differences between local or national RCS norms and RCS norms developed in the United States have led to the conclusion that national norms are necessary for each country in which the RCS is used (for Iberoamerican data, see Vinet, 1998, in press). Special norms have been recommended on the basis of shared cultural differences in personality and as a result of a lack of metric equivalence (Ephraim, 1998, in press). Only by using local norms in countries to which standard tests have been exported can individual psychological status within a group be examined, and valid distinctions between adaptive and psychopathological behaviors be drawn in a particular cultural context.

Cross-cultural and Culture-specific Interpretation

Cross-cultural or culture-specific interpretation assumes that the available norms for standard tests are inadequate. As a consequence, it is necessary to have special norms, either cultural orientation status norms in the United States or national norms for exported tests that have been adequately translated. Of course, in other multicultural nations such as Australia, India, or Great Britain cultural orientation status norms must also be established.

However, a further step is required before these new norms can be applied without the risk of pathologization or caricature. The equivalence of the constructs being measured cannot be taken for granted but has to be demonstrated. For most standard tests, the validity of the constructs in the new cultural or national setting is unknown.

An interim remedy for the paucity of research on construct equivalence will be examined in this section. First, tests requiring low-inference interpretation should precede tests requiring high-inference interpretation. Low-inference interpretation adheres more closely to test scores and is relatively literal as opposed to taking larger jumps from data to inference where the assessor's fantasies, stereotypes, and misinformation can contaminate his or her interpretation (Dana, 1966). For example, if the standard Murray TAT cards are used in Spain, the interpretation should not be dynamic as is typically done in the United States (Rossini & Moretti, 1997) but should instead employ the scoring system with the national norms developed by Avila-Espada (1998, in press). This would permit the TAT to be used with low-inference interpretation.

Second, whenever high-inference interpretation has to be used either because national norms or special norms are unavailable, this process should be controlled in a stepwise manner with the supplementation at each step of culturally relevant information. This is mandatory whenever Anglo assessors process data from multicultural assessees or whenever assessors in other countries are examining persons from immigrant, minority, or linguistically different groups. Table 2 provides a format for suggested steps in the inference process to improve the reliability of interpretation and the accuracy of personality conceptualizations and diagnostic formulations.

During an interview conducted with a culture-specific social etiquette, the assessor examines the feasibility of an assessor-client relationship that will permit sufficient task-orientation to provide an adequate data set. Depending on the adequacy of this relationship, client demographics, and the compatibility of the available tests with a client's cultural orientation status, tests may or may not need to be added to the assessment interview. Acculturation can be explored during the interview by specific questions taken

Table 2
Increasing Reliability of Interpretation During the
Assessment Process with Multicultural Clients

Step	Relevant Information
Interview	Service delivery style (social etiquette). First language? Socioeconomic class /education? Within-group differences. Immigrant? Refugee?
Cultural/Racial Identity Evaluation	Acculturation: Cultural orientation status? Description of cultural self.
Standard Psychological Tests	Are genuine etics available? If not, can emics (or derived test emics) then be used? Is there a translation in client's first language? Has translation been done systematically? Are culture-specific norms available
Culture-specific Tests	If standard psychological tests are inadequate, are emic tests available? Are these measures psychometrically sound?
Interpretation	If low-inference interpretation is not feasible, does assessor have sufficient knowledge and experience of client's culture to attempt high-inference interpretation? Is high-inference interpretation comfortable for assessor? Does assessor understand worldview, values, group identity, self structure, health/illness beliefs, culture-specific personality theory, and relevant research on construct?
Cultural Formulation	Is a diagnosis required? Is there a culture-bound disorder? Can the assessor use the steps to increase reliability of diagnosis suggested in DSM-IV? (i.e., cultural identity, cultural explanation, cultural factors in psychosocial environment and level of functioning, cultural elements of relationship, and overall cultural assessment for diagnosis and care).
Report	How can one describe culture-specific personality characteristics? Are assessment findings to be shared

246 DANA

Table 2 continued

with client and family or others? What are the specific cultural rules and expectations for feedback? Will findings be used as therapeutic assessment or in referral for subsequent treatment?

Note: This table was adapted from Table 18.1, Dana (1998b, p. 340).

from available tests. For younger children and adolescents of lower socioeconomic status and language development, objective tests may be less useful than projective tests, although the projective tests chosen are more likely to require high-inference interpretation. It is advisable to label the cultural orientation status of a client and to describe his or her cultural self before one decides to use particular tests.

The standard psychological tests will ordinarily be mainstream emics used with corrections or adjustments. With a few exceptions later described in this chapter, culture-specific tests are not available. Decisions have to be made about whether or not to use the available norms for the RCS, the MMPI-A, or other tests that have either not been standardized for the client's cultural/racial group or are known to have questionable cross-cultural construct validity. It is possible to use standard tests in the absence of adequate norms if the assessor has explicit expectations for culturally normative behaviors and personality characteristics, although there should be empirical evidence to justify departures from conventional norm-based scores. The cultural identity description obtained earlier in the process becomes another source of data for a decision to use high-inference interpretation.

Table 2 suggests that extensive cultural knowledge and experience is required for high-inference interpretation. This observation is particularly necessary when the assessor uses projective tests in the absence of national norms or lacks sufficient assessment experience with a given cultural/racial population. Detailed recommendations for the projective assessment of Latinos in the United States (Dana, 1998e) and general suggestions for sources of information on other cultural/racial groups are available (Dana, 1998b). The development of cultural formulations requires additional information to increase the reliability of DSM-IV diagnoses. Unfortunately, the diagnostic process is exclusively high-inference, and for that reason, the probability of errors and misclassifications due to the confounding of culture and psychopathology is very high. This is particularly true for personality disorders where the reliability of diagnosis is very low even in the absence of cultural issues (Kirk & Kutchens, 1992) and for the culture-bound disorders contained in the DSM-IV glossary. Castillo (1997) has described the process of doing cultural formulations for each DSM-IV diagnosis and this guide should be used whenever diagnoses are required for multicultural clients.

The preparation of reports for multicultural clients requires a sound knowledge of available interventions, and particular insight into whether or not culture-specific interventions as well as combined culture-specific and culture-general interventions are available for a particular client (see Dana, 1998d). In addition, if feedback is offered to the client and/or family members, the content and manner of presentation will differ across cultural groups and also depend on whether the feedback constitutes a therapeutic assessment or contains content relevant to a referral for subsequent intervention.

DEVELOPMENT OF NEW TESTS

Tests Designed for Multicultural Application

Most tests for children and adolescents constructed in the United States have been geared towards the mainstream population. The normative data for most tests under-represent cultural/racial groups or omit relevant demographic variables for matching purposes. The TEMAS (Tell-Me-A-Story) (Costantino, Malgady, & Rogler, 1988) is a notable exception. The TEMAS is a picture-story test normed for Hispanic and African-American children and adolescents but also includes alternate forms for Anglos and Asian-Americans. The brightly colored pictures present conflict situations. The scoring system includes achievement motivation, affective functions, aggression, anxiety/depression, cognitive functions, and delay of gratification, interpersonal relations, moral judgment, reality testing, self-concept, and sexual identity. This low-inference scoring system and the available standardization data make the TEMAS a unique projective test for certain multicultural populations in the United States.

Emic Tests Developed for Particular Populations

There are only a small number of tests developed exclusively for single cultural/racial populations in the United States with the exception of blacks. For this population, a two-volume handbook, edited by Jones (1996), describes more than 100 instruments, including moderators for standard tests and approaches to the measurement of worldview, physiology-neuropsychology, spirituality, acculturation, life experiences, values, racial identity, stress, racism, coping, service delivery, and others exclusively for black populations. The instruments include 13 measures designed for children and 6 for adolescents. The tests for racial and cultural identity have competent psychometric histories and should be routinely used with black assessees in the United States at the present time. However, to my knowledge, few of these tests are widely used in assessment practice.

For other cultural groups in the United States, there are few available measures. The most notable example is the Hispanic Stress Inventory (HSI) (Cervantes, Padilla, & Salgado de Snyder, 1988, in press), which contains a set of psychosocial stress items tapping six life domains including family, marital, economic, occupational, discrimination, and acculturation. Although developed primarily for adults, the HSI can be used with adolescents because life stress inventories provide relevant data concerning problems. These may be used for an understanding of a client's cultural identity and for the development of cultural formulations if these are needed for diagnostic purposes.

RECOMMENDATIONS FOR MULTICULTURAL ASSESSMENT IN THE UNITED STATES

Multicultural assessment in the United States is not practiced with cultural competence by a majority of Anglo-American and other assessors. In many states the training is piecemeal and available largely through post-doctoral workshops and continuing education courses or workshops which psychologists are asked to take in order to maintain their licensure. As reported in national surveys, most professional psychologists do not feel sufficiently prepared for practice with multicultural populations (Allison et al., 1994, 1996). As a consequence, the quality of assessment services available to these populations is not only insufficient but the poor services also entail misdiagnoses and irrelevant treatment planning, and they ultimately contribute to an underutilization of mental health services. For instance, assessment services for Hispanics in Minnesota—a state with a better than average professional education system and relatively widely available psychological services—are not only inadequate and relatively unavailable, but are often damaging to clients (Carbonell, 1998, in press).

This chapter has considered some of the reasons for this continuing dilemma and some possible remediations have been discussed. The following section will summarize these recommendations for assessment training and practice in the United States.

Assessment Training

Training for cultural competence in providing services cannot be accomplished without a systematic reorganization of professional training programs to avoid what has been described as cultural malpractice (Hall,

1997). Some models for cultural competence training already exist in community-clinical programs that emphasize interdisciplinary training for services and research with multicultural populations. Assessment training should emphasize cultural competencies within the basic courses by exposure of students to multicultural assessees including Anglos and encourage specialized in-depth learning about at least one non-Anglo cultural group. This exposure has to be modeled and supervised by culturally competent instructors. This is particularly important in the preparation of written reports to describe assessees from ostensibly "normal" populations (e.g., college students) as well as multicultural patients in varied clinical settings. Because students should learn competence in these assessment courses, a greater investment of instructor and student time will be required for training. The course objective should be to demonstrate competence in report writing by systematic comparisons of student reports with reports from the same data sets interpreted by culturally competent assessors (Dana, 1998e). This competence pertains to personality description and preparation of cultural formulations for DSM-IV diagnosis. In this process students need immersion in at least one non-Anglo culture that should include an examination of that culture from a variety of academic perspectives and disciplines. During 1998-1999, a two semester assessment course to achieve this objective will be taught at the University of La Verne in California to provide a new model for assessment training and a demonstration of individual student competence in multicultural assessment.

Assessment Practice

Competent assessment services to multicultural populations have some core ingredients, which include (a) a preferred language and service delivery style; (b) use of moderators prior to selection of tests; (c) use standard tests with knowledge of their deficits for cross-cultural applications as well as potential interim remediations; (d) major practice with low-inference tests coupled with experience using high-inference tests when necessary in a context of procedures for increasing reliability of interpretation; (e) preparations of descriptions of cultural identity for personality assessment and preparations of cultural formulations for increasing the accuracy of DSM-IV diagnoses; and (f) preparation of findings to be shared as feedback or therapeutic assessment with clients and significant others using culturally appropriate contents and formats.

250 DANA

SUGGESTIONS FOR APPLICATIONS OF STANDARD
TESTS OUTSIDE OF THE UNITED STATES

Ideally, tests developed in one country should also possess a demonstrated cross-cultural linguistic, construct, and metric equivalence for other countries. However, for those standard tests used by professional psychologists in assessment practice, these equivalencies have only rarely been demonstrated. As a consequence, it is necessary to examine the status of each test for each component of an equivalent area before using it. In this context it is important to determine if the translation has been done using a systematic set of procedures. Although many tests are translated using the steps recommended by Brislin (1976), some versions of standard tests such as the State-Trait Anxiety Inventory for Children (STAIC) (Spielberger & Sharma, 1976) have been translated into many languages for idiomatic equivalency using different systematic procedures. These translations were intended to capture the nuances of feeling conveyed by items with greater fidelity than seem possible using a more literal "Brislin translation."

Secondly, following an adequate translation, it is necessary to demonstrate that the construct has remained consistent across countries. Using the STAI again as an example, confirmatory factor analysis has discovered no major differences in numbers of factors, factor loadings, and errors for men and women in the United States, but there exist gender differences in factors or in the patterns of factor loadings in some European countries. This failure to replicate findings cross-culturally suggests that mean score differences are confounded and may be attributable either to the use of norms developed in the United States or to construct differences between various countries (or to both). In the Spanish version of the STAIC, use of still another systematic process for translation yielded higher scores for Spanish than for Puerto Rican children. Although these differences were explained on the basis of special sample characteristics, there is also the unexamined possibility of construct differences between the two locales.

Construct differences between nations may be suspected on the basis of consistent score differences between United States norms and samples collected in these countries as has been indicated by the RCS Iberoamerican scores reported earlier in this chapter. Construct differences between national samples and the norms collected in the United States always suggest the need for norms from large and representative samples of the national population. To date, for example, national RCS norms have only been established for Portugal (Pires, 1998, in press) and Finland (Mattlear, 1986). If the national norms substantiate the significant score differences obtained in various samples within countries, careful research examination of these imported test constructs is mandatory. Only in this manner can the construct be understood as either a pseudo-etic or as a genuine etic. If the construct is indeed a pseudo-etic, then a different interpretation will be required within the particular country.

Metric differences in standard tests imported and applied in various countries are of secondary importance for European countries where opportunities for test-taking within educational systems are roughly comparable to the United States. In Latin American countries, whenever educational level is comparable, metric differences will also be of minor concern. However, whenever there are gross differences in socioeconomic levels as well as cultural differences attributable to language, worldview, and immigrant status metric differences have to be examined.

EPILOGUE

Our description of the sources of bias in the assessment of multicultural children and adolescents in the United States included proposals for the adaptation of various objective and projective tests to reduce bias and permit a greater utilization of services. Adaptations encompass test translations, constructs, metrics, and the process of test interpretation. Translations need to employ systematic procedures to ensure linguistic equivalence. The constructs in these tests must be examined for cross-cultural validity using a variety of methodologies. The metrics in these tests have to be appraised for use with different cultural/racial groups and in various national contexts. The process of interpretation can use either low- or high-inference procedures, although low-inference norm-referenced procedures are preferable though they are not available for all projective tests.

Any assessment process using these tests must be conducted using an anticipated and acceptable social etiquette in the assessee's first language to assure task orientation and a subsequent response process sufficient to sustain a responsible interpretation of test findings. It is always necessary to ascertain the client's cultural orientation status to permit for the selection of emic, pseudo-etic, or genuine etic tests. Whenever identity issues are paramount in a referral for assessment, an identity description must be developed to better understand the possible presence of psychopathology and to avoid confounding culture and psychopathology by using a cultural formulation to increase the accuracy of any DSM-IV diagnosis. An identity description should also serve as the basis for the decision to use culture-specific interventions or a combination of standard mainstream interventions and cultural components. This will increase the probability that the particular intervention will be both acceptable and effective.

Unfortunately, assessors do not usually recognize bias and the recommendations to reduce bias contained in this chapter have not been incorporated into assessment practice at a time when the United States is being transformed into a multicultural society. Nonetheless, the professional training of assessors can incorporate training for cultural competence. Cultural/racial groups in the United States now exercise increased control over the conditions of their own lives not only within professional psychology but in the political area as their power is augmented by alliances and common concerns.

BIBLIOGRAPHY

Achenbach, T.M., & Edelbrock, C.S. (1978). The classification of child psychopathology: A review and analysis of empirical methods. *Psychological Bulletin, 83*, 1275-1301.

Allen, J., & French, C. (1996). *Northern Plains Bicultural Immersion Scale-Preliminary manual and scoring instructions (Version 5).* Vermillion, SD: University of South Dakota.

Allison, K.W., Crawford, I., Echemendia, R., Robinson, L., & Kemp, D. (1994). Human diversity and professional competence: Training in clinical and counseling psychology revisited. *American Psychologist, 49*, 792-796.

Allison, K.W., Echemendia, R.J., Crawford, I., & Robinson, W.L. (1996). Predicting cultural competence: Implications for practice and training. *Professional Psychology: Research and Practice, 27*, 386-393.

Archer, R.P., Maruish, M., Imhof, E.A., & Piotrowski, C. (1991). Psychological test usage with adolescent clients: 1990 survey findings. *Professional Psychology: Research and Practice, 22*, 247-252.

Arnold, B.R., Montgomery, G.T., Castaneda, I., & Longoria, R. (1994). Acculturation and performance of Hispanics on selected Halstead-Reitan neuropsychological tests. *Assessment, 1*, 239-248.

Avila-Espada, A. (1998, in press). Objective scoring for the TAT. In R.H. Dana (Ed.), *Handbook of cross-cultural and multicultural personality assessment.* Mahwah, NJ: Erlbaum.

Ben-Porath, Y.S. (1990). Cross-cultural assessment of personality: The case for replicatory factor analysis. In J. N. Butcher & C.D. Spielberger (Eds.), *Advances in personality assessment* (Vol. 8, pp. 27-48). Hillsdale, NJ: Erlbaum.

Brislin, R.W. (Ed.). (1976). *Translation: Applications and research.* New York: Wiley.

Butcher, J.N., Williams, C.L., Graham, C.R., Archer, R., Tellegen, A., & Ben-Porath, Y.S. (1992). *MMPI-A manual for administration, scoring, and interpretation.* Minneapolis, MN: University of Minnesota Press.

Campbell, D.T., & Fiske, D.W. (1959). Convergent and discriminant validation by the multitrait-multimethod matrix. *Psychological Bulletin, 56,* 81-105.

Carbonell, S. (1998, in press). A Minnesota assessment practice with Hispanics. In R.H. Dana (Ed.), *Handbook of cross-cultural and multicultural personality assessment.* Mahwah, NJ: Erlbaum.

Carlson, V., & Westenberg, P.M. (1998). Cross-cultural applications of the WUSCT. In J. Loevinger (Ed.), *Technical foundations for measuring ego development: The Washington University Sentence Completion Test* (pp. 57-79). Mahwah, NJ: Erlbaum.

Carson, R.C. (1969). *Interaction concepts of personality.* Chicago, IL: Aldine.

Castillo, R.J. (1997). *Culture and mental illness: A client-centered approach.* Pacific Grove, CA: Brooks/Cole.

Cervantes, R.C., Padilla, A. M., & Salgado de Snyder, N.S. (1998, in press). Assessment of life events: The Hispanic Stress Inventory and other emic measures. In R.H. Dana (Ed.), *Handbook of cross-cultural and multicultural personality assessment.* Mahwah, NJ: Erlbaum.

Charles, K. (1988), *Culture-specific MMPI norms for a sample of Northern Ontarion Indians.* Unpublished master's thesis, Lakehead University, Thunder Bay, Ontario, Canada.

Costantino, G., & Malgady, R.G. (1996). Development of TEMAS, a multicultural thematic apperception test: Psychometric properties and clinical utility. In G.R. Sodowsky & J.C. Impara (Eds.), *Multicultural assessment in counseling and clinical psychology* (pp. 85-136). Lincoln, NE: Buros Institute of Mental Measurements, University of Nebraska-Lincoln.

Costantino, G., Malgady, R.G., & Rogler, L.H. (1988). *TEMAS (Tell-Me-A-Story) manual.* Los Angeles, CA: Western Psychological Services.

Cuéllar, I., Arnold, B., & Maldonado, R. (1995). Acculturation Rating Scale for Mexican Americans-II: A revision of the original ARSMA scale. *Hispanic Journal of Behavioral Sciences, 17,* 275-304.

Cuéllar, I., & González, G. (1998, in press). Cultural identity description and cultural formulations for Hispanics. In R.H. Dana (Ed.), *Handbook of cross-cultural and multicultural personality assessment.* Mahwah, NJ: Erlbaum.

Dahlstrom, W.G., Lachar, D., & Dahlstrom, L.E. (1986). *MMPI patterns of American minorities.* Minneapolis, MN: University of Minnesota Press.

Dana, R.H. (1966). Eisgesis and assessment. *Journal of Projective Techniques and Personality Assessment, 30,* 215-222.

Dana, R.H. (1993). *Multicultural assessment perspectives for professional psychology.* Boston, MA: Allyn & Bacon.

Dana, R.H. (1997). Multicultural assessment and cultural identity: An assessment-intervention model. *World Psychology, 3*(1-2), 121-142.

Dana, R.H. (1998a). Cultural identity assessment of culturally diverse groups: 1997. *Journal of Personality Assessment, 70,* 1-16.

Dana, R.H. (1998b). Personality and the cultural self: Emic and etic contexts as learning resources. In L.E. Handler & M. Hilsenroth (Eds.), *Teaching and learning personality assessment* (pp. 325-346). Mahwah, NJ: Erlbaum.

Dana, R.H. (1998c). Multicultural assessment of personality and psychopathology in the United States: Still art, not yet science, and controversial. *European Journal of Personality Assessment, 14,* 62-70.

Dana, R.H. (1998d). *Understanding cultural identity in intervention and assessment.* Thousand Oaks, CA: Sage.

Dana, R.H. (1998e). Projective assessment of Latinos in the United States: Current realities, problems, and prospects. *Cultural Diversity and Mental Health, 4*(3), 1-20.

Dauphinais, P., & King, J. (1992). Psychological assessment with American Indian children. *Applied and Preventive Psychology, 1,* 97-110.

Díaz-Geurrero, R., & Díaz-Loving, R. (1990). Interpretation in cross-cultural personality assessment. In C.R. Reynolds & R.W. Kamphaus (Eds.), *Handbook of psychological and educational assessment of children: Personality, behavior, and context* (pp. 491-522). New York: Guilford.

Doi, T. (1971). *The anatomy of dependence.* Tokyo: Kodansha International.

Draguns, J.G. (1984). Assessing mental health and disorder across cultures. In P. Pedersen, N. Sartorius, & A.J. Marsella (Eds.), *Mental health services: The cross-cultural context* (pp. 31-57). Beverly Hills, CA: Sage.

Ephraim, D. (1998, in press). Culturally relevant research and practice with the Rorschach Comprehensive System. In R.H. Dana (Ed.), *Handbook of cross-cultural and multicultural personality assessment.* Mahwah, NJ: Erlbaum.

Etzioni, A. (1968). *The active society.* New York: Free Press.

Exner, J.E., & Weiner, I.B. (1995). *The Rorschach: A comprehensive system, Vol. 3* (2nd ed.). New York: Wiley.

Eysenck, H.J., & Eysenck, S.B.G. (1975). *Manual for the Eysenck Personality Questionnaire*. San Diego, CA: Educational and Industrial Testing Service.

Geisinger, K. F. (1994). Cross-cultural normative assessment: Translation and adaptation issues influencing the normative interpretation of assessment instruments. *Psychological Assessment, 6*, 304-312.

Goldman, J., Stein, C.L., & Guerry, S. (1983). *Psychological methods of child assessment*. New York: Brunner/Mazel.

Greene, R.L. (1987). Ethnicity and MMPI performance. *Journal of Consulting and Clinical Psychology, 55*, 497-512.

Hall, C.C.I. (1997). Cultural malpractice. The growing obsolescence of psychology with the changing U.S. population. *American Psychologist, 52*, 642-651.

Hardy, K.V., & Laszloffy, T.A. (1995). The cultural genogram: Key to training culturally competent family therapists. *Journal of Marital and Family Therapy, 21*, 227-237.

Helmes, E., & Reddon, J. R. (1993). A perspective on developments in assessing psychopathology: A critical review of the MMPI and MMPI-2. *Psychological Bulletin, 113*, 453-471.

Holtzman, W.H. (1988). Beyond the Rorschach. *Journal of Personality Assessment, 52*, 578-609.

Holtzman, W.H., Thorpe, J.S., Swartz, J.D., & Herron, E.W. (1961). *Inkblot perception and personality: Holtzman inkblot technique*. Austin, TX: University of Texas Press.

Hsu, F.L.K. (1971). Psychosocial homeostasis and Jen: Conceptual tools for advancing psychological anthropology. *American Anthropologist, 73*, 23-44.

Hui, C.H. (1988). Measurement of individualism-collectivism. *Journal of Research in Personality, 22*, 17-36.

Hy, L.X., & Loevinger, J. (1996). *Measuring ego development* (2nd ed.). Mahwah, NJ: Erlbaum.

Ibrahim, F.A., & Kahn, H. (1987). Assessment of world views. *Psychological Reports, 60*, 163-176.

Irvine, S.H., & Carroll, W.K. (1980). Testing and assessment across cultures: Issues in methodology and assessment. In H.C. Triandis & J. W. Berry (Eds.), *Handbook of cross-cultural psychology: Methodology* (Vol. 2, pp. 181-241). Boston, MA: Allyn & Bacon.

Jones, R.L. (Ed.). (1996). *Handbook of tests and measurements for Black populations* (Vols. 1-2). Hampton, VA: Cobb & Henry.

Kirk, S.A., & Kutchens, H. (1992). *The selling of DSM: The rhetoric of science in psychiatry*. New York: Aldine de Gruyter.

Knoff, H. M. (1986). *The assessment of child and adolescent personality.* New York: Guilford.

Landrine, H., & Klonoff, E.A. (1994). The African American Acculturation Scale: Development, reliability, and validity. *Journal of Black Psychology, 20,* 104-127.

Landrine, H., & Klonoff, E.A. (1996). *African American acculturation: Deconstructing race and reviving culture.* Thousand Oaks, CA: Sage.

Lewis, D.O., Shanok, S.S., Cohen, R., Kligfeld, M., & Frisone, M. (1980). Race bias in the diagnosis and disposition of violent adolescents. *Psychiatry, 137*(10), 1211-1216.

Li-Repac, D. (1980). Cultural influences on perception: A comparison between Caucasian and Chinese-American therapists. *Journal of Cross-Cultural Psychology, 11,* 327-342.

Loevinger, J. (1976). *Ego development.* San Francisco, CA: Jossey-Bass.

Lonner, W.J. (1980). The search for psychological universals. In H.C. Triandis & W.W. Lambert (Eds.), *Handbook of cross-cultural psychology: Perspectives* (Vol. 1, pp. 143-204). Boston, MA: Allyn & Bacon.

Marín, G., Gamba, R.J., & Marín, B.V. (1992). Extreme response style and acquiescence among Hispanics. *Journal of Cross-Cultural Psychology, 23,* 498-509.

Marsella, A.J., & Kameoka, V.A. (1989). Ethnocultural issues in the assessment of psychopathology. In S. Wetzler (Ed.), *Measuring mental illness: Psychiatric assessment for clinicians* (pp. 229-256). Boston, MA: Reidel.

Mattlar, C-E. (1986). Finnish Rorschach responses in cross-cultural context: A normative study. *Jyväskylä Studies in Education, Psychology, and Social Research,* No. 58.

Matsumoto, D., Weissman, M.D., Preston, K., Brown, B.R., & Kupperbusch, C. (1997). Context-specific measurement of individualism-collectivism on the individual level: The Individualism-Collectivism Interpersonal Assessment Inventory. *Journal of Cross-Cultural Psychology, 28,* 743-767.

McNeilly, M.D., Anderson, N.B., Robinson, E.L., McManus, C.B., Armstead, C.A., Clark, R., Pieper, C.F., Simons, C.E., & Saulter, T.D. (1996). Convergent, discriminant, and concurrent validity of the Perceived Racism Scale: A multidimensional assessment of the experience of racism among African Americans. In R.L. Jones (Ed.), *Handbook of tests and measurements for Black populations* (Vol. 2, pp. 359-373). Hampton, VA: Cobb & Henry.

Mjoseth, J. (1998). New diagnostic system could benefit psychologists. *Monitor, 29*(2), 29.

Montgomery, G.T., & Orozco, S. (1985). Mexican Americans' performance on the MMPI as a function of level of acculturation. *Journal of Clinical Psychology*, *41*, 203-212.

Murray, H.A. (1938). *Explorations in personality*. Cambridge, MA: Harvard University Press.

Neighbors, H. W., Jackson, J.S., Campbell, L., & Williams, D. (1989). The influence of racial factors in psychiatric diagnosis: A review and suggestions for research. *Community Mental Health Journal*, *25*, 300-311.

Okazaki, S. (1998). Psychological assessment of Asian Americans: Research agenda for cultural competency. *Journal of Personality Assessment*, *70*, 54-70.

Pinkerman, J., Haynes, J. P., & Keiser, T. (1993). Characteristics of psychological practice in juvenile court clinics. *American Journal of Forensic Psychiatry*, *11*(2), 3-12.

Pires, A. (1998, in press). National norms for the Rorschach Comprehensive System in Portugal. In R.H. Dana (Ed.), *Handbook for cross-cultural and multicultural personality assessment*. Mahwah, NJ: Erlbaum.

Ramirez, M., III. (1983). *Psychology of the Americas: Mestizo perspectives on personality and mental health*. New York: Pergamon.

Rosen, B.M., Badn, A.K., & Kramer, M. (1964). Demographic and diagnostic characteristics of the classification of psychiatric clinic outpatients in the U.S.A., 1961. *American Journal of Orthopsychiatry*, *34*, 455-468.

Rossini, E.D., & Moretti, R.J. (1997). Thematic Apperception Test (TAT) interpretation: Practice recommendations from a survey of clinical psychology doctoral programs accredited by the American Psychological Association. *Professional Psychology: Research and Practice*, *28*, 393-398.

Singelis, T.M. (1994). The measurement of independent and interdependent self-construals. *Personality and Social Psychology Bulletin*, *20*, 580-591.

Spielberger, C.D., & Sharma, S. (1976). Cross-cultural measurement of anxiety. In C.D. Spielberger & R. Díaz-Guerrero (Eds.), *Cross-cultural anxiety* (pp. 13-25). Washington, DC: Hemisphere.

Sue, S., & Zane, N. (1987). The role of culture and cultural techniques in psychotherapy. *American Psychologist*, *42*, 37-45.

Suinn, R.M., Rickard-Figueroa, K., Lew, S., & Vigil, S. (1987). The Suinn-Lew Asian Self-Identity Acculturation Scale: An initial report. *Educational and Psychological Measurement*, *47*, 401-407.

258 DANA

Tuma, J.M., & Elbert, J.C. (1990). Critical issues and current practice in personality assessment of children. In C.R. Reynolds & R.W. Kamphaus (Eds.), *Handbook of psychological and educational assessment of children* (pp. 3-28). New York: Guilford.

Vinet, E. (1998, in press). Use of the Rorschach Comprehensive System in Iberoamerica. In R.H. Dana (Ed.), *Handbook of cross-cultural and multicultural personality assessment*. Mahwah, NJ: Erlbaum.

Watkins, D., & Cheung, S. (1993). Culture, gender, and response bias: An analysis of responses to the Self-Description Questionnaire. *Journal of Cross-Cultural Psychology, 26*, 490-504.

Wyatt, G.E., Powell, G.J., & Bass, B.A. (1982). The survey of Afro-American behavior: Its development and use in research. In B.A. Bass, G.E. Wyatt, & G.T. Powell (Eds.), *The Afro-American family: Assessment, treatment, and research issues* (pp. 13-33). New York: Grune & Stratton.

CROSS-CULTURAL METHODOLOGICAL ISSUES IN DEVELOPMENTAL RESEARCH

Esther Halpern
Tel Aviv University, Israel

INTRODUCTION

A recurrent problem in cross-cultural developmental research arises when attempts are made to devise comparable experimental paradigms and test versions to apply to diverse nationalities and cultures, as can be seen in the developmental studies of anxiety and emotions (Bradshaw, 1987; Charlesworth, 1982; Halpern, 1992; Ujii, 1986).

This paper takes a micro-look at some methodological issues which have arisen in the course of carrying out research on developmental anxieties in five cultural contexts: Hebrew-Israeli, Arab-Israeli, English-Canadian, Australian, and Japanese (Halpern, Ellis, & Marmor, 1987; Halpern & O'Neill, 1989; Halpern, Shirai, Ohtake, & Kuriyama, 1992).

As the research using the Pictorial Experimental Paradigm (PEP) was primarily responsible for bringing many of this paper's issues into focus, this instrument will be briefly described. Subsequently, the cross-culturally "friendly" PEP will be applied (Halpern, 1990).

A BRIEF DESCRIPTION OF THE PEP

The PEP as a Cross-cultural Instrument

The PEP, based on Spielberger's STAIC (Spielberger, Edwards, Lushene, Montuori, & Platzek, 1973), is a multifaceted measuring operation of separation and death anxiety (Halpern, 1990; Hagtvet & Halpern, 1992). In modifying the purely verbal inventories of the STAIC, the PEP adds pictorial materials to the stimulus situation in assessing the anxiety related to death and separation. This allows for the evaluation of the development of anxieties with the same tool over a wide age range (Halpern, Ellis, & Simon, 1990), an important methodological issue in developmental studies (Sugarman, 1987).

The PEP posed only minimal problems in adapting it for use across language and national groups. It does not involve written materials for the child to read in either the instructions which are given verbally, nor in the child's performance, where pointing to pictorial materials is the expected response. Exact word-by-word translation is required only for six words describing positive and negative moods. In the first series of cross-national studies no specific problems were found when these six words were translated from

Part of this research was made possible by a Japan Foundation Fellowship awarded to Esther Halpern, Ph.D.

Hebrew into the closely related language, Arabic (Halpern et al., 1987) nor when using the original STAIC mood adjectives (Spielberger et al., 1973) with Australian-English and Canadian-English children (Halpern & O'Neill, 1989).

Pictorial materials, on which the PEP relies, have been found to be facilitators in cross-cultural studies. Pictures are reported to appeal to a great variety of national groups of all ages. The graphic representations of the child-like PEP cartoon drawings, have only a few specific ethnic characteristics which did not appear to be salient in previous studies (Halpern, 1990; Halpern et al., 1987).

The Pictorially Assisted Separation Narratives

In the PEP-s_1, the brief separation situation is mitigated by adult companionship. It portrays a child (M or F), with a barely visible face, sitting up in bed and waving goodbye to smiling parents in the doorway. Next to the child stands a baby-sitter, also labeled as "minder" or "relative," depending on the subject's sociocultural environment. The narrative emphasizes that during the parent's brief outing, the child is left in adult company.

In the PEP-s_2 the separation situation is unmitigated by adult companionship. It portrays a child (M or F) with a barely visible face, standing in front of the door of a house waving goodbye to smiling parents at the end of a driveway. The narrative emphasizes that the child remains "all alone" at home during the parental outing.

Mood Adjectives

Six mood adjectives describe the feelings of the child depicted in the separation scenes of the PEP-s (s_1 and s_2). The three positive and the three negative moods are counterbalanced; they are presented in an alternate sequence in the fixed order: "pleased, afraid, good, upset, happy, worried." Their intensity is rated by means of the pictorial intensity scale.

Pictorial Intensity Scale

Seven schematic, pastel-colored faces (M or F) ranging in expression from extremely positive, (a broad smile), to extremely negative, (a deep frown), define the intensity of each of the six moods. Pointing to one of these seven schematic faces, the child's response indicates "how pleased ... afraid...etc." the child in the picture is perceived to feel in response to s_1 or s_2, the two separation situations. An increasingly negative face selection operationally defines an increasingly intense level of anxiety. The order of the continuum from smile to frown is alternated with frown to smile, to avoid response set.

Schematic faces were used as early as the 1950s to measure affect. Kunin (1955) found that the pictorial representations yielded more accurate accounts of feelings than verbal reports, when adults' attitudes were measured in conflicting contexts. This method continues to be used in research on emotions in children. Pictorial materials bypass a direct reliance on the child's abilities to verbalize, especially since the recognition of affects through facial expressions emerges earlier than the ability to use verbal labels (Izard, 1982). Facial expressions emerge with invariant regularity in different cultures and are thought to be a universal phenomenon associated with the signaling of emotions (Borke, 1973; Bowlby, 1969; Charlsworth, 1982; Izard, 1971). Developmental studies have found that the curvature of the mouth is one of the salient facial features to convey affect (De Soete & De Corte, 1985). In this context it becomes relevant that the mouth curvature of the schematic face is used in the PEP as the feature indicating such changes. Against this background of developmental studies, the PEP was further assumed to be an appropriate instrument for cross-cultural research.

The PEP's Dimensions

A dimensional analysis specified a componential distinction between the two separation conditions, PEP-s_1 and PEP-s_2 (Hagtvet & Halpern, 1992). The data from developmental studies also showed that even the youngest age group, 3- to 4-year-olds, use comparable variations in intensity scores to the older age groups, as verified by nonsignificant differences in appropriate analyses of variance (Halpern et al., 1990). This indicates that younger age groups do not give random responses to the pictorial derivations of the intensity measures. The process of selecting the six adjectives whose intensity is rated, relied on the high reliability of the standardized Hebrew STAIC words for 5-year-olds (Levkowitch, 1978), the length of the desired list, the 3-year-olds' familiarity with the words as tested in pretrials, and teachers' assessment of their common use even by the youngest age group (Halpern & Palic, 1984). A Cronbach's alpha reliability coefficient of .899 was obtained for s_1 and of .890 for s_2. The item-total correlations for s_1, with a range of .63 to .80 and for s_2, with a range of .66 to .79 are comparable (Halpern, 1990).

EXAMINING ASSUMPTIONS IN CROSS-CULTURAL RESEARCH

A micro-oriented look at the research process encountered when using the PEP highlights some methodological problems in terms of implicit assumptions made in cross-cultural studies. These include: Assumptions of the "cooperative" vs. "collaborative" working relations established at the onset of research projects; assumptions about "cultural distance" between groups studied;

assumptions about the validity of translated verbal materials posing the question of "lexical identity" vs. "psycholinguistic equivalence;" and assumptions about the validity of "culture-free" material and procedures in assessing "experienced," "expressed," and "reported" affect in cultural context.

"COOPERATIVE VS. COLLABORATIVE" WORKING RELATIONS

The type of working relation that develops between an "outsider," a "guest" researcher, and the "host" partners varies in terms of expectations and input into cross-cultural projects. At best such a relationship is "cooperative." The "ready tool," which had been devised exclusively in the "guest's" cultural context, is presented either to the "host" research partners or directly to the subjects who "cooperate" in the endeavor. Such a process of "cooperation" is usually a one-way street, with a one-way flow of information. This may be illustrated in the case of the initial two cross-national investigations employing the PEP. These included an Israeli-Arab-language PEP study carried out with the help of a resident of a "host" Druse village (Halpern et al., 1987) and an English PEP study conducted in Australia, where the "guest" investigator dealt directly with the subjects that the "host" partner had provided (Halpern & O'Neill, 1989). The "cooperation" had been excellent; the rigors of controls and comparable experimental conditions had been thoroughly explained by the "guest" and jealously guarded by the "hosts," and the purpose and the usefulness of this cross-cultural project had been accepted wholeheartedly. The study, which had been exclusively initiated by the "guest," was never questioned by the "host," since neither had any implicit or explicit expectations for giving or receiving feedback.

The resulting one-way flow of information in the "cooperative" working relationship gains additional meaning in cross-cultural research. It reinforces the importing of tools from dominant cultures, an issue of uppermost concern when the internationalization of psychology is considered (Gergen, Gulerce, Lock, & Misra, 1996). These research operations are usually developed and legitimized in the "guest's" cultural context and left unchallenged by the "host" research partners in the "cooperative" working pattern.

"Cooperative" relationships may be contrasted with "collaborative" relationships in cross-cultural studies. Such a pattern was implicit from the onset of the PEP project in Japan (Halpern et al., 1992). Working "collaboratively" on the study was initiated to some extent by the "host" Japanese research team. It included a challenging and problem-solving approach to difficulties encountered, a two-way flow of information, and modifications in the research methods used. This benefited the methodology of the PEP and lead to revisions in all future PEP studies. Many of the questions raised and the attempts at their solution are facilitated in such a "collaborative" framework, but they rarely arise in a "cooperative" framework of cross-cultural research. A pertinent example involves the use of the pictorial intensity scales of the PEP. Here, children are asked to express strong dislikes; that is, negative feelings about "disliked" objects or activities, in an attempt to illustrate the use of the scale in rating the intensity of mood adjectives. Since the "host" "collaborating" team pointed out that very young Japanese children may not have behavioral expressions or linguistic labels for negative affects, it became clear to the "guest" investigator that one major operation of the PEP presented difficulties in this context: Japanese parents and educators rarely use negative labels. What had been assumed to be a minimal cross-cultural test problem for the PEP—the use of the specific six mood adjectives turned out to be a source of great difficulties in this particular culture.

An important aspect of the study could have been easily overlooked, were it not for the "collaborative" nature of the working relation established. The "collaborative" team approach made it possible for the "host" researchers to challenge the "outsider's" assumptions. The trusting relationship within this context allowed not only for the raising of methodological questions, but it also led to attempts at solutions The resulting culturally congruent research operations withstood the tests of the pilot studies and the final data collection procedures In this context, "host" and "guest" researchers traveled a long road of rapprochement to reach such a goal. The "collaborative" working pattern based on a two-way exchange of ideas and a joint problem-solving approach improved the cross-cultural methodology in this and later studies.

Some methodological problems had not come up in previous PEP studies across national groups because certain assumptions had been made regarding their similarities and differences. This brings up the issue of cultural distance.

CULTURAL DISTANCE BETWEEN GROUPS STUDIED

Generally one uses one's own culture as a point of reference when encountering a new milieu. Dichotomous comparisons are then made in terms of obvious similarities and differences. The question of the "amount" of such differences is frequently ignored. In the present case, since our research was based on a search for "universals" in the development of separation anxieties, the important aspect of cultural distance had been ignored. There had been the assumption that the PEP could span the differences among all national groups, given that the samples previously compared had been culturally close. Thus, in the Arab-Israeli study (Halpern et al., 1987), the children were actually culturally close to the Israeli Hebrew-speaking children on which the PEP had originally been standardized (Halpern et al., 1990). Similarly, in the Australian study (Halpern & O'Neill, 1989), the English-language PEP was used. Derived

264 CROSS-CULTURAL METHODOLOGICLAL ISSUES

originally from the American-English STAIC, it had been standardized on a national group that can be considered culturally close to the Australian one. The unanticipated methodological problems that arose with the PEP in Japan can now be viewed in the light of cultural distance: They became salient because the comparison was now made with a culturally distant national group, Japan. The PEP, though previously found adequate, included few assumptions to account satisfactorily for "cultural distance."

LEXICAL IDENTITY VS. PSYCHOLINGUISTIC EQUIVALENCE

In previous studies, the six PEP mood adjectives were translated from English into Hebrew, Hebrew into Arabic, and American English into Australian English. This basically involved the "lexical identity" of words with only some cultural variations in usage: such as "upset" for "disturbed" (Halpern et al., 1987; Halpern & O'Neill, 1989). The validity of the translation was easily proved in these language groups. The first hint that the psycholinguistic characteristics of a language were relevant even for a mere six disparate words, came from Hagtvet's pilot study which proved problematic with respect to the translations into Norwegian. Norwegian has its linguistic roots in a variety of Scandinavian languages; as a result adults use a different form and vocabulary than do children.

The complex Japanese psycholinguistic system presented similar problems affecting the translation of the PEP mood adjectives. A Japanese version of the STAIC for school-age youngsters (Soga, 1983) led to the assumption that one could extrapolate the six translated words for use with the PEP. However, as the "host"-collaborating research team pointed out, different linguistic structures are used by very young Japanese children when compared to older ones whose language increasingly takes on the adult's more formal structure. Hence, "lexical" translations were not valid for the preschool sample of the project. This problem was further compounded in the Japanese context, since very young children are rarely encouraged to use negative labels. The solution arrived at by the team was to combine direct lexical translation with "psycholinguistically equivalent" words/expressions especially for the negative mood adjectives. Their effectiveness in conveying the meaning of the original PEP was tested with each child who had to show the correct application of the word to a concrete situation according to criteria for which 100% agreement was reached among the four research team members.

"EXPERIENCED," "EXPRESSED," AND "REPORTED" AFFECTS
IN CULTURAL CONTEXT

Developmental research in the affective sphere has been faced with methodological issues when trying to assess "experienced," "expressed," and "reported" anxiety (Halpern, Ellis, & Simon, 1989). This has been noted for sex-role determined differences when reporting anxiety, which among adolescents appears to reflect social compliance with cultural norms. It can be seen in the ratings of the intensity of such mood adjectives as "afraid" and "worried" (Halpern, Ellis, & Simon, 1989), even when such self-referent reports about one's feelings were bypassed. Our study presented the methodological challenge of validly assessing "experienced," "expressed," and "reported" affects, as further compounded by the Japanese cultural context.

Pilot-testing revealed problems with the expression and experience of the full range of intensities of both negative and positive moods. Hints of such difficulties appeared during the training sessions in the use of the seven-point pictorial intensity rating scale. Responses such as "like/dislike" are used as a prototype in rating the intensity of preferences for foods, objects, toys. However, the items chosen for this purpose had to be brought within this group's cultural norms. Etiquette prescribes neutral reactions to most foods. A careful search was therefore carried out for items which kids could allow themselves to label as "liked/disliked." Certain insects, such as cockroaches were easily rated by all as extremely "disliked." Most other "liked" and "disliked" items revealed sex differences in 4- to 6-year-olds, in contrast with previous cross-national studies. Girls allowed themselves to rate a TV character-monster and a "rat" as extremely "disliked;" in contrast, a very blond "Barbie doll" and/or a "Snoopy dog" invariably brought a delighted smile to girls' faces and a high-intensity "like" rating. Boys 4- to 6-years-old accepted "Snoopy" only occasionally as the "liked" object. In contrast to the girls, they rated the TV monster with a high "like" intensity. The final solution decided upon was to carry out training at a more impersonal level: by tapping into the highly-valued esthetic appreciation of colors. Japanese children allowed themselves such esthetic judgments when giving ratings of "like/dislike" to pastel colors, without a fear of offending anyone or transgressing etiquette. They demonstrated a grasp of the use of the entire range of intensities of the Pictorial Rating Scale, once the procedure took into account the cultural context and thus allowed the expression and report of the nuances of "like/dislike."

Further difficulties arose when the intensity ratings referred to something more personal than the "like/dislike" prototype introduced during the training sessions. Children reverted to "reporting" low intensities when describing the affects associated with the pictorially aided separation narratives. The experience of a full affective range when separation occurs was shunned by all the subjects in the pilot study, although it is found at this age in most other cultures.

The suspicion arose once again that the Japanese translation of the six mood words was beyond the young child's comprehension. Therefore, an additional step was introduced into the procedure: defining the six words prior to administering the PEP. During this process the previously "inner-calm" children became animated as they gave vivid, affectively loaded examples to illustrate the meaning of the mood adjectives. Once preceded by the definitions of affectively loaded words, the Japanese intensity ratings now showed comparable variations and ranges to those previously found among other national groups.

Within the Japanese cultural context, the process of defining mood adjectives prior to rating the separation situations, facilitated the experiencing of a wide range of positive and negative affects. Implicitly, the change in the experimental procedure may also have given the children the permission and the venue with which to express and report the experienced feelings.

The assumptions made by researchers which guide expectations about behaviors to be found in cross-cultural research are sometimes tinged by generalizations resembling stereotypes. In the case of the Japanese project, the "guest" investigator could have accepted the generalization of "the calm Oriental child," in keeping with some theoretically-derived assumptions of low separation anxiety. However, previous studies with the PEP had underlined certain methodological issues with respect to assessing "experienced," "expressed," and "reported" affects. Being cognizant of the need to adapt experimental procedures to cultural context made it possible for the "guest" researcher to deal with this methodological issue to some extent, rather than to accept at face value the stereotype of low "experienced" intensities of affect as an explanation suggested by the findings of the pilot study. Face validity, however, cannot be ignored; it is another aspect of the PEP that needed to be modified in order for the PEP to fit better into the cultural context.

Even though the PEP's pictorial aides to the separation narratives include child-like cartoon drawings, some features of the personages depicted led to questions about their "culture-free" characteristics and their applicability to the Japanese context. The hair color and some facial expressions of the pictorial representations of the human figures were therefore changed to include Oriental features. This was found satisfactory by the "host" collaborators of the project. A minority viewpoint held by the "guest" investigator proposes that, to a certain extent, these cosmetic changes deal primarily with the "face validity" of the PEP as a cross-culturally friendly instrument. The original PEP had been devised and used with Israeli children, few of whom are blonde and blue-eyed as shown in the pictorial materials. However, raising the face validity of the test materials used in cross-cultural studies probably greatly reduces the experienced "cultural distance" for both "host" experimenters and their subjects, and may thus enhance the validity of the tool.

SUMMARY AND DISCUSSION

An attempt has been made to focus on a few methodological issues in cross-cultural developmental studies. These were highlighted and illustrated by the research process in various national groups which focused on the use of the Pictorial Experimental Paradigm, the PEP. A micro-look at the cross-cultural research problems emphasized the importance of establishing ground rules for working relationships with various national research partners, from the onset of the project. "Collaborative" patterns of interaction were found to be optimal for identifying and solving methodological problems.

The Japanese study brought into focus the issue of the cultural distance between the groups that were compared in our cross-cultural research. Attempts at adapting the PEP to the Japanese cultural context also led to cosmetic changes in its pictorial representations. Subsequently, the necessity of using both lexical identity and its psycholinguistic equivalence in translating the minimal number of words involved in the assessment instrument became salient for this language group. Finally, in order to validly assess "experienced," "expressed," and "reported" affects, the cross cultural research conditions led to a change in the sequence of the steps involved in the PEP administration, including a structured and extended training on how to use the pictorial intensity rating scale. Not only did these latter revisions solve the difficulties encountered in the Japanese cultural context, but they also improved the test's cross-cultural applicability and its effectiveness as an instrument. The obtained test reliabilities in the various national groups, which are depicted in Table 1, illustrate this.

Table 1
Cronbach Alpha for Japanese, Israeli, and Australian
4- to 6-year-old Children on PEP-S_1 and PEP-S_2

National Group	PEP-s_1	PEP-s_2
Japanese original sample (N=41)	.70	.73
Japanese total sample (N=75)	.69	.75
Israeli sample (N=16)	.61	.71
Australian sample (N=20)	.50	.44

Cronbach alpha reliability coefficients for the PEP-s_1 and the PEP-s_2 were calculated using the smaller sample (N=41) which was tested while the "guest" researcher observed the procedure. These were then compared to the entire sample (N=75), which included data collected by the Japanese "host" team without the foreign observer. As can be seen in Table 1, the coefficients are almost identical for the two samples across the two separation conditions. This suggests that the Japanese version of the PEP can now be used as an indigenous instrument for the evaluation of developmental anxieties.

As can be further observed, the Cronbach alpha coefficients of the Japanese study, ranging from .67 to .77, compare favorably with those obtained for this young age range with the Israeli sample, for which the PEP was originally devised. An interesting point for discussion are the considerably lower alpha coefficients obtained for the first cross-cultural adaptation of the PEP in Australia. The Japanese version of the now rigidly explicit training procedure for the pictorial intensity scale is undoubtedly responsible for the higher reliability coefficients obtained in that project. The use of crayons—an important aid for those in the younger age range—in rating the most "liked" to most "disliked" color, further clarified at a cognitive level the distinctiveness of the tested range of intensities.

As a concluding remark, a final assumption about cross-cultural research may now be added: Adapting original tests/experiments to other cultures, in cross-cultural research, is (or should be) a "two-way street." The PEP's Israeli-Hebrew- and English-language versions have been revised as a result of research with the various national groups. Taking into account cross-cultural methodological problems, as was the case in the Japanese project, led to revisions in the experimental operations and to lengthened and more structured training in the use of the pictorial rating scale. This process, in turn, led to improved reliabilities for the younger age groups. Upon returning home we noted a further benefit of the bi-directionality of the collaborative study: the procedural changes made it easier to train experimenters in the use of the Pictorial Experimental Paradigm.

BIBLIOGRAPHY

Borke, M. (1973). Development of empathy in Chinese and American children between 3 and 6. *Developmental Psychology*, *9*, 102-108.

Bowlby, J. (1969). *Attachment and loss: Attachment.* Vol. 1. London: Hogarth Press.

Bradshaw, D.L. (1987). Contributions of research on Japanese infants and mothers in the study of attachment: Annual Report (1985-1986). *Research and Clinical Center for Child Development, Faculty of Education*, Hokkaido University, *9*, 1-10.

Charlesworth, W.R. (1982). An ethological approach to research on facial expressions. In C. Izard (Ed.), *Measuring emotions in infants and children.*

Cambridge, MA: Cambridge University Press.

DeSoete, G., & DeCorte, W. (1985). On the perceptual salience of features of Chernoff faces for representing multivariate data. *Applied Psychological Measurement, 9,* 275-280.

Gergen, J.J., Gulerce, A., Lock, A., & Misra, G. (1996). Psychological science in cultural context. *American Psychologist, 51,* 486-503.

Glasberg, B., & Aboud, F. (1982). Keeping one's distance from sadness: Children's self reports of emotional experience. *Developmental Psychology, 18,* 287-293.

Hagtvet, K.A., & Halpern, E. (1992). A dimensional analysis of a pictorial experimental paradigm measuring children's developmental anxieties. In K.A. Hagtvet & T.B. Johnson (Eds.), *Test anxiety research* (Vol. 7, pp. 175-192). Lisse, The Netherlands: Swets & Zeitlinger.

Halpern, E. (1990). A pictorial experimental paradigm in the assessment of developmental anxieties. In P.J.D. Drenth, J.A. Sergeant, & R.J. Takens (Eds.), *European perspectives in psychology* (Vol. 2, pp. 285-296). New York: Wiley.

Halpern, E., & Palic, L. (1984). Developmental changes in death anxiety in childhood. *Journal of Applied Developmental Psychology, 5,* 163-167.

Halpern, E., Ellis, M., & Simon, F. (1989). Inferred social variables in anxiety assessment: Methodological issues. In R. Schwartzer, H. van der Ploeg, & C.D. Spielberger (Eds.), *Test anxiety research* (Vol. 6, pp. 155-166). Lisse, The Netherlands: Swets & Zeitlinger.

Halpern, E., Ellis, S., & Simon, F. (1990). Developmental changes in separation anxiety in childhood. *Anxiety Research: An International Journal, 2,* 133-146.

Halpern, E., Ellis, S., & Marmor, Y. (1987-August). *Separation and death anxiety in two Israeli subcultures.* Paper presented at the 45th annual meeting of the International Council of Psychologists, New York, U.S.A.

Halpern, E., & O'Neill, M. (1989-June). *Preliminary findings of separation anxiety in Australian day-care children.* Paper presented at the 47th annual meeting of the International Council of Psychologists, Halifax, Canada.

Halpern, E. (1992-July). *Something old, something new, on methodological considerations of cross-cultural research.* Paper presented at the 50th annual meeting of the International Council of Psychologists, Amsterdam, The Netherlands.

Halpern, E., Shirai, T., Ohtake, N., & Kuriyama, Y. (1992-July). *Cross-cultural studies with pictorial materials assessing children's anxieties: The Japanese experience.* Paper presented at the 50th annual meeting of the International Council of Psychologists, Amsterdam, The Netherlands.

Izard, C.E. (1971). *The face of emotion.* New York: Appelton-Century-Crofts.

Izard, C.E. (Ed.). (1982). *Measuring emotions in infants and children.*

Cambridge, MA: Cambridge University Press.

Kunin, T. (1955). The construction of a new type of attitude measure. *Personnel Psychology*, *8*, 65-78.

Levkovitch, V. (1978). *An empirical seminar paper: Adapting the STAIC for young children*. Unpublished manuscript, Psychology Department, Tel Aviv University (in Hebrew).

Soga, S. (1983). A study on the standardization of the Japanese version of the STAIC. *The Japanese Journal of Psychology*, *54*, 215-221.

Spielberger, C.D., Edwards, C.F., Lushene, R.E., Montuori, K., & Platzek, D. (1973). *Preliminary test manual for the State-Trait Anxiety Inventory for Children*. Palo Alto, CA: Consulting Psychologists Press.

Sugerman, S. (1987). The priority of description in developmental psychology. *International Journal of Behavioral Development*, *10*, 391-414.

Ujiie, T. (1986). Is the strange situation too strange for Japanese infants? *Annual Report 1984-1985: Research and Clinical Center for Child Development, Faculty of Education, Hokkaido University*, *8*, 23-29.

SECTION V: CHILDREN AND PARENTS

Numerous variables contribute to the complex relationships among family, culture, and socialization, including cultural context; social beliefs and values; and individual views of children and their place in society, family structure, and parenting styles. However, cross-cultural research on human development shows the significant role that culture plays in socialization at all levels, from birth through the final years of the life span.

Socialization refers to the total set of experiences in which children participate and that allow them to become productive members of their culture. The socialization process is supported by individuals such as parents, grandparents, older siblings, teachers, religious mentors, and so forth. Culture also affects the way in which children are socialized by providing those social settings with which members are expected to become familiar. Children actively explore the world in which they find themselves, and their behaviors partially shape the behaviors of adults and peers who in turn structure the socializing experiences in which parents and children continuously interact.

In her broad review chapter titled *Cross-cultural Study of Infants and Toddlers*, Alice Sterling Honig focuses on the study of infants and toddlers as a catalyst for positive social change. After a historical overview of cross-cultural research on patterns of newborns and on infant care, she examines the problem of hidden variables that co-vary within certain cultures and concludes that the developmental advancement of infants is not exclusively due to culture. Even among newborns cross-cultural differences are witnessed. The author suggests that future cross-cultural developmental research needs to become "more sensitive to the problem of goodness of fit" between care-giving practices, infant temperament, and the goals of the culture in relation to the goals of optimal child development. For instance, varying parental child-rearing practices regarding infants may not have the same long-term effects in developing societies as in more stable societies. Honig goes on to review a considerable amount of cross-cultural research on infants and toddlers from that perspective.

Jaipaul L. Roopnarine, Mellisa A. Clawson, Sylvia Benetti, and Tracey Y. Lewis in *Family Structure, Parent-Child Socialization, and Involvement among Caribbean Families* discuss the parent-child relationships in Caribbean ethnic groups in terms of the sociohistorical context of present-day patterns of socialization and in relation to the diverse beliefs, goals, and practices that guide the socialization of Caribbean children. They provide a) an overview of family structures and different mating arrangements, b) a discussion of mothers' and fathers' involvement with their children and the possible linkages of this involvement to educational and social outcomes, and c) recommendations for future research and family policies. The authors emphasize that Caribbean families are highly diverse and complex in nature, and that any treatment of parent-child relationships and patterns of socialization has to be viewed within the context of family configurations and beliefs about childrearing. In this context, the male's involvement in the family should be an important focus of future research and policy decisions.

The Chinese-Canadian psychologist Xinyin Chen observes in *Growing Up in a Collectivistic Culture: Socialization and Socioemotional Development in Chinese Children* that research on individual socioemotional adjustment has traditionally been neglected in collectivistic cultures such as China. Nevertheless, the available research shows that Chinese children experience equal, or even higher levels of psychological disturbance when compared with children in more individualistic cultures such as the USA. The author's research examines Chinese collectivistic culture and socialization patterns from a contextual cross-cultural perspective. The focus of this integrative approach is on the understanding and systematic assessment of socioemotional and cognitive development within the Chinese cultural context. Chen's research points to some important differences between Chinese and North American studies. Shy children, for instance, prosper in China's collectivistic society, which emphasizes restraint, whereas they tend to suffer from self-esteem and adjustment problems in the more extroverted American society, which demands self-assertion from its members. This suggests, in line with Honig's chapter, that the fit between children's temperament and personality on one hand, and societal expectations on the other, can contribute in important ways to the overall adjustment of children.

In his paper *Social Values: A Comparison of Chinese and American Children*, George Domino reports the results of two studies which compare children from mainland China with those of the United States. Based on a semi-projective story-completion task with 11-13-year-old children, the results of the first study indicate that the Chinese children emphasized a social orientation, affect, moral-ethical rectitude, and natural forces having a quasi-moral character. In contrast, American children were more likely to stress physical aggression and economic considerations. In the second study, 10-12-year-old children from both countries completed an experimental task assessing their productivity to engage in competitive and individualistic rather than cooperative, group-oriented, or egalitarian modes of behavior. Whereas the American children tended to favor individualistic and competitive strategies in the game the Chinese children were more likely to display egalitarian and group-oriented behavior. Individualistic and competitive responses, however, were by no means absent among the Chinese children. The author's results do not only mirror contrasts between a more collectively oriented society (China) and a more individualistically oriented society (USA), but they also mesh well with the findings reported by Chen in the previous chapter.

Edith M. Grotberg indicates in *The International Resilience Research Project* that there are many similarities but also critical differences in the promotion of resilience in children from various cultures. Resilience is defined by her as the human capacity to face, overcome, and even be strengthened by experiences of adversity. The two major conceptual frameworks for studying resilience include a pathological framework and a developmental/life-span framework.

For Grotberg an emphasis on resilience means that we do not focus on disadvantages as problems to be solved or to require compensation; instead we try to look for the strengths that exist within individuals and their environment in order to build upon such disadvantages. In the past, psychologists have tended to focus mostly on pathological behavior, and they therefore know too little about the nature and promotion of adaptive and prosocial behavior.

Grotberg examines international contributions to the study of resilience-promoting behavior and the role of culture/ethnicity in determining what resilience-enhancing strategies are used by children and their parents as well as culturally mediated and personal changes in resilience-promoting behavior. Data from parents and children from 27 sites in 22 countries around the world are examined. Some cross-cultural similarities among international researchers of resilience include common concerns about how children are able to face, overcome, and even become strengthened by experiences of adversity. In contrast, cultural differences include wide variations in age-related expectations. The cultural differences, however, do not prevent the promotion of resilience. Among the unexpected research results is the finding that socioeconomic status had little impact on the amount and kind of resilience-promoting behavior. Perhaps the more important question to ask is which resilience factors are employed by both parents and children and within which particular cultural contexts.

The articles included in this section examine the adaptive, clinical, and educational outcomes of varying patterns of socialization in a wide variety of cultures. Although cross-cultural psychological studies of parents and children may have different aims, the goal is to understand how socialization occurs in the daily lives of individuals in different families and different cultures. We believe, as do the authors represented in this section, that this goal requires a range of different types of investigation. Many of the socialization experiences in which children participate take place within their culture's formal system. An emphasis on resilience means that we do not focus on disadvantages as a problem to be solved or require compensation; instead we try to look for the strengths that exist within individuals and their environment in order to build upon them. In the past, psychologists have tended to focus mostly on pathological behavior, and they therefore know too little about the nature and promotion of adaptive and prosocial behavior. Many of the essays included in the later Sections VII (*Cognitive-developmental Perspectives*) and VIII (*Applications of Cognitive-Developmental Theory: Promoting Role-taking and Reflection*) contain a related emphasis on the promotion of moral and ego-development although from a different theoretical perspective.

CROSS-CULTURAL STUDY OF INFANTS AND TODDLERS

Alice Sterling Honig
Syracuse University, U.S.A.

THE POWER OF CROSS-CULTURAL RESEARCH ON INFANCY

Cross-cultural researches focusing on young children enrich our insights and enlarge our knowledge base of *milestones and sequences* in child development (Kagitçibasi, 1996). As well, we become aware that when immersed in their own cultures, parents tend to take for granted that the procedures they use to care for their infants are "best practices" and perhaps considered more "moral" than methods used by others. Thus, Erikson (1963) reported that Sioux mothers, who nursed on demand, were appalled by the habits of white women who fed babies on schedules. The Native American mothers considered strict time scheduling for nursing to be cruel punishment of a baby. Yet these same Sioux mothers thumped on the head teething babies who bit the breast, and reported that subsequent strong infant crying would make infants grow to be better warriors. In the USA, infants are commonly put to sleep in a crib in their own rooms, yet Mayan mothers view this practice as "tantamount to child neglect" (Morelli, Rogoff, Oppenheim, & Goldsmith, 1992, p. 608).

Cross-cultural studies of infants and their primary caregivers also help us tease out which behaviors may be culture specific and which may be near-universal functional relationships, such as the relationship between infant malnutrition and physical/psychological growth. Kagan (1977) reported Klein's findings that for peoples living on marginal diets in rural farming villages in underdeveloped countries, there is a consistent relationship between a pregnant mother's caloric intake and her infant's likelihood of mortality as well as her preschool child's verbal ability. Cross-cultural study can be of heuristic help in teasing out subtle behavior patterns which may have a biological basis when they are found in very disparate societies.

Across cultures, across centuries, families have invented lullabies and cradlesongs to soothe babies to sleep (Commins, 1967). Thus, the function of the lullaby the world over is quite similar. Yet some lullabies have gentle words, such as the French "Fais dodo, Colin mon petit frère" (which assures baby that papa and mama are cooking up delicious treats for the little one) in contrast to "Rockabye baby in the tree tops" which ends with baby violently crashing down to doom from the tree! Form and content of an infant care technique may differ, but functions may be similar.

Cross-cultural data can also answer questions of whether infant-rearing patterns show greater *variability within cultures than between cultures*. Indeed, infant experiences may differ far more due to social class status despite the fact that the infants live in the same nation.

Confirmation of greater variability of infant experiences within two small-scale preindustrial African societies (Pygmy Aka foragers and Ngandu farmers) is provided by the observational data of Hewlett, Lamb, Shannon, Leyendecker, and Schölmerich (1998). Aka parents hold their infants, keep them close, feed them quite frequently, and respond promptly to infant distress. In contrast, Ngandu care providers hold babies far less and are more likely to let an infant fuss or cry; yet infants in the two cultural groups have equal nutritional and health status and mothers have similar workloads. The researchers note that cultural ideologies, such as the social unity hypothesis, do not explain these great differences. Indeed, the opposite might be expected: Ngandu conformity and patriarchy "would predict greater proximal behaviors" among them than among the more egalitarian, communal Aka people (Hewlett et al., 1998, p. 660).

Used judiciously, insights from cross-cultural findings in the study of infants and toddlers can be a *catalyst for positive social change.* A case in point arises from historical data on institutional care of infants. Early in this century, cross-cultural researches (along with the Iowa orphanage studies by Skeels, 1966) provided evidence of significant developmental delays and retardation that occurred when infants were institutionalized without enrichment opportunities. Spitz's (1953) observations in South American orphanages documented over a year's time a precipitous decline in intelligence from 3 months of age when the babies were left in the institution. His black and white film *Grief, a Peril in Infancy* remains a classic in its vivid depiction of the autistic self-stimulating behaviors and retarded cognition of infants that were cared for physically, but left unstimulated and uncuddled in cribs. Such researches in other cultures have led to widespread rejection of institutional care for infants in the United States.

Given the stringent ethics laws in the United States regarding implementation of experimental enrichment for some infants but not others in situations of grave disadvantage, cross-cultural research has been instrumental and even vital to revealing the importance of such efforts.

Hunt (1980) vividly demonstrated the improvement in infant development that could be achieved by training untrained care providers in orphanages in Teheran. He varied the kinds of stimulation and personalized care provided to the babies. Sometimes he simply improved the ratio of caregivers to infants from 1:10 down to 1:3. In one experimental group, Wave V, Hunt improved the care ratio and also assigned caregivers to specific infants. The adults learned to label their actions, for example, by saying "ear" (in Farsi) as they washed a baby's ear. Hunt provided special toys and taught the caregivers to encourage Piagetian sensorimotor competencies. He modelled the use of vocal imitations of baby sounds to providers who explained that they did not talk with the infants since the babies were not yet verbal! After intervention, the

Teheran infants in Wave V attained the earliest top scores on each of the Piagetian sensorimotor scales; they looked brighter and more animated, and they were subsequently adopted by families.

Increasing the Range of Variability with Cross-cultural Data

By *extending the range of variation* of variables beyond that found in any one culture, cross-cultural research prevents us from drawing incorrect conclusions about the possible covariation of factors in children's lives. Consider the range of variability in fundamental infant behaviors such as nursing and sleeping.

Nursing. In a sample of 80 Kansas City children, Sears and Wise (1950) consistently found more emotional disturbance the later the infants were weaned. Yet the Kansas City sample had a small range of weaning ages (mostly birth to 7 months). To extend the range of weaning, Whiting and Child (1953) coded the relation between weaning practices and emotional health for children from anthropological files for 75 cultures. Their analyses of childrearing practices in five domains (orality, dependency, aggression, sexual, and anal behavior) examined patterns of early indulgence in infancy and later degree of severity of training (such as toilet training or modesty training).

For the cross cultural samples, the longer the nursing, the more emotionally healthy the children. Those nursed for 2 to 5 1/2 years had a mean score of 3.5 (on a 7-point scale) for emotional health compared with a mean score of 2.8 for children in those societies with a mean age for weaning of under two years. However, there is no discrepancy in these findings, because there is almost no overlap in age of weaning between the USA sample and the other cultures studied (the median age of weaning was 2 1/2 years in the other cultures). The few American mothers ($N = 5$) who nursed for longer than 7 months in the Kansas City sample almost a half-century ago, were poor and poorly educated. In the other cultures, weaning was reported as much easier for older toddlers. In the cross-cultural samples, *only* when weaning was relatively early (13-18 months) was there found any relationship between disturbance and age of weaning babies. We may add that cross-societal studies not only increase the range of a variable under investigation, but also permit examination of variables that are "tied" together (such as age and behavior) in one culture but can be viewed un-entangled when a variety of cultures are examined.

Sleep patterns. "Sleep management [is] one of the earliest culturally determined parent-child interactions" (Gardiner, Mutter, & Kosmitzki, 1998, p. 33). Yet, cross-cultural studies have shown wide variation in sleep patterns among different peoples. For instance, while American babies are encouraged to sleep in their own cribs from birth onward, among the Laotian Hmong, children sleep with their parents or grandparents until they are 6 or 7 years old (Muret-Wagstaff & Moore, 1989, p. 322).   Similarly, Japanese children frequently sleep with a parent until age six or seven. Among Kipsigis farming families in rural Kenya in East Africa, a next-to-youngest child continues to sleep with the mother and siblings after the birth of a younger child. But the child now sleeps at the mother's back rather than at her front, where the new baby is now nursing. This change entails a "fundamental shift in the child's physical and social settings of life" (Harkness & Super, 1995, p. 227).

Faith community participation. In some cultures, infants are taught the rudiments of prayer postures and behaviors in their first year of life. For instance, in Buddhist temples in China, I have observed mothers gently shape a baby's hands and body into the prescribed bowing and prostration postures before the statue of Buddha. In other cultures, teaching and expecting participation in religious practices, such as learning catechism, may be formally begun only after a child has learned the rudiments of literacy and achieved concrete operational reasoning.

TESTING THEORETICAL PROPOSITIONS

Developmental theorists frequently make pronouncements about children's development based on research among different social status groups but still within their own culture—most often an industrialized Western society. Cross-cultural study is admirably suited to determining whether some theoretical postulates and predictions are culture-specific or whether they are more likely to occur among families throughout the world.

Psychoanalysis

The important psychoanalytic precept that sole maternal care is essential for normal infant development has been tested by cross-cultural infancy research. Among the Efe foragers in central Africa, for example, infants are passed from one nurturing person to another and not exclusively cared for by the mother (Winn, Tronick, & Morelli, 1989). A more modern natural "experiment" is currently going on as more and more children, from single-parent and dual-career families, are reared in group- care settings from early infancy (prior to one year) on. In western nations such as France and the United States, debate is lively as to the developmental consequences of this "polymatric mothering" pattern (Caldwell, Hersher, Lipton, & Richmond, 1963). Some developmentalists have found no detrimental social effects for infants reared by several caregivers. Others have documented wide variations in infant-maternal interaction patterns for babies enrolled full-time in crèches in France (Balleyguier, 1988). A possible increase in child aggression and noncompliance among USA infants who have experienced full-time nonparental day care during the first year of life has also been reported (Belsky & Rovine, 1988). Studying preschool interactions with peers and teachers in a middle-class American sample, Park and Honig (1991) found a slight increase in both observed and teacher-rated aggression as well as an increase in teacher-rated abstraction ability for children who had been in full-time nonparental care during the first year of life. Thus, Freudian predictions (which are based on clinical experience obtained in "repressed" Viennese society of the early 20th century) that full-time (more than 30 hours per week) nonmaternal care in early infancy would inevitably result in later personality disturbance has only received weak support from USA day-care studies a half-century later.

Early Piagetian Developmental Stages: Universal or Culture Dependent?

Cross-cultural research has been particularly useful in demonstrating the universality of cognitive stages during child development (Price-Williams, 1980). For instance, the sequence and timing of Piagetian sensorimotor learning in infancy appears quite similar across cultures (Dasen, 1977; Super, 1981). Such learning includes: object permanence, the appearance of separation of means and ends (as when a baby pulls a string to obtain a favored toy at the end of the string), the appearance of an active search for causal mechanisms (as baby tries to turn a Jack-in-the-box knob and succeeds in making the jack pop up). African infants are in advance in the development of object permanence in comparison with Western babies, yet within-culture variations are very large (Dasen & Heron, 1981).

Despite the gradual nature of and continuity in early development, cross-cultural studies indicate that there exist discontinuities in the developmental milestones achieved in the early years. For example, the advances in infant intelligence that Piaget, studying his babies in Geneva, labelled "tertiary circular reactions" represent a truly new level of infant cognitive capacity. The toddler, deliberately varying actions to produce new effects and outcomes, carries out "experiments in order to see" (Piaget, 1963, p. 275). Not only in Geneva, but in many other cultures has this impressive new ability been found among infants between about 18-24 months. Thus, research impelled by the Piagetian paradigm has revealed universalities in the orderliness of development of more mature cognitive capacities throughout infancy. With behavior patterns similar to Cambridge infants, Guatemalan Indian babies living in villages near Lake Atitlan showed a lawful, invariant sequence in developing successful responses to object permanence problems (Kagan, 1977). Kagan also found across both cultures that infants nearing one year of age protest separation from the mother. When she leaves, infants can establish a schema for mother, retrieve a schema for her, and hold it in awareness for a longer period of time, while still vulnerable to uncertainty about what will occur next. He attributes this cross-cultural consistency to central nervous system maturation and to "biochemical events that are essential elements in ontogenesis" (p. 283).

Attachment Theory: Cross-cultural Explorations

Attachment in infancy, conceived of as a behavioral-motivational control system whose set goal is for baby to feel secure, was formulated by British psychoanalyst John Bowlby over 40 years ago and enriched splendidly by the work of Ainsworth (1967) among Ganda infants and by child development specialists in many countries. Slowly, over the first year of life, the infant develops an internalized "working model" of the caregiver. Optimally, babies learn confidence in the availability and sensitive responsiveness of their attachment figures (Bretherton & Waters, 1985; Sroufe, 1997; Waters, Vaughn, Posada, & Kondo-Ikemura, 1995). In the United States, the Strange Situation (Ainsworth, Blehar, Waters, & Wall, 1978), a twenty-minute laboratory procedure consisting of three-minute episodes (mother and infant present; infant with stranger; and infant alone prior to re-entry of mother) has been used to tease out the following four patterns: secure attachment (B) and three different insecure patterns, labelled A, C, and D. *Reunion* behaviors of the infant with mother are crucial for categorizing infant attachment status. The baby's ability to approach and take comfort from the mother during reunion, its ability to use the mother as a secure base when frightened or stressed, as well as its ability to explore competently when mother is available nearby characterize behaviors of the secure (B) baby.

American studies show that about 2/3 of babies are *securely attached* (B). About 20% of the babies are classified as *avoidant* (A babies) during reunions with mother in the Strange Situation, while 10-15% of them are classified as *anxious/ambivalent* (C) infants, who seek reassurance on reunion and yet cannot accept or gain comfort from the mother. They may even push away from her, as if they have no confidence that she can be relied on.

Is secure-base behavior of infants universal? Specifically, is attachment a species-based behavior to be observed across cultures? Each of the attachment classifications has been found in other cultures where the Strange Situation procedure has been carried out (Honig, 1998). However, the distribution across groups varies as a function of culture. Thus, in Israel and in Japan, far fewer A babies but more C babies have been reported, but in North Germany, Grossman and Grossman (1990) discovered a far higher proportion of A babies than had previously been found in the USA. The German mothers expressed a preference in the second half of the first year of infants' lives for more infant independence and self-sufficiency. The Grossmans conclude that across cultures, "Individuals with secure attachment histories pay attention to the full range of external causes for conflicting emotions, and they tolerate contradictory emotions…These developmental consequences appear to be universal. Cultural differences may exist in terms of frequency and difficulty of potentially conflicting challenges imposed" (p. 31).

Examining infant attachment in seven different cultures, Posada, Gao, Wu, Posada, Tascon, Schoelmcrich, Sagi, Kondo-Ikemura, Haaland, and Synnevaag (1995) reported a predominance of secure-base behavior. The researchers suggest that "what has been selected for in the course of human evolution can be better understood in terms of a propensity to organize an attachment behavioral system within the context of child-caregiver interactions" (p. 28). However, the absolute similarity of proportions of different infant attachment classifications in different cultures was low.

When reared on a Kibbutz (a communal agricultural settlement in Israel), two infants cared for by the same *metapelet* (infant caregiver) tended to have the same attachment experience and develop similar bonds to that caregiver (Sagi, van IJzendoorn, Aviezer, Donnell, Koren-Karie, Joels, & Harel, 1995). This finding only held true for those infants who had the same *metapelet* for a year and who returned to sleep with their own families at night, rather than sleep in communal arrangements. Thus, Sagi et al.'s Israeli Kibbutzim data provide a caution that cross-cultural researchers need to consider the *quality* and *duration* of nonparental relationships and the long-term development of attachment rather than carry out brief observations of infant attachments in different cultural settings. Handing a baby to kin for pleasurable play until the next nursing may not correspond to leaving the infant with strange baby sitters chosen haphazardly by an employed mother who desperately seeks childcare for her infant (Honig, 1995).

Therapy with infants at risk for insecure attachment. Lieberman (1989) has enriched our understanding of the importance of cultural sensitivity in her report of a year-long intervention which succeeded in improving the relationship between highly stressed Hispanic mothers and their one-year-old babies. These mothers felt that infant disobedience and disrespect should never be allowed.

One mother spoke about how mischievous and disobedient her 15-month-old son was, and how she had begun to spank him to teach him respect. We first empathized with how difficult it was when the child got into everything, particularly since the whole family lived in one small room and it was hard enough to keep things tidy after a long day at work. Then very slowly, as the mother spoke about how hard things were for the family, we sympathetically linked the difficult conditions with the mother's short fuse towards her son…We commented lightly that when one is stressed out it is easy to forget that at 15 months, children have a lot of energy and a very short memory. The mother laughed and said, in a sad tone, that it was easy to use the children as scapegoats. This led to a discussion of children's feelings, and memories about how she was disciplined with a belt. I asked her if she respected her parents when they did that. She said yes, but she was also scared of them...After a silence, she said thoughtfully that she never felt close to her parents, and that she didn't want her son to be scared of her. This opened the door to a recurrent discussion of how best to instill respect in children, and children's natural wish to please their parents as a basic psychological underpinning for obedience and respect. (p. 202)

Therapeutic contexts that are attuned to cross-cultural differences may be more successful in attempts to enlist family support for more facilitative parent-child interactions. When Brazelton was visiting with Zinacanteco Mayan Indian mothers in Mexico, they refused to allow him to see their newborns because of their fear of the "evil eye." Brazelton (1977) asked the interpreter to explain to one mother who quickly covered her five-month-old's face, that he was a "curer" (in his capacity as a pediatrician). Then, he assured the mother that "If I have the evil eye, I know how to cure it" (p. 47). The mother's eyes widened, and after that Dr. Brazelton gained trust and was given the rare opportunity to see deliveries and examine newborns in Mayan villages.

PARENTAL VALUES FOR INFANTS

Parental values and short-term goals for infants and young children may vary not only by culture group, but also depend on the frequency of health and accident threats to infant survival. Holding babies becomes urgent if health hazards, such as open fires or predatory animals, abound in the baby's environment. Kaplan and Dove (1987) suggest that Ache foragers in Paraguay hold their babies all the time because the forest has so many potential hazards. Based on his work among the Gusii in East Africa, LeVine (1994) describes two parenting strategies: agrarian and urban-industrial. He believes that whereas agrarian families hold babies close and indulge them with on-demand feeding to prevent health hazards, urban-industrial parents (in societies with low infant mortality) tend instead to emphasize language and the development of cognitive skills.

Since parents exert the most important influence on children's acquisition of values (Grusec & Kuczynski, 1997), what values do parents want infants and young children to learn? Whiting and Whiting (1975) reported that a primary goal for infants and young children among agricultural peoples they studied was the socialization of respect and obedience. Similarly, Fiji mothers valued respecting property and other rules of proper behavior, learning a service role, avoiding any dangers to health, and amusing the parent with dancing and singing (West, 1988). In fact, Fiji parents would "usually ask children to perform for visitors" (p. 19). By contrast, when questioned about values and goals, 19 out of 20 Boston mothers mentioned the importance of independence. Inner psychological qualities, such as being happy regardless of how materially well-off they become and the goal for children to be generous, honest, and respectful of the rights of others were noted as important by 17 out of 20 Boston mothers (Richman, Miller, & Solomon, 1988).

Prosocial values are not promulgated strongly in some cultures. Indeed, revenge and jealousy seem to have a prominent status among various tribes in Papua, New Guinea (Mead, 1935) and among the Ik mountain people in Africa (Turnbull, 1972). In other cultures, however, instilling prosocial characteristics is highly valued. "Nothing is more important to the Hopi than having a 'Hopi good heart' defined as trust and respect for others, concern for everyone's rights, welfare, and feeling, inner peacefulness, and avoidance of conflict" (Mussen & Eisenberg-Berg, 1977, p. 3). In the United States, Pines (1979), reporting on the work of Yarrow and colleagues, did not find a cultural pattern to promote prosocial values in infants. Empathic responses, such as when a toddler generously hands a cracker (which he loves too!) back to a visiting baby and says "No cry, baby!" were characteristic only in families where a mother strongly modelled caring responses to her own infant's distress and firmly forbade the child to use force for settling social problems.

Parental values may survive movement to another culture. Mexican mothers of toddlers living in the United States behaved quite similar to urban and rural Mexican mothers. They reported balancing the use of affection and authority as they predominantly sought to foster cooperative behaviors and interdependence while encouraging competency (Cabrera, Knauf-Jensen, Pinedo, Burrow, Everett, & DeRosiers, 1997).

Parental Conceptualization of Young Children's Work

In most cultures, young children are required to pitch in and help with family chores at some level (Munroe, Munroe, & Shimmin, 1984; Whiting, 1963). Goodnow's (1989) interviews with Lebanese-born and Anglo-Australian born mothers revealed that Anglo mothers valued such work and required tasks graded by age. They expected a young child to put pajamas on the bed, not on the floor, for example. The chores expected, then, were mainly self-care chores. In contrast, Lebanese-born mothers found it strange to ask five-year-olds to do jobs around the house since they considered them "still babies." But Lebanese-born mothers did agree that "Yes, a five-year-old could mind a young child, or amuse the baby." Minturn and Lambert (1964) noted major responsibilities given to a three-year-old Tarong girl in the Philippines. Her job was "to keep her baby brother from falling off the porch." The parents told her: "You play around where he is and when he goes near the stairs, you pull his shirt so he won't fall" (p. 327). A Hmong girl too is considered competent to take care of babies, "often carrying a young sibling on her back" (Muret-Wagstaff & Moore, 1989, p. 323).

Infant care by young children (5 to 10 years old) seems particularly prevalent in polymatric systems, where many relatives live nearby (Whiting & Whiting, 1975). Rogoff, Mistry, Goncu, and Mosier (1989) comment that "care by siblings may provide infants with special intellectual opportunities...Solomon Island sibling caregiving provides infants with a great diversity of cognitive and social stimulation" (p. 177). Heath (1983) observed that working-class Carolina African-American girls enriched infants' lives with nonsense wordplay, counting, and naming body parts.

The notion of child care "work" as appropriate for very young children seems widespread among many societies. In rural agricultural societies, young children may be asked to fetch water or run errands, that is, to help the daily work of the family. In many societies, even an informal job required of the youngest may be difficult.

[A Papago elder] turned to his little three-year-old granddaughter and asked her to close the door. The door was heavy and hard to shut. The child tried, but it did not move. Several times the grandfather repeated: "Yes, close the door." No one jumped to the child's assistance. No one took the responsibility away from her. On the other hand there was no impatience, for after all the child was small. They sat gravely waiting until the child succeeded and her grandfather gravely thanked her (Erikson, 1963, p. 236).

Erikson concluded that in many cultures "the essential point of such child training is that the child is from infancy continuously conditioned to responsible social participation, while at the same time the tasks that are expected of it are adapted to its capacity. The contrast with our society is very great" (p. 236).

How work is perceived by the young child may make the crucial difference. Guatemalan Mayan toddlers routinely observe home-based economic activities, such as sewing and weaving. Indian tribal toddlers observe their mother's work in the fields or in daily-paid labor outside the home where they routinely accompany their mothers (Rogoff et al., 1989). In Tibetan rug-weaving factories, I have observed toddlers playing for hours near the dusty looms where their mothers were weaving industriously. In middle-class western families, some infants will be exposed to the world of group care; others will have opportunities to watch homemaking activities. Possibly, as they grow older, some children in busy dual-career families in western societies feel resentful doing chores they perceive as the responsibility of a parent. But if the family engenders in the child a sense of accomplishment and pride in helping the family flourish, then cross-cultural data suggest that work chores, judiciously chosen, may add to a young child's deep sense of security and satisfaction in "belonging" within the family.

Research into what values families emphasize from infancy onward can enrich our understanding not only of child development but also the ways in which we might facilitate more intercultural understanding among social groups where there have been traditional hostilities, even within the same nation or state.

PATTERNS OF CHILDREARING: CROSS-CULTURAL
SIMILARITIES AND DIFFERENCES

Cross-cultural studies sometimes strive carefully to research selected variables, while controlling for social class, urban vs. rural or other milieux (desert or forest), maternal education, parity of child, economic situation, prenatal and perinatal risk factors, and "modernity." Holding the above factors constant, researchers search for cultural commonalities and/or differences in parenting beliefs, styles, and practices. They search also for which practices are found occurring together in some cultures but not in others. Some researchers maintain that the key process underlying differences among peoples is learning—unique for each culture. Others believe that, particularly with newborns, the biological needs of the baby constrain patterns of care to meet the infant's biological and physiological needs. LeVine (1977) notes that a culture's caregiving strategy evolves predominantly in response to environmental hazards in order to maximize the child's capacity for reproduction, for economic self-maintenance at maturity, and for instilling the values of its culture. This model suggests that there are no "ideal" parenting practices, since each culture evolves those persons who serve the culture's ecological and evolutionary needs.

Is there a "prototypical system of child care independent of the differences in infant behavior that exists among cultures?" (Winn et al., 1989, p. 89). Bornstein, Tal, and Tamis-LeMonda (1991) observed normal interactions of first-time mothers with 5-month-old infants in natural home settings. All mothers were urban, educated, and middle class in the three cultures studied: USA, France, and Japan. Social interactions, indexed by maternal nurturant and vocally imitative responsiveness tended to occur equally with infants across cultures. The American mothers were more likely to stimulate babies with toys than the French or Japanese mothers. This had been predicted given USA cultural values of wanting children to become autonomous early. Social stimulation and tactile kinesthetic play were found among all mothers, but they covaried positively only in the American sample. Whereas the French mothers displayed high levels of adult conversational speech to infants, the American mothers showed the most frequent use of high-register "Parentese" talk (where vowels are drawn out as in "Pretty baaaaaby!"). Brain research confirms that such talk is optimal for stimulating synaptic connections in the frontal cortex of infants during the first two years of life. "The high-pitched singsong speech style known as Parentese helps babies connect objects with words" (Nash, 1997, p. 54).

Comparing maternal childrearing practices among poor, low-education urban mothers of one- and three-year-olds in five cultures (France, Sweden, India, Korea, and USA), Honig and Chung (1989) noted strong similarities as well as some culturally unique patterns in responses to the IPLET (Implicit Parental Learning Theory) interviews, specific for each age group, and carried out individually with each mother in her home. IPLET (Honig & Caldwell, 1965) assesses via a mother's verbal report the array of behaviors in an infant or young child that a parent would either encourage or discourage and the type of technique the parent uses. Across all five cultures, mothers responded overwhelmingly positively if the child behaved positively. They reported smiling, praising, offering tangible rewards, and physical affection. When babies were frightened, mothers across cultures tended to report using positive reassuring techniques. When infants and toddlers behaved negatively toward others, the range of maternal behaviors reported increased markedly. Then positive responses were very rare, and fewer than 15% of mothers reported "doing nothing." Indeed, in response to negative infant/toddler behaviors, mothers in all five culture groups used deprivation of privileges, hitting, scolding, and giving commands. The Korean mothers were most indulgent of negative social acts by one-year-olds (but not 3-year-olds), and they were also most likely to reassure a frightened baby with hugs, food, or toys.

Maternal responses to danger situations, such as running into the road, and to expressed infant neediness showed marked maternal variability regardless of culture group. When puzzled or frustrated by infant behaviors, mothers in all five cultures seemed to try a wider variety of techniques. The low-income African-American mothers (USA sample) reported hitting as their major technique (60%) to handle dangerous behaviors of one-year-olds, but they also reported much use of teaching techniques in response to other infant behaviors.

Across various child behaviors, the French mothers most consistently reported using methodical training or prevention techniques to encourage maturity. One mother boasted to me that she had but to "show the whip" to her toddler for him to improve his behavior. Mothers explained that they sat a toddler frequently and regularly on the potty or used door latches to prevent a tot from entering a forbidden area. During an IPLET interview in an apartment in Paris, I noted that the mother had erected a vertical wooden barrier at the door to the infant's room (which was devoid of toys), so that he could not toddle out of the room and join her in the kitchen as she prepared food. Swedish mothers were more likely than the four other culture groups to report "doing nothing" in response to many categories of infant behavior. Their responses indicated a belief that infants and toddlers would developmentally be expected to outgrow many early behaviors, such as fearfulness or even negative social acts, and that parents need not intervene much for maturing eventually to occur.

The above findings are congruent with Bornstein et al.'s (1991) work in indicating cross-cultural universals as well as culturally-specific differences in maternal responses to infant and toddler behaviors.

Adolescent Parenting

In western societies, adolescent parenting is considered deviant and non-normative. Research on outcomes for young children of adolescent mothers in the USA has shown language delays and later behavior difficulties associated with adolescent parenting, even across generations (Hardy, Astone, Brooks-Gunn, Shapiro, & Miller, 1998). But in many cultures, teenage girls become mothers at very young ages. Thus, cross-cultural studies of infants and young children should provide some evidence of whether the findings for western society hold true across much of the world, where adolescent parenting is more normative. Addressing this problem is difficult, unfortunately, because of "tied" variables that covary together. In many cultures, maternal relatives provide extensive support for the young mother and her infant. In many cultures, unlike in the USA, the teenage mother is likely to be wed in a legal marriage prior to the birth of the infant, rather than living as a single mother supported by public assistance. Thus, outcomes among babies may differ not because of the more normative nature of teenage parenthood in other cultures, but because of kin support systems consistently available to young mothers in those cultures.

Monomatric vs. Polymatric Care

Shared infant care is common across cultures. In Fiji, for example, mother was observed as the caregiver in fewer than half of the observations of weaned infants at each age point between 13 to 50 months (West, 1988). Nonmaternal Fiji caregivers behaved differently and acted more lively and playful with babies.

Who holds babies? How are they held? When awake, Fiji babies have physical contact with someone in 56% of daytime hours. At night, infants sleep with the mother until weaning and then sleep with another member of the household throughout early childhood. "The mean frequencies of infant crying per four hours of observation are 81 (Gusii), 73 (Yucatan) as compared with 190 in the US sample" (Richman et al., 1988, p. 87) where maternal holding is far less frequent. The current USA pattern of extensive use of "plastic holders," such as cribs, car seats, swings, and other baby carriers is atypical in many of today's third-world cultures and probably does not produce as quiet or calm an infant when compared to other cultures emphasizing extensive maternal holding. Navaho babies in the USA, however, were traditionally not carried on the mother's body but on cradleboards, whose last use was "just over 10 months" (Chisholm, 1989, p. 349). Shredded bark of the desert cliffrose was used as an absorbent diapering material. For the first 3 months of life, infants were on the cradleboard 15-18 hours a day. Chisholm reasons that the motor-restraint effect of the cradleboard is intended to lower infant state, provides some protection for the baby, and allows the mother to carry out her work while keeping the infant near her. When the preferred cultural pattern emphasizes the constant holding of babies, this may reflect less a cultural prescription for holding but instead a lack of safety in the environment and the potential for serious accidents, such as a baby toddling into a campfire (LeVine, 1989).

Mothers may hold babies differently for nursing or for social interaction. In some cultures, mothers are more adept at *en-face* orientations and interactions with their babies. Marquesan mothers in the South Pacific usually hold babies facing outward and encourage them to attend to and interact with others, such as an older sibling. They shape the infants' attention toward others and objects and shape their movements towards effective contact and locomotion. By the end of the first year, infants are ...able to accompany and learn from older children in an environment supervised by adults (Martini & Kirkpatrick, 1981, p. 209).

CROSS-CULTURAL RESEARCH ON NEWBORNS

Do Newborns Exhibit Differential Development as a Function of Culture Group?

Because of cultural differences in prenatal care for pregnant women and because of nutritional deficiencies among many low-SES families in poor countries, strong neonatal differences might be expected. Nearly half a century ago, Geber and Dean (1957) observed that 9-hour-old Gandan neonates in Uganda were already advanced in neuromuscular development. Native African babies are advanced beyond western Caucasian babies in skeletal maturation and ossification even at birth. Ainsworth (1967) attributed advanced motor abilities among the Ganda to the physical freedom and nurturing that infants received. Babies from Lusaka, East Africa, carried on their mothers' bodies and allowed to nurse freely, exhibited superior postural control of head and trunk at 10 days (Brazelton, 1977), even though at birth they had shown evidence of dysmaturity, such as dry scaling skin, poor subcutaneous fat stores and floppy bodies, as if malnourished in utero. Kenyan Kipsigis infants were advanced in sitting, standing and walking but retarded in head lifting, crawling, and turning over (Super, 1976). Super noted that over 80% of Kipsigis mothers deliberately taught their infants to sit, stand, and walk. He also observed that African infants reared like European babies lose the muscular advantage of the traditionally reared babies suggesting that psychomotor differences among infants can be influenced by childrearing practices.

Other newborn research points to culturally unique infant-rearing patterns. Among Asian infants, Caudill and Weinstein (1969) observed Japanese infants to be similar to Chinese infants. The Asian babies cried less, were motorically less active, and vocalized less than the Anglo babies. Yet, working with babies of recent Japanese descent in the USA, these researchers recorded patterns of mother-infant behavior more similar to those of mothers and infants in America than in Japan.

The Brazelton BNBAS Scale: Cross-cultural Findings

Recent infancy research across cultures frequently involves collaborations among pediatricians, anthropologists, and child development specialists (Nugent, Lester, & Brazelton, 1989). Devised by T. Berry Brazelton (1973), the Brazelton Neonatal Behavioral Assessment Scale (BNBAS) consists of 27 items. Reflexes are measured as well as habituation to stimuli. Sometimes, the aversive pinprick stimulus item is not administered. Behavior clusters assessed include Habituation, Orientation, Motor Performance, Range of State, Regulation of State, Autonomic Regulation, Response to Stress, and Irritability. Brazelton (1977) has promoted this tool as a way to sensitize parents to the competencies of their infants, and thus enhance the parent-infant relationship from birth onward.

Differences as well as similarities among neonates have been reported. On four separate assessments during the first month of life "Hmong infants born in the USA and compared to Caucasians, scored substantially more favorably on orientation to visual and auditory stimulus" (Muret-Wagstaff & Moore, 1989, p. 329). They were less irritable and more measured on the range of infant states (which include drowsiness, deep sleep, crying, quiet alert, etc.), and quieter motorically with lower scores due mostly to head lag when the baby was raised from supine to sitting position.

But BNBAS scores may not reflect cultural differences among newborns as much as subtle factors associated with poverty and ill health. For example, Malaysian newborns from poor families had a high score on the Irritability factor (corresponding to a high peak state of excitement, rapid build-up to the initial cry, frequent bouts of crying, poor consolability, and ineffective self-quieting). They were born following a longer second stage of labor, were exposed to higher maternal blood pressure during labor, had less exposure to maternal analgesics, and were more likely to be postterm deliveries (Woodson & Da Costa, 1989). Many variables besides culture group can be responsible for neonatal differences on the BNBAS. For the most part, Woodson and Da Costa report that BNBAS scores for Chinese, Malay, and Tamil babies in their comparative study were more alike than different. One must be careful when attributing infant neonatal behaviors differences to culture groups if there are not sufficient research controls for prenatal and perinatal factors, such as maternal nutrition, spacing between births, poverty, and many others.

HEALTH, NUTRITION, RISK FACTORS, AND RESILIENCE IN INFANCY

Prenatal and postnatal nutrition vary widely for babies in different cultures. Furthermore, in some cultures, severe stresses accompany cultural rites such as clitoridectomy for Mali infant girls. Health risk factors show wide cultural differences. How significant are these early differences for later child development?

Discovering long-term effects of early risk factors depends crucially on prospective, longitudinal, cross-cultural studies. Such studies permit us to gain insights into the potential *buffering and remedial supports* some cultural practices provide. Resilience support allows some infants to succeed despite adversity. In Kenya, for instance, where the water supply is contaminated and economic resources to buy milk or food are meager, prolonged nursing is an important health protection practice. Hmong babies in their homeland are traditionally breast-fed for 1 to 4 years (Muret-Wagstaff & Moore, 1989).

Using a longitudinal, cross-cultural approach, Beckwith (1986) studied the development of Hispanic and Anglo infants in the USA that were born prematurely. The appearance of a premature infant violates a parent's expectancies of the "typical" infant. The infant's organization of state arousal, motor tone, coordination in visual processing, and ability to respond to caregiver signals and social stimuli tend to be less adequate. However, when followed to age 5 years, no relationship was found between neonatal medical problems and mental development; yet within-culture group differences were still found.

Infants born preterm to Spanish-speaking families, an immigrant group in the poorest social circumstances, performed similarly to infants in English-language homes during the first year of life, but by two years, DQ scores were below average (mean 93, range 79-104), and they had decreased from nine months. At five years, performance on the Stanford-Binet, administered in Spanish, was also significantly below average (mean 83, range 64-105). The downward trend in Hispanic test scores was even more accelerated than a corresponding trend in the lower-class Anglo sample (p. 34).

This longitudinal study makes clear how carefully cross-cultural research needs to specify powerful variables such as social class as well as the culture groups in which infants are studied.

Other confounding variables that need to be specified by infancy research, regardless of culture, are well illustrated in Werner's impressive longitudinal study of high-risk infants born on the island of Kuaui (Hawai'i). Beginning prenatally, Werner (1989) followed the lives of poor at-risk infants into adulthood 32 years later. Among the multiracial high risk infants, about 25% developed into "competent, confident and caring young adults" (p. 72). At 20 months, the resilient toddlers were temperamentally more cheerful and friendly. They had at least one significant caregiver from whom they had received a great deal of positive nurturing during the first year of life. The risk literature consistently suggests that male infants are more vulnerable to psychosocial stress. Yet, many male Kuaui first born, at-risk children were identified as resilient.

Despite stressful life events for these high-risk infants, the following supporting conditions increased their resilience so that they were *less* likely to have a criminal record or a broken marriage 30 years after they were first assessed:

1. No younger sibling was born less than 24 months after the study child.
2. The infant was raised by a married rather than an unmarried mother.
3. Father was present during infancy and early childhood.
4. The infant did not experience separation from mother during the first year of life; nor were there prolonged disruptions including parental illness, unemployment by the major wage earner, and major moves.
5. The infant had adequate substitute care during the first 20 months of life if mother was employed.
6. A loving caregiver was available for the infant during the first year.

When at-risk births among poor families in other cultures are studied, it is important to look for factors promoting *resilience*, an enterprise that Grotberg (1997, see also her chapter in this volume) has been actively promoting across numerous cultures. Such information can provide useful tools for helping stressed families, whether minority or immigrant, in western societies (Honig, 1989). Among South Indian infants, Landers (1989) describes the following supports: babies are nursed frequently and on demand and swaddled to calm them; women return to their native home for delivery, remaining there from 3 to 6 months; the maternal grandmother plays a major role in the early life of the infant; it is a time when all of the new mother's energies are directed toward the care of her infant and she is comforted and strengthened by the security of her familial environment; from the moment of birth, the Indian infant is greeted and surrounded by constant physical ministrations (p. 179).

Similar social and family support has been reported by Hostetler and Huntington (1971) in the rearing of Amish infants in the USA. The Amish enjoy babies and believe them to be gentle, responsive, and secure within the home and the Amish community, but vulnerable when out in the world. "There is no such thing as a bad baby, although there may be a difficult baby" (p. 17).

Amish babies are rarely alone. They sleep in their parents' room, and in a large family they are held during most of their waking hours. They are diapered and bathed on their mother's lap rather than on a hard, cold table or tub; it is a time of happy sociability. The family attitude is one of sharing its good food with the baby. In addition, they believe that babies as young as five or six months don't eat well if fed alone (p. 17).

Yet when Amish babies are taken outside the home, the baby is tightly wrapped and covered in his mother's shawl. "Even his face may be covered to protect him from the "bad air.""…The way the baby is handled when the mother is shopping or traveling shows the Amish distrust of the outside world and the parents' efforts to protect the baby" (p. 17). Coding responses of infants exposed to other adults must take into account the difference between a baby's exposure to large numbers of ingroup caregivers vs. infant experience with "strangers."

Children with Disabilities: Variations in Parental Beliefs and Care

In some cultures, parents regard child disabilities, retardation, and physical handicaps as something to be hidden from others. For example, among the traditional Hmong, a birth deformity was considered a reflection of the mother's or father's past misdeeds (Potter & Whiren, 1982). Whether parents believe in inborn or ancestral "causes" for children's behaviors or traits or whether they believe that situational interventions can make a difference influences their willingness to work with teachers or health workers. In this context, research provides "substantial support for the principle of the self-serving attributional bias" that serves to enhance the parents' own self-esteem for characteristics and outcomes that parents feel are under their control (Booth, 1997, p. 630).   Cross-cultural research that increases our understanding of parental beliefs can broaden the framework for understanding behaviors and offer intervention strategies by bolstering parental beliefs that positive changes are something parents *can* accomplish.

In Beijing, Mao (1989) began a private boarding school for retarded Chinese preschoolers after learning from the parents how strong were their feelings of shame and despair. Developmental outcomes for children attending the FORTUNE school (so named to change the fortunes of the preschoolers) attest to the possibility of changing a culture of shame to a culture of hopefulness for retarded youngsters. Today, many resources exist for helping families and for improving childcare facilities so that they can enhance the lives of typical and atypical children from diverse cultural and linguistic backgrounds (Honig, 1997; Lynch & Hanson, 1998).

LANGUAGE DEVELOPMENT

A primary concern in cross-cultural language research is whether there is orderliness in the learning of language, whether in phoneme acquisition or syntactic and semantic competence, among infants and toddlers. If early babbling and one-word holophrastic speech are mostly *biologically* rather than culturally driven, then diverse linguistic experience should not result in differential development of babbling. It has been found in this context that infants of deaf parents do babble like infants of hearing parents until about six months of age. Similarly, infants learning Spanish, Japanese, or English are mostly alike in their basic repertoires of sound production. Thus, babbling is initially biologically primed and seems less a product of cultural experience (Nakazima, 1975; Oller & Eilers, 1982).

Of course, babies born into different language communities learn the language of their caregivers—and cultures differ markedly in the importance they place on language in communicating with and teaching young children. In many cultures, adults prefer that young children learn by watching others and consequently, language interactions may be sparse. For instance, Kaluli mothers in Papua New Guinea rarely engage infants in dyadic verbal interactions before the babies speak real words (Ochs & Schieffelin, 1984). In contrast, Kwara'ae mothers from the Solomon Islands (Melanasia) believe that babies can understand adult speech long before they can talk themselves (Watson-Gegeo & Gegeo, 1986). Thus, they engage in direct language teaching through "calling out and repeating routines" which begin when the baby is 6 months of age. In the USA, larger productive vocabularies have been reported for those 17-month-olds whose mothers spoke and read a great deal with them and provided "optimal" intellective stimulation (Clarke-Stewart, 1973). Thus, *parental beliefs* about the importance and efficacy of promoting early language skills differ widely both across and within cultures. Perhaps mothers who engage in less verbal interaction have more basic priorities, such as infant survival and protection from illness.

Social class differences have frequently been reported to account for differences in language competence. In this context, SES differences may be confounded with culture if the focus is on a cultural group where lack of education and poverty are entrenched. When families of low- and middle-socioeconomic status (SES) with one- to three-year-olds were observed at home in the USA, parents of language-competent children were more likely to be from middle-SES homes. Middle-class parents were more involved in activities of an educational nature, provided more educational toys and books, and read and conversed more extensively with their infants and toddlers (Carew, Chan, & Halfar, 1976).

SES differences in language have also been reported among toddlers assessed at a Bilan de Santé health clinic in Paris. Language retardation was more prevalent for French toddlers from low- SES rather than middle-SES families. Significantly, language adequacy related to parental variables. *Parental stress* was revealed as an important predictor of optimal vs. delayed vs. retarded language development among the French, North African, and African toddlers whom the clinic served (Honig & Park, 1989). When mothers and fathers reported being overwhelmed with stress, then 45% and 57% of the toddlers, respectively, exhibited language problems. In contrast, only 24% and 28% of those toddlers, respectively, whose mothers and fathers felt optimal about their life situation had problems with language development.

These mothers also reported on their interpersonal relationships with their toddlers. Whereas 24% of the toddlers whose mothers reported optimal relationships with them had language problems, 48% of the toddlers had language problems if the mother reported a poor relationship with them. The *quality* of the mother-toddler relationship influenced toddler language regardless of whether the infants came from North African, African, or French families. Significantly, mean language scores were higher for the toddlers whose mothers did not graduate from high school, but who reported no life stress in comparison with lower scores for toddlers whose mothers were high school graduates, but who also reported more life stress. Language deficit was related to the mother-toddler relationship and to paternal education in all three cultural groups.

GENDER DIFFERENCES

According to UNESCO reports (United Nations, 1985) most of the world's illiterates are female. In many cultures, a male is the child of choice and females are less preferred. Thus, it would be no surprise to find sex differences in cross-cultural studies of childrearing practices with male and female infants and young children. Modesty training differs, for instance, with typically more stringency for girls (Whiting & Child, 1953). Among cultural groups such as the Taliban in Afghanistan, where women's opportunities are severely restricted with few chances for employment or education, maternal depression is high, and detrimental psychosocial effects on very young children are thus a likely outcome.

Sharp gender differences characterize the beliefs and customs of many cultures. For example, Yi (1993) describes traditional Korean society as follows:

"A house was separated into two sectors, an outside sector for men and an inside sector for women...Direct contact between males and females was prohibited...Exterior behaviors of males included: leading the family members, deciding important issues such as education of their sons, and worshipping the ancestors. Interior work included: nurturing children, teaching a daughter how to be a wise mother and good wife, and managing households and maids" (p. 19).

Although gender effects in research on infant rearing in both industrial and nonindustrial societies may be uncommon (Hewlett et al., 1998), this does not mean that such effects will not be found for the later toddler and preschool years.

TEMPERAMENT: THE INTERPLAY OF NURTURE AND NATURE

Thomas, Chess, Birch, Hertzig, and Korn (1963), working with New York families from Puerto Rican and Caucasian backgrounds, identified nine child temperament traits. These traits clustered into three personality types: the easy baby (average activity level, moderate bodily rhythmicity, adaptable, moderate in response to distress, positive mood, long attention span, adaptable); the fearful child (withdrawing from new stimuli, slow in adapting, low-key mood, irregular in bodily functions); and the intense, difficult child (low threshold for distress, intense response to stress, irregular body rhythms, high activity level, low in adaptability). Sometimes the easy baby may get neglected, and in harsh rearing environments this may pose a threat to survival. Yet among the Masai in Kenya, fussy, irregular, unadaptable, and intense four-month-old infants tended to survive draught and malnutrition especially well. In this context, DeVries and Sameroff (1984) hypothesized that the demandingness of difficult babies is advantageous in a hostile living environment because parents are alerted to provide even more nurturance in order to prevent morbidity. However, in an industrial Western society, stressed parents may respond with anger in such situations, thus increasing the possibility for child abuse of difficult infants and the possibility that these infants may develop insecure attachments (Helfer, Kempe, & Krugman, 1997).

The cross-cultural study of infant temperament has generated strong interest among researchers who strive to find similarities and differences soon after birth in infants' temperament characteristics across different cultures. If differences exist among neonates in different cultures, then possibly infants shape caregiving cultural practices (as well as the reverse). For instance, the slow liquid movements of Zinacanteco infants in southern Mexico are quiet; their motor activity is controlled and well organized; and they experience strikingly long periods of alert state. Brazelton (1972) noted that these characteristics were present in the adults' personalities as well and they were valued culturally. Consequently, he argued that a culture's beliefs and practices are in part shaped by the temperamental traits and behaviors of its infants.

In contrast, the relatively greater impact of mothers in modulating their infants' interactions and galvanizing their development has been emphasized by Tamis-LeMonda and Bornstein (1989). They analyzed in detail how intricately the mother takes the lead, and how by her subtle, sensitive interactions during early infancy she supports later optimal toddler development.

Nepalese infants with poor and average Ponderal Index (PI is a weight-to-length measure of prenatal malnutrition) have been shown to have better regulation of autonomic functions and of state (e.g., transitions from sleep to quiet alert awake state rather than strong crying) when compared with American infants regardless of their nutritional (PI) status. Nepalese mothers provide their swaddled infants with frequent stimulation as they lie next to them in an *en-face* position. A baby's entire body is daily massaged with oils to mold the infant physically and to "convey the mother's love and affection" (Escarce, 1989, p. 81). A Nepalese mother also provides the baby with liberal on-demand breast-feeding. "In turn, the Nepalese baby brings to this exchange high motoric competence, mature physiological organization, and high responsiveness, all of which are expected to reinforce the mother's doting" (p. 83).

Other infancy specialists do emphasize the importance of the infant's contribution. Some culture groups with low PI babies do not treat them similarly. In contrast with Nepalese mothers, West Bengali mothers with undernourished infants were generally *less* responsive to them through 18 months of age (Graves, 1978). Low-income, high school dropout single American mothers with low PI babies also became increasingly less involved in their interactions with their infants over the first few years of life (Ramey & Gowen, 1986). Indeed, a discouraging spiral appeared to operate among these North Carolina low PI control babies. Their mothers paid less and less attention to them. By 36 months, low PI babies in the control group had a mean IQ of 70.6 compared to the average PI control infant mean IQ of 84.7. It is important to note that all control group infants received free pediatric care and formula. The researchers hoped then that differences between controls and the babies enrolled in the Abecedarian Project (an educational program for infants at high risk for later school failure) could be attributable to cognitively enriching infancy experiences rather than to health or nutrition factors, since the respective IQs of average and low PI babies enrolled in the Abecedarian program were respectively 98.1 and 96.4. Ramey and Gowen conclude in this context:

"These results illustrate the chain-of-events principle of the General Systems Model...Mothers of the fetally malnourished infants in the control group were significantly less involved with their infants at ages 18 and 30 months than were mothers of average PI infants and mothers of infants receiving educational daycare. One can speculate that the supportive and enriching day-care environment facilitated development of child characteristics which, in turn, promoted more positive maternal interaction" (p. 21).

The remarkable ability of South Indian low PI babies to overcome by 3 months high perinatal risk factors, such as unmonitored deliveries by small-stature mothers with poor weight gain during pregnancy has been attributed by Landers (1989) to the effectiveness of cultural rearing patterns. These infants receive an elaborate daily bath and massage and are nursed at the slightest signal of discomfort.

"The mother's responses to the demands of her infant reflect both her deeply rooted emotional stance ...toward her infant and the culture's perception and value of the children. The Indian mother's psychosocial commitment to her child emerges out of an extended family system which instructs, regards, and supports her in these efforts...As reflected in the popular devotional Krishna mythology, the child is traditionally perceived as a completely innocent being, a gift of the gods, towards whom one is expected to show deepest protection, affection and indulgence" (p. 204).

These findings confirm LeVine's (1977) precept that we must always assess the adaptive component and significance of adult childrearing practices. Freedman, Olafsdottir, Guoan, Park, and Gorman (see their chapter in this book) also emphasize the biological function of the persistence of early social patterns, and they postulate that there is a species advantage to such behavioral patterns.

Temperament and attachment. Another important impetus for temperament researches has been the puzzle as to whether temperament and attachment are in some way related. As Waters, Vaughn, Posada, and Kondo-Ikemura (1995) have noted: "Temperamental variability among infants might influence interpretation of attachment assessments... Infant temperament during the first year of life may influence the nature of parent-child interactions that are important in shaping the development of attachment patterns" (p. 168).

Efe infants in Central Africa are cared for and even nursed by a large number of others in addition to mother. However, infants who fuss more at 3 and 7 weeks spend more time with their mothers. Other persons pass fussy babies back to their mothers more often (49% of the time). Fussy infants are comforted within 10 seconds. Temperament affects *who* the caregiving person is among the Efe, and the number of care providers, in a culture where multiple caregiving is quite frequent. Fewer caregivers take care of low-birthweight, fussy babies, who therefore receive more care by their own mothers (Winn, Tronick, & Morelli, 1989).

Therapeutic Work with Mothers of Highly Irritable Infants

Can interventions in one culture provide insights for therapists in other nations? In Holland, this question was answered positively by a fascinating therapeutic intervention with 100 highly irritable first-born babies from low-SES families (van den Boom, 1994). Half the infant-mother dyads were randomly assigned to intervention and half to a control group. Half the babies received a pretreatment assessment and half did not. During 6-month home visits by interviewers (blind to group status), maternal sensitivity and responsiveness were coded. Every three weeks for three months, the intervention moms received home visits focused on enhancing maternal sensitive responsiveness. Moms were taught how to adjust their behaviors to the baby's unique cues, and how to select and carry out effective appropriate responses.

Particularly, moms were taught to become accurate observers of their babies' signals and encouraged to imitate baby behaviors such as vocalizations, while respecting infant gaze aversion by nonintrusiveness. The importance of soothing a crying infant was highlighted and individualized for each mother. Playful interactions with toys were promoted. All infants were videotaped in the Ainsworth Strange Situation at one year of age. The results showed that the intervention infants were more sociable, more able to soothe themselves, and engaged in cognitively more sophisticated exploration than the control babies. *More intervention babies (62%) were securely attached at one year compared with control babies (28%).*

FATHERING

The cross-cultural investigation of fathering roles has only recently been emphasized. Roopnarine, Lu, and Ahmeduzzaman (1989) and Roopnarine, Talukder, Jain, Joshi, and Srivastav (1990) have focused on fathers' play interactions, such as rough housing, tossing, tickling, bouncing, object-mediated play, and "peekaboo" games with infants in Malaysia and India. In their studies, the Indian fathers were gentle play partners with infants and treated female and male infants equally in play.

Among low-education North African (Tunisian, Moroccan, and Algerian) immigrant families in Paris, fathers of toddlers contributed significantly to increased maternal stress (Honig, Gardner, & Vesin, 1987). North African mothers who reported feeling overwhelmed by stress were also far more likely to report high father stress and major problems in the father-toddler relationship.

Hewlett (1992) provides a fascinating glimpse into the hunter-gatherer culture of the Aka Pygmies in African tropical rain forests. Aka fathers are very much invested in infants. Although mothers provide most of the care, fathers hold babies, entertain them, and help carry them for miles when the parents go on a hunt to net animals. Babies are carried on a parent's side when the parents dance and sing. Hewlett concludes that the intimate affectionate relationships of Aka fathers and mothers with babies account for their precocious skills and competence with digging tools, and use of a small ax.

By 18-24 months, infants usually know how to cook some foods on the fire. I have seen 1-year-olds roast nuts and bananas and wrap meat in a leaf and put it on the fire. All of these experiences contribute to the development of the infant's autonomy and understanding of cooperation (Hewlett, 1992, p. 235).

Degree of father interaction with 9- to 10-month-old infants has been related in India to household size. That is, when the household is organized around an extended family system, there are multiple female caregivers as well as the mother, and then "fathers and uncles withdraw from taking care of children since their contribution is not seen as essential," whereas in smaller households, fathers are active participants with infants (Sharma & LeVine, 1998, p. 65). Thus, patterns of father involvement may be quite heterogeneous, varying not only due to culture group but also reflecting family household size and composition.

CONCLUSIONS

The problem of hidden variables that covary within certain cultures makes it difficult to conclude definitively that infant developmental lags or advances are exclusively or predominantly due to culture. Neonatal assessments, for example, have shown how powerfully a pregnant mother's high blood pressure (more frequent in some cultures characterized by extreme poverty) or living at high altitude, or number of repeat pregnancies, may affect neonatal assessments, more than membership in a specific culture group.

The increasing attention of cross-cultural research to studying infants in preindustrial societies in transition to becoming more industrial and literate will no doubt provide fascinating data on the stresses that culture groups encounter and the ingenuity they show in retaining values, beliefs, practices that can make transitions more optimal for their small children.

Even when cross-cultural differences are found among newborns, or in parental patterns of childrearing with infants, these patterns may not have the same effects for future development in rapidly changing cultures as in more stable societies. "This evolutionary view of culture as an environmental tracking mechanism [may] account for the empirical findings in developmental psychology that early experience seems to affect later behavior only when the developmental environment is most stable" (Chisholm, 1989, p. 346).

The "rigidity" of men's roles vis-à-vis infant/toddler care has been well documented (see Roopnarine in this volume). Cross-cultural research of the future may well want to focus on how, where, and with what supports the roles of fathers begin to change toward more egalitarian participation in infant/toddler care or to document the ways in which cultural mores continue patterns of noninvolvement in some societies.

Females are treated less optimally than male infants in some third-world societies. Yet in an increasingly technology-driven world, increasing demands for technological skills will require more education. Thus, patterns of prejudice and even physical mutilation of female infants will hopefully become subject to great pressures for cultural change.

Longitudinal study and a cross-cultural focus on infants in interactions with peers and families will continue to be heuristically important and offer an exciting window on the beginnings of and the variations in human development. A special challenge for cross-cultural research will be to create measures of those values and beliefs that can subtly or not so subtly affect parental involvement in and cooperation with programs that encourage parenting practices designed to enhance early language, cognitive, and emotional competence.

Future cross-cultural researches in infant-toddler development need to become ever more sensitive to the problem of "goodness of fit" between caregiving practices, social strategies and social values that support those practices, infant temperament, and the goals of a given culture group in relation to the general goal of optimal child development.

BIBLIOGRAPHY

Ainsworth, M.D.S. (1967). *Infancy in Uganda: Infant care and the growth of love*. Baltimore, MD: Johns Hopkins University Press.

Ainsworth, M. D. S., Blehar, M. C., Waters, E., & Wall, S. (1978). *Patterns of attachment: A psychological study of the Strange Situation*. Hillsdale, NJ: Erlbaum.

Balleyguier, G. (1988). What is the best mode of day care for young children? French study. *Early Child Development and Care*, *33*, 41-66.

Beckwith, L. (1986). Parent interaction with their preterm infants and later mental development. In A. S. Honig (Ed.), *Risk factors in infancy* (pp. 27-40). London: Gordon & Breach.

Belsky, J., & Rovine, M. J. (1988). Nonmaternal care in the first year of life and infant-parent attachment. *Child Development*, *59*, 157-167.

Booth, C. L. (1997). Are parents' beliefs about their children with special needs a framework for individualizing intervention or a focus of change? In M. J. Guralnick (Ed.), *The effectiveness of early intervention* (pp. 625-639). Baltimore, MD: Brookes.

Bornstein, M. H., Tal, J., & Tamis-LeMonda, C. (1991). Parenting in cross-cultural perspective: The United States, France, and Japan. In M.H. Bornstein (Ed.), *Cultural approaches to parenting* (pp. 69-90). Hillsdale, NJ: Erlbaum.

Brazelton, T. B. (1972). Implications of infant development among the Mayan Indians of Mexico. *Human Development*, *15*, 90-111.

Brazelton, T. B. (1973). *Neonatal Behavioral Assessment Scale*. London: Heinemann Medical Books.

Brazelton, T. B. (1977). Effects of maternal expectations on early infant behavior. In S. Cohen & T.J. Comiskey (Eds.), *Child development: Contemporary perspectives*. (pp. 44-52). Itasca, Il.: Peacock.

Bretherton, I., & Waters, E. (Eds.). (1985). Growing points of attachment theory and research. *Monographs of the Society for Research In Child Development*, *50*(1-2, Serial No. 209).

Cabrera, E., Knauf-Jensen, D. E., Pinedo, J. D., Burrow, R., Everett, J.R., & DeRosiers, F. (1997, April). *A comparison of child-rearing methods: Mexican and Mexican-American mothers tell us about raising toddlers.* Poster presented at the biennial meeting of the Society for Research in Child Development, Washington, DC.

Caldwell, B. M., Hersher, L., Lipton, E. L., & Richmond, J. B. (1963). Mother-infant interaction in monomatric and polymatric families. *American Journal of Orthopsychiatry*, *33*, 653-654.

Carew, J., Chan, I, & Halfar, C. (1976). *Observing intelligence in young children*. Englewood Cliffs, NJ: Prentice Hall.

Caudill, W., & Weinstein, H. (1969). Maternal care and infant behavior in Japan and America. *Psychiatry*, *32*, 12-43.

Chisholm, J. S. (1989). Biology, culture, and the development of temperament: A Navaho example. In J. K. Nugent, B. M. Lester, & T. B. Brazelton (Eds.), *The cultural context of infancy* (pp. 341-364). Norwood, NJ: Ablex.

Clarke-Stewart, A. (1973). Interactions between mothers and their young children. *Monographs of the Society for Research in Child Development*, *38*, (No. 153).

Commins, D. B. (1967). *Lullabies of the world*. New York: Random House.

Dasen, P. R. (Ed.). (1997). *Piagetian psychology: Cross-cultural contributions*. New York: Gardner Press.

Dasen, P. R., & Heron, A. (1981). Cross-cultural tests of Piaget's theory. In H. C. Triandis & A. Heron (Eds.), *Handbook of cross-cultural psychology* (Vol. 4, pp. 295-341). Boston, MA: Allyn & Bacon.

DeVries, M. W., & Sameroff, A. (1984). Culture and temperament: Influences on infant temperament in three East African societies. *American Journal of Orthopsychiatry, 54*, 83-96.

Erikson, E. (1963). *Childhood and society*. New York: Norton.

Escarce, M. E. W. (1989). A cross-cultural study of Nepalese neonatal behavior. In J. K. Nugent, B. M. Lester, & T. B. Brazelton (Eds.), The *cultural context of infancy* (Vol. 1, pp. 65-86). Norwood, NJ: Ablex.

Freedman, D., Olafsdottir, V., Guoan, Y., Park, L., & Gorman, J. (2000). (See this volume).

Gardiner, H.W., Mutter, J. D., & Kosmitzki, C. (1998). *Lives across cultures: Cross-cultural human development.* Boston, MA: Allyn & Bacon.

Geber, M., & Dean, R. (1957). The state of development of newborn African children. *Lancet, 1,* 1216-1219.

Goodnow, J. (1989). Family life: The place of children's work around the house. In A. S. Honig (Ed.), Cross-cultural aspects of parenting normal and at-risk children. (Special issue). *Early Child Development and Care, 50*, 121-130.

Graves, P. (1978). Nutrition and infant behavior: A replication study in the Kathmandu Valley, Nepal. *American Journal of Clinical Nutrition, 31*(3), 541- 551.

Grossman, K.E., & Grossman, K. (1990). The wider concept of attachment in cross-cultural research. *Human Development, 33*, 31-47.

Grotberg, E. (1997). The International Resilience Project: Findings from the research and the effectiveness of interventions. In B. Bain (Ed.), *Psychology and education in the 21st century: Proceedings of the 54th annual convention, International Council of Psychologists* (pp. 118-128). Edmonton, Canada: ICPress.

Grusec, J.E., & Kuczynski, L. (1997). *Parenting and children's internalization of values: A handbook of contemporary theory.* New York: John Wiley.

Hardy, J., Astone, N.M., Brooks-Gunn, J., Shapiro, S., & Miller, T. (1998). Like mother, like child: Intergenerational patterns of age at first birth and associations with childhood and adolescent characteristics and adult outcomes in the second generation. *Developmental Psychology, 34*(6), 1220-1232.

Harkness, S., & Super, C. M. (1995). Culture and parenting. In M. Bornstein

(Ed.), *Handbook of parenting* (Vol.2, pp. 211-234). Hillsdale, NJ: Erlbaum.

Heath, S. B. (1983). *Ways with words: Language, life, and work in communities and classrooms.* Cambridge, UK: Cambridge University Press.

Helfer, M. E., Kempe, R. S., & Krugman, R. D. (Eds.). (1997). *The battered child* (5th ed.). Chicago, IL: University of Chicago Press.

Hewlett, B. S. (1992). Husband-wife reciprocity and father-infant relationship among Aka Pygmies. In B. S. Hewlett (Ed.), *Father-child relations: Cultural and biosocial perspectives* (pp. 153-176). New York: Aldine De Gruyter.

Hewlett, B. S., Lamb, M. E., Shannon, D., Leyendecker, B., & Schölmerich, A. (1998). Culture and early infancy among central African foragers and farmers. *Developmental Psychology, 34*(4), 653-661.

Honig, A. S. (Ed.). (1989). Cross-cultural aspects of parenting normal and at-risk children (Special Issue). *Early Child Development and Care, 50.*

Honig, A. S. (1995). Choosing child care for young children. In M. Bornstein (Ed.), *Handbook of parenting* (Vol. 4, pp. 411-435). Hillsdale, NJ: Erlbaum.

Honig, A. S. (1997). Creating integrated environments for young children with special needs *Childhood Education Journal, 25*(2), 93-100.

Honig, A.S. (1998, August 20). *Attachment and relationships: Beyond parenting.* Television presentation for the Head Start Quality Network Research Satellite Conference, East Lansing, Michigan.

Honig, A. S., & Caldwell, B. M. (1965). *The Implicit Learning Theory (IPLET)* (interviews for caregivers of young children). Unpublished manuscript, Syracuse University.

Honig, A. S., & Chung, M. (1989). Childrearing practices of urban poor mothers of infants and three- year-olds in five cultures. In A. S. Honig (Ed.), Cross-cultural aspects of parenting normal and at-risk children (Special Issue). *Early Child Development and Care, 50,* 75-98.

Honig, A. S., Gardner, C., & Vesin, C. (1987). Stress factors among overwhelmed mothers of toddlers in immigrant families in France. *Early Child Development and Care, 28,* 37-46.

Honig, A. S., & Park, K. (1989). Correlates of language competence among toddlers in French, North African, and African families in France. In D. M. Keats, D. Munro, & L. Mann (Eds.), *Heterogeneity in cross-cultural psychology* (pp. 392-402). Amsterdam: Swets & Zeitlinger.

Hostetler, J. A., & Huntington, G. E. (1971). *Children in Amish society: Socialization and community education.* Orlando, FL: Holt, Rinehart, & Winston.

Hunt, J. M. (1980). *Early psychological development and experience.*

Worcester, MA: Clark University Press.

Kagan, J. (1977). The uses of crosscultural research in early development. In P.H. Leiderman, S. R. Tulkin, & A Rosenfeld (Eds.), *Culture and infancy: Variations in the human experience* (pp. 271-285). New York: Academic Press.

Kagitçibasi, C. (1996). *Family and human development across cultures: A view from the other side.* Mahwah, NJ: Erlbaum.

Kaplan, H., & Dove, H. (1987). Infant development among the Ache of Eastern Paraguay. *Developmental Psychology, 23,* 190-198.

Landers, C. (1989). A psychobiological study of infant development in South India. In J. K. Nugent, B. M. Lester, & T. B. Brazelton (Eds.), *The cultural context of infancy* (Vol.1, pp. 169-208). Norwood, NJ: Ablex.

LeVine, R. A. (1977). Child rearing as cultural adaptation. In P.H. Leiderman, S. R. Tulkin, & A. Rosenfeld (Eds.), *Culture and infancy: Variations in the human experience* (pp. 5-27). New York: Academic Press.

LeVine, R. A. (1989). Cultural environments in child development. In N. Damon (Ed.), *Child development today and tomorrow* (pp. 52-68). San Francisco, CA: Jossey-Bass.

LeVine, R. A. (1994). *Child care and culture: Lessons from Africa.* Cambridge, UK: Cambridge University Press.

Lieberman, A. (1989). What is culturally sensitive intervention? In A. S. Honig (Ed.), Cross-cultural aspects of parenting normal and at-risk children. (Special Issue). *Early Child Development and Care, 50,* 197-204.

Lynch, E. W., & Hanson, M. F. (1998). *Developing cross-cultural competence: A guide for working with children and their families.* Baltimore, MD: Paul H. Brookes.

Mao, Y.Y. (1989). The FORTUNE training school in China: A support for mentally retarded children and their parents. In A. S. Honig (Ed.), Cross-cultural aspects of parenting normal and at-risk children. (Special Issue). *Early Child Development and Care, 50,* 189-196.

Martini, M., & Kirkpatrick, J. (1981). Early interaction in the Marquesas Island. In T. M. Field, A.M. Sostek, P. Vietze, & P.H. Leiderman (Eds.), *Culture and early interactions* (pp. 189-213). Hillsdale, NJ: Erlbaum.

Mead, M. (1935). *Sex and temperament in three primitive societies.* New York: Morrow.

Minturn, L., & Lambert, W. W. (1964). *Mothers of six cultures.* New York: Wiley.

Morelli, G. A., Rogoff, B., Oppenheim, D., & Goldsmith, D. (1992). Cultural variation in infant sleeping arrangements: Questions of independence. *Developmental Psychology, 28,* 604-613.

Munroe, R. L., Munroe, R. Y., & Shimmin, H. (1984). Children's work in four cultures: Determinants and consequences. *American Anthropologist*, *86*, 342-348.

Muret-Wagstaff, S., & Moore, S. G. (1989). The Hmong in America: Infant behavior and rearing practices. In J.K. Nugent, B. M. Lester, & T. B. Brazelton (Eds.), *The cultural context of infancy* (Vol.1, pp. 319-340). Norwood, NJ: Ablex.

Mussen, P., & Eisenberg-Berg, N. (1977). *Roots of sharing, caring, and helping: The development of prosocial behavior in children.* San Francisco, CA: Freeman.

Nakazima, S. (1975). Phonemicization and symbolization in language development. In E. H. Lenneberg & E. Lenneberg (Eds.), *Foundations of language development: A multidisciplinary approach* (Vol. 1, pp. 181-187). New York: Academic Press.

Nash, J. M. (1997, February 3). Fertile minds. *Time*, 49-56.

Nugent, J. K., Lester, B. M., & Brazelton, T. B. (1989). *The cultural context of infancy.* Norwood, NJ: Ablex.

Ochs, E., & Schieffelin, B. (1984). Language acquisition and socialization: Three developmental stories. In R. Shweder & R. A. Levine (Eds.), *Culture theory: Essays on mind, self, and emotion* (pp. 276-320). New York: Cambridge University Press.

Oller, D. K., & Eilers, R. E. (1982). Similarity of babbling in Spanish and English-learning babies. *Journal of Child Language*, *9*, 565-577.

Park, K., & Honig, A. S. (1991). Infant child care patterns and later teacher ratings of preschool behaviors. *Early Child Development and Care*, *68*, 89-96.

Piaget, J. (1963). *The origins of intelligence in children.* New York: Norton.

Pines, M. (1979). Good samaritans at age two? *Psychology Today, 13*, 66-74.

Posada, G., Gao, Y., Wu, F., Posada, R., Tascon, M., Schoelmerich, A., Sagi, A., Kondo-Ikemura, K., Haaland, W., & Synnevaag, B. (1995). The secure base phenomenon across cultures: Children's behavior, mothers' preferences, and experts' concepts. In E. Waters, B. E. Vaughn, G. Posada, & K. Kondo-Ikemura (Eds.), Caregiving, cultural, and cognitive perspectives on secure-base behavior and working models: New growing points of attachment theory and research. *Monographs of the Society for Research in Child Development, 60*(2-3, Serial No. 244), 27-48.

Potter, G. S., & Whiren, A. (1982). Traditional Hmong birth customs: A historical study. In B. T. Downing & D. P. Olney (Eds.), *The Hmong in the West: Observations and reports* (pp. 48-62). Minneapolis, MN: University of Minnesota, Center for Urban and Regional Affairs.

Price-Williams, D. R. (1980). Anthropological approaches to cognition and their relevance to psychology. In H.C. Triandis & W. Lonner (Eds.), *Handbook of cross-cultural psychology* (Vol. 3, pp. 155-184). Boston,

MA: Allyn & Bacon.

Ramey, C.T., & Gowen, J.W. (1986). A General Systems Approach to modifying risk for retarded development. In A. S. Honig (Ed.) *Risk factors in infancy* (pp. 9-26). London: Gordon & Breach.

Richman, A. L., LeVine, R. Q., New, R. S., Howrigan, G. A., Welles-Nystrom, B., & LeVine, S. E. (1988). Maternal behavior to infants in five cultures. In R. A. LeVine, P.A. Miller, & M. M. West (Eds.), *Parental behavior in diverse societies* (pp. 81-98). San Francisco, CA: Jossey-Bass.

Richman, A. L., Miller, P. M., & Solomon, M. J. (1988). The socialization of infants in suburban Boston. In R. A. LeVine, P.A. Miller, & M. M. West (Eds.), *Parental behavior in diverse societies* (pp. 65-74). San Francisco, CA: Jossey-Bass.

Rogoff, B., Mistry, J., Goncu, A., & Mosier, C. (1989). Cultural variation in the role relations of toddlers and their families. In M. H. Bornstein, M. H. (Ed.), *Cultural approaches to parenting* (pp. 173-184). Hillsdale, NJ: Erlbaum.

Roopnarine, J., Clawson, M.A., Benetti, S., & Lewis, T.Y. (2000). (See this volume).

Roopnarine, J., Lu, M., & Ahmeduzzaman, M. (1989). Parental reports of early caregiving, play, and discipline in India and Malaysia. In A. S. Honig (Ed.), Cross-cultural aspects of parenting normal and at-risk children. (Special Edition). *Early Child Development and Care, 50*, 109-120.

Roopnarine, J. L., Talukder, E., Jain, D., Joshi, P., & Srivastav, P. (1990). Characteristics of holding, patterns of play, and social behaviors between parents and infants in New Delhi, India. *Developmental Psychology, 26*, 667-673.

Sagi, A., van IJzendoorn, M.H., Aviezer, O., Donnell, F., Koren-Karie, N., Joels, T., & Harel, Y. (1995). Attachments in a multiple-caregiver and multiple-infant environment: The case of the Israeli Kibbutzim. In E. Waters, B. E. Vaughn, G. Posada, G., & K. Kondo-Ikemura (Eds.), Caregiving, cultural, and cognitive perspectives on secure-base behavior and working models: New growing points of attachment theory and research. *Monographs of the Society for Research in Child Development, 60*(2-3, Serial No. 244), 71-94.

Sears, R.R., & Wise, G. W. (1950). Relation of cup feeding in infancy to thumb-sucking and the oral drive. *American Journal of Orthopsychiatry, 20*, 123-138.

Sharma, D., & LeVine, R. A. (1998). Child care in India: A comparative developmental view of infant social environments. In D. Sharma & K. W. Fischer (Eds.), *Socioemotional development across cultures* (pp. 45-68).

San Francisco, CA: Jossey-Bass.

Skeels, H. M. (1966). Adult status of children with contrasting early life experience. *Monographs of the Society for Research in Child Development*, *31*(3, Serial No. 105).

Spitz, R. (1953). Hospitalism: An inquiry into the genesis of psychiatric conditions in early childhood. *The Psychoanalytic Study of the Child*, *1*, 45-74.

Sroufe, L. A. (1997). On the universality of the link between responsive care and secure base behavior. *ISBD Newsletter*, *1*(31), 3-5.

Super, C. M. (1976). Environmental effects on motor development: The case of "African infant precocity." *Developmental Medicine and Child Neurology*, *18*, 561-567.

Super, C. M. (1981). Behavioral development in infancy. In R. Munroe, R. L. Munroe, & B. B. Whiting (Eds.), *Handbook of cross-cultural human development* (pp. 181-270). New York: Garland.

Tamis-LeMonda, C. S., & Bornstein, M. H. (1989). Habituation and maternal encouragement of attention in infancy as predictors of toddler language, play, and representational competence. *Child Development*, *60*, 738-751.

Thomas, A., Chess, S., Birch, H.G., Hertzig, M. E., & Korn, S. (1963). *Behavioral individuality in early childhood*. New York: New York University Press

Turnbull, C. M. (1972). *The mountain people*. New York: Simon & Schuster.

United Nations (1985). *United Nations demographic yearbook*. New York: Oxford University Press.

van den Boom, D. C. (1994). The influence of temperament and mothering on attachment and exploration: An experimental manipulation of sensitive responsiveness among lower-class mothers with irritable infants. *Child Development*, *65*, 1457-1477.

Waters, E., Vaughn, B. E., Posada, G., & Kondo-Ikemura, K. (1995). Caregiving, cultural, and cognitive perspectives on secure-base behavior and working models: New growing points of attachment theory and research. *Monographs of the Society for Research in Child Development*, *60*(2-3, Serial No. 244).

Watson-Gegeo, K., & Gegeo, D. (1986). Calling out and repeating routines in Kwara'ae children's language socialization. In B. B. Schieffelin & E. Ochs (Eds.), *Language socialization across cultures*. Part 1 (pp. 17-50). New York: Cambridge University Press.

Werner, E. E. (1979). *Cross-cultural child development: A view from the planet earth*. Monterey, CA: Brooks-Cole.

Werner, E. E. (1989). High-risk children in young adulthood: A longitudinal study from birth to 32 years. *American Journal of Orthopsychiatry*, *59*(1), 72-81.

West, M. M. (1988). Parental values and behavior in the outer Fiji Islands. In R. A. LeVine, P.A. Miller, & M. M. West (Eds.), *Parental behavior in diverse societies* (pp. 13-26). San Francisco, CA: Jossey-Bass.

Whiting, B. B. (Ed.). (1963). *Six cultures: Studies in child rearing*. New York: Wiley.

Whiting, J. W., & Child, I. (1953). *Child training and personality*. New Haven, CT: Yale University Press.

Whiting, B.B., & Whiting, J. W. (1975). *Children of six cultures: A psychocultural analysis*. Cambridge, MA: Harvard University Press.

Winn, S., Tronick, E. Z., & Morelli, G. A. (1989). The infant and the group: A look at Efe caretaking practices in Zaire. In J.K. Nugent, B. M. Lester, & T. B. Brazelton (Eds.), *The cultural context of infancy* (Vol.1, pp. 87-109). Norwood, NJ: Ablex.

Woodson, R. H., & Da Costa, E. (1989). The behavior of Chinese, Malay, and Tamil Newborns from Malaysia. In J.K. Nugent, B. M. Lester, & T. B. Brazelton (Eds.), *The cultural context of infancy* (Vol.1, pp. 295-317). Norwood, NJ: Ablex.

Yi, S. H. (1993). Transformation of child socialization in Korean culture. In A. S. Honig (Ed.), Perspectives on Korean child care, development, and education. (Special Issue). *Early Child Development and Care*, *85*, 17-24.

FAMILY STRUCTURE, PARENT-CHILD SOCIALIZATION, AND INVOLVEMENT AMONG CARIBBEAN FAMILIES

Jaipaul L. Roopnarine
Mellisa A. Clawson
Sylvia Benetti
Tracey Y. Lewis
Syracuse University, U.S.A.

Any discussion of parent-child relationships in the Caribbean must consider the diverse ethnic groups and family structures that exist, the sociohistorical context of present patterns of socialization, and the diverse beliefs, goals, and practices that guide the socialization of children (Roopnarine & Brown, 1997; Senior, 1991). The Caribbean is a vast region that is made up of diverse groups of families who speak English, French, French Creole, Patois, Spanish, Hindi, and Chinese among other languages, and who have been variously affected by slavery, colonization, indentured servitude, harsh economic conditions, religion, and more recently by internal and external migration. The polyglot nature of the Caribbean and the nontraditional family structures that are evident among families permit only a handful of broad statements about parent-child relationships and involvement. We are particularly mindful of this in our present discourse.

In this essay, we attempt to provide a synopsis of a disparate and fragmentary literature on parent-child relationships in the English-speaking Caribbean—mainly Guyana, Trinidad and Tobago, Jamaica, Grenada and other countries such as Antigua, Dominica, St. Kitts, and St. Vincent. More specifically, we hope to: (a) provide an overview of family structures and different mating arrangements, (b) discuss patterns of socialization—including beliefs, practices, and goals that parents employ in raising/minding children, (c) examine mothers' and fathers' involvement with children and their possible links to educational and social outcomes in children, and (d) make some recommendations for future research and family policies. The reader should be aware that psychological studies of parent-child relationships in the Caribbean are rather sparse and historically much of what has been written about families in the region has been couched within a deficit structure/dysfunctional perspective (Roopnarine, Snell-White, & Riegraf, 1993). Quite often this has led to an overly negative portrayal of Caribbean family life. This view still predominates despite newer research (Roopnarine & Brown, 1997) that presents a more balanced view of families. Both descriptive and empirical accounts presented herein refer primarily to African-Caribbean and East Indian families, but occasionally we refer to data on indigenous people and other ethnic groups (e.g., Chinese, Amerindians, and Black Caribs).

FAMILY STRUCTURES AS CONTEXT FOR SOCIALIZATION

Without doubt, one of the most studied features of Caribbean family life is the context for mating and childrearing. It is well established that mating and childrearing in the English-speaking Caribbean occur in diverse family structural-functional arrangements. Progressive mating outside of marriage, in which men and women bear children from multiple partners, is a common practice. Acknowledging the diverse economic circumstances and belief structures of people within the Caribbean, scholars have discerned four major family/mating forms: visiting, common-law, marital, and single (Leo-Rhynie, 1997; Roopnarine, 1997; Senior, 1991). Although visiting and common-law relationships have been in existence for over 150 years, they have been criticized on moral and social grounds as being incompatible with European norms of family composition and as inadequate for raising children. These criticisms aside, our understanding of the impact of being raised in different family configurations in the Caribbean is limited.

Herewith are the structural dynamics of the four most predominant family or mating unions in which Caribbean children are raised. In the past, social and moral judgments about the legitimacy of non-marital unions for raising children have led to the pathologizing of Caribbean families. Regrettably, there has been a lack of concern for the basis of the evolution of such family forms and their adaptive strategies and formulas for raising children. Strong statements about the ability of families in nonmarital unions to meet young children's social and intellectual needs are avoided because of how little we know about these families at the moment.

Visiting Unions

Among low-income African-Caribbean families, most sexual relationships and childbearing begin in visiting unions or visiting relationships. In these unions, men and women do not live together; they meet at a pre-arranged location for sexual and social relations. These unions are tenuous as the man's financial and other obligations to his mating partner and children are unclear and most women see the union as transitory (Powell, 1986). Further, there is no legal recognition of visiting unions despite their pervasiveness. There is some indication that in visiting unions the man is considerably older and the woman younger, usually in her teenage years (Sharpe, 1997). The prevalence of visiting unions vary by ethnicity. Whereas 17.4% of rural African-Caribbean Jamaicans and 34.3% of urban African-Caribbean Jamaicans are in visiting unions, only 2.7% of East Indians in Guyana are in such unions (Brown, Newland, Anderson, &

Chevannes, 1997; Smith, 1996). An overwhelming majority of women in visiting unions do not see this type of relationship as an impediment to their personal desires in life and view marriage as a distinct possibility in the near future (Powell, 1986). Nevertheless, the African-Caribbean marriage rate has been conspicuously low for decades (Roberts & Sinclair, 1978).

Common-law Unions

Women usually enter a common-law union after bearing children in visiting relationships. This type of union appears more stable than visiting relationships because the couple shares living space and resources and there is deeper commitment to the husband-wife role. Women are expected to assume responsibility for domestic tasks, while men are expected to assume the instrumental breadwinning role. With the exception of Barbados, there is little legal protection accorded women in common-law relationships. However, some countries (e.g., Guyana, Jamaica, St. Vincent) do have legislation in place that mandates the support of children after paternity is established (Senior, 1991). By and large, though, the legal rights of women and children in common-law unions are nebulous. Again, among East Indians there are far fewer common-law relationships than among African-Caribbean people (in some estimates 8.9% vs. 20.7% respectively) (Smith, 1996).

Married Couples

Marriage among African-Caribbean families usually occurs later after progressive mating (between 35-54 years of age) (Powell, 1986). Generally, marriage rates have been low among African-Caribbean people (e.g., 4 per 1,000 among Jamaicans) but higher for East Indians and Chinese in Guyana (88.4% among East Indians in Guyana), Trinidad and Tobago, and among Amerindians in Belize (Roberts, 1975). In these latter societies, marriage occurs at much younger ages and family forms are more likely to resemble that of the European ideal. Despite later marriages among African-Caribbean couples, most women believe that marriage would be a positive step for them (Powell, 1986). However, they do not necessarily see marriage as a way to salvation and happiness. Caribbean women accept the notion of "partnership" regardless of the type of union (Clarke, 1957).

Single Parent

It should be pointed out that "single" may not refer to conjugal but rather union status—women who are not currently in any union (Senior, 1991).

Note that a significant number of Caribbean women are the head or de facto head of the household. Female-headed households are often more common in Caribbean countries with predominantly African-Caribbean populations than those with large numbers of East Indians or Amerindians. It is estimated that 22.4% of women in Guyana, 27% in Trinidad and Tobago, 33.8% in Jamaica, 42.9% in Barbados, and 45.3% in Grenada are the head of their households (Massiah, 1982; Powell, 1986). About 50% of household heads have never been married, have low educational attainment, and are less likely to be employed. While among African-Caribbean women being the household head may be tied to economic factors and progressive mating, East Indian women who are the head of their households are more likely to be widows (34.1% in Guyana) than single parents (Massiah, 1982). The probability of single women not being in a union is rather small (less than 3%).

As is clear from the above discussion, the family context for the socialization of Caribbean children does not quite conform to the European ideal of the nuclear family. Nor is there evidence for the global assumption that men are the head of the household or are present in children's lives. Consequently, scholars of Caribbean family life (e.g., Leo-Rhynie, 1997; Senior, 1991) have highlighted the diverse family forms—multi-generational female-headed units, married couples, common-law and visiting relationships—as adaptive and to different degrees functional for childrearing. In the next section, we delve into some core beliefs and practices that guide parent-child relationships.

PATTERNS OF SOCIALIZATION: BELIEFS AND PRACTICES

Not unlike families in other societies around the world, Caribbean families place a high value on children. Of course, one could debate whether premium is placed on utilitarian over psychological value, given the tendency of Caribbean parents of different ethnic backgrounds to emphasize the role of children to care and provide economic support for them in their older years and the unreasonable behavioral expectations some parents have of their children. The salience of a utilitarian value of children is endemic to a number of other societies such as the Philippines, Thailand, Taiwan, and Turkey as well (Kagitçibasi, 1996). Irrespective of the outlook parents may have on children, there are some key childrearing practices and beliefs that set Caribbean parents apart from those in other cultures.

It is widely accepted that parents' beliefs, ideas, or ethnotheories about socialization and development assist in charting the course for parent-child relations (Harkness & Super, 1996; Kagitçibasi, 1996). In essence, parents' internal working models about child development and parenting guide socialization practices and expectations about childhood development. Thus, there is tremendous promise for understanding the meaning of parental practices if we explore parental beliefs, perceptions of children and their role in society, folk beliefs and practices, religious practices, parental strategies employed in socialization, and the social-structural organization of members of a society. Undoubtedly, by tapping into the formulas specific cultures have devised for childrearing over time (Ogbu, 1981), we are in a better position to decipher what drives parenting and successful and unsuccessful developmental outcomes.

Several causal models have been proposed on the influence of the cultural context within which the family is situated and the family structure on socialization values and family interaction and socialization (e.g., Coll, Lamberty, Jenkins, McAdoo, Crnic, Wasik, & Garcia, 1996; Kagitçibasi, 1996). It is not the goal of this essay to review these models here. We call attention to them because those paradigms emphasizing context offer greater hope in assisting us to tease out the impact of being raised in different family configurations in the Caribbean and simultaneously may help us lay bare parental ethnotheories about childrearing that are central to the socialization process. To this end, we identify a set of global beliefs and practices that are key to childhood socialization in the Caribbean.

Parental Beliefs

1) Beliefs about parenting style vary by socioeconomic status, gender of parent, and ethnic group. Even though Caribbean parents prefer a more authoritarian and restrictive parenting style–high degree of control and expectations of compliance on the part of children–families in the higher socioeconomic groups (Ricketts, 1982) and East Indian mothers appear more permissive (Roopnarine, Snell-White, Riegraf, Wolfsenberger, Hossain, & Mathur, 1997). Thus, as Leo-Rhynie (1997) wrote, parenting in the Caribbean context is a mixture of authoritarian/punitive control and indulgence and protectiveness.

2) There is a strong belief that children should be obedient, compliant, and show unilateral respect for parents and other adult members of society. In a study of low-income households across the Caribbean, Grant, Leo-Rhynie, and Alexander (1983) found that 100% of parents in Antigua, 96% in St. Kitts, 85% in St. Lucia, 94% in St. Vincent, 82% in Barbados, and 95% in Jamaica believe that children should "obey their parents and behave themselves." It is generally held that parental success in childrearing is measured by the compliance children display in the community, being tidy, and the ability of children to sit still for long periods of time.

3) Parents believe in harsh discipline. African-Caribbean parents believe in the biblical injunction of "Spare the rod and spoil the child." After the early childhood period, East Indian parents also believe that leniency and too much praise may "spoil" children and therefore favor stricter measures of disciplining children (see Table 1).

Table 1
Parental Beliefs in Selected Caribbean Countries

	Countries					
Measures	Antigua	St Kitts	St Lucia	St Vincent	Barbados	Jamaica
1. Don't spare the rod and spoil the child	96%	95%	74%	83%	31%	88%
2. Too much love and attention will spoil the child	50%	40%	43%	67%	8%	31%
3. Children must be seen and not heard	47%	51%	37%	29%	4%	27%

Note: Numbers refer to percentage of parents who agreed with each statement. The information is taken from Grant et al. (1983).

4) Both African-Caribbean and East Indian parents recognize the utilitarian value of children. Parents believe that children (and in many cases especially boys) should provide economic support and care for their aging parents particularly in East Indian families. In low-income African-Caribbean families, however, mothers prefer girls over boys because they believe that daughters will care for them in their old age and believe that boys are too difficult to raise anyway (Leo-Rhynie, 1997). Due to poverty, children are involved in economic activities early in their lives in order to support parents and siblings.
5) Parents believe that religious indoctrination is a central force in raising children. Christian, Rastafarian, Hindu, and Muslim parents all emphasize grounding children in spiritual experiences and celebrations (Roopnarine & Brown, 1997).

Several prominent psychologists (Goodnow & Collins, 1990; Harkness & Super, 1996; Sigel, 1985) have suggested that parental beliefs or the "inner psychologies" of parents serve as a compass for parental practices. Parental beliefs push the cognitive structuring of behavior and action and have been shown to be associated with child development outcomes (McGillicuddy-DeLisi, 1985). We see parental practices as reflecting an uptake of society-wide beliefs regarding parenting. Accordingly, the practices outlined below are inextricably tied to the beliefs discussed in the preceding section.

Parental Practices

1) In different ethnic groups, multiple caregiving is common; grandparents, aunts, uncles and other relatives are centrally involved in children's lives. For example, Flinn (1992) in his work on families in Trinidad observed that during infancy and early childhood, care of children was distributed across several individuals: 44.2% by mothers, 10.3% by fathers, 16.3% by siblings, 17.6% by grandparents, 4.5% by aunts/uncles, and 7.2% by distant kinship members and nonrelatives. Likewise, in the *Women in the Caribbean Project* (1979-1982), a survey of 1,600 households in the eastern Caribbean revealed that 50% of children were cared for by relatives (Brodber, 1986). Rodman (1971) reported that mothers in Trinidad experience no guilt in sharing childcare responsibilities with others.

2) Discipline techniques employed by parents are harsh and often in the form of denigration and/or severe physical punishment but may be tempered by level of schooling. Families with higher educational achievement are less strict and more permissive (Ricketts, 1982) and less likely to use physical punishment than those with lower educational and economic status (Grant et al., 1983). Others (Arnold, 1993) argue that physical punishment is so ubiquitous that it pervades socioeconomic status. Fully 83.5% of children in one survey received a "beating" for doing something wrong; only 9.8% had privileges taken away from them (Arnold, 1993).

3) Child-shifting is widespread and may be done for the convenience of the parent without taking into full account the needs of the child. It is a practice that involves "giving" children (informal adoption) to be raised by others. Dann (1987) found that about 15% of men in Barbados were raised by neither a father nor mother, and Powell (1982) calculated that in Jamaica 33% of the teenage mothers in her sample were raised by grandmothers. An earlier report (Roberts & Sinclair, 1978) confirms that about 15% of Jamaicans under 15 were shifted to other dwellings.

4) Parents do not dispense praise or reward regularly, and public displays of affection are uncommon. An analysis of parental expressions of approval and disapproval when children please them indicates that 36.6% provided no response, 23.6% used praise only, and 5.4% used praise and affection. Only 3.7% used affection (Leo-Rhynie, 1997).

STRICT OR ABSENT FATHER, RESPONSIBLE MOTHER

As one of us (Roopnarine, 1998) has written elsewhere, Caribbean mothers' and fathers' relationships with children may span several unions/partners. This adds to the complexity of men's and women's social, intellectual, and economic obligations to children. For the most part, the mother is the primary caregiver to children, while men appear distant or are physically absent during the early and middle childhood periods. This summation does not tell the whole story, however. To get a more lucid picture of parental involvement with children, it is necessary to delve separately into motherhood and fatherhood in the different ethnic groups in the Caribbean.

Steeped in beliefs about patriarchy, the roles of mothers and fathers in East Indian families in Guyana and Trinidad and Tobago are driven by religious and sociocultural edicts that can be traced back to ancient spiritual/religious texts (e.g., *Upanishads, Ramayana, Mahabharata,* and *Qu'ran*). The ideological bases of these texts enjoin an androcentric and authoritarian posture regarding the roles and responsibilities of Indian men and women (Chekki, 1988). Although these beliefs are challenged today, women are expected to assume a subordinate and subservient position to men in the family and to be loyal to their husband (*pativrata*) and their husband's family. Men are expected to display filial loyalty within the concept of *Shravan Kumar*—the devoted son. They have strong allegiances to their father and brothers. The eldest son is called upon to perform religious sacraments and to care for his aging parents (Kakar, 1991; Roopnarine et al., 1997).

Within the structural demands of patriarchy, mothers appear indulgent and permissive in the childrearing role. From infancy through middle childhood the East Indian mother and other women are primarily involved in caring for children and meeting their emotional needs. Physical contact is intense during the infancy period; mothers hold infants close to the body, provide extensive massages to them, and most infants and young children co-sleep with parents and grandparents. Mothers may nurse young children way beyond toddlerhood (Roopnarine et al., 1997). Indian mothers serve as a liaison between children and fathers and other adult members of the society. The mother-son relationship may be characterized as a blend of maternal care, subservience, and parental authority, while the mother-daughter relationship is governed by greater parental control and scrutiny (Jayawardena, 1963).

Historically Caribbean East Indian fathers have been viewed as strict and distant from children, especially daughters. Fathers engage in sporadic care (bathing, feeding, cleaning) of young children. They are seen as austere, an authority figure who should be revered and respected (Jayawardena, 1963). Both ethnographic and survey research (Roopnarine et al., 1997; Wilson, 1989) seem to signal that father involvement with children may be increasing, but early caregiving remains perfunctory to men. As children get older, sons are expected to show deference to the father and avoid expressions of familiarity; girls are expected to remain subservient to the wishes of the father. The nature of the father's relationship with children is built on the premise that emotional distance and the lack of familiarity will thwart challenges to paternal authority and reduce social conflicts later on (Jayawardena, 1963).

The structural dynamics of African-Caribbean families have already been laid out in a previous section. We now turn to a treatment of the specific involvement patterns of African-Caribbean mothers and fathers with children. Like their East Indian sisters, African-Caribbean women have been the primary caregivers to children. These women have always found room in their lives for their own children and those of others—a phenomenon that Brodber (1986) terms "emotional expansiveness." Candidly, then, despite the fact that a sizable number of African-Caribbean women share childrearing with other kinship and nonkinship females, they find currency in motherhood—a strong desire to have and care for children (Senior, 1991).

Quite often, with assistance from other kinship and nonkinship members and with very little economic support from fathers, low-income African-Caribbean women tackle parenthood with vaunted spirit. They appear fiercely maternal, in some countries engaging in formal infant handling routines that include massage, stretching, and motor exercises (Hopkins & Westra, 1988), being physically close to children and attending to their fretfulness, crying, and interrupted sleep patterns in a very relaxed manner (Landman, Grantham-McGregor, & Desai, 1983). Mothers are quite resourceful in tapping into community support for childrearing. For instance, in her work on community life in the yards of Kingston, Jamaica, Brodber (1975) showed that Jamaican women developed relationships with other women in the "yard" who became significant sources of support for childcare, child-watching, and general companionship. In other parts of the Caribbean, too, single-handedly or with the help of others, women must ensure that their children are fed, groomed, and sent to school (Powell, 1986).

In assuming broad responsibility for childrearing, it is not surprising that Caribbean women have been viewed as "fathering children" (Clarke, 1957). The famed Caribbean writer George Lamming in his novel, *In the Castle of my Skin*, lamented about his mother who fathered him. Not unexpectedly, in the absence of fathers, African-Caribbean mother-son bonds are close since boys are expected to become the protector of the family, carry on the family name, and care for their aging parents. Mothers offer boys greater latitude to engage in activities outside the home; girls receive constant scrutiny, are kept closer to parents, and are raised to be resourceful helpmates to partners (Brown et al., 1997).

Although African-Caribbean fathers have frequently been portrayed in a negative light as "drunken," "irresponsible," and "marginal" to family life, most men aspire to be good fathers (Brown et al., 1997). The findings of studies conducted over the last decade lend credence to such an assertion. In an interview study (Roopnarine et al., 1995) conducted in Jamaica and in a survey study (Wilson, 1989) conducted in Guyana, it was reported that African-Caribbean men showed levels of involvement in caring for young children that were comparable to those found for fathers in the industrialized countries of North America and Europe (see Table 2).

Table 2

Mean Number of Hours per Day African-Caribbean Parents in Kingston, Jamaica and African-American Parents in Syracuse, U.S.A., Engaged in Two Basic Caregiving Activities and Play With Infants

Measures	African-Caribbean (N=86)		African-American (N=63)	
	Mothers	Fathers	Mothers	Fathers
Feeding	2.31	.94	2.89	1.22
Cleaning	1.90	.52	2.01	.92
Playing	3.63	2.75	3.05	2.41

Note: The African-Caribbean fathers were from low-income common-law unions and resided in Kingston, Jamaica. The African-American fathers were from two-parent, middle-income families residing in Syracuse, New York. The same instrument was used to assess paternal and maternal involvement with infants in both groups of families. No direct comparisons are intended nor were there any computed. The data are used for illustrative purposes only. In our other work on African-American families with preschool-aged children (Ahmeduzzaman & Roopnarine, 1992), we found that fathers spent on average 2.8 hours per day in basic caregiving activities. Comparable hours of involvement with children have been noted for Euro-American families (Lamb, 1997).

Two large-scale qualitative studies completed by Brown and her colleagues (Brown, Anderson, & Chevannes, 1993; Brown et al., 1997) reveal similar findings. The first, conducted on men in Jamaica, showed that most fathers felt responsible for the moral education of their children, and were actively involved in tidying, playing, and helping children with their homework. The second, conducted in Guyana, Jamaica, and Dominica, provided insights into conceptions of fatherhood and paternal responsibility. Men in Guyana and Jamaica perceived manhood/fatherhood to mean the provision of financial support to "mind" children, to protect the family, and to exercise authority over women. These beliefs can lead to an unequal distribution of childcare responsibility, and they are sometimes said to precipitate alienation, distrust, and disillusionment between partners (e.g., Brown et al., 1997).

The scant information on other ethnic groups in the Caribbean points to similar levels of maternal and lower levels of paternal involvement with children as those determined for women and men in East Indian and African-Caribbean families. Among Amerindians in a coastal village in Guyana, fathers' economic and food production activities keep them away from children during the early childhood period. Fathers, however, do integrate sons into economic and assorted male activities as they get older and teach them how to fish, hunt, and make bows, arrows, and baskets (Sanders, 1973). Particularly troublesome is the indication that Carib men in Dominica are very distant from children. They provide very little economic support for children and spend little time in the natal or conjugal residence (Roopnarine et al., 1993).

In short, whether it is the East Indian, Carib, Amerindian, or African-Caribbean family, mothers and other women shoulder a majority of the responsibility for the socialization of children during the childhood years. Fathers, when present, are austere or seem preoccupied with exercising power over family members, and they are not as involved in the day-to-day care of children as mothers and other female figures are. Yet previous characterizations of Caribbean fathers as irresponsible and distant are unreasonable. Our suspicion is that with increased economic opportunities and educational attainment, Caribbean fathers are apt to show keener involvement in family life in general.

DIFFERENTIAL TREATMENT AND EXPECTATIONS OF BOYS AND GIRLS

The gender cleavage that is noticeable in the socialization of children in the Caribbean also has been observed in a number of pre-industrialized and developing societies around the world (Katgitçibasi, 1996; Lamb, 1987;

Roopnarine & Carter, 1992; Whiting & Edwards, 1988). Across the Caribbean, boys and girls are subjected to differential socialization experiences from parents and society-wide institutions (see Leo-Rhynie, 1997 for a discussion of the treatment of boys and girls in school). Not only do parents dress boys and girls differently and provide them with gender-differentiated toys (Leo-Rhynie, 1995), they exercise different levels of control and vary the severity of punishment dispensed to them. That is, boys are permitted more self-expression and self-assertion and are the recipients of more severe punishment from mothers and fathers than girls (Brown et al., 1997). The punishment is seen as necessary to toughen boys up so they can meet the challenges of the "rough outside world." In poorer urban settings, boys are involved in street activities and are in the company of other men early in their lives. They express "bravado" (slapping hands and aggressive displays) in greeting each other, and crying is reserved for serious loss, such as death. Boys view hugging and holding hands as unacceptable behaviors and too much "petting" is considered inimical to developing tough boys with a heterosexual orientation (Brown et al., 1997).

By comparison, girls display affection openly, and they are more likely to be involved in schoolwork and domestic activities closer to home. Girls are offered greater protection and are expected to assist with childcare very early in their lives, whereas boys are given heavy, outdoor tasks such as chopping wood, fetching water, and caring for animals (Justus, 1981; Rodman, 1971). While obedience and manners are valued for both, these expectations are more lax for boys than for girls. When exhibited by girls, feisty and disrespectful behaviors receive more negative sanctions than when manifested by boys. Parental affection is more common toward girls than boys; paternal affection toward girls diminishes, however, as girls grow older. Affection from men towards girls is seen as inappropriate and should be avoided (Brown et al., 1997).

SOCIALIZATION OF RACIAL-ETHNIC IDENTITY

The economic and political impact of White colonization in the Caribbean has been articulated by many individuals (Jagan, 1966; Smith, 1996; Vervotec, 1991; Williams, 1991). It is less clear what influence White standards of beauty may have had on the ethnic identity development and self-worth of non-White children in the Caribbean. Within the United States children are aware of racial differences as early as 3 years of age (Katz, 1982), and racial attitudes toward self and others have been outlined in classic studies (Clark, 1955). While the findings are not as clear cut as those reported for children in the United States, some data suggest that

Caribbean parents and children favor individuals with lighter over those with darker complexion (Grant, 1974).

Proceeding with commentary from the colonial period, Braithwaite (1953) observed that Caribbean mothers explicitly used terminology such as "good skin," "nice complexion," and "good and bad hair" when instructing their children about those who might be desirable playmates. Research from the post-independence period (after the 1960s) indicates that both parents and children continue to gravitate toward a preference for lighter skin. A prime example involves parents blaming children's misdeeds on their dark skin and "ugly Negro features" (Grant, 1974). An obvious question is: Do these beliefs and attitudes shake children's perceptions about the self and sabotage ethnic identity development? A dated study by Miller (1969) sheds light on the phenomenon. Adolescent African-Caribbean girls listed Caucasian features as the ideal for body image and denounced some of their own features in the process. This dissatisfaction was also present among East Indian and Chinese girls.

Are children getting these messages from parents only? Senior (1991) and Leo-Rhynie (1997) discussed the central role "nannies" play in instilling beliefs concerning light-skinned preference in children whose parents are better educated and are of the upper socioeconomic groups. Additionally, these authors implicate popular songs and novels as conveying messages that indicate the preference for lighter-skinned individuals (*Wide Sargasso Sea* by Jean Rhys; *The Orchid House* by Phyllis Shand Allfrey; cited in LeoRhynie, 1997). What this boils down to is that Caribbean children are bombarded with messages about the increased status that accompanies having lighter skin. But not all signs point to an enchantment with lighter skin. One study conducted in the early 1980s (Richardson, 1982) suggests that adolescents showed some movement toward more positive views pertaining to personal and national identities than they had in previous decades. Nonetheless, skin color remains a strong force in the lives of Caribbean children.

CLINICAL AND EDUCATIONAL OUTCOMES
OF PATTERNS OF SOCIALIZATION

Harsh economic conditions notwithstanding, three factors have been identified as having serious implications for Caribbean children's mental health and schooling: mate-shifting and its sequel child-shifting, harsh discipline, and distant or absent fathers. It is often difficult, though, to distinguish between the impact of these factors and the impact of economic conditions on children's mental health and educational outcomes. Of relevance is the finding that with greater economic resources come increased family stability and greater paternal involvement with children,

322 ROOPNARINE, CLAWSON, BENETTI, & LEWIS

with men having fewer "outside children." (Brown et al., 1997). Perhaps poor economic conditions destabilize men's roles within the family (Ahmeduzzaman & Roopnarine, 1992).

Father absence has received a good deal of attention in both literary works and sociological studies (Roopnarine et al., 1993). Unfortunately, much of what has been published is largely descriptive and speculative. There have been few systematic investigations of the impact of father absence or minimal father contact on children's intellectual and social development. What we do know shows that juvenile delinquents had fathers who were poor role models, but they were no more likely to come from father-absent homes (53%) than juveniles in a control group (49%) (Crawford-Brown, 1997). Students who were enrolled at the University of the West Indies report significant hostile feelings toward their absent or distant fathers (Allen, 1985), and males in Barbados, a country in which one in five males is raised in a married household, report anger toward their absent fathers (Dann, 1987). In addition, the school enrollment and achievement patterns of African-Caribbean Jamaican children living only with their mothers are not significantly different from those of East Indian Jamaican children living in two-parent households (Miller, 1991).

Paradoxically, father absence may not have the same negative consequences on Caribbean children's intellectual and social development as it does for children in other societies (see Lamb, 1997). Interestingly, it has not been determined to what extent Caribbean children who are from "father absent" homes have social contacts with other men or "father figures" who may influence their lives in important but as yet undocumented ways. A great advantage is that Caribbean children grow up in a cultural milieu that embraces the notion of multiple caregivers and fosterage. These social networks may buffer some of the more dramatic effects of father absence observed in post-industrialized societies where children are likely to be raised in smaller isolated units (see Furstenburg, 1991 for a discussion of teenage childbearing).

When we consider the consequences of child-shifting on childhood development, the data are equally as murky. Results from a recent project in Jamaica (Crawford-Brown, 1997) paint a disturbing picture about the effects of child-shifting on conduct problems among juvenile boys. Juvenile delinquents were more likely to have multiple residences (92% had between 2 and 6 changes in residences) and low social contact with parents when compared to non-delinquents. In a related fashion, children whose parents left them in the care of relatives and other adults during their migration to Canada and Great Britain experienced severe transitional difficulties. These were linked to reestablishing attachment bonds, cultural and ethnic identity confusion, and abuse (daCosta, 1985; Robertson, 1997;

Sharpe, 1997). But not all studies provided negative testimony on the consequences of child-shifting. Qualitative accounts of families in Barbados suggest positive associations between economic activity and social functioning in families and the practice of child-shifting (Russell-Brown, Norville, & Griffith, 1997). In this context we may ask: Do these positive associations translate into better outcomes for children later on? This question remains unanswered.

Rounding out this section, we examine the effects of harshness and severity of physical punishment on children's development. Although deeply embedded in the childrearing practices of Caribbean families, the psychological consequences of "beating" children with a belt or stick have not been fully explored. From research conducted in North America (e.g., Rohner, Bourque, & Elordi, 1996; Turner & Finkelhor, 1996), it can be said that physical punishment is associated with aggressive tendencies, delinquency, poorer psychosocial adjustment, lower self-esteem, and more emotional problems in children. In spite of these associations, the influence of severe punishment on children's well-being is a contentious issue. Rohner et al. (1996) and Baumrind (1996) argue that the love and rejection children receive from parents may be more strongly correlated with children's well-being than corporal punishment. Moreover, a threshold concept of the severity of physical punishment has been proposed (Rohner et al., 1996). It was reported that children's psychological adjustment does not appear to be compromised as much if they were punished once a week and the punishment was not hard. Those who were punished more than three times a week and perceived the punishment to be either "a little hard" or "hard" were at greater risk for psychological maladjustment (Rohner et al., 1996).

A major concern with the physical beatings that Caribbean children endure at the hands of adults—parents, parent surrogates, and teachers—is that in some instances it is so severe as to constitute abuse. Yet parents seem unaware of this possibility. In her clinical work with Caribbean children, Sharpe (1997) concluded that those children who were maltreated by parents were prone to depression, conduct disorder, and running away from home. Similarly, Sharpe and Bishop (1993) found that the mental health problems of teenage mothers in Trinidad preceded the pregnancy and were frequently connected to, among other things, physical beatings, abandonment, and severe neglect during different periods of childhood. To date, we cannot say whether the severity of the punishment meted out to Caribbean children may have led to the level of maladjustment discerned.

CONCLUDING REMARKS AND SOME RECOMMENDATIONS

Caribbean families are complex and diverse, and as such, any treatment of parent-child relations and patterns of socialization must be viewed within the context of family configurations, economic conditions, and emerging and reconstituted beliefs about childrearing. Families should not be seen in static terms, as there is a life course pattern of mating and childrearing. To researchers in the post-industrialized world, common-law unions may seem nontraditional and out of the realm of what constitutes "a family" in the Eurocentric definition. However, as stated before, these family forms have been in existence for over a century and have taken on adaptive meaning. How children fare in these different family configurations and what their eventual psychological and educational destinies may be remain largely unexplored.

In this regard, much more research is needed to map basic processes of socialization in the different family configurations. In view of the large number of Caribbean children who are raised without or with limited social contacts with fathers, it is imperative that we determine the impact of father absence/presence and multiple caregiving on children's mental health and educational achievement. So far, there have been speculative claims about levels of father involvement and children's development. And, there have been bold proposals that basically espouse the notion that poor non-White men may show a biological predisposition toward "CAD" reproductive strategies in which there is greater interest in mating than parenting (Belsky, Steinberg, & Draper, 1991). As Silverstein (1993) so cogently states, however, paternal involvement with children in non-White families may have a lot to do with environmental factors such as economic resources, racism, and the political and social climate, rather than reflecting a biological predisposition toward "CAD" reproductive strategies.

Finally, there should be legal recognition of common-law relationships. Caribbean men should be held responsible for the social, economic, and intellectual well-being of their children. Along with the implementation of laws, community programs should focus on male parenting and family responsibility. In particular, stereotypes men harbor about their role in the family and conceptions about "manhood" need to be reframed. Programs that focus on these issues seem to have benefited men who have been attending a fatherhood group in Kingston, Jamaica (Brown et al., 1997). The reality is that most countries in the Caribbean are so strapped economically that resources are being spent on meeting the basic nutritional and educational needs of families. Thus, governments would have to be judicious in implementing policies that have a more immediate impact on children's lives. It appears that a high priority policy goal would entail enlisting men's involvement in family life.

FAMILY STRUCTURE, PARENT-CHILD 325

Ahmeduzzaman, M., & Roopnarine, J.I. (1992). Sociodemographic
factors, functioning style, social support, and fathers' involvement with
preschoolers in African-American families. *Journal of Marriage and
the Family*, *54*, 699-707.
Allen, A. (1985). Psychological dependency among students in a "cross-
roads" culture. *West Indian Medical Journal*, *34*, 123-127.
Arnold, E. (1997). Issues in re-unification of migrant West Indian children
in the United Kingdom. In J.L. Roopnarine & J. Brown (Eds.),
Caribbean families: Diversity among ethnic groups (pp. 243-258).
Norwood, NJ: Ablex.
Arnold, E. (1993, January). The use of corporal punishment in child
rearing in the West Indies. *Servol News*, *8*, 34.
Baumrind, D. (1996). The discipline controversy revisited. *Family
Relations*, *45*, 405-414.
Belsky, J., Steinberg, L., & Draper, P. (1991). Childhood experience,
interpersonal development, and reproductive strategy: An evolutionary
theory of socialization. *Child Development*, *62*, 647-670.
Braithwaite, L. (1953). *Social stratification in Trinidad*. Institute of Social
and Economic Research. Mona, Jamaica: University of the West Indies.
Brodber, E. (1975). *A study of yards in the city of Kingston*. Mona,
Jamaica: Institute for Social and Economic Research, University of the
West Indies.
Brodber, E. (1986). Afro-Jamaican women at the turn of the century.
Social and Economic Studies, (Special Issue: Women in the Caribbean
Project, Pt. 2), *35* (3), 25-30.
Brown, J., Anderson, P., & Chevannes, B. (1993). *The contribution of
Caribbean men to the family*. Report for the International Development
Centre, Canada. Caribbean Child Development Centre, Mona:
University of the West Indies.
Brown, J., Newland, A., Anderson, P., & Chevannes, B. (1997).
Caribbean fatherhood: under-researched, misunderstood. In J.L.
Roopnarine & J. Brown (Eds.), *Caribbean families: Diversity among
ethnic groups* (pp. 85-113). Norwood, NJ: Ablex.
Chekki, D.A. (1988). Recent directions in family research: India and
North America. *Journal of Comparative Family Studies*, *19*, 171-186.
Clark, K. (1955). *Prejudice and your child*. Boston, MA: Beacon.
Clarke, E. (1957). *My mother who fathered me: A study of family in three
selected communities in Jamaica*. London: George Allen & Unwin.
Coll, C.G., Lamberty, G., Jenkins, R., McAdoo, H., Crnic, K., Wasik,
B., & Garcia, H. (1996). An integrative model for the study of

developmental competencies in minority children. *Child Development*, *67*, 1891-1914.

Crawford-Brown, C. (1997). The impact of parent-child socialization on the development of conduct disorder in Jamaican male adolescents. In J.L. Roopnarine & J. Brown (Eds.), *Caribbean families: Diversity among ethnic groups* (pp. 205-222). Norwood, NJ: Ablex.

daCosta, E. (1985). *Reunion after long-term disruption of the parent-child bond in older children: Clinical features and psychodynamic issues.* Toronto: Clark Institute of Psychiatry.

Dann, G. (1987). *The Barbadian male: Sexual beliefs and attitudes.* London and Bassingstoke: Macmillan.

Flinn, M. (1992). Paternal care in a Caribbean village. In B. Hewlett (Ed.), *Father-child relations: Cultural and biosocial contexts* (pp. 57-84). New York: Aldine de Gruyter.

Furstenburg, F. (1991). As the pendulum swings: Teenage childbearing and social concern. *Family Relations*, *40*, 127-138.

Goodnow, J., & Collins, W.A. (1990). *Development according to parents.* Hove: Erlbaum.

Grant, D.R.B. (1974). *Living conditions of some basic school children: Pointers to disadvantage.* Kingston: Bernard Van Leer Foundation-Centre for Early Childhood Education.

Grant, D.B.R., Leo-Rhynie, E., & Alexander, G. (1983). *Life style study: Children of the lesser world in the English speaking Caribbean: Vol 5, Household structures and settings.* Kingston: Bernard Van Leer Foundation-Centre for Early Childhood Education.

Harkness, S., & Super, S. (Eds.). (1996). *Parental cultural belief systems: Their origins, expressions, and consequences.* New York: Guilford.

Hopkins, B., & Westra, T. (1988). Maternal handling and motor development: An intercultural study. *Genetic, Social, and General Psychology Monographs*, *114*, 377-408.

Jagan, C. (1966). *The west on trial.* London: Michael Joseph.

Jayawardena, C. (1963). *Conflict and solidarity in a Guianese plantation.* London: (University of London) Athlone.

Justus, J. (1981). Women's role in West Indian society. In F. Steady (Ed.), *The Black woman cross-culturally* (pp. 421-430). Cambridge, MA: Schenkman.

Kagitçibasi, Ç. (1996). *Family and human development across cultures.* Mahwah, NJ: Erlbaum.

Katz, P. (1982). Development of children's racial awareness and intergroup attitudes. In L. G. Katz (Ed.), *Current topics in early childhood education* (pp. 17-54). Norwood, NJ: Ablex.

Kakar, S. (1991). *The inner world*. New Delhi, India: Oxford University Press.

Lamb, M. (Ed.). (1987). *The father's role: Cross-cultural perspectives*. Hillsdale, NJ: Erlbaum.

Lamb, M. (Ed.). (1997). *The role of the father in child development* (3rd ed.). New York: Wiley.

Landman, J., Grantham-McGregor, S.M., & Desai, P. (1983). Child rearing practices in Kingston, Jamaica. *Child: Care, Health, and Development*, *9*, 57-71.

Leo-Rhynie, E. (1995). *Girls' toys, boys' toys: Toys as a factor in gender socialization of Jamaican children*. Unpublished manuscript.

Leo-Rhynie, E. (1997). Class, race, and gender issues in child rearing in the Caribbean. In J.L. Roopnarine & J. Brown (Eds.), *Caribbean families: Diversity among ethnic groups* (pp. 25-55). Norwood, NJ: Ablex.

Massiah, J. (1982). *Women who head households*. WICP. Institute of Social and Economic Research, Cave Hill, Barbados: University of the West Indies.

McGillicuddy-DeLisi, A. (1985). The relationship between parental beliefs and children's cognitive level. In I. Sigel, A. McGillicuddy-DeLisi, & J. Goodnow (Eds,), *Parental belief systems: The psychological consequences for children* (2nd ed.) (pp. 7-24). Hillsdale, NJ: Erlbaum.

Miller, E. (1969). Body image, physical beauty and colour among Jamaican adolescents. *Social and Economic Studies*, *18*, 72-89.

Miller, E. (1991). *Men at risk*. Kingston: Jamaica Publishing House.

Ogbu, J. (1981). Origins of human competence: A cultural-ecological perspective. *Child Development*, *52*, 413-429.

Powell, D. (1982). Network analysis: A suggested model for the study of women and the family in the Caribbean. *Women and the family*. Cave Hill, Barbados: Institute for Social and Economic Research, University of the West Indies, WICP, Vol. 2.

Powell, D. (1986). Caribbean women and their responses to familial experience. *Social and Economic Studies*, *35*, 83-130.

Richardson, M. (1982). Socialization and identity. *Social and Economic Studies*, *31*, 1-33.

Ricketts, N. (1982). *Disciplinary home climate and social adjustment of selected second year basic school students*. Unpublished bachelor's thesis, Faculty of Education, University of the West Indies, Mona, Jamaica.

Roberts, G. (1975). *Fertility and mating in four West Indian populations*. Mona, Jamaica: Institute of Social and Economic Research, University of the West Indies.

Roberts, G., & Sinclair, S. (1978). *Women in Jamaica*. New York: KTO Press.

Robertson, E. (1975). *Out of sight—Not out of mind. A study of West Indian mothers living in England, separated for long periods from their children through leaving them behind when migrating and subsequently reunited.* Unpublished master's thesis, Sussex University, UK.

Rodman, H. (1971). *Lower-class families: The culture of poverty in Negro Trinidad.* New York: Oxford University Press.

Rohner, R., Bourque, S., & Elordi, C. (1996). Children's perceptions of corporal punishment, caretaker acceptance, and psychological adjustment in a poor, biracial community. *Journal of Marriage and the Family, 58,* 842-852.

Roopnarine, J.L. (1997). Fathers in the English-speaking Caribbean: Not so marginal. *World Psychology, 3* (1-2), 191-210.

Roopnarine, J.L., & Brown, J. (Eds.). (1997). *Caribbean families: Diversity among ethnic groups.* Norwood, NJ: Ablex.

Roopnarine, J.L., & Carter, B. (Eds.). (1992). *Parent-child socialization in diverse cultures.* Norwood, NJ: Ablex.

Roopnarine, J., Snell-White, P., & Riegraf, N. (1993). *Men's roles in family and society: Dominica, Guyana, and Jamaica.* UNICEF and University of the West Indies, Kingston, Jamaica.

Roopnarine, J.L., Brown, J., Snell-White, P., Riegraf, N. B., Crossley, D., Hossain, Z., & Webb, W. (1995). Father involvement in child care and household work in common-law dual-earner and single-earner families. *Journal of Applied Developmental Psychology, 16,* 35-52.

Roopnarine, J., Snell-White, P., Riegraf, N., Wolfsenberger, J., Hossain, Z., & Mathur, S. (1997). Family socialization in an East Indian village in Guyana: A focus on fathers. In J. L. Roopnarine & J. Brown (Eds.), *Caribbean families: Diversity among ethnic groups* (pp. 57-83). Norwood, NJ: Ablex.

Russell-Brown, P., Norville, B., & Griffith, C. (1997). Child shifting: A survival strategy for teenage mothers. In J.L. Roopnarine & J. Brown (Eds.), *Caribbean families: Diversity among ethnic groups* (pp. 223-242). Norwood, NJ: Ablex.

Sanders, A. (1973). Family structure and domestic organization among coastal Amerindians in Guyana. *Social and Economic Studies, 22,* 440-478.

Senior, O. (1991). *Working miracles: Women's lives in the English-speaking Caribbean.* ISER, University of the West Indies, Barbados. London: James Curry and Bloomington, IN: Indiana University Press.

Sharpe, J. (1997). Mental health issues and family socialization in the Caribbean. In J. L. Roopnarine & J. Brown (Eds.), *Caribbean families: Diversity among ethnic groups* (pp. 259-273). Norwood, NJ: Ablex.

Sharpe, J., & Bishop, J. (1993). *Situation analysis of children in especially difficult circumstances in Trinidad and Tobago*. New York: UNICEF.

Sigel, I. (1985). A conceptual analysis of beliefs. In I. Sigel, A. McGillicuddy-DeLisi, & J. Goodnow (Eds.), *Parental belief systems: The psychological consequences for children* (2nd ed.) (pp. 345-371). Hillsdale, NJ: Erlbaum.

Silverstein, L. (1993). Primate research, family politics, and social policy: Transforming "CADS" into "DADS". *Journal of Family Psychology, 7*, 267-282.

Smith, R.T. (1996). *The matrifocal family: Power, pluralism, and politics*. London: Routledge.

Turner, H.A., & Finkelhor, D. (1996). Corporal punishment as a stressor among youth. *Journal of Marriage and the Family, 58*, 155-156.

Vervotec, S. (1991). East Indians and anthropologists: A critical review. *Social and Economic Studies, 40*, 133-169.

Whiting, B.B., & Edwards, C. (1988). *Children of different worlds: The formation of social behavior*. Cambridge, MA: Harvard University Press.

Williams, B.F. (1991). *Stains on my name, war in my veins: Guyana and the politics of cultural struggle*. Durham, NC: Duke University Press.

Wilson, L.C. (1989). Family and structure and dynamics in the Caribbean: An examination of residential and relational matrifocality in Guyana. Unpublished doctoral dissertation, University of Michigan.

GROWING UP IN A COLLECTIVISTIC CULTURE: SOCIALIZATION AND SOCIOEMOTIONAL DEVELOPMENT IN CHINESE CHILDREN

Xinyin Chen, University of Western Ontario, Canada

INTRODUCTION

Individual socioemotional adjustment and problems have traditionally been neglected in Chinese and perhaps many other collectivistic cultures in which the welfare and interests of the collective are considered more important than those of individuals. Pursuing personal social status and expressing individual feelings and emotions, particularly of a negative nature, are frequently considered selfish and socially inappropriate (Luo, 1996). This may be particularly the case in children since they are typically expected to concentrate on their school performance (Ho, 1986; Stevenson, Lee, Chen, Stigler, Hsu, & Kitamura, 1990). Indeed, Chinese parents and teachers appear highly insensitive to children's socioemotional problems such as social isolation and depressed affect (Chen & Kaspar, in prep.).

Nevertheless, the neglect of personal social and emotional problems in Chinese culture does not imply that children in China do not experience socioemotional distress. In fact, it has been found that Chinese children experience an equal, or even higher, level of psychological disturbance, when compared with their North American counterparts (Chen, Rubin, & Li, 1995a, 1995b; Cheung, 1986; Crystal, 1994; Dong, Yang, & Ollendick, 1995; Shek, 1991). Moreover, a high rate of "malicious incidents" such as suicide in Chinese children and adolescents has been reported in the media (e.g., *China Youth Daily*, July 14, 1994; *China New Digest*, January 26, 1998). Unfortunately, there is little research extant concerning the developmental process of social and emotional functioning in Chinese children, and thus it is largely unknown what factors may be responsible for adjustment problems. On the other hand, given the dramatic differences regarding socialization beliefs, norms, and values in Chinese and Western cultures, it may be inappropriate to generalize Western-based theories and findings to Chinese culture without a careful examination of children's social and emotional development in their

The research projects described in this chapter were supported by grants from the Social Sciences and Humanities Research Council of Canada and a faculty award from the William T. Grant Foundation. I would like to thank Bo-shu Li, Dan Li, Zhenyun Li, and Guozheng Cen, at Shaniahai Teachers' University, and Huichang Chen and Qi Dong, at Beijing Normal University, who aided in data collection. I also thank the children and their parents and teachers in Shanghai and Beijing, P. R. China, who participated in these longitudinal projects.

cultural context. Culture not only affects the production of specific behaviors, but also imparts the meanings and directs the developmental patterns of socioemotional functioning.

In the past 10 years, my colleagues in China and Canada and I have been conducting several longitudinal cross-cultural projects concerning children's social relationships and socioemotional adjustment (Chen, Rubin, & B. Li, 1995a; Chen, Rubin, & Z. Li, 1995; Chen, Rubin, & D. Li, in press). In these studies, we have been interested in (1) the prevalence of social behaviors, including sociable-prosocial, aggressive-disruptive, and shy-inhibited behaviors, and emotional adjustment and maladjustment such as feelings of insecurity, loneliness, and depression, in Chinese children; (2) the cultural and contextual aspects that define the "meanings" of socioemotional functioning, particularly in social interactions and relationships; and (3) the developmental patterns of socioemotional functioning. These projects will serve as the major source of information for the following discussion of socioemotional development in Chinese children.

CHINESE COLLECTIVISTIC CULTURE AND SOCIALIZATION PATTERNS

Achieving and maintaining social order and stability are the primary concerns in both traditional and contemporary collectivistic Chinese societies. According to collectivistic principles, the interests of the individual must be subordinated to those of the collective. Selfishness, including seeking individual benefit at the expense of group interests and indifference to group interests, is regarded as a cardinal evil (Ho, 1986). The expression of individuals' needs or strivings for autonomous behaviors is considered socially unacceptable. Individual behaviors that may threaten the group functioning and the well-being of the collective are strictly prohibited.

In Chinese collectivistic culture, maintaining harmonious relationships with others is an index of individual social maturity. Interpersonal harmony is considered an ideal social condition for the achievement of individual mental health or "internal peacefulness." According to the theory of harmony (Luo, 1996), the degree of concordance and compatibility among different psychological components, including dispositional conditions, intellectual abilities, and social desires, determines one's psychological well-being. Socioemotional disturbances or disorders result from the lack of internal concordance and balance among the different elements and the lack of effective coping and regulatory mechanisms. Moreover, the theory of harmony states that the degree of harmony or goodness of fit at the intraindividual level may be affected by one's situation at the interpersonal or social level. Discord or disorganization in interpersonal relationships will eventually be reflected in individual socioemotional maladjustment. Interpersonal harmony plays a critical role in the mediation and moderation of the connection between contextual factors and psychological characteristics (Luo, 1996). Specifically, the influence of cultural and ecological conditions on children's socioemotional functioning may be mediated by the quality and the process of social relationships. Moreover, harmonious interpersonal relationships may serve as social and affective resources for children who are coping with adversities in life.

In contemporary Chinese society, developing harmonious social relationships and maintaining stable group functioning are the basic contents of school moral education, which are reflected in various political, social, and academic activities in the school. Students in Chinese schools, from kindergarten to graduate school, are required to attend regular political-moral classes in which collectivistic principles and requirements are systematically illustrated. In addition, children are frequently required to participate in extensive extracurricular group activities that are organized by formal organizations such as the Young Pioneers and the class committee. During these activities, children are encouraged to cooperate with each other and to develop positive relationships in the peer group. Moreover, children are expected to learn skills and behaviors required for group functioning such as obedience, conformity, and interdependence.

The emphasis on interpersonal relationships and group achievement in Chinese culture is reflected in socialization patterns. In many Western individualistic cultures, the goal of socialization is to help children develop social and cognitive competence for personal adaptation and achievement. Accordingly, acquiring personal social status and maintaining positive self-perceptions and feelings are major indices of developmental accomplishment. In contrast, the tasks of socialization in Chinese culture are (1) to help children learn how to control individualistic acts and reduce unique individual characteristics, (2) to develop collectivistic ideologies and cooperative skills and behaviors, and finally (3) to become an integral part of the group and to make contributions to the well-being and harmony of the collective (Chen & Kaspar, in prep).

The cross-cultural differences in socialization goals and values constitute a significant conceptual and methodological challenge to developmental researchers. On the one hand, specific cultural features serve as a context for children's adjustment and development; development cannot be completely and accurately understood without taking into account cultural factors. On the other hand, cultural influences on children's social and emotional functioning should be examined from a developmental perspective. Regardless of the culture, for example, common developmental tasks and requirements in socialization, such as learning to understand and respond appropriately to social and cultural standards (Whiting & Edwards, 1988), may lead to some cross-culturally similar patterns in human development. A focus on interactions between cultural context and developmental factors may help us understand complex processes in which children with particular dispositional features grow in various culturally created socioecological settings. Consistent with this view, we have applied an integrative methodology, the contextual cross-cultural approach, to examine developmental processes of social and emotional functioning in the Chinese collectivistic cultural context.

THE CONTEXTUAL CROSS-CULTURAL APPROACH: A METHODOLOGICAL NOTE

Researchers have attempted to examine cultural factors in human development from different perspectives, using different strategies. Two major approaches commonly used include the cross-cultural and the cultural approach, with the former emphasizing comparisons across cultures and the latter arguing for the understanding of processes within the culture. (See the chapters by Triandis and Kagitiçibasi in this volume.) In the cross-cultural approach, culture is frequently considered a "variable" in research design and data analysis; the focus is on comparisons between samples that represent different cultures on specific dimensions of psychological functioning such as intelligence, academic achievement, moral judgment, and aggression. Such a "variable-oriented" research in cross-cultural comparisons provides little information concerning the culturally bound developmental significance, functions, and processes of the phenomenon that are critical in the developmental field. The neglect of developmental processes and contextual factors may lead to misunderstanding and misinterpretation of the phenomenon and the construct (e.g., Chen & Kaspar, in prep.). Due to specific cultural conventions, norms, and socialization goals and expectations, underlying psychological constructs may be reflected or expressed in different forms across cultures (Bornstein, 1995). The cross-cultural approach appears insensitive to this issue.

The cultural approach, on the other hand, represents a contextual, and to a great extent, a relativistic perspective on development. The cultural approach focuses on the understanding of developmental processes as seen from a within-culture perspective; culture is considered a context that constantly interacts with individual behavior. The interactive relations between context and behavior pose methodological difficulties in collecting, analyzing, and interpreting information concerning the role of culture in development. At this time, interpretive methods such as ethnographic techniques are often advocated and applied by cultural psychologists. However, the judgmental nature of ethnographic methods remains a major concern for many researchers who pay attention to the scientific validity of the procedure and the replicability and generalizability of the findings.

A contextual yet cross-cultural approach has been adopted in our research. The focus of this integrative approach is on the understanding and assessment of social, cognitive, and psychological development in a systematic manner while, at the same time, the involvement of cultural context is taken into consideration. First, this approach indicates the role of contextual factors in social and emotional development and thus emphasizes the recognition and appreciation of sociohistorical, cultural, and ecological conditions for development. At the same time, on the basis of the understanding of social and cultural context, cross-cultural comparisons, either explicit or implicit, may provide valid, systematic information concerning the covariation between culture and child functioning. Second, according to this approach, it is important to investigate not only the production and prevalence of the behavior, but also the "meanings" of the behavior in the culture. In other words, culture may not only have main effects on social, behavioral, and emotional functioning, but also interact with individual functioning in determining developmental pathways and outcomes and, thus, serve as a moderator of developmental patterns. Third, psychological functions do not operate in isolation. The correlated constraints across different functions and dysfunctions mean that "person-oriented" comprehensive assessments may provide more complete information about how children develop in the context. Finally, it is essential to examine the developmental history and the course of social, cognitive, and emotional functioning in a paradigmatic manner. Information on the antecedents and outcomes of socioemotional functioning may lead to a better understanding of its significance and meaning in the culture.

To achieve the goals as proposed by the contextual cross-cultural approach, we have used integrative strategies and analyses in our research. Specifically, we have engaged constantly in "informal" communications and discussions among research members, local "experts," and participants, a process which helps us to locate the issues of interest in the culture, in terms of their relevance and significance. We have attempted to gather information concerning contextual factors including social, cultural, and ecological conditions such as family economic and educational status, socialization beliefs and values, and family functioning. The information about context is used not only for a better understanding of the adolescents' background, but also for purposes of data analysis. In addition, we have collected data from multiple sources using multiple methods including standardized measures, ethnographic interviews, naturalistic observations, and archival data, such as school records. Convergent information on multiple indicators concerning the construct may increase our confidence in both the validity of the procedure and the validity of the results while reducing concerns about measurement biases and errors.

Finally, we are using multivariate programmatic strategies in our analyses, usually of longitudinal data sets. The focus of our research is on the identification of general developmental patterns and the connections between psychological functions and contextual factors.

SOCIOEMOTIONAL FUNCTIONING: CULTURAL MEANINGS AND DEVELOPMENTAL SIGNIFICANCE

Developmental researchers have long been interested in the role of social functioning in children's social and psychological adjustment (Paker, Rubin, Price, & DeRosier, 1995). It has been found that socially competent functions are associated with indices of adjustment including social status in the peer group, school-related competence, and emotional well-being (Rubin, Bukowski, & Parker, 1998). Children who are socially assertive, cooperative, and friendly are likely to perform well in social and academic areas and to be psychologically resilient (Masten, Coatsworth, Neemann, Gest, & Tellegen, 1995; Rubin, Chen, McDougall, Bowker, & McKinnon, 1995). It has been suggested that, in addition to its direct effects, social competence may serve as a protective factor helping to buffer the negative influences of risk factors on development (Garmezy & Masten, 1991; Masten & Coatsworth, 1995).

In contrast, deviant behaviors such as aggression-disruption are associated with, and predictive of, adjustment problems including low social status, school-related difficulties, and juvenile delinquency (Caspi, Elder, & Bem, 1987; Rubin et al., 1995). It has also been found that children who are shy and socially withdrawn may be rejected or isolated by peers in social situations and experience emotional distress such as negative perceptions of competence and feelings of loneliness and depression (Hoza, Molina, Bukowski, & Sippola, 1995; Rubin, Chen, & Hymel, 1993; Rubin et al., 1995). It has been argued that, whereas aggression and disruption may be behavioral manifestations of underlying externalizing disorders, shyness and social withdrawal may reflect internalizing problems including fearfulness, social anxiety, and emotional distress (Rutter & Garmezy, 1983).

Similar behavioral patterns reflecting constructs of sociability, aggression-disruption, and shyness-inhibition have been found in Western and non-Western cultures (Hayashi, Toyama, & Quay, 1976; Kagan & Moss, 1962; Weisz, Sigman, Weiss, & Mosk, 1993). However, it has been argued that cultural values and social conventions may influence the judgment and evaluation of social behaviors as adaptive or maladaptive (Benedict, 1934; Chen & Kaspar, in prep.). Behaviors that are perceived as deviant and abnormal in Western cultures may be acceptable in other cultures. And, behaviors that are valued in the West may be regarded as maladaptive in other cultures. These arguments have been supported by findings, from our cross-cultural studies, that social behaviors may have similar or different adaptive "meanings" in Chinese and Western cultures (e.g., Chen, Rubin, & Sun, 1992; Chen, Rubin & Z. Li, 1995).

Social Competence: A Two-dimensional Model

We have generally found that in Chinese children prosocial, cooperative, and friendly behaviors are associated with, and predictive of, various indices of adjustment in social, school, and emotional areas (Chen, Rubin, & D.Li, in press). Consistent with the Western literature, socially competent children are liked by peers and adults, have high social status, and perform well in academic achievement. However, we have identified two overlapping but distinct aspects of social competence, sociable and prosocial functions, and these may play different roles in Chinese children's adjustment. Sociability or level of social participation represents the motivation and the capacity to initiate and maintain social interactions (Rubin & Asendorpf, 1993). Sociable children are often active in social settings and tend to establish extensive social contact with peers. On the other hand, being prosocial, cooperative or socially appropriate, including helping, caring or taking responsibility for another (Radke-Yarrow, Zahn-Waxler, & Chapman, 1983), represents how smoothly or properly children engage in social interactions. It involves self-regulatory skills or self restraint and social judgment of one's behaviors according to social norms and values. It is believed that prosocial-cooperative children are sensitive to others' distress and needs, and that they tend to follow rules and provide instrumental assistance and emotional support to others (Radke-Yarrow et al., 1983). Relative to sociability, prosocial attitudes and behaviors more likely represent an outcome of socialization because they are based on children's understanding and internalization of social norms and values (Eisenberg & Babes, 1998). Given the distinction between sociable and prosocial functions, it is conceivable that sociability may not always be expressed in socially appropriate or acceptable manners and that prosocial behaviors may not necessarily be displayed in sociable manners.

Consistent with the two-dimensional model, our research first revealed two clear factors, representing the sociable and prosocial dimensions in Chinese children, but interestingly, not in North American children (Chen, Liu, & Li, 1998). The differences between sociable and prosocial functions may be particularly salient in cultures such as China in which sociable and prosocial behaviors are viewed and valued differently. Since children are encouraged to learn how to control individualistic acts and to develop prosocial and cooperative attitudes and behaviors, it is not surprising that prosocial-cooperative behaviors are associated with social status and school adjustment. In contrast, sociability is not so highly appreciated or valued in Chinese culture. Although children are encouraged to interact and to maintain harmonious relationships with others, it is believed that social interactions and activities must be guided by prosocial or "right" orientations (Luo, 1996). Sociability itself does not bear much relevance to social and school adjustment, although sociable functioning may be associated with, and predictive of, emotional adjustment including feelings of loneliness, depression, and perceived self-worth.

In our Shanghai Longitudinal Project, it was found that, in addition to their common contributions to adjustment, sociable and prosocial functions each made unique contributions to the prediction of concurrent and later adjustment in specific areas (Chen, Liu, & Z. Li, 1998). Being prosocial was positively associated with, and predictive of, social and school adjustment and negatively associated with, and predictive of, externalizing problems. In contrast, functioning in sociable ways made unique contributions to the prediction of emotional adjustment including perceived self-worth, loneliness, and depression. The effects of sociability on social and school adjustment were moderated by prosocial orientation. Specifically, it was found that having a sociable reputation was significantly and positively associated with social and school adjustment and significantly and negatively associated with learning problems for children who had high scores on prosocial reputation; however, the associations were nonsignificant for children who had low prosocial scores. Furthermore, it was found that sociability was positively associated with, and predictive of, externalizing problems when its commonality or overlap with prosocial behavior was partialled out, suggesting that sociable children might be disruptive and aggressive if their behavior is not directed toward socially appropriate orientations Finally, it was found that the prosocial behavior served as a protective factor in the development of emotional difficulties. Thus, although sociability was significantly associated with, and predictive of, perceived self-worth and low levels of loneliness and depression, it may be an effective strategy to help children with emotional problems learn social norms and skills and develop socially appropriate behaviors. By displaying prosocial and cooperative behaviors children may improve their relationships with peers and their status in the group. This process, in turn, may change their negative perceptions and attitudes toward self and the world.

In short, the results indicate that, although sociable and prosocial functions are associated with each other, they make differential contributions to the social, school, and psychological adjustment of Chinese children. The results suggest that prosocial and cooperative children are clearly accepted by peers and adults and likely to be competent and well adjusted in social and school performance. In contrast, although sociable children tend to have positive self-perceptions and self-feelings, their social and school status depends on whether their sociable behaviors are directed by their prosocial or their antisocial orientations. The "two-factor" model indicates that sociability and a prosocial orientation, as the reflection respectively of individual reactivity and of constraint in social settings, may mutually regulate or "mediate" each other in their influences on children's adjustment in various domains.

Aggressive and Disruptive Behaviors

Aggressive, disruptive, and delinquent behaviors are common forms of externalizing problems in children and adolescents across cultures (Weisz, Sigman, Weiss, & Mosk, 1993). These behaviors are prohibited in Chinese society because they may cause damage to the welfare and harmony of the collective. It has been found that the level of aggressive and disruptive behaviors in Chinese children is roughly the same as that found among Western children (e.g., Chen, Chen, and Kaspar, in press). Moreover, consistent with the Western literature, aggressive behavior is significantly associated with, and predictive of, low social status and poor quality of peer relationships in Chinese children (Chen, Rubin, & Z. Li, 1995; Chen, Rubin, & D. Li, in press). Aggressive-disruptive children and adolescents are likely to be rejected by peers, rated by teachers as socially incompetent, and enjoy little respect and status in school.

It was found in a longitudinal study that aggressive behavior was strongly associated with learning problems in Chinese children and that early aggression and acting-out were negatively associated with later academic achievement (Chen, Rubin, & D. Li, 1997). Further analysis revealed that the relation between aggressive-disruptive behavior and achievement was unidirectional. While aggression-disruption significantly predicted low academic achievement, academic performance did not predict aggression once the stability of the latter variable was statistically controlled. Thus, although academic success or failure might not affect aggressive behavior, aggressive and disruptive behaviors were likely to hinder academic achievement, a process which might have been mediated by difficulties in learning processes and negative attitudes toward one's school.

In Western cultures, aggressive children and adolescents frequently fail to report internalizing difficulties such as feelings of loneliness and depression (e.g., Hoza et al., 1995; Rubin et al., 1995). It has been found that aggressive children tend to have biased self-perceptions and that they overestimate their social competence (e.g., Asher, Parkhurst, Hymel, & Williams, 1990). However, unlike their Western counterparts, aggressive children in China perceive themselves negatively. Furthermore, aggressive children report higher levels of loneliness, social dissatisfaction, and depression than non-aggressive children do (Chen et al., 1995a, 1995b). In fact, aggressive children are the most depressed group in China. This may be because children's social behavior and performance is regularly and publicly evaluated by teachers, peers, and self in Chinese schools, which may make it difficult for aggressive children to develop inflated or "inaccurate" self-perceptions of their social status.

Shyness and Social Inhibition

Social inhibition, which is often manifested in shy, withdrawn, and sensitive behaviors, has been conceptualized as being derived from conflictive approach-avoidance motives (Rubin & Asendorpf, 1993). The notion of shyness, or *Hai Xiu* in Mandarin (*Modern Chinese Dictionary*, 1986), as an anxious and reticent reaction to stressful novel situations or social evaluations, is virtually identical to that described in the Western literature (e.g., Rubin & Asendorpf, 1993). Nevertheless, the phenomenon may be viewed, and responded to, differently across cultures.

Shy and inhibited behaviors are regarded as socially immature and maladaptive in Western, and particularly in North American, individualistic cultures (Rubin & Asendorpf, 1993). Due to the widespread endorsement of assertive and competitive behaviors in these cultures, socially inhibited children may be at a distinct disadvantage relative to their more assertive age-mates. In contrast, since shy-inhibited behavior is unlikely to cause negative outcomes for the group, peers and adults in the collectivistic Chinese culture may not regard this behavior as maladaptive. Furthermore, since harmonious group functioning requires behavioral restraint, obedience, and submission, shy-inhibited behavior may be positively valued and encouraged. Indeed, in Confucian philosophy, inhibition and self-restraint are considered indices of accomplishment, mastery, and maturity (Feng, 1962; King & Bond, 1985); consequently shy, reticent, and inhibited children are believed to be well behaved and understanding (Ho, 1986; Tseng & Hsu, 1969-1970). Children are trained by adults to control their emotions and behaviors at an age as early as four years (King & Bond, 1985).

Positive evaluations of shy and inhibited behavior in China may also be related to the generally stable social environment. For example, the extensive peer contact that Chinese children have in the stable school and neighborhood environment may reduce the stress of interpersonal interactions and provide multiple opportunities for children to establish intimate social relationships and support systems. These social conditions may be particularly beneficial for shy-inhibited children who frequently experience difficulties interacting with others and exhibiting competent behaviors in stressful situations (Fox, Rubin, Calkins, Marshall, Coplan, Porges, Long, & Stewart, 1995). Given this background, it may not be difficult to understand that shy-inhibited Chinese children do not have problems in adjustment. On the contrary, the social acceptance and positive feedback that shy-inhibited children receive may increase their confidence and reinforce their competent performance, which ultimately leads to adaptive development.

Consistently, we have found that shy-anxious children in *Canada* experience social and adjustment difficulties including peer rejection, teacher-rated school problems, and negative self-perceptions and feelings. Shy-inhibited children in *China*, however, are accepted by peers and well adjusted to the social environment (Chen, Rubin, & Sun, 1992). Moreover, shy Chinese children are less likely than others to report loneliness and depression (Chen et al., 1995b). Finally, shyness-sensitivity in childhood was positively predictive of indices of adolescent adjustment such as teacher-assessed competence, leadership, and academic achievement (Chen, Rubin, & D. Li, in press).

Taken together, the results of our cross-cultural studies have indicated that Chinese culture clearly values children's behaviors that are beneficial to interpersonal harmony and group functioning including prosocial and cooperative behavior and inhibited-restrained behavior. In contrast, the behaviors that may threaten group harmony, particularly externalizing behaviors such as aggression and disruption, are strictly prohibited in the culture and, thus, associated with pervasive difficulties in social, school, and psychological adjustment. The associations between prosocial and shy-inhibited behaviors and self-reported social satisfaction and perceived self-worth, and the associations between aggression-disruption and feelings of loneliness and depressed mood support our view concerning the connection and interface between intrapersonal adjustment and interpersonal functioning.

DISPOSITION, SOCIALIZATION, AND CULTURE

Tracing the roots of children's social competence and problems has been one of the central themes in developmental psychology. It has generally been believed that both dispositional characteristics and socialization practices contribute, independently and interactively, to later social functioning. This belief has been supported by findings from a number of research programs in North America (see Kagan, 1989; Rubin et al., 1998, for comprehensive reviews). Nevertheless, it is important to note that the operation of dispositional and social-relational factors in development takes place in a cultural context. Culture influences socialization modes and strategies, personal traits, and the way in which they interact with each other (Chen & Kaspar, in prep.). Moreover, cultural context determines, to a great extent, how early factors can lead to adaptive or maladaptive development.

Dispositional   Characteristics: Inhibition,   Emotion-regulation,   and
Compliance

It has been reported that Chinese infants and children are more timid, shy,
and fearful in social situations than their Western counterparts (Gong, 1984;
Kagan, Kearsley, & Zelazo, 1978; see also the chapter by Freedman et al. in
this volume). For example, Kagan et al. (1978) found that, compared with
their Caucasian counterparts, Chinese infants and toddlers were more inhibited
behaviorally, less vocal and active, more apprehensive in novel situations, and
more likely to cry in the laboratory during maternal departure.

In April of 1995, my collaborators and I initiated a longitudinal project in
China and Canada to investigate developmental antecedents of social
functioning in Chinese and Canadian children. Two hundred and fifty toddlers
at 2 years of age, randomly selected in Beijing and Shanghai, China, and 120
toddlers at the same age, randomly selected in Ontario, Canada, participated in
the study together with their mothers. Data on temperament were collected
both from a videotaped laboratory visit and from parental reports. During the
laboratory visit, the children were brought to a novel room and tested for
cooperation and compliance, self-regulation and frustration tolerance, and
behavioral inhibition, using procedures adopted from the work by Fox and
Calkins (1993).

It was found first that, compared with their Canadian counterparts, Chinese
infants clearly demonstrated a higher level of inhibition and fear. They were
more vigilant and more likely to show high anxiety in novel social situations;
they often refused to engage in play behavior with unfamiliar adults, and they
stayed in close proximity to their mothers during free play and stressful
situations. These results were consistent with Kagan's et al. report (1978) cited
earlier. It was also found that Chinese toddlers were more compliant and
cooperative with adults during free play sessions and on clean-up tasks.
Chinese children were more likely than Canadian children to cooperate and to
comply when the mother initiated a command, request, or suggestion.
Moreover, a higher proportion of Chinese children completed the clean-up
tasks voluntarily and willingly. Finally, Chinese children tended to be less
expressive emotionally and had higher scores on emotion regulation during
frustration sessions (Chen, Hastings, Chen, & Cen, 1996). The findings
concerning behavioral inhibition, compliance, and regulation in Chinese and
Canadian infants and toddlers indicate that there may be different dispositional
conditions for socialization and cultural influences on socioemotional
development.

Behavioral functioning in the early years such as inhibition to novelty is
often considered dispositionally or biologically rooted (Kagan, 1989, 1998). It
is unclear at this time how the cross-cultural differences in compliant,

impulsive, and inhibited behaviors are reflected at the biological-physiological level. Some initial evidence has indicated that Chinese and European-American children differ in autonomic nervous system functioning as, for instance, indicated by heart rate variability in novel situations (Kagan et al., 1978). However, it remains to be examined whether there are differences in regulatory processes such as frontal brain activities (Fox et al., 1995), which may be particularly relevant to socialization experiences.

Child-rearing Attitudes and Practices

It has been argued (Chao, 1994; Ekblad, 1986; Ho, 1986) that socialization processes in Chinese culture are different from those found in Western cultures. Cross-cultural differences in socialization may be reflected in both parental ideologies concerning child-rearing, including socialization goals, expectations, and values, and parenting practices and strategies. In traditional Chinese culture, for example, "filial piety" is a Confucian doctrine dictating that children pledge obedience to and exhibit reverence for parents (Ho, 1986). Chinese parents, in turn, are responsible for "governing" (i.e., teaching, disciplining) their children, and they are held accountable for their children's failures. In this context, it has been consistently reported that, compared to Western parents, Chinese parents are more controlling and protective in child-rearing (Kriger & Kroes, 1972; Lin & Fu, 1990). For example, Chinese parents often encourage their children to stay close to them and to be cautious and dependent (Ho, 1986). Most Chinese infants and toddlers are allowed to sleep in the same bed or in the same room as their parents.

We have examined, in several studies, parenting attitudes and practices in Chinese culture, using multiple methods including parental reports and observations. It was found that, compared with North American parents, Chinese parents were more concerned with children's achievement and emotion control. However, Chinese parents were less likely to use reasoning and induction in parenting and appeared to be more authoritarian. They were also less likely to encourage their children to be independent, curious, and exploratory. Finally, we found that Chinese parents were more rejecting of and less affectionate toward their children than Canadian parents. Chinese parents were likely to use high-power strategies such as physical punishment in child-rearing (Chen, Hastings, Rubin, Chen, Cen, & Stewart, in press).

Given the Chinese emphasis on parental authority and child obedience, parenting styles and practices such as parental warmth and authoritarianism that were initially conceptualized in Western contexts (Baumrind, 1971), may possess adaptive "meanings" different from those found in Western cultures (Steinberg, Dornbusch, & Brown, 1992). In other words, given the cultural background, these parenting practices may not be relevant to social, cognitive, and emotional adjustment in Chinese children (Steinberg et al., 1992). Inconsistent with this argument, however, our recent studies have clearly demonstrated that parental authoritarian and authoritative parenting practices and parental acceptance and rejection serve virtually identical functions for child social, school, and psychological adjustment in Chinese and Western cultures (Chen, Dong, & Zhou, 1997). Specifically, it was found that authoritarian parenting was associated positively with aggression and negatively with peer acceptance, sociability-competence, distinguished studentship, and school academic achievement. In contrast, parental authoritative style was associated positively with indices of social and school adjustment and negatively with adjustment problems. Thus, regardless of cross-cultural differences in average levels of parental authoritativeness and authoritarianism, the adaptive meanings of these parenting styles in Chinese culture are similar to those found in the Western literature (Baumrind, 1971; Maccoby & Martin, 1983). Given that coercive, power assertive, and prohibitive strategies may lead to the child's negative emotional and behavioral reactions such as fear, frustration, and anger, it is not surprising that authoritarian parenting is associated with maladaptive social and academic development. In contrast, since authoritative parenting provides explanation, guidance, and communication of affect, it is associated with the child's feelings of confidence and security in the exploration of the world and with positive parent-child relationships, which in turn are associated with children's social and scholastic competence.

In addition, it has been found that, consistent with the Western literature (Rohner, 1986), parental warmth and acceptance, particularly in mothers, constitutes a social and emotional resource that allows children to explore their social and nonsocial environments. Moreover, parental warmth is a protective factor in the development of socioemotional functioning. In contrast, parental rejection and punitive strategies may have detrimental effects on children's social and school adjustment. In the Shanghai Longitudinal Project, for example, we found that maternal acceptance made significant and unique contributions to the children's development of social competence and behavioral functioning (Chen, Rubin, & B. Li, 1997). Children who were rejected by their mothers were likely to develop social and behavioral problems as well as depressive symptoms in later years. The similar effects of parental acceptance and rejection on social and emotional development in Chinese and Western children may indicate the universal significance of this "classical" dimension of parenting (Rohner, 1986).

Interactions and Transactions Between Parenting and Disposition in Cultural Context

Our research has revealed that Chinese children may display certain dispositional behaviors such as compliance and inhibition in the early years and that Chinese parents may use distinct strategies such as high power assertion in child-rearing. Given this background, how do dispositional and socialization factors contribute to socioemotional development in Chinese culture? The findings of our research projects have demonstrated that disposition and socialization may interact with each other in determining developmental pathways and outcomes. Moreover, the interactions between dispositional characteristics and child-rearing ideologies and practices may be constrained by cultural norms and values.

For example, it has been found that, whereas behavioral inhibition was associated with parental rejection, disappointment, and punishment in Western cultures, inhibition was associated with parental acceptance and encouragement of achievement in China (Chen, Hastings, Rubin, Chen, Cen, & Stewart, in press). The different parental attitudes toward inhibited behavior in Chinese and Western children may be derived from different cultural values regarding the behavior, and, at the same time, lead to different parental emotional and behavioral reactions to inhibited children. Whereas in Western cultures inhibited children are under pressure from their parents to change their behavior, inhibited Chinese children are encouraged by their parents to continue their behavior. This, in turn, may positively influence their perceptions of self-worth and their attitudes toward parents and others. Consequently, Chinese children are more likely to maintain their inhibited behavior and to remain wary, restrained, and cautious in social situations in the later years.

Similar processes have been found in the development of aggression and disruption in boys and girls. As we indicated earlier, aggressive-disruptive behavior is prohibited in Chinese culture because it may cause serious damage to group functioning. Compared with boys, girls may receive even greater sanctions against aggressive behavior because they are traditionally expected to behave in a compliant and passive manner. Thus, aggressive behavior in girls may be perceived as more deviant and abnormal and lead to more negative reactions from others. Consequently, it has been found that, although aggression-disruption was relatively stable from childhood to adolescence for Chinese boys, aggressive girls were likely to change their aggressive behavior and become socially competent (Chen, Rubin, & D. Li, in press).

The interaction between children's adaptive and maladaptive functioning and socialization practices has been observed also at the intracultural level. Specifically, and consistent with the Western literature (e.g., Rubin, Lemare,

& Lollis, 1990), it has been found that young children's even-tempered and easy temperament, accompanied by sensitive and responsive parenting styles and harmonious family relationships, predict the development of sociable, competent, and cooperative behavior in Chinese children. In contrast, children who are temperamentally difficult, easily frustrated, and emotionally unregulated are likely to become disruptive, impulsive, and hostile in their social interactions; these children tend to develop adjustment problems such as rejection by peers and academic difficulties (Chen & Rubin, 1994). However, consistent with the interactive perspective on the development of social functioning (Patterson, 1982), we have found that the associations between difficult temperament and later problems may be moderated by parental behavior and other socialization factors (Chen, Rubin, & B. Li, 1997). For example, the association is stronger for children who experience insensitive and inconsistent parenting and family stress than for children who enjoy warm and responsive parents and a supportive family environment. Parental warmth and acceptance may create "buffers" that protect disruptive and aggressive children from developing adjustment difficulties. Specifically, children who are aggressive but have warm parents and a positive family environment are less likely to exhibit behavioral and adjustment problems in later years than those aggressive children who have rejecting and neglecting parents and a stressful family environment (Chen, Rubin, & B. Li, 1997). Similarly, early timid, fearful, and inhibited temperament is associated with shy and wary behavior in childhood. This relation is exacerbated by a highly protective, directive, and anxious parenting style. However, wary and inhibited temperament and strong parental protectiveness appear to fit the Chinese culture and thus lead to adaptive outcomes in Chinese children.

THE EMERGENCE OF DEVELOPMENTAL PATHWAYS

Reflecting the pressures both of long-term cultural context and of biological processes, Chinese children appear to carry with them certain biologically based dispositional characteristics when they enter the world. The early dispositional biases may immediately be given cultural meanings and subsequently interact with culturally prescribed socialization forces such as parental child-rearing practices. As a result, culture influences not only specific behavioral functioning, but also the general patterns of social and emotional development.

Several pathways have been revealed in our research concerning socioemotional development in Chinese children. The first pathway starts with easy, even-tempered infants. Most infants may have this kind of easy-going, calm, and pleasant disposition. They are likely to receive positive responses from, and establish warm and secure relationships with, their parents. During infancy and toddlerhood, they cooperate and comply with parents on many training and learning activities, and perhaps, are socialized to be more compliant and obedient than their Western counterparts. During school years, these children are likely to display competent, particularly prosocial and cooperative, behaviors and are consequently accepted by their peers. At the same time, they have positive relationships with teachers, perform well in academic areas, and develop positive images and confidence about their general self-worth, all of which lead to desirable conditions for their adolescent lives.

On the other hand, for infants with a difficult and fussy temperament, the developmental pathway is quite different. Difficult temperament tends to elicit parental disappointment, rejection, and power-assertion, which in turn may collectively contribute to children's hostile and noncompliant behaviors. The negative attitudes toward the world and the undercontrolled, poorly regulated behaviors that the child carries into the school setting may lead to peer and teacher rejection. Together, the negative relationships with parents, peers, and teachers may further facilitate the development of pervasive social, academic, and psychological problems. Given the cultural norms and the school social circumstances such as the public evaluation process, aggressive and disruptive children may develop externalizing as well as internalizing problems. Of course, not all children starting with a difficult temperament follow this developmental pattern. A supportive family and school environment including parental acceptance and inductive child-rearing practices may moderate the developmental processes and thus buffer aggressive children from developing maladaptive behaviors.

The third emerging pathway starts with a wary and inhibited infant. Chinese children seem to be more anxious and inhibited in novel and challenging situations than Western children are. Whereas inhibited children are regarded as incompetent and immature in the West, inhibited children in China are both accepted by their parents and encouraged to maintain their behavior. Consistently, since shy-inhibited behavior is positively perceived and evaluated by peers and teachers in the school, shy-inhibited children are liked by peers and teachers and function well in the school. Moreover, given the continuous positive feedback they receive during childhood and adolescence, shy-inhibited children gradually develop positive perceptions of their competence and their intimate social relationships and support systems, and thus continue to adjust well to their adolescent environments (Chen, Rubin, & D. Li, in press).

ISSUES AND DIRECTIONS

Our research represents an initial effort in the exploration of the socioemotional development of Chinese children. Many issues remain to be examined. For example, in a recent study based on observations of social interactions in the home situation, we found that many grandparents were involved in child-rearing. Some grandparents even take on the primary responsibilities for childcare, training, and education. Research that focuses mainly on parenting attitudes and behaviors of parents and ignores the influences of other social relationships such as grandparent-child relationships may not tap some of the most important aspects of socialization and development in Chinese children.

Most Chinese children live in rural areas where the social conditions, cultural norms, and family structure and organization may differ from those prevailing in the major cities. However, our research has been conducted mainly in the urban areas because it is practically difficult to gain access to and collect data from rural populations. Although cross-cultural comparisons between urban Chinese children and their counterparts in Western cultures are theoretically meaningful, interesting and methodologically appropriate, it remains an open issue how far the findings of our studies also apply to the rural areas of China. Thus, it will be our next step to examine this issue.

Finally, like many other countries in the world, China is undergoing dramatic changes. Western values and ideologies have been introduced into the country along with advanced technology. In addition, Chinese family structure and organization and child-rearing beliefs and values have been changing (Chen, 1997). Thus, in the future years, it will be important to investigate how societal and family changes may influence socialization patterns and child development.

BIBLIOGRAPHY

Asher, S., Parkhurst, J.T., Hyniel, S., & Williams, G.A. (1990). Peer rejection and loneliness in childhood. In S.R. Asher & J.D. Coie (Eds.), *Peer rejection in childhood* (pp. 253-273). New York: Cambridge University Press.

Baumrind, D. (1971). Current patterns of parental authority. *Developmental Psychology Monograph, 4* (1, pt. 2).

Benedict, R. (1934). Anthropology and the abnormal. *Journal of General Psychology, 10*, 59-82.

Bornstein, M.H. (1995). Form and function: Implications for studies of culture and human development. *Culture and Psychology, 1* (l), 123-138.

Caspi, A., Elder, G.H. Jr., & Bem, D.J. (1987). Moving against the world: Life-course patterns of explosive children. *Developmental Psychology, 23*, 308-313.

Chao, R.K. (1994). Beyond parental control and authoritarian parenting styles: Understanding Chinese parenting through the cultural notion of training. *Development*, *65*, 1111-1119.

Chen, X. (1997). The changing Chinese family: Resources, parenting practices, and children's socioemotional problems. In U.P. Gielen & A.L. Comunian (Eds.), *The family and family therapy in international perspective* (pp. 150-167). Trieste, Italy: Edizioni Lint.

Chen, X., Chen, H., & Kaspar, V. (in press). Social, emotional, and school adjustment in Chinese adolescents. *International Journal of Group Tensions*.

Chen, X., Dong, Q., & Zhou, H. (1997a). Authoritative and authoritarian parenting practices and social and school adjustment in Chinese children. *International Journal of Behavioural Development*, *20*, 855-873.

Chen, X., Hastings, P., Chen, H., & Cen, G. (1996, May). *Emotion regulation in Chinese and Canadian toddlers*. Presented at the 9th Waterloo Biennial Conference on Child Development, Waterloo.

Chen, X., Hastings, P., Rubin, K.H., Chen, H., Cen, G., & Stewart, S.L. (in press). Child-rearing attitudes and behavioral inhibition in Chinese and Canadian toddlers: A cross-cultural study. *Development Psychology*.

Chen, X., & Kaspar, V. (in prep). Cross-cultural research on childhood. In U.P. Gielen (Ed.), *Childhood and adolescence in cross-cultural perspective*.

Chen, X., Liu, M., & Li, Z. (1998), *Sociable and prosocial reputations in Chinese children: Relations with social, academic and psychological adjustment*. Manuscript submitted for publication.

Chen, X., & Rubin, K.H. (1994). Family conditions, parental acceptance and social competence and aggression. *Social Development*, *3*(3), 269-290.

Chen, X., Rubin, K.H., & Li,B. (1995a). Social and school adjustment of shy and aggressive children in China. *Development and Psychopathology*, *7*(2), 337-349.

Chen, X., Rubin, K.H., & Li, B. (1995b). Depressed mood in Chinese children: Relations with school performance and family environment. *Journal of Consulting and Clinical Psychology*, *63*, 938-947.

Chen, X., Rubin, K.H., & Li, B. (1997). Maternal acceptance and social and school adjustment in Chinese children: A four-year longitudinal study. *Merrill-Palmer Quarterly*, *43* (4), 663-681.

Chen, X., Rubin, K.H., & Li, D. (1997c). Relation between academic achievement and social adjustment: Evidence from Chinese children. *Developmental Psychology*, *33*, 518-525.

Chen, X, Rubin, K.H., & Li, D. (in press). Adolescent outcomes of social functioning in Chinese children. *International Journal of Behavioral Development*.

Chen, X., Rubin, K.H., & Li, D. (1997). Relation between academic achievement and social adjustment: Evidence from Chinese children. *Developmental Psychology, 33*, 518-525.

Chen, X., Rubin, K.H., & Li, Z. (1995c). Social functioning and adjustment in Chinese children: A longitudinal study. *Developmental Psychology 31*, 531-539.

Chen, X., Rubin, K.H., & Sun, Y. (1992). Social reputation and peer relationships in Chinese and Canadian children: A cross-cultural study. *Child Development, 63*, 1336-1343.

Cheung, F.M.C. (1986). Psychopathology among Chinese people. In M.H. Bond (Ed.), *The psychology of the Chinese people* (pp. 171-211). New York: Oxford University Press.

Crystal, D.S., Chen, C., Fuligni, A.J., Hsu, C.C., Ko, H.J., Kitamura, S., & Kimura, S. (1994). Psychological maladjustment and academic achievement: A cross-cultural study of Japanese, Chinese, and American high school students. *Child Development, 65*, 738-753.

Dong, Q., Yang, B., & Ollendick, T.H. (1994). Fears in Chinese children and adolescents and their relations to anxiety and depression. *Journal of Child Puchology and Psychiaatry, 35*, 351-363.

Eisenberg, N., & Babes, R.A. (1998). Prosocial development. In N. Eisenberg (Ed.), *Handbook of child psychology: Vol 3. Social, emotional and personality development* (pp. 701-778). New York: Wiley.

Ekblad, S. (1986). Relationships between child-rearing practices and primaryschool children's functional adjustment in the People's Republic of China. *Scandinavian Journal of Psychology, 27*, 220-230.

Feng, Y.L. (1962). *The spirit of Chinese philosophy.* (Translated by E.R. Hughes). London: Routledge & Kegan Paul.

Fox, N., & Calkins, S. (1993). Relations between temperament, attachment, and behavioral inhibition: Two possible pathways to extroversion and social withdrawal. In K.H. Rubin & J. Asendorpf (Eds.), *Social withdrawal, inhibition, and shyness in childhood* (pp. 81-100). Chicago, IL: University of Chicago Press.

Fox, N., Rubin, K.H., Calkins, S., Marshall, TR., Coplan, R.J., Porges, S.W.,Long, J.M., & Stewart, S. (1995). Frontal activation asymmetry and social competence at four years of age. *Child Development, 66*, 1770-1784.

Garmezy, N., & Masten, A.S. (1991). The protective role of competence indicators in children at risk. In E.M. Cummings, A.L. Greene, & K.H. Karraker (Eds.), *Life-span developmental psychology: Perspectives on stress and coping* (pp. 151-174). Hillsdale, NJ: Erlbaum.

Gong, Y. (1984). Use of the Eysenck Personality Questionnaire in China. *Personality and Individual Differences, 5*, 431-438.

Hayashi, K., Toyama, B., & Quay, H. C. (1976). A cross-cultural study concerned with differential behavioral classification. I. The Behavior Checklist. *Japanese Journal of Criminal Psychology*, 2, 21-28.

Ho, D.Y.F. (1986). Chinese pattern of socialization: A critical review. In M. H. Bond (Ed.), *The psychology of the Chinese people* (pp. 1-37). New York: Oxford University Press.

Hoza, B., Molina, B.G., Bukowski, W.M., & Sippola, L.K. (1995). Peer variables as predictors of later childhood adjustment. *Development and Psychopathology*, 7, 787-802.

Kagan, J. (1989). Temperamental contributions to social behavior. *American Psychologist*, 44, 668-674.

Kagan, J. (1998). Temperament and the reactions to unfamiliarity. *Development*, 68, 139-143.

Kagan, J., Kearsley, R B., & Zelazo, P.R. (1978). *Infancy: Its place in human development*. Cambridge, MA: Harvard University Press.

Kagan, J., & Moss, H.A. (1962). *Birth to maturity: A study in psychological development*. New York: Wiley.

King, A.Y.C., & Bond, M.H. (1985). The Confucian paradigm of man: A sociological view. In W.S. Tseng & D.Y.H. Wu (Eds.), *Chinese culture and mental health* (pp. 29-45). New York: Academic Press.

Kriger, S.F., & Kroes, W.H. (1972). Child-rearing attitudes of Chinese, Jewish, and Protestant mothers. *Journal of Social Psychology*, 86, 205-210.

Lin, C.C., & Fu, V.R. (1990). A comparison of child-rearing practices among Chinese, immigrant Chinese, and Caucasian-American parents. *Child Development*, 61, 429-433.

Luo, G. (1996). *Chinese traditional social and moral ideas and rules*. Beijing, China: The University of Chinese People Press.

Maccoby, E.E., & Martin, J.A. (1983). Socialization in the context of family: Parent-child interaction. In E.M. Hetherington (Ed.), *Handbook of child psychology: Vol. 4. Socialization, personality and social development* (pp. 1-102). New York: Wiley.

Masten, A.S., & Coatsworth, J.D. (1995). Competence, resilience, and psychopathology. In D. Cicchetti & D.J. Cohen (Eds.), *Developmental psychopathology: Vol. 2. Risk, disorder, and adaptation* (pp. 715-752). New York: Wiley.

Masten, A., Coatsworth, J.D., Neemann, J., Gest, S.D., Tellegen, A., & Garmezy, N. (1995). The structure and coherence of competence from childhood through adolescence. *Child Development*, 66, 1635-1659.

Parker, J.G., Rubin, K.H., Price, J.M., & DeRosier, M.E. (1995). Peer relationships, child development, and adjustment: A developmental psychopathological perspective. In D. Cicchetti & D.J. Cohen (Eds.), *Developmental psychopathology: Vol. 2. Risk, disorder, and adaptation*

352   CHEN

(pp. 96-161), New York: Wiley.

Patterson, G.R. (1982). *A social learning approach to family intervention: III. Coercive family process.* Eugene, OR: Castalia.

Radke-Yaffow, M., Zahn-Waxler, C., & Chapman, M. (1983). Children's prosocial dispositions and behavior. In E.M. Hetherington (Ed.), *Handbook of child psychology: Vol. 4. Socialization, personality, and social development* (pp. 469-546). New York: Wiley.

Rohner, R.P. (1986). *The warmth dimension: Foundation of parental acceptance-rejection theory.* Newbury Park, CA: Sage.

Rubin, K.H., & Asendorpf, J. (1993). *Social withdrawal inhibition, and shyness in childhood.* Hillsdale, NJ: Erlbaum.

Rubin, K.H., Bukowski, W., & Parker, J.G. (1998). Peer interactions, relationships, and groups. In N. Eisenberg (Ed.), *Handbook of child psychology: Vol. 3. Social, emotional, and personality development* (pp. 619-700). New York: Wiley.

Rubin, K.H., Chen, X., & Hymel, S. (1993). Socio-emotional characteristics of aggressive and withdrawn children. *Merrill-Palmer Quarterly, 39,* 518-534.

Rubin, K.H., Chen, X., McDougall, P., Bowker, A., & McKinnon, J. (1995). The Waterloo Longitudinal Project: Predicting internalizing and externalizing problems in adolescence. *Development and Psychopathology, 7,* 751-764.

Rubin, K.H., LeMare, L., & Lollis, S. (1990). Social withdrawl in childhood: Developmental pathways to peer rejection. In S.R. Asher & J.P. Coie (Eds.), *Peer rejection in childhood* (pp. 217-249). New York: Cambridge University Press.

Rutter, M., & Garmezy, N. (1983). Developmental psychopathology. In E.M. Hetherington (Ed.), *Handbook of child psychology: Socialization, personality, and social development* (pp. 775-911). New York: Wiley.

Shek, D.T. (1991). Depressive symptoms in a sample of Chinese adolescents: An experimental study using the Chinese version of the Beck Depression Inventory. *International Journal of Adolescent Medicine and Health, 5,* 1-16.

Steinberg, L., Dornbusch, S., & Brown, B.B. (1992). Ethnic differences in adolescent achievement: An ecological perspective. *American Psychologist, 47* (6), 723-729.

Stevenson, H.W., Lee, S., Chen, C., Stigler, J. W., Hsu, C., & Kitamura, S. (1990). Contexts of achievement. *Monographs of the Society for Research in Child Development, 55,* (Serial N. 221).

Tseng, W.S., & Hsu, J. (1969-70). Chinese culture, personality formation and mental illness. *International Journal of Social Psychiatry, 16,* 5-14.

Weisz, J.R., Sigman, M., Weiss, B., & Mosk, J. (1993). Parent reports of behavioral and emotional problems among children in Kenya, Thailand, and the United States. *Child Development*, *64*, 98-109.

Whiting, B.B., & Edwards, C.P. (1988). *Children of different worlds.* Cambridge, MA: Harvard University Press.

SOCIAL VALUES: A COMPARISON OF CHINESE AND AMERICAN CHILDREN

George Domino, University of Arizona, U.S.A.

INTRODUCTION

The genesis of the two studies to be reported here occurred in September of 1982 when, as a member of a delegation of psychologists headed by Dr. Shelley Korchin, I had the opportunity to visit Mainland China for approximately a month. The trip was a unique life-long experience, filled with visits to universities and mental hospitals, schools and communes, major cities and the country side; among the many and confused impressions I brought back with me were the exquisite beauty of the vast land and its people, and the close melding of political, moral, and personal values.

When I returned to the United States, I tried to make better sense of my experience by sharing enthusiastic reminiscences with others who had also visited the People's Republic of China, and by immersing myself in the psychological literature related to China. One result was an annotated bibliography (Domino, 1985) of what I considered to be 54 basic studies of interest to the Western social scientist about to embark on a China odyssey. A second result (Domino, Affonso, & Slobin, 1987) was a paper trying to synthesize our varied impressions on the role of community psychology in China. Still a third result was the somewhat surprising realization that on the one hand there *is* a vast Western literature on the Chinese written from anthropological, sociological, and psychological points of view, but that there are actually very few empirical studies that provide comparative data between Americans and mainland Chinese; what empirical studies are available are often based on Chinese residing in San Francisco or New York Chinatowns, or Chinese living in highly Westernized settings such as Hong Kong and Taiwan, or in multiethnic settings such as Hawaii. I have attempted to remedy this in a very small way in the area of cancer imagery (Domino & Lin, 1991; 1992) and attitudes toward suicide (Domino, Lin, & Chang, 1995; Domino, Shen, & Su [in press]; Domino & Su, 1994; Domino, Su, & Shen [in press])

The present studies then, were undertaken to begin the exploration of basic psychological phenomena that might be reflective of the differences and similarities between Chinese and American, and might give us a "behavioral photograph" by which better to understand human behavior as influenced by cultural milieu. Perhaps it should be mentioned here that these studies emanate from what was once called "dustbowl empiricism" that is, an attempt to assess what the evidence is, without the benefits and disadvantages of a well formulated theoretical framework such as the stage theory of Kohlberg (1983) or the balance theory of Heider (1958). At the same time, I have had enough experience doing empirical studies to know that theory, implicit or explicit, always lies not far below the surface; and so the classical work of Kluckhohn and Murray (1953) as well as the writings of Bagby (1953) might be identified as having had a theoretical influence on the present studies.

Social Values

A perusal of the available literature (e.g., Bond, 1996; Bond & Wang, 1983; Ho, 1981; Hsu, 1970; Kessen, 1975; Murphy & Murphy, 1968; Scofield & Sun, 1960; Wilson, 1970) indicates that Chinese society is marked by several salient social values which stress close family ties, mutual dependence of one another, a culture rich in tradition and conformity, an emphasis on group solidarity, and an almost total acceptance of authority as authority; at the same time, a number of changes in these and other aspects seem to be occurring (Yang, 1996).

The presence of these values is well documented by observational and anecdotal accounts, but substantially less so by empirical data. In trying to develop a study that would focus on social values we were stymied by a multitude of factors; these included the fact that paper-and-pencil questionnaires so common in American schools are rather alien to the Chinese; that Chinese psychologists are few in number and though fully cooperative were not in a position to carry out an investigation instigated by an unknown American; that for practical reasons, the data needed to be collected within a short time span; and that most questionnaires developed by Western psychologists seemed quite inappropriate.

Almost serendipitously we came upon a story completion technique developed by Metraux (1955) in the context of a study of ten- and eleven-year-old West German children. Metraux utilized a series of six story plot situations, all variations on the theme of loss and accidental damage. The story plots or stems are presented to the individual child who is asked to complete each story, to give each story an ending. In her study, Metraux discussed the resulting completions in a qualitative manner, with no statistical analyses, and no American comparison group.

METHOD OF STUDY 1

Materials

For this study, only five of Metraux's (1955) stories were utilized, as one story was deemed inappropriate. Minor revisions were made in the five stories so that each would be pertinent to both Chinese and American cultures; for example, "playing football" was changed to "playing ball" and "going to the butcher's to buy some sausage" was changed to "going to the store to buy some meat." These are the five stories:

1. Peter and Frank are walking to school. Suddenly Frank grabs Peter's cap and throws it high into the nearest tree, so that Peter cannot get it down. Frank has never done this before, and Frank and Peter did not argue before this. Why did Frank do this? What does Peter do? What does Frank think? What does Peter think? What will happen?

2. The mother sends Michael to the store where he is to buy some meat for supper. On the way home Michael lays the package down and plays with his friends for a little while. Suddenly a dog runs up and pulls some pieces of meat out of the package and runs away with them. Michael wraps up the rest of the meat and goes home. What does Michael say to his mother? What does the mother do? What does Michael think then? What happens?

3. The teacher (a man) suddenly discovers that some money has disappeared from his desk. He looks up and sees that the whole class is quietly working on their arithmetic lesson. He considers what has happened to the money and what he should do. What does the teacher do? End this story with some sentences. Tell what happened to the money, and also exactly what the teacher thinks and what he does.

4. Elizabeth is sitting at home doing her schoolwork. She thinks about her mother's new coat. She would like to see how the coat looks on her and tries it on. When she takes it off, she notices that she has got ink spots on her mother's new coat. Just as Elizabeth is rubbing out the spots, her mother comes in the door. What does her mother say? What does each think? What does Elizabeth say? What does each do?

5. John and Bill are playing ball. They know that they should not kick the ball on the little street in front of the house. John kicks the ball and it flies into the window, which gets a big crack. Bill thinks someone came to the window. No one could have seen who kicked the ball into the window. End this story with some sentences and tell what you think both boys thought and did.

The stories were translated into Chinese using the back-translation method (Brislin, 1979) with common Chinese names such as Yong, Wei, and Yan substituted for Peter, Frank, and Elizabeth. The translation process went through several iterations with its focus on what Brislin (1986) calls decentering - moving back and forth between languages so no one language is the "center" of attention.

The Pilot Studies

Several pilot studies were carried out with both Chinese and American children to determine if the story completion technique was psychometrically and experimentally sound. Some difficulties were encountered with children younger than nine years of age, but children 11- to 13-years-old seemed relatively at ease with the procedure, able to keep in mind the various elements of each story plot, and able to respond to the multiple questions without much prompting.

A more formal pilot study was then conducted with 53 American and 12 Chinese children 11- to 13-years-old. These children generated 248 story completions and these completions, together with Metraux's (1955) discussion were used to develop a content analysis schema eventually covering 121 elements. For example, story completions to Story #1 were scored along the following dimensions:

A. *Main solution given to story:*

1. Frank gets the cap down.

2. Peter gets the cap down.

3. The situation becomes a joke (there is denial of seriousness).

4. Natural forces (such as the wind) provide a positive solution (e. g., the cap is retrieved).

5. Natural forces (such as the wind) provide a negative solution (e.g., the cap is blown away).

6. The incident reflects a bigger issue (e.g., the boys are enemies; getting even; etc.).

7. No solution is given.

B. *Adults*

1. Do adults show up?

2. If yes, are they punitive? (e.g., Frank is spanked).

3. If yes, are they helpful? (e.g., they retrieve the cap).

4. If yes, are they authoritarian? (e.g., the principal tells Frank to get the cap or else).

5. If yes, are they problem-solvers? (e.g., tell the children where to get a ladder).

C. *Other children*

1. Do other children show up?

2. If yes, do they help with the hat?

3. Are they playmates, not related to retrieval of the hat?

4. Do the other children solve the situation?

D. *Emotions expressed*

1. Is the main interplay between Peter and Frank intellectual? (e.g. how do we get the cap down?).

2. Is the main interplay emotional? (e.g., one or both are very angry, upset, delighted, etc.).

3. Is the main interplay physical? (e.g., they hit each other).

4. Does Peter: __get angry? __cry? __insult Frank? __get physical? __get hurt? __avoid confrontation by denial?

5. Does Frank: __make amends? __apologize? __pay for cap? __ get the cap down? __turn situation into a joke? __get hurt in   process of amends? (e.g., falls from the tree). __ get punished as a direct result? __ get punished indirectly? (e.g., the next day he gets hit by a car).

6. Do Peter and Frank get into a fight?

7. Is jealousy expressed? (e.g., Frank would like a cap of his own).

8. Does teamwork occur? (e.g., Peter holds the ladder while Frank retrieves the cap).

E. *Other aspects*

1. Degree of humor present (1 = none; 3 = average; 5 = high).

2. How original is plot (1 = not original; 3 = average; 5 = very original).

3. Is there a moral to the story? If yes, is the moral explicit (i.e., spelled out), or implicit?

4. Is the story resolution generally positive (rate on a 1 to 5 scale from 1 = somewhat to 5 = extremely positive) or is the story resolution generally negative (rate on a 1 to 5 scale as above).

5. Does the victim (Peter) get even?

6. Does the friendship survive or break down (must be explicitly stated)?

Subsets of the 248 story completions were then independently rated by three research assistants who had been trained on the stories collected during the more informal pilot phases. Percentage of agreements were computed and elements were modified or eliminated (if below 70% agreement) on the basis of the results obtained. Computed percentage of agreements indicated satisfactory reliability, with a median of 92%, and a range of 70% to 100% agreement.

Participants

Story completions were then obtained from two samples of children, ages 11- to 13-years-old. One sample consisted of 80 Chinese children, 40 boys and 40 girls attending a primary school in Beijing. A second sample consisted of 80 American children, 40 boys and 40 girls, attending a primary school in Los Angeles, California.

Initially, the intent was to match the two groups not only on age and gender, but also on socioeconomic level and academic achievement. Practical and theoretical difficulties however, prevented the kind of experimental matching one usually expects in such studies. Not only were objective academic achievement records not available to us for the Chinese sample, but occupational status (of parents) in China is simply not related to the myriad differences present in the United States as to type of housing, amount of spendable income, community prestige, etc. Impressionistic evidence however, suggests that the two samples represented average middle-class children living in large urban areas, and were roughly comparable within the limitations imposed by the two cultures.

All the children were native speakers in their respective cultures and were tested individually by native speakers. Children were told that the examiner was compiling children's stories and that the child's assistance was needed to complete some stories. For each story the child was asked to tell what would happen, to suggest what each protagonist would think and do, and to provide a realistic ending to the story. Each child was assured that story endings would not be shared with school personnel and that this was not an assessment of the child's intellectual or school abilities. Emphasis was placed on giving a story ending that might reasonably happen. The examiner tape recorded the story endings in an unobtrusive manner and later transcribed them.

Theoretically, 400 story endings should have been obtained from each sample. A number of exigencies ranging from malfunctioning tapes to mumbled responses, resulted in 338 story endings generated by the Chinese children and 363 by the American children.

The obtained story endings were quite variable, but the following two will give the reader a bit of a feeling for the type of responses obtained:

Story ending to Story #4 by a Chinese girl age 12:

The mother asks Yan what she is doing and why. Yan begins to cry and tells the mother she got ink on her coat. Yan's grandmother comes in the room and tells Yan that she will clean the spots, but she must be very careful in the future. At suppertime, Yan's father tells the whole family that Yan will be getting a new coat just like her mother's.

Story ending to Story #4 by an American girl age 12:

Her mother asked Elizabeth what she was doing. Elizabeth told her. She told her mom about the ink spot. Her mom scolded her and sent her to her room. When the father came home he was very angry and told Elizabeth she would get no allowance for two months. The coat was sent to the cleaners and the spot came out.

The Chinese story endings were translated into English and where possible without distorting the story ending, Chinese names and references were removed and replaced by American names and references. Both American and Chinese story endings were then coded and individually typed on 5 x 8 cards, so that story endings could be scored in as blind a manner as possible. The story endings were independently scored by three undergraduate students, after undergoing some training sessions on stories from the pilot studies. Medians (or modes) were computed as appropriate.

RESULTS

The story endings were first checked to determine if they differed on verbal fluency, as assessed by length of story, as a function of either gender or ethnic background; they did not. The 121 scoring elements were then collapsed into 30 a priori categories that reflected themes across most or all of the five stories; for example, the presence of helpful adults, intellectual exchanges between protagonists, and the explicit statement of a moral. This was done in order to increase the reliability of the content analysis, by depending on thematic composites rather than individual elements. Thus, for each child 30 scores were available, prorated where necessary. These scores were then submitted to a factor analysis using a principal component solution with normalized Varimax rotation (Kaiser, 1958) for the Chinese children and the American children separately. These analyses yielded four factors judged to be common to both Chinese and American story endings, as judged by Cattell's S index (Cattell, Balcar, Horn, & Nesselroade, 1969); these factors accounted for 68.31% and 74.52% of the total variance, respectively. In addition, one unique factor was found for the Chinese sample and two for the American sample. The results are presented in Table 1. For each child, scores on the four common and three unique factors were computed using variable scores. A stepwise discriminant function analysis was then performed using the four common factors as predictors of membership in the four groups (Chinese boys, Chinese girls, American boys, and American girls). Three discriminant functions were calculated, with a combined $X^2(9)$ of 208.39, $p < .001$. After the first function was removed, there was no additional significant discriminating power [$X^2(4) = 8.31$, $p =$ ns]. Therefore, only the first function which accounted for 92.8% of the between-group variability was interpreted. This function maximally separated the Chinese children from the Americans, but did not discriminate between the sexes of either nationality. The function produced a very high degree of separation as indicated by the final Wilks' lambda of .18 and a canonical correlation of .86.

Table 2 shows a loading matrix of correlations between predictor variables and the first discriminant function which suggests that the primary factors distinguishing Chinese from American children were social orientation ($r = 48$), and concern with authority ($r = .43$).

The discriminating power of these two factors is supported by results from the stepwise procedure, which selected predictor variables based upon the minimization of Wilks' lambda. After all variables were entered, and adjusting for the discrimination among the groups contributed by the other factors, these two predictors showed the highest Fs-TO-REMOVE (3, 156): 14.58 ($p < .01$) social orientation, and 9.86 ($p < .01$) for concern with authority. Group means shown in Table 3 for both common and unique factors indicate that American

Table 1
Result of Factor Analysis of 30 Content Dimensions

(N = 80 per group)

Common Factors	Chinese	American	Highest Loading Items
I. Social orientation	.79	.42	Teamwork is expressed
	.68	.59	Helpful adults show up
	.65	.61	Helpful children show up
	.61	.59	Playmates are present
	.58	.40	Positive relationship continues
II. Presence of Affect	.65	.46	Strong emotions expressed
	.61	.38	Jealousy is shown
	.59	.51	Truth is told
III. Moral-ethical rectitude	.73	.32	Moral explicitly stated
	.51	.49	Perpetrator makes amends
	.47	.45	Incident reflects bigger issue
	.47	.51	Promise of correct future behavior
	.46	.38	Public shame
IV. Concern with authority	.64	.43	Authority figure introduced
	.61	.62	Adults show positive traits
	-.43	-.51	Adults show negative traits
	-.38	-.56	Punishing adults appear

Unique Factors			
V. Natural Forces	.73		Natural forces solve situation
	.58		Luck plays a part
	.41		Denial of intentionality
	.38		Victim makes amends
VI. Economic orientation		.63	Amend consists of payment
		.58	Price explicitly mentioned
VII. Physical Aggression		.58	Main interplay is physical
		.46	Punishment is physical
		.44	Punishment involves restriction

Table 2
Correlations Between Predictor Variables and Discriminant Function

(*N* = 160)

Predictor Variables	*r*	Univariate *F*s-TO-REMOVE (*df* = 3, 156)
Factor I: Social Orientation	.48	14.58**
II: Presence of Affect	.39	5.91**
III: Moral-ethical rectitude	.38	6.73**
IV: Concern with Authority	.43	9.86**

** $p < .01$

children's story completions showed a stronger focus upon physical aggressiveness and economic orientation than did those of Chinese children; the Chinese, on the other hand, placed more emphasis upon natural forces, social orientation, affect, moral-ethical rectitude, and concern with authority than did the Americans. Separate sex analyses in each ethnic group revealed that none of the factors, either singly or in combination, significantly distinguished Chinese boys from Chinese girls. When the two American groups were contrasted, however, the single discriminant function derived in this analysis showed significant separation between boys and girls [$X^2(6) = 49.3$, $p < .001$]. After adjusting for overlapping variance among the seven factors that entered into the analysis the strongest predictors of membership in the two American groups were Physical Aggression ($F[1,73] = 18.3$, $p = <.001$) and Moral-Ethical Rectitude ($F[1, 73] = 14.6$, $p = <.001$). Mean scores for the American boys focused more upon elements of physical aggression than those of girls while American girls' stories reflected more concern with moral and ethical correctness than those of boys. With the use of a jackknifed classification procedure for the total sample of 160 children, 71.8% were classified into the correct group. For each subgroup, the percentage of correct classifications were: Chinese boys 67.5%; Chinese girls, 70%; American boys, 82.5%; American girls, 67.5%.

Although this study began from a strictly empirical basis, the available literature suggested that seven hypotheses could be clearly stated, before data collection began. These hypotheses were that Chinese story completions should (1) evidence greater social orientation, as reflected primarily by such aspects as a greater number of story characters introduced, the presence of more social interactions, a greater emphasis on public shame as an arbiter of behavior, fewer interpersonal confrontations, and more instances of teamwork; (2) indicate the more prominent concern with and role of authority, particularly as reflected in the greater number of authority figures and

Table 3
Means and SDs for Each of the Seven Factors

(*N* = 40 each)

Factor	Chinese males		Chinese females		American males		American females		F (df = 3,156)
	M	SD	M	SD	M	SD	M	SD	
I. Social Orientation	56.2	8.3	55.8	8.1	46.2	6.4	45.3	6.1	12.35**
II. Presence of Affect	54.8	7.9	53.9	7.6	45.7	5.8	46.3	5.9	9.86**
III. Moral-ethical rectitude	59.4	6.9	58.6	6.3	41.3	5.3	45.6	4.9	18.88**
IV. Concerns with authority	51.1	7.5	52.3	7.3	40.8	6.9	41.3	7.1	10.36**
V. Natural forces	51.8	5.4	53.1	4.9	42.6	6.5	43.8	6.6	11.38**
VI. Economic orientation	40.3	3.8	39.2	3.8	53.7	5.2	52.9	4.5	15.39**
VII. Physical aggression	41.1	6.3	40.9	5.2	59.9	6.8	50.0	5.6	12.35**

**p<.01

DISCUSSION

references to authority; (3) reflect a greater preoccupation with moral and ethical rectitude; (4) show a stronger belief in chance or luck and in the influence of natural forces, such as wind and water, upon one's daily environment; (5) contain more affective elements, such as direct expressions of sorrow and happiness, and less rationality or cognitive aspects; (6) contain fewer instances of physical aggression, as reflected in mentions of physical punishment or the use of physical means to settle differences; (7) show a lesser economic orientation, as indicated by fewer instances of payment for damages, reduction of allowance as punishment, or economic jealousy as a motivational theme.

These hypothesized thematic differences are given substantial support by the obtained data. As with any other study however, there are a number of limitations that need to temper our conclusions. One central issue is the comparability of the two samples. The Chinese children were a sample of convenience, assessed because they were available; the American sample was selected from several potential schools because it seemed most similar in socioeconomic level and academic competence. A second issue involves the realization that no two samples could be representative of two countries so vast and diverse in population.

Another issue centers on the demand characteristics of the story completion task. Tseng and Hsu (1972) have pointed out that Chinese parents tell their children stories of filial piety and other moral teachings, and that stories are used to educate rather than entertain. Thus, the same technique of story completion may represent quite different tasks for American versus Chinese children. On the other hand, it was the impression of the experimenters in both countries that children cooperated with the task in a straightforward manner.

Still a fourth issue is that, given the numerous unspecified variables on which the two groups possibly contrast, it is difficult, if not impossible, to locate the source of the observed variation. One approach (Shweder, 1973) is to support any between-culture findings by within cultural comparisons. Pragmatic restrictions in the present study (e.g., relative homogeneity of socioeconomic status within each sample) as well as space limitations preclude such analyses.

What do these results then mean?

The story completions given by the Chinese children clearly reflect a greater social orientation, and are consonant with the characterization given by Hsu (1970) that Chinese children are introduced into the adult world earlier and in a more comprehensive manner than American children. As Wilson (1980) and others have pointed out, in Chinese society the group is the ultimate standard for approval or rejection of behavior. This characteristic is clearly reflected in many of the story completions given by the Chinese children. In Story 1, for example, other children are introduced into the story in 25% of the Chinese responses, but only in 7% of the American story completions. Similarly, in Story 3, none of the American children mention public shame, but 12 (21%) Chinese children do. The Chinese stories often reflect the idea that, since group unity is to be highly sought after, deviant behavior violates group goals and causes shame for all. Such undesirable behavior needs to be altered through peer pressure or, if necessary, severe punishment and ostracism. Thus in a number of Chinese stories, the prescribed punishment seems, at least to a Western observer, to be quite severe (e.g., a child who steals money from the teacher's desk has his right hand hacked off, another has the word thief branded on his forehead).

The role of authority in Chinese culture has been well-documented (Hsu, 1970; Kessen, 1975) and the current results are in agreement with both observational and experimental reports. Sidel (1972) comments that Chinese childrearing methods emphasize expectations of good behavior, cooperation, and obedience, while Breiner (1980) pointed out the tremendous emphasis on discipline and conformity to peer demands. Chu (1979) found Taiwanese children to be more conforming and socially dependent than American children, and specifically to be more responsive to experimental manipulations of modeling based on high or lower status of the role model. As Tseng and Hsu (1972) indicate, authority is not to be defied; even when authority is malevolent, it triumphs in the end. The greater concern with authority is reflected in the Chinese story completions in which more adult figures are introduced, especially of policemen, storekeepers, and school principals. Often these authority figures are given more than average powers, as when the teacher of Story 3 is omniscient as to who took the money (in 21% of the Chinese, but 1% in the American story completions).

The Chinese story completions also reflect a greater concern with moral and ethical rectitude. A major cultural force in Chinese society is that of *Tao*, a continuous search for the appropriate conduct of one's intrapersonal and interpersonal life (Lin, 1980). Western observers have been uniformly impressed by the inculcation of such precepts in everyday schooling (Kessen, 1975), and the story completions reflect this preoccupation with right conduct. For example, in Story 5, 50% of the American children give stories that involve the two boys running away from the broken window, and often with impunity; only 13% of the Chinese children give such stories, but in every single case the boys are subsequently caught, tell the truth, or are afflicted with serious consequences (in one story, both boys eat poisoned food).

Bronfenbrenner (1962b) discusses Communist ideology in terms of character education. Both Chinese and Russian emphasize group commitment, but one major difference is the Russians' emphasis on competition between groups as the basic mechanism for achieving behavior norms. Bronfenbrenner also hypothesizes that internalization of moral standards appears to be maximized when both parental affection and discipline are high; it is my observation that the Chinese family system is high in both, and the present results support Bronfenbrenner's hypothesis. There is some empirical evidence to support the observation of a high degree of discipline in the Chinese family (e.g., Kriger & Kroes, 1972) but I am not aware of studies in the area of affection.

The saliency of the physical environment is also reflected in the Chinese story completions, where a number of times the plot resolution is a function of the wind or of fate. This agrees with the observations of Hsu (1970) that because of differential childrearing practices, Chinese children are more sensitive and responsive to the natural environment, while American children tend to control or change that environment. An interesting aspect is that more Chinese completions to Story 2 (dog eats meat) contain a denial on the part of the mother that the action was intentional (26% vs. 12%), that is, the mother perceives the loss of the meat as an accident rather than a willful disobedience by the child. While the flavor of most American stories is one of rationality, with an emphasis upon cause and effect, many of the Chinese stories bring in elements that reflect the forces of nature, or of a quasi-spirit world.

Chinese story completions contain more affective elements, as reflected by direct emotional expressions, and fewer cognitive elements, such as rational exchanges between story protagonists. The significance of this can be interpreted in a number of ways. For example, Borke and Su (1972) found that Taiwanese and American second graders differed in their perception of emotional responses to stories, with Taiwanese children perceiving more angry reactions and fewer sad reactions. These authors postulate that the results reflect childrearing practices: American parents begin socializing their children earlier and, consequently, these children internalize adult standards earlier. As a result, American children experience guilt when they feel or act out of anger. They also postulate that it is more socially acceptable in the American culture to feel sad rather than angry in response to frustration.

Scofield and Sun (1960) also proposed that personality differences between Chinese and American college students, including greater emotional insecurity, reflected childrearing practices. Although the specific conclusions of these authors may be debated, what is available in the literature does suggest significant differences in affect between Chinese and Americans (Russell & Ylk, 1996).

Pascal and Kuo (1973) pointed out that the results of their study comparing Taiwanese and American college students on a variety of measures, as well as the results of other investigators (Shen, 1936; Sun, 1968) support the contention that Chinese are more emotionally "unstable" than their American counterparts. If instability can be interpreted to mean emotional expressiveness, then the present results are quite consonant. At the same time, a number of writers (e.g., Bond & Wang, 1983) have agreed quite persuasively that the Chinese socialize their children to exhibit emotional restrain as promotive of group harmony, and there is some evidence to indicate that Chinese-American newborns are less emotionally reactive than European-American newborns (Freedman, 1971; see also the chapter by Freedman et al. in this volume). Certainly the question of cultural differences in emotional expressivity is an open one that needs to be explored further, particularly in the distinction of intensity vs. frequency. It is interesting to compare the Chinese polar terms *Yin* and *Yang* -- cultural descriptions of inherently contrasting elements of the universe -- with the more rational and technical descriptions offered by Western society. This *Yin-Yang* dimension, which is applied to such diverse aspects as disease and diet, can be characterized by affective adjectives like cold-hot, passive-active, and soft-hard (Lin, 1980). This affective emphasis is underscored by the observation that in Chinese culture fear of loss of affection or of approval from significant others is highly accentuated.

Stories by Chinese children contain substantially fewer elements of physical aggression; this difference may be related to a number of Chinese cultural features. For example, Wilson (1980) indicates that the most powerful source of Chinese socialization is the mother; not only does she have the largest impact on the child in shaming and punishment situations, but she is primarily involved with the giving of affect, while the father is the rule enforcer. Thus physical aggressiveness, characteristically labeled a more masculine trait, may be less saliently modeled for the child, if not in the family, certainly in the school setting where the emphasis is on discipline and cooperation (Sidel, 1972). In a study of Chinese-American parents, Sollenberger (1968) concluded that withdrawal of rewards and exclusion from the social life of the family were used more frequently than physical punishment.

Finally, Chinese stories contained far fewer economic elements, perhaps reflective of current economic differences between the two countries. In a number of American stories, the story plot was resolved by the child protagonist paying for the damage, typically with no recognition of the moral malfeasance involved. American stories also often mentioned the price of an object (e.g., the cost of a new coat), or involved making amends through monetary means (e.g., the child's allowance being restricted as a punishment) whereas such themes were rare in the Chinese stories.

In general, the story completions given by the American children reflect themes highly similar to those obtained by Metraux (1955) with German children, although no statistical comparisons are possible since Metraux did not present quantitative data. There is in general an expectation that wrongdoing is to be followed by punishment, though such an expectation seems less prevalent than what Metraux (1955) reported. There is also a relatively high value placed on voluntary confession, often with the result that punishment is avoided. Adults are not pictured as omniscient; indeed they are often irrational and inappropriately punitive. Hsu (1970) argued that the situation centered way of life of the Chinese contrasts with the self-reliance centered American way of life, but that the American way of life reflects a more general Western pattern. In the present study, the similarity between American and German themes seems to support Hsu's contention; for example the Chinese focus upon approval from others and the power of the environment contrasts with those of both Germans and Americans who placed less emphasis upon the omnipotence of authorities but underscored the individual's ability to alter situational outcomes.

The obtained thematic differences presumably reflect significant cultural differences, in turn composed of different approaches to childrearing, socialization, religious-ethical practices, the role of the family, etc., and are assumed to be widely shared within each culture. In this context, it is worth noting the two major theoretical approaches to understanding the process of socialization. Cognitive development theorists (e.g., Kohlberg, 1964, 1969) focus on cognitive maturation through a series of culturally invariant stages reflective of a universal development from egocentrism to autonomy, while social learning theorists (e.g., Bandura & Walters, 1963; Bronfenbrenner, 1962a; Whiting & Child, 1953) argue that socialization is more reflective of cultural variance and culturally related variables. The present results, though not designed to test these two differing points of view, would seem more consonant with a social learning approach (Wilson, 1980). China is currently undergoing tremendous cultural and economic changes; it would be of interest to assess whether such changes will be mirrored in story completions years hence. At the same time, it needs to be reiterated that the obtained results should not be taken as reflective of individual personality factors; as Shweder (1979) has so cogently argued, to talk of personality differences, one must first observe behavioral differences in equivalent situations.

Although the focus of this study is on the cross-cultural aspects, the obtained cultural sex differences are rather striking. The lack of statistically significant differences between Chinese boys and Chinese girls is highly consonant with the impression of Western visitors (e.g., Kessen, 1975) that Chinese children are treated equally in the school, and sex differences are minimized, despite the strong cultural tradition that male children are economically more desirable, while the significant sex differences in the American children are congruent with the literature that indicates greater aggression in boys and a greater strength of moral code in girls (Maccoby, 1974).

A SECOND STUDY: COMPETITION AND COOPERATION

The study reported above represents a rather broad exploratory study, using a semi-projective technique, with the focus on group trends. By contrast, the second study to be reported is much more specific, uses a well validated experimental procedure, and focuses more on individual variation rather than nomothetic results.

A substantial amount of research has been done in the area of cooperative, competitive, and individualistic social values, with current research focusing both on information-processing capabilities (Knight, Dubro, & Chao, 1985) and ethnic background (Kagan, 1977, 1984; Knight & Kagan, 1977).

Participants

The participants were 76 children (38 boys and 38 girls) attending school in the city of Guangzhou, and 76 children (38 boys and 38 girls) attending school in Phoenix, Arizona. All children were between the ages of 10 and 12 and in regular school programs. Guangzhou, known to the Western world for many years as Canton, is the capital of Guangdong Province, and is an important industrial and foreign trade center; Phoenix is the capital of Arizona and a major tourist center.

Social Value Apparatus

The procedure used is one utilized by Knight and his students and is described in greater detail in his studies (Knight et al., 1987).

Each child is individually asked to complete a task in which he or she can obtain some tokens to be traded for some desirable prize, such as puzzles, games, small toys, or colored pens, with "better" prizes related to larger number of tokens. The task involves making a decision between two alternatives, with both alternatives offering some tokens for the child and for an unspecified classmate, but in varying proportions. The materials consist of 36 white poster board cards (approx. 20 x 25 cm.) on which are glued a number of colored poker chips (tokens) to the top and bottom half of each card. The child is instructed that the bottom half of the card represents the number of tokens that the child may obtain, while the top half represents the number of tokens the unspecified classmate will obtain. The choice the child must make is between the left side of the card and the right side of the card. Figure 1 illustrates two such cards.

In card A the choice is between getting three tokens for oneself *and* two for the other child, versus one token for oneself *and* two for the other child; this choice can be abbreviated 3/2:1/2. In card B, the choice is between two tokens for oneself and one for the other child, versus three tokens for oneself and two for the other child, or 2/1:3/2.

For each card the possible number of tokens can vary from 1 to 3 for each child, and the 36 cards represent all the possible combinations of pairs, presented to the child in a random order.

Based upon the patterning of the child's choices, six patterns of outcome preferences can be distinguished:

(1) *Individualism*: the individualistic child prefers getting 3 tokens for himself more than 2 tokens, or 2 tokens more than 1, with little attention paid to the number of tokens that the other child receives.

(2) *Competition*: the competitive child prefers getting 2 more tokens than the other child (i.e., the 3/1) more than getting one more than the other child (the 3/2 and 2/1 outcomes), which are preferred more than equal outcomes (3/3, 2/2, and 1/1).

(3) *Equality*: the child who shows this pattern of responding prefers an equal division of tokens (i.e., the 3/3, 2/2, and 1/1 outcomes) more than those outcomes that give either child an advantage of one token (i.e., the 3/2, 2/3,

Figure 1
Example of Knight Technique

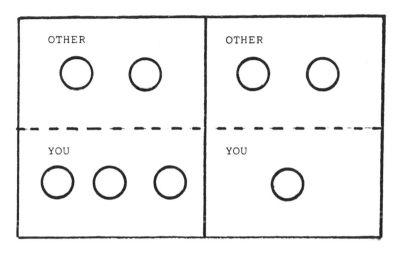

CARD A

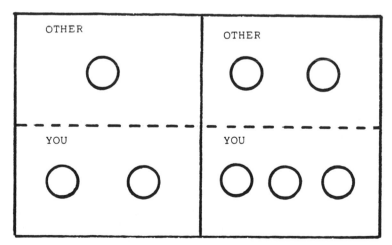

CARD B

2/1, and 1/2 outcomes) and these are selected over the outcomes that result in an advantage of two tokens for either child (i.e., the 3/1 and 1/3 outcomes).

(4) *Group-enhancement or cooperation*: the cooperative child selects the outcome that totals 6 tokens (i.e., 3/3), then the outcomes that total 5 tokens (3/2 and 2/3), then those that total 4 tokens (3/1, 2/2, 1/3) etc., irrespective of the specific division of tokens.

(5) *Competition and individualism*: the child who exhibits this response pattern prefers getting 3 tokens for himself more than 2 tokens, and 2 tokens are preferred more than 1. Within each of these groupings, the child prefers those outcomes that maximize his relative advantage (or minimize the disadvantage): i.e., 3/1 more than 3/2, and 3/2 more than 3/3; 2/1 more than 2/2, and 2/2 more than 2/3; and 1/1 more than 1/2, and 1/2 more than 1/3.

(6) *Equality and individualism*: the child prefers an equal division of tokens (i.e., the 3/3, 2/2, and 1/1 outcomes) more than those outcomes that give either child an advantage of one token, and these are preferred over outcomes that give either child an advantage of two tokens. Within each of these groupings, the child prefers to maximize his rewards: thus the 3/3 is preferred over 2/2, and 2/2 over 1/1; the 3/2 is preferred over the 2/3 and 2/1 outcomes, and these are preferred over the 1/2; the 3/1 outcome is preferred over the 1/3 outcome.

Results

The results are presented in Table 4.

For the United States children the most common preference shown is individualism, with 32 out of 76 children (42%) showing this pattern, and the second most common pattern is competition, shown by 28 (37%) out of the 76 children. Equality is shown by only 10 (13%) children, group enhancement by 2 (3%) and competition-individualism by 3 (4%). None of the children fall into the equality-individualism pattern, and only 1 child exhibited a pattern of response that does not fall into one of the six identified patterns.

By contrast, for the Chinese children the most common response pattern is equality chosen by 27 of the 76 children (36%), and the second most common response pattern is group enhancement, shown by 18 (24%) children. Competition is shown by 16 (21%) children and individualism by 13 (17%) children. No Chinese children fell into the last two response categories, and two children gave response patterns that could not be categorized. Thus the patterns exhibited by the two groups are significantly different. Considering only the first four groupings of response patterns, a rank order correlation for the two samples yields a coefficient of -.80, confirming statistically the divergence of results.

Despite these striking differences, it is of interest to note that even in the

Table 4
Response Patterns Shown by Chinese and American Children

Response pattern:	Chinese Boys	Girls	Total	American Boys	Girls	Total
1. Individualism	7	6	13	18	14	32
2. Competition	6	10	16	16	12	28
3. Equality	12	15	27	2	8	10
4. Group enhancement	11	7	18	0	2	2
5. Competition & Indiv.	0	0	0	2	1	3
6. Equality & Indiv.	0	0	0	0	0	0
Not interpretable	2	0	2	0	1	1

Chinese sample, there is a considerable number of children who respond in an individualistic and competitive manner. Wilson (1975) and other sociobiologists have suggested a genetic basis for reciprocally altruistic acts, but these results might suggest that a certain amount of competitive behavior is ingrained in the organism regardless of what the culture teaches.

These results confirm what the literature already suggests and what Western observers have reported anecdotally (Breiner, 1980; Kessen, 1975), namely that the school environments for Chinese children and for American children are substantially divergent in the types of social values that they promote (see Gow, Balla, Kember, & Hau, 1996). These results are also congruent with other studies that have used similar methodologies. For example, Kagan and Knight (1984) found that Mexican-American children were significantly more cooperative than Anglo-American children in that they more often selected the group enhancement and equality alternatives. Care should be exercised however, when comparing results from different studies, since even the Knight Technique has undergone substantial modifications from study to study.

There are of course a number of possible explanatory hypotheses that can be generated to attempt to explain the above findings. To do so however, would be prematurely speculative, but at least some major themes can be identified. Clearly, the obtained findings are probably the result of myriad influences, of which school and family are but two pivotal points. In this context the study by Steward and Steward (1973) should be mentioned. They observed a small number of Anglo-, Mexican-, and Chinese-American mothers teaching their preschool age sons a sorting and a motor skill game. An analysis of the videotaped interactions between mother and child, indicated that the Chinese mothers used significantly more positive feedback than Mexican and Anglo mothers, and that their feedback was more contingent upon the child's responses. The Chinese-American mothers also considered teaching to be an important component of their maternal role.

As Wu (1989) has demonstrated, one characteristic function of preschool in both mainland China and Taiwan has been the explicit and implicit inculcation of moral values that reflect both political ideology and Chinese cultural tradition. This inculcation continues throughout a Chinese child's schooling in a much more deliberate and calculated manner than that given to American children. Thus the results of this study may be but a reflection of the degree to which the two cultures emphasize such moral training.

Still another possibility to be considered is that the task used in this study may simply not be an appropriate one for use with Chinese children. The task assumes, from a Western framework, that external rewards dictate at least in part, personal behavior. Such a "behavioristic" assumption may well be at odds with the Confucian traditions that are at the basis of Chinese education where self-discipline and benevolence towards others are the guiding principles.

As LeVine (1970) so clearly states, knowing that the frequency of a particular behavior varies with nationality is the beginning not the end of the investigation, and so what is presented here is but a modest beginning. As China becomes more accessible to both its own and foreign social scientists, the basic first steps that are needed will be taken and be augmented by more sophisticated second and subsequent steps.

BIBLIOGRAPHY

Bagby, P. H. (1953). Culture and the causes of culture. *American Anthropologist, 55*, 535-554.

Bandura, A., & Walters, R.H. (1963). *Social learning and personality development*. New York: Holt, Rinehart and Winston.

Bond, M.H. (Ed.) (1996). *The handbook of Chinese psychology*. Hong Kong: Oxford University Press.

Bond, M.H., & Wang, S.H. (1983). China: Aggressive behavior and the problem of maintaining order and harmony. In A.P. Goldstein & M.H.Segall (Eds.), *Aggression in global perspective* (pp. 58-74). New York: Pergamon Press.

Borke, H., & Su, S. (1972). Perception of emotional responses to social interactions by Chinese and American children. *Journal of Cross-Cultural Psychology, 3*, 309-314.

Breiner, S. J. (1980). Early childhood development in China. *Child Psychiatry and Human Development, 11*, 87-95.

Brislin, R.W. (1979). Back translation for cross-cultural research. *Journal of Cross-Cultural Psychology, 1*, 185-216.

Brislin, R.W. (1986). The wording and translation of research instruments. In W.J. Lonner & J.W. Berry (Eds.), *Field methods in cross-cultural research.*(pp. 137-164). Beverly Hills, CA: Sage.

Bronfenbrenner, U. (1962a). The role of age, sex, class and culture in studies of moral development. *Religious Education, 57*, 3-17.

Bronfenbrenner, U. (1962b). Soviet methods of character education: Some implications for research. *American Psychologist, 17*, 550-564.

Cattell, R.B., Balcar, K.R., Horn, J.L., & Nesselroade, J.R. (1969). Factor matching procedures: An improvement of the S index; with tables. *Educational and Psychological Measurement, 29*, 781-792.

Chu, L. (1979). The sensitivity of Chinese and American children to social influences. *Journal of Social Psychology, 109*, 175-186.

Domino, G. (1985). Psychology and psychiatry in the People's Republic of China: An annotated bibliography. *Professional Psychology, 16*, 529-539.

Domino, G., Affonso, D., & Slobin, M. (1987). Community Psychology in the People's Republic of China. *Psychologia, 30*, 1-11.

Domino, G., & Lin, J. (1991). Images of cancer: China and the United States. *Journal of Psychosocial Oncology, 9*, 67-78.

Domino, G., & Lin, W.Y. (1992). Cancer metaphors: Taiwan and the United States. *International Journal of Psychology, 28*, 45-56.

Domino, G., Lin, J., & Chang, O. (1995). Attitudes toward suicide and conservatism: A comparison of Chinese and United States samples. *Omega, 31*, 237-252.

Domino, G., Shen, D., & Su, S. (in press). Acceptability of suicide: Attitudes in Taiwan and in the United States. *Omega.*

Domino, G., & Su, S. (1994). Conservatism and attitudes toward suicide: A study of Taiwanese-American and U.S. adults. *Omega, 30*, 131-143.

Domino, G., Su, S., & Shen, D. (in press). Cross-cultural investigation of a new set of scales for the Suicide Opinion Questionnaire. *Omega.*

Freedman, D. G. (1971). An evolutionary approach to research on the life cycle. *Human Development, 14*, 87-99.

Gow, L., Balla, J., Kember, D., & Hau, K.T. (1996). The learning approaches of Chinese people. A function of socialization processes and the context of learning? In M.H. Bond (Ed.), *The handbook of Chinese psychology* (pp. 109-123). Hong Kong: Oxford University Press.

Heider, F. (1958). *The psychology of interpersonal relations.* New York: Wiley.

Ho, D. Y. F. (1981). Traditional patterns of socialization in Chinese society. *Acta Psychologica Taiwanica, 23*, 81-95.

Hsu, F.L.K. (1970). *Americans and Chinese: Purpose and fulfillment in great civilization*. Garden City, NY: Natural History Press.

Kagan, S. (1977). Social motives and behaviors of Mexican American and Anglo American Children. In J.L. Martinez (Ed.), *Chicano psychology* (pp. 45-86). New York: Academic Press.

Kagan, S. (1984). Interpreting Chicano cooperativeness: Methodological and theoretical considerations. In J.L. Martinez, Jr. & R.H. Mendoza (Eds.), *Chicano psychology* (2nd ed., pp. 289-333). Orlando, FL: Academic Press.

Kagan, S., & Knight, G. P. (1984). Maternal reinforcement style and cooperation-competition among Anglo-American and Mexican-American children. *The Journal of Genetic Psychology, 145*, 37-47.

Kaiser, H. (1958). The Varimax criterion for analytic rotation in factor analysis. *Psychometrika, 23*, 187-200.

Kessen, W. (Ed.). (1975). *Childhood in China*. New Haven, CT: Yale University Press.

Kluckhohn, C., & Murray, H. (1953). *Personality in nature, society, and culture*. New York: Alfred Knopf.

Knight, G.P., & Kagan, S. (1977). Development of prosocial and competitive behaviors in Anglo-American and Mexican-American children. *Child Development, 48*, 1385-1394.

Knight, G.P., Berning, A.L., Wilson, S.L., & Chao, C. (1987). The effects of information processing demands and social/situational factors on the social decision-making of children. *Journal of Experimental Child Psychology, 43*, 244-259.

Knight, G.P., Dubro, A., & Chao, C. (1985). Information processing and the development of cooperative, competitive and individualistic social values. *Developmental Psychology, 21*, 37-45.

Kohlberg, L. (1964). Development of moral character and moral ideology. In M.L. Hoffman & L.W. Hoffman (Eds.), *Review of child development research* (Vol. 1, pp. 383-431). New York: Russell Sage Foundation.

Kohlberg, L. (1969). Stage and sequence: The cognitive developmental approach to socialization. In D.A. Goslin (Ed.), *Handbook of socialization theory and research* (pp. 347-480). Chicago: Rand McNally.

Kohlberg, L. (1983). *Moral stage: A current formulation and a response to critics*. New York: Karger.

Kriger, S.F., & Kroes, W.H. (1972). Child-rearing attitudes of Chinese, Jewish, and Protestant mothers. *Journal of Social Psychology, 86*, 205-210.

LeVine, R.A. (1970). Cross-cultural study in child psychology. In P.H. Mussen (Ed.), *Carmichael's Manual of Child Psychology*, 3rd ed. (Vol. 2, pp. 559-612). New York: Wiley.

Lin, K. (1980). Traditional Chinese medical beliefs and their relevance for mental illness and psychiatry. In A. Kleinman & T.Y. Lon (Eds.), *Normal and abnormal behavior in Chinese culture* (pp. 95-111). New York: D. Reidel.

Maccoby, E.E. (1974). *The psychology of sex differences.* Stanford, CA: Stanford University Press.

Metraux, R. (1955). The consequences of wrongdoing: An analysis of story completions by German children. In M. Mead & M. Wolfenstein (Eds.), *Childhood in contemporary cultures* (pp. 306-323). Chicago: University of Chicago Press.

Murphy, G., & Murphy, L.B. (1968). *Asian psychology.* NY: Basic Books.

Paschal, B.J., & Kuo, Y.Y. (1973). Anxiety and self-concept among American and Chinese college students. *College Student Journal, 7,* 7-13.

Russell, J.A., & Yik, M.S.M. (1996). Emotion among the Chinese. In M.H. Bond (Ed.), *The handbook of Chinese psychology* (pp. 166-188). Hong Kong: Oxford University Press.

Scofield, R.W., & Sun, C.W. (1960). A comparative study of the differential effect upon personality of Chinese and American child training practices. *Journal of Social Psychology, 52,* 221- 224.

Shen, E. (1936). Differences between Chinese and American reactions to the Bernreuter personality inventory. *Journal of Social Psychology, 7,* 471-474.

Shweder, R.A. (1973). The between and within of cross-cultural research. *Ethos, 1,* 531-545.

Shweder, R.A. (1979). Rethinking culture and personality theory. *Ethos, 7,* 255-311.

Sidel, R. (1972). *Women and child care in China.* New York: Hill & Wang.

Sollenberger, R.T. (1968). Chinese-American child-rearing practices and juvenile delinquency. *Journal of Social Psychology, 74,* 13-23.

Steward, M., & Steward, D. (1973). The observation of Anglo-, Mexican-, and Chinese-American mothers teaching their young sons. *Child Development, 44,* 329-337.

Sun, C.W. (1968). A comparative study of Chinese and American college students on the 16 personality factor test. *Psychological Testing, 8,* 33-37. (Cited by Paschal & Kuo, 1973).

Tseng, W.S., & Hsu, J. (1972). The Chinese attitude toward parental authority as expressed in Chinese children's stories. *Archives of General Psychiatry, 26,* 28-34.

Whiting, J.W.M., & Child, I.L. (1953). *Child training and personality: A cross-cultural study.* New Haven, CT: Yale University Press.

Wilson, E.O. (1975). *Sociobiology: The new synthesis.* Cambridge, MA: Harvard University Press.

Wilson, R.W. (1970). *Learning to be Chinese: The political socialization of children in Taiwan.* Cambridge, MA: The MIT Press.

Wilson, R.W. (1980). Conformity and deviance regarding moral rules in Chinese society: A socialization perspective. In A. Kleinman & T.Y. Lin (Eds.), *Normal and abnormal behavior in Chinese* culture (pp. 117-136).New York: D. Reidel.

Wu, D.Y.H. (1989). *Explicit and implicit moral teaching of preschool children in Chinese societies.* Paper presented at the CCU-ICP International Conference on Moral Values and Moral Reasoning in Chinese Societies, Taipei, Taiwan, R.O.C.

Yang, K. (1996). The psychological transformation of the Chinese People as a result of societal modernization. In M.H. Bond (Ed.), *The handbook of Chinese psychology* (pp. 479-498). Hong Kong: Oxford University Press.

THE INTERNATIONAL RESILIENCE RESEARCH PROJECT

Edith H. Grotberg, University of Alabama, Birmingham, U.S.A.

PURPOSE

The primary purpose of the International Resilience Research Project (IRRP) was to address the question: What actions do parents or other caregivers and children themselves take that seem to promote resilience in the children up to age 12? Secondary questions were: 1. What are the differences in the promotion of resilience as a function of the age and gender of the child; and, 2. What are some cultural/ethnic similarities and differences in the promotion of resilience in children?

DEFINING RESILIENCE

The definition of resilience used in this research stated: Resilience is the human capacity to face, overcome, and even be strengthened by experiences of adversity. However, defining resilience is a continuing problem (Kaufman, Cook, Arny, Jones, & Pittinsky, 1994), and there is still a lack of consensus about the domain covered by the construct of resilience; i.e., its characteristics and dynamics (Gordon & Song, 1994). Furthermore, some languages do not yet have an equivalent word in the behavioral sciences (Kotharenco, 1993). Spanish, for example, has no word for resilience in the psychological literature; instead, the term "la defensa ante la adversidad" (defense in the face of adversity) is used (Grotberg, 1993). French, on the other hand, has the word. However, the concept as used in the behavioral sciences is frequently understood, not only as a western, but more specifically, as an Anglo-American term. Its increasing international acceptance is also recognized (Manciaux, 1995).

There is currently sufficient agreement on many of the factors that contribute to resilience or define resilience in certain populations for discussion and study. These factors began to emerge from the early studies by researchers such as E. Werner and R. Smith (1982), N. Garmezy (1985, 1987), and M. Rutter (1987, 1991). These factors have been rediscovered, reinforced, or added to by other researchers. For example, S.J. Wolin and S. Wolin (1993) reinforced Werner and Garmezy's resilience factor of trusting relationships; F. Loesel (1992) reinforced Werner's resilience factor of emotional support outside the family; and R. Brooks (1992) and Wolin and Wolin (1993) reinforced the resilience factor of self-esteem. J. Segal and H. Yahraes (1988) added the resilience factor of encouragement of autonomy, and D. Mrazek and P. Mrazek (1987) added hope, responsible risk taking, and a sense of being lovable. Loesel (1992), A. Osborn (1990), and M. Wang, D. Haertel, and H. Walberg (1994) added school achievement as a resilience factor. J. Garbarino

(1993) added belief in God and morality, and U. Bronfenbrenner (1979) had already contributed the resilience factor of unconditional love from someone. These contributions are not listed in chronological order, but they have emerged and reemerged over time. The earlier contributors are referenced from more recent publications.

However, there is more to the problem of definition, because the genetic makeup and temperament of a child are also important aspects for understanding and defining resilience. The genetic makeup and temperament of a child are continuing forces that contribute to the process of becoming resilient. Whether a child is more or less vulnerable to anxiety, challenges, stress, and unfamiliarity, whether the child is inhibited or uninhibited, determines how a child perceives himself or herself, how he or she interacts with others, and how he or she addresses adversities (Kagan, 1991). Closely related to Kagan's definition of temperament is that of J.H. Block and J. Block (1980). They examined ego-resilience and indicated that there are ego-overcontrollers and ego-undercontrollers, by referring respectively to Kagan's inhibited and uninhibited definitions of temperament. They point out that for children in functional settings, either may serve the child, but in dysfunctional settings, the ego-overcontrollers may have a better chance for developing resilience by controlling their reactions to family problems.

WAYS TO STUDY RESILIENCE

An equally important concern is how to study resilience. There have been two primary ways for studying resilience: retrospective studies and concurrent studies. While the retrospective studies provided the large base for identified resilience factors noted above, the concurrent studies tended to look for those resilience factors in children and adolescents in school settings (Loesel; Osborn; and Wang, Jaertel, & Walberg, as referenced), or in extreme situations: such as a detention setting (McCallin, 1993). The present study drew from the resilience factors originally identified in the retrospective studies and reinforced by the concurrent studies, but addressed the new question: How do children become resilient?

The two major conceptual frameworks for studying resilience include a pathological framework examining psychopathology or social pathology, and a developmental/life-span framework. While more research has used the pathological framework for study, there is now a growing body of literature focusing on the developmental/life-span model (Staudinger, Marsiske, & Baltes, 1993). This shift is particularly important for the present study, which is concerned with the promotion of resilience in children as they develop over time, with or without some kind of pathology in the family or in the child.

A constant element in all of the studies, however, was to view the child in a context; i.e., the family, the social group, the school, the larger community. The child in context was also the basic unit for the present study.

INTERNATIONAL CONTRIBUTIONS

A growing international interest in resilience became evident through a series of conferences and meetings which began in 1986. An early one was held in Durango, Colorado (Frankenburg, 1987); another was held in Lesotho, Africa, in November, 1991 (Bernard van Leer Foundation, 1994); one was held in Washington, D.C., in December, 1991 (Institute for Mental Health Initiatives, 1991); a meeting held in Paris, France, in 1993, was related to the present study; another conference was held in New York, 1993 (Vanistendael, 1996); one in Santiago, Chile in 1995 (Kotliarenco, Caceres, & Alvarez, 1996); and another one in Lisbon, Portugal, 1995 (Joao Gomes Pedro, no publication to date).

This series of international conferences and meetings, joined with the literature, suggested the definition of resilience used in the present study: Resilience is a universal human capacity to face, overcome, and even be strengthened by experiences of adversity. Resilience may be found in a person, group or a community and may make stronger the lives of those who are resilient. The resilient behavior may be in response to adversity in the form of maintenance of normal development, despite the adversity, or as a promoter of growth beyond the present level of functioning. Furthermore, resilience may be promoted not necessarily because of adversity, but, indeed, may be developed in anticipation of inevitable adversities. Resilience is promoted as part of the developmental process of a child over time.

This universal capacity for resilience develops out of and is nurtured by: 1. factors of *external* supports and resources; i.e., trusting relationships; access to health, education, welfare, and security services or their equivalent; emotional support outside the family; structure and rules at home; parental encouragement of autonomy; stable school environments; stable home environments; role models; and religious organizations/morality (labelled I HAVE (Grotberg, 1995c); 2. *inner*, personal strengths; i.e., a sense of being lovable; autonomy; appealing temperament; achievement oriented; self-esteem; hope, faith, belief in God, morality, trust; empathy/altruism; and locus of control (labelled I AM (Grotberg, ibid.); and 3. *social*, interpersonal skills; i.e., creativity; persistence; humor; communication; problem solving; impulse control; seeking trusting relationships; intellectual skills (labelled I CAN (Grotberg, ibid.). Definitions of each of these factors vary, often depending on the author conducting the research. However, whatever precise definitions may be accepted or rejected, the common thrust is that resilience is promoted by factors *provided* around the child (I HAVE), by factors promoted and *developed* within the child (I AM), and by factors *acquired* by the child (I CAN). The facing of adversity requires a dynamic and balanced interaction of these factors; i.e., no one factor, one source or one way, is sufficient.

FOCUS OF THE STUDY

The present study represented a departure from the previous lines of research. The intent was to examine what parents, caregivers or children do; i.e., how they use resilience factors, to promote resilience in the children. Osborn reported (1990) that mothers who are optimistic tend to have more resilient children than mothers who are not or are, indeed, depressed. However, specific actions on the parts of mothers were not identified. Garbarino (1993) stressed the primary importance of keeping a family intact to help children become resilient or at least deal with adversity, but does not indicate what it is about an intact family that promotes resilience in children.

The present study examined resilience promoting behavior in many nations around the world. This international perspective seemed appropriate to determine similarities and differences in ways to promote resilience; the role of culture/ethnicity in determining what resilience factors are used as well as their dynamics; and the changes in resilience promoting behavior that arise as a function of the age of the child.

THE ADVISORY COMMITTEE

To assure the international focus of the study, an Advisory Committee made up of international organizations was formed, including Civitan International Research Center, University of Alabama, Birmingham, the sponsor of the study; United Nations Education Scientific and Cultural Organization (UNESCO); Pan American Health Organization (PAHO); World Health Organization (WHO); International Children's Center (ICC); International Catholic Child Bureau (ICCB); and the Bernard van Leer Foundation. The Advisory Committee was to provide suggestions and criticisms to the International Resilience Research Project (IRRP).

THE RESEARCH

Selection of Design, Instruments, and Participants

The design and instruments used in the IRRP incorporate the following assumptions:
a. Resilience factors that are used in response to structured Situations of adversity and in the reporting of a Personal Experience of adversity involving

the target child are, in fact, used in the promotion of resilience in the children.
b. Adversity is not limited to man-made disasters, such as war, famine, poverty, confinement, refugee status, etc., or to natural disasters such as earthquakes, hurricanes, floods, fires, droughts, etc. Adversity also occurs in everyday life in the form of divorce, abandonment, abuse, alcoholism, stabbing, illness, death, robberies, loss of home or job, moving, accidents, murder.
Further, resilience may be promoted not necessarily because of adversity but, in fact, may be developed in anticipation of inevitable adversities.
c. The earlier years of development are accepted as a critical time for acquiring many of the basic skills, attitudes, and values that tend to remain over the lifespan. Werner (1993) specifically stated that children 11 years of age and under are the most likely age group to develop many resilience factors.
d. The Erikson developmental model is an appropriate model to use internationally, in spite of its lack of addressing gender or cultural/ethnic differences. And while there is concern about using western models for cross-cultural research (Grotberg & Badri, 1987; Wade, 1993), many studies (Grotberg & Badri, 1992; Sparling, 1992) have found such models useful when: a. applied without rigid age division lines; b. using flexibility in noting behaviors in observation; c. using culturally adapted measurements of developmental status; and d. being flexible in intervention activities. Many measurement instruments lend themselves quite readily to translation and cultural adaptation (Badri & Grotberg, 1984).

The Design

The design for the IRRP was based on the use of 15 constructed Situations of adversity. Each of the Situations included a child or children and adults, involved or nearby. (The Situations are presented below in Table 2.) The first 9 Situations were used with parents of children 6 and under; the remaining 6 Situations were used with parents and/or children where the children were between 9 and 11. When a child in the age group 4-6 was able to communicate, that child also responded to Situations. The age groupings, birth-3; 4-6; and 9-11, were within Erikson's developmental levels and permitted more reliable analysis of data than age by single years or larger age groupings. The Situations were further divided into two sets of 3 for each age group, and respondents answered questions relating to no more than 3 Situations.
The questions for adults were: What did the adult do?; how did the adult feel?; what did the child do when the adult did that?; how did the child feel?; how did things come out or how are things now?

The questions for children were: What did the adult do?; what did the child do when the adult did that?; how did the child feel?; how did things come out or how are things now?

The one question, "how did the adult feel?" was left out because of concern by the Advisory Committee about arousing anxiety in the child or the adult by asking the question requiring assessment of the adult's feelings. The same questions were used whether the adult or the child reported a recent Personal Experience of adversity that involved the target child, except that the questions were personalized.

The 15 Situations, developed by the Project Director, were critiqued and modified through consultation with members of the IRRP Advisory Committee and through field testing by graduate students at the University of Maryland School of Nursing, under the supervision and training of Peggy Parks.

Instruments

Instruments used in addition to the Situations and Questions consisted of one non-standardized test and several standardized tests.

The non-standardized test was the Checklist for Children, developed by the Project Director. There were no tests of resilience in the literature and it seemed desirable to develop an initial test and to field test it as part of the research design. The items on the Checklist required a response of Yes or No to a descriptive statement that indicated resilience in the child. The Checklist included such statements as: The child is praised for doing things on his/her own; The child believes things will turn out all right; The child feels that what she/he does makes a difference in how things come out; etc. The Checklist was dropped from the research after examining responses in the earlier data. The responses were erratic in that parents too often saw all of these characteristics in their child or none. Further, interviewers had frequently left unclear whether they were asking the parents or the children to respond.

The following standardized tests were employed: The Social Skills Rating System: SSRS-Student Form, Elementary Level; and the Parent Form, Preschool Level (Gresham & Elliot, 1990); The Nowicki-Strickland Locus of Control Test (1973); and the Parental Bonding Inventory (PBI) (Parker, Tupling, & Brown, 1979).

Each of these tests was used in North America to validate the selection of resilience factors that were assumed to measure social skills in the interpersonal area, locus of control as an inner strength, and the parental contribution to resilience from external supports. The resilience factors were validated by the tests, with the Parental Bonding Inventory validated in Canada (Hiew & Cormier, 1994); and in cross-cultural groups (Arindell, Hanewald, & Kolk, 1989).

Participants

The participants of the IRRP were selected because of their professional status and work and because of their interest in resilience. They held positions as directors of research at their institutions; professors; medical doctors in health services; directors of training programs; and practicing psychologists. Some of the participants trained students at graduate or undergraduate levels to gather data for the IRRP. The director of the project, in consultation with the Advisory Committee and Dr. Parks, developed a *Guidance for the Research Process* and a *Manual for the Training of Interviewers*.

The names of the participants came from members of the Advisory Committee; colleagues sharing membership in international associations; and requests by prospective participants themselves as they heard or read about the IRRP. Participants from 30 countries expressed interest in joining the IRRP. However, the data reported here were received from 22 countries at 27 sites. The research was replicated in each country, so that the data could be examined both within a nation and across nations.

Data received between September, 1993 and August, 1996, are from the 22 countries and 27 sites geographically distributed as follows: *Europe*: Krasnador, Russia; Yerevan, Armenia; Martuni, Azerbaijan; Helsinki, Finland; Vilnius and Kaunas, Lithuania; Prague, Czech Republic; Budapest, Hungary. *Africa*: Khartoum, Sudan; Nairobi, Kenya; Pretoria and Johannesburg, South Africa; Windhoek and Katatura, Namibia. *Latin America*: Sao Paulo, Brazil; Santiago, Chile (2 sites); San Jose, Costa Rica; Panama City, Panama. *North America*: Los Angeles, California; Syracuse, New York; Canada: Fredericton, New Brunswick; Edmonton, Alberta. *Pacific countries*: Taipei, Taiwan; Tokyo, Japan; Bangkok, Thailand; Hanoi, Vietnam; Perth, Australia.

Methodology

The methodology was based on purposeful samples of selected families with children in specific age groups and included structured interviews for parents with children 4-6; 9-11, as well as with the children themselves. Parents of children in the 3 and under age group were also interviewed. To assure similarity in methodology, each participant received a paper summarizing the research on resilience (Grotberg, 1993a); the *Methodology Guidance* and the *Manual for the Training of Interviewers*; a demographic sheet; a packet of the Situations and forms with the Questions to be answered; a request for the report of a Personal Experience of adversity, asking the same Questions; the *Checklist for Children*; and additional standardized tests when requested. The participants were informed that once raw data were standardized, they could use the data any way they wished. They understood they would receive a print-out of their summarized data and a disk with the data for each target child in a form compatible with their processing machines. And, they were asked to provide data from a minimum of 25 target children. Participants returned the initial data for scoring by the project director and data analysis at Civitan. Each participant included a description of the country, city, or area where the study took place and provided information about the cultural setting, especially where the target child lived.

Scoring Responses

The unit of scoring responses to the constructed Situations and Personal Experience was the complete episode of response; i.e., there was a beginning, a process, and an ending, each part of which used resilience factors for promoting resilience in the children. A 3-point scale was used for scoring responses. A score of 3 was assigned to a complete episode promoting resilience. A score of 2 was given to responses mixing resilient and non-resilient promoting behavior, and a score of 1 was given to responses that would prevent the development of resilience in the children.

When a response was scored 3, the resilience factors derived from the literature were used to identify which resilience factors were used in promoting resilience, identifying the specific external supports and resources; the inner factors used; and the social, interpersonal skills used. A score of 3 did not require the use of factors from each of the categories; what was important was the successful process of overcoming the adversity.

The project director scored each response to provide a consistent scoring procedure. An intrascorer reliability check consisted of returning to earlier episodes and rescoring. There was an 85% consistency in scoring. A second reliability check was made with the local scorer of the participants in Canada. Comparing 50 scored episodes, 32 had identical scores of 1, 2, or 3 (64%); and 18 (36%) had a plus or minus one point disagreement. The higher score was given by the senior rater, indicating a perception of more resilience in the responses. However, the high comparability of scoring suggested an acceptable level of interscorer reliability.

Findings

Data provided in the findings came from the 22 countries and 27 sites identified above. The data are presented in Table 1, Description of Population. The population consisted of a total N of 1,225 target children and their families or caregivers; 590 (48%) girls and 635 (52%) boys. Two hundred and thirteen of the children (18%) were 3 and under; 454 of the children (36%) were 4-6 years of age; and 558 (45%) were 9-11 years of age. Health data were not reliable using the WHO standards relating to age and height, because some countries had children far below the standards but who were quite healthy. When questioned, the report was that the people are genetically small. Ninety percent of the children were in some kind of school situation. Eighty-seven percent of the caregiver respondents were parents, with 13% being teachers or other caregivers. Eighty-five percent of the families were in some kind of urban or semi-urban setting, including compounds, suburbs, or separate sections of a town. Seventeen percent of the fathers were absent and 2% of the mothers. Forty-six percent of the target children had one or more older siblings and 45% had one or more younger siblings. The mean size of families, included all who lived in the same residence, was 5.3, with an average family size of 3 to 5. Twenty percent of the fathers had education beyond High School and 22% of the mothers had education beyond High School. Twelve percent of the families reported a serious outside problem and 48% reported a serious intra-family problem within the past five years. The cultural/ethnic identity broke down into 9% with a religious identity; 28% with a national identity; 9% with a racial identity; 23% with a tribal identity; and 10% a mixed national/racial identity.

The 6 major outside problems the family experienced within the preceding 5 years were, in rank order: earthquakes, floods; robberies; war; fires; and riots. The 6 major within-family problems the family experienced within the preceding 5 years, were, in rank order: death of a parent or grandparent; loss of job or income; separation; illness of parent or siblings; and family or a friend moving.

Evidence of Resilience-promoting Behavior

The interviews were conducted between September, 1993 and August, 1996. The percentage of resilience-promoting responses to each of the 15 constructed Situations that provided evidence of resilience promoting behavior, i.e., earned scores of 3, are provided in Table 2. Following that table is an analysis of each constructed Situation to determine the differences in resilience features used and in the responses that indicated behavior limiting the promotion of resilience in children.

There was a total of 2,204 responses to Situations from parents or other caregivers and of 1,194 responses from children aged 4-6 and 9-11. The first 9 Situations were presented to parents of children 6 and under and to children 4-6. Situations 10 to 15 were presented to parents of children 9-11, as well as to children in that age group.

Table 1
Description of Population

Target children: N=1,225	Girls: N=590 (48%)	Boys: N=635 (52%)
Ages 0-3: N=213 (18%)	4-6: N=454 (36%)	9-11: N=558 (45%)

School or Preschool: 90% Parent respondents: 87%   Other caregiver respondents: 13%

Residence: Urban or semi-urban: 85%   Mean family size: 3-5 members

Fathers absent: 17%   Mothers absent: 2%

One or more older siblings: 46%   One or more younger siblings: 45%

Education beyond Grade 12: Fathers: 20%   Mothers 22%
Serious outside problem for family: 12%   Serious within-family problem: 48%

Ethnic/cultural identity: Religious: 9%;
National: 28%; Racial: 9%; Tribal: 23%;
Mixed: 10%

Table 2
Percentage of Resilience-promoting Responses to Situations

Situation	N	Parents % of 3s	N	Children % of 3s	
				Boys	Girls
One	87	75	None	-	-
(Infant cries and screams. Parent does not know what is wrong.)					
Two	236	37	48	9	14
(Infant finds dirty rag on floor and begins to suck on it. Parent sees it and fears illness.)					
Three	38	52	None	-	-
(Infant does not sit up or respond to parents.)					

Table 2 Continued

Four	240	21	59	4	5

(Two year old takes sweet from store and screams when mother tries to take it away.)

Five	231	31	42	9	30

(Two and one-half year old refuses to eat. Screams and kicks when urged to eat.)

Six	76	40	None	-	-

(Three year old cannot walk and wants to go out. Throws things because mother is too busy.)

Seven	181	34	47	14	12

(Boy annoys parents and guests with his playing. Told to stop, and screams in protest.)

Eight	139	28	38	2	4

(Children use scarce food to play store. Father sees them and knows the food is precious.)

Nine	107	65	37	30	42

Six year old is disabled and cannot reach building sticks. Frustrated, he throws them and cries.)

Ten	186	34	136	30	34

(Nine year old is teased and pushed as she walks to school. Is fearful and pretends she is sick.)

Eleven	158	23	143	22	25

(Boy climbs tree in school yard, is being pulled down by others and kicks one in the face.)

Twelve	137	40	153	42	39

(Girl and younger brother are alone. The brother catches his foot, it hurts, and he screams.)

Thirteen	141	49	152	39	43

(Seven year old goes to new school alone. Children tease him. Teacher sees his plight.)

Fourteen	124	29	160	35	32

(Four children 9-11 years old are in the market when they hear gun shots.)

Fifteen	123	18	159	17	12

(Older slow learning children chase younger ones who tease them. Teacher sees the chase.)

Analysis of Responses Promoting Resilience

An overall finding indicated that socioeconomic status had an insignificant impact on amount and kind of resilience-promoting behavior. Resilience was promoted in children as frequently in lower-income families as in higher-income families. The differences were largely in the number of resilience factors used, parents of children from higher-income families using more factors. Resilience was also promoted in children who were considered less intelligent or, indeed, intellectually impaired. Many were taught how to reach out for help when faced with difficulties.

Further analysis indicated that parents of children 6 and under had a 42% average in scores of 3 in response to the first 9 constructed Situations, ranging from 21% to 75%. The higher percentages of scores of 3 involved dealing with situations of an infant crying (One), a disabled child needing help in building a house (Nine), and a child who is developmentally delayed (Three). Each of these involved a relatively helpless child needing support, receiving empathy, building confidence in the child, and helping the child acquire skills of self-calming and mastery of a task. The higher percentages of resilience-promoting behavior had themes of children making fewer demands on the parents in terms of conflict or challenging authority, and in which parents had a clear opportunity to help.

The lower percentages of scores of 3 involved children making a scene at a market (Four), children taking food without permission (Eight), and a child who refuses to eat (Five). Each of these involved anger, frustration, rather severe punishment, and leaving the children in a state of no resolution, learning, or reconciliation. The lower percentages of resilience- promoting behavior had themes of loss of parental control, need to punish, and unresolved feelings of anger and helplessness.

The children aged 4-6 who were able to respond to the constructed Situations had a 7% average in scores of 3 in response to 6 of the same 9 Situations. (There were no resilience responses to Situations 1, 3, or 6.) The percentages ranged from 1% to 32%. The higher percentages involved a disabled child needing help in building a house (Nine), a child not eating (Five), and a child building a road and annoying company in the house (Seven). Both parents and children had one Situation (Nine) in common in terms of scores of 3 and with similar responses, i.e., helping, showing empathy, and encouraging the child to accomplish a task.

The higher percentages of resilience promoting behavior had themes of helping others, negotiating solutions to problems, and displaying a sense of autonomy and caring. The lower percentages involved a child creating a scene in the market and the children taking food without permission. Both of these Situations were the same as those in which parents had low percentages and with the same behaviors—anger and frustration, rather severe punishment, and no resolution, learning, or reconciliation. The lower percentages of resilience-promoting behavior had themes of resistance to controls, feelings of anger and frustration, and being punished severely and unfairly, with no resolution or reconciliation.

Parents of children 9-11 had a 31% average in scores of 3 in response to constructed Situations 10-15, ranging from 23% to 49%. The higher percentages involved a child going to school alone (Ten), and a girl taking care of her brother who became injured (Twelve). Both of these involved a relatively helpless child needing care and support, empathy, and resolution of a problem. The higher percentages of resilience promoting behavior had themes of using outside supports to help family members, fostering a sense of autonomy in children, and expressing empathy for the victim.

The lower percentages involved developmentally delayed children protecting themselves from teasing by others (Fifteen), and a child in a tree protecting himself from being pulled down by kicking at those who were pulling at him (Eleven). Both of these involved punishing the victims rather than the perpetrators, absence of concern for the children's self-esteem and need for understanding, and an arbitrary resolution of the problem by an authority figure. The lower percentages of resilience promoting behavior had the themes of misdirected punishment, ignoring the need for communication, lack of sharing of feelings, and no resolution or reconciliation.

Children aged 9-11 had a 31% average in scores of 3 in response to the same Situations: 10-15, ranging from 15% to 49%. The higher percentages involved a girl taking care of her younger brother who became injured (Twelve), and a group of children in a market where gun shots are heard (Fourteen). Both involved a need for autonomous action, seeking of help, calming themselves and finding a solution.

The higher percentages of resilience promoting behavior had themes of self-esteem, confidence, autonomy, and problem solving. The lower percentages involved the developmentally disabled children and the boy in the tree and included blaming and punishing the wrong persons, and absence of concern for the children's self-esteem and need for understanding. The lower percentages of resilience-promoting behavior had the themes of being unfairly treated and punished, feeling helpless and misunderstood, and finding no satisfaction in the outcome.

Results from reports of Personal Experiences of adversity were not incorporated into this report because they tended to show the same average percentages of resilience scores of 3 as in the Constructed Situations and drawing on the same resilience factors.

Age and Gender Differences

Table 2 also provides information on age and gender differences in the promotion of resilience. Children 4-6 demonstrated minimum use of factors promoting resilience and relied primarily on their parents for its promotion. The parents of those younger children, in fact, demonstrated more promoting of resilience (42%) than parents of children 9-11 (31%). When the younger children promoted resilience, the girls used resilience-promoting behavior more than boys in the situations involving the young child refusing to eat and the disabled child trying to reach the building sticks. They showed empathy and helpfulness in both situations.

Children 9-11, both boys and girls, had average resilience scores of 31%. The differences between the children and their parents were not in the overall promotion of resilience, but rather in the resilience factors used. Parents drew on trusting relationships, role modeling and promoting autonomy from external resilience factors; seeing their children as being lovable, showing empathy, having self-esteem, feeling autonomous, and being confident from internal resilience factors; and communication, problem-solving behavior from interpersonal resilience factors. Overall, children 9-11 drew on role modeling and encouragement of autonomy less than their parents; drew on being lovable or showing empathy less than parents; and managing their own behavior less than parents. The only resilience factor these children used more than their parents was seeking trusting relationships for help.

Further analysis by gender indicated that girls drew on trusting relationships and receiving help in becoming autonomous more than boys from the external factors. Girls drew on internal factors of being lovable, being autonomous, having self-esteem, feeling confident, and showing empathy more than boys. Girls also relied more on communication, problem solving, and relating to others than boys. No differences indicated that boys used a resilience factor more than girls. Both boys and girls used, with the same frequency, having services available; receiving emotional support and having a role model; feeling a sense of control; managing their own behavior; and reaching out for help.

Boys generally drew on fewer resilience factors to deal with adversities, while having the same overall percentage of resilience-promoting responses as girls. Apparently the ones they did use were sufficient to deal with the adversity.

Table 3
Resilience Promoting Behavior in Three Countries

Sudan		Namibia	Armenia

Parents

External:	role model	trusting relationship	role model trusting relationship encourage autonomy
Internal:	autonomy	lovable responsible empathy problem solving	lovable confidence, hope empathy problem solving
Social:	problem solving	communication seeking help	communication seeking help

Children 9-11

External:	trusting relationship	trusting relationship	trusting relationship encourage autonomy
Internal:	autonomy	responsible	confidence, hop lovable self-esteem
Social:	problem solving seeking help	problem solving	problem solving seeking help communication

Cultural/Ethnic Similarities and Differences

In examining the cultural/ethnic similarities and differences in the resilience in children from 22 countries and 27 sites, the following overall descriptions summarize the findings: The similarities involve some common concerns about children being able to face, overcome, and even be strengthened by experiences of adversity. These include: providing loving support, being role models, seeking help, recognizing the child's need to be responsible for his or her own behavior, and having rules. The differences include wide variations in children, the degree to which punishment is viewed as strengthening children, the resources available to draw on, the presence of hope and faith in outcomes, skills in communication, and problem solving.

Data from a sampling of three countries provide examples of these similarities and differences in the promotion of resilience, and they are presented in Table 3. Analyses and comparisons for other sites are to be presented in a future document.

The sites compared are metropolitan Khartoum, Sudan; Windhoek, Namibia; and Yerevan, Armenia. Children 9-11 from each country and their parents responded to Situation 10, the girl walking to school alone, being harassed, and refusing to go to school, claiming illness, when her mother knew she was well.

Parents in each country used similar and/or different resilience factors in promoting resilience in their children. The Sudanese children from metropolitan Khartoum are expected to be autonomous and self-reliant in facing adversities; Namibian children receive more empathy and communication, are seen as lovable, and are encouraged to seek help. Parents from Yerevan, Armenia, use resilience factors of each of the other sites, but, in addition, encourage autonomy and foster confidence.

Children 9-11 from each site drew on the resilience factor of trusting relationships, but in Yerevan, Armenia, the children also expect help in becoming more autonomous. From the resilience factors of inner strengths, children from each site drew on different factors. In Sudan the children rely heavily on autonomy; in Namibia, the children rely on being responsible for their behavior; and in Armenia, the children drew from confidence and hope, seeing themselves as lovable, and having self-esteem. The interpersonal skills resilience factors included the common one of problem solving in each country, with the children in Sudan and Armenia drawing on seeking help, and in Armenia, alone, communicating feelings and alternative solutions.

The cultural differences do not prevent the promotion of resilience in children. More important seems to be which resilience factors are used within the cultural context. In Sudan, for example, the children are expected to be more autonomous than in the other two countries; in Namibia, there is a good deal of support, but an expectation that the child will be responsible; in Armenia, there is more interaction with the child facing an adversity and a greater availability of support as the resolution of the adverse situation proceeds.

SUMMARY

Data from parents and children from 27 sites in 22 countries around the world indicated that about one-third are promoting resilience in children up to age 12. Resilience, however, is promoted more in situations in which helplessness and need are perceived and where supportive help seems feasible. Resilience is promoted less in situations where there is a perceived threat to authority, blame and punishment seem more important than understanding or communication, and the person who could promote resilience is more concerned with feelings of frustration.

Younger children (4-6) rely more on help and guidance from parents to face, overcome, and even be strengthened by experiences of adversity; older children (9-11) promote resilience with the same frequency as their parents. When younger children do promote resilience (7%), the girls drew more on empathy and helpfulness than the boys. For the older children, even though the average score on resilience promoting behavior was the same for girls and boys (31%), the girls drew more on trusting relationships and encouragement of autonomy; all of the internal resilience factors, except a sense of control; and all interpersonal skills except managing impulsive behavior and seeking help, which were used with the same frequency as boys. Both boys and girls drew on having services available, receiving emotional support and having role models from external resilience factors. It is not clear why these gender differences occur. Is it the fact that girls are more open in talking about what they draw on for dealing with adversities or is it that boys do not need to draw on so many resilience factors to achieve the goal of overcoming the adversity? However, the children's consistent drawing on trusting relationships for most responses to situations of adversity, suggests the significance of the basic need for such trusting relationships for optimal human development.

The variability in ways to promote resilience involve not only age, sex, and familial differences, but also cultural/ethnic differences. It appears that parents and children draw on similar and different resilience factors and both fewer or more factors to promote resilience. The cultural/ethnic differences and similarities do not mitigate against the promotion of resilience. Examples from Sudan, Namibia, and Armenia suggest some differences and similarities in successful ways to promote resilience.

An unexpected finding was that socioeconomic status had an insignificant impact on the promotion of resilience, the difference being primarily in the number of resilience factors used. Also, many respondents who were intellectually limited, as indicated by parent information, knew how and when to reach out for help.

Resilience is being promoted around the world without intervention or, indeed, without the word in the vocabulary. However, there is much room for giving greater attention to promoting resilience in children for them to be able to face, overcome, and even be strengthened by experiences of adversity. About two-thirds of the participants in the International Resilience Research Project would benefit from such information. No one is spared adversities and the paradigm of I HAVE; I AM; I CAN (Grotberg, 1995c) is a useful guide for learning how to promote resilience in children.

BIBLIOGRAPHY

Arindell, W.A., Hanewald, G.J., & Kolk, A.M. (1989). Cross-national constancy of dimensions of parental rearing styles: The Dutch version of the Parental Bonding Instrument (PBI). *Personality and Individual Differences, 10* (9), 949-956.

Badri, B., & Grotberg, E. (1984). Adapting and validating the Denver Prescreening Developmental Questionnaire for the Sudan. *The Ahfad Journal, 1*, 27-33.

Bernard van Leer Foundation (1994). *Building on people's strengths: Early childhood in Africa*. The Hague: Bernard van Leer Foundation.

Badri, G. (1978). *Child rearing practices in the Sudan: Implications for parent education.* Unpublished dissertation, University of California at Santa Barbara.

Block, J.H., & Block, J. (1980). The role of ego-control and ego-resiliency in the organization of behavior. In W.A. Collins (Ed.), *Minnesota symposia on child psychology: Development of cognition, affect, and social relationships, 13*, 39-101. Hillsdale, NJ: Erlbaum.

Bronfenbrenner, U. (1979). *The ecology of human development*. Cambridge, MA: Harvard University Press.

Brooks, R. (1992). Self-esteem during the school years. *Pediatric Clinics of North America, 39* (3).

Cheong, A.C.S. (1996). A study of collectivism/individualism among Singapore teachers. In E. Miao (Ed.), *Proceedings of the 53rd Annual Convention of the International Council of Psychologists: Cross-cultural encounters* (pp. 315-330). Taipei, Taiwan: General Innovation Service.

Chia, R., Lytle, T., Borshiung, C., & Jen, C.C. (1997). Differences in source and modes of Locus of Control for Chinese and Americans. In B. Bain, et al. (Eds.), *Psychology and education in the 21st century: Proceedings of the 54th Annual Convention, International Council of Psychologists* (pp. 67-72). Edmonton, Canada: ICPress.

Frankenburg, W. (1987). *Fifth International Conference: Early identification of children at risk: Resilience factors in prediction*. University of Colorado, Denver, CO.

Garbarino, J., Kostelny, K., & Dubrow, N. (1993). *No place to be a child.*

Lexington, MA: Heath.

Garmezy, N. (1985). Stress-resistant children: The search for protective factors. In J.E. Stevenson (Ed.), Recent research in developmental psychopathology. *Journal of Child Psychology and Psychiatry Book Supplement No. 4* (pp. 213-233). Oxford: Pergamon Press.

Garmezy, N. (1987). Stress, competence, and development: Continuities in the study of schizophrenic adults, children vulnerable to psychopathology, and the search for stress-resistant children. *American Journal of Orthopsychiatry, 57* (2), 159-174.

Gordon, E., & Song, L.D. (1994). Variations in the experience of resilience. In M. Wang & E. Gordon (Eds.), *Educational resilience in inner-city America* (pp. 27-43). Hillsdale, NJ: Erlbaum.

Greesham, F., & Elliot, S. (1990). *The Social Skills Rating System.* Circle Piner, MN: American Guidance Service.

Grotberg, E. (1993a). Promoting resilience in children: A new approach. *The Ahfad Journal, 10* (2), 5-14.

Grotberg, E. (1993b). Promocion de la "defensa ante la adversidad" en los ninos: Nueva aproximacion. *Medicina y Sociedad, 10* (1-2).

Grotberg, E. (1995a). *The International Resilience Research Project: How resilience is promoted in children.* Paper presented at the International Symposium· Stress e Violencia, Liahon, Portugal, September 27 30.

Grotberg, E. (1995b). *The International Resilience Project: Promoting resilience in children.* ERIC ED 383424.

Grotberg, E. (1995c). *A guide to promoting resilience in children: Strengthening the human spirit.* The Hague: The Bernard van Leer Foundation.

Grotberg, E. (1996a). The International Resilience Project: Research and application. In E. Miao (Ed.), *Proceedings of the 53rd Annual Convention, International Council of Psychologists: Cross-cultural encounters*, Taipei, Taiwan: General Innovation Service.

Grotberg, E. (1996b). Promoviendo la resiliencia en niños: Reflexiones y stratagias. In M. Kotliarenco (Ed.), *Resiliencia: Construyendo en adversidad* (pp. 33-48). Santiago, Chile, CEANIM.

Grotberg, E. (1996c). *Guia de promocion de la resiliencia en los niños para fortalecar el espiritu humano* (Transl. by N.S. Ojeda). The Hague: Fundacion Bernard van Leer.

Grotberg, E. (1997). The International Resilience Project: Findings from the research and the effectiveness of interventions. In B. Bain, et al. (Eds.), *Psychology and education in the 21st Century: Proceedings of the 54th Annual Convention, International Council of Psychologists* (pp.118-128). Edmonton: ICPress.

Grotberg, E., & Badri, G. (1987). Changing child-rearing practices in Sudan:

An early stimulation experience. *Notes, Comments. N. 178.* Paris: UNESCO/UNICEF/WFP Cooperative Program.

Grotberg, E., & Badri, G. (1992). Sudanese children in the family and culture. In U.P. Gielen, L.L. Adler, & N.A. Milgram (Eds.), *Psychology in international perspective* (pp. 213-232). Amsterdam: Swets & Zeitlinger.

Grotberg, E., Badri, G., & King, A.D. (1987). Changing child-rearing practices in Sudan: An early stimulation demonstration program. *Children Today,* January-February 26-29.

Hiew, C.C., & Cormier, N. (1994). *Children's social skills and parental relationship in promoting resilience.* Paper presented at the annual conference of the International Council of Psychologists. Lisbon, Portugal, July, 1994.

Kagan, J. (1991). *Temperament and resilience.* Paper presented at the Fostering Resilience Conference. Washington, DC: Institute for Mental Health Initiatives.

Kaufman, J., Cook, A., Arny, L., Jones B., & Pittinsky, T. (1994). Problems defining resilience: Illustrations from the study of maltreated children. *Development and Psychopathology, 6,* 215-247.

Kotliarenco, M.A., Caceres, I., & Fontecilla, M. (1997). *Estasdo del arte en resiliencia.* Santiago, Chile: CEANIM.

Kotliarenco, M.A., & Duenas, V. (1993). *Vulnerabilidad versus "resilience:" Una propuesta de accion educativa.* Paper presented at the seminar: Pobreza y desarrollo humano: Legitmidad y validez del diagnostico y evaluacion convencional. Santiago, Chile: November l992.

Loesel, F. (1992). *Resilience in childhood and adolescence: A summary for the International Catholic Child Bureau.* Geneva, November 26, l992.

Loesel, F., & Biesener, T. (1990). Resilience in adolescence: A study on the generalizability of protective factors. In K. Hurrelmann & F. Loesel (Eds.), *Health hazards in adolescence* (pp. 299-320). New York: Walter de Gruter.

Manciaux, M. (1995). *De la vulnerabilité à la resilience: du concept à l'action.* Paper presented at the International Symposium: Stress e violencia. Lisbon, Portugal, September 27-30.

McCallin, M. (1993). *Living in detention: A review of the psychosocial well-being of Vietnamese children in the Hong Kong detention centres.* Geneva: International Catholic Child Bureau.

Mrazek, D.A., & Mrazek, P.J. (1987). Resilience in child maltreatment victims: A conceptual exploration. *Child Abuse and Neglect, 11,* 357-366.

Norwicki, S.J., & Strickland, B.R. (1973). A locus of control scale for children. *Journal of Consulting and Clinical Psychology, 40,* 148-154.

Osborn, A.F. (1990). Resilient children: A longitudinal study of high achieving socially disadvantaged children. *Early Childhood Development and Care, 62,* 23-47.

Parker, G., Tupling, J., & Brown, L.B. (1979). A parental bonding instrument. *British Journal of Medical Psychology, 52,* 1-10.

Phinney, J.S. (1996). When we talk about American ethnic groups, What do we mean? *American Psychologist, 51* (9), 918-930.

Rutter, M. (1987). Psychosocial resilience and protective mechanisms. *American Journal of Orthopsychiatry, 57,* 316-331.

Rutter, M., (1991). *Some conceptual considerations.* Paper presented at the Fostering Resilience Conference. Washington, DC: Institute for Mental Health Initiatives.

Segal, J., & Yahraes, H., (1988). *A child's journey.* New York: McGraw Hill.

Shure, M.B. (1991). *Resilience as a problem-solving skill.* Paper presented at the Fostering Resilience Conference. Washington, DC: Institute for Mental Health Initiatives.

Sparling, J. (1992). *A program of screening and intervention in a Romanian orphanage.* Sixth International Conference on Children at Risk, Santa Fé, NM.

Staudinger, U., Marsiske, M., & Baltes, P. (1993). Resilience and levels of reserve capacity in later adulthood: Perspectives from life-span theory. *Development and Psychopathology, 5,* 541-566.

Truant, G.S., Donaldson, L.A., Herscovitch, J., & Lohrenz, J.G. (1987). Parental representations in two Canadian groups. *Psychological Reports, 61,* 1003-1008.

Vanistendael, S. (1996). *Growth in the muddle of life: Resilience: Building on people's strengths* (2nd ed.). Geneva: International Catholic Child Bureau.

Wade, C. (1993). The impact of gender and culture on our conception of psychology. *The General Psychologist, 29* (3).

Wang, M., Haertel, D., & Walberg, H. (1994). Educational resilience in inner cities. In M. Wang & E. Gordon (Eds.), *Educational resilience in inner-city America* (pp.45-72). Hillsdale, NJ: Erlbaum.

Werner, E. (1994). Risk, resilience, and recovery: Perspectives from the Kauai Longitudinal Study. *Development and Psychopathology, 5,* 503-515.

Werner, E., & Smith, R.S. (1982). *Vulnerable but invincible: A longitudinal study of resilient children and youth.* New York: McGraw Hill.

Wolin, S.J., & Wolin, S. (1993). *The resilient self.* New York: Villard Books.

SECTION VI: ADOLESCENCE

Each culture presents its adolescents with a different set of beliefs that are shaped by ecological conditions, overall worldviews, the schooling systems, family, and the peer group. Adolescents look to adults and peers as possible models for adult roles and behavior. However, adolescents in different cultures seem to perceive their social networks quite differently. The socialization of adolescents is largely influenced by factors other than the family and peers within the larger cultural context. The larger cultural influences include school, community, media, the larger social system, and general cultural beliefs. Adolescents from traditional cultures appear to place emphasis on issues relating to the family, whereas those living in more modern and industrialized cultures are more concerned about higher education and career choices. Nonetheless, young people across cultures share general concerns about the world, their lives, and their future.

Judith L. Gibbons, in *Personal and Social Development of Adolescents: Integrating Findings from Preindustrial and Modern Industrialized Societies* integrates research on adolescents living in different kinds of societies and demonstrates that such studies can test the generality of psychological theories. Considering a variety of approaches including ethnographic studies and more quantitative psychological studies, her review addresses identity development and autonomy, future orientation, self-concept, self-esteem, and civic identity among adolescents from widely varying cultural settings. Research addressing adolescence in cross-cultural and cross-national perspective as well as those psychological theories and practices that are based on indigenous concepts of development can be particularly useful. Comparative studies need to be made of and greater attention has to be paid to adolescents' perception of important issues in their lives. Several of these issues were revealed as shared by adolescents living in very different contexts, while some developmental issues appear only to be applicable in the industralized world.

T.S. Saraswathi, in *Adult-child Continuity in India: Is Adolescence a Myth or an Emerging Reality?* provides a developmental profile of a majority of Indian adolescents and delineates some general trends that are related to the economic development and modernization of Indian society: From a complete absence of adolescence in girls who were betrothed during childhood and married before puberty, to prolonged adolescence in well-educated Indians that extends beyond the teenage years; from no formal schooling and direct integration within the work sphere to highly specialized education with parental support; from sexual restraint to occasional sexual permissiveness. For the present in India, a complex society in transition, wide disparities prevail. Nevertheless, with increasing economic development, adolescence may emerge as a distinctive phase cutting across class and gender. In the context of Indian society, Saraswathi's central thesis is that adolescence is the invention of a technological, industrial society that is marked by a discontinuity between childhood and adulthood. She supports her thesis on the basis of a wide-ranging review of the research already available.

Pedro R. Portes, Richard Dunham, and Kent Del Castillo, in *Identity Formation and Status Across Cultures: Exploring the Cultural Validity of Eriksonian Theory,* explore the cross-cultural validity of Erikson's psychosocial model through research on identity and status substages across the social context. They compare literature relating to mediating cultural factors and compare pilot data from different countries using the Ego Identity Personality Questionnaire. In addition to exploring the psychometric properties of the EIPQ, they explore the construct of "cultural validity." Cross-cultural research suggests that the formation of ethnic/cultural identity tends to resemble the formation of ego identity as outlined by Erikson. Since the larger cultural context influences the specific context of adolescents self-concepts and personal identities, culture also plays an important role in the progression of social identity formation and its psychological consequences. In this chapter, it is shown that adolescence assumes different forms in different societies and that shifts in adolescent identity are directly linked to rapid social changes and to a variety of cultural contexts.

The contributions in this section share a common concern for the exploration of variability in the lives of adolescents. As Saraswathi demonstrates in her essay, social class and gender exert such a decisive influence on the life course of young Indians that poor girls in India may be said to have no adolescence at all. One wonders whether this might not also have been true for the poor girls of many historical societies including those of medieval Europe, traditional China, and so on. Other researchers such as Offer, however, have found more commonalities across societies and even used the term "universal adolescent" to describe the numerous youngsters in their cross-cultural study who reported positive self-concepts and good relationships with their families. One may wonder, however, whether Offer's observations would also hold true for those poor Kashmiri girls who spend their childhood in front of a carpet-making loom and who will later be asked by their families to accept as their husband a man whom they have never seen before.

PERSONAL AND SOCIAL DEVELOPMENT OF ADOLESCENTS: INTEGRATING FINDINGS FROM PREINDUSTRIAL AND MODERN INDUSTRIALIZED SOCIETIES

Judith L. Gibbons, Saint Louis University, U.S.A.

INTRODUCTION

Adolescents grow up in diverse social, economic, historical, and political contexts. Differences in the adolescent experience are more apparent than the commonalities. Cross-cultural and cross-national differences are well established, and within nations, adolescents differ in terms of ethnicity, gender, economic advantage and disadvantage, physical and cognitive abilities, age, family structure, educational opportunity, sexual preference, place of residence (urban or rural), and exposure to international media. All of these factors affect adolescents' lives, values, and expectations for the future. Even among relatively homogeneous groups such as the Inuit of northern Canada, it would be difficult to describe the typical adolescent without specifying that teenage girls assume more household responsibilities than do boys, and that younger adolescents are more likely to attend school (Condon, 1987). In more heterogeneous cultures, special issues may emerge for immigrant or refugee adolescents, rural adolescents, and adolescents with disabilities (e.g., Copeland & Harvey, 1989; Resnick, 1986; Rodriquez & Santiviago, 1991; Sam, 1991; Southern & Spicker, 1989). National demographics such as gross national product (GNP), the proportion of the population who are of adolescent age, and public policies may also affect the lives of adolescents (Aptekar, 1988; Offer, Ostrov, Howard, & Atkinson, 1988). Cultural changes such as industrialization and modernization have important consequences for adolescents (e.g., Cederblad, 1984; Condon, 1990), both because adolescents may be the first to embrace change (e.g., Rosenthal & Feldman, 1990) and because their successful entry into adulthood demands adaptation to the changing social

Author Notes: The author would like to thank Uwe P. Gielen, Aaronette White, Michael Ross, Raymond Senuk, Honore Hughes, Deborah Stiles, Hardin Collins, and James Korn who provided comments on a earlier draft of this manuscript and Lana Larsen, David Shocklee, Kelly Wadeson, Berna Guroglu, and Maria Lynn who helped obtain bibliographic references. Preparation of this paper was supported, in part, by the Beaumont Faculty Development Fund of Saint Louis University. Requests for copies should be directed to Judith L. Gibbons, Department of Psychology, Saint Louis University, 221 North Grand Blvd., St. Louis, MO 63103, USA.

conditions (Ogbu, 1981). As has been pointed out by a number of theorists and researchers, cross-cultural and cross-national research are important in the study of adolescence because such studies can test the generality of theories, expand the range of variables, and identify phenomena which are widespread or universal (Offer et al., 1988). These purposes might be best achieved by integrating research on adolescents living in different kinds of societies, both industrialized and pre industrial, and research from a variety of approaches, including ethnographic studies and more quantitative psychological studies.

In the present chapter, the literature on adolescents who are growing up in pre-industrial societies or in Western industrialized societies is reviewed and integrated with respect to the definition of the adolescent life stage and adolescent personal and social identity development. The focus is on issues related to the adolescent self-esteem, and political and social identity. The development of the self, including the social self, is central to a number of theories and numerous empirical studies of adolescence; however, this focus excludes a great deal of important current research on adolescent time use, coping and adjustment, and education and schooling.

DEFINING ADOLESCENCE CROSS-CULTURALLY

Most definitions of adolescence recognize the onset of the physical changes of puberty as defining the beginning of adolescence (e.g., Whiting & Whiting, 1987). However, even this biological transition has cultural antecedents as well as consequences. The timing of puberty varies cross-culturally and historically. For example, the average age of menarche had been declining for European and North American girls, and is now leveling off (Brooks-Gunn, 1991). In addition, menarche occurs earlier for girls living in urban areas than for girls living in rural areas (Tanner, 1978). Nutrition, body weight, and exercise appear to be the most important determinants of age variations in the onset of puberty (Brooks-Gunn, 1991). There are also gender differences in that girls on the average experience an earlier pubertal growth spurt than do boys (Whiting & Whiting, 1987). The experience of puberty and its meaning for individuals and cultures vary greatly, ranging from elaborate celebration in some cultures to concealment and embarrassment in others (Brooks-Gunn & Reiter, 1990; Schlegel & Barry, 1979). When puberty rituals occur, their purpose, according to John Whiting (1990), is to help young people understand and accept adult identity.

The end of the stage of adolescence occurs when a person attains adulthood, a state which is culturally defined, and culturally variable. Full participation in the adult roles usually includes marriage and procreation

(Schlegel & Barry, 1991), but other social criteria may be included. In contemporary industrialized societies, a major criterion is participation in the work force and economic independence. For adolescents in Morocco, an important behavioral criterion for adulthood is the acquisition of "*aql*: learning to interact with the wider society in an appropriate way, and learning the complex process of maneuvering skillfully among various relationships" (Davis & Davis, 1989, p. 156). For Mescalero Apaches in the United States, the qualities required of adults include honesty, generosity, pride, and bravery (Farrer, 1987). These are celebrated in puberty rituals for adolescent girls. And, among the Sambia of Papua New Guinea, full adulthood (*aatmwunu*) is obtained by a man only when he has two children (Herdt, 1990).

While the social stage of adolescence may be approximately linked to chronological age (that is, it usually occurs between ages 10 and 20), the age range is extremely variable as described above, and it can only be considered a rough estimate. Moreover, the end of adolescence may be more variable than the onset. Thus, for the current review, early and middle adolescence (approximately ages 11 through 18) will be emphasized, and only a few selected studies of late adolescence will be mentioned.

Some authorities have questioned the universal existence of a life stage of adolescence (e.g., Ariès, 1962; Saraswathi, this volume; Sebald, 1984). They argue that adolescence is a creation of modern industrial societies in which the transition from childhood to adulthood is prolonged. A tempered version of this argument has been presented by Castelnuovo (1990) who argues that what is commonly conceived of as adolescence is a consequence of a societal change away from a traditional agrarian society and toward urbanization and modernization. Others have argued that historically the nature of the adolescent stage has drastically changed, so that, for example, during the latter part of the 19th century, adolescents in North America and Europe became more economically dependent on their parents while at the same time being allowed more choice regarding marriage partners and occupations (Baumeister & Tice, 1986). Whereas few would dispute the impact of historical setting and factors such as urbanization and modernization on the adolescent stage, the more extreme statement, that adolescence is the product of industrialization, has been rather convincingly challenged (Schlegel & Barry, 1991).

In the most comprehensive study of adolescence in pre industrial societies to date, Schlegel and Barry (1991) have found that recognition of a life stage of adolescence (that is, a stage between childhood and adulthood) is widespread. "Adolescence as a social stage with its own activities and behaviors, expectations and rewards, is well recorded in the history and literature of earlier times" (Schlegel & Barry, 1991, p. 2). Of the 186 preindustrial societies of the Standard Cross-Cultural Sample (Murdock & White, 1980), sufficient data were available to assess the existence or nonexistence of a socially defined adolescent stage for boys in 173 societies and for girls in 175 societies. All of the 173 societies defined a social stage of adolescence for boys, and all but one for girls. In that culture, the Gros Ventre, girls were married before the onset of menstruation and were expected to perform all the social roles of adulthood from marriage onward (Schlegel & Barry, 1991).

Although social recognition of a stage of adolescence may be widespread, the duration of the stage varies widely (Schlegel & Barry, 1991), and societal changes can lead to changes in the length of the adolescence stage (Burbank, 1988; Condon, 1990). For example, Burbank (1988) has suggested that the abandonment of a nomadic lifestyle, the expectation of universal schooling, and the imposition of Australian law prohibiting marriage until age sixteen have created a stage of adolescence for Aboriginal girls who traditionally had married prior to menarche. Those same factors decreased the adolescent stage for boys who traditionally had not married until their 20s or even 30s. Among preindustrial societies, the length of adolescence appears to be greatest in those practicing neolocal residence (Schlegel & Barry, 1991). That is, societies which require a young couple to move to a separate residence rather than live with either set of parents have a longer adolescent stage. In addition, Schlegel and Barry determined that the adolescent stage for boys was frequently longer than that for girls because of the tendency for girls to marry younger (Schlegel & Barry, 1991). Thus, it appears that the onset, duration, and termination of the adolescent life stage are closely linked to social and cultural factors.

PERSONAL AND SOCIAL DEVELOPMENT DURING ADOLESCENCE

What appears to be consistent is that adolescence is a period of transformation from the social role of child to the more complex and socially integrated role of adult. The transformation seems to be most substantial in the realms of personal and social development. Some of the important social developmental tasks of the adolescent stage include establishing an identity, orienting to the future, constructing a socially integrated self-concept and self-image, maintaining self-esteem, and committing to a political and civic ideology.

Adolescent Identity

The major developmental task of adolescence according to Erikson (1950, 1968) and many subsequent thinkers (e.g., Marcia, 1966; Harter, 1990; Rosenberg, 1965) is the establishment of a unique individual identity. While not denying cultural and societal influences on the developing adolescent, Erikson (1950, 1968) emphasized the separate *autonomous* self as the successful outcome of the identity crisis. In the same vein, Marcia (1966) has described identity statuses as falling into four categories— identity achievement, moratorium, foreclosure, and identity diffusion. The identity status approach implies that successful development involves exploration and commitment, processes that demand independent, autonomous actions. For example, the foreclosed identity status (the acceptance of a life plan and self definition dictated by others rather than an exploration and attainment of one's unique identity) is often considered a less than optimal identity solution in industrialized countries (Marcia, 1966).

Although there have been significant attempts to describe identity and personality development in indigenous and non-Western perspectives (e.g., Asthana, 1988; Church, 1987; de Silva, Stiles, & Gibbons, 1992; Diaz-Guerrero, 1975; Nsamenang, 1992; Sinha, 1982), these concepts have not permeated research on identity development and the adolescent self. As Gardiner, Mutter, and Kosmitzki (1998) have pointed out, empirical cross-cultural studies of identity development are "surprisingly scarce" (p. 124— but see Portes, Dunham, and Del Castillo in this volume). On the other hand, identity has played a central role in studies of immigrant adolescents (e.g., Camilleri & Malewska-Peyre, 1997; Liebkind & Kosonen, 1998; Sam, 1991, 1994; Stiles, Gibbons, Lie, Sand, & Krull, 1998) and ethnic minority adolescents (e.g., Kvernmo, 1998; Phinney, 1990; Phinney & Chavira, 1992).

Among the authors of the Harvard Adolescence series, the issues of identity and autonomy have been taken up by Hollos and Leis (1989), Davis and Davis (1989), and Condon (1987). These authors note that autonomy may be construed differently in preindustrial societies than in the industrialized Western world. Among the Ijo of Nigeria, an increasing ability to make choices and to take responsibility are seen as central to development; at the same time, a fully realized adult has an identity based on being part of the community (Hollos & Leis, 1989).   Similarly, Moroccan adolescents do not seem to strive for independence from others, but rather strive to achieve a balance of meeting social responsibilities and their own psychological needs (Davis & Davis, 1989). In contrast, Condon (1987) noted that Inuit adolescents experience a great deal of autonomy in terms of freedom to schedule their own lives and to make their own decisions about education and sexuality. Parents do not require responsible behavior as the price of autonomy, but instead, freedom for children and adolescents is taken for granted. While traditional Inuit culture had relied on a balance of cooperation and self-reliance, the recent changes seem to have shifted the balance toward self-reliance, a quality acquired through the exercise of freedom (Condon, 1987).

Self and identity were addressed in the Schlegel and Barry (1991) study of preindustrial societies in terms of the character traits, which are inculcated during adolescence. The majority of societies (149 of 186) emphasized both sexual restraint and sexual expression as behaviors to be learned. The next most common traits promoted were obedience and conformity. Thus, in preindustrial societies adolescent socialization was focused on behaviors related to procreation and compliance with authority.

Future Orientation

The identity development of adolescents may also be manifest in related areas, such as adolescents' ideas about the future. There is a growing corpus of research on adolescents' orientation to the future. In their projections into the future, adolescents construct their possible or likely identities in various domains. A major review of adolescents' future orientations (Nurmi, 1991) revealed both similarities among adolescents as well as cultural differences. Internationally in the contemporary world, the major goals and expectations of adolescents concerned future education and occupation (Nurmi, 1991). The next most important concerns were marriage and future family. Other domains that interested teenagers were leisure activities and material acquisitions. Adolescents' worries centered primarily around acquiring a good education, procuring a good job, and starting a family. However, they also exhibited broader societal concerns such as fears about the threat of nuclear war.

More recent studies of future orientation have tended to confirm and extend those findings. Adolescents of three countries—Australia, Finland, and Israel—expressed interest in the major areas associated with normative developmental tasks, including completing an education, entering a career, and founding a family (Nurmi, Poole, & Seginer, 1995). However, Israeli adolescents expressed more hopes and fears concerning military service, girls expressed more hopes and fears related to education, and Australian adolescents expressed more hopes about leisure and more fears about global and political issues. In a comparison of Druze and Jewish adolescents within Israel, Druze adolescents were found to express fewer hopes and fears in the normative domains such as education and career, and more in the personal domains (such as the self) (Seginer & Halabi-Kheir, 1998). In a comparison of the future occupational plans of French and Finnish adolescents, the major difference was that the French students, participants in an early educational tracking system, had firmer plans whereas the occupational plans of the Finnish students were less fixed (Motola, Sinisalo, & Guichard, 1998).

In a recent comparison of the future interests of adolescents from eleven European countries and the United States (Nurmi, Liiceanu, & Liberska, 1999) some clear cross-national differences emerged. Adolescents from Western European countries (Switzerland, Germany, Norway, and Finland) showed greater interest in acquiring a good education and job and in spending leisure time with their peers than did those from Eastern European countries (such as Bulgaria, the Czech Republic, Hungary, Poland, Romania, and Russia). Adolescents from Eastern European countries endorsed more social responsibility (being useful to my country and my parents) and expressed more interest in money, fame, and importance. Although adolescents from the United States were more like the Eastern European adolescents in most domains, like the Western European adolescents they endorsed the importance of education and career. There were also gender differences, with girls, more than boys, expressing interest in a future family and boys, more than girls, expressing interest in wealth and fame. The authors concluded that, "the sociocultural environments related to the current economic and political situation play an important role in young people's lives" (p. 97).

In the Harvard Adolescence Project, the researchers asked adolescents about their future aspirations; Inuit adolescents, Moroccan adolescents, and Nigerian adolescents all expressed hopes concerning future occupations and their future families, providing some evidence that attention to these issues is virtually universal among contemporary adolescents (Condon, 1987; Davis & Davis, 1989; Hollos & Leis, 1989).

Self-concept

Cross-cultural studies of self-concept often start by noting that the basic concept of the person varies cross-culturally (Shweder & Bourne, 1984), and that the self-concept is a particular instance of the person. Miller (1987) has extended the cross-cultural analysis of the concept of the person to a developmental perspective. For Western youth, a hallmark of adolescence has been the transition from concrete specific conceptualizations of the person to more general trait descriptions based on psychological dispositions (e.g., Harter, 1988, 1990; Montemayor & Eisen, 1977). For example, the preadolescent might state, " She helps her mother with the housework and her friends with their homework." The adolescent might say, "She is a kind and helpful person." Miller (1987) hypothesized that Hindu Indian respondents would not follow this pattern, but instead make more self-involved descriptions with increasing age. A self-involved description for the previous example would be, "She often helps me." Participants (8, 11, and 15 years old and adults from the U.S.A. and India) described two peers known well to them and two peers not known well. The hypotheses were supported. Young children (age eight) of both cultures used psychological dispositions infrequently. Adolescents and adults from the U.S.A. used psychological dispositions more frequently than children and two to three times as frequently as did their counterparts in India. While self-involved descriptions decreased with age among U.S.A. respondents they increased with age in Hindu Indian respondents. Two conclusions may be drawn from this study. First, that developmental changes at adolescence do not inevitably lead to an increase in trait descriptions of the person, but may follow a "culturally variable developmental course" (Miller, 1987, p. 317) and second, that adolescents' ways of describing the person vary in cross-cultural perspective.

In a now classic article, Markus and Kitayama (1991) presented convincing evidence that not only the concept of the person, but also the concept of the self varies cross-culturally. They argued that U.S.A. culture fosters an independent construal of the self, with emphasis upon the individual's unique inner qualities. On the other hand, persons from Japan and many other Asian cultures may represent the self as more interdependent, with emphasis on the essential connectedness of the self with significant others.

Adolescents' self-concepts were studied by Cousins (1989) who demonstrated cross-cultural differences in adolescent's descriptions of themselves. High school students from Japan and the United States completed twenty statements beginning with "I am...."; then they did the task again for particular contexts, for example, in the family. In the context-free condition, the U.S. students gave more psychological traits such as, "I am friendly." When the context was given, however, the United States students qualified their answers more (I am sometimes friendly) and the Japanese students used more general traits. These results suggest that the context matters in cross-cultural studies of self.

Using a different measure—the open-ended question "how would you describe yourself to yourself," Stiles, Gibbons, and De Silva (1996) found more similarities than differences between adolescent girls from Sri Lanka and girls from the United States. For girls from both countries the most frequent themes were those of relational style and skills, reflected in statements such as "I open up to people," "I don't want to hurt my mother." On the Twenty Statements Test, however, girls from the United States responded more individualistically than did the girls from Sri Lanka.

The developmental course of adolescent self-concept in different socioeconomic (SES) contexts was investigated in two studies of adolescents living in southern India (Kuebli, Reddy, & Gibbons, 1998; Reddy & Gibbons, in press). School age children (ages 9-11) and adolescents (ages 12-16) wrote open-ended descriptions of themselves in answer to the question, "How would you describe yourself to yourself?" and also completed the twenty statements test. While adolescents from the economically advantaged group showed the developmental changes in self-concept frequently exhibited by adolescents in the Western world (such as decline in references to others and increased individuality with increasing age), this pattern did not hold for the adolescents from the low-SES group. Adolescents from a low-SES background (particularly boys) showed, on the contrary, intensified group and social identifications with increasing age (Reddy & Gibbons, in press).

The *domains* which are important to self-definition and the *dimensions* of the self may also vary in cross-cultural perspective. A study by Watkins (1988) demonstrated clearly that particular cultural groups of adolescents may have very different self-domains than those commonly reported in the literature. Watkins (1988) asked young adolescents from a rural, economically depressed region in the Philippines to describe the most important areas of their lives, and to indicate whether these usually made them feel good or bad. Eight domains of self emerged (food, money, school, friends, family, clothes, religion, and recreation). Three of these domains—food, money, and clothes—are rarely addressed in self-image research.

In summary, there is mounting evidence that the concepts of the person and of the self vary cross-culturally, with Western cultures endorsing a more self-contained independent notion of self, and many Asian, possibly African, and possibly Latin American cultures expressing a more interdependent, role-defined notion of the self. In addition, the dimensions which are important in describing the self may vary cross-culturally. These observations may have profound implications for research with adolescents in cross-cultural perspective in that adolescence may be a critical stage for increased understanding of the self, and thus may be an age in which cultural differences are increasingly important.

Adolescent Self-image

The most comprehensive cross-national study of adolescent self-image was that by Offer and his colleagues (Offer et al., 1988). The instrument used was the Offer Self-Image Questionnaire (OSIQ), a multidimensional measure of adolescent self-image. The OSIQ includes scales on the psychological self (3 scales—impulse control, emotional tone, and body image), the social self (2 scales—social relationships, vocational and educational goals), the sexual self (liberal vs. conservative attitudes), the familial self (family relationships), the coping self (3 scales—mastery, psychopathology, and superior adjustment). Participants included younger (ages 13 to 15) and older (ages 16 to 19) adolescents from ten countries— Australia, Bangladesh, Hungary, Israel, Italy, Japan, Taiwan, Turkey, West Germany, and the United States. They were selected by collaborators to be representative of the adolescents of those countries. Careful translation and back-translation procedures were employed.

Offer and his colleagues found that adolescents in international perspective are characterized by a sense of well-being rather than conflict and stress. They coined the term "universal adolescent" to describe the global young person with a good relationship with family, positive self-concept, and good coping skills. Some items were almost universally endorsed by young people. An example was the item, "I like to help a friend whenever I can," which received very high endorsement among various age, gender, national groups ranging from a low of 86% among younger Italian males to a high of 100% among older Turkish females.

The greatest number of consistent differences among the sample were related to gender. Boys reported more emotional self-control, more happiness, and more pleasure about sexuality than did girls. For example, they were more likely to endorse the statement: "I enjoy life." Girls more often endorsed items of sadness, fearfulness, and unattractiveness. There were also age differences with older adolescents reporting more confidence.

The cross-national differences were complex and sometimes interacted with age and gender. A number of demographic variables were associated with adolescents' responses on the OSIQ. Teenagers who lived in countries with high proportions of teenagers in the population reported significantly more negative moods. On the other hand, gross national product (GNP) was positively correlated with adolescents' mood. The social relationships scale, which taps the quality of teenagers' peer relationships, was positively related to GNP, and negatively to the proportion of the population of adolescent age. Liberal sexual attitudes among adolescents were also associated with a high GNP and a high quality of life index.

The strengths of this substantial study include the large sample sizes, the large number of countries sampled, and the high internal consistencies of the scales internationally. Some limitations, however, are that the majority of adolescent participants were middle class, urban, and literate

(Triandis, 1988). The universality of the findings is also limited by the absence of samples from Africa or Latin America.

In conclusion, although *The Teenage World* is clearly the most comprehensive study of adolescent self-image in cross-national perspective, it seems somewhat premature to speak of the "universal adolescent."

Adolescent Self-esteem or Self-worth

Self-esteem and self-worth represent the evaluative component of the self-concept. The idea of self-worth or self-esteem is central to many definitions of adolescent well-being and adolescent competence (e.g., Buehler, Weigert, & Thomas, 1977; Millstein & Irwin, 1988; Resnick, 1986; Savin-Williams, 1989), as well as to more general theories of human behavior (e.g., Solomon, Greenberg, & Pyszczynski, 1991). However, the evaluative dimension of the self may be less salient to children and adolescents themselves than to the researchers who study them. When USA adolescents describe themselves in an open-ended way fewer than ten percent of their comments are evaluative (McGuire, McGuire, & Winton, 1979, cited in McGuire & McGuire, 1988; McGuire & Padawer Singer, 1976). Moreover, the concept of self-esteem is problematic when viewed in cross-cultural and cross-national perspective.

Self-esteem or self-worth has been defined in a variety of ways. Global self-esteem is often measured by such items as, " On the whole, I am satisfied with myself" (Rosenberg, 1965, p. 17) or, "I'm happy the way I am" (AAUW, 1990, p. 4). On the other hand, some researchers have seen self-evaluations as domain specific and have investigated the contributions of specific domains to overall self-esteem (e.g., Coopersmith, 1959; Marsh, 1986; Offer et al., 1988).

Harter (1988) has articulated a comprehensive theory of adolescent self-worth or regard for oneself as a person. She postulates two major determinants of global self-worth. The first is the perception of success in those domains which are considered to be important. That is, a young person who evaluates herself highly in the sphere of athletics and who also believes that participation in sports is important will hold herself in high regard. The domains that Harter has investigated include physical appearance, social acceptance, scholastic competence, athletic competence, and behavioral conduct (Harter, 1987). Among adolescents in the United States, the most important contribution to self-esteem is perceived physical attractiveness (Harter, 1990).

The second component of Harter's theory is that self-esteem is also a function of the perceived opinions of significant others (Harter, 1988, 1990). This has been referred to as the "looking glass self" (Cooley,

1902). Among the adolescents Harter studied, parents' opinion was most closely related to global self-worth, followed closely by classmates' regard. The regard of close friends and teachers was less important (Harter, 1987).

Harter's theory is based primarily on research with mainstream U.S.A. adolescents. However, even if the theory itself holds true in cross-cultural and cross-national perspective it is still possible that the domains of the self considered important might vary cross-culturally (e.g., Watkins, 1988). In several tests of the contribution of various domains to the self-esteem of adolescents, physical attractiveness was found to be the most important contributor to global self-esteem for adolescents in Northern Ireland (Granleese & Joseph, 1993), Scotland (Hoare, Elton, Greer, & Kerley, 1993), and Norway (Wickstrom, 1998).

Another way that cross-cultural differences might occur is in the identity of the significant others whose regard is essential for self-esteem. This possibility has been demonstrated in the Netherlands. The self-esteem of mainstream Dutch adolescents living in the Netherlands was significantly correlated with the perceived opinions of their siblings, friends, and teachers (Verkuyten, 1986, 1988). However, for immigrant ethnic minority adolescents in the Netherlands, self-esteem was uncorrelated with outsiders' opinions, but instead correlated highly with the perceived opinions of family members, including mothers, fathers, siblings, and other relatives. The overall self-esteem of mainstream and minority immigrant adolescents, however, did not differ.

These results are similar to those obtained among minority youths in the United States. In general, prejudicial opinions held by society may be countered by the positive opinions of the local community, family, peers, and schools (Barnes, 1980; Rosenberg, 1965; Spencer, Dornbusch, & Mont-Reynaud, 1990). In general, ethnic minority status is not linked to lower self-esteem for adolescents   (e.g., AAUW, 1990; Bell-Scott & McKenry, 1986; Harter, 1990; Martinez, Martinez, Olmedo, & Goldman, 1976; Verkuyten, 1986).

Notably, self-esteem and self-worth are not listed in the indexes of the books in the Harvard Adolescence Project, suggesting either that self-esteem was not an important construct among adolescents in the preindustrial societies studied or that the project directors had decided not to address the issue. Sources of self-esteem can only be inferred indirectly, such as through this quote from a troubled adolescent in Zawiya, Morocco, "Living is not just eating, but if you feel that your parents support you and provide you with what you need. That's what parents do. There are parents who have only one son and they are proud of him. They love him a lot and they provide him with all he needs" (Davis & Davis, 1989, p. 150). This quote seems to reflect the looking glass component of self-esteem, that a young person who is well thought of by his parents will experience a sense of well-being. Nevertheless overall, the absence of references to self-esteem among adolescents in the preindustrial societies studied suggest its relative lack of salience.

Another factor which might lead to differences in self-esteem internationally is that the willingness to acknowledge self-esteem may be regarded differently in different cultures. Markus and Kitayama (1991) have amassed persuasive evidence that self-promotion is not valued in cultures with an interdependent construal of the self. For example, Japanese school children evaluated a modest peer more highly than a self-promoting peer and this tendency became more pronounced with increasing age (Yoshida, Kojo, & Kaku, 1982). The false uniqueness effect, or self-serving bias that has been demonstrated among U.S.A. college students was absent among Japanese college students (Markus & Kitayama, 1991). Given these findings, it seems likely that the demand characteristics in completing a self-esteem instrument vary by culture. While Western respondents might be expected to present a self-promoting positive self-image, Eastern respondents might be motivated to present a modest or self-effacing self-image.

There have been many studies comparing the self-esteem of adolescents of different nations and cultures (e.g., Agrawal, 1978; Calhoun & Sethi, 1987; Karim, 1990; Olowu, 1983; Parikh & Patel, 1989; Robinson, Tayler, & Piolat, 1990; Smart & Smart, 1970; Verkuyten, 1986; Watkins, Regmi, & Alfon, 1990). However, these studies are difficult to interpret because of the limitations described above. For example, in many studies, the domains that may be important for self-esteem were assumed to be universal and to be tapped by the instrument used. Thus, for example, if the familial self is the most important and overriding factor in the self-esteem of adolescents growing up in a collectivistic culture, that specific effect may be blurred by the instruments used. Collectivistic adolescents' self-esteem might be judged to be higher (if the instrument includes many family items), or lower (if the instrument includes few family items). There has been some attempt to develop instruments based on adolescent-defined domains (e.g., Juhasz, 1985), but there has not been widespread use of measures which weigh the importance of various domains of self (but see Watkins et. al., 1990).

In the case of Filipino adolescents, Watkins (1982) contends that Western notions of generalized self-esteem or self-worth are related to Philippine indigenous concepts of *amor propio* (self-pride) and *hiya* (shame), and thus Western measures of self-esteem and the study of its correlates are appropriate in the Filipino context. However, analyses such as Watkins' are lamentably rare. More often, Western instruments have been used without consideration for the local relevance (see Kulkarni & Ruhan, 1988 for a discussion of this practice in India). Other problems with the conceptualization and measurement of self-esteem internationally have been addressed by Smith and Bond (1999). They suggest, for example, that "culture may shape the *type* of self-esteem that is emphasized (for example, self-competence versus self-liking), rather than its overall level" (p. 120).

In summary, if adolescents of different cultures hold different concepts of the person (Miller, 1987), consider as important different dimensions of the self (Watkins, 1988), and maintain different criteria for development (Davis & Davis, 1989; Klaczynski, 1990; Ogbu, 1981), direct application of Western ideas of adolescent identity development to diverse groups of adolescents is risky at best. If adolescents of different cultures consider different domains of the self to be important (Watkins, 1988; Markus & Kitayama, 1991), use different significant others to evaluate self-worth (Verkuyten, 1988), and vary in their willingness to describe themselves in a positive light (Markus & Kitayama, 1991), then cross-cultural studies comparing adolescent self-esteem are difficult to interpret.

Another way to evaluate the function of self-esteem for adolescents internationally is to examine its antecedents, correlates, and consequences. This would mean to ask the question: Does self-esteem, independent of its level, play a comparable role in the lives of adolescents from different cultural settings? This approach is analogous to that taken by Van IJzendoorn (1990) for the issue of attachment in infancy and later life.

One antecedent (or correlate) of self-esteem has already been mentioned above. At least for adolescents in the United States, Northern Ireland, Norway, and Scotland (Granleese & Joseph, 1993; Harter, 1990; Hoare et al., 1993; Wickstrom, 1998), the most important contributor to overall self-esteem is perceived physical attractiveness. In general, there is substantial evidence that, cross-culturally, beauty is considered to be positive (Albright, Malloy, Dong, Kenny, & Fang, 1997; Chen, Shaffer, & Wu, 1997; Wheeler & Kim, 1997), although the characteristics that contribute to attractiveness may be culturally variable. Whether attractiveness is the most important contributor to self-esteem among adolescents in non-Western settings remains to be investigated.

Another construct that appears to correlate with self-esteem is a sense of well-being (Grob, 1998). Among adolescents from eleven Eastern and Western European nations and the United States, positive attitudes about life (e.g., "I am happy to live") were correlated with self-esteem (e.g., "I have an overall positive attitude toward myself") in each country. The correlations did vary, however; there was a closer relation between self-esteem and positive attitudes in the U.S. and Russian samples, and a lower correlation between self-esteem and positive attitudes among French-speaking Swiss adolescents (Grob, 1998). As with the contribution of attractiveness to self-esteem, it is not known whether the relation between self-esteem and well-being holds true in non-Western settings.

Another study which investigated the correlates of self-esteem in different cultural settings was that of Bagley and Mallick (1995). They demonstrated that the presence of stressors in the lives of adolescents from three countries (Canada, Britain, and Hong Kong) correlated negatively with self-esteem. Although all four sources of stress—peer relationships, abuse at home, loneliness and isolation, and school and career—were significantly correlated with low self-esteem in each sample, those correlations varied in magnitude.

Other variables may be similarly (or dissimilarly) correlated with self-esteem in cross-cultural perspective. The most useful cross-cultural studies in the future will be those that identify the variables that predict, covary with, and follow from self-esteem in cross-cultural and international perspective.

Political and Civic Identity

Even though political philosophy was a core domain of early identity theory (Erikson, 1950; Marcia, 1966), and political beliefs were among the first issues to be studied among adolescents in cross-national perspective (Gillespie & Allport, 1955), the study of adolescents' civic and national identity and political commitment has only recently seen a resurgence.

The process of making a political and civic commitment is complex in contemporary societies but what adolescents from many countries may have in common is that activities such as participation in school governance and volunteering in the community may lead to political participation in adulthood (Youniss & Yates, 1999).

Perhaps surprisingly, groups of adolescent youth in preindustrial societies are frequently engaged in community service, by enforcing community morals or norms, organizing public events, or entertaining others (Schlegel & Barry, 1991).   For example, among the Palau in Micronesia described by Barnett (1949), groups of boys and girls formed clubs that performed community service under the direction of village chiefs. Similarly, groups of Muria adolescents, from central India, performed tasks such as working on the roads or attending at festivals or weddings (Elwin, 1968, cited in Schlegel & Barry, 1991). Thus, it seems that development of a civic identity may be common for adolescents in preindustrialized societies.

Among adolescent Inuit boys in Holman, groups of boys were most likely to compete in hockey games, often entertaining the whole community (Condon, 1987). A scarcity of adolescent groups was noted by Davis and Davis (1989) for adolescents in Zawiya, Morocco. In contrast, groups of Ijo boys in Nigeria would go on fishing or hunting trips, or sometimes help out at the store of a friend's parents (Hollos & Leis, 1989). These reports suggest great diversity in the community participation of adolescent groups among the non-Western societies studied.

One of the most extensive recent studies of adolescents' civic commitment was conducted by Flanagan, Bowes, Jonsson, Csapo, and Sheblanova (1998) in Australia, the United States, Sweden, Hungary, Czech Republic, Bulgaria, and Russia. Civic commitment, defined as the importance adolescents placed on making a contribution to their country and improving their society, was predicted by their family's emphasis on social responsibility and, to a lesser extent, their sense of membership at school. In several countries, it was also related to participation in volunteer work (United States, Sweden, the Czech Republic, Bulgaria, and Russia) or to democratic school practices (United States and the Czech Republic). These results suggest that adolescents' civic identity is derived primarily from experiences in the family and at school.

Finally, the political development and commitment of adolescents in times of rapid social change or political turmoil has been the focus of a number of studies in recent years. The contexts for these investigations have included political change in central and eastern Europe (Macek, Flanagan, Gallay, Kostron, Botcheva, & Czapo, 1998), Northern Ireland (Whyte, 1998, 1999), South Africa (Finchilescu & Dawes, 1998), Palestinian West Bank and Gaza Strip (Barber, 1999), and the unification of Germany (Kracke, Oepke, Wild, & Noack, 1998; Oswald, 1999). In sum, there is some evidence that the development of a civic and political identity is an adolescent issue across time and space.

CONCLUSIONS AND DIRECTIONS FOR FUTURE RESEARCH

Cross-cultural and international studies of adolescent development can explore the generality of developmental processes. The present review, while not exhaustive, has addressed identity development and autonomy, future orientation, self-concept, self-esteem, and civic identity among adolescents from different national and cultural settings. While identity development may be universal, its dependence on autonomy may be culturally variable. Future orientations of adolescents in the modern world also show certain commonalities, including a concern with future occupation and family. Some cultural variation, especially between adolescents of Western and Eastern Europe, has been demonstrated. The literature on self-concept and self-esteem comes primarily from adolescents living in the industrialized world. Self-esteem, in particular, may not be salient for adolescents growing up in preindustrialized societies. A promising approach for research on self-esteem is the investigation of its antecedents, correlates, and consequences in international perspective. Finally, research into civic and political identity development is flourishing, and there are indications of community service among adolescents in preindustrial societies, as well as the modern world.

This brief review has necessarily omitted much important ongoing international research with regard to adolescence. There are considerable and vital recent studies, particularly in the areas of adolescent time use (Alsaker & Flammer, 1999), conflict and relationships with parents (Nauck, 1994; Rosenthal, Demetriou, & Efklides, 1989; Silbereisen & Schmitt-Rodermund, 1994; Trommsdorff, 1994), coping and adjustment (Gibson-Cline, 1996; Jose, D'Anna, Cafasso, Bryant, Chiker, Gein, & Zhezmer, 1998; Palmonari, Kirchler, & Pombeni, 1991; Seiffge-Krenke, 1990; Scott & Scott, 1989, 1998; Scott, Scott, Boehnke, Cheng, Leung, & Sasake, 1991; Scott, Scott, & McCabe, 1991), delinquency (Hurrelmann & Engel, 1992; Yang, Yue, & Wu, 1991; Yee, Yang, & Barnes, 1990), and education and schooling (Chen, Rubin, & Li, 1997; Kagitçibasi, 1992) that have necessarily been omitted.

Despite the large number of studies addressing adolescence in cross-cultural and cross-national perspective, psychological theory and practice would benefit from additional research of a particular kind. Specifically, a greater sensitivity to the contexts of adolescents' lives is warranted. In addition, research that is based on indigenous, local, or ethnopsychological concepts of development can be particularly useful. Comparative studies need to include at least four samples and use appropriate statistical procedures (van de Vijver & Leung, 1997). In addition, greater attention needs to be paid to adolescents' own perceptions of the important issues in their lives. For example, many studies have looked at adolescents' views of the future without any evidence (to this author's knowledge) that adolescents look to the future more than do adults or children.

In conclusion, the objective of the current literature review has been to perspectives—the ethnographic tradition and the quantitative illustrate how the integration of research in different settings and from two psychological approaches—can provide insights into adolescent development. Specifically, several adolescent developmental issues were revealed as shared by adolescents living in very different contexts, while some developmental issues appear to be applicable only to adolescents growing up in the industrialized world.

BIBLIOGRAPHY

Agrawal, P. (1978). A cross-cultural study of self-image Indian, American, Australian, and Irish adolescents. *Journal of Youth and Adolescence, 7,* 107-116.

Albright, L., Malloy, T. E., Dong, Q., Kenny, D. A., & Fang, X. (1997). Cross-cultural consensus in personality judgments. *Journal of Personality and Social Psychology, 72,* 558-569.

Alsaker, F. D., & Flammer, A. (1999). *The adolescent experience: European and American adolescents in the 1990s.* Mahwah, NJ: Erlbaum.

American Association of University Women (AAUW). (1990). *Shortchanging girls, shortchanging America: Expectations and aspirations, Gender roles and self-esteem.* Washington, DC:Greenberg-Lake.

Aptekar, L. (1988). *Street children of Cali.* Durham, NC: Duke University Press.

Ariès, P. (1962). *Centuries of childhood* (trans. R. Baldick). New York: Vintage Books.

Asthana, H. S. (1988). Personality. In J. Pandey (Ed.), *Psychology in India: The state-of-the-art. Vol. 1: Personality and mental processes* (pp. 153-189). New Delhi, India: Sage.

Bagley, C., & Mallick, K. (1995). Negative self-perception and component of stress in Canadian, British, and Hong Kong adolescents. *Perceptual and Motor Skills, 81,* 123-127.

Barber, B. K. (1999). Youth experience in the Palestinian Intifada: A case study in intensity, complexity, paradox, and competence. In M. Yates & J. Youniss (Eds.), *Roots of civic identity: International perspectives on community service and activism in youth* (pp. 178-204). Cambridge University Press.

Barnes, E. J. (1980). The black community as the source of positive self-concept for black children: A theoretical perspective. In R. Jones (Ed.), *Black psychology* (pp. 106-130). New York: Harper and Row.

Barnett, H. C. (1949). *Palauan Society.* Eugene, OR: University of Oregon Publications.

Baumeister, R. F., & Tice, D. M. (1986). How adolescence became the struggle for self: A historical transformation of psychological development. In J. Suls & A. G. Greenwald (Eds.), *Psychological perspectives on the self* (Vol. 3, pp. 182-211). Hillsdale, NJ: Erlbaum.

Bell-Scott, P., & McKenry, P. C. (1986). Black adolescents and their families. In G. K. Leigh & G. W. Peterson (Eds.), *Adolescents in families* (pp. 410-432). Cincinnati, OH: South Western.

Brooks-Gunn, J. (1991). Maturational timing variations in adolescent girls, antecedents of. In R. M. Learner, A. C. Petersen, & J. Brooks-Gunn (Eds.), *Encyclopedia of adolescence* (vol. 2, pp. 609-613). New York: Garland.

Brooks-Gunn, J., & Reiter, E. O. (1990). The role of pubertal processes. In S. S. Feldman & G. R. Elliott (Eds.), *At the threshold: The developing adolescent* (pp. 16-53). Cambridge, MA: Harvard University Press.

Buehler, C. J., Weigert, A. J., & Thomas, D. (1974). Correlates of conjugal power: A five culture analysis of adolescent perceptions. *Journal of Comparative Family Studies, 5*, 5-16.

Buehler, C. J., Weigert, A. J., & Thomas, D. (1977). Antecedents of adolescent self-evaluation: A cross-national application of a model. *Journal of Comparative Family Studies, 8*, 29-45.

Burbank, V. K. (1988). *Aboriginal adolescence: Maidenhood in an Australian community*. New Brunswick, NJ: Rutgers University Press.

Calhoun, G., Jr., & Sethi, R. (1987). The self-esteem of pupils from India, the United States, and the Philippines. *Journal of Psychology, 121*, 199-202.

Camilleri, C., & Malewska-Peyre, H. (1997). Socialization and identity strategies. In J. W. Berry, P. R. Dasen, & T. S. Saraswathi (Eds.), *Handbook of cross-cultural psychology* (2nd ed.). Vol. 2: *Basic processes and human development* (pp. 41-67). Needham Heights, MA: Allyn & Bacon.

Castelnuovo, A. (1990). La adolescencia como fenomeno cultural [Adolescence as a cultural phenomenon]. *Revista de Psicoanalisis, 47*, 661-672.

Cederblad, M. (1984). Det sarbara barnet—uppvaxtvillkor och psykisk halsa [The vulnerable child: Conditions of growing up and mental health]. *Psykisk Halso, 25*, 3-11.

Chen, X., Rubin, K. H., Li, D. (1997). Relation between academic achievement and social adjustment: Evidence from Chinese children. *Developmental Psychology, 33*, 518-525.

Chen, N. Y., Shaffer, D, R., & Wu, C. (1997). On physical attractiveness stereotyping in Taiwan: A revised sociocultural perspective. *Journal of Social Psychology, 137*, 117-124.

Church, A. T. (1987). Personality research in a non-Western culture: The Philippines. *Psychological Bulletin, 102*, 272-292.

Condon, R. G. (1987). *Inuit youth: Growth and change in the Canadian arctic*. New Brunswick, NJ: Rutgers University Press.

Condon, R. G. (1990). The rise of adolescence: Social change and life stage dilemmas in the Central Canadian Artic. *Human Organization, 49*, 266-279.

Cooley, C. H. (1902). *Human nature and the social order.* New York: Charles Scribner's Sons.

Coopersmith, S. A. (1959). Method for determining types of self-esteem. *Journal of Abnormal and Social Psychology, 58*, 211-215.

Copeland, N. H., & Harvey, C. D. H. (1989). Refugee adaptation: The case of Southeast Asian youth in a Western Canadian city. *Canadian Home Economics Journal, 39*, 163-67.

Cousins, S. D. (1989). Culture and selfhood in Japan and the United States. *Journal of Personality and Social Psychology, 56*, 124-131.

Davis, S. S., & Davis, D. A. (1989). *Adolescence in a Moroccan town.* New Brunswick, NJ: Rutgers University Press.

De Silva, S., Stiles, D. A., & Gibbons, J. L. (1992). Girls' identity formation in the changing social structure of Sri Lanka. *Journal of Genetic Psychology, 153*, 211-220.

Díaz-Guerrero, R. (1975). *Psychology of the Mexican.* Austin, TX: University of Texas Press.

Elkind, D. (1974). *Children and adolescents.* New York: Oxford University Press.

Elwin, V. (1968). *The kingdom of the young.* Bombay: Oxford University Press.

Erikson, E. H. (1950). *Childhood and society.* New York: Norton.

Erikson, E. H. (1968). *Identity: Youth and crisis.* New York: Norton.

Farrer, C. R. (1987). Singing for life: The Mescalero Apache girls' puberty ceremony. In L. C. Mahdi, S. Foster, & M. Little (Eds.), *Betwixt & between: Patterns of masculine and feminine initiation* (pp. 239-263). La Salle, IL: Open Court.

Finchilescu, G., & Dawes, A. (1998). Catapulted into democracy: South African adolescents; sociopolitical orientations following rapid social change. *Journal of Social Issues, 54*, 563-584.

Flanagan, C. A., Bowes, J. M., Jonsson, B., Csapo, B., & Sheblanova, E. (1998). Ties that bind: Correlates of adolescents' civic commitments in seven countries. *Journal of Social Issues, 54*, 457-475.

Gardiner, H. W., Mutter, J. D., & Kosmitzki, C. (1998). *Lives across cultures: Cross-cultural human development.* Boston, MA: Allyn & Bacon.

Gibson-Cline, J. (1996). *Adolescence from crisis to coping: A thirteen nation study.* Oxford: Butterworth-Heinemann.

Gillespie, J. M., & Allport, G. W. (1955). *Youth's outlook on the future: A cross-national study.* Garden City, NY: Doubleday.

Granleese, J., & Joseph, S. (1993). Factor analysis of the Self-perception Profile for Children. *Personality and Individual Differences, 15*, 343-345.

Grob, A. (1998). Adolescents' subjective well-being in fourteen cultural contexts. In J-E. Nurmi (Ed.), *Adolescents, cultures, and conflicts: Growing up in contemporary Europe* (pp. 21-42). New York: Garland.

Harter, S. (1987). The determinants and mediational role of global self-worth in children. In N. Eisenberg (Ed.), *Contemporary topics in developmental psychology* (pp. 219-242). New York: Wiley.

Harter, S. (1988). The construction and conservation of the self: James and Cooley revisited. In D. K. Lapsley & F. C. Power (Eds.), *Self, ego, and identity: Integrative approaches* (43-70). New York: Springer-Verlag.

Harter, S. (1990). Self and identity development. In S. S. Feldman & G. R. Elliott (Eds.), *At the threshold: The developing adolescent* (pp. 352-387). Cambridge, MA: Harvard University Press.

Herdt, G. (1990). Sambia nosebleeding rites and male proximity to women. In J. W. Stigler, R. A. Shweder, & G. Herdt (Eds.), *Cultural psychology: Essays on comparative human development* (pp. 366-400). Cambridge: Cambridge University Press.

Hoare, P., Elton, R., Greer, A., & Kelley, S. (1993). The modification and standardization of the Harter Self-Esteem Questionnaire with Scottish school children. *European Child and Adolescent Psychiatry, 2*, 19-33.

Hollos, M., & Leis, P. E. (1989). *Becoming Nigerian in Ijo Society*. New Brunswick, NJ: Rutgers University Press.

Hurrelmann, K., & Engel, U. (1992). Delinquency as a symptom of adolescents' orientation toward status and success. *Journal of Youth and Adolescence, 21*, 119-138.

Jose, P. E., D'Anna, C. A., Cafasso, L. L., Bryant, F. B., Chiker, V., Gein, N., & Zhezmer, N. (1998). Stress and coping among Russian and American early adolescents. *Developmental Psychology, 34*, 757-769.

Juhasz, A. M. (1985). Measuring self-esteem in early adolescents. *Adolescence, 20*, 877-887.

Kagitçibasi, Ç. (1992). Human development and societal development: Linking theory and application. *Cross-Cultural Psychology Bulletin, 26*, 2-17.

Karim, S. F. (1990). Self-concept: A cross cultural study on adolescents. *Psychological Studies, 35*, 118-123.

Klaczynski, P. A. (1990). Cultural-developmental tasks and adolescent development: Theoretical and methodological considerations. *Adolescence, 25*, 811-823.

424   GIBBONS

Kracke, B., Oepke, M., Wild, E., & Noack, P. (1998). The impact of social change on antiforeigner and antidemocratic attitudes. In J-E. Nurmi (Ed.), *Adolescents, cultures, and conflicts: Growing up in contemporary Europe* (pp. 149-170). New York: Garland.

Kuebli, J. E., Reddy, R., & Gibbons, J. L. (1998). Perceptions of others in self-descriptions of children and adolescents in India. *Cross-Cultural Research, 32*, 217-240.

Kulkarni, S. S., & Ruhan, B. N. (1988). Psychological assessment: Its present and future trends. In J. Pandey (Ed.), *Psychology in India the state-of-the-art*. Vol. 1: *Personality and mental processes* (pp. 19-91). New Delhi, India: Sage.

Kvernmo, S. (1998). Language and ethnic identity in indigenous adolescents. In E. Skoe & A. von der Lippe (Eds.), *Personality development in adolescence* (pp. 123-139). London: Routledge.

Liebkind, K., & Kosonen, L. (1998). Acculturation and adaptation: A case of Vietnamese children and youths in Finland. In J-E. Nurmi (Ed.), *Adolescents, cultures, and conflicts*: Growing up in contemporary Europe (pp. 199-224). New York: Garland.

Macek, P., Flanagan, C., Gallay, L., Kostron, L., Botcheva, L., & Csapo, B. (1998). Postcommunist societies in times of transition: Perceptions of change among adolescents in central and eastern Europe. *Journal of Social Issues, 54*, 547-562.

Marcia, J. E. (1966). Development and validation of ego-identity status. *Journal of Personality and Social Psychology, 3*, 551 - 558.

Markus, H. R., & Kitayama, S. (1991). Culture and the self: Implications for cognition, emotion, and motivation. *Psychological Review*, *98*, 224-253.

Marsh, H. W. (1986). Global self-esteem: Its relation to specific facets of self-concept and their importance. *Journal of Personality and Social Psychology*, *51*, 1224-1236.

Martinez, J. L. Jr., Martinez, S. R., Olmedo, E. L., & Goldman, R. D. (1976). The semantic differential technique: A comparison of Chicano and Anglo high school students. *Journal of Cross-Cultural Psychology*, *7*, 325- 334.

McGuire, W. J., & McGuire, C. V. (1988). Content and process in the experience of self. *Advances in Experimental Social Psychology*, *21*, 97-144.

McGuire, W. J., & Padawer-Singer, A. (1976). Trait salience in the spontaneous self-concept. *Journal of Personality and Social Psychology*, *33*, 743-754.

Miller, J. G. (1987). Cultural influences on the development of conceptual differentiation in person description. *British Journal of Developmental Psychology, 5,* 309-319.

Millstein, S. G., & Irwin, C. E. (1988). Accident-related behaviors in adolescents: A biopsychosocial view. *Alcohol, Drugs and Driving, 4,* 21-29.

Montemayor, R., & Eisen, M. (1977). The development of self-conceptions from childhood to adolescence. *Developmental Psychology, 13,* 314-319.

Motola, M., Sinisalo, P., & Guichard, J. (1998). Social habitus and future plans. In J-E. Nurmi (Ed.), Adolescents, *cultures and conflicts* (pp. 43-73). New York: Garland.

Murdock, G. P., & White, D. R. (1980). The standard cross-cultural sample and its codes. In H. Barry, III & A. Schlegel (Eds.), *Cross-cultural samples and codes* (pp. 3-44). Pittsburgh, PA: University of Pittsburgh Press.

Nauck, B. (1994). Educational climate and intergenerative transmission in Turkish families: A comparison of migrants in Germany and non-migrants. In P. Noack, M. Hofer, & J. Youniss (Eds.), *Psychological responses to social change* (pp. 67-86). Berlin: Walter de Gruyter.

Nsamenang, A. B. (1992). *Human development in cultural context: A third world perspective.* Newbury Park, CA: Sage.

Nurmi, J-E. (1991). How do adolescents see their future? A review of the development of future orientation and planning. *Developmental Review, 11,* 1-59.

Nurmi, J-E., Liiceanu, A., & Liberska, H. (1999). Future-oriented interests. In F. D. Alsaker & A. Flammer (Eds.), *The adolescent experience: European and American adolescents in the 1990s* (pp. 85-98). Mahwah, NJ: Erlbaum.

Nurmi, J-E., Poole, M. E., & Seginer, R. (1995). Tracks and transitions— A comparison of adolescent future-oriented goals, explorations, and commitments in Australia, Israel, and Finland. *International Journal of Psychology, 30,* 355-375.

Offer, D., Ostrov, E., Howard, K. I., & Atkinson, R. (1988). *The teenage world: Adolescents' self-image in ten countries.* New York: Plenum Medical.

Ogbu, J. U. (1981). Origins of human competence: A cultural-ecological perspective. *Child Development, 52,* 413- 429.

Olowu, A. A. (1983). A cross-cultural study of adolescent self-concept. *Journal of Adolescence, 6,* 263 - 274.

Oswald, H. (1999). Political socialization in the new states of Germany. In M. Yates & J. Youniss (Eds.), *Roots of civic identity: International perspectives on community service and activism in youth* (pp. 97-113). Cambridge, UK: Cambridge University Press.

Parikh, J. C., & Patel, M. M. (1989). A cross-cultural study of self-esteem among tribals and non-tribals of Gujarat. *Indian Journal of Applied Psychology*, *26*, 22-25.

Palmonari, A., Kirchler, E., & Pombeni, M. L. (1991). Differential effects of identification with family and peers on coping with developmental tasks in adolescence. *European Journal of Social Psychology*, *21*, 381-402.

Phinney, J. S. (1990). Ethnic identity in adolescents and adults: A review of research. *Psychological Bulletin, 108*, 499-514.

Phinney, J. S., & Chavira, V. (1992). Ethnic identity and self-esteem: An exploratory longitudinal study. *Journal of Adolescence, 15*, 271-281.

Reddy, R., & Gibbons, J. L. (in press). School socioeconomic contexts in adolescents' self-descriptions in India. *Journal of Youth and Adolescence.*

Resnick, M. D. (1986). Sociological and social psychological factors influencing self-image among physically disabled adolescents. *International Journal of Adolescent Medicine and Health*, *2*, 211-221.

Robinson, W. P., Tayler, C. A., & Piolat, M. (1990). School attainment, self-esteem, and identity: France and England. *European Journal of Social Psychology*, *20*, 387-403.

Rodriquez, O., & Santiviago, M. (1991). Hispanic deaf adolescents: A multicultural minority. *Volta Review*, *93*, 89-97.

Rosenberg, M. (1965). *Society and the adolescents' self-image.* Princeton, NJ: Princeton University Press.

Rosenthal, D. A., Demetrious, A., & Efklides, A. (1989). A cross-national study of the influence of culture on conflict between parents and adolescents. *International Journal of Behavioral Development*, *12*, 207-219.

Rosenthal, D. A., & Feldman, S. S. (1990). The acculturation of Chinese immigrants: Perceived effects on family functioning of length of residence in two cultural contests. *Journal of Genetic Psychology*, *151*, 495-514.

Sam, D. L. (1991). Emosjonell tilpasning hos unge innvandrere i Norge [Emotional adjustment among young immigrants in Norway]. *Tidsskrift for Norsk Psykologforening 28*, 789-797.

Sam, D. L. (1994). The psychological adjustment of young immigrants in Norway. *Scandinavian Journal of Psychology, 35*, 240-253.

Savin-Williams, R. C. (1989). Gay and lesbian adolescents. *Marriage and Family Review*, *14*, 197-216.

Schlegel, A., & Barry, H. III. (1979). Adolescent initiation ceremonies: A cross-cultural code. *Ethnology: An International Journal of Cultural and Social Anthropology*, *18*, 199-210.

Schlegel, A., & Barry, H. III. (1991). *Adolescence: An anthropological inquiry*. New York: Free Press.

Scott, W. A., & Scott, R. (1989). Family correlates of high-school student adjustment: A cross-cultural study. *Australian Journal of Psychology*, *41*, 260-284.

Scott, R., & Scott, W. A. (1998). *Adjustment of adolescents: Cross-cultural similarities and differences*. London: Routledge.

Scott, W. A., Scott, R., Boehnke, K., Cheng, S-W., Leung, K., & Sasake, M. (1991). Children's personality as a function of family relations within and between cultures. *Journal of Cross-Cultural Psychology*, *22*, 182-208.

Scott, W. A., Scott, R., & McCabe, M. (1991). Family relationships and children's personality: A cross-cultural, cross-source comparison. *British Journal of Social Psychology*, *30*, 1-20.

Sebald, H. (1984). *Adolescence: A social psychological analysis*. Englewood Cliffs, NJ: Prentice-Hall.

Seginer, R., & Halabi-Kheir, H. (1998). Adolescent passage to adulthood: Future orientation in the context of culture, age, and gender. *International Journal of Intercultural Relations*, *22*, 309-328.

Seiffge-Krenke, I. (1990). Developmental processes in self-concept and coping behaviour. In H. Bosma & S. Jackson (Eds.), *Coping and self-concept in adolescence* (pp. 49-68). Berlin: Springer-Verlag.

Shweder, R. A., & Bourne, E. J. (1984). Does the concept of the person vary cross-culturally? In R. A. Shweder & R. A. LeVine (Eds.), *Culture theory: Essays on mind, self, and emotion* (pp. 158-199). Cambridge: Cambridge University Press.

Silbereisen, R., & Schmitt-Rodermund, E. (1994). German immigrants in Germany: Adaption of adolescents' timetables for autonomy. In P. Noack, M. Hofer, & J. Youniss (Eds.), *Psychological responses to social change* (pp. 105-125). Berlin: Walter de Gruyter.

Sinha, J. B. P. (1982). The Hindu (Indian) identity. *Dynamic Psychiatry*, *15*, 148-160.

Smart, M. S., & Smart, R. C. (1970). Self-esteem and social-personal orientation of Indian 12 and 18 year olds. *Psychological Reports, 27*, 107-115.

Smith, P. B., & Bond, M. H. (1999). *Social psychology across cultures* (2nd ed.). Boston, MA: Allyn & Bacon.

Solomon, S., Greenberg, J., & Pyszczynski, T. (1991). A terror management theory of social behavior: The psychological functions of self-esteem and cultural worldviews. *Advances in Experimental Social Psychology*, *24*, 93-159.

Southern, W. T., & Spicker, H. H. (1989). The rural gifted on line: Bulletin boards and electronic curriculum. *Roeper Review*, *11*, 199-202.

Spencer, M. B., Dornbusch, S. M., & Mont-Reynaud, R. (1990). Challenges in studying minority youth. In S. S. Feldman & G. R. Elliott (Eds.), *At the threshold: The developing adolescent* (pp. 123-146), Cambridge, MA: Harvard University Press.

Stiles, D. A., Gibbons, J. L., & de Silva, S. (1996). Girls' relational self in Sri Lanka and the U.S.A. *Journal of Genetic Psychology, 157*, 191-203.

Stiles, D. A., Gibbons, J. L., Lie, S., Sand, T., & Krull, J. (1998). "Now I am living in Norway:" Immigrant girls describe themselves. *Cross-Cultural Research, 32*, 279-298.

Tanner, J. M. (1978). *Fetus into man: Physical growth from conception to maturity*. Cambridge, MA: Harvard University Press.

Triandis, H. C. (1988). Commentary. In D. Offer, E. Ostrov, K. I. Howard, & R. Atkinson (Eds.), *The teenage world: Adolescents' self-image in ten countries* (pp.127-128). New York: Plenum Medical.

Trommsdorff, G. (1994). Parent-adolescent relations in changing societies: A cross-cultural study. In P. Noack, M. Hofer, & J. Youniss (Eds.), *Psychological responses to social change* (pp. 189-218). Berlin: Walter de Gruyter.

Van de Vijver, F., & Leung, K. (1997). *Methods and data analysis for cross-cultural research*. Thousand Oaks, CA: Sage.

Van IJzendoorn, M. H. (1990). Developments in cross-cultural research on attachment: Some methodological notes. *Human Development, 33,* 3-9.

Verkuyten, M. (1986). Impact of ethnic and sex differences on global self-esteem among adolescents in the Netherlands. *Psychological Reports*, *59*, 446.

Verkuyten, M. (1988). General self-esteem of adolescents from ethnic minorities in the Netherlands and the reflected appraisal process. *Adolescence*, *23*, 863-871.

Watkins, D. (1982). Antecedents of self-esteem, locus of control, and academic achievement: A path analytic investigation with Filipino children. *International Review of Applied Psychology*, *1*, 475-491.

Watkins, D. (1988). Components of self-esteem of children from a deprived cross-cultural background. *Social Behavior and Personality*, *16*, 1-3.

Watkins, D., Regmi, M., & Alfon, M. (1990). Antecedents of self-esteem of Nepalese and Filipino college students. *Journal of Genetic Psychology, 151*, 341-347.

Wheeler, L., & Kim, Y. (1997). What is beautiful is culturally good: The physical attractiveness stereotype has different content in collectivistic cultures. *Personality and Social Psychology Bulletin, 23,* 795-800.

Whiting, J. W. M. (1990). Adolescent rituals and identity conflicts. In J. W. Stigler, R. A. Shweder, & G. Herdt (Eds.), *Cultural psychology: Essays on comparative human development* (pp. 357-365). Cambridge: Cambridge University Press.

Whiting, B. B., & Whiting, J. W. M. (1987). Foreword to Adolescents in a Changing World series. In R. G. Condon (Ed.), *Inuit youth: Growth and change in the Canadian Arctic* (pp.xiii-xxii). New Brunswick: Rutgers University Press.

Wickstrom, L. (1998). Self-concept development during adolescence: Do American truths hold for Norwegians? In E. Skoe & A. von der Lippe (Eds.), *Personality development in adolescence* (pp. 98-122). London: Routledge.

Whyte, J. (1998). Young citizens in changing times: Catholics and Protestants in Northern Ireland. *Journal of Social Issues, 54,* 603-620.

Whyte, J. (1999). Political socialization in a divided society: The case of Northern Ireland. In M. Yates & J. Youniss (Eds.), *Roots of civic Identity: International perspectives on community service and activism in youth* (pp. 156-177). Cambridge, UK. Cambridge University Press.

Yang, K-S., Yue, D-H., & Wu, E-C., (1991). Normal and delinquent syndromes of Chinese youth in Taiwan: Quantitative differentiation and psychological profiles. *Proceedings of the National Science Council, Part C: Humanities and Social Sciences, 1,* 260-279.

Yee, D-H., Yang, K-S., & Barnes, B. K. (1990). An inquiry into Confucian socialization related to the development of juvenile delinquency. *Chinese Journal of Psychology, 32,* 75-94.

Yoshida, T., Kojo, K., & Kaku, H. (1982). A study on the development of self-presentation in children. *Japanese Journal of Educational Psychology, 30,* 30-37.

Youniss, J., & Yates, M. (1999). Introduction: International perspectives on the roots of civic identity. In M. Yates & J. Youniss (Eds.), *Roots of civic identity: International perspectives on community service and activism in youth* (pp. 1-15). Cambridge, UK: Cambridge University Press.

Youniss (Eds.), *Roots of civic identity: International perspectives on community service and activism in youth* (pp. 178-204). Cambridge, UK:Cambridge University Press.

ADULT-CHILD CONTINUITY IN INDIA:
IS ADOLESCENCE A MYTH OR AN EMERGING REALITY?

T.S. Saraswathi
Maharaja Sayajirao University of Baroda, India

In January 1979, at a seminar entitled "Identity and Adulthood," delivering the Vikram Sarabhai Memorial lecture, Erik Erikson commented on a lighter note that adolescence as a stage of development finds no place either in the Hindu scriptures that delineate the stages of human life cycle or in Shakespeare's famous list of seven ages in *As You Like It*. To quote, "But is it not strange that this playwright mentions no play age, this passionate genius no stage of adolescence, this creator no stage of parenthood? Instead, he depicts in seven acts the entire world's stage: the "mewing and puking" infant, the "whining schoolboy creeping like snail unwillingly to school," and then, "the lover," the "soldier," and "the justice," followed by two rapidly declining oldsters, one marked by "childishness" (Erikson, 1979, p. 15). Also noteworthy here is that the first "real" stage of development highlighted in the Hindu *Ashramadharmas* is that of apprenticeship (*brahmacharya*). It is characterized by industry and the acquisition of competence, to be followed by the householder stage of *grahashya*, equivalent to Erikson's stage of young adulthood and characterized by achievement of intimacy, gratification of sexual urges, and acquisition of wealth.

In the context of the contemporary Indian society, my central thesis is that adolescence is the invention of a technological, industrial society marked by a discontinuity between childhood and adulthood. Undoubtedly, puberty is a distinct physiological landmark across cultures and in almost all cultures the social transition from childhood to adulthood has some observable markers. But whether this is necessarily accompanied by the intermediate phase of adolescence that links childhood to adulthood is a matter of cultural construction. My argument is that the greater the continuity between childhood and adulthood, and the greater the similarity in life course and continuity in expectations from childhood to adulthood, the greater the possibility that a distinct phase or life stage called adolescence will be absent.

Furthermore, cross-sectional and longitudinal studies of Indian children and youth ranging from those in the pre-puberty years to those in their mid-

or even late-twenties (Garg & Parikh, 1981, 1993; Kakar, 1979a; Kakar & Chowdhry, 1970; Paranjpe, 1975; Saraswathi & Dutta, 1988; Sharma, 1996) clearly highlight the gendered and class-based nature of the presence of an adolescence marked by a psychosocial moratorium and a search for one's identity and own place in the larger scheme of things.

Child-adult continuity is most clearly evident among girls, cutting across all social classes, except in the highest socioeconomic groups. It is somewhat less marked in the case of those males, (although still evident as will be elaborated later), whose exposure to higher education and preparation for career roles prolongs the period of dependency upon their parents, delays marriage and the establishment of sustained heterosexual relationships, and exposes them to possible alternative life choices.

Females in all social classes are groomed to become good wives and mothers. Even the increasing career options of middle-class girls are subsumed under the primary goals of marriage and motherhood, typically leading to consensus rather than conflict in parent-child relations. In a culture where chastity is cherished as more precious than life itself, girls are oversocialized from childhood on to accept their subservient role in a patriarchal set-up, to learn modesty and self-denial, and to develop proficiency in household tasks and child care through intensive participation in the natal home where they are considered guests till they marry and leave. As phrased by M.N. Srinivas, a leading Indian sociologist, in India "girls learn to be mothers even before they are wives" (1960), hereby referring to the sibling care assigned to girls in the natal home.

In the case of the males, the picture is more ambiguous and mixed. For the 40% of all children belonging to the lower economic strata, the compelling need to earn before one can learn obliterates the possibility of adolescence or of even the phase of late childhood, the play age. Much has been already written about the lost innocence of child laborers (see, e.g., Blanchet, 1996; Burra, 1987, 1995). In discussing this issue, it may be apropos to borrow from Ananthamurthy's (1979) poignant description of identity and adulthood, "As his senses were actively engaged with the world outside him, he had no time to reflect on the luxury of the existentialist problem of whether life was meaningful" (p. 110).

Higher up in the socioeconomic ladder, the social setting of male middle-class children and youth is characterized by high parental control and involvement, a highly competitive academic environment, and high career aspirations set by parents. Having spent a major portion of their lives with "their nose to the grindstone" as it were, youth even in their late twenties evince signs of being torn between family obligations and individual needs. A continued emotional dependence on parents, especially the mother (Kakar, 1978), an ultimate reliance on the parents for mate selection, and an expectation of nurturance and continued reliance on reinforcement from the management in one's job situation, have led psychoanalysts to posit the possibility of an unresolved identity crisis and delayed adolescence into early adulthood. Supportive evidence comes from organizational psychologists who point to the success of the paternalistic, nurturing task leader, in contrast to the more Western democratic, participatory leader, for example, in Indian organizational settings (Sinha, 1980). This observation is substantiated in a comparative study of Caucasian-American, Chinese-American, Chinese, and Indian adolescent males aged 12-14, which assessed the effect of authoritarian and democratic leadership on morale, productivity, and quality of product. Meade (1985) observed that Caucasian-Americans responded consistently better to the democratic mode of leadership, Chinese and Indians responded best to authoritarian leadership, and Chinese-Americans responded equally well to either style of leadership.

In the following section an attempt is made to portray the life of girls and boys in the three major socioeconomic groups in India. The composite picture is derived from literature spanning twenty-five years. It includes ethnographic studies (Bhattacharjee, in press; Sarangapani, 1997) in school settings and in the village settings and urban slums of Gujarat (Saraswathi & Dutta, 1988); case studies of 120 adolescent girls from three different social classes—including the lower, middle, and upper socioeconomic classes—in the urban metropolis and two social classes in the rural areas of Punjab and Uttarpradesh (Sharma, 1996); longitudinal case studies of middle-class youth in Maharashtra (Paranjpe, 1975); and longitudinal follow-up studies of several hundred management trainees and their life histories based on in-depth interviews (Garg & Parikh, 1981, 1993; Kakar & Chowdhry, 1970), and representing various regions of the subcontinent. Comments from the interdisciplinary participants of the Seminar on Adulthood and Identity, led by Sudhir Kakar and Erik H. Erikson (Kakar, 1979a) are drawn upon for interpretation, supplemented by selected references.

CHILDHOOD AND YOUTH IN THE LOWER SOCIAL CLASS

The Female Child

At birth, the female child receives, at best, a reluctant welcome if she is the first born and expressions of disappointment and even grief, if she happens to be the second or third girl child in the family. The early years are cushioned by the presence of other children, siblings, and cousins in the extended family or neighborhood and by the presence of adults other than parents. Participation in the adult household chores and child care of younger siblings is initiated before or around 8-9 years of age (Saraswathi & Dutta, 1988; Sharma, 1996), depending on the mother's employment status. Schooling is a luxury, which can be indulged in only if the parents can spare the girl from full-time household responsibilities (Sarangapani, 1997). There are minimal expectations regarding school education, (i.e., in terms of functional literacy), so that girls can "read bus numbers or write a postcard after they marry and leave home." The prime goal of socialization is to prepare the girl to be a good daughter-in-law in another house. Girls tend to be highly acceptant of their comparatively inferior status, and they unquestioningly trust that parents would know best how to select a marriage partner for them and when to get them married.

The identity of girls is submerged in clear-cut, prescribed roles, and is marked by limited aspirations (to be a good daughter-in-law and wife), selflessness, and a network of relationships defining their role and their self-esteem. The role of peers is almost absent and even when present, minimal, carefully monitored, and barely significant when compared with the pervasive influence of the immediate and extended family. Assessments of the self-esteem of adult women in the same social class (Kapadia, 1996) confirms their self-definitions in terms of roles, relationships, and self-fulfillment through role performance and role achievement vis-à-vis close relatives such as husband, sons, brothers, and children.

Transition from childhood to adulthood is marked by continuity. In this social matrix, "even though adolescence as a phase [is] not recognized, the passage from childhood to the adult stage [is] guided through a series of what Erikson would call "situations" in the establishment of an individual in his [or her] adult role" (Ramanujam, 1979, p. 38). The question of the emergence of an independent adult role does not arise in such a setting. In fact, "subordinating one's individual needs to the interests of the group, be it a family, a kinship group, a clan or a class is upheld as a virtue. The linear structure of authority distribution reinforces and sustains this paradigm. Thus, self-assertion becomes selfishness, independent decision making is perceived as disobedience" (Ramanujam, 1979, p. 54).

The life course development of the young girl in the urban lower-class setting is not too different from that of the rural girl. The urban slums in any case have been aptly described as urban villages by Indian sociologists. Educational aspirations as expressed by both the parents and the girls themselves, are only slightly higher than those prevailing in the rural areas, i.e., completion of primary grades or even elementary school so "she can supervise her own children's schooling and also manage household expenses and accounts" (Saraswathi & Dutta, 1988; Sharma, 1996). In addition, marriage is delayed by a couple of years, i.e., to 16 years of age (though the legal age for marriage is 18 years). Otherwise, the constraints and restrictions imposed to protect the pre- and post-pubescent girl's chastity are even greater than those prevailing in the rural settings. At least in the village, the girls can enjoy a certain degree of freedom till they are married, for they are "daughters of the village" and thus will be safe. But in the uncertainty of the urban setting, girls have to be watched and regulated more carefully. As noted by Schlegel and Barry III (1991) in their cross-cultural study, "Even when a puberty ceremony at or around menarche marks the girl's new adolescent status, the social setting of her daily life differs little from that of earlier years. In fact, in those cases in which her freedom is more restricted and she cannot roam about as she could as a younger child, her setting becomes even more hierarchical" (p. 184).

The Male Child

As one shifts from the rural to the urban scene, one witnesses, even in the lower social class, the beginnings of what may be termed an adolescent phase, consequent to a slightly lengthened period of schooling and postponement of marriage. And this shift is more evident in the case of urban LSES boys than girls. For those boys who do not choose the path of continuing school education after the primary grades, for want of competence, motivation, or both, wage earning is the only option. Those who do continue with schooling do so with the clear awareness of the sacrifices the family needs to make to keep them in school. Hence, there is the expectation of having to perform well without any distractions and maintain a sense of obligation to family responsibilities once they finish school and acquire jobs. These responsibilities range from ensuring the education of younger brothers, getting younger sisters married, and providing care for elderly parents (Kapadia, 1980).

The picture of the daily life of LSES male children and prepubescent boys differs from that of the girls only to the extent that a larger percentage of them stay in primary schools and enjoy at home the privileges of being a male child in a patriarchal society (Saraswathi & Dutta, 1988). They are allowed more freedom, more play time, and must meet only minimal expectations in terms of participation in household chores. In the rural areas, however, and with a few exceptions, boys are expected to contribute to their family's income by the time they are 13-14 years of age, either by participating in their family's traditional occupation, such as agricultural labor, cattle rearing, pottery, basket weaving, or as manual laborers. Even school children participate in seasonal work such as cotton-picking or the harvesting of vegetables alongside their parents. The parents and family arrange marriages by the time children are 18, even though the couple may be permitted to cohabit only a year or two after the young bride-to-be has attained puberty.

One can hardly characterize the life of Indian teenage boys from a lower socioeconomic background in the context of a psychosocial moratorium and a search for identity. In a majority of cases, schooling ends before puberty, participation in income generation is initiated soon after or even concurrent to puberty, marriage is socially prescribed and orchestrated, and there is little scope to experiment with alternative roles. Moreover, parental influence and control supersedes that of the peer group, and participation in or involvement with the peer group is constrained by adult supervision.

GROWING UP IN THE MIDDLE SOCIOECONOMIC CLASS

In terms of education, age of marriage, and career aspirations, the middle social class presents a distinctly different picture from that of the lower social class. Education is prioritized as a prime goal by children of both sexes and by parents, and it is clearly seen as a pathway to success in life (Kakar & Chowdhry, 1970; Paranjpe, 1975; Sharma, 1996). Career aspirations are closely linked to education and great significance is attached to careers in medicine, engineering, and the administrative services. Since the stakes are high and competition is keen for limited seats in the professional colleges, practically every minute of the 15-18-year-old youngsters' waking hours are closely monitored with a heavy curriculum load in school, intensive out-of-school tutoring, and extensive homework under the parents' watchful eyes and even with their full involvement.

While both boys and girls are encouraged to prepare for a career through the pursuit of higher education, gender discrimination in favor of boys is more evident in the lower-middle class. In general, when resources are limited, boys are favored to enter training in prestigious (and hence more expensive) professional programs of study such as medicine, engineering, and management.

It is only when young people have ensured a place in a program of study of their own—and often their parents'—first or second choice, or when they come to terms with the compromise entailed in alternative choices such as majoring in the sciences, arts, or commerce, that they can attend to developmental tasks such as a search for self-identity. In fact, because many of the professional programs are very demanding, students continue to slog in professional colleges in order to maintain their place and grade. Thus, only those enrolled in the liberal arts and commerce programs can afford to indulge in the luxury of a psychosocial moratorium via peer group activities or engage in student unrest and rebellion on campus. Once again, the expression of moving through a psychosocial moratorium is gendered, being more characteristic of boys than of girls.

Historically, despite the class related shift in the educational and career goals of girls many of whom now have a clear expectation that they will be employed, gender socialization even in the upper-middle social class remains unambiguous.   Girls continue to be socialized to subsume their personal aspirations to the goals of marriage and to the expectations of the family into which they will marry.

Peer interaction, though substantially more prevalent than in the case of the LSES girls, is secondary to family involvements, especially in terms of their influence.   In a large majority of cases both children and parents expect that the parents will arrange their children's marriage though the children may be consulted in the final selection.

Evidence gathered both by psychoanalysts (Kakar, 1978; Ramanujam, 1979) and through follow-up studies of lower- and upper-middle class college students (Garg & Parikh, 1981, 1993; Kakar & Chowdhry, 1970; Paranjpe, 1975) points to signs of unresolved identity crises. During the young adulthood years, these crises are frequently expressed through problems in the work environment and through the manifestation of psychosomatic disorders, especially among males. Several family variables contribute to the complexity of the problem and its uneasy/incomplete resolution.   These include the intense mother-son bond resulting from the mother's own uncertain status in the house of the stranger to whom she is married; the cultural expectation that the son is the parent's "savior," both now and in their next lives; and the stringent demand and expectation that the son must repay his parents, supporting them both financially and socioemotionally in return for all the sacrifices they made for his education. As a rule, the socialization of girls in both lower and middle social classes, as well as that of lower-class boys relies on firm social and family control, a near absence of choices, and unambiguous expectations. Changes in the life experience of middle class-boys, especially when they are sent for higher education to a different town, include the experience of hostel life, sustained peer company, and exposure to alternative lifestyles.   Yet, as mentioned earlier, the emotional hold of the family and the prescribed expectations and anticipated obligations act as deterrents to exploration and experimentation leading to what is described by psychoanalysts and therapists as delayed adolescence and identity confusion in young adults.   Once again the picture shifts rather dramatically in the case of upper-class boys and girls. The comments that follow are based on the author's naturalistic observations and first hand experience with students on college campuses and in metropolitan cities throughout various regions of India.   No systematic data can be presented in this case as evidence.

CHILDHOOD AND YOUTH IN THE UPPER SOCIAL CLASS

A distinct difference in life style, expectations, and life-course development can be seen in the case of children and youth from the upper class. Several factors play a role in bringing into prominence a distinct phase of adolescence in this social class. Education, while seen as important, is not the only pathway to career and economic success as is the case for the middle class. Hence, there are options and the freedom to experiment without the pressure to succeed. Furthermore, in contrast to the prevailing family control in the other social classes, children and young people of the upper class enjoy a good amount of freedom from parental supervision. Many factors contribute to this: both parents lead a busy professional and/or social life, leaving much of the housekeeping and child care to paid help; living quarters are much more spacious and provide for the privacy of independent rooms for children (something unheard of in the other social classes); access to vehicles such as powerful motorbikes or cars permits independent mobility; and cash can be spent on consumer goods without necessarily having to account for it. In fact, parents in this group play an active role in promoting adolescent consumerism in order to keep up with their own peers. All these pave the way for a greater relevance and importance of peer groups and the consequent emergence of a peer culture characterized by a kind of consumerism that both mimics and parallels the American adolescent culture. A visit to some of the fast-food joints in cities like Delhi and Bombay makes one wonder whether one is in India or in the West.

The above observation leads one to conclude that, "these kids can afford to indulge in the luxury of being adolescents, can afford a phase of psychosocial moratorium, freedom to experiment with alternatives and to deal with their identity crisis," [a luxury not permitted in the more constrained and socially prescribed life trajectories of the young people from the lower and middle social classes]. The social world of adolescents is indeed "... shaped, constructed and constrained by "messages" from the macro context—social, cultural, temporal, historical as to which are possible and acceptable social pathways, behaviors, and aspirations..." (Poole, 1989, p. 68).

TRANSITION FROM CHILDHOOD TO ADULTHOOD:
CONTINUITY AND DISCONTINUITY

It may be appropriate to summarize at this juncture the arguments presented in the previous pages. It is maintained that in view of the prevailing socioeconomic constraints, the marked sociocentric emphasis on interdependence and interrelatedness, and the prescriptive mode of child-rearing in the Indian setting, adolescence as a life stage is both gendered and class-based. Except in the case of the upper social class, wherein economic, social, and personal options are both feasible and affordable, in all other social classes the transition from childhood to adulthood is marked more by continuity than by discontinuity, leaving little scope for the emergence of an adolescent culture. Conformity to adult "prescriptions" is more pronounced for girls than for boys in all social classes including the middle social class wherein a dramatic social transformation in terms of women's education and employment is evident. Submerging the self for the sake of one's family and of society has its costs. This is particularly evident in the case of young men from the upper-middle social class who taste independence during their professional training away from home, and yet remain tied down by family obligations and emotional bonds with parents and siblings.

Depending upon the demands of the setting, societies regulate the status of upper-middle-class youth, either integrating them as responsible members into the in-group or treating them as members of a temporarily troublesome out-group. In this context one recalls the American studies of Barker and his associates on teen culture in big and small towns. Their research highlighted the small town teenagers' active participation in socially useful behaviors because the settings needed their contributions when compared to settings in big towns or in big schools where their services were irrelevant and perhaps not even wanted (Barker & Gump, 1964; Schoggen & Barker, 1989).

When there is an absence of segregation of youth and adults because education is gained through apprenticeship by participating in adult activities, when socialization into work follows a continuous process such as in artisan families or agricultural laborers, and when leisure time is programmed by the entire village community, then the specification of an adolescent stage has little meaning. Even in the Euro-American context, adolescence is the historical produce of the bourgeois middle class as it emerged from the industrial revolution (Hurrelmann, 1989).

From a sociological viewpoint, adolescence represents a period of transition from the family of orientation to the family of procreation. The developmental tasks to be achieved during the period of transition from puberty to adulthood include: coping with the increasing sexual urges and bodily changes accompanying puberty; choice of and training in an occupation; finding a marriage partner; and incorporating oneself into the economy, political structure, and community of adult society (Paranjpe, 1975). Continuity or discontinuity in this transition is dependent upon how the "... world of the adolescents is shaped, constructed, and constrained by messages from the macro-context social, cultural, temporal, historical..." (Poole, 1989, p. 68).

Adolescence as a distinct stage emerges under the following conditions: a learning process (education) that is divorced from practice; delayed experience of one's own social usefulness; later choice of job or career; prolonged economic dependence on parents; more leisure time that can be spent with same-age group members; and longer time spent in individual development rather than in a collective mode of performance. All these experiences are leading to a lengthening of the psychosocial moratorium (Baethge, 1989). The social structures of economically advanced societies such as those in the West, and of selected sections of a larger society, such as are the case for upper-class Indian youth, provide such an ecology, and hence facilitate self-definition and self-exploration. However, under conditions of socioeconomic constraints, "... self assertion becomes selfishness, independent decision-making is perceived as disobedience. The response from the in-group is tacit disapproval if not outright condemnation" (Ramanujam, 1979, p. 54).

Viewed in the broader social context of the nature of the adult roles, for which the young are being prepared, child-adult continuity makes good sense. The Hindu *Dharmasastras* that constitute India's normative "sociology" (Kakar, 1979b) and detail the duties prescribed to the adult householder, highlight the individual's embeddedness in relationships. According to Kakar (1979b) "The adult of the *Dharmasastras*, consistent with the social focus of these texts, is not an isolated being but an individual embedded in a multiplicity of relationships. He is a partner (to the spouse), a parent to his children (and a child to his parents), and a link in the chain of generations and in the history of the race" (p. 122). Erikson (as cited in Vasudev, 1984) views the concept of *dharma* as both personal "determining what we call identity," and communal, "If individuals depend on each other for a maximum and optimum of mutual activation, *dharma* is a consolidation of the world through the self-realization of each individual within a joint order" (p. 37).

In this context it is interesting to note a comment by Western scholars on the nature of self-absorption in present-day Western culture. Huebner and Garrod (1991) argue that "Issues of self-sacrifice, selfishness, and selfhood take center stage ... Discovering, or reclaiming oneself is considered vital to healthy adulthood" (p. 348). Such a preoccupation with self definition stands in stark contrast to the Buddhist philosophy that denies the existence of self and the Hindu concept of *Ahambhava*, which points to the need to control egoism through submerging the self in other human beings and finally in Ultimate Reality. It is significant that many "contemporary scholars are claiming that the self does not exist apart from relationships, that one is interconnected with others in essential ways, and that the moral ideal includes responsibility towards others, connection, and compassion" (Huebner & Garrod, 1991, p. 349).

The arguments presented so far reiterate the prevalence of a prescriptive mode of socialization, a sociocentric emphasis on interdependence, and the importance of negative sanctions for deviation from the accepted code of conduct, all of which foster adult-child continuity.

In focusing on the adult-child continuity in the Indian context, one cannot completely overlook the presence of social change, social conflict in a transitional phase, and the forms of conflict resolution. The presence of a distinct and prolonged phase of adolescence, and hence adult-child discontinuity, as prevalent in the Indian upper social class, was discussed in the earlier sections of this paper. The increasingly evident consequences of social change in the upper-middle class deserve special mention here. Two factors play key roles in this regard. First, there is the fairly long period of exposure to the peer group and to alternative life styles and independent living during the period of stay in hostels for purposes of higher education and professional training. Secondly, there is the bombardment of the mass media, which bring a vision "of a new world order" of youth culture and consumerism to the living rooms of the middle-class homes.

As stated by the present author in her recently published work on *Socialization in the Indian Context*, "One of the significant characteristics is...the experience of approach-avoidance conflict in terms of stability and change" (Saraswathi & Pai, 1996, p. 90). Something akin to a "cold feet" syndrome is evident in upper-middle class parents' attempts to adopt more indulgent and permissive child-rearing practices as a reaction to their own strict upbringing. However, when young people transgress basic social values, parents take recourse to the old values and practices to draw the line. Similarly, youth in their conflict to break away from the stronghold of tradition either resort to "... passive aggressive behavior or regression into total passivity..." (Ramanujam, 1979, p. 54) or they resolve the conflict by either seeking identity in family togetherness or by deciding to build their separate lives while retaining a sense of emotional continuity through a ritualistic observation of role obligations (Garg & Parikh, 1993). The cleavages in traditional socialization precipitated by industrialization and its concomitants (a prolonged period of education, economic dependency, and delayed marriage) and the inroads made by the market economy are further aggravated by the mass media. The extent of the impact of the mass media on the home, especially via the kind of television that daily brings exaggerated pictures of youth culture, consumerism, and insular nuclear family goals right into the living room, is yet to be ascertained.

IN THE LARGER PICTURE: A CROSS-CULTURAL COMPARISON

This chapter has so far focused mainly on the social class and gender differences in developmental continuities and discontinuities from childhood to adulthood. The complex anthropological inquiry of adolescence in 186 preindustrial societies by Schlegel and Barry III (1991) makes it possible to contextualize the observations in a cross-cultural scenario and to draw some comparisons. Unlike the present paper, which focuses on the psychosocial continuities in adolescent development, Schlegel and Barry's III work addresses the issue of a near universal presence of adolescent discontinuity as a social phenomenon.

Several observations by Schlegel and Barry's III regarding gender differences in the duration of adolescence, the social protection of female sexuality, and the forms of mate selection and marriage are pertinent here. Four topics directly relevant to the present essay have been singled out for discussion.

Presence or Absence of an Adolescent Social Stage

Schlegel and Barry III note that in all the 173 societies for which data were available for boys and in 174 of the 175 societies for which data were available for girls, adolescence as a social stage was present. The only exception was the Gros Ventre (Flannery, 1953, cited in Schlegel & Barry III, 1991), "Where girls are married by about age 10. Because the Gros Ventre believe ... marriage must occur before menarche" (p. 34). Their general observation is that "The frequency distribution of the data strongly suggests that an adolescent social stage is very widespread and possibly universal for boys" (p. 42), but comparatively rather brief in the case of girls. Viewed from this perspective, the data from India reiterate the importance of gender differences and also highlight the social class differences, given that the continuity in transition from childhood to adulthood is far more marked in the lower social class than in the upper classes. Even among the lower-class village girls whose shift from childhood to adulthood is marked by a high degree of continuity, one perceives the presence of a brief transitional stage before marriage when girls assume greater responsibility in the home, relieving the mother of many household responsibilities.

Adolescents' Relations with their Parents

A second inference of interest in the anthropological study by Schlegel and Barry III (1991) relates to parent-child relations. "Across the societies in the sample, girls have more contact and greater intimacy with the mother than boys do with parents of either sex. Brought ... into the company of women, girls participate in multigenerational groups. Boys, even when they work alongside their fathers, have less contact and intimacy with them and other men than do girls with women" (p. 182). While the observation is pertinent to the Indian situation in terms of mother-daughter and father-son relationships, a striking divergence is observed in the case of mother-son relations. Schlegel and Barry III argue that as a rule and in all societies mothers extrude boys more than they do girls. In the context of the Indian family, wherein the mother-son bond assumes a special sociological and psychological significance (Kakar, 1978), such an extrusion is unlikely. As elaborated by Kakar, in accordance with the exogamous marriage arrangements and the patrilineal family system, a large majority of women (particularly in Northwest India) marry a stranger with whom intimacy in the psychological sense may evolve only over a long period of time. The birth of a son, which is also much welcomed by the otherwise hostile family of in-laws, is a reprieve for the Indian woman in many ways. These include an improved status in the family for continuing the lineage; a promise of care in old age; possible salvation after death as the funeral pyre will be lit by a son; and above all, the scope for emotional intimacy denied in the natal home where she was treated as a guest and in her marriage where her role is mainly that of a sex partner and a vehicle for procreation. In fact, psychoanalysts have speculated on the possibility of ambiguous resolution of identity in boys because of the intense mother-child bond which resurfaces again when the son in turn marries and the cycle repeats itself (Kakar, 1978; Ramanujam, 1979).

Adolescent Sexuality and Taboos

Socialization for sexuality in India leans clearly toward the restrictive end of the continuum, with more permissiveness for boys, especially at the lowest and uppermost ends of the class continuum. Chastity for girls is considered an essential virtue, as the reputation of not only the girl but also of the entire family is contingent on the girl's chastity.

Since the Islamic code for chastity is even more stringent and applicable in major regions of the Middle East and South Asia, the observation that nearly 68% of the 162 societies examined by Schlegel and Barry III did permit premarital sex among girls comes as a surprise (Kagitçibasi, 1997).

In India, heterosexual interactions are generally discouraged, especially once the girl approaches puberty. This applies even to interactions between father and daughter, brother and sister, and among cousins of the opposite sex (but not between mother and son as noted earlier in the discussion of parent-adolescent relationships).

As Schlegel and Barry III argue, this is a way of achieving sexual separation and preventing incest. In fact, in communities wherein such segregation is not enforced there have been reports of incestuous relations (Khandekar, personal communication, 1988 based on a TISS survey). Krishnakumar's (1986) observations on growing up as a male in the Indian setting are relevant here. "This sudden separation from the girls (i.e., after primary grades), made no sense at first; a little later it led us to see girls as enigma; and finally, we accepted it as a protection that society had offered us against the danger of coming in contact with a female human before we were ready for such contact. This rationalizing took years; it was a tedious process, demanding tremendous amounts of psychic energy, and of course we never had access to an adult to ask any questions about the great mystery of girls and their separation from us" (p. 22).

Guarding the girl's chastity and thereby protecting the family honor is acknowledged as unambiguously significant by parents and children, the scriptures, the media, literature, and the school. Transgressions are dealt with severely especially in the middle class, though since the late 1980s gynecologists and counselors have been reporting out-of-wedlock pregnancies and covert (but legal) abortions in about 5% to 10% of the urban girls. Unambiguous supportive data are not available.

Mating, Marriage, and the Duration of Adolescence

One of the main ideas elaborated in the present paper relates to social class differences (and similarities) in the Indian context, in terms of mate selection, age of marriage, and concomitantly, the duration of adolescence. In terms of mate selection, even in contemporary India, arranged marriages remain the predominantly preferred form of finding a mate. Though self-selection has never been absolutely absent, and inter-caste and inter-regional marriages through self-selection are increasing in number, young people, including college students, consider it wiser to let parental wisdom prevail. A common refrain is: "Parents know best; they are experienced and can weigh several factors in selecting a suitable partner. We have limited opportunities to meet the right kind of girls/boys even on the college campus and do not wish to be carried away by emotions that can lead to regrets later." And few are in a great hurry to get married. Girls are willing to wait till 23 or even 25 years of age and young men till their late twenties, until they have settled themselves career wise. Among the lower classes, marriage is earlier: by 14-16 years of age among rural girls; by 18 for rural boys; by 16 for urban girls; and by 20-22 for urban males.

As one moves up the socioeconomic scale, boys and girls have clearer ideas regarding the kind of partner they would like to have chosen for them. These refer to qualities such as family background, level of education, economic status, and physical appearance. In a large number of families, horoscopes are compared by both families, who consult specialists in astrology, and once the horoscopes match, the short-listed prospective partners' families meet, and the girl and boy are allowed to see or even talk to each other (under adult supervision) and give their consent.

An interesting recent development is the jet set arranged marriages of expatriate Indian men, especially from the USA and the UK, who still prefer a mate from "back home." Their marriages are often arranged while they are on home leave for 10-15 days with a high rating for "green cards" (work permits) and/or an even higher one for citizenship abroad.

Besides the traditional way of arranging marriages through known intermediaries or marriage brokers, another practice for mate selection that has attracted the attention of sociologists is matchmaking through advertisements in newspapers. These advertisements usually provide a basic description of the advertising prospective bride or bridegroom and the qualities desired in the partner (and they can offer amusing reading material). In recent years, regional and caste-based organizations have sprung up to play the role of matchmakers, using computer technology to building a data bank of horoscopes of young people of specified caste and community. The network extends across the country, at times including overseas Indian families also. These are becoming increasingly popular.

Marriage in India is clearly a family affair—a union of families and not a union of only two individuals. Establishing the pair bonding between two individuals is viewed not only as a partnership for their lifetime, but also as "sowing the seeds for a thousand years," implying its link to successive generations of progenies. "The assumption underlying this link between marriage and mating is that most biological reproduction occurs within marriage" (Schlegel & Barry III, 1991, p. 93), an assumption still ecologically valid in India today (or so we like to believe!).

Despite the strict and regimented code for mate selection and marriage with its focus on family relationships and procreation, romantic love still has a definite foothold. Paradoxically, while romantic love is frowned upon in real life, Indian films, with their tremendous mass appeal are invariably based on romantic love. Religion and mythology provide another rich source of exemplars in the forms of gods and goddesses who fall in love and choose their own partners after interesting interludes.

Contrary to the observation that "... very early marriage is a custom of the elite and those who emulate them ... (and) it is hardly surprising that poorer families ... (are) not ... eager to hasten the marriage of daughters ..." (Dumont, 1970, pp. 110-111, cited in Schlegel & Barry III, 1991, p. 102), Indian marriages by and large take place earlier among the poor than among the well-to-do families. And dowry giving is becoming a near universal pattern regardless of the economic standing of the parents.

CONCLUSION

It may be appropriate to conclude at this juncture with a caveat that while an attempt has been made to provide a developmental profile of a majority of Indian adolescents and to delineate a general trend, it remains true that—as can be expected in a complex society like India—a wide range of alternative patterns do prevail. These range from the complete absence of adolescence in girls who are betrothed in childhood and married before puberty, to a prolonged adolescence that extends beyond the teens; from no schooling and direct integration into the work force to extended and highly specialized expensive education with parental support; from sexual restraint as a rule to sexual permissiveness as an exception. Woven into these variations are the dynamics of a society in transition, with a trend indicating that in the decades to come, with greater access to schooling and economic prosperity, adolescence may emerge as a distinct phase cutting across class and gender. For the present, wide disparities prevail.

BIBLIOGRAPHY

Ananthamurthy, U.R. (1979). Search for an identity: A viewpoint of a Kannada writer. In S. Kakar (Ed.), *Identity and adulthood* (pp. 105-117). Delhi : Oxford University Press.

Baethge, M. (1989). Individuation as hope and as disaster: A socioeconomic perspective. In K. Hurrelmann & U. Engel (Eds.), *The social world of adolescents. International perspectives* (pp. 27-41). Berlin: de Gruyter.

Barker, R.G., & Gump, P.V. (1964). *Big school, small school; high school size and student behavior.* Stanford, CA: Stanford University Press.

Bhattacharjee, N. (in press). Through the looking glass: Socialization in a primary school. In T.S. Sarawathi (Ed.), *Culture, socialization and human development: Theory, research and applications in India.* New Delhi: Sage.

Blanchet, T. (1996). *Lost innocence: Stolen childhood.* Dhaka, Bangladesh: University Press.

Burra, N. (1987). Sight unseen: Reflections on the female working child. *Report of the National Workshop on the Girl Child.* New Delhi: National Institute of Public Cooperation and Child Development.

Burra, N. (1995). *Born to work: Child labor in India.* Delhi: Oxford University Press.

Erikson, E. (1979). Report to Vikram: Further perspectives on the life cycle. In S. Kakar (Ed.), *Identity and adulthood* (pp. 13-34). Delhi: Oxford University Press.

Garg, P.K., & Parikh, I.J. (1981). *Profiles in identity: A study of Indian youth at the crossroads of culture.* Ahmedabad: Academic Book Centre.

Garg, P.K., & Parikh, I.J. (1993). *Young managers at the crossroads: The Trishanku Complex.* New Delhi: Sage.

Huebner, A., & Garrod. A. (1991). Moral reasoning in a karmic world. *Human Development. 34*, 341-352.

Hurrelmann, K. (1989). The social world of adolescents: A sociological perspective. In K. Hurrelmann & U. Engel (Eds.), *The social world of adolescents· International perspectives* (pp. 3-26). Berlin: de Gruyter.

Kagitçibasi, Ç. (1997). *Concluding comments.* Symposium on Adolescence in Cross-cultural Perspective: Cross-cultural Perspectives on Human Development, Regional Conference of the International Council of Psychologists, Padua, Italy, July 21-23, 1997.

Kakar, S. (1978). *The inner world: A psycho-analytic study of childhood and society in India.* Delhi: Oxford University Press.

Kakar, S. (1979a). *Identity and adulthood.* Delhi: Oxford University Press.

Kakar, S. (1979b). Relative realities: Images of adulthood in psychoanalysis and the yogas. In S. Kakar (Ed.), *Identity and adulthood* (pp. 118-130). Delhi: Oxford University Press.

Kakar, S., & Chowdhry, K. (1970). *Conflict and choice: Indian youth in a changing society.* Bombay: Somaiya.

Kapadia, S. (1980). *Understanding children in their ecological setting.* Unpublished master's thesis, Maharaja Sayajirao University of Baroda, India.

Kapadia, S. (1996). *Women's empowerment: Identifying psychosocial linkages.* Unpublished doctoral dissertation, Maharaja Sayajirao University of Baroda, India.

Khandekar, M. (1988). *Personal communication.* Baroda, May 1988.

Kumar, K. (1986). Growing up male. *Seminar, 318*, 21-73.

Meade, R.D. (1985). Experimental studies of authoritarian and democratic leadership in four cultures: American, Indian, Chinese and Chinese-American. *High School Journal*, *68* (4), 293-295.

Paranjpe, A.C. (1975). *In search of identity*. Delhi: Macmillan.

Poole, M.E. (1989). Adolescents' transitions: A life-course perspective. In K. Hurrelmann & U. Engel (Eds.), *The social world of adolescents: International perspectives* (pp. 65-85). Berlin: de Guyter.

Ramanujam, B.K. (1979). Toward maturity: Problems of identity seen in the Indian clinical setting. In S. Kakar (Ed.), *Identity and adulthood* (pp. 37-55). Delhi: Oxford University Press.

Sarangapani, P. (1997). *Social experience and the children's construction of knowledge*. Unpublished doctoral dissertation, University of Delhi, India.

Saraswathi, T.S., & Dutta, R. (1988). *Invisible boundaries: Grooming for adult roles*. New Delhi: Northern Book Centre.

Saraswathi, T.S., & Pai, S. (1996). Socialization in the Indian context. In H. Kao & D. Sinha (Eds.), *Asian perspectives in psychology* (pp. 74-92). Sage Methodology Series. New Delhi: Sage.

Schlegel, A., & Barry III, H. (1991). *Adolescence: An anthropological inquiry*. New York: Free Press.

Schoggen, P., & Barker, R.G. (1989). *Behavior settings: A revision and extension of R.G. Barker's ecological psychology*. Stanford, CA: Stanford University Press.

Sharma, N. (1996). *Identity of the adolescent girl*. New Delhi: Discovery Publishing.

Sinha, J.B.P. (1980). *The nurturant task leader*. New Delhi: Concept Publishing.

Srinivas, M.N. (1960). *India's villages*. Bombay: Media.

Vasudev, J. (1984). *Kohlberg's claim to universality: An Indian perspective*. Paper presented at the Second Ringberg Conference. Ringberg, West Germany, July 1984.

IDENTITY FORMATION AND STATUS ACROSS CULTURES: EXPLORING THE CULTURAL VALIDITY OF ERIKSONIAN THEORY

Pedro R. Portes
University of Louisville, KY, U.S.A.
Richard Dunham
Florida State University, U.S.A.
Kent Del Castillo
University of Louisville, KY, U.S.A.

INTRODUCTION

The relationship between culture and the construction of social identities has become a popular topic in the psychological literature, a topic that extends now into the realms of various other disciplines. Social and individual identities and their formation seem to relate directly to cultural processes intertwined with gender, ethnicity, and other factors. Erik Erikson's psychosocial model continues to serve as a cornerstone for research on the identity formation process, particularly with the extensions made by Marcia's (1966) identity status typology model. The life-cycle of an individual has been regarded by Erikson (1968) as following a progression through a series of developmental stages and their defining psychosocial crises. The individual's ego becomes defined through relationships with family members, peer groups, significant others, and through interactions with the larger society.

Marcia (1966) conceptualizes identity formation especially in late adolescence as a dialectical process between exploration and commitment that defines four statuses: diffusion, foreclosure, moratorium, and achievement before intimacy is achieved. Identity achievement requires exploration and commitment, while diffusion denotes an absence of both of these. Moratorium is marked by exploration with a lack of commitment, while foreclosure is the opposite. Each status is associated with a number of personality correlates that are summarized in Marcia (1993).

Erikson (1968) notes that an individual's identity development is largely defined by his or her social context. It would seem then that culture contrasts are important in understanding variations in identity development. Research on relationships between identity and culture, however, is mostly limited to findings that contrast the identity statuses of mainstream and

Acknowledgments: The authors thank Regine Dupuy for sharing her data for his study.

minority university students. The findings suggest that among those to be predominant. Abraham (1986) found that Mexican-Americans tend to cluster more in the foreclosed status than do Anglo-Americans, who were more evenly distributed across various identity statuses. Markstrom-Adams and Adams (1995) suggested that the familial styles of ethnic minority groups might lead toward more passive forms of identity, such as foreclosure or diffusion. A further analysis of the data showed that this clustering effect occurred only in the ideological but not in the interpersonal domains. Other research (Abraham, 1983; Streitmatter, 1988) has also found that members of minority groups are more likely to cluster in the foreclosed status. An important question here concerns whether the difference is due to cultural value differences or whether it reflects the history and circumstances confronting those of minority status in relation to a given dominant culture.

Although some culture-related research exists with respect to the identity status model (McClain, 1975; Ochse & Plug, 1986) the validity of the model outside the culture in which it was conceptualized and developed remains problematic. Identity research tends to conceptualize ego development from a fairly traditional Freudian point of view and sees the development of the self and the human mind within a broad perspective cutting across more specific domains of functioning. The extent to which a given identity is developed or constructed from the culturally variable settings, beliefs, and opinions available to the individual poses a challenge to psychological models in search of universal patterns and their formation.

What little research exists regarding identity formation in United States subcultures tends to fall into one of two categories: 1) Either the research contrasts the identity status of mainstream youth to the status of minority youth without controlling for important and potentially confounding factors, or 2) it attempts to explain the development of ethnic identity as an additional component in the identity formation of minority group persons. The first category fails to distinguish between cultural differences emerging in either national or intranational groups and ethnicities. The second category poses a different sort of problem that cannot be addressed here.

The problem of cultural differences in identity formation has been addressed by some studies focusing on subcultures within the U.S. sharing minority status and below average SES (Abraham, 1986; Spencer & Markstrom-Adams, 1990). Although Erikson recognized the influence of culture in his later work, current theory has not formally addressed the problem of cultural influences. For example, a cultural or ethnic component in identity achievement may be context specific mainly because it emerges in multicultural contexts. Identity status research, like most research investigating the psychosocial model, needs to venture further into the litmus test offered by cross-cultural research. One exception is Ochse and Plug's (1986) study in South Africa which did not focus on identity status per se, but rather investigated broader aspects of Erikson's theory.

Other Differences

Studies of gender differences in identity formation have suggested that women develop more quickly than men (Abraham, 1986; Marcia, 1993; Markstrom-Adams & Adams, 1995; Streitmatter, 1988), although in pencil-and-paper studies using identity assessment measures other than the OMEIS, EOMEIS, or EOMEIS-2, gender differences failed to emerge (Marcia, 1993). These studies have also found commonalities between groups. When comparing grade levels, Rotheram-Borus (1989) found that certain ethnic groups have a similar rate of development across grade levels. Markstrom-Adams and Adams's (1995) results also support this conclusion.

Many problems exist in the available research on culture, ethnicity, and identity. The available definitions of culture and ethnicity are very diverse making it difficult, if not impossible, to compare different studies (see review by Phinney, 1990). In much of the research, important variables such as SES are not controlled (Abraham, 1983; Streitmatter, 1988). Other types of variables unique to this type of research such as prejudice may also need to be considered. Rotheram-Borus (1989), for example, worked with an ethnically balanced high school group to minimize the effects of prejudice. Phinney (1990; Phinney & Alipuria, 1990) has argued that self-definition and a person's views toward his or her group of origin constitute important mediating factors. The effects of acculturation are another factor to be considered (Gil et al., 1994; for review see Phinney, 1990), as are effects that geographic location may have upon a particular ethnic groups.

Identity exploration may be constrained not only by SES and cultural values, but may also have different consequences concerning a person's adaptation, depending on context and individual will. A number of cultural mediating factors appear to test the generalizability of this epigenetic model; for instance, the extent to which exploration partially defines identity achievement may be culturally relative. A "masked foreclosure identity" may be the more adaptive, intelligent, and healthy strategy in cultural contexts outside North America and Europe. Nevertheless, the process of individuation seems to be universal enough to attract investigations concerning the prevalence of exploration, crisis, and commitment across many cultural groups.

Purpose of the Study

The present study reports preliminary results concerning the identity status of youth from three cultural groups, the U.S., Haiti, and Colombia. It is part of a larger data collection effort aimed at examining the validity of the identity status model. Because the instrument employed, the Ego Identity Process Questionnaire, is new, the present study is also intended to contribute to its validation. It is part of a research agenda that will eventually include other groups. This is essentially a descriptive study. The main research question is: To what extent do SES, gender, and culture shape differences in identity status after age differences have been taken into account? It is predicted that a) cultural differences will remain significant after SES and age are controlled, and b) that exploration is less prevalent in traditional, Third-World societies which, instead, value collectivism and foreclosure relative to the individualism that tends to prevail in the U.S. and in most other postindustrial societies.

METHOD

The Ego Identity Process Questionnaire (Balistreri, Busch-Rossnagel, & Geisinger, 1995) was administered to 50 Colombians, 187 high school and younger U.S. youth, and 59 Haitians, along with a demographic information form. The average age of the respondents was 18 years of age, with a range from 12 to 26 years of age. Although the Haitians were significantly older, age differences were controlled in subsequent analyses along with gender and SES to explore potential cultural differences in identity formation. The Haitian group (X=22.4, SD=1.5) differed in social class composition (upper and middle) from the other groups, and this provided a reference point for this study. The U.S. sample included mostly high school students (X=16.6, SD=1.6), for whom social class information was collected (parental occupation, education, and income). The Colombian group mostly included younger adolescents (X=17.4, SD=3.8), but also some university freshmen from an urban university.

Instruments and Procedure

The Ego Identity Personality Questionnaire (Balistreri et al., 1995) was translated and administered to university and high school students. The EIPQ provided commitment and exploration scores that were employed as the dependent variables. Based on these scores, respondents can be classified into four status categories. The reliability and validity data are satisfactory in the original study by Balistreri et al. (1995).

RESULTS

In order to explore separately the potential effects of SES and age, a MANCOVA with SES, gender, and cultural condition as the independent variables and age as a covariate was performed.

The multivariate F-ratios were significant for gender ($F[2, 259] = 4.30$, $p < .01$) and culture ($F[2, 260] = 10.28$, $p < .00$) only. There were no significant age or SES differences among the groups, nor were the interactions significant. In the follow-up univariate tests, cultural differences were most pronounced for commitment scores ($F[2, 260] = 5.301$, $p < .01$). The Haitian and U.S. samples had significantly higher commitment scores than the Colombian sample in follow-up contrasts (see Table 1). Cultural differences in exploration scores were also marginally significant after controlling for the other factors ($F [2, 260] = 2.525$, $p < .08$). The U.S. and Haitian students again had higher exploration scores than the Colombians.

Gender differences were found for commitment scores only ($F[1,260] = 7.191$, $p < .01$), with females receiving significantly higher commitment scores. Although age and SES did not show significant effects, they helped account for some cultural group differences. The adjusted variance accounted for was 5% for the commitment scores and less than 2% for the exploration scores.

Table 2 depicts means for exploration and commitment scores separately by gender and by cultural origin. As a follow-up for examining identity status, the overall sample was classified on the basis of both scores and produced a pattern that is consistent with the above findings (see Figure 1). The younger Colombians were especially likely to occupy a diffused identity status. Like the older Haitians, the Colombians were also likely to occupy a foreclosed identity status. Identity achievement was most frequently observed in the U.S. sample.

DISCUSSION

Our findings suggest that cultural context is predictive of variations in identity formation. In controlling for SES and age, which is rare in the relevant scientific research literature, more conservative estimates were provided in terms of culture and gender. Our results concerning ethnicity and gender are relevant to a number of studies in the field concerning ethnic differences in identity formation. It should be noted that our results are based on samples living in their country of origin. This situation remo-

Table 1
ANCOVAS for Exploration and Commitment by Ethnicity, SES, Gender with Age

Source	Dependent Variable	df	Mean Square	F	p
Corrected Model	Exploration	5	143.424	1.793	.115
	Commitment	5	342.036	3.613	.004
Intercept	Exploration	1	10191.370	127.392	.000
	Commitment	1	11965.545	126.404	.000
Ethnicity	Exploration	2	201.970	2.525	.082
	Commitment	2	501.752	5.301	.006
Gender	Exploration	1	20.142	.252	.616
	Commitment	1	680.752	7.191	.008
SES	Exploration	1	190.502	2.381	.124
	Commitment	1	9.246	.098	.755
Age	Exploration	1	8.511	.106	.745
	Commitment	1	1.302	.014	.907
Error	Exploration	260	80.000		
	Commitment	260	94.661		
Total	Exploration	266			
	Commitment	266			
Corrected Total	Exploration	265			
	Commitment	265			

Table 2
Exploration and Commitment Scores by Country and Gender

	Ethnicity	Gender	Mean	Standard Deviation	N
Exploration	Colombians	Male	55.30	6.14	20
		Female	57.81	6.77	27
		Total	56.74	6.56	47
	Americans	Male	59.90	10.44	90
		Female	60.64	7.32	70
		Total	60.23	9.18	160
	Haitians	Male	61.23	10.60	30
		Female	59.90	9.14	29
		Total	60.58	9.85	59
	Total	Male	59.53	10.08	140
		Female	59.87	7.69	126
		Total	59.69	9.01	266
Commitment	Colombians	Male	60.45	7.48	20
		Female	60.96	5.64	27
		Total	60.74	6.41	47
	Americans	Male	64.07	9.90	90
		Female	67.09	10.88	70
		Total	65.39	10.42	160
	Haitians	Male	63.63	9.91	30
		Female	69.59	9.98	29
		Total	66.56	10.30	59
	Total	Male	63.46	9.62	140
		Female	66.35	10.16	126
		Total	64.83	9.97	266

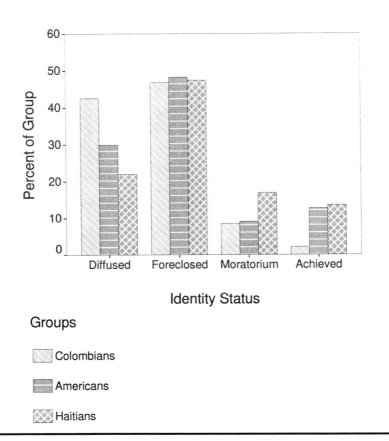

Figure 1
Distribution of Groups Across Identity Statuses

Groups

Identity Status

☐ Colombians

■ Americans

☒ Haitians

ves the confounding influence of minority group status upon identity status when comparing cultural-national groups.

Although two of the three samples are too small to support any strong conclusions, the study does provide a frame of reference for addressing various conceptual and methodological problems in the field. Based on these data, it appears that even after controlling for age and SES, cultural and gender differences in exploration and commitment remain significant. Females tend to report more commitment across groups, a finding that is consistent with some of the literature and theory developed within the cultural psychology framework (Cole, 1996). It is clear that, in general, societies pressure females more to restrict their exploration. Commitment is generally associated with responsibility, and the higher scores of females suggest that they are more responsibility-oriented and mature than males. However, gender differences in identity achievement, particularly those based on Eriksonian theory and measured with the present methodology remain a problematic issue.

Cultural differences in commitment scores appear to be pronounced when comparing younger Colombians with older Haitians. It may be that differences in maturation underlie the ethnic differences found thus far. While we attempted to control for age, context differences may nevertheless remain important. Female Haitians had the highest commitment scores of any subgroup. With respect to exploration, the American students had considerably higher scores than the younger Colombians. The special economic and political situation of present-day Colombian society apparently supports ideological rather than vocational exploration among university students. The Americans and older upper-class Haitians tended to be intermediate in exploration.

The EIPQ appears to be sensitive to cultural processes, including those concerning gender. The translation of the EIPQ adds a useful tool for future research. However, the sample sizes and characteristics of the Colombian and Haitian groups preclude any conclusion that in traditional, developing countries, identity achievement is less likely to be found. Two possibilities appear plausible. In less individualistic societies, ego identity development may be considered to be achieved when exploration is curtailed and commitment is manifested. Adaptation in these contexts may favor this developmental sequence in light of limited options. The second possibility is that research with more representative samples from a variety of countries might reveal greater exploration than was found in this study. In general, cultural differences were more pronounced for commitment scores than for exploration scores. It may be that for Colombian students, college participation begins earlier and carries different implications than for United States students. For the Haitian groups, it should be recalled that the present results are only generalizable to middle- and upper-class groups in that country.

Besides an increased emphasis upon longitudinal designs, future research will need to include larger and more diverse samples with respect to age and SES. It should be noted that many adolescents were included in the study who did not attend college. By adding new cultural groups to the predominantly North American research literature, we could provide evidence suggesting that ego identity develops through a fairly predictable process that is influenced by cultural values and educational/vocational opportunities as well as by prevailing cultural and historical conditions.

The gender differences point to culturally mediated effects that are more pronounced in traditional, developing countries than in modern, economically well-off societies.

Future research also needs to include similar data from older respondents to explore the prevalence of identity achievement in other age and cultural contexts. The characteristics of the present sample leave questions regarding identity achievement in later age open, along with several other factors concerning the influence of cultural history and cultural values on identity development.

BIBLIOGRAPHY

Abraham, K. G. (1983). The relation between identity status and locus of control among rural high school students. *Journal of Early Adolescence, 3,* 257-264.

Abraham, K. G. (1986). Ego-identity differences among Anglo-American and Mexican-American adolescents. *Journal of Adolescence, 9,* 151-166.

Adams, G. R., Shea, J. A., & Fitch, S. A. (1979). Toward the development of an objective assessment of ego-identity status. *Journal of Youth and Adolescence, 8,* 223-237.

Archer, S. L. (1982). The lower age boundaries of identity development. *Child Development, 53,* 1551-1556.

Balistreri, E., Busch-Rossnagel, N., & Geisinger, K. F. (1995). Development and preliminary validation of the Ego Identity Process Questionnaire. *Journal of Adolescence, 18,* 179-192.

Bennion, L. D., & Adams, G. R. (1986). A revision of the Extended Version of the Objective measure of Ego Identity Status: An identity instrument for use with late adolescents. *Journal of Adolescent Research, 1,* 183-198.

Erikson, E. (1968). *Identity: Youth and crisis.* New York: Norton.

Gil, A. G., Vega, W. A., & Dimas, J. M. (1994). Acculturative stress and personal adjustment among Hispanic adolescent boys. *Journal of Community Psychology, 22,* 43-54.

Grotevant, H. D., & Adams, G. R. (1984). Development of an objective measure to assess ego identity in adolescence: Validation and replication. *Journal of Youth and Adolescence, 13,* 419-438.

Kroger, J. (1985). Separation-individuation and ego identity status in New Zealand university students. *Journal of Youth and Adolescence, 14,* 133-147.

Marcia, J. E. (1966). Development and validation of ego identity status.

Journal of Personality and Social Psychology, 3, 551-558.

Marcia, J.E. (1993). The ego identity approach. In J.E. Marcia, A.S. Waterman, D.R., Matteson, S.L. Archer, & J.L. Orlofsky (Eds.), *Ego identity: A handbook for psychosocial research* (pp. 3-41). New York: Springer-Verlag.

McClain, E.W. (1975). An Eriksonian cross-cultural study of adolescent development. *Adolescence, 10,* 527-541.

Markstrom-Adams, C., & Adams, G. R. (1995). Gender, ethnic group, and grade differences in psychosocial functioning during middle adolescence? *Journal of Youth and Adolescence, 24,* 397-417.

Ochse, R., & Plug, C. (1986). Cross-cultural investigation of the validity of Erikson's theory of personality development. *Journal of Personality and Social Psychology, 50* (6) 1240-1252.

Phinney, J.S. (1990). Ethnic identity in adolescents and adults: Review of research. *Psychological Bulletin, 108,* 499-514.

Phinney, J. S., & Alipuria, L. L. (1990). Ethnic identity in college students from four ethnic groups. *Journal of Adolescence, 13,* 171-183.

Rotheram-Borus, M. J. (1989). Ethnic differences in adolescents identity status and associated behavior problems. *Journal of Adolescence, 12,* 361-374.

Spencer, M.B., & Markstrom-Adams, C. (1990). Identity processes among racial and ethnic minority children in America. *Child Development, 61,* 290-310.

Streitmatter, J. L. (1988). Ethnicity as a mediating of early adolescent identity development. *Journal of Adolescence, 11,* 335-346.

Zuschlag, M. K., & Whitbourne, S. K. (1994). Psychosocial in three generations of college students. *Journal of Youth and Adolescence, 23,* 567-577.

SECTION VII: COGNITIVE-DEVELOPMENTAL PERSPECTIVES

With increased social participation throughout childhood and adolescence, youngsters begin to understand how to relate to others in moral and socially desirable ways. Developmental psychologists have proposed that moral development progresses in stages, each stage representing a more mature form of reasoning about moral problems and moral conduct. The most influential theoretical model is Kohlberg's theory of moral development: It proposes that there are six stages of moral development and that these stages are present in every culture, although the stage at which individuals complete their development and the time it takes for its completion may vary considerably. While Kohlberg's definition and assessment of moral reasoning maturity have been challenged by several of his students and collaborators, the work of cognitive development theorists has changed our basic understanding of the process of human growth and development, and it has provided applied psychologists with an important set of directing constructs.

Among the most important innovations offered by some of Kohlberg's followers have been two objective tests designed to measure moral judgment: Lind's *Moralisches-Urteil-Test (MUT)* or Moral Judgment Test *(MJT)* and Rest's Defining Issues Test *(DIT)*. This section contains two papers that are based on these tests and report some challenging data gathered respectively in Germany and in Taiwan.

In his chapter *Are Helpers Always Moral? Empirical Findings from a Longitudinal Study of Medical Students in Germany*, Georg Lind argues that helping behavior and moral competence should be closely related, but then goes on to question whether helping behavior determines moral development. He asks whether participation in an institution with high prosocial aims and values furthers the moral development of its members and whether the intensive exposure to helping behavior and its daily exercise have a positive impact on people's moral development. To answer these questions, Georg Lind studied a group of German medical students who have chosen helping as their profession and career. By employing his *Moralisches-Urteil-Test (MUT)*, he was able to distinguish clearly between the affective and the cognitive aspects of moral judgment behavior. The author also maintains that his test is able to provide an unconfounded assessment of moral judgment competence. The results of his study indicate that medical training over several years did not lead to improved moral judgment competence, unlike in many other disciplines. Thus, being involved in medical helping situations does not appear to support the development of moral judgment competencies—a troublesome result throwing some doubt on the moral dimensions of medical training in

Germany and perhaps elsewhere.

It has frequently been claimed that Kohlbergian theories contain a fundamental western or American bias reflecting an individualistic emphasis on moral autonomy at the expense of more collectivistic and feminine concerns for care and responsiveness to others and their expectations. In their article, *Perceived Parental Behavior and the Development of Moral Reasoning in Students from Taiwan*, Uwe P. Gielen and Emily S.C.Y. Miao test this proposition by applying Rest's DIT to a representative sample of Chinese high school and university students from Taiwan. Taiwan sees itself as a bastion of Chinese culture, which to a considerable degree is based on the Confucian heritage. Contrary to the claims advanced by critics of the Kohlbergian enterprise, the Taiwanese students (and especially the females) received very high scores on the DIT, suggesting that principled and autonomous forms of moral reasoning are fully compatible with collectivistic, holistic Chinese ethics. In contrast to these findings, perceived parental behavior was only rarely related to the students' moral judgment scores. Similarly to the argument advanced by Kagitçibasi in her earlier chapter (see Section II), Gielen and Miao conclude that there is a widespread tendency to confuse moral autonomy (i.e., guidance by inner principles) with individualism and separateness although these constitute two conceptually and empirically separate dimensions of thought and action. While western societies such as the United States endorse more individualistic value systems and East Asian societies such as Taiwan more collectivistic goals, moral autonomy has been an important developmental goal in both ancient and modern Chinese culture.

The two studies included in Section VII suggest that there is still a lot of "mileage" left in the cognitive-developmental approach to the study of morality. Unlike most other cross-cultural psychology approaches, cognitive-developmental theories emphasize general structural patterns rather than the diverse contents of culturally variable value systems. This distinction has direct implications for the global debate on human rights. Whereas cognitive-developmental theories have proposed some distinct theoretical ideas about the nature of universal human rights and moral goals, the more relativistically oriented approaches to cross-cultural psychology have instead tended to focus on cross-cultural differences among moral ideas and ideals. Respect for cultural differences, however, remains an empty and even dangerous ideal unless it is accompanied by a clear understanding of moral principles that can be shared across cultural boundaries. A predominant focus on cross-cultural differences will prove insufficient for the development of a global psychology of the future.

ARE HELPERS ALWAYS MORAL?
EMPIRICAL FINDINGS FROM A LONGITUDINAL STUDY OF
MEDICAL STUDENTS IN GERMANY

Georg Lind, University of Konstanz, Germany

INTRODUCTION

This paper is part of a series of studies into the relationship between moral development and (prosocial) behavior. In general, many of us believe that morality and helping behavior are similar, if not identical. Helping behavior and moral competence are seen as so closely related to each other that sometimes these two terms are used interchangeably and the one is taken as a sign for the other. For example, we believe that a test of moral development must clearly distinguish between those who help and those who do not help. Indeed, some carefully designed studies, as the one by Shari McNamee (1977), support this view. McNamee found that there was a close linear relationship between subjects' level of moral development, as measured by Kohlberg´s Moral Judgment Interview, and their helping behavior in a laboratory situation (for an overview see Sprinthall et al., 1994). In that study, the subjects' real helping behavior was more closely related to moral development than their intention to help.

In another very sophisticated experiment, Kathryn Jacobs (1975) found a strong relationship between moral development and prosocial behavior. She studied cooperative behavior and emotional responses of subjects in a series of prisoner-dilemma-situations. She found that subjects with a high P-score, derived from Rest's (1979) Defining Issues Test (DIT) tended first to respond egotistically to their confederates' seemingly non-cooperative moves, just like subjects with low P-scores did. Yet, after a while, in contrast to the low-scorers, the highly developed subjects settled their inner conflict by resuming their cooperative behavior.

In spite of these supportive studies, the relationship between moral development and helping behavior is far from being perfect. Many studies found also low or zero correlations between moral development and prosocial behavior (Blasi, 1980). These low correlations may in some instances be merely due to bad research design. Yet, the research evidence showing low correlations is massive, indicating that this relationship is more complex than we used to believe and that we need to do more research to understand how moral development affects prosocial behavior and how prosocial behavior affects moral development.

The first part of this question, whether the level of moral judgment competence accounts for adolescents' intention to help, I addressed in another study (Lind, 1997). In that study, we found that moral judgment competence was *not* related to secondary school students' prosocial intentions. There was only a weak, non-linear relationship between the adolescents' MJT score and their willingness to help. However, we found that moral judgment competence very much influences the sort of factors that trigger helping intentions. Low scoring students helped when they were asked to do so by an authority (e.g., the teacher), or when they believed that others would also help, whereas students with high moral judgment competence were much less dependent on such external triggers but intended to help when they felt responsible. This finding can be taken as a confirmation of Kohlberg and Candee's (1984) theory about the mediating role of responsibility judgments.

In the present study, I focus on the second question, whether helping behavior determines moral development. Various theories predict such a causal relationship. From a psychoanalytic theory point of view, a person who is continually exposed to an environment that demands prosocial behavior, will eventually incorporate prosocial values in his or her super-ego. From a social learning theory point of view, a person will always adopt the values of the group to which he or she belongs (Hogan & Emler, 1995). Even cognitive-developmental theorists can be understood in this way. So for Kohlberg (1984/1969) moral development depends strongly on role-taking opportunities. Hence, we could hypothesize that people, who live in an environment that provides them with many opportunities to help other people, will reach a higher level of moral competence than people with little opportunities will. Kohlberg postulated some kind of "match" between a person's moral ideology and the moral ideology of the institution in which he or she lives.

The question we want to answer then is: Does the participation in an institution with high prosocial aims and value—either through internalization, or through social pressure, or through role-taking opportunities—increase the moral development of its members?

Our dual-aspect theory of moral development (Lind, 1993, 1995) requires us to be more specific. We must ask: Does the fact that one lives and works and learns in a "moral" institution increase the moral attitudes of its member, or his/her moral competencies or both? We have shown in many studies a) that moral attitudes and competencies can be clearly discriminated and independently measured, b) that both aspects are not separable into different domains of behavior but are attributes of the same pattern of behavior, c) that, in many instances, both aspects are highly correlated with one another, but d) that both aspects behave also different in a predictable way (Lind, 1985, 1993, 1995). For example, while people can fake their moral attitudes in any direction, they cannot pretend to have a higher moral judgment competence than they actually have.

To answer these questions we will study a group of people who are highly exposed to a prosocial environment and whose status makes them especially prone to influences from this institution, namely medical students. Medical students have chosen helping as their profession and career. Through their status as students they should be especially open for the prosocial values of the health care system. Moreover, they entered this social institution voluntarily and, as many studies show, they bring with them a high level of moral development already at the beginning of their study (Self & Baldwin, 1994).

The German medical students, on whom I will report here, may stand for medical students all over the world. However, as medical schools and the health care system differ profoundly from one country to another, they may also show some particularities. In Germany, attendance of university is (still) for free. Yet, because only a limited number of students are admitted to medical school, the students are highly selected. Their grade point average in high school is unusually high. This does not mean that medical students are merely "cold intellectuals." Most medical students chose this profession for highly prosocial reasons. Their motivation to help is higher than that of most other students. Indeed, this helping orientation is a better predictor for their admittance to medical schools than any other variable, including academic achievement (Bargel & Ramm, 1994; Lind, 1981). Moreover, many medical students made their career plans at a younger age than the students of most other fields of study did (Lind, 1981). Through this early career decision, even those with a low grade point average often manage to meet the academic requirements right in time to get admitted. Finally, as we will see, beginners at medical school, exhibit a higher level of moral judgment competence than beginners in most other fields of study.

Furthermore, we were surprised when we found in our longitudinal study that, in contrast to all other students that we have studied so far, medical students do not increase in their moral development but seem to even regress.

METHODS

Although the data reported here were collected in the early 1980s, they have not been previously analyzed or published, nor do they seem outdated in any sense. In his presentation at the Padua conference, Helkama (1997) reported on a more recent longitudinal study in Finland using Kohlberg's Moral Judgment Interview, which shows a very similar phenomenon (see also Helkama, 1987). In a series of representative surveys of medical (and other) students in Germany, conducted every two year, medical students, more than any other group of university students, express great concern that their study fails to provide them with social and communicative competencies needed in their profession (Bargel & Ramm, 1994).(1)

Respondents

The medical students (as well as the other students who will be taken as a comparison group) have been surveyed four times: in their first, fifth, and ninth semesters and in their 13th semester when many of them had already graduated and did their internship.(2) Here I will analyze only those students who have participated in all four surveys (N=746 out of 1673 students who participated in the first-semester survey). Among these were 104 medical students and 604 students from other fields of study. Because of the selection of fields of studies, many more male (N=563) than female respondents (N=183) were sampled.

Independent Variable

Moral judgment competence and moral attitudes were measured using the *Moral Judgment Test* (MJT) by Lind (1978, 1985, 1995; Lind & Wakenhut, 1985). The MJT measures both moral attitudes and moral competencies (or cognition) simultaneously though as logically independent aspects of a person's judgment behavior. Moral attitudes are operationalized in the MJT as the average rating of arguments pertaining to a particular stage of reasoning. Moral judgment competence is defined in the MJT, following Kohlberg (1964), as "the capacity to make decisions and judgments which are moral (i.e., based on internal principles) and to act in accordance with such judgments" (p. 425). The MJT measures the degree to which subjects rate other people's moral arguments with respect to their moral quality rather than with respect to amoral considerations like the arguments' opinion agreement.

Because the MJT has been described at length in various places, a short overview may suffice. The standard version of the MJT consists of two sub-tests, each containing a dilemma-story and questions regarding this story. The unique feature of the MJT is the fact that it contains both arguments in favor and arguments against the presented solution of the dilemma. So the test-taker is confronted with moral reasons that are inconsistent with his or her opinion. In fact, many people find it hard to understand and appreciate the moral quality of arguments that oppose their opinion. Some people are even unwilling (or unable) to read through such arguments. Hence, the MJT provides a good *task* for observing subjects' moral judgment competence, that is, their ability to judge in accordance to moral principles. This ability is indexed by the so-called C score. The C score can range from zero, indicating absence of any moral judgment competence, to 100, indicating perfect judgment competence.

In contrast to other tests of moral development, the MJT provides a pure measure of moral judgment competence (and, of course, also pure measures of moral attitudes). A high C score indicates that the subject can rate arguments consistently from a moral point of view. This does not mean that he or she must prefer stage 5 or 6 reasoning to get a high C score. The C index is logically independent from an individual's moral ideology. Because of these features, one may hypothesize that persons with high C scores are unable to take a stance on a moral issue (DuBois, 1997a). We will provide data on this hypothesis below.

In order to include as many subjects as possible in the analysis, I substituted missing data through empirical means if, and only if, no more than one out of 24 items was missing in a dilemma. For substitution, the individual mean rating of the other 23 items in a dilemma was used.

As a second set of information, the MJT provides scores for subjects' attitudes toward each of the six stages of moral reasoning as defined by Kohlberg (1984/1969). These attitudes can be looked at individually stage by stage, and in total, as profiles. So we can assess both a) the absolute degree of acceptability of each stage of moral reasoning, and b) the order or hierarchy that these stages form in the subjects' minds.

Statistical Analysis

My statistical analysis will focus mainly on frequencies, means and correlations, and report statistical significance only by ways of convention. On the one hand, our sample is so large that almost any difference becomes statistically significant even though it may be psychologically insignificant.(3) On the other hand, as all of know of course, statistical significance testing is biased against the null hypothesis since it totally ignores Type-II errors.

FINDINGS

Four findings pertain to our question. To get a general idea about what impact higher education has on students' moral development; we will first look at the change of their moral attitudes and of their moral competencies.

Figure 1
Affective Aspect: Moral Attitudes of German University Students
by Semester
$(F[15, 6975] = 5.03, r = .03)$

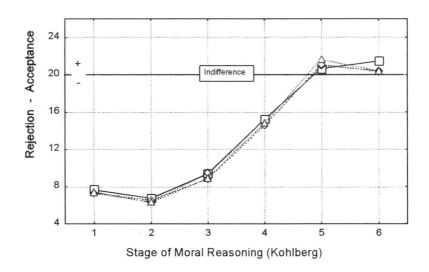

-□- 1st Sem
-◇- 5th Sem
··◇·· 9th Sem
-△- 13th Sem

Moral Attitudes

The findings in Figure 1 show that higher education has almost no impact on students' moral *attitudes*. Over the whole range of seven years, from first to 13th semester, the mean moral attitudes are almost invariant. Students clearly prefer stages 5 and 6 over all other stages, as the most adequate levels of moral reasoning for solving the two dilemmas presented in the MJT, the dilemma of the doctor who is asked to help a terminally ill woman to die, and of two workers who break the law in order to enforce law abiding.

It seems that young adults' moral ideology is not influenced by such a mighty social institution as a medical school. Our data do not support social learning theory, which claims that persons of all ages are influenced by the social institutions of which they are members. For other theories, the findings presented in Figure 1 are not relevant. Psychoanalytic theory would predict such influence only for early childhood. With regard to Kohlberg's theory the data on people's moral attitudes seem not relevant as this theory claims moral cognition to be at the heart of moral development.

Moral Judgment Competence

In regard to moral judgment competence scores of university students, we found a strong developmental trend. Figure 2 depicts the data for all students except medical students. While first semester students show a

Figure 2
Longitudinal Change of Moral Judgment Competence in German University Students (without Medicine)
$(F[3, 1212] = 10.14, p < .000)$

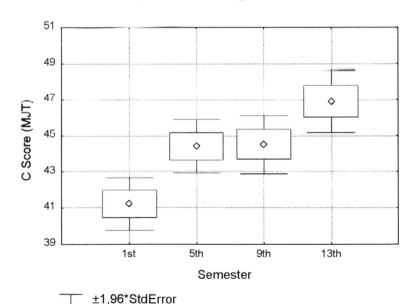

mean C score of about 41, the mean C score of 13th semester students (or graduates) is about 6 points higher, namely 47, that is, well above the standard sampling error shown in the whisker-box-plot.

Very similar changes have been found in studies using Kohlberg's Moral Judgment Interview (Colby, Kohlberg, et al., 1987) or Rest's Defining Issues Test (Rest, 1979). However, the studies using these two measures, could not differentiate between moral attitudes and cognition, as the MJT does. The MJT studies help us clarify this issue. Those findings seem to reflect changes of moral competence rather than of moral attitudes. Thus it seems fair to conclude that higher education promotes students' ability to make judgments consistent with their moral principles rather than presses students to change their moral attitudes.

Figure 3
Longitudinal Change of Moral Judgment Competence in German Medical Students
(F[3, 1383] $= 1.84, p < .14$; min. N $= 592$, max. N $= 719$)

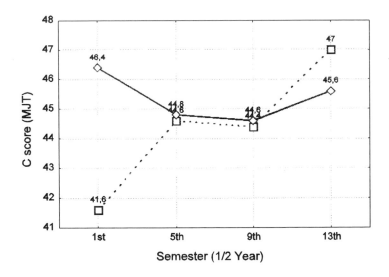

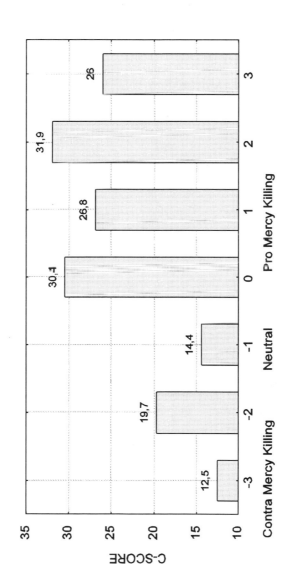

Figure 4
Opinion of Medical Personnel on Mercy Killing by Moral Judgment Competence (MJT)
($F[6, 178] = 7.59$, $p < .000$)

The Impact of Medical School

The impact of *medical* education differs markedly from this. As Figure 3 shows, first semester medical students start on a high level. Yet over their time of study, their moral judgment competence stagnates or even regresses. This is, as far as I know, the only field of study in which such a phenomenon has ever been observed.

Moral Judgment, Competence, and Helping

In a study by DuBois (1997) of approximately 200 medical doctors and nurses in Austria and Saudi-Arabia, moral judgment competence was correlated with doctor's opinions on how to help other people in need (Figure 4). A majority expressed a strong opinion on ethical issues like mercy killing.

This figure also shows that helping can mean quite different things. It can mean to deny mercy killing, and it can mean to help a terminally ill persons die to shorten their suffering. The opinion on this problem is split among medical personnel, implying that even among them there is no clear answer on the question, which decision is moral and which is immoral. It is interesting to note though that there is a tendency for doctors and nurses with high C scores to allow mercy killing.

Data on Theoretical Validity

To check on the validity of these data from different cultures, we analyzed the relationship of the C-score to gender (no differences were expected) and to other indicators. As in most other studies on gender differences (Walker, 1986), there was hardly any differences in moral judgment competence between male and female students (Lind et al., 1987). The small differences that we found were in favor of female students, whose scores were somewhat higher (C=44.2) than the score of the male students (C=41.5).

Lind (1985) proposed three other criteria for checking on the theoretical validity of MJT data from various cultures. The MJT data meet all these criteria: a) As we saw in Figures 1, the preferences for the six stages are ordered in the predicted way, b) the stage inter-correlations form an almost perfect quasi-simplex structure, and c) the six moral attitude scores on the one hand, and the moral competence score on the other, are nearly perfectly inter-correlated and support the notion of affective-cognitive parallelism in all four longitudinal surveys.

DISCUSSION

Our initial question was whether helpers are always moral. That is, does the intensive learning of helping behavior and its daily exercise as professional, impact people's moral development?

After our study, this question seems rather naive and needs rewording. For example, we must say which aspect of moral development we mean, the change of moral attitudes or the change of moral competencies? Yet, even when we make this distinction, the answer remains negative. Medical students, who enter medical school with high moral development scores, and with a strong motivation to help other people, neither change their moral ideals (which could only be to the worse), nor improve their moral judgment competence. While their peers in other fields of study also do not change their moral attitudes during their study, they clearly profit from the opportunities for role-taking and guided reflection that their education seems to offer (Lind, 1996).

Various checks for evidence which could attenuate this finding, are negative, that is, they do not alter this conclusion. The MJT data proved to be highly valid from a theoretical point of view. Moral judgment competence, as measured through its C score, seems to really reflect an ability rather than merely a moral ideology (Lind, 1993). Although this score is defined in a rather formal way, that is, independently from a person's moral ideology, subjects with high scores exhibit strong opinions on ethical issues. This is so because the C score is defined independently only from a particular moral stage of reasoning but not from the moral point of view. The C score reflects the fact that respondents judge arguments in respect to their moral principles, whatever kind they may be.

So it seems safe to conclude that medical education offers too little, if any role-taking opportunities and opportunities for guided reflection in the domain of sociomoral competencies. Such a conclusion is clearly supported by the reports that German medical students give about their learning environment (Bargel & Ramm, 1994). More than students from any other field, medical students report that they must study very hard and feel highly pressured to achieve good grades, but that they are hardly taught to understand the basic principles of their profession, to cooperate with their peers, to develop their own areas of interest, or to evaluate critically the information they rely on in their work.

What are the implications of our findings for theories of moral development? They seem to clearly refute social learning theory, which predicts that medical students would change their moral attitudes. They also partly refute Kohlberg's stage theory of moral development, which predicts that there is always increase but no regression in moral judgment competence. However, our findings strongly support Kohlberg's notion of moral *competencies*, which are at the heart of moral development. I believe that this notion is much more important than the assumption of invariant sequence, and that we must not do away with the competence assumption when we refute the invariant sequence assumption.

In respect to practical questions, our findings together with others, I believe, point at a deep crisis of medical education, which calls for a profound change in the way in which we train our doctors and nurses. I do not believe that courses in medical ethics, as they are widely practiced in the United States and elsewhere, will help much to improve the situation. Many of these courses contain little ethics, and if they do, the subject matters taught are too remote from the real moral tasks with which medical doctors are confronted everyday. I believe that we must take problems and conflicts that a doctor may run into, as the focus of their ethical training. I also believe that we need not teach doctors moral ideals or moral attitudes. These they already have to such a high degree that such teaching would mean "carrying coal to Newcastle." Rather, such ethical education should foster future doctors' ability to translate their moral ideals into proper moral action and to solve the conflicts and dilemmas that they will inevitably experience when they try to help other people.

In regard to the more general question of this study how morality and prosocial behavior are related with one another, this study demonstrates that careful distinctions are in place. We need to clearly distinguish between affective and cognitive aspects of moral judgment behavior. Otherwise, we will confound these two distinct yet inseparable aspects of moral behavior. We also need to look more carefully at the meaning of "helping behavior." People do not only differ very much in how they define "helping" but also in regard to how to help someone who is in need. For example, some believe that helping a terminally ill persons implies that one must preserve such persons' biological lives regardless of the quality of their lives, while others believe that, in this case, helping means to fulfill people's will to die and to shorten their unbearable pain. Which side is morally right? Each of us may have a personal opinion on this question but can we, as scientists, decide this question in an objective way? Surely, we cannot. All that we can do as scientist, is to take an Aristotelian point of view by defining that reasoning as more morally mature which takes the most perspectives into account. This is the truly universalistic point of view, proposed by philosophers like Immanuel Kant and John Rawls, as well as by educators like John Dewey. This point of view commands us to judge the morality of another person not by his or her concrete decision but by the way he or she arrived at this decision.

BIBLIOGRAPHY

Bargel, T., & Ramm, M. (1994). *Das Studium der Medizin. Eine Fachmonographie aus studentischer Sicht* [The study of medicine. A description of a field from students' point of view]. Bonn: Federal Ministry of Education and Science.

Blasi, A. (1980). Bridging moral cognition and moral action: A critical review of the literature. *Psychological Bulletin, 88,* 1-45.

Carver, R.P. (1993). The case against statistical significance testing, revisited. *Journal of Experimental Education, 61* (4), 287-292.

Colby, A., Kohlberg, L., & Collaborators (1987). *The measurement of moral judgment* (Vols. 1-2). Cambridge: Cambridge University Press.

DuBois, J. (1997a). *The moral judgment of medical personnel. A crosscultural study about brain death and organ explanation.* Unpublished doctoral dissertation, University of Vienna.

DuBois, J. (1997b). *Secondary analysis of the data from DuBois (1997a) by the author.*

Framhein, G., & Langer, J. (Eds.). (1984). *Student und Studium im internationalen Vergleich* [Students and study in an international perspective]. Klagenfurt: Karntner Druck- u. Verlagsanstalt.

Helkama, K. (1987). *The fate of moral reasoning in medical school: A twoyear longitudinal study.* Unpublished manuscript. University of Helsinki, Finland.

Helkama, K. (1997). *A longitudinal study of the moral reasoning of Finnish medical students.* Paper presented at the Regional Meeting of the International Council of Psychologists, Padua University, July 21-23, 1997.

Hogan, R., & Emler, N. (1995). Personality and moral development. InW.M. Kurtines & J.L. Gewirtz (Eds.), *Moral development: An introduction* (pp. 209-227). Boston, MA: Allyn and Bacon.

Jacobs, M.K. (1975). *Women's moral reasoning and behavior in a contractual form of prisoner's dilemma.* Unpublished doctoral dissertation, University of Toledo.

Kohlberg, L. (1964). Development of moral character and moral ideology. In M.L. Hoffman & L.W. Hoffman (Eds.), *Review of child Development research* (Vol. 1, pp. 381-431). New York: Russel Sage Foundation.

Kohlberg, L. (1984). Stage and sequence. In L. Kohlberg, *Essays on moral development,* Vol. 2, *The psychology of moral development* (pp. 7-169). San Francisco, CA: Harper & Row (originally published 1969).

Kohlberg, L., & Candee, D. (1984). The relationship of moral judgment to moral action. In L. Kohlberg, *Essays on moral development,* Vol. 2,

The psychology of moral development (pp. 498-582). San Francisco, CA: Harper & Row.

Lind, G. (1981). *Fachinteressen im Prozeß der Ausbildungsentscheidung am Beispiel des Medizinstudiums* [The effects of interest in medical studies on the choice of medicine as a career. A follow-up study of "Gymnasium" graduates who enter medical school]. Special Research Unit 23, Mimeographed report. Konstanz, Germany.

Lind, G. (1985). *Inhalt und Struktur. Theoretische, methodologische und empirische Untersuchungen zur Urteils- und Demokratiekompetenz bei Studierenden* [Content and structure of moral judgment behavior. Theoretical, epistemological, and empirical investigations of moral and democratic competencies of students]. Mimeographed doctoral dissertation. University of Konstanz.

Lind, G. (1993). *Moral und Bildung* [Morality and education]. Heidelberg: Asanger. (2nd. ed.: http:www.uni-konstanz.de/ ZE/Bib/ habil/lind/ lind.htm)

Lind, G. (1995). *The meaning and measurement of moral development competence revisited—The dual aspect approach..* Invited paper, Moral Development and Education, 1995 Meeting of the American Educational Research Association, San Francisco. (http:www.uni-konstanz.de/ag-moral/mjt-95.htm)

Lind, G. (1996). *Educational environments which promote self-sustaining moral development.* Paper presented at the meeting of the American Educational Research Association, April 1996, New York. www. (http://uni-konstanz.de/selfsust.htm)

Lind, G., Grocholewska, K., & Langer, J. (1987). Haben Frauen eine andere Moral? Eine empirische Untersuchung von Studentinnen und Studenten in Österreich, der Bundesrepublik und Polen. [Do women have a different morality? An empirical study of female and male students in Austria, Germany, and Poland]. In L. Unterkirchner & I. Wagner (Eds.), *Die andere Hälfte der Gesellschaft* [The other half society] (pp. 394-406). Wien: Verlag des Österreichischen Gewerkschaftsbundes.

Lind, G., & Wakenhut, R. (1985). Testing moral judgment competence. In G. Lind, H.A. Hartmann, & R. Wakenhut (Eds.), *Moral development and the social environment* (pp. 79-105). Chicago, IL: Precedent.

McNamee, S. (1977). Moral behavior, moral development and motivation. *Journal of Moral Education*, 7 (1), 27-31.

Peisert, H., & Framhein, G. (1994). *Das Hochschulsystem in der Bundesrepublik Deutschland. Aktualisierte Fassung* [The system of higher education of the Federal Republic of Germany: The most recent version]. Bonn: Bundesministerium für Bildung und Wissenschaft.

Rest, J.R. (1979). *Development in judging moral issues*. Minneapolis, MI: University of Minnesota Press.

Self, D.J., & Baldwin, D.C. (1994). Moral reasoning in medicine. In J.Rest & D. Narvaez (Eds.), *Moral development in the professions* (pp.147-162). Hillsdale, NJ: Erlbaum.

Sprinthall, N.A., Sprinthall, R.C., & Oja, S.N. (1996). *Educational psychology: A developmental approach* (6th ed.). New York: McGraw-Hill.

Walker, L. (1986). Sex differences in the development of moral reasoning: A critical review. *Child Development, 57*, 677-691.

ENDNOTES

1. The reader may wonder why these data remained unpublished for so long. The group that conducted this research at the University of Konstanz (Tino Bargel, Barbara Dippelhofer-Stiem, Gerhild Framhein, Hans Gerhard Walter), had to dissolve before the major body of data from this longitudinal, cross-cultural study could be analyzed and published. While the funding agency, *the Deutsche Forschungsgemeinschaft*, was willing to continue this research, the hosting university was not. The author privately funded the present analysis. I would like to thank my former colleagues who helped to design this study and to collect the data.

2. It should be noted that the German educational system differs markedly from the US-American and other systems. As I already noted, there are no fees for studying at a university. There are no colleges in Germany, although in some English-speaking institutions of higher education (*Fachhochschulen*) are called colleges. They do not offer a liberal arts curriculum as in the US, and, therefore, can more be compared to institutes of technology. The undergraduate curriculum of American colleges is largely integrated in German high schools, which prepare students for entry into university. The high schools are called "Gymnasium." (For further information on the German educational system, see Peiser & Framhein, 1994; the study design is reported in more detail in Framhein & Langer, 1984).

3. "There is no good excuse," as Carver (1993) notes, "for saying that a statistically significant result is significant because this language erroneously suggests to many readers that the result is automatically large, important, and substantial" (p. 288).

PERCEIVED PARENTAL BEHAVIOR AND THE DEVELOPMENT OF MORAL REASONING IN STUDENTS FROM TAIWAN

Uwe P. Gielen
St. Francis College, USA

Emily S.C.Y. Miao
Chinese Culture University, Taiwan, R.O.C.

INTRODUCTION

The psychological study of moral reasoning has for several decades been dominated by Kohlberg's stage theory. Kohlberg (1984) has proposed that children, adolescents, and adults everywhere transverse a series of increasingly adequate, differentiated, abstract, and comprehensive stages of moral reasoning. These stages reflect a sequence of moral philosophies or schemes of cooperation that persons in all societies are said to develop as a function of age, education, and various forms of social experience. While the sequence of stages is fixed, the various forms of role-taking opportunities will determine how fast a person progresses in the stage hierarchy, and what end point in his or her development the person reaches. Kohlberg's theory has been especially challenging to cross-cultural psychologists, since it postulates universal forms of moral reasoning and thus opposes cultural relativism (Gielen & Markoulis, in press). Among the many social institutions influencing the rate of adolescent moral development, the family has often been singled out as being of greatest importance. Families provide numerous role-taking opportunities that may facilitate or hinder the development of moral reasoning.

A considerable amount of research inside and outside the USA has attempted to link parental childrearing practices to adolescent moral development (Ahmed, Gielen, & Avellani, 1987; Dickinson, 1979; Gielen, Ahmed, & Avellani, 1992; Gielen, Markoulis, & Avellani, 1994; Hoffman, 1970; Holstein, 1972; Parikh, 1975; Speicher-Dubin, 1982; Thorlindsson, 1978). In light of this research and cognitive-developmental theory, the following working hypotheses were formulated.

The first research hypothesis suggested that parental warmth contributes to the growth of moral reasoning in children because children who feel accepted rather than neglected by their parents are more responsive to parental influence. Since parents usually reason in more complex ways than their children, acceptance supports the development of increasingly complex forms of moral reasoning in children, while parental neglect or rejection interfere with the moral development of children. The rationale for this first hypothesis was in part provided by Rohner (1984). He has suggested that parental variations in parental acceptance, warmth, neglect, and hostility influence children's behavior to a great extent, and he has provided a considerable amount of cross-cultural evidence supporting this viewpoint (Rohner, 1975).

The second research hypothesis in this study proposed that strong conflict between parents interferes with the development of role-taking abilities, since it leads to emotional and cognitive confusion in children and adolescents. Children have difficulty taking the perspective of parents who argue with each other constantly, since the parents themselves are unable to do so. At the same time, complex schemes of cooperation do not develop in children whose parents demonstrate an unwillingness to cooperate in a reasonable way on a daily basis.

The third research hypothesis in this study stated that adolescent children develop autonomous, principled forms of moral reasoning if their parents encourage them to behave autonomously and responsibly. In other words, parents who adopt democratic strategies of childrearing (e.g., sharing of decision-making with their adolescent children; emphasizing equality; responding to children's viewpoints) further the development in their children of more equilibrated forms of thinking.

These hypotheses suggest that the following factors contribute to the growth of moral reasoning in children and adolescents: parental warmth and acceptance; absence of parental rejection and/or neglect; absence of parental conflict; and democratic childrearing practices which encourage autonomous behavior. However, the postulated relationships between parental behavior and adolescent reasoning skills may not be very strong, since many other, extra-familial factors are also likely to influence these moral reasoning skills.

The cross-cultural empirical validation of Kohlberg's approach and related approaches to the study of moral reasoning has made considerable progress in recent years (Eckensberger & Zimba, 1997; Edwards, 1981, 1986; Gielen, 1991, 1996; Gielen & Markoulis, in press; Lind, 1986; Moon, 1986; Snarey, 1985; Snarey & Keljo, 1991; Vine, 1986). Researchers have typically applied either Kohlberg's moral judgment interview (MJI), Rest's Defining Issues Test (DIT), or Lind's *Moralisches-Urteil-Test* (MUT). While Kohlberg's interview method constitutes a production test, Rest's DIT and Lind's MUT are preference/recognition tests. The DIT, as employed in this study, asks a person to read through five moral dilemmas and subsequently to evaluate 60 moral arguments that are relevant to the moral decision stories. The moral arguments are designed to reflect different moral stages. The stages include the morality of instrumental egoism (stage 2), the morality of interpersonal concordance (stage 3), the morality of law and duty to the social order (stage 4), the morality of alienation from the social order (stage 4½ or stage A), the morality of societal consensus and internalized conscience (stages 5A and 5B), and the morality of non-arbitrary cooperation among equal, rational, impartial persons (stage 6) (Rest, 1983). It should be noted here that in several North American studies, Rest's moral judgment scores were only moderately correlated with Kohlberg's moral maturity scores. In two Chinese studies, correlation coefficients between Rest's index of moral maturity and Kohlberg's moral maturity score reached only $r = +.49$ and $r = +.20-.29$ respectively (Tsaing, 1980; Ma, 1980). Clearly, the two tests measure two related, yet different, aspects of moral judgment development.

Cross-cultural research on moral reasoning includes a number of studies conducted in countries with a Confucian heritage. These include Hong Kong (Hau & Lew, 1985; Ma, 1985, 1988a), South Korea (Park & Johnson, 1984), and Taiwan (Cheng, 1979; Gielen, 1987; Lei, 1981, 1984; Lin & Shan, 1987; Tsaing [Shan], 1980). These studies give moderate to good support to some of Kohlberg's and Rest's claims. Moral stage scores and Rest's index of principled moral reasoning tend to increase with increasing age and education. However, Lin and Shan (1987) have recently pointed out that their Chinese version of Rest's DIT did not always sufficiently discriminate between high school and college/university students. Additional research evidence concerning Chinese adaptations of the DIT is much needed.

In the following, a study is described that investigated the validity of the DIT in a Taiwanese setting. In addition, the research focused on possible relationships between perceived parental behavior and the development of moral reasoning in two groups of high school and college/university students from Taiwan. Data from the present study are compared to data from other studies, including those conducted in the USA, in Taiwan, and elsewhere in the East Asia.

Setting. Taiwan is a rapidly developing country with about 21 million predominantly Chinese inhabitants. It has a developed market economy. It's literacy and life expectancy rates are comparable to those of other industrialized countries. Education is compulsory and free for students between the ages 6-15 in primary and junior high schools, and there are 28 universities and colleges. The present research was conducted in and around T'ai-pei, the country's capital.

Chinese value systems have been influenced by Confucianism and Neo-Confucianism, Daoism, Mahayana Buddhism, and recent exposure to Western, especially North American, ideas. At the heart of Confucianism and Neo-Confucianism lies a concern for broad ethical principles (Confucius [551-479 B.C.E.], 1979; Mencius [372-281 B.C.E.], 1970; Miao, 1982; Roetz, 1993, 1996). The moral values embodied in the teachings of Confucius and Mencius emphasize *jen* or *ren* (human-heartedness, benevolence, a feeling for the dignity of human life), *ji* (righteousness, justice), *chung* (loyalty and responsibility in relationship to family and other institutions), *hsin* (trustworthiness as the bedrock of one's sense of commitment), *ho* (harmony and unity between the spiritual, social, and physical aspects of human existence; harmony between "heaven" and humanity, between people, and between humans and the material world), *hsiao* (filial piety), *hsiu-shen* (self cultivation), and *chung jang* (the doctrine of the golden mean).   The Chinese people have traditionally avoided extreme and absolutistic doctrines (Hsu, 1981).   *Ren-ching-wei* (the flavor of human feelings) permeates many social relationships in Taiwan and demands that human considerations should take precedence over logic or legalistic considerations.

Several authors have argued that the traditional "Confucian view of man as an integral part of an orderly universe with an innate moral sense to maintain harmony" is fundamentally incompatible with Kohlberg's emphasis on autonomous human beings making free and rational choices (Dien, 1982; see also Bloom, 1977).   The present research disagrees with this criticism of Kohlberg's theory and implies that an integration between traditional Chinese thought and modern Western conceptions such as Kohlberg's universalistic theory of moral reasoning is both possible and fruitful (Ma, 1988b; Roetz, 1993, 1996).

METHOD

Participants

The sample consisted of 330 female and 191 male students selected from four high schools and four universities in the greater Taipei area: Shyu-Huey High School (Catholic, boys), Tzu Shiu High School (private, boys and girls), Foh-Chung High School (public, boys and girls), Wesley High School (Protestant, girls), Chinese Culture University (private), Tam Kang University (private), National Chung-Shing University (public), and National Taiwan Normal University (public).   Table 1 describes the backgrounds of the students included in the study. 63% of the students attended junior or senior high schools and 37% attended universities.   The mean age of the students was 17 years and 8 months, with 512 of the 521 participants falling in the 15-25-age range. 28.4% of the students' fathers held blue collar jobs, 56.4% held white collar jobs, 10.2% were professionals or managers, and 5% were retired or their occupation was unclear. 63.2% of the mothers were housewives, 29.2% held white-collar jobs and 7.6% were professionals.   The overall sample of 521 students thus represented a broad cross-section of students from quite varied backgrounds.

Questionnaire

The questionnaire was translated from English into Mandarin Chinese and adapted to Taiwanese circumstances by the second author and a panel of qualified judges (see below). It consisted of background questions and five separate scales: A "Parents and Children" scale, "Mother" and "Father"

Table 1
Origin of Students Participating in the Study

School	Females	Males	All
Shyu-Huey High School (Catholic-Boys)	-	69	69
Tzu Shiu High School (Private)	39	35	74
Foh-Chung High School (Public)	73	28	101
Wesley (Protestant-Girls)	83	-	83
Chinese Culture University (Private)	32	24	56
Tam Kang University (Private)	18	6	24
National Chung-Shing University (Public)	55	13	68
National Taiwan Normal University (Public)	30	16	46
	330	191	521 Total

Note: The 521 participants were selected from a larger sample of 640 students. Participants were excluded, if their responses were incomplete or if they did not pass the standard DIT inconsistency check. The excluded students did not differ in background characteristics from the present sample.

scales, a "Parental Conflict" scale, and the "Defining Issues Test" (DIT), an objectively scored moral judgement questionnaire. The "Parents and Children" scale contained 24 items about perceptions of child-related parental behavior. These items were adapted from a longer scale by Coopersmith (1967) and used a 4-item Likert answering format ranging from "Always True" to "Never True." The 24 items were scored individually, and in addition, various items were combined to form subscales measuring perceived "Acceptance," "Autonomy" and "Democracy." These three subscales combined to form an overall measure of perceived parental "Childrearing Quality."

The "Mother" and "Father" scales each contained 31 items describing perceived maternal and paternal behavior. The items were selected and adapted from longer scales provided by Rohner (1984). All items used a Likert answering format and were scored individually. Following Rohner, items were also combined to form subscales for perceived "Warmth," "Aggression," "Indifference-Neglect," and "Rejection" on the part of a mother and father. In addition, all 31 items were combined to create an overall "Parental Acceptance-Rejection" (PARQ) index separately for mothers and fathers.

The "Parental Conflict" scale contained 24 items concerning parental conflicts about "Finances," joint "Family Activities" and "Childrearing Practices." These items were adapted from a more extensive scale by Schwarz and Getter (1980). The 24 items were combined to form an overall measure of "Parental Conflict."

Moral judgement was measured by Rest's (1986b) Defining Issues Test (DIT). The test consisted of the following moral dilemmas: (1) Should a poor husband steal a drug in order to save the life of his very sick wife if he cannot get the drug any other way? (2) A man escapes from prison and subsequently leads a model life. Should a neighbor who years later recognizes him report him to the police? (3) A woman is in terrible pain and is dying of cancer. She asks the doctor to kill her in order to end her suffering. Should the doctor do this? (4) Should the owner of a gas station hire a highly qualified but physically ugly mechanic, when he is afraid that many of his prejudiced customers will take their business elsewhere? (5) Should a high school principal stop the publication of a highly controversial student newspaper?

A sixth story—students occupy a university building in order to protest a ROTC program—was not included in the questionnaire, since its cross-cultural applicability appeared to be limited. The moral reasoning test used in the present study constituted a revised version of Tsaing's (1980) translation of the DIT into Chinese.

Following each dilemma, 12 arguments were provided that could be used to solve the conflict. The arguments reflected different moral stages. Respondents were asked to rate the importance of each argument. In addition, the participants were asked to select the four most important arguments.

The DIT was objectively scored following procedures recommended by Rest (1986b). The test provided moral stage scores for stages 2, 3, 4, 4½, 5A, 5B, and 6. Preferences for principled thinking (stages 5A, 5B, 6 combined) were expressed by the P-Score. The P-Percentage Score indicated the percentage of respondents' rankings which fell in the principled range.   In addition, an overall weighted indicator of moral judgement development was available in the D-score.   The D-Score reflected a person's relative preference for principled reasoning (stages 5A, 5B, and 6) over conventional reasoning (stages 3 and 4) and preconventional reasoning (stage 2).   The D-Score was based upon a complex mathematical formula that took into account and weighed a respondent's ratings of the 60 moral arguments provided by the five- story version of the DIT (Rest, 1986b).   All students included in the present study passed a standard consistency check proposed by Rest (1986b), indicating that the students were conscientious and understood the nature of the task provided by the test.

Translation and Adaptation of the Questionnaire: The DIT was translated by a team of Chinese researchers into Mandarin Chinese, pretested and revised between August 1979 and April 1980 (Lin & Shan, 1987).   The overall questionnaire was translated by the second author and a team of qualified Chinese judges.   The team also revised the previous Chinese version of the DIT.   Wherever necessary, details of the questionnaire (including the DIT) were adapted to cultural circumstances in Taiwan. This included changing the names of the characters in the moral dilemmas and changing various details in the dilemmas.

RESULTS

Distribution of Moral Stage Scores

Table 2 contains the distribution of DIT moral stage scores for the 521 Taiwanese participants in this study.   For comparison purposes, the moral stage scores of 203 high school and college students from the USA were also included in the table.   The stage scores for the USA sample were taken from Gielen, Swanzey, Avellani and Kramer (1986b).   The average ages for the two samples were quite similar.   The results for the Taiwanese students indicated that they preferred conventional moral arguments (Stages 3 and 4=47.74%) over principled arguments (Stages 5A, 5B, and 6=38.17%) and preconventional arguments (Stage 2=6.88%). However, it should be noted that the DIT contained more conventional than principled or preconventional arguments.   The obtained results, therefore, reflected in part the overall construction of the DIT.   Students from Taiwan were considerably more likely to select principled moral arguments (P%=38.17%) than students from the USA (P%=28.26%). This held true for all three stages included in the principled moral reasoning category, namely stages 5A, 5B, and 6. At the same time, students from Taiwan selected fewer Stage 2 and Stage 4 arguments, but more Stage 3 arguments than the American students. The Taiwanese students also selected fewer meaningless items, indicating their conscientiousness and understanding of the task requirements.

Table 2
Distribution of DIT Stage Scores for Taiwan and the USA

Stage	Taiwan (*N*=521) Mean %	SD	USA (*N*=203) Mean %	SD	*t*	*df*	*p*
Stage 2	6.88%	5.68%	9.48%	5.80%	5.50	722	.000
Stage 3	2 2.67%	11.14%	19.80%	9.84%	3.40	414*	.001
Stage 4	25.07%	10.18%	33.47%	10.08%	-10.00	722	.000
Stage 4½	3.56%	4.18%	3.21%	3.96%	1.05	722	n.s.
Stage 5A	24.66%	9.38%	18.79%	8.55%	7.75	722	.000
Stage 5B	7.15%	5.52%	5.78%	5.08%	3.07	722	.002
Stage 6	6.36%	4.87%	3.21%	3.87%	9.11	460*	.000
Meaningless	3.64%	3.76%	4.47%	3.58%	-2.73	722	.007
P%-Score	38.17%	12.12%	28.27%	11.71%	9.96	722	.000
D-Score	22.08	5.23	-	-	-	-	-

Mean Age   17 years, 8 months   18 years, 1 month

Note: All participants passed the standard DIT consistency check. The data for the USA are taken from Gielen et al. (1986b). With the exception of D-Scores, moral judgment scores are expressed in percentages. *=*df* adjusted for separate variance estimates.

Relationships between Educational Level and Moral Stage Scores

The DIT claims to measure the development of moral understanding. To investigate this claim, the moral stage scores of the Taiwanese students were correlated with their educational backgrounds. The backgrounds ranged from junior high school level to university level. Table 3 indicates the correlations separately for female students, male students, and all students. The important correlation between educational level and P%-Score was positive and statistically significant for both female and male students. The correlations between educational level and Stages 5B and 6 were also significant, but the correlation between educational level and Stage 5A failed to reach statistical significance for the female students. For the D-Score, the correlation was positive and significant for male students and the overall sample, but failed to reach significance for the female students. Correlations between educational level and Stages 2, 4, and 4½ were negative for both female and male students. No relationship existed between educational level and endorsement of Stage 3 arguments. The more highly educated students (especially males) were more likely than less educated students to endorse sophisticated sounding, yet meaningless moral arguments.

Table 3
Correlations between Educational Level and Stage Scores

	Females (N=330)	Males (N=191)	All (N=521)
Stage 2	-.098**	-.182***	-.133***
Stage 3	+.001	-.005	-.001
Stage 4	-.107**	-.216***	-.154***
Stage 4½ (A)	-.121**	-.117*	-.122***
Stage 5A	+.013	+.095*	+.057*
Stage 5B	+.113**	+.189***	+.144***
Stage 6	+.201***	+.242***	+.222***
Meaningless	+.102**	+.213***	+.141***
P% (Principled)	+.146	+.245***	+.198***
D	+.052	+.194***	+.122***

$*=p<.10$; $**=p<.05$; $***=p<.01$
All correlations are Pearson product-moment correlation coefficients.

Educational Level and P%-Score

Figure 1 depicts the relationship between educational level and P%-Scores. P%-Scores increased from the junior high school level to the senior high school level and on to the university/college level. Starting with the first year of college, the P%-Scores began to level off. To facilitate comparisons with other Chinese studies employing the DIT (see Discussion section), three groups of students were formed and their P%-Scores were established. The three groups included students attending junior high school (N=26), students attending senior high school (N=306), and university students (N=194). The mean P%-Scores were Mean=30.38 for junior high school students, Mean=36.80 for senior high school students, and Mean=41.35 for university students. University students received significantly higher P%-Scores than the senior high school students ($t[375]=4.06$, $p<.001$; *df* adjusted for heterogeneous variances) and the junior high school students ($t[218]=4.19$, $p<.001$). The senior high school students received higher P%-Scores than the junior high school students ($t[325]=2.80$, $p=.005$).

Figure 1
Educational Level and P%-Score (N=521)

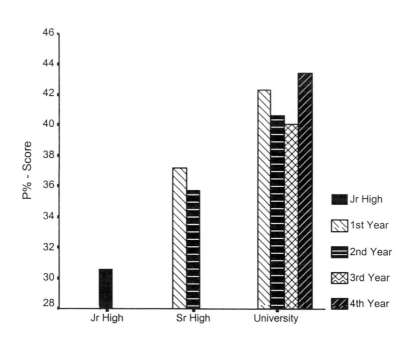

Gender Differences

Table 4 contains mean P%-Scores for female and male students grouped by three educational levels. The female students received higher P%-Scores than the male students at the senior high school and university levels. To establish more precise statistical comparisons between the moral judgment scores of female and male students, partial correlation coefficients controlling for age differences between the two sexes were computed. Female students received significantly higher P%-Scores ($r[503] = +.16$, $p < .001$ with age controlled), Stage 6 Scores ($r[503] = +.09$, $p = .002$ with age controlled), and Stage 5A Scores ($r[503] = +.14$, $p = .001$ with age controlled) than the male students. Female students received lower Stage 3 Scores ($r[503] = -.08$, $p < .04$) and M-Scores (Meaningless items; $r[503] = -.06$, $p < .08$) than the male students. There were no other significant differences in stage scores between the sexes.

Table 4
Average P%-Scores for Female and Male Students
at Three Levels of Education

Educational Level	Females (N=330)	Males (N=191)	All (N=521)
Junior High	-	30.38%	30.38%
Senior High	37.98%	34.62%	36.80%
University Students	42.15%	39.53%	41.35%

Correlations between Age and Moral Stage Scores

Correlations were also established between age and all moral stage scores. These correlations are depicted in Table 5 for female students, male students, and all students. The pattern of correlations between age and moral stage scores closely mirrored the pattern of correlations between educational level and moral stage scores. In other words, age and educational level appeared to influence moral stage scores in almost identical ways. The important P%-Score was positively correlated with age for both the female and male students, as were Stage 5B and Stage 6 Scores. Stage 2 Scores, Stage 4 Scores, and Stage 4½ Scores (males only) tended to decline as the age of the students increased. D-Scores increased significantly with age among male students, but not among female students.

Table 5
Correlations between Age and Stage Scores

	Females (N=329)	Males (N=191)	All (N=520)
Stage 2	-.107**	-.139**	-.119***
Stage 3	-.037	+.107*	+.002
Stage 4	-.105**	-.272***	-.170***
Stage 4½ (A)	-.024	-.116*	-.066*
Stage 5A	+.012	+.038	+.019
Stage 5B	+.105**	+.171***	+.129***
Stage 6	+.247***	+.194***	+.222***
Meaningless	+.078*	+.194***	+.124***
P%(Principled)	+.163***	+.176***	+.162***
D	+.050	+.176***	+.096**

$*=p<.10;$ $**=p<.05;$ $***=p<.01$
All correlations are Pearson product-moment correlation coefficients.

Correlations between Background Characteristics and the P%-Score

In order to establish possible connections between various background characteristics and moral judgment development, partial correlation coefficients between P%-Scores and the following variables were established: Father's and mother's occupation, father's and mother's education, family income, self reported social class, place of growing up, length of absence of a parent due to death or divorce/separation, number of brothers and sisters, and involvement in a variety of organizations. All of the partial correlation coefficients controlled for the effects of age. Many of the background characteristics were unrelated to P%-Scores. Thus, mother's occupation (r[507]=.02, n.s.), father's education (r[506]=.00, n.s.), mother's education (r[508]=.02, n.s.), family income (r[499]=.00, n.s.); place of growing up: village vs. small town vs. big city (r[516]= -.01, n.s.), number of sisters (r[516]=-.04, n.s.) were not related to the students' P%-Score. Two indicators of SES were weakly, but significantly related to the students' P%-Score: Father's occupation (r[491]=.074,

$p = .05$) and self reported social class ($r[499] = .073$, $p = .053$). Students reporting a large number of brothers appeared to receive slightly higher P%-Scores than students reporting fewer brothers ($r[516] = .06$, $p = .084$). Students reporting involvement in social organizations received higher P%-Scores than students reporting less involvement in social organizations ($r[513] = .08$, $p = .03$).

Correlations between Perceived Parental Behavior and the P%-Score

In order to establish possible connections between perceived parental behavior and moral judgment development, partial correlation coefficients between parental behavior scales and P%-Scores were computed separately for female and male students. The partial correlation coefficients controlled for age, since age had an independent influence upon P%-Scores. Table 6 contains these correlation coefficients. Most of the correlation coefficients were statistically insignificant and thus provided no support for the authors' experimental hypotheses. No significant associations were found between the overall quality of parental childrearing, the level of parental conflict, the fathers' overall level of acceptance and the students' moral judgment skills.

For female students only, mother's overall level of acceptance (Mother PARQ) and mother's warmth were negatively correlated with moral judgment development, while mother's aggression, indifference, and neglect were positively related to moral judgment development. Father's overall acceptance (Father-PARQ) and parental democracy were negatively related to the P%-Scores of female students ($p < .10$), while father's rejection tended to have a positive association with the P%-Scores of female students ($p < .10$). These surprising findings contradicted the authors' experimental hypotheses.

DISCUSSION

In our discussion, we will first focus on the moral reasoning scores obtained with the DIT in the present study, comparing them with moral reasoning scores from similar studies conducted in East Asia and elsewhere. Subsequently, the discussion will shift to a consideration of the results obtained with the parental behavior scales.

The overall distribution of moral reasoning scores in the present study resembles the distributions of moral reasoning scores previously found for high school and university students from Hong Kong, South Korea, and Taiwan. Table 7 summarizes the P%-Scores obtained in seven studies, including the present one. The table reports P%-Scores separately for junior high school students, senior high school students, and college/university students. The studies included in the table come from

Table 6
Partial Correlations between Perceived Parental
Behavior and P%-Score with Age Controlled

Parental Behavior Scales	Females (df=323-326)	Males (df=184-188)
Mother - PARQ	-.119**	+.036
Mother - Warmth	-.125**	-.021
Mother - Aggression	+.099**	-.060
Mother - Indifference	+.118**	+.017
Mother - Rejection	+.080*	-.052
Father - PARQ	-.052	-.030
Father - Warmth	+.080*	-.026
Father - Aggression	+.007	+.022
Father - Indifference	+.012	+.027
Father - Rejection	+.077*	+.082
Parents - Childrearing Quality	-.028	+.040
Parents - Democracy	-.071*	+.012
Parents - Autonomy	+.047	+.024
Parents - Acceptance	-.048	+.058
Parental Conflict	+.032	-.002
Parental Conflict - Childrearing	+.045	-.040
Parental Conflict - Finances	+.001	-.048
Parental Conflict - Family Activities	+.008	+.019

$*=p \leq .10$; $**=p \leq .05$; $***=p \leq .01$

Note: High scores on PARQ indicate high levels of overall acceptance. High scores on "Aggression" indicate high levels of aggression, etc.

Taiwan (Tsaing, 1980; Gendron, 1981; and the present study), Hong Kong (Hau, 1983; Ma, 1988a), South Korea (Park & Johnson, 1984), and the USA (Rest, 1986b). The data for the USA represent the composite results of a number of American studies. It should be noted that the seven studies summarized in Table 7 employed various versions, translations, and adaptations of the DIT.   The number of moral dilemmas included in the studies ranged from three to six.

Table 7
Distribution of P%-Scores in Seven Studies

COUNTRY	JUNIOR HIGH	SENIOR HIGH	COLLEGE/ UNIVERSITY	DIT VERSION EMPLOYED
TAIWAN (Present Study)	30.4%	36.8%	41.4%	5-story
TAIWAN (Tsaing, 1980)	20.4%	26.8%		5-story + 1 new story
TAIWAN (Gendron, 1981)	-	28.9% (Sample 1) 31.7% (Sample 2)	33.4% (Sample 1) 37.9% (Sample 2)	3-story
HONG KONG (Hau, 1983)	25.3%	29.3% (9-10th grade) 34.5% (11-12th grade)	37.9%	6-story
HONG KONG (Ma, 1988a)	-	28.1%	35.4%	4-story
SOUTH KOREA (Park & Johnson, 1984)	25% (6th grade) 30.2% (8th grade)	37.4% (11th grade)	41.5%	3-story
USA (Composite Sample - Rest, 1986)	21.9%	31.8%	42.3%	Mixed (?)

Table 7 shows that in all seven studies increasing levels of education are associated with increasing levels of the P%-Score.   This increase in P%-Scores is especially pronounced for the American composite sample.   In general, correlations between age or education and P%-Scores tend to be lower for Chinese samples (Gendron, 1981; Hau & Lew, 1985; Lei, 1981; Lin & Shan, 1987; Ma, 1980, 1985, 1988a; Tsaing [Shan], 1980; see also

Tables 3 and 5 for the present study) than for American samples (summarized in Rest, 1986b). This is *not* due to higher levels of principled reasoning in the American samples. In fact, P%-Scores for younger high school students from the East Asian societies tend to be as high or higher than the P%-Scores of corresponding American high school students. This is clearly the case for the present study (see Tables 2 and 7). The P%-Scores of Taiwanese high school students in the present study lie somewhat higher than the P%-Scores of Chinese students from Hong Kong and Taiwan obtained in previous studies. They resemble, however, quite closely the P%-Scores of South Korean students in Park and Johnson's (1984) study.

It has often been claimed that principled patterns of moral thinking, as understood by Kohlberg and Rest, merely reflect Western or more specifically North American ways of thinking. Kohlberg's and Rest's theories and methods are said to incorporate fundamental liberal, male, upper-class ethnocentric biases (Vine, 1986). In contrast, Chinese patterns of moral thinking have been characterized as situation centered and as lacking a concern for broad, absolutistic, universal principles (Bloom, 1977; Dien, 1982; Hsu, 1981). The results of the present study as well as those of previous studies conducted in Taiwan (Lei, 1994 employing the MJI) and South Korea (Park & Johnson, 1984 employing the DIT) do not support these generalizations. DIT and MJI scores indicating principled forms of moral reasoning are as high in the East Asian studies as in comparable North American studies (Edwards, 1981, 1986; Gielen & Markoulis, in press; Snarey, 1985; Moon, 1986). At the same time, studies employing the MJI or DIT in Third-World countries have usually found much lower moral reasoning scores than studies conducted in the USA, West Europe, or in East Asian societies influenced by Confucian and Neo-Confucian value systems (Gielen & Markoulis, in press). This suggests that for moral reasoning scores, the crucial distinction is *not* between Western and Non-Western cultures, but between complex modern, industrialized societies supporting rigorous educational institutions, and less complex, less industrialized societies supporting less demanding educational institutions (Gielen, Cruickshank, Johnston, Swanzey, & Avellani, 1986). In addition, it should be emphasized that modernized, Neo-Confucian ideologies appear to be quite able to support structurally advanced forms of moral reasoning in students from East Asian countries.

Bloom's (1977) and Dien's (1982) doubts about the applicability of Kohlbergian theories to the holistic, collectivistic, situationally oriented moral thinking of the Chinese people rest on several basic misunderstandings. These include a failure to distinguish between American individualism and autonomous moral principles, a failure to recognize the importance of moral autonomy in Confucian and Neo-Confucian thought, the underestimation of the importance of cooperation in cognitive-developmental accounts of moral reasoning, and the failure to distinguish between structural moral action schemes and reflective ethical philosophies.

Kohlberg's philosophical-psychological concept of moral autonomy does not at all coincide with rugged, masculine, rule-oriented American individualism.   Moral autonomy refers to an orientation towards internalized, shareable moral principles.   These principles reflect schemes of cooperation (Rest, 1983) rather than the arbitrary preoccupation with self-expression in the service of individualistic goals.   The very purpose of principled moral thinking is to create just solutions to moral problems based upon shareable values and ideal role-taking.

Moral autonomy (but not individualism) has traditionally been valued in Confucian and Neo-Confucian thought (Roetz, 1993).   The Confucian philosopher Tu (1984) has emphasized that moral growth, according to the inner logic of Confucian philosophy, includes both a deepening and a broadening process.   The broadening process leads from the self to an expanding universe of relationships: to the family, the community, the country, the world, and ultimately the universe.   The *chün-tzu* (the noble gentleman, the ideal moral person) identifies with "heaven, earth, and the myriad things."   The deepening process focuses upon moral transformation based upon *hsiu-shen* (self-cultivation), self-awareness, self-realization, and the integration of body, mind, heart and spirit.   In this broadening and deepening process, the *chün-tzu* is, above all, beholden to "heaven."   He is thus morally autonomous in relationship to society, but certainly not individualistic (Tu, 1984, 1985).   Chinese history includes a good number of moral heroes who chose to die rather than to give up their moral principles.   In this context the German sinologist Heiner Roetz (1993, 1996) has recently presented a detailed Kohlbergian analysis of Chinese philosophy during its Golden Age (i.e., during the 5th-3rd centuries B.C.E.).   In his difficult but fascinating book *Confucian Ethics of the Axial Age: A Reconstruction under the Aspect of the Breakthrough Towards Postconventional Thinking*, he demonstrates the postconventional features of much of classical Chinese philosophy during China's "Axial Age" (Jasper, 1949).   Given that Confucian and Neo-Confucian thought is regularly taught in Taiwan's schools and universities we should not be surprised that postconventional moral arguments are frequently endorsed by Taiwanese students.   It should be added that principled forms of moral reasoning can also be easily recognized in the ethical theories of some ancient as well as modern Hindu and Buddhist philosophers/theologians. The idea that Kohlberg's conception of principled moral thinking merely represents a manifestation of Western individualism (and nothing more) is a myth.

A further misunderstanding of Kohlbergian theories by Bloom (1977) and Dien (1982) is based upon their failure to differentiate moral reasoning from broad ethical and metaethical theorizing. Moral reasoning, as understood in the Kohlbergian tradition, refers to the coordination of mental action systems as they are applied to concrete moral dilemmas. In contrast, broad ethical and metaethical theorizing focuses on the reflective integration of general moral theories. Such theories may cover the nature of human beings, moral virtues, moral emotions, psychological processes leading to ethical behavior, the nature of morality as such, etc. Kohlbergian stage theories attempt to identify the deep structure of mental schemes, while Confucian and other philosophical systems attempt to construct broad ethical and metaethical theories. These two perspectives on morality cannot be reduced to each other, although many critics of moral stage theories and cross-cultural research on moral reasoning continue to confuse the two perspectives.

We now turn to a discussion of gender differences. Gilligan (1982) has forcefully argued that Kohlbergian theories and methods misrepresent the moral thinking of women, downgrading them to the status of children. To evaluate some of her claims, Walker (1984, 1991) has reviewed a large number of North American studies employing Kohlberg's MJI. He found little evidence for Gilligan's much publicized contentions. Thoma (1986) employed meta and secondary analyses in order to trace gender differences on the DIT. His study integrated the results from 56 samples with more than 6,000 North American female and male students. Contrary to Gilligan's claims, female respondents at all age levels received slightly higher P%-Scores than male respondents do. The present study extends Thoma's findings to Chinese students from Taiwan and again finds somewhat higher P%-Scores for female students. Similar results have also been reported by Tsaing (1980) for Taiwanese high school students, by Hau (1983) for Chinese students from Hong Kong, and by Park and Johnson (1984) for students from South Korea. Ma (1988a), however, failed to find clear gender differences for Chinese students from Hong Kong. The evidence from East Asia, then, suggests that on the whole the DIT tends to slightly favor female students over male students. This conclusion supports Thoma's (1986) findings and contradicts some of Gilligan's (1982) claims.

The present study found only fairly weak (though significant) correlations between age/education and P%-Scores and D-Scores. As Tables 3 and 5 demonstrate, this finding is due to two major reasons. On the one hand, Stage 5A Scores are only very weakly related to education, and they are unrelated to age. Since Stage 5A Scores contribute importantly to P%-Scores and D-Scores, this lack of a clear relationship between Stage 5A and age/education also weakens correlations between P%-Scores, D-Scores, and age/education. On the other hand, Stage 3 is unrelated to age/education, while Stage 4 is negatively related to age/education. This again weakens associations between the D-Score and age/education. The patterns of correlations described in Tables 3 and 5 do not always conform to Rest's theoretical predictions. The patterns suggest that the DIT does not work as "cleanly" in Taiwan as in the USA. The developmental status of the DIT in Taiwan appears to be weaker than the developmental status of the DIT in the USA. More work on Chinese adaptations of the DIT needs to be done (Gielen, 1987; Lin & Shan, 1987).

The present study did not establish any clear relationships between perceived parental behavior and the development of moral reasoning skills in Taiwanese students. Most relationships tested in the present study were statistically insignificant. Furthermore, the few obtained relationships between parental behavior and the moral reasoning scores of female students were weak and contradicted our experimental hypotheses. Three previous studies from Taiwan have attempted to link parental behavior with students' moral reasoning scores. Tsaing (1980) used a forerunner of the present Chinese version of the DIT. He failed to find any clear relationships between parental behavior and students' moral reasoning scores. More recently, Cheng (1987) attempted to connect parental behavior to students' moral reasoning scores, as measured by Kohlberg's recent version of the MJI. He found that students reporting inconsistent childrearing practices by their parents also received lower moral reasoning scores than students reporting more consistent parental childrearing practices. However, his other findings concerning parental attitudes and students' moral reasoning scores were unclear. Su (1975) based her work on Hoffman and Saltzstein's (1967) conceptualizations of parental discipline and moral development. She distinguished between a less mature external moral judgment orientation and a more mature internal judgment orientation. In her study, lower-class boys reporting power assertive discipline by their mothers were relatively externally oriented. However, the same relationship did not hold true for lower-class girls, middle-class boys, or middle-class girls. Parental childrearing styles based upon love withdrawal or induction (= reasoning with the adolescent) did not have significant effects upon the adolescents' moral orientation.

The three studies cited above and the present study employed a considerable variety of methods to link parental behavior to adolescents' or children's moral reasoning scores. The methods included two Chinese adaptations of Rest's DIT, a Chinese adaptation of Kohlberg's MJI, and a

Chinese adaptation of Hoffman's external-internal orientation measure. The studies also employed a variety of childrearing scales, including a set of scales specifically developed in Taiwan. In all four studies, Chinese researchers were involved. Yet in spite of the variety of approaches and adaptations, the following conclusion appears to be inescapable: At present, there exists no convincing scientific evidence that can link the behavior and attitudes of Taiwanese parents in a systematic manner to the moral reasoning scores of their children. One may ask: Is this failure to find systematic links a failure of our theories, a failure of our methodologies, or does it actually reflect reality?

We will shortly discuss two possible reasons why various indices of parental behavior have failed to correlate with adolescent moral reasoning scores. The first explanation suggests that the DIT and the MJI measure changes of moral reasoning that occur mainly due to the adolescents' exposure to extra-familial societal institutions, such as schools, the mass media, peer groups, etc. In the present study, parental characteristics such as family income, mother's education and occupation, father's education and occupation, etc. contributed little or nothing to the adolescents' moral reasoning scores. In other words, neither general parental characteristics such as SES, nor specific parental childrearing behaviors were related in a systematic fashion to adolescent moral reasoning scores, because parental influences were overridden by extra-familial influences.

The second explanation suggests that structures of adolescent moral reasoning will directly influence adolescent perceptions of family members and the self. Hayes (1987) has shown that individuals employing more concrete levels of moral reasoning identify more strongly with, and attribute more influence to, familial figures when compared to individuals using more abstract moral judgements. This explanation suggests that adolescents with more advanced moral judgment scores are also more critical (objective?) of both family members and the self. Therefore, studies such as the present one may depend too much on perceptual measures of parental behavior rather than observational measures of parent-adolescent interaction sequences.

BIBLIOGRAPHY

Ahmed, R. A., Gielen, U. P., & Avellani, J. (1987). Perceptions of parental behavior and the development of moral reasoning in Sudanese students. In Ç. Kagitçibasi (Ed.), *Growth and progress in cross-cultural psychology* (pp. 106-206). Lisse, Holland: Swets Zeitlinger.
Bloom, A. (1977). Two dimensions of moral reasoning: Social principledness and social humanism in cross-cultural perspective.

Journal of Social Psychology, 101, 29-44.

Cheng, B. S. (1987). *Relationships between moral reasoning, parental attitudes, and personality characteristics.* Unpublished master's thesis, Chinese Culture University, Taipei, Taiwan (In Chinese).

Cheng, H. W. (1979). *A Chinese version of the Standard Form Moral Judgment Interview.* Unpublished manuscript, National Taiwan University, Taipei, Taiwan (In Chinese).

Confucius. (1979). *The analects (Lun yü).* Translated by D. C. Lau. London, UK: Penguin.

Coopersmith, S. (1967). *The antecedents of self-esteem.* San Francisco, CA: Freeman.

Daedalus. (1975). *Wisdom, revelation, and doubt: Perspectives on the First Millennium B.C.* (Vol. *104* [2]).

Dickinson, M. (1979). *A study of the development of moral judgment in relationship to commonly used sample characteristics and family factors in an Australian setting.* Unpublished doctoral dissertation, Macquarie University, North Ryde, Australia.

Dien, D. S. F. (1982). A Chinese perspective on Kohlberg's theory of moral development. *Developmental Review, ?,* 331-341.

Eckensberger, L. H., & Zimba, R. (1997). The development of moral judgment. In W. Berry, P. R. Dasen, & T. S. Saraswathi (Eds.), *Handbook of cross-cultural psychology.* Vol. 2. *Basic processes and human development* (pp. 299-338). Needham Heights, MA: Allyn & Bacon.

Edwards, C. P. (1981). The comparative study of the development of moral judgment and reasoning. In R. H. Munroe, R. L. Munroe, & B. B. Whiting (Eds.), *Handbook of cross-cultural human development* (pp. 501-528). New York: Garland Publishers.

Edwards, C. P. (1986). Cross-cultural research on Kohlberg's stages. The basis for consensus. In S. Mogdil & C. Mogdil (Eds.), *Lawrence Kohlberg: Consensus and controversy* (pp. 419-430). London: Falmer Press.

Gendron, L. (1981). *An empirical study of the Defining Issues Test in Taiwan.* Unpublished manuscript, Fujen Catholic University, Hsinchuang, Taiwan.

Gielen, U. P. (1987). Conference report: The Sino-American Colloquium on Moral Cognition. *Moral Education Forum, 12* (1), 27-32.

Gielen, U. P. (1990). Some recent work on moral values, reasoning, and education in Chinese societies. *Moral Education Forum, 15* (2), 3-22.

Gielen, U. P. (1991). Research on moral reasoning. In L. Kuhmerker with U. P. Gielen & R. L. Hayes, *The Kohlberg legacy for the helping professions* (pp. 39-60). Birmingham, AL: R.E.P. Books.

Gielen, U. P. (1996). Moral reasoning in cross-cultural perspective: A review of Kohlbergian research. *World Psychology*, *2* (3-4), 313-333.

Gielen, U. P., Ahmed, R. A., & Avellani, J. (1992). The development of moral reasoning and perceptions of parental behavior in students from Kuwait. *Moral Education Forum*, *17* (3), 20-37.

Gielen, U. P., Cruickshank, H., Johnston, A., Swanzey, B., & Avellani, J. (1986). The development of moral reasoning in Belize, Trinidad-Tobago and the USA. *Behavior Science Research*, *20* (1-4), 178-207.

Gielen, U. P., & Markoulis, D. C. (in press). Preference for principled moral reasoning: A developmental and cross-cultural perspective. In L.L. Adler & U.P. Gielen (Eds.), *Cross-cultural topics in psychology* (2nd ed.).

Gielen, U. P., Markoulis, D. C., & Avellani, J. (1994). Development of moral reasoning and perceptions of parental behavior in Greek students. In A. L. Comunian & U. P. Gielen (Eds.), *Advancing psychology and its applications: International perspectives* (pp. 107-124). Milan: FrancoAngeli.

Gielen, U., Swanzey, B., Avellani, J., & Kramer, J. (1986). *Moral judgment and parental behavior*. Unpublished manuscript, St. Francis College, Brooklyn, N.Y.

Gilligan, C. (1982). *In a different voice. Psychological theory and women's development*. Cambridge, MA: Harvard University Press.

Hau, K. T. (1983). *A cross-cultural study of a moral judgment test (DIT)*. Unpublished master's thesis, The Chinese University of Hong Kong, Shatin, N.T., Hong Kong.

Hau, K. T., & Lew, W. J. (1985). *Moral development of Chinese students in Hong Kong*. Unpublished manuscript, The Chinese University of Hong Kong, Shatin, N.T., Hong Kong.

Hayes, G. E. (1987). *The relationships between moral reasoning and sources of moral authority*. Unpublished doctoral dissertation, Columbia University.

Hoffman, M. (1970). Moral development. In P. H. Mussen (Ed.), *Carmichael's handbook of child psychology* (Vol. 2, pp. 261-360). New York: Wiley.

Hoffman, M. L., & Saltzstein, H. D. (1967). Parent discipline and the child's moral development. *Journal of Personality and Social Psychology*, *5*, 45-57.

Holstein, C. (1972). The relation of children's moral judgment level to that of their parents and to communication patterns in the family. In R. Smart & M. Smart (Eds.), *Readings in child development and relationships*. New York: MacMillan.

Hsu, F. (1981). *Americans and Chinese. Passage to differences* (3rd ed.).

Honolulu: The University Press of Hawaii.

Jaspers, K. (1949). *Vom Ursprung und Ziel der Geschichte* [*About the origin and goal of history*]. Munich: Piper. Translated by Michael Bullock as: *The origin and goal of history* (1953; New Haven, CT: Yale University Press).

Kohlberg, L. (1984). *The psychology of moral development*. San Francisco, CA: Harper and Row.

Lei, T. (1981). The development of moral, political and legal reasoning in Chinese societies. Unpublished master's thesis, University of Minnesota, Minneapolis, MN.

Lei, T. (1984 August). *Socialization and moral development in Taiwan*. Paper presented at the Conference on Child Socialization and Mental Health: The Case of Chinese Culture. Honolulu: East-West Center.

Lei, T. (1994). Being and becoming moral in a Chinese culture: Unique or universal? *Cross-Cultural Research, 28* (1), 58-91.

Lin, P. C., & Shan, P. W. J. (1987, January). *Chinese translation and explanation of the DIT*. Paper presented at the Sino-American Colloquium, Taipei, Taiwan. (In Chinese; abbreviated English version available).

Lind, G. (1986). Cultural differences in moral judgment competence? A study of West and East European university students. *Behavior Science Research, 20* (1-4), 208-225.

Ma, H. K. (1980). *A study of the moral development of adolescents*. Unpublished master's thesis, University of London, London, United Kingdom.

Ma, H. K. (1985). Consistency of stage structure in objective moral judgment across different samples. *Psychological Reports, 57,* 987-990.

Ma, H. K. (1988a). Objective moral judgment in Hong Kong, Mainland China, and England. *Journal of Cross-Cultural Psychology, 19* (1), 78-95.

Ma, H. K. (1988b). The Chinese perspectives on moral judgment development. *International Journal of Psychology, 23,* 201-227.

Mencius. (1970). *Mencius*. (Translated by D. C. Lau). London, UK: Penguin.

Miao, E. (1982, September). *Report of Taiwan, Republic of China. Toward a better quality of life: A cultural perspective*. Paper presented at Interim Conference of the Federal Asian Women's Associations, Singapore.

Moon, Y. L. (1986). A review of cross-cultural studies on moral judgment development using the Defining Issues Test. *Behavior Science Research, 20* (1-4), 147-177.

Parikh, B. S. (1975). *Moral judgment development and its relation to family environmental factors in Indian and American upper middle class families.* Unpublished doctoral dissertation, Boston University, Boston, MA.

Park, J. Y., & Johnson, R. C. (1984). Moral development in rural and urban Korea. *Journal of Cross-Cultural Psychology, 15,* 35-46.

Rest, J. (1979). *Development in judging moral issues.* University of Minnesota Press, Minneapolis, MN.

Rest, J. (1983). Morality. In P. Mussen (Ed.), *Handbook of child psychology* (Vol. 4, pp. 556-629). New York: Wiley.

Rest, J. (1986a). *Moral development: Advances in Research and theory.* New York: Praeger.

Rest, J. (1986b). *Manual for the Defining Issues Test: An objective test of moral judgment development* (3rd ed.). Minneapolis, MN: Minnesota Moral Research Projects.

Roetz, H. (1993). *Confucian ethics of the axial age: A reconstruction under the aspect of the breakthrough towards postconventional thinking.* Albany, NY: SUNY Press.

Roetz, H. (1996). Kohlberg and Chinese moral philosophy. *World Psychology, 2* (3-4), 335-363.

Rohner, R. (1975). *They love me, they love me not. A worldwide study of the effects of parental acceptance-rejection.* New Haven, CT: HRAF Press.

Rohner, R. (1984). *Handbook for the study of parental acceptance and rejection.* Storrs, CT: University of Connecticut, Center for the Study of Parental Acceptance and Rejection.

Schwarz, J. C., & Getter, H. (1980). Parental conflict and dominance in late adolescent maladjustment: A triple interaction model. *Journal of Abnormal Psychology, 89,* 573-580.

Snarey, J. (1985). Cross-cultural universality of social-moral development: A critical review of Kohlbergian research. *Psychological Bulletin, 97,* 202-232.

Snarey, J., & Keljo, K. (1991). In a *Gemeinschaft* voice: The cross-cultural expansion of moral development theory. In W. Kurtines & J. Gewirtz (Eds.), *Handbook of moral behavior and development: Theory* (Vol. 1, pp. 395-424). Hillsdale, NJ: Erlbaum.

Speicher-Dubin, B. (1982). *Relationships between parent moral judgment and family interaction: A correlational study.* Unpublished doctoral dissertation, Harvard University, Cambridge, MA.

Su, C. W. (1975). Parental childrearing practices as related to moral behavior in adolescence. *Acta Psychologica Taiwanica, 17,* 109-124 (In Chinese, with English summary).

Thoma, S. J. (1986). Estimating gender differences in the comprehension and preference of moral issues. *Developmental Review, 6,* 165-180.

Thorlindsson, T. (1978). *Social organization, role-taking, elaborated language and moral judgment in an Icelandic setting.* Unpublished doctoral dissertation, University of Iowa, Iowa City.

Tsaing (Shan), P. W. J. (1980). *Moral judgment development and familial factors.* Unpublished master's thesis, National Taiwan University, Taipei, Taiwan (In Chinese).

Tu, W. M. (1984). *Confucian ethics today: The Singapore Challenge.* Singapore: Federal Publications.

Tu, W. M. (1985). *Confucian thought: Selfhood as creative transformation.* Albany, NY: State University of New York Press.

Vine, I. (1986). Moral maturity in sociocultural perspective: Are Kohlberg's stages universal? In S. Modgil & C. Modgil (Eds.), *Lawrence Kohlberg: Consensus and controversy* (pp. 431-450). Philadelphia, CA: The Falmer Press.

Walker, L. J. (1984). Sex differences in the development of moral reasoning: A critical review. *Child Development, 55,* 677-691.

Walker, L. J. (1991). Sex differences in moral reasoning. In W. M. Kurtines & J. L. Gewirtz (Eds.), *Handbook of moral behavior and development* (Vol. 2, pp. 333-364). Hillsdale, NJ: Erlbaum.

AUTHOR NOTES

The authors are grateful to the many students from the Chinese Culture University, Tam Kang University, National Chung Shing University, Taiwan National Normal University and four high schools who so patiently filled out a lengthy questionnaire. We also which to acknowledge our indebtedness to our late colleague Joseph Avellani, who performed many statistical analyses for our research report. The research was supported by much appreciated grants from the Pacific Cultural Foundation (T'ai-pei, Taiwan, R.O.C.) and the H. F. Guggenheim Foundation to the first author.

SECTION VIII: APPLICATIONS OF COGNITIVE-DEVELOPMENTAL THEORY: PROMOTING ROLE-TAKING AND REFLECTION

Historically, the cognitive-developmental approach originated in the work of three American scholars, the philosopher-scientist James Mark Baldwin, the educational philosopher-psychologist John Dewey, and the sociologist George Herbert Mead. It was then taken up by the Swiss epistemologist Jean Piaget who, in turn, strongly influenced the work of the American psychologist-philosopher-educator Lawrence Kohlberg. On his part, Kohlberg had a guiding influence on a younger generation of scholars including Georg Lind, Uwe P. Gielen, Alan Reiman, Sharon Nodie Oja, and Sandra DeAngelis Peace. Their work is represented in Sections VII and VIII.

The three chapters included in Section VIII share a common concern for the application of Kohlbergian and Vygotskyian ideas to the training of teachers, school counselors, psychologists, and social workers. Consequently, the authors adopt an approach that integrates a concern for social role-taking with an emphasis on active reflection through the use of diaries, log books, dialogue between mentors and novice teachers or counselors, and so on.

Alan Reiman in *Promoting Reflective Practice within a Cognitive-structural Framework: Theory, Research, and Practice* examines reflection and developmental principles within a Vygotskyian framework (guided reflection and the zone of proximal development, activities as mediated through tools); reflection and development principles within a Piagetian framework (equilibrium and disequilibrium); and cognitive-structural growth for adults, presenting models of intervention such as guided reflection based on written discourse. He discusses the strengths and limitations of written reflective discourse from a cross-cultural perspective and outlines the implications for cross-cultural and interdisciplinary research and practice. Helping activities such as teaching, monitoring, and tutoring requirements are suggested. He argues that reflection must be adaptive and differentiated according to the needs of the learner. In his research review, the author establishes a significant basis for the claim that teachers are neither born nor made, but that they instead develop by adopting new social roles and by engaging in higher-order guided reflection. An evolving model of role-taking and reflection is summarized with special emphasis given to how guided reflection can promote structural cognitive growth in the conceptual, moral, and ego-development domains. Attention is given to the "zone of proximal development" and how cognitive disequilibrium is mediated through the reflective process.

In her chapter, *The Unique Place of Role-taking and Reflection in Collaborative Action Research,* Sharon Nodie Oja reviews recent social role-taking/reflection research with experienced teachers who have assumed the complex new role of "teacher as action researcher." The author focuses on action research as a better method to supervise beginners by helping them explore their developmental needs and by challenging them to reach new levels of growth in a supportive but demanding environment. Action research can provide extraordinary opportunities for intensive analysis of and reflection on the teaching/learning enterprise. Cognitive-developmental theories together with a variety of research studies suggest that collaborative action research can lead to effective programs for promoting the personal and professional growth of novice teachers who become more responsive to the concerns and developmental needs of their students.

Sandra DeAngelis Peace, in *Role-taking and Reflection: Promoting the Development of School Counselors, Psychologists, and Social Workers as Supervisors* describes an educational program that prepares experienced school counselors, psychologists, and social workers for their new role as supervisors. The program aims at promoting the cognitive development of professionals and their behavioral competence. A summary of quantitative results and qualitative data from the program's structured activities for guided reflection is presented. The author outlines the rationale for training experienced counselors in their new role as supervisors with a focus on the development rather than the evaluation of new, less experienced supervisors. Promoting higher levels of cognitive, ego, and moral development opens up opportunities for counselors to bridge cultural divisions and social and class inequities, and enables them to advocate for a fairer school climate.

It is interesting to compare the cognitive-developmentally oriented chapters in this volume with some of the other contributions. Whereas a good part of modern cross-cultural psychology contains a relativistic flavor, the Kohlbergian chapters are based on a developmental stage model that provides clear directions for psychological and moral growth. The research reviewed in the chapters suggests that this growth can be seen not only on various paper-and-pencil-tests, but also in the professional activities of teachers, school counselors, psychologists, and social workers. While the relevant research evidence stems mostly from western countries, there are signs that the cognitive-developmental model with its emphasis on educational and psychological action research may in some form be suitable for application in many nonwestern countries. Consequentially, there are now journals specifically publishing action research for a worldwide audience of researchers-practitioners. A future challenge is to integrate cultural perspectives into action research so as to achieve a better match between cultural prescriptions, societal realities, and developmentally oriented training programs.

PROMOTING REFLECTIVE PRACTICE
WITHIN A COGNITIVE-STRUCTURAL FRAMEWORK:
THEORY, RESEARCH, AND PRACTICE

Alan J. Reiman
North Carolina State University–Raleigh, U.S.A.

INTRODUCTION

Reflective practice, which has received attention in recent years from psychologists and educators (Copeland & Birmingham, 1993; Harrington & Hathaway, 1994; Kitchener & King, 1994; Schon, 1987; Zeichner & Liston, 1987) is increasingly recognized as a central process and benchmark disposition of the teacher as she or he engages in the teaching/learning process. Yet, as Copeland and Birmingham (1993) point out in their review, the "movement" in education is "in danger of being drawn beyond our knowledge base to the employment of practices that are founded only in assumptions, rhetoric, and belief in what should be" (p. 347). The purposes of this article are to summarize important elements of Vygotsky's theory and Piaget's theory as they relate to reflection and praxis, to present a cognitive-structural framework for guiding reflection and role-taking, to synthesize recent research that has applied and extended the guided reflection and action framework, to review strengths and limitations of the action reflection framework from a cross-cultural perspective, and to suggest implications for cross-cultural and interdisciplinary research and practice.

Engaging in reflective practice involves a process of problem solving and reconstructing meaning. Reflecting upon one's experiences permits new learning to occur. In its absence one runs the risk of relying on routinized teaching and stabilized development. Reflective teaching means the ability to analyze the process of what one is doing while simultaneously adapting one's practice so that it best matches the needs of students. Thus, it connotes a conceptually complex, ethical, and flexible person who can engage in social perspective taking and who can consider alternative viewpoints.

Considered a milestone skill for professional practice (Schon, 1987), reflection is not, however, necessarily automatic. In fact, ever since Dewey (1933), at least, educators and psychologists have grappled with the problems of how to learn from experience, and how to identify experiences that are educative. The difficulty is the sophisticated and subtle problem of how to extract complex meaning from experience. Earlier intervention programs had shown that conceptual complexity determines how deeply persons can both perceive and analyze (Oja & Sprinthall, 1978). In fact, it reminds one of Perry's opening chapter (1970) in which he describes college students at three levels of complexity with widely differing interpretations of the same test question. Obviously the examination question was the same but the ability to interpret the meaning was governed by the level of complexity of the perceiver. Thus, a current challenge and question for educators and psychologists interested in promoting development is the creation and testing of interventions that can guide reflection according to the needs of the learner. Just as instruction can be adapted to the different needs of students, so reflection needs to be encouraged, differentiated, and guided according to the learning and developmental needs of the adult learners as they engage in significant new roles (Sprinthall, Reiman, & Thies-Sprinthall, 1996).

REFLECTION AND DEVELOPMENTAL PRINCIPLES WITHIN A VYGOTSKIAN FRAMEWORK

Vygotsky's work (1986) has received increasing attention in recent years but has received little attention in the reflection literature (Copeland & Birmingham, 1993). Among the interpreters of Vygotsky's work three of the most prominent are Wertsch (1985), Kozulin (1990), and Cole (1996). However, there are many other scholars who have made significant contributions to a large body of theoretical and empirical research that has addressed a broad range of topics related to psychological, sociological, and educational issues. Volumes edited by Rogoff and Lave (1984), Moll (1990), Wertsch, Rio, and Alvarez (1995), and Wozniak and Fischer (1993), contain the work of many of these scholars. Once referred to as "the Mozart of Psychology" (Toulmin, 1981), it should be noted that Vygotsky's work would have undergone further development and elaboration if he had lived longer. For example, although Vygotsky studied children's concept formation and development, he never extended his theory to the adult learner. However, his intentions for the future were to develop successful methods of instruction across the life-span.

Interdependence of Language and Thought

At the core of all of Vygotsky's work was his belief in the primacy of culture in shaping development and, in particular, the importance of language in mediating thought. Words are the means through which thought (and consciousness) is formed and reified. Since words are dynamic rather than static, the relationship of thought to word constantly changes, undergoing a continual process from thought to word and word to thought. "The relation between thought and word is a living process; thought is born through words. A word devoid of thought is a dead thing and a thought unembodied in words remains a shadow" (Vygotsky, 1986,

p. 255). Luria and Yudovich (1959) note that speech plays a decisive role in the formation of mental processes.

Most importantly, Vygotsky recognized that a person may have an unconscious understanding of a concept before being able to express it in language. Concepts are formed, he believed, not by an interplay of associations or by repeated experience but by an intellectual construction. Putting things into words centers attention, clarifies thinking, provides a means of symbolizing thought, and is an integral part of the process of concept formation. The development of conscious awareness through the use of language propels thinking forward toward conceptual understanding. Thus, the construction of meaning requires personal activity by students as they acquire competence across a variety of developmental domains.

Applying Vygotsky's concept to a concrete example in teaching and teacher education, we can take the word motivation as a case in point. Motivation probably has a narrower meaning for the undergraduate student who has just begun his or her preparation to become a teacher than for the instructor; the meaning of the word, however, changes as the student interacts with the faculty and the students, and the concept of motivation gradually acquires a larger and more complex meaning closer to the one held by the instructor. The student will learn that motivation can be intrinsic or extrinsic, that it is affected by teacher's pedagogical decisions, home, and students' locus of control, and that self-determination or competence motivation may actually grow and develop over time. The change in the understanding of the meaning of the word is therefore inseparable from conceptual development. The relationship between the Vygotskian principle of language mediating thought and reflection is direct. The pedagogy of reflection and keeping journals can therefore frame language in new ways and promote deeper understanding in the student.

Guided Reflection and the Zone of Proximal Development

Vygotsky conceived instruction as interaction with adults or more advanced peers, believing the interaction to be essential for development. In contrast to Piaget, who believed that instruction does not influence development but must wait on it or, in Piaget's words, "development explains learning" (Piaget, 1967, p. 171), Vygotsky submits that teaching is a form of "support and challenge" that leads development. Within this perspective, he articulated a "zone of proximal development (ZPD)" within which instruction is most productive. In Vygotsky's words, the ZPD is:

> ...the distance between the actual developmental level as determined by independent problem solving and the level of potential development as determined through problem solving

under adult guidance or in collaboration with more capable peers (Vygotsky, 1978, p. 86). And the ZPD is bi-directional. Although the more capable person usually provides assistance in the co-construction of a child's or colleague's zone of proximal development, there are instances when the child or colleague provides assistance in the co-construction of a zone of proximal development for the more capable peer. But Vygotsky's emphasis was always on the idea that development comes about through social interaction.

Davydov (1995), a prominent Vygotsky scholar, describes the social interaction as a true collaboration between persons, in which the teacher guides, directs, and encourages a student's activity and reflection. This should not be confused with forcing or dictating the teacher's will on students. Thus, the zone of proximal development and Vygotsky's explication of the role of language in development has implications for the study of guided reflection and professional discourse. An instructor (or peers) must provide new information that is just beyond the current preferred system of problem solving. Thus the word guided, in guided reflection, implies active consideration of persons' ZPD or current preferred ways of solving complex problems.

Activity is Mediated through Tools

Because Vygotsky theorized that teaching/learning and upbringing assume personal activity and collaborative activity by students, the tools or processes that promote such activity become important. Wartofsky (1979) proposes several kinds of tools that mediate activity or experience. From his perspective, hammers, pencils, telephones, journals, microcomputers, and telecommunication networks are examples of primary tools which enable one to interact with others and to modify the environment. When a student (or students) uses telecommunications, writing, or dialogue journals to formulate thoughts and makes explicit what one is learning or what one knows, he or she is constructing personal meanings and explanations that lead to a heightened level of consciousness about what he or she knows. Subsequently, knowledge domains are given richer and more deepened structures, and they are more retrievable for transfer in other contexts (Davydov, 1995).

Secondary tools include language, ideas, complex new experiences, and modes of action like coaching. If language is the "tool of tools," carrying the cultural code for tool use (Wartofsky, 1979), complex new roles are like a "tool box" providing an array of personal activities that can shape development. George Herbert Mead's (1934) concept of social role-taking suggested that complex new social role-taking experiences could positively affect human growth. Such role-taking was a bridge, a necessary condition leading to conceptual or moral growth. Thus, a complex new experience is an example of a secondary tool. However, as research suggests, when the new experience involves "helping others and taking the perspective of others," it becomes a very powerful and complex activity that can promote learning and development across a variety of professions, as well as a variety of interpersonal and intrapersonal domains (Oja & Sprinthall, 1978; Peace, 1992; Reiman & Thies-Sprinthall, 1993). For example, selecting a complex helping experience in a real world context like tutoring or mentoring, the new complex helping role (action) precedes and shapes the intellectual consciousness (reflection) that grows out of it.

REFLECTION AND DEVELOPMENTAL PRINCIPLES
WITHIN A PIAGETIAN FRAMEWORK

In contrast to Vygotsky, Piagetian thought is characterized by the view that the driving force in development is internal. For Piaget maturation was the central factor in development while for Vygotsky the social world was central. Piaget recognized social-linguistic interaction as an important factor in the development of knowledge (i.e., equilibration and person-environment interactions), but only if cognitive structures necessary for assimilation were already present. Piaget's view was that the mechanisms for development reside within the child and that learning is subordinated to development (Piaget, 1972; Flavell, 1992).

Equilibration and Disequilibrium

The first element of Piaget's theory that has implications for reflection and subsequent development is the focus on internally driven mental activity. Piaget submitted that persons can only know the world through mental activity that organizes and transforms their perceptions. That is, each individual must construct knowledge and meaning for himself or herself. The construction of meaning requires internal changes in mental structures (equilibration) as new experiences are encountered. Piaget called this change process equilibration because he thought new experiences forced disequilibrium (cognitive dissonance) in the functioning of mental structures that subsequently motivate the person to make the structure more complex and more applicable to the introduced abstraction.

The conception of psychological adaptation described by Piaget includes the process called assimilation, which involves trying to make the characteristics of a situation fit existing action patterns. At the same time, one may adjust those patterns to the unfamiliar characteristic of the new experience. This process involves accommodation, a bending of the existing structure in an attempt to take account of new aspects of an object or situation. Piaget argued that assimilation and accommodation work together and are normally in balance in successful intellectual acts. However, when one encounters a complex experience, the balance is upset, thus causing disequilibrium. To reestablish equilibrium, the person's effort to accommodate the existing mental structure to the additional dimension must become balanced with the assimilation of the problem to the existing scheme. This new equilibrium can only be established when the "deep mental structure" has itself been enlarged.

The implications of Piaget's concept of equilibration for reflection are direct. For example, if an instructor requires students to engage in a more complex new helping role with greater responsibility, disequilibrium results. And the disequilibrium or knowledge perturbation includes stress. In fact, the author has found that structural growth through accommodation does not come cheaply for adults. The feelings of personal "loss" can be significant as young adults move to more complex levels of development. In fact, giving up an "old friend" of one's current preferred method of problem solving has been greatly neglected in the literature (Sprinthall, Reiman, & Thies-Sprinthall, 1993). Practicing "developmental responsiveness," an instructor who uses journals or computer conferencing to encourage reflection and dialogue, must "read and flex" (Hunt, 1976) his or her reflective responses to the student's zone of proximal development, offering support and acknowledgment of feelings of stress, yet not eliminating the challenge.

Matching and Mismatching

Concepts related to Piaget's theory of equilibration are matching and graduated mismatching (Hunt, 1976). The instructor, hoping to guide reflection, must skillfully match and mismatch written responses according to the unique needs of the student or adult. Matching means "starting where the learner is." Conversely, "mismatching" implies providing additional challenge. For example, if a novice teacher writes in his or her journal about a proposed lesson, and the instructor who reads the journal entry notes that the novice teacher has neglected to consider the implications of a lesson on student learning, a written response to the student might include several questions and/or directions that require the novice teacher to account for the learning of students in the creation of lessons. The challenge for the instructor is knowing when to support (match) and when to challenge (mismatch). This process will be discussed shortly as it relates to guided reflection, and it is the most complex pedagogical requirement of our system.

Level of Complexity as a Predictor of Behavior

A final element from the Piagetian perspective is the assumption that cognitive development proceeds in stages or plateaus that are universal and predictable. Thus, when planning instruction, designing curriculum, or guiding written or oral social discourse, one must take into account the developmental level of students when deciding which concepts are appropriate for students. In contrast to Vygotsky, neither previous experience, the social context, nor individual interests are thought to override the primacy of the person's cognitive level or stage in determining what can be learned, and what should be instructed (Piaget, 1972). Cautions to this interpretation are that levels of complexity can vary across a series of domains, that persons in a state of disequilibrium will appear to be at less complex levels, and that predictions must be based on repeated and careful observations.

COGNITIVE-STRUCTURAL GROWTH FOR ADULTS, OR IS HIGHER BETTER?

Over the past twenty years there have been a series of studies and meta-analyses which validate this question, yet only under certain circumstances. For example, Blasi (1980) has shown a steady positive relationship between moral levels of development and moral behavior in a meta-analysis of some 80 studies. Other reviews by Rest and Narváez (1994), Lind (1993), and Oser (1994) report consistently positive relationships across a variety of ages and professions. In each case, the task, providing help to another person or persons in a humane atmosphere where the goal is to enhance the other persons' growth toward autonomy, requires higher levels of complexity by the professional. Teachers who process experience more complexly have a greater ability to "read and flex" with pupils, to take the emotional perspective (empathy) of others, and to think on their feet and find alternative solutions (less "functional fixedness") (O'Keefe & Johnston, 1989). In general, then, higher levels of cognitive development predict performance in complex tasks. Conversely, more conventional indices such as grade point average, standardized intelligence/achievement measures, or static personality traits do not (Sprinthall & Thies-Sprinthall, 1983).

In reviewing the work of Vygotsky and Piaget, the author has coordinated the sociological/cultural perspective and the psychological perspective. With the research base clearly outlining the advantages of cognitive-developmental level as a predictor of behavior, can developmental level become the object of educational programs? In other words, can educators promote development? In the next section, a framework is reviewed that explicates conditions for development.

TOWARD A MODEL OF INTERVENTION

With the cognitive-structural research clearly outlining the advantages of higher levels of complexity as predictors of performance in complex human-helping tasks (Sprinthall, Reiman, & Thies-Sprinthall, 1996), the next question is whether cognitive-structural growth can become the object of educational programs, e.g., as the dependent variable? A series of field-based studies over fifteen years have examined those conditions that appear to be needed for adult structural growth in the moral, conceptual, and ego domains to take place. Drawing on George Herbert Mead's (1934) concept of social role-taking, a framework with five conditions has been described and tested. The conditions include:

1. *Role-taking (not role-playing)*. Role-taking is a selected complex new helping experience in a real-world context such as mentoring, counseling, tutoring, action research, or a community internship. The role-taking (action) precedes and shapes the intellectual consciousness (reflection) that grows out of it. In the absence of social interaction within a complex new role, the person is unlikely to initiate the actions required to change (accommodate) new ideas.

2. *Reflection*. Reflection includes sequenced readings, dialogue journals, and ongoing discussions of the new role-taking experiences. Some of the research that will be reviewed in the next section, has clarified three issues. The first is that new experiences that are devoid of reflection make no impact on the cognitive-structural level of the adult learner (Conrad & Hedin, 1981; Sprinthall & Scott, 1989). The second point is that reflection needs to be guided (Reiman, 1988). As Vygotsky illustrated, what persons can do with the assistance of others is more indicative of their mental development potentials than what they can do alone (Davydov, 1995). And thirdly, educators cannot assume a sophisticated capacity for reflection. Rather, reflection requires educating (Reiman & Thies-Sprinthall, 1993).

3. *Balance*. It is important that action (new role) and reflection remain in balance or praxis. Usually this means that the helping experience is supported by weekly dialogic and guided reflection. Too great a time lag between action and reflection or the other way around halts the growth process.

4. *Continuity*. This concept, originally addressed by Dewey, also mirrors a learning truism that spaced practice is superior to massed practice. The research suggests that when cognitive-structural growth in conceptual, moral, or ego domains is the goal, a continuous interplay of action and reflection is needed. Usually, at least one semester and preferably two are needed for significant structural growth to occur (Sprinthall & Thies-Sprinthall, 1983).

5. *Support and Challenge*. Essentially, Vygotsky's Zone of Proximal Development has been applied to adult growth. Both support (encouragement) and challenge (new learning) must be provided; however, the amount of each is dependent on the adult learner's current preferred mental system of solving complex problems associated with the new experience. Thus, the pedagogy requires the instructor to match (start where the learner is) and constructively mismatch, according to the learner's developmental and individual particularities. Hence, although a pedagogy of matching and mismatching reflection can be outlined, it must be creatively applied; therefore the guided reflection on the new experience (activity) cannot be uniform. Furthermore, the dialogic reflection promotes a form of authentic teaching/learning through collaboration.

REFINING GUIDED REFLECTION: WRITTEN DISCOURSE

Ever since John Dewey (1933), at least, educators and psychologists have grappled with the problem of how to extract meaning from experience, and a number of contemporary scholars have begun to explore this question (Comunian & Gielen, 1997; Lind, 1993; Schon, 1987). And, as was mentioned previously, external verbalization through written reflection is an example of an initial tool for processing and structuring new information (Vygotsky, 1978). Also recall that Vygotsky suggested that student verbalization with peers or an instructor problem solving at a slightly higher problem-solving level can maximize growth. Furthermore, the distance between an individual's problem-solving level and the individual's potential problem-solving level with assistance represents the "zone of proximal development."

Earlier studies (Mosher & Sullivan, 1976; Thies-Sprinthall, 1984) suggested that the rather generic method of responding to journals each week was not as effective as it might be, and it certainly was not sufficiently developed to the point where it could be taught to someone else (e.g., supervisor, mentor, teacher educator). Thus, how to refine the guided reflection process became the issue. How can guided reflection start where the adult learner is, and then gradually mismatch according to the learner's zone of proximal development? Specifically, could a flexible framework to guide and differentiate reflection be developed as an intervention? Also recall that journals are a primary tool (Wartofsky, 1979) and represent a valuable individual and collaborative activity

Based on the work of Flanders (1970) in studying teaching, his system was adapted as a means for responding to the narrative in student journals and written coursework (Reiman, 1988).   Flanders essentially outlined seven types of instructional influence, and provided an extremely large set of studies to validate teaching effectiveness as a ratio of direct versus indirect methods. If those forms worked in the classroom (Gage, 1978), could an altered version work in providing written feedback and dialogue in the journal and/or written coursework format?

A related problem to solve was how to use the categories of response differently.   For example, if the learner has difficulty in the journal describing and discussing feelings about self and others, the instructor must share in his or written responses feelings which the learner may be experiencing.   On the other hand, the instructor would remain less active and more indirect (accepting and perhaps clarifying emotional themes) when responding to more complex written narratives.

The goal of the intervention, then, was to explicate how each type of Flander's influence might be reframed as a differentiated response that could be uniquely crafted as a response to the developmental and individual characteristics of the learner. The goal for the creation of the guided reflection framework was a type of interactive lesson plan for written reflection that can permit greater developmental responsiveness as the instructor systematically guides reflection. Table 1 outlines the categories of the guided reflection framework.   As one can see, the system permits differentiated responses for feelings, encouragement (support), clarification of ideas, questioning, information sharing, directions, and problem solving based on individual dispositions toward critical thinking and complex problem solving.

Recent Research

A more recent set of studies has focused on facilitating structural growth of pre-service and in-service teachers employing the more carefully guided reflection with role-taking. These studies meet all five developmental conditions, but the more systematic method for guided reflection yields greater gains in cognitive-structural growth across the conceptual, moral, and ego domains. For example, a study by Reiman (1988) compared two groups of supervising teachers (mentors). The

Table 1
Summary of Categories Guiding Written Reflections

Interaction	Journal Pattern	Instructor Response
1. Accepts Feelings	1a. Teacher has difficulty discerning feelings in both self and others.	Share own feelings.
	1b. Teacher discerns feelings in both self and students.	Accept feelings.
2. Praises or Encourages	2a. Teacher doubts self when trying new instructional strategies.	Offer frequent encouragement.
	2b. Teacher has confidence when attempting new instructional strategies.	Offer occasional support.
3. Acknowledges and Clarifies Ideas	3a. Teacher perceives knowledge as fixed and employs a single "tried and true" model of teaching.	Relate ideas to observed events and clarify how ideas affect students' lives.
	3b. Teacher perceives knowledge as a process of successive approximations and employs a diversity of models of teaching.	Accept ideas and encourage exam- ination of hidden assumptions of pedagogy.
4. Prompts Inquiry	4a. Teacher rarely reflects on the teaching/learning process.	Ask questions about observed events in teaching/learning .
	4b. Teacher consistently reflects on diverse aspects of the teaching/ learning	Ask questions that encourage analysis,

Table 1 Continued

	process.	Evaluation, divergent thinking and synthesis of theory of theory/practice and broader societal issues.
5. Provides Information	5a. Teacher disdains theory, prefers concrete thinking and has difficulty recalling personal events.	Offer information in smaller amounts, observed practice, and review regularly.
	5b. Teacher employs abstract thinking shows evidence of originality in adapting innovations to the class and is articulate in analysis of his or her own teaching.	Relate information to relevant theory and contrast with competing theories.
6. Gives Directions	6a. Teacher needs detailed instructions and high structure, is low on self-direction, and follows curriculum as if it were "carved in stone."	Offer detailed instructions, but encourage greater self-direction.
	6b. Teacher is self-directed and enjoys low structure.	Offer few directions.
7. When Problems Exist	7a. Teacher has difficulty responsibility for problems and blames students.	Accept feelings and thoughts, use "I" messages and arrange a

Table 1 Continued

	conference.
7b. Teacher accepts responsibility for actions.	Accepts feelings and thoughts.

teachers were learning to become mentors and supervisors to novice teachers through a one-year training program. The independent variable was the guided reflection process, and the dependent measures of cognitive-structural growth were moral and conceptual growth. Both groups of teachers showed gains, but the experimental group which received the systematic reflection method demonstrated greater gains on both measures. A replication of this study showed similar gains for the quasi-experimental group (Reiman & Thies-Sprinthall, 1993).

Peace also replicated the study with in-service school counselors. The overall problem was the same, to teach counselors how to serve as supervisors for newly hired inexperienced counselors (Peace, 1992). The role-taking was to learn the difference between counseling pupils and supervising a new counselor. Too often the counselors tended to use the same approach to both problems. A year-long sequence of meetings in an action-guided reflection framework with the five conditions was implemented. Systematic guided reflection through journals and weekly assignments was included. The results were highly similar. Moral reasoning increased after one semester and conceptual development after two semesters.

A fourth study focused on undergraduates in a pre-service teacher education program. In this case the goal was the same, i.e., cognitive-structural growth, but with undergraduates in the process of leaving adolescence and becoming adult professionals. The effects of a standard undergraduate teacher education program were compared with a program that included the developmental conditions (i.e., role-taking, guided reflection, balance, support and challenge, and continuity). The students, in this case, were all in a special teaching fellow program including full four-year scholarships with high grade point averages and high general standardized test scores. A sub-group was involved in role-taking experiences (tutoring) for two semesters complete with systematic reflection in their journals. Pretests were administered during the first year with posttests four years later. The results indicated that both groups improved on their conceptual level measure (a measure of preferred style of problem solving in complex situations), but only the experimental group improved on the assessment of moral reasoning (Reiman & Parramore, 1993).

A fifth study focused on undergraduates in a pre-service teacher education program. In this case the undergraduate students were participating in an introductory course for prospective teachers. The students were pretested at the beginning of the semester and again at the end of the semester on measures of cognitive-structural growth (i.e., moral reasoning—Defining Issues Test or DIT, and conceptual level—Paragraph Completion Test). The role-taking required the students to observed teachers and tutor a student. The systematic guided reflection process was used weekly throughout the semester. The comparison group was a comparable course at a nearby university. Results indicated that the experimental group significantly improved in both moral reasoning level and conceptual level (Watson, 1994). The experimental group also showed improvement in teaching skills.

A sixth study (Arrendondo & Rucinski, 1997) focused on prospective supervisors in an educational leadership graduate class. The role-taking involved principals and assistant principals mentoring novice teachers. The mentoring role was undertaken for one semester. Guided reflection was offered weekly during the intervention. Pretest-posttest measures (beginning and end of the semester) included the Defining Issues Test (moral reasoning) and the Epistemological Questionnaire (Schommer, 1989), which assesses changes in epistemological beliefs. Strong trends were observed regarding the moral reasoning of the mentors (supervisors), and significant differences on six of the ten subset scores for mentors were found.

A seventh study focused on 97 undergraduate Italian students (Comunian & Gielen, 1997). The experimental group consisted of 67 students and the control group of 30 students. The experimental group participated in an intensive cooperative group format throughout the semester which provided opportunities for student-student guided reflection and student-instructor guided reflection. Changes were measured by the ORIGIN/u, a questionnaire developed by Lind and Heberich (1996), which assesses opportunities for role-taking and guided reflection (e.g., syllabus-bound learning opportunities—class discussions, syllabus-related learning opportunities—tutoring, extra-curricular learning opportunities—student government, and non-curricular learning opportunities—church, clubs). The ORIGIN/u provides summary scores for each domain of learning environment, and for both types of learning opportunities (role-taking, guided reflection). Significant effects for the experimental group were found with respect to guided reflection ($F[1,66] = 14.67, p < .001$) and to role-taking scores ($F[1,66] = 14.98, p < .001$).

Table 2
Role-taking Studies that Include Guided Reflection

Study	Sample	Measures	Outcomes
Reiman (1988)	Mentor Teachers	Moral Reasoning	+
		Conceptual Level	+
		Skill: Teaching Repertoire	+
Reiman (1991)	Mentor Teachers	Moral Reasoning	+
		Conceptual Level	+
		Skill: Indirect Supervision	+
Peace (1992)	Counselor Mentors	Moral Reasoning	+
		Conceptual Level	+
		Skill: Indirect Supervision	+
Reiman & Parramore (1991)	Undergraduates in Teacher Education	Moral Reasoning	+
		Conceptual Level	+
		Ego Level	0
Oja & Smulyan (1989)	Teachers as Action Researchers	Moral Reasoning	+
		Conceptual Level	+
		Ego Level	+
Watson (1993)	Undergraduates in Teacher Education	Moral Reasoning	+
		Conceptual Level	+
		Skill: Effective Teaching	+
Arrendondo & Rucinski (1997)	Educational Leaders	Moral Reasoning	0
		Epistemological Beliefs	+
Comunian & Gielen (1997)	Undergraduates	Role-taking	+
		Guided Reflection	+

Finally, work by Lind and Heberich (1996) with a sample of 271 German undergraduate students has confirmed the potential of promoting moral development through role-taking and guided reflection. Using the Moral Judgment Competence test as the assessment, Lind found role-taking and guided reflection to be important conditions for the growth of moral competence.

From these studies, one can conclude that cognitive-structural interventions that include role-taking and guided reflection show promise for promoting moral and conceptual growth across a number of nationalities, professions, and age spans (see Table 2).

STRENGTHS AND LIMITATIONS OF WRITTEN REFLECTIVE DISCOURSE FROM A CROSS-CULTURAL PERSPECTIVE

As has been mentioned previously, the concept of social role-taking with concomitant guided reflection, as outlined in this chapter, has been shown to effect moral/ethical development in samples of undergraduate students and novice and experienced educators in the United States, Germany, and Italy. Although samples have been small, the trends in moral and cognitive growth that result from placing persons in new roles with guided reflection are consistently positive. However, the question remains whether the action/reflection sequence outlined in this paper comprehends a model of praxis that also contains the seeds of growth for all cultures.

A number of scholars and educators have acknowledged the importance of action and guided reflection. For example, the famous Brazilian educator Paulo Freire (1983) has noted that action without reflection leads to activism while reflection without action leads to pedantry. In Freire's writings, guided reflection is a necessary condition for helping persons extract meaning from experience. Similarly, a contemporary scholar of multiculturalism, James Banks (1993), has noted in research on equity issues, intergroup relationships, and the achievement and intellectual and social-emotional development of minority students, that persons' multicultural perspective-taking occurs at increasingly complex levels, and that the cultivation of more complex perspectives requires critical thinking and reflection as persons engage in new roles as data gatherers, studying crime, poverty, or pollution.

A limitation is the focus of the interventions described. All studies utilized written dialogic reflection that was differentiated for the young adult learners. Thus, the model gives primacy to written interaction, and ignores the rich nonverbal (non-written) communication that can occur within cultures. For example, Reilly's cross-cultural study of spoken and paralinguistic effects (1992) (gestural and facial) has shown that preschoolers make far more use of paralinguistic means for expressing affect than do school age children and adults.

But perhaps the most important issue from a cross-cultural perspective is the differentiated reflection taxonomy. The construct uses an adaptation of the Flanders model as a framework for guiding written dialogic reflection. Flanders' construct and the subsequent adaptation of the construct to written interaction, is based on direct observation of thousands of K-16 classrooms in the United States. We may ask: What evidence is there that the elemental strands making up the construct of differentiated guided reflection (e.g., acceptance of feelings, praise or encouragement, accepting or clarifying ideas, asking questions, providing information, giving directions, and statements of concern) exist in some or many schools and teacher education programs in the world? At present, there is no direct answer to this question. In fact, the very consideration of the question alerts the author that guided reflection at a deep structural level requires the educator to translate the written language and implied meanings of the student or a colleague. Such interpretations and *translations* can miss the many textual layers and meanings of discourse that may be shared. Further, some of the processes described in the model are designed to accommodate to Western notions of learning. Is written narrative conveyed differently in various cultures?

This question of how written narrative varies among cultures has been taken up by Burman and Slobin (1994) in an exhaustive cross-linguistic study. In their analyses of child and adult language, they asked children and adults to provide words to a wordless picture book devoted to a quest for a runaway frog. Underlying their inquiry was their own quest for a better understanding of the development of more complex linguistic, cognitive, and communicative abilities that underlie human capacity to capture and convey experience in words. The decade-long inquiry included data from children and adults in five cultures, i.e., German, Spanish, Hebrew, Turkish, and English, with additional independent analysis from researchers conducting similar inquiry in Australia, Chile, Iceland, China, Turkey, Russia, and Japan.

To date, there are 150 researchers, collecting "frog stories" in 50 languages—not only in the field of standard spoken language development, but also in the development of sign languages, in a range of language impairments, and in both spoken and written modes. The methodology of the study required different age groups to tell a story about a missing frog. All stories were transcribed, coded, and analyzed. Three conclusions of the study were that across the five cultures: 1) experiences are filtered through choice of perspective which becomes increasingly complex (multiple perspectives) as the child ages; 2) narrative is packaged into hierarchical constructions, rather than simply a linear chain of successive events located in time and space, and 3) younger children take fewer expressive options because: (a) cognitively, they cannot access a full range of perspectives; (b) communicatively, they cannot fully assess the listener's viewpoint; and (c) linguistically, younger children do not command the full range of formal devices.   The study found that narrative development increases in the hierarchical organization of the narrative with age, and older children will more often account for emotional, cognitive, and physical causes.

Most importantly, Berman and Slobin (1994) find that each culture's language plays an important and unique role in shaping its own array of expressions, while at the same time representing but one variant of a familiar and universally human pattern of development in complex linguistic, cognitive, and communicative abilities.   The Berman and Slobin study provides indirect evidence that the action/reflection framework described can be adapted to different cultures because the patterns of linguistic, cognitive, and communicative expression are similar across a range of cultures.

IMPLICATIONS FOR CROSS-CULTURAL AND INTERDISCIPLINARY RESEARCH AND PRACTICE

One major implication of this work is toward the question of theory and practice for teacher education.   One of the long-standing problems in this area has been the lack of directing constructs and research for the professional education of teachers. The role-taking and guided reflection framework described in this paper attempts to resolve this problem. However, it requires substantial commitment of time and continuity, and careful attention to how persons' reflections are guided.   The "one size fits all" approach to guided reflection ignores the unique needs of the adult learner, and it underestimates the sophisticated and subtle challenge of how to assist others in extracting complex meaning from experience.   As mentioned previously, a person's moral, ego, and conceptual complexity determines how deeply he or she can perceive, analyze, and reflect on experience.   The pedagogical vision of "developmental responsiveness" outlined by Kohlberg and Mayer (1972) in their germinal work represents the other half of their coinage, so to speak.   If development is the aim, then what pedagogies can be identified that promote such growth? The flexible framework to guide reflection that itself can be differentiated according to the developmental preferences of adult learners represents an important step toward actualizing Kohlberg and Mayer's vision.

A second implication is that "dialogue journaling," which can include substantive written interactions about assignments and can occur between students or between student and instructor, should be considered as an important tool in learning and development. The joining of written dialogue to complex new activities makes possible the development of abstract intelligence. Words shape activity into a structure. Consequently, dialogue journaling which requires students to use the planning function of language, (that is, to evaluate proposed actions in terms of both future goals and past activities), holds promise as a developmental tool.

As mentioned previously, instructor responses should lead development. That is, they should provide opportunities for students to initiate and acquire competence in intellectual functions that are, in Vygotsky's words (1978, p. 86), on the verge of coming to life. Most importantly, the adult learner must have a means of crossing over from what one knows to what is new knowledge. Journaling, as a type of highly interactive and differentiated dialogue that complements complex new experiences and activities, awakens life functions which are in a stage of maturing and lie in the zone of proximal development (Vygotsky, 1978).

Finally, as it relates to mentoring and leadership programs, teacher education, and supervision initiatives, mastering new pedagogical skills like higher-level questioning can be facilitated by the guided reflection process described in this article. Such learning provides the basis for the development of complex internal thinking. The Zone of Proximal Development (ZPD) is created in the interaction between the expert or mentor and the novice. Recognizing that novice teachers, for example, may be more receptive at certain periods, a goal for future research is to determine when the sensitive periods arise.

A third implication is that the flexible guided reflection framework described in this paper offers a type of pedagogical scaffold for the instructor. Scaffolding describes the role of tutors or mentors in enabling novices to solve a problem that is beyond their individual ability. Scaffolding is the process of structuring the task (matching and constructively mismatching) or the task elements that initially may be beyond the learner's capacity, so that the adult learner can concentrate on and complete those new elements. This shared activity or written discourse is a means of transferring control to the novice.

A fourth implication is that disequilibrium needs to be better understood as a central process in development. Substantial learning occurs in periods of conflict, confusion, surprise, and over long periods of time. How this disequilibrium or "cognitive dissonance" is resolved becomes a central issue. Certainly the guided reflection framework described in the paper gives attention to acknowledging feelings and knowledge perturbations.

However, as Flanders found, teachers typically respond at an affective level in only 1 out of every 1,000 teacher/student interactions (Flanders, 1970). Clearly, developmental interventions and developmental education programs must create better ways to acknowledge dissonance of learners within professional preparation programs.

In sum, a helping activity (new role) such as teaching, mentoring, or tutoring requires guided reflection. However, guided reflection must itself be adaptive and differentiated according to the needs of the adult learner. The research reviewed here establishes a significant basis for the claim that teachers (and adults) are neither born nor made, but that they may be developed through new roles and higher-order guided reflection (Sprinthall & Thies-Sprinthall, 1983).

BIBLIOGRAPHY

Arrendondo, D., & Rucinski, T. (1997, March). *Use of reflection and structured journaling within complex helping relationships as a stimulus for cognitive-structural growth*. Paper presented at conference of the American Educational Research Association, Chicago.

Banks, J. (1993). *Approaches to multicultural curriculum reform in multicultural education: Issues and perspectives*. Boston, MA: Allyn & Bacon.

Blasi, A. (1980). Bridging moral cognition and moral action. Psychological Bulletin, 88, 1-45.

Burman, R. A., & Slobin, D. I. (1994). *Relating events in narrative: A crosslinguistic developmental study*. Hillsdale, NJ: Erlbaum.

Cole, M. (1996). *Cultural psychology: A once and future discipline*. Cambridge, MA: Harvard University Press.

Comunian, A., & Gielen, U.P. (1997, July). *The effects of guided reflection on academic role-taking in young Italian adults*. Paper presented at the International Council of Psychologists Regional Conference, Padua, Italy.

Conrad, D., & Hedin, D.(1981). Natural assessment of experiential Education. *Experiential Education*, 7, 6-20.

Copeland, W.D., & Birmingham, C. (1993). The reflective practitioner in teaching: Toward a research agenda. *Teaching and Teacher Education*, 9 (4), 347-359.

Davydov, V.V. (1995). The influence of L.S. Vygotsky on education: Theory, research, and practice. *Educational Researcher*, 24 (3), 12-21.

Dewey, J. (1933). *How we think: A restatement of the relation of reflective thinking to the educative process*. Chicago, IL: Henry Regnery.

Flanders, N.A. (1970). *Analyzing teacher behavior*. Reading, MA: Addison-Wesley.

Flavell, J. (1992). Cognitive development: Past, present, and future. Developmental Psychology, *28*, 998-105.

Freire, P. (1983). *Pedagogy of the oppressed*. New York: The Seaburg Press.

Gage, N.L. (1978). *The scientific basis for the art of teaching*. New York: Teachers College Press.

Harrington, H., & Hathaway, R. (1994). Computer conferencing, critical reflection, and teacher development. *Teaching and Teacher Education*, *10* (5), 543-554.

Hunt, D. (1976). Teachers' adaptation: Reading and flexing to students. *Journal of Teacher Education*, *27*, 268-275.

Kitchener, K., & King, P. (1994). *Developing reflective judgment*. San Francisco, CA: Jossey-Bass.

Kohlberg, L., & Mayer, R. (1972). Development as the aim of education. *Harvard Educational Review*, *42*, 449-496.

Kozulin, A. (1990). *Vygotsky's psychology.* Cambridge, MA: Harvard University Press.

Lind, G., & Heberich, S. (1995). *The ORIGIN/u questionnaire for assessing opportunities for roletaking and guided reflection in the learning environments of college/university students*. University of Constance, Germany.

Lind, G. (1993). *Moral und Bildung* [*Morality and education*]. Heidelberg: Roland Asanger Verlag.

Luria, A., & Yudovich, F. (1959). *Speech and the development of mental processes in the child*. Hammondsworth, England: Penguin Books.

Mead, G.H. (1934). *Mind, self, and society*. Chicago, IL: University of Chicago Press.

Moll, L. (Ed.). (1990). *Vygotsky and education: Instructional implications and applications of sociohistorical psychology*. Cambridge: Cambridge University Press.

Mosher, R., & Sullivan, P. (1976). A curriculum in moral education for adolescents. *Journal of Moral Education*, *5*, 159-172.

O'Keefe, P., & Johnston, M. (1989). Perspective-taking and teacher effectiveness: A connecting thread through these developmental literatures. *Journal of Teacher Education*, *40* (3), 14-20.

Oja, S.N., & Sprinthall, N.A. (1978). Psychological and moral development of teachers. In N.A. Sprinthall & R.L. Mosher (Eds.), *Value development as the aim of education* (pp. 117-134). Schenectady, NY: Character Research Press.

Oser, F. (1994). Moral perspectives on teaching. In L. Darling-Hammond (Ed.), *Review of research in education* (pp. 57-128). Washington, DC: American Educational Research Association.

Peace, S. (1992). *A study of school counselor instruction: A cognitive-developmental mentor/supervision training program.* Unpublished doctoral dissertation. North Carolina State University, Raleigh, NC.

Perry, W. (1970). *Forms of intellectual and ethical development in the college years.* New York: Holt.

Piaget, J. (1967). Cognitive development in children: Development and learning. *Journal of Research in Science Teaching*, *2*, 176-186.

Piaget, J. (1972). Intellectual evolution from adolescence to adulthood. *Human Development*, *15*, 1-12.

Reilly, J.S. (1992). How to tell a good story: The intersection of language and affect in children's' narratives. *Journal of Narrative and Life History*, *2*, 335-377.

Reiman, A.J. (1988). *An intervention study of long-term mentor training: Relationships between cognitive-developmental theory and reflection.* Unpublished doctoral dissertation, North Carolina State University, Raleigh, NC.

Reiman, A.J., & Parramore, B. (1993). Promoting preservice teacher development through extended field experience. In M. O'Hair & S. Odell (Eds.), *Teacher education yearbook I: Diversity and teaching* (pp. 111-121). Forth Worth, TX: Harcourt Brace Jovanovich.

Reiman, A.J., & Thies-Sprinthall, L. (1993). Promoting the development of mentor teachers: Theory and research programs using guided reflection. *Journal of Research and Development*, *26* (3), 179-185.

Rest, J., & Narváez, D. (1994). *Moral development in the professions: Psychology and applied ethics.* Hillsdale, NJ: Erlbaum.

Rogoff, B., & Lave, J. (Eds.). (1984). *Everyday cognition: Its development in social context.* Cambridge, MA: Harvard University Press.

Schommer, M. (1989). Effects of beliefs about the nature of knowledge on comprehension. *Dissertation Abstracts International*, *50*, 8A.

Schon, D. (1987). *Educating the reflective practitioner.* San Francisco, CA: Jossey-Bass.

Sprinthall, N.A., & Thies-Sprinthall, L. (1983). Teacher as an adult learner: A cognitive-developmental view. In G.A. Griffin (Ed.), *Staff development: Eighty-second yearbook of the National Society for the Study of Education* (pp. 24-31). Chicago, IL: University of Chicago Press.

Sprinthall, N.A., & Scott, D. (1989). Promoting psychological development, math achievement, and success attribution of female students through deliberative psychological education. *Journal of Counseling Psychology*, *36* (4), 440-446.

Sprinthall, N.A., Reiman, A.J., & Thies-Sprinthall, L. (1993). Roletaking and reflection: Promoting the conceptual and moral development of teachers. *Learning and Individual Differences*, *5* (4), 283-299.

Sprinthall, N.A., Reiman, A.J., & Thies-Sprinthall, L (1996). Teacher professional development. In J. Sikula (Ed.), *Second handbook of research on teacher education* (pp. 666-703). New York: Macmillan.

Thies-Sprinthall, L.(1984). Promoting the developmental growth of supervising teachers: Theory, research programs, and implications. *Journal of Teacher Education*, *35* (3), 53-60.

Toulmin, S. (1981). Motsart v psikhologii [A Mozart in psychology]. *Voprosy psikhologii* [*Questions of Psychology*], *10*.

Vygotsky, L. (1978). *Mind in society: The development of higher psychological processes*. Cambridge, MA: Harvard University Press.

Vygotsky, L. (1986). *Thought and language* (A. Kozulin, Trans.). Cambridge, MA: MIT Press.

Wartofsky, M. (1979). *Models*. Dordrecht, Netherlands: D. Reidel.

Watson, B. (1994). *Early field experiences in teacher education: A developmental model*. Unpublished doctoral dissertation. North Carolina State University, Raleigh, NC.

Wertsch, J. (Ed.). (1985). *Vygotsky and the social formation of mind*. Cambridge, MA: Harvard University Press.

Wertsch, J., Rio, del P., & Alvarez, A. (Eds.). (1995). *Sociocultural studies of mind*. Cambridge: Cambridge University Press.

Wozniak, R., & Fischer, K. (Eds.). (1993). *Development in context*. Hillsdale, NJ: Erlbaum.

Zeichner, K., & Liston, D. (1987). Teaching student teachers to reflect. *Harvard Educational Review*, *37*, 23-48.

THE UNIQUE PLACE OF ROLE-TAKING AND REFLECTION IN COLLABORATIVE ACTION RESEARCH

Sharon Nodie Oja
University of New Hampshire, U.S.A.

INTRODUCTION

It is commonly acknowledged that teacher research is a form of teacher knowing and staff development aimed at classroom improvement and school change. Educators argue that action research and collaborative inquiry bolster professional development and result in more caring and just school environments. Consequently, action research has been integrated into teacher preparation and teacher supervision activities at some universities (e.g., Atweh, Kemmis, & Weeks, 1998; Calhoun, 1994; Hollingsworth, 1997; Lytle & Cochran-Smith, 1992; Noffke & Stevenson, 1995; Zeichner & Liston, 1987). The last decade has witnessed a variety of action-research articles in numerous major refereed journals including new journals that are published for a world-wide audience and are devoted expressly to action research (e.g., *Educational Action Research: An International Journal*). Increasingly, conferences in various parts of the world have focused on collaborative inquiry and action research, and a variety of collaborative action research networks (e.g., CARN) have gained increasing attention and participation from a worldwide audience.

Collaborative action research is useful to universities and schools that are trying to establish partnerships for the improvement of education. The research summaries that follow examine action research and collaborative inquiry as the vehicles for reflection and significant new role-taking. They may facilitate the development of cognitive-structural growth (moral reasoning, conceptual level, ego/self development) in experienced teachers who are working together in collaborative action research groups in what today is termed school-university partnerships.

Studies of teachers-as-researchers have measured teacher-researchers' increased problem-solving skills, continuous learning, enhanced self-confidence, increased self-efficacy, as well as increased reflective, analytical, and critical understanding of their own teaching (Henson, 1996); and these outcomes seem contingent upon teacher-researchers being equal partners with experienced university researchers in collaborative inquiry in the action research studies.

The effects of social role-taking and social interactions in the context of action research, however, have been less frequently studied. Literature on collaborative action research that focuses on the cognitive-structural development of teachers along ego, moral, conceptual, and interpersonal development dimensions is scarce. The research that follows investigated action research and collaborative inquiry as a complex new role assumed by teachers. Using a cognitive-structural framework this research studied how sustained participation in action research changed teachers' conceptual complexity, empathy, and perspective taking. In these studies key elements of effective action research and collaborative inquiry are analyzed. Theories on group dynamics and adult development have helped to explain how individual teacher-researchers and collaborative action research groups develop.

DEFINITION OF COLLABORATIVE ACTION RESEARCH AND TEACHERS' NEW ROLES

In the new role of teacher-researcher, teachers are helping to redesign teaching and schooling in line with goals for restructuring schools toward outcomes that will be needed in the 21st century. For example, Joyce and Showers (1995) emphasized teachers' need to investigate and try out new teaching roles that best teach students to develop intellectual independence, reasoning and problem-solving capabilities, the competence needed to absorb and manipulate complex information and data, and the ability to successfully navigate the information age. In addition, teachers are asked to take on numerous new roles requiring collaboration with other adults and with pupils. For example, teachers are expected to guide pupils' social construction of knowledge through cooperative forms of learning. Teachers are expected to collaborate with other adults in the classroom (e.g., student teachers, aides, special educators, parent volunteers), with university faculty in professional development schools and school-university partnerships, and to collectively plan with peers, administrators, and parents to improve their schools.

Action research and collaborative inquiry are providing a mechanism for teachers to investigate and try out these new roles. Collaborative action research is particularly important today at a time when there is a call for universities and schools to collaborate in the structural reform of education. Collaborative action research is an important strategy for change because it identifies the role of the teacher in defining and solving school problems, emphasizes collaboration between school teachers and university faculty, and focuses on problem-solving which encourages reflection on practice. In collaborative action research groups, teachers-as-researchers provide practical knowledge of the problems chosen for study. University researchers become democratic facilitators (Oja & Smulyan, 1989) who help the group to approach problems from multiple perspectives. Collaboration of school and university educators recognizes and utilizes the unique skills and insights provided by each participant. Leadership in this type of action research group involves a democratic process that encourages others to lead the group when they have the relevant skills and confidence. Leadership is a collaborative effort; group members share the task and maintenance functions of group processes that allow the group to meet its goals. The outside university researcher may, however, have a unique place in this process, often providing the initiative, questions, and support necessary to allow the group to meet its goals. Using a developmental approach to leadership, this outsider may also help address the needs of the group and its members by offering developmentally appropriate guidance, support, and challenge. Consensus in decision-making can encourage each participant to voice his or her perspective while attempting to understand and take the perspective of others.

Collaborative action research proposes alternatives in the conventional roles of both school and university participants. All are asked to take on significant new roles and are provided with the support to do so. Teacher-researchers learn and use action research skills to reflect on their practice and experiment with a range of new teaching, leadership, or supervision roles. University researchers become sensitive to the complexities of classrooms and/or school leadership functions while they learn how to collaborate more effectively with schools.

A collaborative action research group of school and university educators is sensitive to the school in which the research takes place. Participants work together to understand the school and its influence on the teachers' development as well as the limitations and opportunities for personal and professional growth. Discussions in collaborative action research groups frequently center on the real-life dilemmas prevalent in the schools. There is a level of moral complexity in the group setting that satisfies rather than frustrates those using higher stages of moral reasoning, and it can be challenging for those using lower stages of moral reasoning. These knowledge perturbations in the interactions of the collaborative action research group resemble Piaget's concept of disequilibrium in cognitive development that stimulates growth to greater understanding and problem solving.

RELATING THE "HIGHER IS BETTER" STAGE CONCEPT TO COLLABORATIVE ACTION RESEARCH: COGNITIVE-STRUCTURAL DEVELOPMENT OF TEACHERS

"Higher is better" is a cognitive-structural stage concept suggesting that the more advanced stages of development are necessary for persons operating in a complex society. The movement from earlier to more advanced stages of development is activated by cognitive dissonance or disequilibrium. The Vygotskyan (1978) zone of proximal development and sociocultural theory adds to earlier Piagetian theories and to what David Hunt terms the arena for a constructive mismatch in describing new approaches to learning. The key seems to be the concept of "reading and flexing" also called matching and graduated mismatching (Sprinthall, Sprinthall, & Oja, 1998, p. 407). For example, reviews of research in teaching show that teachers at higher stages can manage group instruction and respond to individual and small-group differences, and they are better able to adopt and implement strategies for higher-order thinking and cognitively guided instruction (Oja & Reiman, 1998; Sprinthall, Reiman, & Thies-Sprinthall, 1996).

The objective of cognitive-structural teacher development is to structure adult personal development along dimensions of ego maturity, moral judgment, and conceptualization, and to increase professional competence and efficacy in models of teaching, supervising, and school improvement. Increasing *ego maturity* is defined as the development of more complex, differentiated, and integrated understandings of the self and others; the development moves away from manipulative, exploitative, self-protective attitudes toward self-respect, mutual respect, and identity formation. *Moral maturity* is defined as development toward principled moral judgments; it represents a shift away from unquestioned conformity to peer, social, or legal norms and toward self-evaluated standards within a world environment where individual human rights and mutual interpersonal responsibilities coexist. *Conceptual growth* is defined as the development of more complex modes of understanding, that departs from thinking in terms of simple stereotypes and clichés and moves toward constructed knowledge, recognition of individual differences in attitudes, interests, and abilities and increased tolerance of paradox, contradiction, and ambiguity. *Professional competence* and efficacy in models of teaching, supervising, and school improvement are defined as a more complex understanding of many diverse models, and as moving beyond rigid adherence to a single model toward flexible application of various models depending upon the needs (stages) of the learners, supervises, or school improvement participants. Those who call for the restructuring of education expect that teachers would be able to take on these new roles.

REFLECTION AND COLLABORATIVE ACTION RESEARCH

Action research by definition includes cycles of action and reflection. Reflection in the cognitive-structural studies of collaborative action research has been influenced by research on individual reflection or "guided reflection" (Reiman & Thies-Sprinthall, 1993) and joint reflection or "meta-reflection" through discourse within small groups (Oser, 1994). The strategy of collaborative action research is well suited to the notion of guided reflection in small groups. For example: a) In collaborative action research groups teachers build supportive interpersonal skills and relationships that create a supportive environment which is necessary for further development and learning; b) they research new skills or practices and investigate prior understandings of theories which are needed for their new roles; c) new and more complex roles are used in teaching, supervising, or school improvement; d) there is consistent reflection on new behaviors and responsibilities in the classroom or school and teachers act as advisors, consultants, or listeners when the new roles are creating periods of disequilibrium; and e) collaborative action research groups are on-going; time is allowed for the necessary cycles of action and reflection in the research. These five elements fit the five conditions of the cognitive-structural teaching/learning framework as identified by Sprinthall, Reiman, and Thies-Sprinthall (1996) and as tested in a number of studies over the past fifteen years.

ROLE-TAKING AND COLLABORATIVE ACTION RESEARCH

Teachers in the cognitive-structural studies started by designing action mini-units for their own new roles in teaching in their own classrooms, such as indirect teaching, managing cross-age teaching, organizing peer teaching, individualizing instruction, contracting with pupils, and designing cooperative learning activities. In subsequent studies teachers-researchers took on new roles in school improvement projects. Next, they moved to study teachers as researchers of their new supervisory roles, as cooperating teacher for student teachers, and their subsequent leadership in school–university partnerships. The studies were premised on the basic cognitive-structural conditions for promoting development and learning: role-taking (action), social interaction, and reflection. George Herbert Mead (1934) described the importance of *role-taking* as a catalyst for growth. Specifically, he maintained that active participation in a complex "real world" activity as opposed to role-playing or simulated experience offers tremendous potential for development. *Social interaction* has its roots in the work of Vygotsky who stressed the importance of discourse for development. As an example, teachers involved in collaborative action research meet regularly to discuss their new roles as researchers. Such discussion or social interaction presents the adult learner with a variety of perspectives and new problems to resolve, thus encouraging individuals to develop a number of domains or frameworks for thinking or resolving problems. In a Vygotskyian sense, the teacher in collaborative action research can perform at a developmentally more advanced level than when acting alone because others provide assistance and coaching. Dewey (1933, 1963) elaborated on the important interplay between action and *reflection*. He recognized that there are major differences inherent in the content of experience; for instance, working on a school bus is not equivalent to researching one's teaching practice with the goal of providing adequate education for students. In the process of collaborative action research a colleague's functioning is "stretched" slightly beyond his or her preferred style of problem solving. All developmental theorists agree that this stretching component allows new cognitive-structural learning to begin as a result of a perturbation or knowledge disturbance. This idea was perhaps most central to Piaget's (1985) final reformulation of equilibration theory. In particular, Piaget tried to describe more specifically how equilibration could lead to new and more complex forms of thought, a process of reflective abstraction.

ROLE-TAKING/REFLECTION AS EXPERIENCED TEACHERS RESEARCH NEW TEACHING ROLES IN THE CLASSROOM

Initial studies showed that it was possible to design an intervention program that resulted in teachers' personal growth in ego maturity as measured by the Loevinger Test, moral reasoning as measured by the Rest Defining Issues Test, and cognitive complexity as measured by the Hunt Conceptual Level Test. These early studies are summarized below.

In a large midwestern school district in the U.S.A., a team of three university faculty and six doctoral students worked with 37 experienced elementary and secondary school teachers during a summer session and the following school year. The group was divided into three teams each facilitated by two of the university doctoral students. The program design incorporated the five conditions needed for cognitive-structural development: role-taking (not roleplaying), reflection, balance, continuity, and support/challenge. The teams of school and university participants who met daily during the summer as all learned and practiced new skills related to the new roles of teacher as individualizer of instruction, supervisor of peer and cross-age teaching, and contractor with students for behavior change. During the fall semester of the following school year the teams met weekly to reflect on teachers' action mini-units (subsequently termed action research units in later studies) to try out significantly new teaching roles. All teachers used the action research strategy to design, try out, and refine curriculum units focused on their new teaching roles. Teachers were also responsible for the new teacher role (new to most) of being an effective facilitator of discussions in one's classes thereby helping the pupils to make sense of their new learnings. There were significant differences pre- to post-test between the experimental group (N=37) and the two comparison groups (N=25, N=23) on all three cognitive-structural tests, favoring the experimental group of teachers who carried out action research mini-units in their classrooms (Oja & Sprinthall, 1978). The teachers' journals reflected their risk-taking to learn the new skills needed for the new roles, their initial hesitancy to open up with colleagues for feedback in the small groups, and their successes and failures in applying the new skills in their new roles to the classroom via the action research units.

Equally important, the journals substantiated changes found in teachers' levels of ego maturity, moral reasoning, and cognitive complexity, in particular their increasing ability to reason more abstractly, gain an awareness of alternatives, choose multiple perspectives, and become more sensitive to the emotions of self and others. The teachers in the experimental group significantly increased their ability to accurately identify and respond to human emotions (as measured by a Reflection of Feeling test). In addition, significant improvement was found in elementary school teachers' ability to employ dimensions of indirect teaching that involved accepting and using students' ideas, asking questions, accepting feelings, and praising or encouraging students (measured by Flanders' Interaction Analysis of videotaped classes).

Subsequently, this model, focusing on action research as a cognitive-structural strategy for teacher development was initiated with 20 experienced teachers employed at the same northeastern, United States school that had previously begun a school-wide improvement program. This study adhered to the same design described above, incorporating the five conditions for adult development. Meeting within small-sized collaborative groups teachers and university instructors built supportive interpersonal relationships. They investigated models of teaching and practiced more complex teaching skills associated with the new teacher roles of individualizing instruction, increasing pupils' interpersonal skills through cooperative learning-type activition, supervising peer teaching or cross-age teaching in their own classes, and contracting with students for behavioral improvement. Acting in their new teacher role teachers tried out the skills in their classrooms using cycles of action research. The pre-test scores on the Loevinger, Rest, and Hunt tests for these 20 teachers were similar to pre-test data in the previous study conducted with 85 elementary and secondary school teachers from many different schools. At the end of the 16-week experience, post-test scores indicated significant growth in moral judgment, as indicated by an increase from 42% to 52% on the principled thinking measure of Rest's DIT. In case studies of individual teachers whose growth in moral judgment was matched by increases in ego stage, changes occurred in the direction from the Conformist to the Conscientious Stage on Loevinger's Test. The changes were similar to the ego development test results in the previous study. In this study the average ego test scores of the group remained stable pre to post at the self-awareness ego level, and the average CL test score for the group also remained stable pre to post-test, at moderately high CL. On the underlying dimension of moral judgment, however, significant changes occurred for this group of 20 teachers, in the 16-week period.

ROLE-TAKING/REFLECTION WITH EXPERIENCED TEACHERS COLLABORATIVELY RESEARCHING SCHOOL IMPROVEMENT

The next cognitive-structural study in this series was a two-year case study of two collaborative action research groups of junior high teachers, each group at a different school, one in the midwest and one in the northeast U.S.A. In this study teachers-as-researchers worked on a collaborative group project related to improvement in their schools instead of individual action research units on new teaching roles for their classrooms. This multi-case study design focused on ten teachers, representing a range of ego, moral, and conceptual test scores. The multi-case study documented each teacher's reactions, attitudes, and behaviors in the collaborative action research process. Each collaborative action research group consisted of five teachers and two university researchers. Each group chose its own area of research; one group focused on teacher morale and the other on middle school block scheduling. The university researchers worked closely with teachers in the collaborative action research groups in the two middle/junior high schools over the period of two years. The overall framework of the collaborative action research groups included regular opportunities for the participants to meet and discuss ideas and feelings in a relaxed mode using the Vygotsky, Furth, and Freire instructional principles. Transcripts of these meetings over the two years of the project permitted careful observation and analysis of the five teachers in each group over the duration of the project. The findings showed that teachers who scored at different stages of development reacted differently to the reflective inquiry and to the group process of the collaborative action research. Teachers who scored at different developmental stages exhibited different patterns in their attitudes toward decision-making and change, perception of group organization and group process, perceptions of leadership, and perceptions of school administrators. The university researchers took on the role of democratic facilitators of the collaborative action research group. The meta-analysis of the workings of the collaborative action research groups documented the role-taking and reflection in the group as the teachers became collaborative researchers. The teacher's cognitive-structural stage perspective defined a meaning system through which the teacher interprets and acts on issues related to the reflective inquiry and processes of collaboration in the group during the research. The findings of this multi-case study suggest that the same basic structures that shape a teacher's meanings and attitudes toward change also operate in his or her conceptions and behavior regarding the group dynamics, the research process, the group leadership, the school principal's relation to the group, and the goals and outcomes of the research.

In particular, at the conformist and self-awareness ego stages, we documented the teacher's tendency to act from external rather than self-evaluated standards. They showed little appreciation of multiple possibilities in the problem-solving situations of the collaborative action research process. At the conscientious ego stage, the teacher-researcher shifted toward more self-evaluated standards, and demonstrated a fuller recognition of individual differences in the attitudes, interests, and abilities of other people on the action research team. Finally, at the transition between the individualistic and autonomous stages of ego development, the teacher-researcher assumed multiple perspectives, used a wider variety of coping behaviors in response to school pressures and action research issues, employed a larger repertoire of group process and change strategies, and was very self-reflective and highly effective in the collaborative action research (Oja & Smulyan, 1989). The strength of the cognitive-structural approach in this multi-case study was as a model for understanding the underlying patterns and changes in teachers' thinking and problem-solving on the collaborative action research team.

The role of teacher-researcher is still new to many schools and teachers; it may be a stimulating experience for teachers, and, at times, overwhelming. By observing closely the natural process in this study over two years, we were more able to understand how collaborative action research could be best put into practice. In relation to the school organization we noted that the collaborative action research group became a temporary system in the school that differed from the permanent system of the school in a number of ways. For example, the action research group was characterized by the following conditions: non-hierarchical and self-managed; norms of collegiality and experimentation; power diffused among the teachers on the team; teachers develop their own tasks and flexibly take on a variety of new roles and responsibilities; a setting for reflective thinking and cognitive expansion is created; participatory and collaboratively shared decision-making (Oja & Pine, 1987).

ROLE-TAKING/REFLECTION IN COLLABORATIVE ACTION RESEARCH BY COOPERATING TEACHERS: PROJECT ATTRACTS HIGH-STAGE TEACHERS AND HAS LONG-TERM EFFECTS ON SCHOOL-UNIVERSITY PARTNERSHIPS FOR TEACHER PREPARATION

The final study to be reviewed is a longitudinal study involving cooperating teachers of pre-service teaching interns who took on significantly new roles in their supervisory responsibilities with student teaching interns. The more active teachers in the collaborative action research process have a more vested interest in the group's problem-solving and consequently more motivated by a need to reconcile the perturbations or contradictions to their current or preferred ways of understanding and solving problems. Knowledge disturbance and its role in equilibration has been a major focus of developmental inquiry, in general. The previous studies extended the cognitive-structural framework to investigations of the strategy of action research and of collaborative action research. In this study we investigated the teacher taking on the newer role of cooperating teacher to student teaching interns, and how these cooperating teachers use their collaborative action research groups to get support to deal with problems which their current cognitive structures cannot adequately resolve alone. This study resulted in significant new leadership roles for teachers in a school-university partnership that led to restructured programs for internship placement and supervision in the teacher preparation program at the university.

Cooperating teachers, the school principals, and the university supervisors of the interns met in action research groups to investigate theories of development and models of supervision. Participants were drawn from three communities in the northeastern United States; one was a state university community and the other two were more rural communities within 30 miles of the state university. These three communities represented the types of schools and teachers that this state university works with for the preparation of teachers. This sample afforded an excellent opportunity to study what we thought were powerful factors involved in collaborative action research that could promote the cognitive-structural growth of those teachers taking on significant new cooperating teacher roles. (Although student teaching interns were interviewed, they were not involved in the original three-year study; our focus was on the cooperating teachers and their cognitive-structural development [Oja, 1990-1991]). A few years later, however, we were able to study the cognitive-structural growth of interns in one of the schools in the recently formed school-university partnership (Oja, Struck, Chamberlain, & Moran, 1997).

Prior to the beginning of the project the superintendent of the district that included all three communities had asked his staff to rethink their supervisory practices for teachers in the schools. At the beginning of the project the presenting reality was that of schools in the very early phases of restructuring from an industrial model to a model emphasizing the nature of learning communities. In the schools some teachers were organized in teams, taught in an interdisciplinary manner, some were in teams but taught separately, and others remained separate and taught alone. For instruction, in some classes and subjects pupils were heterogeneously mixed and for others, they were homogeneously sorted. The constructivist theory of learning was just beginning to take root in the form of the writing process which has its roots in constructivist learning principles. So some teachers were changing from teaching at the front of the room with more direct teaching styles to guiding learning through use of more indirect teaching strategies (see direct versus indirect teaching according to Flanders' Interaction analysis in Sprinthall et al., 1998). Students' learning was becoming an active rather than a passive process. Classrooms in the schools were generally uniform in size but some had movable walls that were occasionally opened to create larger spaces. Some teachers shared planning time; others were accustomed to planning alone and teaching in more typical self-contained classrooms. The faculty in the three communities were predominantly veteran groups. Many had begun their teaching careers in these communities. In terms of personal life changes, some of the teachers were marrying, starting families, and raising children, some were divorcing, and some were remaining single; some were experiencing the excitement of becoming grandparents while others were experiencing the pain of caring for ill parents or losing their parents altogether.

Of increasing interest to our investigation was the way these school communities responded to the university teacher preparation program during the placement process for internships and during the cooperating teachers' work with the interns. The existing university framework for supervising interns exhibited many aspects of what is now being called for in restructured teacher preparation (Oja, Diller, Corcoran, & Andrew, 1992). The university already had a long-standing extended five year program culminating in a 30 credit master's degree that required a post-BA full-year internship for a teaching license. The university selected its teacher candidates from the top half of the university population, requiring competitive scores on the GREs and GPAs averaging 3.2 on a 4.0 scale. The university teacher education program already emphasized extensive commitment of its faculty toward supervision of interns. Every faculty in teacher education was required to supervise in field experience courses. Faculty loads in internship exhibited the university's financial commitment to the five-year teacher education program. Six interns per year for one faculty member were the equivalent of two courses out of a five-course faculty load. Placement of interns, however, still followed a fairly traditional model. The Director of Field Experiences called the school principal and the principal placed the intern with the cooperating teacher. Little input came from teachers. So the internship placement and supervision structure was still predominately based on hierarchical decision-making, and while not singularly top-down, it involved teacher input more than actual teacher participation. The same was true of prospective interns who generally were allowed choices only about the geographical area of their placement. Although the triad relationship of university supervisor, intern, and cooperating teacher was recognized as important, cooperating teachers felt they had few supervisory responsibilities. Cooperating teachers had input more than being actual participants in the supervising process.

Procedures

A variety of data sources were used to record and monitor the process of collaborative action research as cooperating teachers in the study researched and tried out alternative supervisory practices with their teaching interns. These included: 1) audio recordings of all team meetings and transcripts of selected meeting tapes; 2) written summaries of all school and university meetings connected with the project; 3) journals by cooperating teachers of their supervisory interactions with their teaching interns; 4) pre/post questionnaires and surveys with participants; 5) three empirical measures of participants' cognitive-structural stages; and 6) interviews conducted at crucial points in the research process with school and university participants. In addition, a self-assessment inventory of supervisory competencies was designed by the teams and used by cooperating teachers in the 2nd and 3rd year of the project.

At the close of the project, audio tapes, year-end surveys, and minutes of supervisory group meetings were analyzed to assess the knowledge base of teachers in three areas: theories of teacher development, models of supervising teaching, and the process of collaborative action research. An outside evaluator interviewed selected participants individually and in small groups; she looked for instances in which teachers recalled their knowledge of teacher development and supervisory models, articulated their knowledge of these areas, and recognized instances in which they effectively understood and responded to the attitudes and behaviors of the teaching interns. Performance was also measured by way of journals, supervisory logs, audio and videotapes, year-end surveys, and direct observations of interactions among cooperating teachers and teaching interns. These same data sources were used to assess the attitudes of cooperating teachers regarding educational research and school-university collaboration. Teachers completed written assessments in the areas of ego/self development, moral judgment, and conceptual level. The scores in year three were compared to those from the instruments used in year one. Project staff analyzed performance data focusing on teacher characteristics that specifically related to growth in complex thinking, increased ability to clarify instructional processes, skill in determining alternative supervisory solutions, willingness to take risks, flexibility in responding to the needs of individual teaching interns, and interpersonal relationships within the collaborative action research groups.

Intervention

Full-year teaching interns were placed in clusters of six to a school. School-based collaborative action research groups consisted of six cooperating teachers, the university supervisor, and often the school principal who met at least once a month. The knowledge bases in supervision and teacher development were neither prescribed nor interpreted in a limited fashion. Instead, each collaborative action research group negotiated the scope of the two areas and formed initial boundaries for the topics, concerns, problems, and issues to be further investigated. All participants were active in the beginning of the project to examine, reflect, and evaluate the knowledge bases and their own practice, so that both informed each other. Cooperating teachers learned about developmental theory, investigated alternative supervision strategies, and attempted to vary their supervision practices according to the capabilities, variety, and flexibility observed in their student teaching interns. Cooperating teachers attempted to support the intern in new learning experiences and challenge the intern's development to new levels; this followed Hunt's match-and-graduated- mismatch concepts. Practical and theoretical knowledge interacted continuously as participants worked through the cycles of action research to further analyze, understand, and evaluate their supervisory behaviors with the teaching interns. The cooperating teachers reflected on these experiences through journals, logs, interviews, consultations, and the on-going collaborative action research meetings.

Measures of Cognitive-structural Learning

Three formal measures of developmental stage were administered to cooperating teachers: the Defining Issues Test (DIT), the Washington University Sentence Completion Test (WUSCT), and the Conceptual Level (CL) Test. The DIT was scored by project staff, and the WUSCT and CL test were scored by trained raters who had reached high levels of reliability. Summaries of the developmental test scores in year one were made available to individual project participants shortly after the data were scored. At the end of year three, post-test results were given to individuals during an interview session that investigated to what extant and how each participant made use of his or her first set of developmental test scores during the course of the project. The Defining Issues Test (DIT) of moral judgment (Rest, 1974) is an objective test of moral reasoning that assesses the basic conceptual frameworks by which a person analyzes a social/moral problem (dilemma) and judges the proper course of action. The DIT presents a moral dilemma and a list of definitions of the major issues involved. It uses a multiple-choice rating and ranking system instead of a moral judgment interview. It can be easily administered to groups and objectively scored, and has been researched with firm reliability and validity levels (Rest, 1986; Rest & Narvaez, 1994). We used the shortened version of the DIT consisting of three dilemmas. The Washington University Sentence completion Test of ego development (Loevinger, 1976) is based on the assumption that each person has a core level of ego functioning. The purpose of the test is to determine this core level by assigning an ego level based on the distribution of a person's ratings or responses to the thirty-six items on the test. Reliability and validity data for the WUSCT are strong as reported in Redmore and Waldman (1975) and reviewed further in Hauser (1976). Hunt's (1978) Conceptual Level test is designed to tap an individual's manner of dealing with conflict and response and orientation toward authority and rules. Miller's (1981) meta-analysis of over 60 studies of conceptual level supported the construct of CL and concluded that persons functioning at higher stages of conceptual level exhibited behaviors such as: reduction in prejudice, greater empathy in communication, greater focus on internal control, longer decision latencies, more flexible teaching methods, and/or more autonomy and more interdependence.

Results

This collaborative action research project attracted and sustained the involvement of cooperating teachers who scored at higher stages of development. This finding is important. Twenty-four of twenty-eight participants scored at Conscientious, Individualistic, and Autonomous stages of development. Of these 24, two-thirds scored at the post-conventional (Individualistic and Autonomous) stages on the Loevinger Test. Sixty-one percent (61%) of the cooperating teachers scored at moderately high and high levels of moral judgment on the DIT, and ninety percent (90%) of the cooperating teachers scored at moderately high and high conceptual levels on the CL test. The average pre-test score on Loevinger's Ego test was the post-conventional Individualistic ego level (N=28, mean score 7.8, s.d.=1.36) which represents the transition between the Conscientious and Autonomous stages. The average pre-test score on the Hunt CL test was 2.28 (N=20, s.d.=.45) indicating the ability for using abstract, internal principles and multiple viewpoints, which is categorized as high conceptual complexity. The DIT pre-test of moral judgment showed a mean P-score (principled thinking) of 60.4% (N=18, s.d.=14.99).

These pre-test results from teachers participating in the collaborative action research in the supervision study are much higher than the pre-test data in the earlier studies summarized in this paper. Individuals functioning at fairly high developmental stages may not exhibit vertical stage change in just two years, so it is not surprising that we found no significant vertical change in teachers' developmental scores. Loevinger claims that at least five years is needed for stage change. We believe this is true, particularly at the higher postconventional stages. Our work in both this study and the prior studies has indicated that vertical stage change is more likely to occur within the conventional scorers, with the higher stage teachers experiencing horizontal growth within their postconventional stages.

Discussion with Implications for School–University Partnerships

What is important about this collaborative action research project with cooperating teachers is that teachers who self-selected to be involved because of their interest in a new role as cooperating teachers and who maintained their involvement throughout the two years were teachers at higher stages of development. The benefits and outcomes experienced by these cooperating teachers went beyond their individually developing supervisory roles as cooperating teachers. All of the cooperating teachers indicated collaboration with the university had improved. Eighty-seven percent indicated that collaboration among teachers within their schools had improved, although this was not a stated goal of the supervision project. All of the cooperating teachers reported the discovery of new ways of looking at people, in particular, that at different developmental stages persons have different strengths and weaknesses, capacities, and limitations. Teachers reported an increased sense of efficacy. Over three-fourths of the group reported significant changes in their school's recruitment, placement, supervision, and assessment of interns. Cooperating teachers perceived benefits from the collaborative action research process in terms of the opportunities for sharing and support among their colleagues. Eighty percent appreciated the sense of common purpose and common challenges. Ninety-five percent reported a feeling of mutual support, and 85% liked the open sharing in supervisory team meetings. We observed an increased sense of professionalism. Action research group discussions often focused on larger school improvement issues and concerns beyond the specific supervision of interns but which affect the climate of the school. In this project, the context of the collaborative action research groups had supported and challenged higher stage teachers who wished to take on significantly new supervisory roles with student teaching interns.

COLLABORATIVE ACTION RESEARCH PRACTICE AND SCHOOL RESTRUCTURING

Recent reports in education call for restructuring and change from present-day traditional schools to the learning communities of the future. They envision restructuring as a total system overhaul involving changes in organizational structures, practices, beliefs, and values. They recognize and acknowledge that the process of restructuring engenders anxiety in some teachers and administrators which leads them to resist, avoid, or withdraw from the restructuring effort. As a means for helping to reduce anxiety, increase commitment, and encourage participation, they suggest the use of a collaborative process for developing shared visions, missions, goals, and strategies for change (e.g., Covey, 1990; Senge, 1990; Sergiovanni, 1990).

The cognitive-structural theories and research findings suggest the use of interactive challenges and supports to facilitate teachers' participation, inquiry, and reflection and to reduce anxiety in their new role-taking experiences in the classroom and the school community. As the contrast between the vision for learning communities and the reality of the traditional schools would suggest, the changes necessary for restructuring to a learning community are numerous and extensive and would significantly impact the lives of teachers. The specific number, nature, and scope of these changes and their specific impact on teachers in any given school is dependent upon the presenting reality of the school and the cognitive-structural levels of the teachers. The success of a school's restructuring efforts depends to a great extent on the appropriateness and the adequacy of the challenges and support available to teachers throughout the process. Appropriate challenges and adequate supports keep teacher anxiety at constructive, manageable levels and facilitate both teacher development and the restructuring process. School restructuring programs may need to offer options which differentially attract teachers at different stages of development. The collaborative action research process seems to invite and support the participation of teachers at the conscientious, individualistic, and autonomous stages of development. This chapter reviewed recent role-taking/reflection research with experienced teachers who have assumed complex new roles. Collaborative action research, under certain conditions, can be an effective program for promoting the personal and professional (e.g., cognitive-structural) growth of teachers. Collaborative action research offers an extraordinary opportunity for new role-taking and intensive reflection in the teaching/learning/school restructuring enterprise.

BIBLIOGRAPHY

Atweh, B., Kemmis, S., & Weeks, P. (1998). *Action research in practice: Partnerships for social justice in education*. London: Routledge.

Calhoun, E.F. (1994). *How to use action research in the self-renewing school*. Alexandria, VA: Association for Supervision and Curriculum Development.

Covey, S.R. (1990). *Principle-centered leadership*. New York: Simon & Schuster.

Dewey, J. (1933). *How we think: A restatement of the relation of reflective thinking to the educative process*. Chicago, IL: Henry Regnery.

Dewey, J. (1963). *Experience and education*. New York: Collier.

Furth, H. (1981). *Piaget and knowledge*. Chicago, IL: University of Chicago Press.

Hauser, S.T. (1976). Loevinger's model and measure of ego development: A critical review. *Psychological Bulletin, 83*, 928-955.

Henson, K.T. (1996). Teachers as researchers. In J. Sikula (Ed.), *Handbook of research on teacher education* (2nd ed.) (pp. 53-64). New York: Simon & Schuster/Macmillan.

Holligsworth, S. (1997). *International action research: A casebook for educational reform*. London: Falmer Press.

Hunt, D.E., Butler, L.F., Noy, J.E., & Rosser, M.E. (1978). *Assessing conceptual level by the paragraph completion method*. Toronto: The Ontario Institute for Studies in Education.

Joyce, B., & Showers, B. (1995). *Student achievement through staff development: Fundamentals of school renewal* (2nd ed.). White Plains, NY: Longman.

Loevinger, J. (1976). *Ego development*. San Francisco, CA: Jossey-Bass.

Lytle, S.L., & Cochran-Smith, M. (1992). Teacher research as a way of knowing. *Harvard Educational Review, 62* (4), 447-474.

Mead, G.H. (1934). *Mind, self, and society*. Chicago, IL: University of Chicago Press.

Miller, A. (1981). Conceptual matching models and interactional research in education. *Review of Educational Research, 51* (1), 33-84.

Noffke, S.E., & Stevenson, R.B. (1995). *Educational action research: Becoming practically critical*. New York: Teachers College Press.

Oja, S.N. (1990-1991, Winter). The dynamics of collaboration: A collaborative approach to supervision in a five-year teacher education program. *Action in Teacher Education, 12* (4), 11-20.

Oja, S.N., Diller, A., Corcoran, E., & Andrew, M.D. (1992). Communities of inquiry, communities of support: The five-year teacher education program of the University of New Hampshire. In L. Valli (Ed.),

Reflective teacher education: Cases and critiques (pp. 3-23). New York: SUNY.

Oja, S.N., & Pine, G.J. (1987). Collaborative action research: Teachers' stages of development and school contexts. *Peabody Journal of Education, 64* (1), 96-115.

Oja, S.N., & Reiman, A.J. (1998). Supervision for teacher development across the career span. In G.R. Firth & E.F. Pajak (Eds.), *Handbook of research on school supervision* (pp. 463-487). New York: Macmillan.

Oja, S.N., & Smulyan, L. (1989). *Collaborative action research: A developmental process*. London: Falmer Press.

Oja, S.N., & Sprinthall, N.A. (1978). Psychological and moral development of teachers. In N.A. Sprinthall & R.L. Mosher (Eds.), *Value development as the aim of education* (pp. 117-134). Schenectady, NY: Character Research Press.

Oja, S.N., Struck, M.H., Chamberlain, E., & Moran, M.J. (1997). Supporting the "teacher as learner:" Interns and cooperating teachers in a cluster site. *SRATE Journal, 6* (2), 30-38.

Oser, F. (1994). Moral perspectives on teaching. In L. Darling-Hammond (Ed.), *Review of research in education* (pp. 57-128). Washington, DC: American Educational Research Association.

Piaget, J. (1985). *The equilibration of cognitive structures*. Chicago, IL: University of Chicago Press.

Redmore, C., & Waldman, K. (1975). Reliability of a sentence completion measure of ego development. *Journal of Personality Assessment, 39* (3), 236-243.

Reiman, A.J., & Thies-Sprinthall, L. (1993). Promoting the development of mentor teachers: Theory and research programs using guided reflection. *Journal of Research and Development, 26* (3), 179-185.

Rest, J. (1974). *Manual for the Defining Issues Test: An objective test of moral judgment*. Minneapolis, MN: University of Minnesota.

Rest, J. (1986). *Moral development: Advances in research and theory*. New York: Praeger.

Rest, J., & Narvaez, D. (1994). *Moral development in the professions: Psychology and applied ethics*. Hillsdale, NJ: Erlbaum.

Selman, R. (1980). *The growth of interpersonal understanding*. New York: Academic Press.

Senge, P.M. (1990). *The fifth discipline: The art and practice of the learning organization*. New York: Currency/Doubleday.

Sergiovanni, T.J. (1992). *Moral leadership: Getting to the heart of school improvement*. San Francisco, CA: Jossey-Bass.

Sprinthall, N.A., Reiman, A.J., & Thies-Sprinthall, L. (1996). Teacher professional development. In J. Sikula (Ed.), *Handbook of research on teacher education* (2nd ed.) (pp. 666-703). New York: Simon & Schuster Macmillan. London: Prentice Hall International.

Sprinthall, R.C., Sprinthall, N.A., & Oja, S.N. (1998). *Educational psychology: A developmental approach.* Boston, MA: McGraw-Hill.

Vygotsky, L. (1978). *Mind in society.* Cambridge, MA: Harvard University Press.

Zeichner, K., & Liston, D. (1987). Teaching student teachers to reflect. *Harvard Education Review, 57* (1), 23-48.

ROLE-TAKING AND REFLECTION: PROMOTING THE DEVELOPMENT OF SCHOOL COUNSELORS, PSYCHOLOGISTS, AND SOCIAL WORKERS AS SUPERVISORS

Sandra DeAngelis Peace, North Carolina Central University, U.S.A.

INTRODUCTION

Counselors are valuable members of school teams in the United States who provide a variety of services to students, teachers, and families (Baker, 1996; Schmidt, 1996). Individual and group counseling helps students to cope better with emotional and behavioral problems, similar to the therapeutic services provided by psychologists in other settings. School counselors also conduct prevention activities to promote students' social, psychological, and educational development. These activities include peer tutoring programs which enhance study and social skills, facilitating moral discussion groups, and consulting with teachers and parents (Paisley & Peace, 1995). Among the most current issues facing school counselors today is the challenge to facilitate the development of an increasingly diverse student population. There are increased numbers of Asian/Pacific Islanders and Hispanic students enrolling in American schools, while African American students are still expected to be the second largest racial/ethnic group by the year 2005 (Lee, 1995). It is imperative that counselors, therefore, have a pluralistic education perspective and are competent in the area of multicultural counseling (Pedersen & Carey, 1994).

Because of these challenges and as a result of the increased national interest in the quality of schooling (Goodlad, 1990; Stallings, 1995), the importance of the continued professional development of teachers and counselors becomes evident. For example, because of an increase in professional performance requirements for teachers, many states have now instituted a two- to three year probationary status period for training and supervision beyond university requirements. Such efforts have encouraged the creation of extensive in-service training to prepare experienced teachers for the role of being a mentor and supervisor to new teachers (Sprinthall, Reiman, & Thies-Sprinthall, 1993). Similarly, in part due to the increased complexity of the school counselor's role, there is also a need for the creation of systematic in-service programs to train experienced school counselors to take on the role of mentor and supervisor to beginning counselors. Unfortunately, the current state of supervision of school counselors is problematic. Recent studies have indicated that clinical supervision from trained peers remains a rare occurrence for school counselors (Borders & Usher, 1992; Roberts & Borders, 1994).

Recent reviews have also indicated that there is a need to view the supervision of beginning counselors from a broader perspective than simply thinking in terms of an evaluation for a license or for employment purposes

(Borders, 1991; Schmidt, 1990). In fact, many new counselors in schools receive very little support and technical assistance from qualified peers; instead, they are expected to perform all the roles of an experienced counselor as a "finished product" (Matthes, 1992).

This paper outlines the rationale for training experienced counselors in a new role as supervisors with a focus on the development rather than the evaluation of their new, less experienced colleagues. This is followed by a summary of the curriculum objectives. Examples of guided reflection activities as a means of promoting growth are highlighted. An analysis of results and program implementation is also presented. School psychologists and social workers have also participated in this training. For the purpose of this paper, only the term counselor is used.

RATIONALE

In order to meet the challenges of an increasingly diverse society and address the problems facing many children and their families, the need to develop higher levels of thinking, problem-solving, and empathy among educators is greater than ever. Competent educators can be defined as those with the ability to see the social and political implications of their actions and who can use their skills to promote greater equality, justice, and humane conditions in schools and society (Holmes Group, 1990; Valli, Cooper, & Frankes, 1997). Kohlberg recognized that high levels of counseling competency "aids in the development of counselor as well as client because listening requires the empathy and role-taking that is important for both moral and psychological growth" (Kohlberg & Wasserman, 1980, p. 563). Unfortunately, counselor in-service programs have not focused on developing those qualities. Instead, they have tended to consist of short-term or episodic workshops (Brown, 1989). Even more extensive training with an emphasis only on skill development has had limited effects (Baker, Daniels, & Greely, 1990).

A massive meta-analysis of graduate-level counselor training programs revealed that most skill-training was positive yet modest in its effects on the counselors during graduate school. There was, however, very little, if any, transfer of training effects (Baker, Daniels, & Greely, 1990). Thus, the expectation that skill training in graduate school will continue to inform counseling practice for the experienced counselor and that it will become the basis for a supervisor model for a beginning counselor appears unlikely to be fulfilled. At the same time, extensive research has shown that experienced teachers can become an effective resource for the supervision of their new colleagues (Sprinthall, Reiman, & Thies-Sprinthall, 1996). Experienced school counselors then have the same potential for effective supervision of beginning counselors, yet the vehicle for actualizing that potential has been missing.

DIRECTING CONSTRUCTS: ADULT DEVELOPMENT

A supervisor training program was designed and based on the conception of the counselor as an adult learner. Arlin (1984) has shown that cognitive-developmental stage theory can be applied to adults. Human growth for adults depends on changes in cognitive structures, which manifest themselves as sequential, irreversible, and hierarchical stages. A large body of studies supporting the predictive qualities of the stage theory (Blasi, 1980; Miller, 1981; Rest, 1986) has shown a positive relationship between cognitive stage and altruistic behavior in adults. Even more relevant is the research linking higher developmental stage with more effective counseling skills (Borders, 1989; Holloway & Wampold, 1986; Strohmer, Biggs, Haase, & Purcell, 1983). Such research findings support the rationale for applying cognitive-developmental theory to the goals of promoting counselor growth. These studies of counselors are highly consistent with research in other professions, such as, public administration, accounting, medicine, and dentistry (Rest & Narváez, 1994).

The link between stage of development and professional behavior is crucial since there is often a misunderstanding in the literature that cognitive-developmental structural growth has only a very tenuous connection to behavior (Kahn, 1991). The issue that is usually missed in this controversy is the question of higher stages of cognitive complexity in relationship to the task demands of the activity itself. Thus, higher is better only in situations, which require complex performance, like counseling and supervising. When the task requires the ability to conceptualize, to place one's self in the emotional "shoes" of another, to respond based on principles of equity, and to behave in a consistently humane manner, then higher stages predict higher levels of professional effectiveness and vice versa. Though frequently not mentioned, there is a downside to these findings, namely that professional counselors, accountants, doctors, dentists, and public administrators who process experience at more modest stages of development also perform their professional tasks less adequately. For example, Strohmer, Biggs, Haase, and Purcell (1983) reported that counselors at lower levels of conceptual complexity were less competent in providing a therapeutic environment for students with special needs.

Cognitive Developmental Stage: From Predictor to Curriculum Goal

From the standpoint of professional education, of course, an important question arises. If higher levels of development predict more complex behaviors, can training/education positively affect stage? In other words, can developmental stage and behavior become the object of intervention, a dependent variable rather than a predictor or independent variable? Holloway and Wampold (1986) found some but not much evidence to support the idea that counselor training programs could effect cognitive stage. On the other hand more recent studies of teachers (Paisley, 1990) and teacher supervisors (Reiman & Thies-Sprinthall, 1991; Thies-Sprinthall, 1984) have shown that developmental growth and behavior can be positively affected by a systematic approach to training. This means that the goals of such development are two-fold: professional skill development, e.g., methods of supervision; and cognitive structural growth, e.g., upward movement toward more complex levels of thinking, empathy, and reasoning.

THE INDEPENDENT VARIABLE: COUNSELOR SUPERVISOR TRAINING

Basically, the training involved a careful balance of role-taking, reflections, readings, and discussions, carried out over a two-semester sequence in an atmosphere that was both supportive and challenging. Each activity in the sequence was presented through the skill development method of Joyce and Weil (1980). Skills were taught in a sequence of (a) providing a rationale, (b) modeling, (c) peer practice, and (d) generalization. Complete details describing the curriculum for the training can be found in Peace (1995).

In the first semester, the focus was on theory and practice in supervision. The goals were to enhance the participants' counseling skills as an effective model for the beginning counselor and to build an understanding of developmental supervision techniques. The topics included:
1. Needs of beginning counselors and building a helpful supervision relationship
2. Renewing effective counseling skills
3. Clinical supervision: Cycles of assistance (conferencing and collecting observation data)
4. Adult development theory: differentiating supervision
5. Analyzing supervisor-supervisee interactions

ROLE-TAKING: Supervising a Beginner

The second semester of the treatment was focused on applying the theory and skills from the first semester to actual supervision. Counselors were asked to learn and then to perform a significant new role as a supervisor, distinctly different from counseling students. The role required taking on a new perspective and functioning at a somewhat higher level, involving complex tasks. This included regular tape-recorded supervision sessions of cycles of assistance with either an intern from a university master's degree program or a first year counselor. Each week there was a review and analysis of such tapes including a structured self analysis of the tape and a review by the instructor. Also, it became obvious that the actual involvement in real-life supervision became much more demanding than the practice experience with a peer from the course in the first semester. The overall action-reflection cycle continued for the second semester with weekly journals and written feedback from the instructor.

The Role of the Interventionist

The action-reflection cycle was critical to the dual goals of the curriculum, namely, to promote cognitive structural complexity and the acquisition of effective supervisory behaviors. Neither by itself could be considered sufficient. Structural growth without skills could be too reflective. Skills without structural growth could be too action-oriented.

This approach is an intensive form of instruction because it involves reviewing tapes, journals, and providing supportive or corrective feedback, which was varied according to the developmental level of the trainee. For example, some of the counselor supervisors grasped the model and moved into effective methods during the earlier part of the second semester. They received and enjoyed low-structure and challenging open-ended commentary by the instructor, the interventionist. In a sense, they moved through the Stoltenberg and Delworth (1987) phases of counselor supervisor development smoothly. From a developmental perspective, they were capable of processing experience at a complex level. Others, however, were much slower to pick up on the model and required concrete feedback, very high structure, high levels of positive support, and very modest amounts of challenge. It also means that such a differentiated approach is really at the heart of the developmental model. The instructor is required, in David Hunt's words to "read and flex" with the participants and to provide different learning environments in accord with the developmental needs of the learner, for example, high, moderate, or low structure (Hunt, 1974). This approach to individualizing was based on the instructor's ability to assess the participants' developmental level through a continuous analysis of their classroom performance and journal entries. Examples of counselor's behaviors as indicators of stage level are found in Table 1. The variable structure provides a bridge to each level, starting where the learner is at the moment, the initial preferred stage of functioning. Then, through a process of graduated mis-matching the learner is guided to greater complexity in thoughts, feelings, and action. Table 2 illustrates a system of strategies for differentiating the instructional process.

Table 1
Counselor Behaviors–Hunt's Levels*

STAGE A
Shows strong evidence of concrete thinking
Exhibits compliance and expects the same from clients
Is low on self-direction and initiative; needs detailed instructions
Nonverbals are often incongruent
Counsels in a robot fashion
Needs immediate reinforcement
Difficulty in tracking clients. Inaccurate on active listening
Enjoys highly structured activities for self and for clients
Is very uncomfortable with ambiguous assignments—prone to anxiety
Verbalizes feelings at a limited level
Is reluctant to talk about own inadequacies; low on self-reflection, high on
anxiety

STAGE B
Separates facts, opinions, and theories about counseling
Employs some different models in accord with client differences
Shows some resistance to some models
Shows some evidence of systematic "matching and mismatching"; can vary
structure
Is open to innovations and can make some appropriate adaptations; evidence of
self reflection
Shows sensitivity to emotional needs—responds to a variety of client feelings
Enjoys some level of autonomy and self-directed learning as a goal for self
Accurate on active listening with most clients
Appropriate ratio of content/feeling responses
Non-verbals are usually congruent

STAGE C
Understands counseling as a process of successive approximations
Non-verbals are congruent
Shows evidence of originality in adapting innovations to the client's needs
Is comfortable in applying all appropriate models
Is most articulate in analyzing his or her own counseling in both content and
feeling
Has high tolerance for ambiguity and frustration; can stay on task in spite of
major distractions
Does not automatically comply with directions—asks supervisor's reasons
Fosters an intensive exploratory approach with clients when appropriate

Responds appropriately to the emotional needs of all clients. Can move "up" & down on the Active Listening scale
Can "match and mismatch" with expert flexibility
Appropriate balance of support and challenge

*Hunt, D. E. (1974). *Matching models in education.* Toronto, Ontario: Institute for Studies in Education. Adapted for counselors by Norman A. Sprinthall, North Carolina State University.

Table 2
Differentiating the Instructional Process

Factors	High Structure	Low Structure
Concepts:	Concrete	Abstract
Time Span:	Short	Long
Time on Task:	Multiple practice	Single practice
Advance Organizers:	Multiple Use	Few organizers needed
Complexity of Learning Tasks:	Divided into small steps and recycled	Learning tasks are clustered into wholes
Theory:	Concretely matched with experiential examples	Generalized including research
Instructor Support:	Consistent and frequent	Occasional

Guiding Reflection

The instructor established a personal dialogue with each of the participants by responding to all self-assessments and journals. A flexible framework for guiding each individual's reflections (Reiman, 1988) was used to differentiate feedback. Three examples of the counselor journal entries are provided, as indicators of different stage levels. As the counselors began the process of assimilating and accommodating training and supervision experiences, they often felt "stretched;" and a state of disequilibrium was apparent.

The first example is from an entry by a counselor who initially functioned at a very modest level of development. He became highly anxious when completing basic skill practice assignments and processed experiences at a concrete level. His counseling skills were not responsive to student clues and he was not aware of his inadequacies. While overly conscientious, in this example he missed the purpose of the taping assignment.

"I am pleased with my counseling skills. I modeled:
• accurate questioning skills, with appropriate use of open-ended/ closed questions
• positive reinforcement
• appropriate nonverbal behaviors."

In response to this entry and critiquing the tape, the instructor provided support while giving structured directions:

> "You sounded satisfied with your questioning skills. I agree that your closed questions produced information about the student and your use

of praise was effective. My suggestion is to strive for more of a

balance between open and closed questions with more eliciting feelings in addition to content.

> "Since the purpose of this assignment was to practice active listening, I am sending one of my tapes for you to review along with a rating scale. Then please call me to meet so we can discuss any questions or role-play this skill before you make another tape. I know you are working hard and I am impressed with your eagerness to contribute in class. I look forward to seeing you soon."

The second entry is by a counselor who moved to a more moderate level of functioning, vacillating between dependency and autonomy. Her counseling skills improved but her listening was not consistently accurate. This is a reflection on her taping of a counseling session intended for a critique by a peer. She recently began expressing her emotions more openly.

> "This taping was very stressful, knowing it would be analyzed by an experienced counselor. I was very cautious at first and thought the session had no direction. But then I really focused on active listening and stayed with the student. When I listened to the tape, I think the student was helped."

The following instructor's response focused on support, positive reinforcement, and suggestions:

> "I understand your tense feelings about sharing your work with a peer. Your openness in expressing your feelings will be a plus in helping you to be empathic toward a beginning counselor's anxiety about critiquing tapes. You seem eager to increase your active listening-skills and to support that goal I've indicated which responses were accurate. I suggest you submit another tape and focus more on responding to student feelings. I believe you are ready to accomplish this, since most of your paraphrases were accurate. In your reflections, please let me know what you noticed about the differences in the two tapes, and I look forward to hearing how you felt also."

In contrast, the next entry was from a counselor (whose self-evaluation of her counseling skills was congruent with her competent performance), a more complex thinker, who focused on broader issues:

> "I felt confident about the work I'm doing with this student and pleased after rating the tape to see my indirect behaviors along with client talk were high. Computing the ratios of direct to indirect behaviors as

well as client talk percentages could be a useful tool for helping novice counselors. Often one of the major pitfalls of new counselors is acting out the desire to "fix" things for their clients. Therefore, as a mentor, I would perhaps address this issue from not only a personal point of view by listening to the feelings behind the "need to fix" but also a fairly analytical one by helping the new counselor compute an indirect/direct ratio. During the assignment, I wondered how the ratios might appear for people using various theoretical orientations. Any studies ever done on this?"

The instructor's response provided challenge by encouraging advanced activities:

"This is another example of your ability to view course content from the beginner's perspective and to make important connections to your future work as a mentor. Enclosed is an article speaking to some of the issues you brought up. How about analyzing your future tapes by comparing different ratios with different client issues or, with a video tape, compare nonverbal cues during indirect vs. direct behaviors and during client talk? I'll be interested in your reactions and perhaps you can share results in class."

RESULTS

The purpose of this study was to evaluate the counselor supervisor education program, the independent variable, designed to focus on promoting the developmental growth of the experienced counselors and the acquisition of supervision skills. This field research project used one experimental group composed of eleven experienced counselors employed in three school systems. Lack of a comparable group due to the dearth of counselor mentor training programs prevented the use of a formal comparison group. Initial results from the first semester of the in-service program follow; the complete details of the study are described in Peace and Sprinthall (1998).

Cognitive Data

Both the Hunt et al. (1977) and the DIT (Rest, 1986) measures were used on a pretest- posttest basis in the first semester and the Hunt PCM only for the second semester. Since the DIT is a recognition test, it is useful as a pre-post measure but inappropriate to administer it a third time in the one-year time span. The Hunt procedure, on the other hand, requires participants to construct their own meaning for the stems each time and is, therefore, less subject to confounding by content familiarity and consequently less subject to a reactive effect of testing. Table 3 presents the results of both developmental measures.

For the Hunt measure, there was a modest but statistically insignificant trend in the level of conceptual development (mean gain score of +.16) from 1.87 to 2.03 in the first semester. By the end of the second semester, however, the gain of +.35, from 1.87 to 2.2, was significant ($t=$ 2.76, $p<.025$). In stage terms, the gain is just over one-third of a stage on a 3-point scale (1.0, 2.0, 3.0), and it can be considered an important increase in the level of conceptual complexity. The pretest-posttest results for the Rest DIT indicate that the experimental group increased from a mean of 33 to 40.9 in the amount of Principled reasoning ("P" score) in the first semester.

Table 3
Developmental Measures: Mean Scores of Hunt CL
(Semesters One and Two) and Rest DIT (Semester One)

| | Semester One | | | Semester Two | |
	Pretest (1)	Posttest (2)	Gain (from 1 to 2)	Posttest (3)	Gain (from 1 to 3)
Hunt (N=11)	1.87	2.03	.16	2.22 ($t=1.29$)* (N=9)[+]	.35 ($t=2.76$)***
Rest (N=11)	33P	40.9P	7.9 ($t=1.63$)**	____	____

Notes: * $p<.11$; ** $p<.07$; *** $p<.025$
[+] In semester two, 2 counselors had to drop the class because of schedule conflicts.

Supervisor Skill Development

The results of the analysis of four clinical supervision conferences, using the Flanders Interaction Analysis Scale-Adapted for Counselor Supervision, are shown in Table 4. An adapted version of the Flanders (1970) Interaction Analysis Scale (FIAS-S) was used to categorize their verbal behaviors into two modes of supervisory influence, Direct and Indirect. There was a substantial gain, over the time series, in the use of the 4 Indirect categories from 55% to 74%. This showed an increase in levels of higher order skills, accurate empathy, and building on the content of the supervisee's communications.

Qualitative Analysis: Reflecting on the Reflection Process

The third estimate of outcome was derived from the subjective journal accounts of the participants.Such a qualitative measure provided a "voice" for each of the

Table 4
Ratings of Supervisor Skill Behaviors: Average Percentages Using
Flanders Interaction Analysis System-Adapted for Counselor Supervision
(FIAS-S) to Analyze Supervision Conferences

| | Time Series of Conferences | | | |
| | Semester One (N=11) | | Semester Two (N=9) | |
	Time 1	Time 2	Time 3	Time 4
Ratio*				
Categories 1 through 4 =	55.5%	67%	73%	74%
Categories 1 through 7				
# of observations	337	287	283	286
Accepting Feelings &				
Ideas Ratio*				
Categories 1 through 3 =	15.5%	29.5%	32%	30%
Categories 1 through 7				
# of observations	337	287	283	286

Note:* Ratios were computed by dividing the following categories of supervisor behaviors on the Flanders Interaction Analysis System-Adapted for Supervision (FIAS-S):
1. Accepts supervisee's feelings.
2. Praises or encourages: Positive comments about supervisee's contributions.
3. Accepts or uses supervisee's ideas: Clarifies, develops, or refers to supervisee's contributions.
4. Asks questions.
5. Gives information and analyzes data.
6. Gives directions and states procedures.
7. Confrontation.

counselor supervisors to describe their own ideas and feelings about the program in an individualistic mode. These data, collected from journals and evaluations of all training activities disclosed participants' perceptions about renewed counseling effectiveness and the acquisition of useful supervisory skills (Peace, 1995). The following comments are a representative sample of the participants' evaluations of the reflection component of the training program:

"Writing reflections—processing the use of new material (learned in class) in my work at school—was of great value to me. It allowed me to reexamine my own thinking and ways of doing things."

"Discussion of concerns and sharing ideas in class provided other points of view and new strategies for helping the novice counselor."

"Critiquing my mentee's counseling tapes was often an emotionally charged experience—for both of us. Reflecting on it in my journal really helped me look at my supervision more objectively and critically."

During the role-taking experience as supervisors, they learned to use the Reiman (1988) method for responding to their supervisees' journals. The supervisors reacted positively to this system for promoting their beginners' growth:

"The reflections unit was helpful because being aware of their (supervisees) concerns and feelings and the way you convey your reactions are both important."

"Communicating through the journals was less threatening than critiquing tapes and beneficial to both of us. My intern was open and asked questions when she wasn't sure. I enjoyed responding to her reflections because I learned a variety of strategies."

This counselor's comments indicated an understanding of how her responses employed matching and mis-matching strategies:

"In responding to Katie's reflections, I found it best to first accept her feelings and thoughts. Then I'd try to "turn it up a notch" by offering a broader perspective than the individual child or situation to which she referred. Also in conversations, we occasionally took different points of view, purposely, so she could see situations from different viewpoints."

While the process did not come naturally to many of the counselors, they left the training with reflection as a useful tool, transferable to their work setting:

"I have never experienced writing reflections in a journal. I wish I were better at it. I will continue to reflect more and try to improve my learnings about things that I do."

"Learning how to respond to mentees' reflections was also useful for my work with students. I am doing that with several of my students and try to include as many aspects of response writing as possible when I write back to them in their journals."

Discussion

Caution is needed in drawing broad conclusions from this study's findings because of the small number of participants and the lack of a contemporaneous comparison group. However, extensive research has demonstrated that developmental levels remain stable during adulthood and change is unlikely with traditional short-term training (Hunt, 1974; Rest, 1986). Measures such as the Hunt conceptual level test require significant increases in cognitive complexity by the participants if a statistically significant gain in the assessed level is to occur. The trend evident at the first posttesting shifted to a stronger indicator of growth at follow-up. Thus, the practicum, which included additional instruction, role-taking, and reflection activities, appears to have provided the participants with enough praxis to promote significant structural growth. Further research, including larger samples, is needed, however, to clarify the current study's findings.

PROGRAM IMPLEMENTATION

This program has evolved through a series of steps, starting as a pilot program in 1991. Since then, 87 culturally diverse counselors have been trained as supervisors. As a "turnkey" model, first counselors were trained at the university level by the first author, and then selected counselors were prepared to educate counselors in their own school systems. During their first year of teaching the coursework, these school-based counselor educators participated in an internship with the first author for assistance and support. Recently, school social workers and psychologists have also participated in the supervisor education program.

CONCLUSION

School counselors reach out to a variety of diverse audiences—students, parents, and teachers. A profession, committed to nurturing the potential of others, must continually ask itself, "Are there sufficient and adequate efforts for addressing school counselors' personal and professional development?" The counselors in this study did master the fundamentals of developmental supervision and their levels of conceptual and moral development were enhanced. Of course, it is important to underscore that this intervention strategy is intensive well beyond the weekly three hours of classroom work for two semesters. The process of guiding reflection and with helpful feedback is certainly as crucial as the management of the course tasks. Thus there is no viable short-cut to such an approach that seeks to promote stage growth and professional skills.

Equally important is the potential that exists for this program to facilitate the growth of novice counselors and to enhance the psychological maturity of their supervisors. Promoting higher levels of cognitive and moral development opens up opportunities for counselors to bridge cultural divides, disentangle social and class inequities, and be advocates for a fair school climate. Both the novice and the experienced counselors' gains apply to a common goal: to succeed in the mission of encouraging and promoting the development of *all* students in their care.

BIBLIOGRAPHY

Arlin, P. (1984). Adolescent and adult thought: A structural interpretation. In C. Armon, M. Commons, & F. Richards (Eds.), *Beyond formal operations: Late adolescent and adult cognitive development* (pp. 258-271). New York: Praeger.

Baker, S.B. (1996). *School counseling for the twenty-first century*. Englewood Cliffs, NJ: Prentice Hall.

Baker, S., Daniels, T., & Greely, A. (1990). Systematic training of graduate-level counselors: Narrative and meta-analytic reviews of three major programs. *The Counseling Psychologist, 18*, 355-421.

Blasi, G. (1980). Bridging moral cognition and moral action. *Psychological Bulletin, 38*, 1-45.

Borders, L.D. (1989). Developmental cognitions of first practicum supervisees. *Journal of Counseling Psychology, 36*, 163-169.

Borders, L.D. (1991). Supervision/evaluation. *The School Counselor, 38*, 253-255.

Borders, L.D., & Usher, C.H. (1992). Post-degree supervision: Existing and preferred practices. *Journal of Counseling and Development, 70*, 594-599.

Brown, D. (1989). The perils, pitfalls, and promises of school counseling program reform. *The School Counselor, 23*, 47-53.

Flanders, N. (1970). *Analyzing teacher behavior*. Reading, MA: Addison-Wesley.

Goodlad, J. (1990). *Teachers for our nation's schools*. San Francisco, CA: Jossey-Bass.

Holloway, E.L., & Wampold, B.E. (1986). Relation between conceptual level and counseling related tasks: A meta-analysis. *Journal of Counseling Psychology, 33*, 310-319.

Holmes Group (1990). *Tomorrow's schools*. East Lansing, MI: Author.

Hunt, D.E. (1974). *Matching models in education*. Toronto, Ontario: Institute for Studies in Education.

Hunt, D.E., Butler, L.F., Noy, J.E., & Rosser, M.E. (1977). *Assessing conceptual level by the paragraph completion method*. Toronto, Ontario: Institute for Studies in Education.

Joyce, B., & Weil, M. (1980). *Models of teaching*. Englewood Cliffs, NJ: Prentice-Hall.

Kahn, P. (1991). Bounding the controversies: Foundational issues in the study of moral development. *Human Development, 34*, 325- 340.

Kohlberg, L., & Wasserman, E. (1980). The cognitive-developmental approach and the practicing counselor: An opportunity for counselors to rethink their roles. *Personnel and Guidance Journal, 58*, 559-567.

Lee, C. (1995). *Counseling for diversity*. Boston, MA: Allen & Bacon.

Matthes, W.A. (1992). Induction of counselors to the profession. *The School Counselor*, *39*, 245- 250.

Miller, A. (1981). Conceptual matching models and interactional research in education. *Review of Educational Research*, *51*, 33-84.

Paisley, P.O. (1990). Counselor involvement in promoting the development of beginning teachers. *Journal of Humanistic Education and Development*, *29*, 20-29.

Paisley, P.O., & Peace, S.D. (1995). Special Edition on Developmental Issues. *Elementary Guidance & Counseling, 30*.

Peace, S.D. (1995). Addressing school counselor induction issues: A developmental counselor mentor model. *Elementary School Guidance & Counseling*, *29*, 177-190.

Peace, S.D., & Sprinthall, N.A. (1998). Training school counselor supervisors to supervise beginning counselors: Theory, research, and practice. *The Professional School Counselor*, *1*, 2-8.

Pedersen, P., & Carey, J.C. (1994). *Multicultural counseling in schools*. Boston, MA: Allyn & Bacon.

Reiman, A.J. (1988). *An intervention study of long-term mentor training: Relationships between cognitive-developmental theory and reflection*. Unpublished doctoral dissertation, North Carolina State University, Raleigh.

Reiman, A. J., & Thies-Sprinthall, L. (1991). Promoting the development of reflection. *Journal of Research and Development in Education*, *26*, 179-185.

Rest, J.R. (1986). *Moral development: Advances in research and theory*. New York: Praeger.

Rest, J.R., & Narváez, D. (1994). *Moral development in the professions*. Hillsdale, NJ: Erlbaum.

Roberts, E.B., & Borders, L.D. (1994). Supervision of school counselors: Administrative, program, and counseling. *The School Counselor*, *41*, 149-157.

Schmidt, J.J. (1990). Critical issues for school counselor performance appraisal and supervision. *The School Counselor*, *38*, 86-94.

Schmidt, J.J. (1996). *Counseling in schools: Essential services and comprehensive programs*. Boston, MA: Allyn & Bacon.

Sprinthall, N.A., Reiman, A.J., & Thies-Sprinthall, L. (1993). Role-taking and reflection: Promoting the conceptual and moral development of teachers. In P.K. Arlin (Ed.), Special Issue: *Learning and Individual Differences* (No. 5, pp. 283-299).

Sprinthall, N.A., Reiman, A.J., & Thies-Sprinthall, L. (1996). Teacher professional development. In J. Sikula (Ed.), *Handbook of research in teacher education* (pp. 666-703). New York: Macmillan.

Sprinthall, N.A., & Thies-Sprinthall, L. (1983). The teacher as an adult learner: A cognitive-developmental view. In G. Griffin (Ed.), *Staff development: Eighty-second yearbook of the National Society for the Study of Education* (pp. 13-35). Chicago, IL: University of Chicago Press.

Stallings, J.A., (1995). Ensuring teaching and learning in the twenty-first century. *Education Researcher, 24,* 4-8.

Stoltenberg, C.D., & Delworth, U. (1987). *Supervising counselors and therapists: A developmental approach.* San Francisco, CA: Jossey-Bass.

Strohmer, D.C., Biggs, D.A., Haase, R.F., & Purcell, M.J. (1983). Training counselors to work with disabled clients: Cognitive and affective components. *Counselor Education and Supervision, 23,* 132-138.

Thies-Sprinthall, L. (1984). Promoting the developmental growth of supervising teachers: Theory, research, programs, and implications. *Journal of Teacher Education, 35,* 329-336.

Valli, L., Cooper, D., & Frankes, L. (1997). Professional development schools and equity: A critical analysis of rhetoric and research. *Review of Research in Education, 22,* 251-303.

SECTION IX: CROSS-CULTURAL VIEWS ON AGING

The world is turning gray. Except for some Muslim countries in the Middle East and North Africa, the percentage of the aged is growing rapidly in both the industrialized and the industrializing countries around the globe. The contributions contained in this section address the aging process from a global perspective and investigate those factors that make for feelings of well-being or unhappiness among the aged.

Throughout life each individual faces biological, psychological, and social changes that require adaptation to homeostasis or wellness. In this context one may ask: How do cultural beliefs influence one's well-being and ill health during later adulthood? In this section cultural differences in health care beliefs and cross-cultural comparison of the elderly are examined along with cultural practices.

In their broadly conceived review chapter, *Aging in a Cross-Cultural Perspective,* the German psychologists Ursula Lehr, Elisabeth Seiler, and Hans Thomae state that while international and intercultural research on aging has been increasing, systematic cross-cultural research on aging is less forthcoming. Lehr et al. discuss the meaning of old age in different cultures, varying social support systems, styles of family interaction, and the cross-cultural validity of both the disengagement theory and the modernization theory.

Successful aging in terms of life satisfaction or well-being is a central issue of gerontological studies. Investigations of the psychological and psychosocial correlates of longevity and the influence of cultural factors suggest one major conclusion: No single variable can independently explain longevity and well-being in old age. Psychosocial factors (socialization practices, cultural and ecological influences, personality factors, social status, and special lifestyles) interact with each other and are part of a complex reciprocal causal network. In cross-cultural research projects investigating well-being in late adulthood, only a few gender differences have emerged regarding the degree of life satisfaction. However, men and women advance divergent reasons for overall life satisfaction (i.e., women frequently focus on social and familiar networks, whereas men tend to stress material issues and economic security). The authors also describe various studies that point to generally high levels of life satisfaction among the aged.

Eva Sandis, in *The Aging and Their Families: A Cross-national Review*, asks how global trends affect the role of the family in meeting the needs of the aging, and then analyzes the development of policies that can assure equity between the generations among the world's aging societies. The author compares changes in societies from both developing and industrialized regions based on global population trends related to family changes and to aging. While the proportion of the aged varies considerably across the regions of the world, there exists an unmistakable global trend toward an increasingly aging population. This situation generates the need for social policies designed to ensure a satisfactory quality of life for the elderly and their families. Such policies need to consider at least six considerations: a) the aging engaging in self-care, with a preference for independence and "intimacy at a distance;" b) the aging as caregivers to both older and younger family members; c) the aging exercising both self-care and other-care roles; d) women needing to become aware of their unfair share in family caregiving; e) increasing gender equity to ensure adequate access to educational job training and work opportunities for women, and finally f) increasing intervention and support by governments, non-governmental organizations, and local communities.

In her chapter titled *Gender, Health, and Behavior among Aging North Americans*, Margot B. Nadien analyzes how global trends affect the role of the family in meeting the needs of the aging and the development of policies that assure equity between the generations. Primary aging, gender differences in physical health, factors involved in health-behavior relationships leading to personality changes, gender differences and similarities in personality, and the question of stability vs. change in old age are some of the topics under investigation.

Three central questions emerge in the chapter. The first concerns some major gender similarities and differences found among aging North Americans, the second, the narrowing of various psychosocial gender differences among older persons, and the third, certain less desirable outcomes. When unfavorable genes and a stressful life history culminate in many secondary aging processes, the last year of life may bring a sharp decline in physical and mental health, and also in the general well-being of the aging individual. Nevertheless, the author concludes that many aging people can look forward to a largely satisfying stage in their lives. This is especially true of those aging women and men who actively seek to satisfy their needs and sense of well-being within the constraints of their situation and their physical and psychological limitations.

Guido Amoretti in *The Assessment of Cognitive Abilities in Old Age: Construction of a Battery of Tests, Normative Data, and Results in Normal and Pathological Italian Respondents* discusses a battery of tests that assess cognitive abilities in old age. The importance of the effects of level of education on test performance (including culture-free subtests) has been the most significant finding of studies of normal aging populations. A short form of the battery was constructed in order to establish its diagnostic usefulness and the appropriateness of cognitive rehabilitation training on the basis of meta-cognitive techniques and through various cognitive activities is demonstrated.

The international team of Leonore Loeb Adler, S. Patricia Clark, Florence L. Denmark, Ramadan A. Ahmed, TaeLyon Kim, Suneetha S. de Silva, and Steven Salbod, in *Cross-cultural Investigation Comparing Attitudes Toward Living and Dying,* have investigated some research questions about important and challenging aspects of living and dying. Their study focused on four countries: Kuwait before the Iraqi invasion, South Korea, Sri Lanka, and the USA. The respondents were asked questions about loneliness, opportunities to discuss one's problems with others, and how one would deal with an incurable illness. In spite of some interesting cross-cultural differences in the respondents' replies, the results suggest that there are some nearly universal questions and considerations that arise in the "business of living."

While the process of aging is universal, the specific behavior of the older adult is influenced by complex interactions between age, biological changes, various psychological factors, social structural variables, and evolving cultural belief systems and practices. With increased research across cultures, new solutions to problems associated with aging can be more readily found and used to promote positive and creative adjustment during the last phase of life. Everywhere, the aging interpret their lives in terms of a shifting balance of gains and losses. While physical impairments of some kind are common most adults adapt successfully to these and other kinds of challenges. They continue to live active lives and to find meaning in the face of the inevitability of death.

The inevitability of physical death may nevertheless be accompanied by a firm belief in the survival of the soul after the body has decayed. The varying means of the death are indeed the topic that Pittu Laungani discusses in his chapter titled *Death: The Final End or a New Beginning? Cross-Cultural Evaluations.* Laungani, who grew in Bombay but has been residing in London for many years now, compares typical notions regarding death now prevailing in the mind of the West with those that have informed Hindu beliefs and practices over centuries. Under the influence of secular and humanistic ideologies Western societies such as England and the U.S.A. have become death-denying societies. They have handed death over to the doctors and to the funeral directors whose function is to remove death from our midst. In contrast, death among Hinds remains a family and communal affair (as indeed it was in the West during earlier centuries). Laungani's chapter ends with an analysis of the psychologically protective mechanisms that may help Hindus to cope better with some of the primeval fears associated with the idea of death since times immemorial.

AGING IN A CROSS-CULTURAL PERSPECTIVE

Ursula Lehr
University of Heidelberg, Germany
Elisabeth Seiler
University of Heidelberg, Germany
Hans Thomae
Bonn University, Germany

INTRODUCTION

The Meaning of Old Age

Aging and its final state, old age are universal phenomena for all humans throughout the world. But this statement does not imply that old age has the same meaning everywhere. At first glance, old age seems to be a natural category that is primarily determined by biological processes. But a closer look reveals that the concept of old age is also a social construction, differing widely between cultures and societies. The meaning of old age is closely linked to the organization of the life course which to a great extent is determined by cultural factors.

In Western industrialized societies age is largely conceived of as a chronological entity, signifying the time that has elapsed since birth. The life course is determined by many normative age markers: entry into school, work, retirement. Kohli (1985) points out that it was industrialization that led to an institutionalization of the life course based on chronological time. Old age in Western societies is usually perceived as beginning with retirement, around the age of 65.

In non-industrialized cultures life is not organized by counted time. In these societies we observe different meanings attached to old age, which may be similar or dissimilar for men and women in a given society. People around the age of 45, who from our point of view are thought to be middle aged, are considered to be old in these societies.

In premodern cultures functional capacity plays a vital part in human life. People do hard physical labor, and the individual's ability to contribute to his (her) own, his family's, and society's well-being depends on good health and functioning. Here we find a functional concept of old age: aging is viewed as a decline in physical capacity, and old age means that a person is no longer able to accomplish the full range of physical tasks.

In many societies the life course especially for women is ordered by status of marriage and motherhood. Old age begins with certain events, for example when a woman has her first grandchild from her oldest son. Therefore, in these societies unmarried and childless women may never be considered as belonging to the elderly (Elwert, 1992).

In age-set societies age confers entry into a formal group of age mates in the succession of generations. Age is viewed in a relative sense, and it refers to acquiring seniority in relation to the following generation. Chronological age can differ considerably within one group. The members of a particular age set proceed together, accompanied by formal ceremony, through a series of age grades. Each transition is marked by role shifts and an increase in status and power.

Problems of Research in Cross-cultural Studies

Cross-cultural research on aging was initiated in cultural anthropology. Simmon's (1945) classical study on the aged in primitive societies pointed to the impact of culture on the attitudes toward the aged. This was even more true for the work of Cowgill and Holmes and their "modernization theory" (1970) which continues to be one of the most frequently quoted approaches even if it was disconfirmed and modified in several studies.

Disengagement theory as formulated by the sociologists Cumming and Henry (1961) became the topic of many evaluations and modifications and was tested in a cross-national study in which social and behavioral scientists from American and European countries cooperated. It is an example of using cross-cultural research to demonstrate some of the commonalties in aging—at least for Western societies.

Today, different foundations and international organizations are stimulating cross-cultural or cross-national research for the testing of theories and for the development of policies for the aged.

Empirical studies in cross-cultural research comparing directly different cultures are time- consuming and expensive. Moreover, they pose many methodological problems. Most importantly, in order to allow comparison, they require the use of the same research instruments in the different cultural settings. But even if this is done, these same research instruments can have very different meanings in various cultural contexts. Even a formal interview situation, for example, may be experienced as a strange and artificial situation by research participants of a specific cultural background and will not lead to any useful results in this context. Field research, implying residence in the studied culture over a prolonged period of time, is therefore widely used in anthropological research. Relying on observation, unstandardized interviews, and informal contacts, however, confounds results with many uncontrollable variables, including researchers' bias.

Many studies referring to cultural contexts of aging are "one-country-studies," describing and evaluating specific cultural, economic, and/or political aspects of the situation of the aged, especially in non-Western societies. Cross-cultural comparison then requires a meta-analysis, relating different studies with results obtained under different conditions and frequently employing different research methodologies. This again poses many problems for an interpretation of the results.

This paper focuses on the discussion of cross-cultural studies based on theories such as disengagement theory and modernization theory. Subsequently, a very important concept in recent gerontological research will be discussed in a cross-cultural perspective: successful aging in terms of life satisfaction or well-being. Before this discussion two other aspects are considered: first the differences in life expectancy (or the different ways of demographic changes) in industrialized and non-industrialized countries—and secondly, the complex network of influences regarding psychophysical and psychosocial correlates of longevity.

THE DIFFERENT WAYS OF DEMOGRAPHIC CHANGES

Dramatic demographic changes have occurred during the last decades which are defined not only by an increase of the proportion of the elderly but also by the extension of the lifespan which differs in different cultures. These changes were first observed in industrial societies, but they have also taken place in the developing countries.

Today, we are living in a graying world. Never before in the world could so many people reach such an advanced age. There is an enormous extension of the lifespan in all European countries, as well as in many other countries of the world. In summary, the proportion of the under-20s and the over-60s in the population has changed drastically. This demographic change poses a challenge to every aspect of living—affecting the society at large, the economy, politics, and science.

Relevant aspects of population change should be considered especially under the following aspects:

The Rise of Individual Life Expectancy

The life expectancy of a newborn child in Europe one hundred years ago was 45 years; today it is in Germany 72.7 years for men and 79.7 for women. In Singapore it is 74.1 years for men and 78.4 years for women. However, in developing countries the life expectancy is much lower.

Today in Germany, 60-year-old women can expect to live 23 more years; 60-year-old men 19 more years. This means: after retirement a person will live about 20 more years—one fourth of his entire life!

The Aging Population

We are living in a "graying world." One hundred years ago, the percentage of persons 60 years old and older in Germany was 5%, today it is 21%. In Singapore it is 9%. In the year 2000, it will be 26% in Germany and 11% in Singapore. In 2030, when the students of today will be retired persons, about 37% of the whole population of Germany will be 60 years and older; in Singapore 26%.

One hundred years ago, the ratio of persons 75 years and older in Germany was 1:79; in 1925 the ratio was 1:67; in 1936 1:45; in 1950 1:35; in 1970 1:25, in 1994 1:14.8; and in the year 2020 it will be 1:8.7, in 2040 1:6.2.

But there is also an increase in the group of the 80-, 90-, and 100-year-old persons. Twenty-five years ago, we had only 385 centenarians in our country; in 1994, our Bundespräsident congratulated 4,602 persons on their birthday of one hundred and more years, 582 men and 4,020 women. For the year 2000, more than 12,000 centenarians are to be expected. Scientists of all disciplines and faculties, and administrators, practitioners, and politicians, too, have to discuss the question of longevity in connection with psychophysical well-being. What can be done to assure healthy aging? What can be done to assure the quality of life in old age?

Household Structures

There has been an important trend in Germany and in the industrialized countries which has moved families away from the three-generation-household to the two-generation-household and then to the one-generation-household, and from there to the one-person-household. Only 1.1% of all households are three-generation-households. In the developing countries three-generation-households are very common—but this may change in the future.

Of all persons 65 years old and older in Germany, nearly 40% are living in a one-person-household. Sixty-three percent of all women 75 years and older are living in a one-person-household. In Singapore, 85% of the elderly are living with their families and only 3% in a one-person-household. But, we already observe in some Asian countries the same trend as in Europe: that old people tend to live separate from their families. It should be remembered, however, that according to studies conducted in many countries in Europe, this change in household-structure should not be identified with isolation of the elderly, as frequent intergenerational contacts are reported independent from the household structure.

Four percent of the population 60 years and older in Germany live in nursing homes or homes for the aged; even more in the Northern European countries, but less in Southern Europe (in Greece the figure is only 1.5%).

From the Three-generation Family to the Four- or Five-Generation Family

In former times, a newborn child seldom had the opportunity of knowing his four grandparents. Today, a child frequently gets to know all of her/his four grandparents, and very often two or three great-grandparents as well. Persons in their sixties with great-grandchild(ren) are quite common—and also persons, 60-years-old and older who are caring for their own parents (about 20%). Due to this fact, since some years, gerontologists have argued that discussions of three-generation-families are no longer relevant for the contemporary demographic situation, as there is a remarkable increase of four-(and five-) generation-families.

Even if the majority of the very old persons in the industrialized countries are active and competent, these changes in the household and family structure should be considered whenever the problems of caring for the aged are discussed.

Consequences of Demographic Changes

Given the worldwide demographic evidence for an increasing life expectancy and for population-aging, one needs to understand the biological and cultural components of aging which are influencing this process. Such an understanding has consequences also in regard to caring for the disabled elderly.

Lower fertility rates, which eventually accompany population aging, imply that fewer children will be available to care for elderly parents. Because elders tend to live with children in developing countries (Kinsella & Taeuber, 1992), decreasing family size represents a potential threat to elders in need of care.

Martin (1988) indicates that in Asia about 75% of elders share a household with children, but this percentage is changing. Fewer elders are living with their children and more older couples and older women are living alone. This trend is especially apparent in Japan, but there is evidence in other Asian countries of an increase of older women living alone or in institutions. Whatever the living circumstances of the elderly, "changes in attitudes about aging will be essential; all older people, both the healthy and the sick, will need a chance to contribute meaningfully to society" (Holmes & Holmes, 1995, p. 34).

PSYCHOPHYSICAL AND PSYCHOSOCIAL CORRELATES OF
LONGEVITY:
THE INFLUENCE OF CULTURAL FACTORS

In the early days of psycho-gerontology, age was introduced as the only independent variable, e.g., for predicting performance on cognitive or psychomotor tests. In the last decade a great amount of insight into the complex network of influences on behavior and achievement in old age was attained. This is illustrated by Figure 1 (see below) which suggests a variety of psychophysical and psychosocial correlates of longevity.

There are many determinants which influence longevity and well-being in old age. From the results of many studies we can conclude that no single variable can independently explain longevity. Although biogenetic and physical factors are very influential, they are not sufficient in explaining longevity. Cultural factors are very important, too.

The results of international longevity research point to a number of interesting relationships. And yet, considering the present state of research, it still seems premature to derive theories or even lawful relationships which may be related to long life expectancy. It should be stressed, especially, that possible factors influencing increased life expectancy typically interact with each other. Such interactions point to the existence of complicated reciprocal causal networks. A possible model of these interacting influences upon longevity is presented in Figure 1.

Genetic, physical, and biological factors can be regarded as having a direct influence upon longevity (Arrow 1) and also on the personality development (2) of an individual (personality, intelligence, activity, morale, adaptation, self-esteem, etc.). Personality development, moreover, is determined by socialization processes which are influenced by culture to a remarkable extent: child-rearing practices, the teachers, significant others, and the social environment in general determine the experience and behavior of an individual; historical factors also play a role in this socialization process (3). In addition, ecological determinants such as physical environment, living in urban or rural areas with their specific forms of stimulation, and living in different cultural and climatic conditions all have an impact on personality development (4). A number of studies have demonstrated direct connections between personality and longevity (5). Correlations between ecological factors and longevity (6) are frequently referred to in studies with centenarians. Personality variables, on the other hand, have an impact on education and occupational training, on occupational activities, and thus, on socioeconomic status (7). Correlations between social status and longevity (8) have been determined primarily from vital statistics and demographic analyses and also

Figure 1
Correlates of Psychophysical Well-being and Longevity

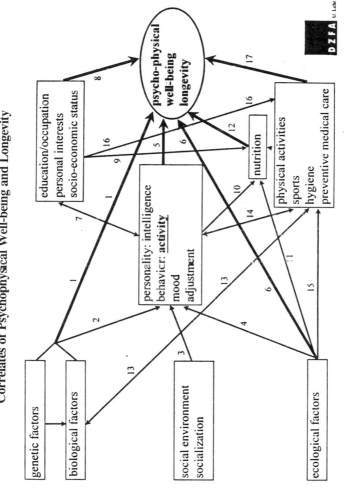

by follow-up and longitudinal studies finding increased life expectancy for persons with a high socioeconomic status (SES).

Social status (9) and personality (10) as well as cultural and ecological factors (11) influence nutritional habits. Moreover, a direct correlation between nutrition and longevity (12) is claimed to exist. The role of nutrition on diabetes in relation to age and of nutritional aspects of atherosclerosis and stroke have to be mentioned here. Smoking and the use of alcohol must also be considered.

Genetic and biological factors (13), personality (14), ecological variables (15), and socioeconomic status (16) have been found to influence physical activities and sports, as have been preventive medical care, and hygiene. Correlations of all these variables with longevity (17) have been demonstrated.

Our model includes, by no means, all variables that may possibly influence longevity. It is merely meant to stimulate further empirical studies and to provide encouragement for future modification, elaboration, and differentiation (Lehr, 1982.)

The analysis of the data of the Bonn Longitudinal Study on Aging (Lehr & Thomae, 1987; Thomae 1976, 1983) confirms many findings concerning the correlates of longevity and healthy aging. They point to one major conclusion: no single variable can independently explain longevity and well-being in old age. What must receive primary consideration is the fact that a series of psychosocial factors (socialization, cultural influences, personality, ecological stimulation, social status, and special lifestyles) which can possibly influence increased life expectancy, interact with each other and seem to be part of a complicated reciprocal causal network.

DISENGAGEMENT THEORY IN A CROSS-CULTURAL PERSPECTIVE

The theory of disengagement was one of the first approaches to the conceptualization of "successful aging." Contrary to more recent definitions of this concept which emphasize objective criteria like good health or optimal cognitive functioning (Baltes & Baltes, 1990), Havighurst and his colleagues from the Committee on Human Development (1963) of the University of Chicago emphasized life satisfaction as the decisive measure of successful aging. The ability to restore at least some degree of emotional well-being even in depriving or difficult situations is measured by the different variations of the Life Satisfaction Scale.

According to the disengagement theory of aging (Cummings & Henry, 1961), life satisfaction is attained or increased in old age if the individual withdraws from close ties with his/her social network, especially by severing the ties to the extra-familial network.

In a cross-national study on adjustment to retirement, initiated by Havighurst in 1963, this theory was compared with the contrasting activity theory of aging, which proposes that life satisfaction depends on the maintenance of social activity. The participating nations were selected on the basis of the prevalence of different traditions concerning continued activity after the age of 65-70 years. From this point of view, apart from the United States and Israel, six European countries were included in the study: France, Italy, The Netherlands, Poland, the United Kingdom, and West Germany. Using the original interview schedule of the Kansas City Study (which led to the disengagement theory), two age-groups were studied at each of the eight centers: one with an average age of 55 years, expecting retirement in 5-10 years, and a second one with an average age of 70 years, i.e., 5-10 years after retirement. From each center one sample of steelworkers and one of teachers was drawn.

Due to the efforts of Robert J. Havighurst and Bernice Neugarten, an interdisciplinary team of psychologists and sociologists from all of the participating countries cooperated in this project. In four preparatory sessions the adaptation of the interview schedule and the rating scales to the different languages was achieved. There was a long training process for the interviewers and the independent raters.

The findings of this study disconfirmed the disengagement theory in all countries. This was true for all the different samples, the younger and the older ones, the steelworkers and the teachers. Life satisfaction was significantly higher when intra- and extra-familial role activity was high. Hence, the activity theory of aging received full support from this study.

There were some slight divergences, however, in some of the countries. For example, we found that in some cases, the disengagement theory—i.e., a higher level of satisfaction goes together with a decreasing number of social contacts and a lower activity level—may be meaningful but only for a short period within the entire length of the aging process. Appropriately, the adjustment to a new life situation, as in the case of recent retirement, could begin with some sort of "withdrawal"—a kind of concentration on one's self. This might perhaps be compared to what some writers see as an inevitable "turning toward one's inner self" at the beginning of adolescence, followed by a "turning toward the outer world."

In connection with the problem of retirement, disengagement might be understood as a reaction to the stress brought about by the necessity for reorientation. This would imply an exogenous component. Although there are individual differences in reaction to stress, temporary disengagement seems to be the most frequent way of coping with the problems of retirement.

We do not propose that disengagement is a form of satisfactory aging. On the basis of our research results we conclude that after a certain transition period a renewed form of engagement is possible, as seen in our 70-75 year old sample where an increase of social activity and a strong feeling of being needed are correlated with life satisfaction and a positive morale.

Cesa-Bianchi summarized his findings for Italy as follows: "First of all we can advance the hypothesis that for the Milanese groups disengagement is not a pervasive process at 70 to 75 years. When it takes place in certain roles, it is compensated by activity in other roles. Teachers seem to compensate more in family and formal associations; steelworkers in the informal social relations.... The retirement behavior of teachers shows more variability than that of steelworkers, perhaps because their educational and cultural experience gives them greater potential for individual choice.

We can hypothesize that the tendency to activity and the tendency to disengagement coexist in each person at every stage of his life. The social environment influences the dynamic relationship between the two tendencies. If the actual equilibrium between the two tendencies is acceptable to the individual he will maintain a high level of satisfaction. His level of satisfaction will depend on the extent that his biological, psychological, and social needs are met by the actual balance of activity and disengagement in his own life" (in Havighurst et al., 1969, p. 84).

Generally speaking, this study is an example for cross-cultural research in the context of searching for commonalities in aging—at least in industrial societies. Findings were summarized by Havinghurst, Neugarten, and Tobin in the statement: "The older person who ages optimally is the person who stays active and who manages the shrinking of his social world" (1963, p. 414). The validity of this finding for other regions of the world was confirmed as well as disconfirmed by Zimmer and Lin (1996) in an Asian setting. A study of Taiwanese elderly showed that leisure-time activity, in the form of physical activity, not social activity, had the strongest influence on well-being for men. The only leisure-time activity left for women in this culture, namely contemplative activity, had negative effects on their emotional well-being. Based on findings like these the authors stress the need to take into account cultural variations in terms of different role expectations when testing the competing disengagement and activity theories of aging.

It seems that disengagement theory is strongly embedded in the cultural background of Western industrialized societies with their invention of retirement and their orientation toward individualism. In cultures which stress corporate kinship and generational reciprocity and where children are raised in this spirit (Simic, 1990) there is no disengagement because people are engaged in important family roles throughout life.

In pre-industrial societies disengagement is rare and when it occurs, it usually results from physical or mental disability. In these societies everybody has to do his (her) share of work as long as he is able to do it, and he does it in a social context. The duties may become less and hard physical labor is gradually taken over by the younger members of one's family. For the elderly there are often role shifts from production-oriented work to advisory or spiritual duties (e.g., Gutman, 1976; Vatuk, 1980), but there is no disengagement without role substitution. Again, these findings fail to support disengagement theory, but are in line with activity theory.

MODERNIZATION THEORY

Another commonality in the aging process was claimed by modernization theory. It was influenced by Simmon's (1945) notion about an inverse relationship between the level of technological development of a society and the situation of the aged in this society. Cowgill and Holmes (1972) extended this idea to a generalizing statement about a decline of the status of older people through health technology, economics, urbanization, and formal education. In agricultural societies where the elderly are in control of important resources and are engaged in a system of roles with progressively higher authority and responsibility, old people enjoy a high status (Press & McKool, 1972). According to modernization theory, the changes associated with the transition from agricultural to industrialized societies resulted in a rapid decline of the status of the aged. In its original form, modernization theory received sharp criticism (Finley, 1982; Fry, 1996). The following arguments were raised:

The view of high status of the elderly in traditional and low status in modern societies leads to a dichotomy of good vs. bad and thus to a romanticizing perception of a "golden age" for old people. It overlooks the great diversity of traditional cultures and tends to consider the aged as a homogenous group. As Glascock (1990) points out, in many pre-industrial cultures a sharp distinction is made between healthy elderly who are treated well and enjoy a high status and frail and decrepit old people who are often neglected, abandoned, or even killed.

The concept of status was criticized for its imprecise definition. Most importantly, the theory does not differentiate between images of and attitudes toward the aged and their actual treatment (Glascock & Feinman, 1981). These two aspects are not always in congruence with each other.

The view of a linear relationship between modernization and declining status of old people was rejected. Instead, a cyclical relation was proposed with the status of old people rising from the simple cultures of the gatherers and hunters to a peak in agricultural societies, then declining until at the highest stages of modernization as in the United States and Western Europe the status of the old people rises again (Finley, 1982; Palmore, 1976).

Behavioral scientists also raised several methodological problems concerning the comparability of the samples used for the confirmation of the theory, and the nature of the tests, questionnaires, and inventories used. Fry (1996) requested that at least two measures should be used to uphold the distinction between attitudes and behavior and for the assessment of affective qualities in attitudes toward the aged.

Requests of this kind have been met in a study by Esther Contréras De Lehr (1984) on attitudes toward the aged in Germany and Mexico. Using a combination of interview techniques and attitude scales for the analysis of attitudes toward different stages of the life cycle, she showed that in both countries adolescents were perceived in the most negative way and persons in middle adulthood in the most positive way. Old age was evaluated in a rather negative way in Germany, in a more positive way in Toluca, Mexico, and in the most positive way in Mexico City. These findings disconfirm modernization theory, especially since the German sample consisted of citizens of small towns, such as Gießen. De Lehr also asked for a description of the different age groups. The German respondents stated more often than those from Mexico that aged people are active and competent. But they also perceived the elderly as more anxious, lonely, and helpless compared to the respondents from Mexico. In addition, by using discriminant analysis, de Lehr (1984) showed that the image of the aged is less homogeneous in Mexico than in Germany. This is explained by the great diversity of socioeconomic conditions as they exist in developing countries.

Some of de Lehr's German findings about the image of old age are valid also for the United States. In a comparative study on attitudes toward the aged comparing an American sample with Eskimo (Inuit) and Samoa samples, Holmes (1995) found that although the United States are most capable of supporting the elderly, "the old of this society are no doubt the most anxious and apprehensive among the three groups."

Disconfirmation of modernization theory was also the conclusion of Olson (1990) who analyzed the situation of the elderly in Mainland China. The author states that modernization in China had the effect of raising the status of the aged due to influences and programs initiated by the various state and government policies. A modification of modernization theory is suggested by Kiefer (1990) from an analysis of the situation of the elderly in Japan: She argues for a more differentiated analysis of the effects of modernization. According to her data, Japanese elderly still enjoy traditional respect, but following modernization they suffered losses in terms of influence and self-determination.

LIFE SATISFACTION IN CROSS-CULTURAL PERSPECTIVE

One of the most common characteristics of old age as well as of human life in general is the search for satisfaction. Many studies point to a high degree of life satisfaction in the aged. For the European Community this was shown in a multinational survey in 1993 (Eurobarometer, 1993). In most countries 75-80% of the respondents reported a high degree of life satisfaction, percentages that were rather independent of their socioeconomic situation.

Several writers believe that the elderly use some form of cognitive restructuring in order to gain satisfaction even in situations which from an objective point of view have less satisfying aspects. Tornstam (1975) pointed to the high degree of satisfaction of aged people with their own health which very often is less satisfying from a medical point of view. Social comparison processes in which one's own status is evaluated in contrast to disabled or chronically sick persons may be involved in this cognitive restructuring. We observed divergences between subjective and objective health in both directions (Lehr, 1987, 1997). Only one third of the sample studied perceived their health in agreement with their medical assessment.

Carp (1975) found out that elderly people living in very poor housing conditions in San Francisco, California, perceived their homes as satisfactory as long as there was no way of moving to another place. Similarly, in one of our earlier studies with aged women living below the poverty line, these women reported a high degree of satisfaction with their economic situation. This finding was confirmed by Maderna (1977) in a survey conducted in Northern Italy twenty years ago.

One of the most ambitious cross-cultural projects concerned with well-being in late life is the AGE Project (Keith, Fry, Glascock, Ikels, et al., 1994). It includes samples from Swarthmore, Pennsylvania; Momence, Illinois; Blessington, Ireland; Clifton, Ireland; Hongkong, China; the Herero from Botswana; and the !Kung from Botswana. The socioeconomic situation ranged from rather high in Swarthmore to very low among the !Kung population.

In the evaluation of well-being scores two clusters emerged: the low self-raters (!Kung, Herero, and Hong Kong Chinese) and the high self-raters (the Irish and U.S. populations). Both economic and cultural differences explain these results. Where age is defined by physical capacity (as in the African sites), the decline of physical functioning associated with aging leads to low self-perceptions of well-being in old age.

In none of the samples were significant gender differences regarding the degree of life satisfaction observed. Age contributed in different ways to the variance. In both U.S. samples life satisfaction correlated in a positive direction with age. This may be explained by the fear of younger people about an insecure future. In contrast, older people tend to experience a feeling of satisfaction about having achieved many of their objectives in life.

The reasons which the respondents advanced for their self-rated life satisfaction were classified in four categories: health/physical functioning, material issues, social (familial) networks, personal goals, and values. In the two U.S.-samples as well as in Blessington, Ireland, the reasons given were divided about equally among these four categories. Only there the domain of "personal goals" was mentioned by a substantial number of persons. For the African and Hong Kong Chinese samples the most important domain for the evaluation of well-being was the domain of material resources, followed by health and physical functioning in the African samples, and by social networks in the Hong Kong sample. Interestingly, in Hong Kong social reasons were given especially by low self-raters for their lack of well-being, a fact that points to the importance of the family for supporting old people. Low well-being depended upon a lack of familial support or at least the fear of it.

Whereas no gender differences emerged regarding degree of life satisfaction they showed up very clearly in the reasons given for satisfaction. While women mentioned more often social and familial networks, men gave reasons in terms of material issues and economic security.

Although decisive cross-cultural differences emerged from this study, its authors emphasized the universal role played by basic needs for physical and economic security. Only if these needs are satisfied, can people follow personal goals, as has also been emphasized by Maslow. Seen from a world-wide perspective this seems to be a rare event. The authors conclude their discussion as follows: "Not until material and physical issues can be put in the background do people relax enough to contemplate the affective as opposed to the instrumental dimensions of their personal relationships or to speculate on the likelihood of attaining a desirable mental state or realizing their personal goals" (Keith et al., 1994, p. 143). Thus, in a world-wide perspective, life satisfaction in old age seems to be equivalent with freedom from physical and material problems.

For developing countries this was confirmed by Doll (1997) in a study comparing elderly living in Brazil and in Germany. In both samples well-being was most closely correlated with subjective health—a finding supported by a majority of scientists from different Western societies. In Doll's study next to subjective health, income was associated with well-being in Brazil. In Germany, this was true for the familial and (to a smaller degree) for the extra-familial networks; in contrast, income was ranked lower by the German sample. The idea that well-being is created by freedom from material problems was confirmed only for the Brazil sample.

Another study comparing German elderly women with those from Colombia showed no differences regarding the respondents' high degree of life satisfaction (Lopez, 1997). There were differences, however, in area-specific satisfaction scores in different roles. Satisfaction with one's spouse-role and one's neighbor-role was higher in Germany, while satisfaction with one's children, grandchildren, and the extended family members was higher in

Colombia.

Very striking but meaningful differences emerged in this study when the subjects had to define what makes life worth living. In Colombia happiness in marriage, to love and to be loved, and having children were the most frequently mentioned values. In Germany, this was true for happiness in marriage, autonomy, financial independence, and enjoying trips into nature. The latter was mentioned very rarely in Colombia; the same was true for autonomy and for economic independence, which ranked very high in Germany, but very low in Colombia.

It should be mentioned that Lopez used the method of control twins. She selected control persons for German respondents from the Interdisciplinary Longitudinal Study on Aging of Germany (Schmitt, 1997).

For the developed countries there is a tendency to conceptualize well-being in terms of Abraham Maslow's humanistic psychology or in terms of Erik Erikson's psychosocial theory. Ryff and Essex (1991) defined well-being as a complex experience including positive encounters, satisfaction of both primary and secondary needs, openness to the situation, belief in one's own control over the situation, and a positive attitude toward the future. A recent study on "young-old" retired persons from East and West Germany has confirmed such a complex view of well-being (Schmitt, 1997).

Evidence for a conceptualization of subjective well-being has been presented also in a study on older Israeli adults (Shmotkin & Hadari, 1996). A factorial analysis of data from the Life Satisfaction Index of the Philadelphia Geriatric Center Morale Scale revealed a multifaceted structure including components such as "reconciled aging," defined as dissociation from negative feelings, and having a positive outlook on the present and future. A second factor, labeled as "unstrained affect," is related to both denial or suppression of negative affect and anxiety together with general contentment and "present happiness." The "past fulfillment" factor is related to the conceptualization of Ryff and Essex. It reflects the congruence between one's personal expectations and one's actual achievements in the past. In this way the concept of well-being is extended far beyond that of "freedom of problems." It also includes personal values and goals which, however, become important only if the basic needs are satisfied.

For ethnic minorities in developed countries, however, an extended conceptualization of well-being seems to lack validity. For African Americans life satisfaction is associated almost exclusively with income and social status (Jackson, Bacon, & Peterson, 1977). For three Hispanic minorities living in the United States, namely Mexican, Cuban, and Puerto Rican Americans, satisfaction is related first of all to health and to freedom from stress in one's own family. Impairments in the ability to perform the activities of daily living, poor subjective health, and unmet needs in social relationships were the main predictors of perceived stress in all three groups. Especially for the aged Cuban Americans, fears about dependency on others and living alone contributed significantly to perceived stress (Ward, 1979).

CONCLUSION

The studies reported in this paper reflect a pattern of cultural differences existing at a given point in time. While the results are valid for the last decades of the 20th century, our world is changing rapidly.

An important future topic is that of demographic and cultural change. Changes influencing the status and the treatment of the aged can originate within or outside a culture and they may be caused by technical, social, and medical factors and interventions, but also by the aged themselves, and by the graying population.

Furthermore, this graying of the population in both developed and undeveloped countries, can cause changes in the status of the aged, as well as in the attitudes of the younger generation towards them. Relationships between culture and the individual have never been fixed and static; but today these relationships are becoming dynamic in a way which will bring new challenges to societies, the labor market, families, and the individual—and last but not least to scientists, including those who do cross-cultural research.

BIBLIOGRAPHY

Baltes, P.B., & Baltes M.M. (1990). Psychological perspectives on successful aging: The model of selective optimization with compensation. In P.B. Baltes & M.M. Baltes (Eds.), *Successful aging* (pp. 1-34). Cambridge, UK: Cambridge University Press.

Carp, F.M. (1975). Ego-defense or cognitive consistency effects on environmental evaluation? *Journal of Gerontology*, *30*, 707–711.

Cowgill, D.O., & Holmes, L.D. (1972). *Aging and modernization*. New York: Appleton-Century-Crofts.

Cumming, E., & Henry, W.E. (1961). *Growing old: The process of disengagement*. New York: Basic Books.

De Lehr, C.E. (1984). *Zum Altersbild in Mexiko und Deutschland* [About the image of aging in Mexico and Germany]. München: Fink.

Doll, J. (1997). *Einflussfaktoren auf die Lebenszufriedenheit im Alter in Deutschland und Brasilien* [Influences on life satisfaction in old age in Germany and Brazil]. Unpublished masters thesis, University of Heidelberg.

Elwert, G. (1992). Alter im interkulturellen Vergleich. [Aging in cross-cultural comparison]. In P.B. Baltes & J. Mittelstrass (Eds.), *Zukunft des*

Alterns und gesellschaftliche Entwicklung [The future of aging and the development of societies] (pp. 261–281). Berlin: de Gruyter.

European Commission (1993). *Eurobarometer.*

Finley, G.E. (1982). Modernization and aging. In T.M. Field, A. Huston, H.C. Quay, L. Troll, & G.E. Finley (Eds.), *Review of human development* (pp. 511-523). New York: Wiley.

Fry, C.L. (1996). Age, aging, and culture. In R.H. Binstock & L.K. George (Eds.), *Handbook of aging and the social sciences* (4th ed.) (pp. 117-136). New York: Academic Press.

Glascock, A.P. (1990). By any other name, it is still killing: A comparison of the treatment of the elderly in America and other societies. In J. Sokolovsky (Ed.), *The cultural context of aging* (pp. 43–56). New York: Bergin & Garvey.

Glascock, A.P., & Feinman, S.L. (1981). Social asset or social burden: Treatment of the aged in non-industrial societies. In C.L. Fry (Ed.), *Aging, culture, and health: Comparative viewpoints and strategies* (pp. 13-31). New York: J.F. Bergin.

Gutman, D. (1976). Alternatives to disengagement: The old men of the Highland Druze. In J. Gubrium (Ed.), *Time, roles, and self in old age* (pp. 232-245). New York: Human Science Press.

Havighurst, R.J., Munnichs, J.M.S., Neugarten, B.L., & Thomae, H. (Eds.). (1969). *Adjustment to retirement: A cross-national study.* Assen: van Gorcum.

Havighurst, R.J., Neugarten, B.L., & Tobin, S.H. (1963). Disengagement, personality, and life satisfaction in the later years. In P. Hansen (Ed.), *Age with a future* (pp. 419–425). Copenhagen: Munksgaard.

Holmes, E.R., & Holmes, L.D. (1995). *Other cultures, elder years* (2nd ed.). London: Sage.

Jackson, J., Bacon, J., & Peterson, J. (1977). Life satisfaction among black urban elderly. *International Journal of Aging and Human Development, 8,* 169-180.

Keith, J., Fry, Ch., Glascock, A., Ikels, Ch., et al. (1994). *The aging experience: Diversity and commonality across cultures.* Thousand Oaks, CA: Sage.

Kiefer, C.W. (1990). The elderly in modern Japan: Elite, victims, or plural players? In J. Sokolovsky (Ed.), *The cultural context of aging* (pp.181-195). New York: Bergin & Garvey.

Kinsella, K., & Taeuber, C.M. (1992). *An aging world II* (U.S. Bureau of the Census, P-25, 92-3). Washington, DC: Government Printing Office.

Kohli, M. (1985). Die Institutionalisierung des Lebenslaufes [The institutionalization of the lifespan]. *Kölner Zeitschrift für Soziologie und Sozialpsychologie, 37,* 1–29.

Lehr, U. (1982). Socio-psychological correlates of longevity. *Annual Review of Gerontology and Geriatrics, 3,* 102-147.

Lehr, U. (1987). Subjektiver und objektiver Gesundheitszustand im Licht von Längsschnittstudien [Subjective and objective health in the light of longitudinal studies]. In U. Lehr & H.Thomae (Eds.), *Formen seelischen Alterns* [Ways of psychological aging] (pp. 153-159). Stuttgart: Enke.

Lehr, U. (1997). Gesundheit und Lebensqualität im Alter [Health and quality of life in old age]. *Zeitschrift für Gerontopsychologie und -psychiatrie, 10,* 277-287.

Lehr, U., & Thomae, H. (Eds.). (1987). *Formen seelischen Alterns: Ergebnisse der Bonner Gerontologischen Längsschnittstudie* [Ways of psychological aging: Results of the Bonn Gerontological Study of Aging]. Stuttgart: Enke.

Lopez, M.E. (1997). *Lebenszufriedenheit im Alter: Eine Vergleichsuntersuchung deutscher und kolumbianischer älterer Frauen* [Life satisfaction in old age: A comparative study of German and Colombian elderly women]. Unpublished masters thesis, University of Heidelberg.

Maderna, A.M. (1977). *Medical and psychological problems of aging and senility.* Paper presented at the 4th Biennial Meeting, ISSBD, Pavia, Italy.

Martin, L.G. (1988). The aging of Asia. *Journal of Gerontology, 43,* (4), 99-113.

Mui, A.C. (1996). Correlates of psychological distress among Mexican, Cuban, and Puerto Rican elders living in U.S.A. *Journal of Cross-Cultural Gerontology, 11,* 131-147.

Olson, P. (1990). The elderly in the People's Republic of China. In J. Sokolovsky (Ed.), *The cultural context of aging* (pp. 143-161). New York: Bergin & Garvey.

Palmore, E. (1976). The future status of the aged. *Gerontologist, 16,* 297-302.

Press, I., & McKool, M. (1972). Social structure and status of the aged: Toward some valid cross-cultural generalizations. *International Journal of Aging and Human Development, 3,* 297-306.

Ryff, C.D., & Essex, M.J. (1991). Psychological well-being in adulthood and old age: Descriptive markers and explanatory processes. *Annual Review of Gerontology, 11,* 144-171.

Schmitt, M. (1997). *Komponenten des Wohlbefindens. Abschlußbericht des 1. Untersuchungsdurchgangs der Interdisziplinären Langzeitstudie über Bedingungen zufriedenen und gesunden Älterwerdens* [Components of well-being. Final report of the first measurement point of the Interdisciplinary Longitudinal Study on Adult Development and Aging]. Unpublished manuscript. Heidelberg: University of Heidelberg.

Shmotkin, D., & Hadari, G. (1996). An outlook on subjective well-being in older Israeli adults. *International Journal of Aging and Human Development*, *42*, 271–290.

Simic, A. (1990). Aging, world view, and intergenerational relations in America and Yugoslavia. In J. Sokolovsky (Ed.), *The cultural context of aging* (pp. 89–108). New York: Bergin & Garvey.

Simmons, L. (1945). *The role of the aged in primitive society.* New Haven, CT: Yale University Press.

Thomae, H. (1976). Patterns of "successful aging." In H. Thomae (Ed.), *Patterns of aging* (pp. 147–161). New York: Karger.

Thomae, H. (1983). *Alternsstile und Alternsschicksale. Ein Beitrag zur differentiellen Gerontologie.* [Styles and destinies of aging: A contribution to a differential gerontology]. Bern: Huber.

Tornstam, L. (1975). Health and self perception. *The Gerontologist*, *15*, 264–270.

Vatuk, S. (1980). Withdrawal and disengagement as a cultural response to aging in India. In C.L. Fry (Ed.), *Aging in culture and society: Comparative viewpoints and strategies* (pp. 126–148). New York: J.F. Bergin.

Ward, R. (1979). *Minority aging: Double jeopardy or levelling?* Paper presented at GSA Meeting, Washington, DC.

Zimmer, Z., & Lin, H.S. (1996). Leisure activity and well-being among elderly in Taiwan. *Journal of Cross-Cultural Gerontology*, *11*, 167–186.

THE AGING AND THEIR FAMILIES: A CROSS-NATIONAL REVIEW

Eva Sandis, Fordham University, U.S.A.

This paper examines world population trends among the elderly, their impact on family structures and functions, and the implications for social policy. It uses a comparative framework, examining these changes in societies belonging both to the developing and the industrialized world regions.

GLOBAL POPULATION TRENDS

Population aging is a phenomenon experienced by all countries. By the year 2025, it is expected that the elderly population will be 58 million in the U.S.A.; 119 million in India; and 194 million in China, according to a report prepared for the United Nations International Conference on Aging by the United Nations Secretariat (UN Secretariat, 1994, pp. 81, 101). As Luiz Ramos has aptly put it, longevity is no longer today's concern; rather, it is the quality of life of the aging (UN Secretariat, 1994, p. 66).

Although older populations are growing both in absolute and relative numbers, these trends vary by world region. In 1995, those aged 65 and above comprised 6% of the world's population. For the various world regions, the percentages were: Africa, 3%; Latin America, 5%; Asia, 5%; North America, 13%; Europe, 14%; and Oceania, 10% (UN Demographic Yearbook, 1995, Table 2).

While these variations are real, the figures may not accurately describe the situation of individual societies, because the measures employed in the studies reflect Western, rather than universal, definitions of aging. For example, Khasiani (1994) has pointed out that the dependency ratio in East African societies is overstated because it is based on those 60 years and above, in accordance with retirement practices prevailing in the formal sectors of the economy of the world's industrialized societies. But most East Africans work in the informal sectors of their economies which are characteristic of the world's developing regions, and many of them continue to be productive until they are much older. Data on labor force participation of the elderly in four Latin American countries support this contention (Schulz, 1991, p. 9, Table 1).

In fact, the whole concept of age has to be viewed in cultural context. In regions where people have completed little schooling, chronological age is not meaningful; and age grades may instead be defined according to local community perceptions and customs. For example, in East Africa, age is graded according to whether the person is a parent, grandparent, or great-grandparent (Khasiani, 1994, p. 61).

The global aging trend has some specific features with significant implications for family and policy issues. First, there is a growing tendency for the world's elderly to be concentrated in the world's developing regions. Second, in both the developed and developing regions, the segment of very old persons (80 years or over) will continue to grow faster than the elderly group as a whole. Third, there will be a greater increase in the number of older women than of older men, given women's greater longevity. Finally, the dependency ratio (inactive over active/working population) will increase (Schulz, 1991).

Aging populations are the result of declining fertility and mortality. Immigration is no solution to aging populations, because migrants themselves age, as the United Nations conference report on aging and the family concludes (1994, p. 10). The question is whether families, including those of migrants, will be able to cope with the challenges posed by aging societies (Sandis, 1996; United Nations, 1994).

FAMILY CHANGES

Countries differ in their family systems. Therefore, population aging has a differential impact on the structure of the family; the family's capacity to serve the needs of its members; and the requirements of social policies supportive of the aging and their families.

Changing Family Structures

As Goode's careful analyses have confirmed (1963, 1982, p. 176), historically, the structure of families has tended toward being nuclear, either prior to, concurrently with, or subsequent to, industrialization. Today, the nuclear family, consisting of husband, wife, and their dependent children, is being transformed into other family structures, as demonstrated by developments occurring in various world regions. Structurally, the emerging types of families may be classified as: spouses or partners living alone with one another; single parents living with their children; and elderly parents moving in with their children and grandchildren. The predominance of particular family types varies according to world region, and this has a differential impact on family functions and social policy needs.

Contemporary aging trends are also associated with the following factors: a rise in the number of households; a decrease in the size of households; an increase in the number of elderly who choose to live independently if their economic and health situation permits it; and an increase of elderly who co-reside with kin in multigenerational households out of economic or physical necessity (UN Secretariat, 1994, p. 87).

Although household composition is not identical with family composition (see Lehr, Seiler, and Thomae in this volume), data collection on household distribution by generation far exceeds that on distribution of families according to generations (Hagestad, 1994). Therefore, family structure must often be inferred from household composition, even though family organization frequently crosses household boundaries. Fortunately, revised data collection methods are now being developed which will provide more accurate indicators of family composition trends.

Institutionalization is still, globally, a "strategy of last resort" for the very old. Only between 5% and 7% of the population aged 65 and over in the developed societies are institutionalized, and only 0.5% to 2% of this age group in the developing countries. (Japanese figures may slightly undercount the institutionalized population because they do not include those who spend extended periods of time in hospitals and chronic-care centers [UN Secretariat, 1994, p. 89; and Footnote 5, p. 102]).

Family Care-giving and Care-receiving Trends

As the global data on institutionalization indicate, the family is still the primary caregiving and care-receiving institution for its members. The family fulfills this service despite the strains imposed on it by the structural changes it is undergoing. These changes have been in response to societal pressures such as economic developments, migration, and urbanization.

The same pressures which are producing structural family changes are also producing new family relations both within and across generations, as well as new roles, rights, and obligations among family members (Hareven, 1996; United Nations, 1994, p. 13;). Aging family members are increasingly assuming caregiving roles for themselves, the young, and the very old members of their households. Aging women usually care for their elderly husbands and their very old parents. Frequently, they also take care of the children of their own offspring. Adult children recognize their obligations to very old parents. At the same time, they are busy bringing up their own children while often also working full-time. This places considerable burdens on family members, especially women, who are generally the culturally designated family caregivers (*United Nations Bulletin on Aging*, 1995, Nos. 2 & 3).

The elderly themselves, across world regions, tend to show a preference for self-care and independent living when finances and health allow it. They realize the stress produced on intergenerational relations when their situation makes them dependent on the care of family members. Some may even prefer institutionalization under such conditions (Ramos, 1994).

Summarizing the prospects for intergenerational relations in aging societies, Bengtson believes several factors will allow for increased conflict, while others will facilitate increased solidarity (Bengtson, 1994, p. 184). Among the positive developments are: formation of benign cultural norms and practices consonant with the realities of an aging society; a growing acceptance of intergenerational reciprocity throughout the lifespan; and the availability of new roles for the aging which recognize the elderly as valuable resources to their societies.

AGING AND FAMILY TRENDS BY WORLD REGIONS

Developed Countries of the West

In a review of family types in Northwestern Europe and North America, Hoehn (1994, p. 30) concludes that whatever the societal ideals regarding extended families, in actuality the nuclear family has been the dominant structure. High mortality rates have prevented the extension of families, and low fertility rates have encouraged the formation of nuclear families. Patterns of late marriage also contribute to the prevalence of nuclear households.

Denuclearization has been the modern trend in the West. Concomitant with the decline in nuclear families composed of husband, wife, and dependent children there occurred a diversification of family forms and living arrangements, including persons who live alone, single parent households due primarily to divorce, and persons living in consensual unions. This diversification is evident today in Europe, North America, Australia, and New Zealand (Hoehn, 1994, pp. 30-31).

As to family care, today only a "negligible fraction" of the very old are institutionalized in the West. Their wives care for most old men and old women (usually widows) live mostly near their adult children. However, in the future, family caretaking is likely to become more problematic (United Nations, 1994, p. 5).

For the senior generations, the outlook in the West is, according to Hoehn, that there will be more old people; a larger proportion will be living alone, because they never married or are divorced; and fewer old people will be living near adult children who can take care of them, either because they are childless, or their children have moved, or they themselves have moved. Meanwhile, the middle-aged generations will have to take care of their elderly at the same time as of their youth; pay for the pensions of the old; work longer to pay for these pensions; and save for their own. These scenarios must be taken into account when trying to adjust social policies in aging societies (Hoehn, 1994, pp. 31-32).

Developed Countries of the East

Multigenerational co-residence still exists in Japan and in the newly industrialized Asian societies of Korea, Hong Kong, Singapore, and Taiwan, but the corresponding trends vary from country to country. In Taiwan, Korea, and

Hong Kong, the aged frequently continue to live with their married sons and daughters despite modernization and economic development. Nevertheless, the decline in co-residence appears ineluctable and irreversible, as Shigemi Kono notes (1994, p. 43).

The gradual decline of co-residence is also occurring in Japan, although it remains to be seen whether this augurs a convergence with the Western type of "nuclear and individual-oriented living" arrangement (Kono, 1994, p. 43). Be that as it may, data on household structures for Japan from 1955 to 1985 suggest a diversification pattern similar to that in the West. The pattern includes a decrease in families composed of husband, wife, and children, an increase in families composed of husband and wife only, and an increase of one-person households (Kono, 1994, p. 39, Table 6).

While the family remains the primary caretaking institution in the developed countries of Asia, the residential patterns of the elderly give an indication of a generalized preference for self care and independent living where finances and health permit. As Kono observes, the aged in Japan do not necessarily live with their children throughout their life, but may begin to co-reside with their close kin upon the death of a spouse or when they become incapacitated (1994, p. 43).

With respect to the future, it is probable that Japanese families and those of the newly industrialized Asian societies will become smaller, because of fertility declines, increased migration, changes in traditional values, and increasingly high ages of marriage.

Developing Societies of Africa

In the past, extended families were organized into clans who resided in a given territory and assigned land tenure rights to family heads. Women held indirect land tenure rights through their husbands, sons, and brothers. However, the clan system broke down with colonization, and now the nuclear family is considered the operative organizational unit (Khasiani, 1994, p. 62). It is also the unit that is perceived as responsible for the care of its elderly family members. This task falls foremost on spouses, next on adult children (especially sons, who alone can re-establish a widowed mother's land tenure rights), and finally on siblings. Community assistance is mostly symbolic, and governmental assistance virtually nonexistent, according to Khasiani (1994, pp. 63-64).

Elderly people prefer to care for themselves as long as they are able to do so. Old people in East Africa remain productively engaged "into extreme old age." Women especially contribute to their own and their household's welfare well into their seventies. Elderly women not only take care of themselves, but also of their spouses and the rest of their household. They provide food and care for the children of their married and unmarried sons and daughters. The elderly therefore "form a very small percentage of the dependent population compared to their size," and the strain placed on the working population through caring is "minimal" (Khasiani, 1994, pp. 64-65).

But the modernization of African societies has put at risk certain categories of elderly, particularly women. Increased life expectancy has increased both the number of widows and the length of widowhood, but declines in fertility are producing a scarcity of sons to ensure widows' rights to land tenure. A decline in polygamy and increased opportunities for remaining single also put women at risk since such patterns reduce the availability of husbands or male children to secure their rights (Khasiani, 1994, p. 64).

As to implications for social policy, the needs of the elderly are likely to be much greater in the future than they are today. Whereas the cohorts of elderly are increasing in number many individuals are not getting married, others are in unstable relationships, and as fertility declines, many remain childless. The family is still the most appropriate caregiving institution for the elderly, Khasiani maintains, but it needs to be supplemented in ways that are sensitive to the different needs of various categories of elderly: the younger elderly who must be recognized as providers of family care; the very old and disabled who need to receive care in their communities; and women who need to be provided with the economic resources for leading an independent life (Khasiani, 1994, p. 65).

Developing Societies of Latin America

Aging decisively influences household structure, often leading to more numerous co-resident families in developing societies. In Brazil, for example, the majority of the elderly live in multigenerational households. This is the result of economic necessity rather than choice, as the results of Ramos' 1987 household survey of elderly persons residing in the metropolis of Sao Paulo show (Ramos, 1994).

According to the Sao Paulo survey, 12% of the elderly lived alone; 32% resided with a spouse or another person of the same generation; and 56% lived in multigenerational households. Among the latter, half resided with their children in a two-generation household, while the other half lived with their children and grandchildren in a three-generation household. Poverty, the study found, was strongly associated with co-residence in multigenerational households (Ramos, 1994, p. 67).

In the three-generation household, Ramos notes, "the elderly are usually in a marginal situation because their children have to take care of their own children and give the elderly less priority," a situation easily creating dissatisfaction. He surmises that the decline in the prevalence of three-generation households in Sao Paulo between 1984 and 1989 may be an expression of the problems engendered by this kind of household arrangement. It may augur a shift toward institutionalized care, spearheaded by dissatisfied elderly in multigenerational households (Ramos, 1994, p. 71).

No matter what the household type, it is always one family member, usually a woman (daughter or wife) who is principally in charge of family caregiving activities. According to Ramos, this means that the care provided to an elderly person is not shared among all members of the household, even in those composed of three generations. This points to a potential weakness of the multigenerational household as an insurance of well-being in old age, namely that the burden of co-residence tends to have a detrimental effect on the care that caregivers may provide.

Some elderly in Latin America, particularly in the wealthier strata, hesitate to depend on the good will of particular family members to take care of their needs. Like the elderly in the developed societies of the West and the East, they tend to opt for the "intimacy-at-a-distance" habits characteristic of the affluent classes (Ramos, 1994, p. 71).

In the light of findings such as those of the Sao Paulo household survey, policy makers will have to reconsider the role of the multigenerational household in Latin America and its ability to service the growing elderly population. The family will have to be supported and strengthened to carry out its role in caring for the aged.

SUMMARY AND CONCLUSIONS

While the proportion of the aged in the world's societies varies across regions, there is an unmistakable *global trend toward an increasingly aging population.* This aging trend, largely due to declining mortality and fertility rates, *affects both the structure and the function of families.* Historically, the structure of families has tended toward being nuclear, either prior to, concurrently with, or subsequent to, industrialization. Today, the nuclear family of husband, wife, and dependent children is declining, while other types of family structures and household forms are becoming predominant. Among these are families composed of spouses or partners living in one-generation households; of single parents and their children living in two-generation households; and of grandparents moving in with their children and grandchildren to form multigenerational households. The formation of these family types and household forms affects the care-receiving and caregiving functions of families, the family roles of women, and the intergenerational relations among family members. *These changes generate social policy needs* to ensure a satisfactory quality of life for the elderly and their families.

These social policy needs include recognition of the following: First, the aging are engaged in self-care, with a preference for independence and "intimacy-at-a-distance" in so far as their finances and health permit; second, the aging are caregivers to both older and younger family members; third, the aging exercise both self-care and other care-roles for a much longer part of their lifespan than conventional dependency measures assume; fourth, women bear an unfair share of the family caregiving function because of outmoded cultural conventions about gender roles; fifth, gender equity is needed in access to educational, job training, and work opportunities so that elderly women can acquire the resources needed to lead an independent life; and finally, there is a great need for intervention and support by governments, Non-Governmental Organizations (NGOs), and local communities so that families are not left to cope all by themselves with the stresses and burdens of caring for their aging members.

BIBLIOGRAPHY

Bengtson, V.L. (1994). Aging and the problem of generations: Prospects for a new generational contract. In United Nations (Eds.), *Aging and the family* (pp. 178-185). New York: United Nations.

Goode, W.J. (1963). *World revolution and family patterns*. New York: Free Press.

Goode, W.J. (1964/1982). *The family*. Englewood Cliffs, NJ: Prentice-Hall.

Hagestad, G. (1994). The changing balance of young and old: Norwegian families in the post-war era. In United Nations (Eds.). *Aging and the family* (pp. 169-177). New York: United Nations.

Hareven, T. (1996). *Aging and generational relations*. New York: Aldine De Gruyter.

Hoehn, C. (1994). Aging and the family in the context of Western-style developed countries. In United Nations (Eds.), *Aging and the family* (pp. 29-33). New York: United Nations.

Khasiani, S. (1994). The changing role of the family in meeting the needs of the aging population in the developing countries, with particular focus on Eastern Africa. In United Nations (Eds.), *Aging and the family* (pp. 61-65). New York: United Nations.

Kono, S. (1994). Aging and the family in the developed countries and areas of Asia: Continuities and transitions. In United Nations (Eds.), *Aging and the family* (pp. 34-44). New York: United Nations.

Ramos, L.R. (1994). Family support for the elderly in Latin America: The role of the multigenerational household. In United Nations (Eds.), *Aging and the family* (pp. 66-72). New York: United Nations.

Sandis, E. (1994). *Elderly on the move*. Invited paper presented at the 52nd annual meeting of the International Council of Psychologists, Lisbon,

Portugal, July 10-14.
Schulz, J.H. (1991). *The world aging situation, 1991.* New York: United Nations.
United Nations (1994). *Aging and the family.* New York: Author.
United Nations (1995a). *Bulletin on Aging,* Nos. 2 & 3. New York: Author.
United Nations (1995b). *Demographic yearbook.* New York: Author.
United Nations Secretariat (1994). Overview of recent research findings on population aging and the family. In United Nations (Eds.), *Aging and the family* (pp. 79-104). New York: United Nations.

GENDER, HEALTH, AND BEHAVIOR AMONG AGING NORTH AMERICANS

Margot B. Nadien, Fordham University, U.S.A.

Because the elderly in the U.S. and Canada are more similar than different in their development and the factors which shape them, we shall focus on a related topic; namely, the surprisingly similar *differences* which typify the physical and psychosocial functioning of aging females and males in both countries, and the genetic and environmental influences which underlie them. In examining these issues, we shall start with a brief review of the current age-sex structures in the U.S. and Canada. Thereafter, we shall turn first to the physical health of North Americans in terms of their primary and secondary aging processes, and then to their cognitive and personality functioning. Throughout our discussion, we shall seek to explain dissimilarities between the sexes in terms of differences in their past history of health and socialization, and in the context of their lives during old age.

AGE-SEX STRUCTURE IN THE U.S.A. AND CANADA

In turning to a few statistics about life expectancy and the age-sex structure in North America, we discover that, as of the 1980s and 1990s, the elderly form almost 13% of the U.S. population (American Psychological Society, 1993), but less than 10% of the Canadian population (Statistics Canada, 1985).

In developed countries, the estimate at birth of how long people will live, called *life expectancy*, favors females over males. In North America, life expectancy rates in the 1990s are about 78 years for females and 71 years for males. The male's lesser longevity of about seven years traces to two factors: genes and social influences.

Genes

In term of life expectancy, males are disadvantaged by their genetic makeup. For, unlike females, who have two X chromosomes, males normally receive only one X chromosome along with a Y chromosome. The latter, being only one-fifth the size of the X chromosome, accommodates far fewer genes, and thus lacks many counterpart genes to those carried along the X chromosome. For example, immunoglobin M, a substance which confers some immunity against disease, is found in the X chromosome but not in the Y chromosome (Turner, 1982). This lesser amount of protective immunoglobin M may contribute to a male's greater predisposition to infectious disease and earlier death, both in infancy and after age 35 (Preston, 1976).

Social Factors

Social factors may also contribute to the male's lesser longevity. More males than females have a Type A personality, a set of personality traits that increases the risk of coronary attacks. Several factors contribute to this risk. Firstly, males are more prone to aggression, partly because of all the testosterone conferred by their Y chromosome, and partly because of their childhood training in aggression and competitiveness. Secondly, males reared in Canada and the U.S. are likely to be socialized to repress their emotions, deny feelings of physical and emotional pain, and prove their courage through such risky behaviors as car and motorboat racing, contact sports, and mountain climbing (Graney, 1979). Thirdly, unlike women, who prefer low-risk activities and jobs (Ballau & Buchan, 1978; Gee & Kimball, 1987; Root & Daley, 1980), North American males seek and attain a higher proportion of the more lucrative—but also the more dangerous—jobs in heavy industry, construction, railroads, and in police, fire fighting, and military forces.

Having noted some broad bases for gender differences in longevity, we shall now consider physical health in old age, and some factors that affect the speed of aging.

AGING

For both Americans and Canadians, old age brings less stable health than is enjoyed during earlier life phases. Nevertheless, the quality of health among the elderly varies greatly owing to two sources of biological change—that of primary aging and of secondary aging.

Primary Aging

Primary aging is the universal, gene-determined process which contributes toward the slow but continuing decline in many of the body's tissues starting in early adulthood. Joints and tendons become more brittle. Muscles and bones weaken. Food and oxygen metabolize more slowly into energy and new tissue. The lungs' vital capacity lessens. The heart's output of blood declines each year, and the blood vessels, heart, and other tissues become less elastic and resilient. These and other changes, starting in our 30's, contribute to an almost imperceptible yet inexorable decline in our dexterity and our overall strength and stamina. In addition, a weakening immune system renders us more prone to infections, and slower to recover from them (Busse, 1977).

Primary aging also involves a general "slowing" of bodily processes. Blood circulates more slowly, thus taking longer to reach and nourish our body's tissues. Reaction time is also slower because of the need for more intense stimulation in order to activate our sense receptors, and more time for nerve impulses to travel to and from the brain and then to culminate in motor responses.

Overall, these primary aging processes are determined mainly by our genes, and are only minimally retarded by exercise, an appropriate diet, and other fitness measures. By contrast, features of secondary aging are subject to the interactive influence of both genes and environment (Busse, 1977).

Secondary Aging

Secondary aging processes are outcomes of various influences. They result from diseases, such as flu and vascular disorders. They come from the nonuse of one's body, as when a failure to exercise causes our muscles to atrophy and our joints to stiffen. They arise from the abuse of our body, as occurs when we smoke, drink too much, eat unwisely, abuse drugs, and overexpose ourselves to the sun and various air and sound pollutants. Secondary aging also stems from the excessive or prolonged stress that occurs when we fail to establish a good balance between activity and rest or when we fail to draw on known measures of reducing emotional tension.

Since these sources of secondary aging are the product not only of genes but also of environmental factors, they can often be minimized by "wellness" measures. In other words, for people who have good genes and have practiced good health habits for much of their lives, secondary aging is minimal and hence optimal physical and mental functioning may continue well into a person's 70s or 80s. Indeed, the fact that persons over age 79 represent the fastest-growing age group in North America (American Psychological Society, 1993) suggests that increasing numbers of these "oldest-old" persons use wellness measures and advanced techniques of medical and health care.

In sum, aside from a slowing of biological functioning, many elders in the U.S. and Canada have extended their life span and thus enjoy some functional independence through their 70s or 80s, but only if they have observed good health habits, have had access to the continuing advances in health care, and have been genetically resistant to conditions which impair their vital organs.

GENDER DIFFERENCES IN PHYSICAL HEALTH

Turning now to the topic of gender differences in physical health among North Americans, we find that the most striking differences are those that arise not between residents of the U.S. and Canada, but between females and males in both countries. For example, studies of disease and death among older people in the United States and Canada show that males are more prone than females to early death from such major disorders as cancer, pneumonia, or heart disease (Statistics Canada, 1981), whereas the life expectancy of females exceeds that of males by seven years (Verbrugge, 1976). However, for those males and females who survive until age 65, the projected gender difference in longevity narrows to 4.2 years for whites and 3.8 years for nonwhites (Huyck, 1990). Thus, if still alive at age 65, the average North American male may expect to survive until about age 80, and the average female until roughly age 84.

In North America, why do twice as many males as females expire from heart disease? Might it be traced partly to the possession by males of more testosterone, the hormone linked to aggression, and partly to their early childhood training to be assertive and achieving? And might this interplay between the male's inherited and acquired tendencies to aggress and compete predispose males toward a higher incidence of type A personality and, hence, a greater risk of coronary heart disease (Huyck, 1990)?

Aside from this gender difference, a seeming paradox inheres in the data concerning elderly males and females. As noted in an earlier paper (Nadien, 1996a), even though males in North America are genetically more prone than females to infection and early death, females display more sick-related behaviors, such as consulting a physician, using medications, and staying home from work when ill (Nathanson, 1975).

In seeking to explain the greater chronic illness in females but the earlier death in males, Verbrugge (1976) raises the following questions. Might women have more acute and non-lethal illnesses, while men have more of the life-threatening conditions that terminate in early death? Or, might females exhibit more sickness-related behaviors because their childhood socialization encourages them to notice their symptoms and seek care when ill? When their chief activities are home-making and child-rearing, might women suffer more stress from their nurturant role? Might they also be more prone to infections and, when ill, have more time to consult physicians (Gove, 1984; Verbrugge, 1976)?

By contrast, might the childhood training of North American males have led them to view complaints about physical symptoms as signs of weakness? If true, might this have fostered a life-long tendency either to repress or deny physical symptoms or, if aware of them, to delay medical treatment until stricken with life-threatening disorders? And might it even account for North American males being less apt than females to comply with medical advice? Finally, might a combination of these innate and acquired tendencies explain why North American males are more prone than females to suffer and die from grave physical disorders by early old age—i.e., between the ages of 65 and 75?

Having considered some innate and acquired tendencies which may contribute to gender differences in ill health and mortality, let us now explore how some aging health changes may affect the cognitive and personality functioning of elderly North Americans.

HEALTH-BEHAVIOR RELATIONSHIPS

Cognitive Functioning

We noted earlier that aging brings a rise in sensory thresholds and a slower transmission of information from activated sense organs to the brain and from there to the muscles and glands that initiate a response. This decrease in the speed of physical movement becomes reflected in slower cognition. For example, there is a slowing in the speed of new learning and memory, and in the performance of those features on intelligence tests known as *fluid items*, namely, the skills governed more by innate capacities and less by past learning. Thus, even when healthy, the elderly show a slower reaction time, a shorter memory, and a decline in the speed of perceptual-motor tasks, reasoning, judging, and forming concepts (Horn, 1982).

These minor decrements in fluid intelligence are relatively unimportant because effectiveness in the tasks of daily living, our careers, and our social relationships is governed largely by mental processes known as *crystallized features* of intelligence. These processes relate to acquired knowledge, verbal and mathematical skills, and the decision-making processes that depend on complex thought and the integration of diverse types of information and experience (Horn, 1982). Fortunately, healthy older people often remain effective in their crystallized features of cognition through their 60s; and, when well-educated, relatively free of economic and other worries, and mentally and physically active as well as healthy, they sometimes improve their crystallized features of intelligence up through their 70s (Schaie, 1983). Indeed, some research even shows that the elderly, when emotionally and socially mature, may surpass young adults in sociocentrism, the synthesis of ideas, and the complexity of their thought (Boswell, 1978; Labouvie-Vief & Schell, 1982; Zelinski, Gilewski, & Thompson, 1980).

Effects of Severe Forms of Ill Health

Unfortunately, the effective cognitive functioning which characterizes the healthy elderly becomes erased for those stricken with severe disorders. Severe hypertension, atherosclerosis, and diabetes—conditions which often precede heart, brain, and kidney disorders—may undermine cognitive performance directly, or else indirectly, as when medication or depression slows mental processes and impairs attention and memory (Hertzog, Schaie, &

Gribbin, 1978).

Of course, the chief basis for severe and progressive mental deterioration is some form of dementia. This stems most often from Alzheimer's disease, less often from the multi-infarct dementia that occurs when an embolism or atherosclerosis blocks blood vessels, and least often from advanced Parkinson's disease. Whatever its source, dementia undermines a person's memory and judgment; produces disorientation with respect to time, place, and person; disrupts the sense of identity and the recognition of familiar persons; impairs control over emotions and impulses; and causes confusion about appropriate social behavior and the performing of daily-life tasks (Hutton, 1987; Marsden, 1984).

Because dementia is associated with the loss of independence and psychosocial well-being, we can draw comfort from two statistics that concern North Americans. One is that, among persons over age 64, only 15% suffer from any of the 60-odd known mental afflictions. The other fact is that roughly 10 to 20% of all mentally ill elders can be treated because their problems stem from the reversible medical conditions caused by toxins, metabolic or endocrine imbalances, or functional psychiatric problems such as clinical depression (Gurland & Toner, 1982; Hutton, 1987).

As to the influence of gender, there is no clear-cut evidence of gender differences in cognitive functioning even though aging males are more prone to the heart and vascular disorders that undermine learning, memory, and other mental processes involved in problem solving.

Having discussed some ways in which the biological functioning of aging North Americans affects their cognitive stability or decline, let us now consider psychological health and personality in old age, and the gender issues that relate thereto.

FACTORS WHICH MAY LEAD TO PERSONALITY CHANGES

Much of the life-span research suggests that broad personality domains, such as extroversion, neurosis, and openness to new-experience, persist to and through old age (Conley, 1985; Costa & McCrae; 1984), at least among those North Americans who do not succumb to severe circulatory, heart, and brain disorders (Siegler, George, & Okun, 1979). Yet conditions that are not incapacitating may nevertheless evoke personality change. For example, when chronic illness or frailty leads to dependency on others, the elderly may lose confidence and self-esteem, especially if trained as children to be independent. Dependency may also bring the possibility of neglect or abuse or institutionalization by caregivers, conditions that are often followed by sharp declines in both physical and psychological health (Nadien, 1995, 1996b). Moreover, even when free of maltreatment and institutionalization, the sheer loss of mobility when frail or ill may lessen opportunities for social interaction and thus increase a sense of isolation.

Of course, personality change in old age may be the outcome not only of physical decline, but of other losses as well. There may be a loss of income and of meaningful activities upon retirement, and there may be increasing social losses as loved others die or move away.

Gender Differences and Similarities in Personality Stability or Change: The Example of Depression

Loss, whether it be of health or income or loved others, can lead to differing outcomes. One of the most pernicious effects, *depression*, is found more often in females than in males, and may trace to gender differences in socialization.

In contrasting the childhood background of today's elderly North Americans, one discovers that, as children, males were apt to have been rewarded for assertion and aggression, and to have received little or no punishment for impulsive or acting-out behaviors. Might this explain why, as adults, males are more prone than females to the antisocial acts and/or the drug and alcohol abuse that may foreshorten a person's life? Might it also explain why a male's maladjustment arises less often from intropunitive responses and more often from the extrapunitive or acting-out behaviors that may lead to incarceration for criminal acts that has been noted by Gove (see Walsh, 1987)?

Conversely, when considering the childhood training of today's elderly females, might disapproval of their childhood displays of aggression have fostered guilt feelings and the later repression of their anger and aggressive drives? If true, might it explain why, all through adulthood, women are twice as likely as men to suffer depression as well as other signs of repressed anger, such as anxiety, hysteria, and functional disorders?

These male-female differences in childhood training may explain the clear-cut empirical evidence noted by several researchers (Dohrenwend & Dohrenwend, 1976; Gove, 1987; Johnson, 1987) of a higher incidence of depression and mental illness in North American women, and of higher rates of personality disorders, sociopathy, and criminal behavior in men.

Of course, depression in North American males does occur, although less frequently than in females, and may trace to different antecedent events. So as to illustrate this point, let us turn to the relationship between marital adjustment and depression found in Tower and Kasl's (1996) study of elderly married couples. In this study, marital adjustment was assessed in terms of three factors: (1) the perception of the spouse as a *confidant* (i.e., as someone in whom one can confide problems); (2) the perception of the spouse as a source of *emotional support*, (i.e., as someone who, in the face of unmet dependency needs, affords comfort, security, and support; and (3) whether one's own estimate of *marital closeness* (or distance) was perceived to be shared by one's partner. In terms of these factors, the investigators found differing bases for depression in the female and male partners of the 317 community-based married couples whom they examined every three years over a nine-year interval. For the elderly married women, depression was *not* linked to a need for the spouse as a confidant provided that someone else fulfilled this role. Instead, emotional closeness with the husband was a key factor in that depression arose when the husband was perceived to be emotionally distant (Tower & Kasl, 1996).

By contrast, a husband suffered depression only when he perceived a disjunction between the wife's two roles as confidant and as emotional supporter. In other words, the husband was *free* of depression (1) when the wife served both as a confidant and an emotional support, thereby affording the husband a desirable sense of attachment, or (2) when the wife was neither a confident nor an emotional support, in which case the husband could feel the psychological well-being of a preserved sense of autonomy (Tower & Kasl, 1996).

Another explanation of gender differences in marital depression was linked to dissimilar bases for the sense of self and identity. Starting in childhood, North American females are socialized to value themselves for their interpersonal competency and intimacy. Hence, a disrupted emotional relationship undermines their sense of identity and self-worth. In the case of North American males, however, even though satisfaction in old age may derive from attachment to the wife, the absence of a close marital relationship is *not* a cause of depression. Why? North American males, having been socialized to value themselves for independence and achievement (and not for interpersonal sensitivity), suffer depression from the loss of personal autonomy, and not from the loss of a personal relationship (Beck, 1983; Blatt & Zuroff, 1992).

Beyond the implications of this study is the more general finding that, in North America, women suffer more depression than males because they endure greater amounts and sources of loss. Why is this so?

Firstly, while men often deny physical symptoms, women are sensitized to their physical ailments. This means that aging females are more susceptible to the depression that follows from a perceived loss of physical health. Secondly, the widowhood that afflicts so many women often brings other disadvantages in its wake, such as becoming impoverished and having to live alone or with a relative or in an old-age home.

Other Personality Tendencies in Old Age

Despite the fact that physical and social losses may cause depression in some elderly people, the vast majority of older North-American women and men suffer neither physical incapacitation nor chronic depression. Rather, they retain a fairly healthy personality. Moreover, aging people reveal one of three personality trends in old age. One trend shows that reasonably healthy elders retain some of the dominant traits and adjustment patterns of their earlier years. Such patterns, however, show gender differences in certain broad personality tendencies that extend from middle age through old age, such as more extroversion and psychological well-being in males, but a little more neurosis and low life satisfaction in females (Costa & McCrae, 1984).

A second aging trend is a shift toward androgyny, with many females and males adopting some of the preferred traits of the opposite sex, while either retaining or dropping the preferred traits of their own sex (Wainrib, 1992). For example, the six-year Kansas City Studies of middle- and working-class people conducted by Neugarten and her colleagues (1964, 1968) found that, starting in their fifties, there was an increase in some men in the stereotyped feminine traits of nurturance and receptiveness and, in some women, of the stereotyped masculine traits of aggression and impulsivity without feelings of guilt (Neugarten, 1964, 1973).

A third general trend involves similar old-age personality changes in both sexes. For example, as compared with middle-aged persons, many females and males start in their 60s to show more caution, more failure-avoidance, more conservatism, and a greater tendency to perceive the world as a complex and dangerous place to which they must accommodate (Neugarten, 1964). Many aging women and men also become more introspective and reflective, more self-centered and selfish, more preoccupied with physical and sensory functioning, and more focused on health and good interpersonal relationships than on wealth and high status (Neugarten, 1964, 1973).

CONCLUSION

Let me conclude by reviewing three central points raised in this chapter. The first concerns some major gender similarities and differences found among aging North Americans. For example, as to the effects of genes and socialization on longevity, females appear to have an advantage over males. As to questions of intellect, if one disregards the greater incidence in males of heart and blood-vessel disorders—and of the negative impact this has on the male's mental functioning—then cognitive activity in elderly females and males can be viewed as roughly similar. And, as to overall adaptation in old age, present-day research suggests more optimism and psychological well-being in males, and a little more pessimism and neurosis in females (Costa & McCrae, 1984).

A second general pattern concerns the narrowing of gender differences in older persons because of an increasing tendency toward androgyny in members of both sexes. Thus, when favorable genes combine with good physical and mental habits, both elderly females and males tend to maintain some degree of independence for much or all of their old age, enjoying not only adequate physical health and psychological well-being, but also good cognitive functioning, wherein minor declines in learning and fluid features of intelligence are often compensated by stable or improved crystallized and qualitative features.

A third pattern entails outomes that are somewhat less desirable. Certainly, when unfavorable genes or a stressful life history culminates in many secondary aging processes, the last years of life may bring sharp decrements in physical and mental health and well-being. Yet, even people who are at risk for this less desirable pattern can draw comfort from the fact that ongoing research may lead, some day soon, to methods of retarding or even curing most of the vascular and cardiac disorders, and may even avert many of the forms of dementia.

In sum, many people who grow old in Canada and the United States—and in other countries as well—can probably look forward to a largely satisfying old age. This is especially true if, within the constraints of their situation and of their physical and psychological limitations, aging women and men actively seek to satisfy their needs and assure a sense of well-being.

BIBLIOGRAPHY

Author (1993). Vitality for life: Psychological research for productive aging. *Observer*, American Psychological Society. Human Capital Initiative, Report 2. Washington, D.C.

Ballau, R.L., & Buchan, R.M. (1978). Study shows that gender is not a major factor in accident etiology. *Occupational Health and Safety*, *48*, 54-58.

Beck, A.T. (1983). Cognitive therapy of depression: New perspectives. In P.J. Clayton & J.E. Barrett (Eds.), *Treatment of depression: Old controversies and new approaches* (pp. 265-290). New York: Raven Press.

Blatt, S.J., & Zuroff, D.C.(1992). Interpersonal relatedness and self-definition: Two prototypes for depression. *Clinical Psychology Review*, *12*, 527-562.

Boswell, D.A. (1978). *Metaphoric processing in the mature years*. Paper presented at the 1978 annual meeting of the Gerontological Society, Dallas.

Busse, E.W. (1977). Theories of aging. In E.W. Busse & E. Pfeiffer (Eds.),

Behavior and adaptation in late life (pp. 8-30). Boston, MA: Little, Brown.

Conley, J.J. (1985). Longitudinal stability of personality traits: A multitrait-multimethod-multioccasion analysis. *Journal of Personality and Social Psychology, 49*, 1266-1282.

Costa, P.T., & McCrae, R.R. (1984). Personality as a lifelong determinant of well-being. In C.Z. Malatesta & C.E. Izard (Eds.), *Emotion in adult development* (pp. 141-157). Beverley Hills, CA: Sage.

Dohrenwend, B., & Dohrenwend, B. (1976). Sex differences and psychiatric disorders. *American Journal of Sociology, 81*, 1447-1454.

Gee, E.M., & Kimball, M.M. (1987). *Women and aging.* Toronto, Canada: Butterworths.

Gove, W.R. (1984). Gender differences in mental and physical illness: The effects of fixed roles and nurturant roles. *Social Science and Medicine, 19*, 77-91.

Gove, W.R. (1987). Mental illness and psychiatric treatment among women. In M.R. Walsh (Ed.), *The psychology of women: Ongoing debates* (pp. 102-118). New Haven, CT: Yale University Press.

Graney, M.J. (1979). An exploration of social factors influencing the sex differential in mortality. *Sociological Symposium, 28*, 1 26.

Gurland, B.J., & Toner, J.A. (1982). Depression in the elderly: A review of recently published studies. In C. Eisdorfer (Ed.), *Annual review of gerontology and geriatrics* (Vol. 3, pp. 228-265). New York: Springer.

Hertzog, C., Schaie, K.W., & Gribbin, K. (1978). Cardiovascular diseases and changes in intellectual functioning from middle to old age. *Journal of Gerontology, 33*, 872-883.

Horn, J.L. (1982). The theory of fluid and crystallized intelligence in relation to concepts of cognitive psychology and aging in adulthood. In F.I.M. Craik & S.E. Trehub (Eds.), *The 1980 Erindale Symposium* (pp. 237-278). Beverly Hills, CA: Sage.

Hutton, J.T. (1987). Evaluation and treatment of dementia. *Texas Medicine, 83*, 20-24.

Huyck, M.H. (1990). Gender differences in aging. In J.E. Birren & K.W. Schaie (Eds.), *Handbook of the psychology of aging* (pp. 124-132). New York: Academic Press,

Johnson, M. (1987). Mental illness and psychiatric treatment among women: A response. In M.J. Walsh (Ed.), *Psychology of women: Ongoing debates* (pp. 119-126). New Haven, CT: Yale University Press.

Labouvie-Vief, G., & Schell, D. (1982). Learning and memory in later life. In B.B. Wolman (Ed.), *Handbook of developmental psychology* (pp.828-846). Englewood Cliffs, NJ: Prentice-Hall.

Marsden, C.D. (1984). Neurological causes of dementia other than Alzheimer's disease. In D.W.K. Kay & G.D. Burrows (Eds.), *Handbook of studies on psychiatry and old age* (pp. 145-167). Amsterdam, The Netherlands: Elsevier.

Nadien, M.B. (1995). Elder violence (maltreatment) in domestic settings: Some theory and research. In L.L. Adler & F.L. Denmark (Eds.), *Violence and the prevention of violence* (pp. 177-190). Westport, CT: Praeger.

Nadien, M.B. (1996a). *Gender differences in aging in the U.S. and Canada.* Paper presented at the 1996 New York State Psychological Association Convention in Buffalo.

Nadien, M.B. (1996b). Aging women: Issues of mental health and maltreatment. In J.A. Sechzer, J.A., Pfafflin, F.L. Denmark, A. Blumenthal Griffin, & S.J. Blumenthal (Eds.), *Women and mental health* (pp. 129-145). New York: Annals of the New York Academy of Sciences, Vol. 789.

Nathanson, C.A. (1975). Illness and the feminine role: A theoretical review. *Social Science and Medicine, 9,* 57-62.

Neugarten, B.L. (1968). Adult personality: Toward a psychology of the life cycle. In B.L. Neugarten (Ed.), *Middle age and aging* (pp. 137-147). Chicago, IL: University of Chicago Press.

Neugarten, B.L. (1973). Personality change in later life: A developmental perspective. In C. Eisdorfer & M.P. Lawton (Eds.), *The psychology of adult development and aging* (pp. 311-335). Washington, DC: American Psychological Association.

Neugarten, B.L. (1977). Personality and aging. In J.E. Birren & K.W. Schaie (Eds.), *Handbook of the psychology of aging* (pp. 626-649). New York: Van Nostrand Reinhold.

Neugarten, B.L., & Associates (1964). *Personality in middle and later life.* New York: Atherton.

Preston, S.H. (1976). *Mortality patterns in national populations.* New York: Academic Press.

Root, N., & Daley, J.R. (1980). Are women safer workers? A new look at the data. *Monthly Labor Review, 103,* 3-10.

Schaie, K.W. (1983). The Seattle Longitudinal study: A 21-year exploration of psychometric intelligence in adulthood. In K.W. Schaie (Ed.), *Longitudinal studies of adult psychological development* (pp. 64-135). New York: Guilford.

Siegler, I.C., & Costa, Jr., P.T. (1985). Health behavior relationships. In J.E. Birren & K.W. Schaie (Eds.), *Handbook of the psychology of aging* (2nd ed., pp. 144-166). New York: Van Nostrand Reinhold.

Siegler, I.C., George, L.K., & Okun, M.A. (1979). Cross-sequential analysis of adult personality. *Developmental Psychology, 15,* 350-351.

Statistics Canada (1981). *The health of Canadians: Report of the Canada Health Survey.* Ottawa: Statistics Canada Catalogue No. 82-538E.

Statistics Canada (1985). *Income distributions by size in Canada, 1983.* Ottawa: Statistics Canada Catalogue No. 13-207.

Tower, R.B., & Kasl, S.V. (1996). Gender, marital closeness, and depressive symptoms in elderly couples. *Journal of Gerontology: Psychological Sciences, V, 51B* (3), 115-129.

Turner, B.F. (1982). Sex related differences in aging. In B.B. Wolman (Ed.), *Handbook of developmental psychology* (pp. 912-936). Englewood Cliffs, NJ: Prentice-Hall.

Verbrugge, L.M. (1976). Sex differentials in morbidity and mortality in the United States. *Social Biology, 23,* 276-296.

Wainrib, B.R. (Ed.). (1992). *Gender issues across the life cycle.* New York: Springer.

Walsh, M.R. (Ed.). (1987). *The psychology of women: Ongoing debates.* New Haven, CT: Yale University Press.

Zelinski, E.H., Gilewski, M.J., & Thompson, L.W. (1980). Do laboratory tests relate to self-assessment of memory ability in the young and the old? In L.W. Poon, J.L. Fozard, L. Cermak, D. Arenburg, & L. Thompson (Eds.), *New directions in aging and memory: Proceedings of the George Talland Memorial Conference* (pp. 519-544), Hillsdale, NJ: Erlbaum.

THE ASSESSMENT OF COGNITIVE ABILITIES IN OLD AGE: CONSTRUCTION OF A BATTERY OF TESTS, NORMATIVE DATA, AND RESULTS IN NORMAL AND PATHOLOGICAL ITALIAN RESPONDENTS

Guido Amoretti, University of Padua, Italy

The assessment of cognitive abilities in the elderly is generally focused on both diffuse pathologies such as dementia and on specific cognitive impairments. In Italy, we usually perform global evaluations employing the Mini Mental State Examination (MMSE; Folstein, Folstein, & McHugh, 1975), or the Milan Overall Dementia Assessment (MODA; Brazzelli, Capitani, Della Sala, Spinnler, & Zuffi, 1994), or the Quick Mental State Examination (QMSE; Florenzano, 1989).

The MMSE is employed in numerous countries and has been shown to possess cross-cultural validity (Magni, Binetti, Bianchetti, & Rozzini, 1996; Lindsay, Jagger, Mlynik-Szmid, Sinorwala, Peet, & Moledina, 1997; Medical Research Council, 1998). It allows one to evaluate the degree of impairment, specifically dementia, using only a few test items. Tests like the MMSE provide a quick screening device for a wide range of dementias, but only if the patients already display at least some symptoms of a given dementia.

There also exist neuropsychological tests for the assessment of specific cognitive abilities, and these tests provide scores that are adjusted by age and by level of education. Because these tests focus on finding pathologies, the resulting scores provide an accurate assessment of those persons whose abilities rank below the population mean but not of those whose abilities rank them above the population mean. Therefore, these tests reliably describe cognitive impairments, but they do not account for normal cognitive functioning. For this reason they are not useful in identifying early cognitive impairments when selective attention is focused on the normal aged and the aim is to detect an early decline which is nevertheless still falling within the range of normal aging.

The battery of tests discussed in this chapter assesses cognitive abilities in old age and has been employed as part of a longitudinal-cross-sectional study. Assessments are conducted every three years and focus on four cohorts of healthy elderly people (N=246) who reside in two different Italian cities. The participants in the study were born between 1915 and 1924, and at the first time of assessment they were from 66- to 77-years-old. Participants in the four cohorts were matched by sex, age, and level of education (Table 1).

Table 1
Normative Sample

Level of Education	Age					Total
	40-49	66-68	69-71	72-74	75-77	Total
Primary School	10	18	18	18	18	82
Junior High School	10	18	18	18	18	82
High School/ University	10	18	18	18	18	82
Total	30	54	54	54	54	

The test battery attempts to measure selective attention, working memory capacity, speed of learning, short- and long-term memory for visual and verbal stimuli, visuo-spatial memory, memory for historical events, verbal fluency, and logical reasoning. Table 2 describes the subtests included in the C.F.A. Battery for Cognitive Functions in the Aged.

The importance of the effects of level of education on test performance and on the culture-free subtests has been the most impressive finding in our study of a normal population of the aged. The participants with a higher level of education demonstrated fewer age-related changes in cognitive abilities (Andreani, Amoretti, & Ratti, 1992). Given this finding, we established normative data standardized by sex, age, and level of education together with computerized procedures providing for graphical representation of individual profiles. The standardization was based on correction coefficients derived from a regression analysis (Spinnler & Tognoni, 1987). First, we found for each dependent variable the best linear model that would fit the cognitive performance of the participants taking into account characteristics such as sex, age, and level of education. By means of this model we computed the expected performance for each participant and arrived at the weight of each independent variable. The corrected scores were then obtained without the confounding influence of the independent variables. Corrected scores have been standardized using equivalent scores (range 0-7) where 0 identifies performances under nonparametric levels of tolerance for 95% of the population with a 95% level of confidence, while the other equivalent scores represent a proportional split in the distribution of corrected scores. Equivalent scores are provided for the whole distribution and these allow one to identify a person's cognitive performance when it is above the population mean. In

Table 2
C.F.A. Battery for Cognitive Functions in the Aged: Subtests

Test	Type of Material	Measured Abilities
Misprints test	Visual/verbal	Selective attention
Learning and recall of 12 words (immediate and delayed after 15 min.)	Verbal	STM and LTM of unstructured verbal material
Learning and recall of a story (immediate and delayed after 15 min.)	Verbal	STM and LTM of structured verbal material
Learning and recall of 12 pictures (immediate and delayed after 15 min.)	Visual	STM and LTM of unstructured visual material
Visual span (Block Tapping Test)	Visual-spatial	Visual-spatial memory span
Learning and recall of Visual supraspan (immediate and delayed after 15 min.)	Visual-spatial	Visual-spatial STM & LTM
Span forward and backward (numbers)	Verbal	Memory Span
Memory for public events (MLT'88)	Verbal & visual concrete	LTM of public events
Verbal fluency (letters)	Verbal	Lexical access
Verbal fluency (categories)	Verbal	Lexical access
Sentences generation	Verbal	Verbal productivity
Raven Matrices (PM 38 set A, B, C, D)	Visual abstract	Nonverbal reasoning

addition, this procedure provides indices representing the cognitive functions measured by the battery. Table 3 describes the longitudinal sample that was employed in one of the two cities and that was retested after 3 years.

Table 3
Longitudinal Sample

Level of Education	Age 69-71	72-74	75-77	78-80	Total
Primary School	6	6	2	3	17
Junior High School	9	5	7	2	23
High School/ University	5	4	5	2	16
Total	20	15	14	7	56

We found a substantial test-retest stability over a 3 year-period with respect to selective attention, memory span, block tapping test, visuo-spatial supraspan, and Raven matrices. Short-term memory for pictures decreased as did speed of learning, delayed recall, and maintaining information. There was also a loss of efficiency in long-term memory for public events when pictures were used as the stimuli. Based on these results, we conclude that aging is associated with a reduced speed of learning that impairs encoding processes and particularly those involving pictures. This impairment leads to increased losses of information in the delayed recall task and to decreased long-term memory for public events.

Normative data and our longitudinal results suggest that our battery is useful in a wide range of experimental situations. Nevertheless, the battery is too cumbersome to administer for a quick examination of cognitive functioning in screening situations and with pathological participants. To create a short form of the battery, we employed separate cognitive functioning indices to obtain a general index of cognitive efficiency, and we also computed the weight of each measure in determining general cognitive efficiency. We then reduced the original test battery to a short form having good reliability and requiring less time to administer. The subtests contained in the C.F.A. Short Form are described in Table 4.

The short form of the battery has been studied in order to establish its diagnostic usefulness. This form provides some cognitive indices that

Table 4
C.F.A. Short Form: Composition

Test	Type of Material	Measured Abilities
Learning and recall of 12 pictures (immediate and delayed after 15 min.)	Visual	STM and LTM of unstructured visual material
Learning and recall of a story (immediate and delayed after 15 min.)	Verbal	STM and LTM of structured verbal material
Learning and recall of visual supraspan (immediate and delayed after 15 min.)	Visual-spatial	Visual-spatial STM & LTM
Memory for public events (MLT'88)	Verbal & visual concrete	LTM of public events

measure short-term memory, speed of learning, delayed memory, loss of information, and memory for public events as outlined in Table 5. This short form was administered to two pathological groups of participants including respectively those suffering from cardiovascular diseases and alcoholics.

Table 5
C.F.A. Short Form: Indices

Indices	Measures
Short-term memory	Pictures: immediate recall Visual supraspan: immediate recall
Speed of learning	Pictures and Visual supraspan: number of presentations used to obtain two consecutive corrected recalls
Delayed memory	Pictures: delayed recall Visual supraspan: delayed recall
Loss of information	Pictures: difference between higher number of pictures recalled during learning phase and number of pictures recalled after 15 min. Visual supraspan: difference between higher score during learning phase and score after 15 min.

Ten patients admitted to a hospital suffering from high blood pressure or heart deterioration were included in the cardiovascular group. The participants were over 65 years old and demonstrated no cognitive impairment on the Mini Mental State Examination (Score >24), and in addition, they received a score of less than 10 on the Geriatric Depression Scale. We chose cardiovascular patients because changes in blood pressure might reduce the flow of blood in cerebral areas inducing slight cognitive impairment. In this context, we were interested in verifying the ability of the short form of the battery to identify slight cognitive impairment. The indices of cognitive functioning established by our testing procedures showed no differences between the group of cardiovascular patients and the normative sample in terms of short-term memory, speed of learning, and loss of information. We observed a slight impairment in long-term memory, particularly for public events. These results suggest that changes in blood pressure associated with mild cardiovascular diseases may damage the retrieval of information from long-term memory but do not affect learning and short-term memory.

The two most important hypotheses about cognitive impairment related to alcohol abuse are the diffuse cortical atrophy hypothesis (Elias & Kinsbourne, 1974) and the right hemisphere hypothesis (Kaplan, 1980). The first hypothesis suggests that alcohol abuse leads to diffuse cognitive impairment because of general cortical atrophy. The second hypothesis states that alcohol abuse leads to a deterioration of the right hemisphere, which is reflected in impaired performance on visuo-spatial tasks involving this hemisphere. Ryan (1982) has proposed an analogy between cognitive impairment in alcoholics and intellectual decline among the elderly. While the diffuse cortical atrophy hypothesis is quite similar to the global intellectual decline hypothesis, results confirming the right hemisphere hypothesis are congruent with findings in normative cross-sectional studies of intelligence using tests like the WAIS. Given the analogy between the aging process and impairments in alcoholics we arrive at two different hypotheses to explain the effects of alcohol abuse on cognitive functioning: the rapid aging hypothesis and the increased vulnerability or age-sensitivity hypothesis. According to the first hypothesis, cognitive impairment in alcoholics would be similar though occurring more rapidly when compared to cognitive impairments in the elderly, while the second hypothesis suggests that the higher the age the greater the damage produced by alcohol abuse.

Nevertheless, some research results are not consistent with the hypothesis of an earlier aging process due to alcohol abuse. For instance, alcoholics show impairments in long-term memory for public events (Albert, Butters, & Levin, 1979), while the elderly do not (Andreani, Amoretti, & Ratti, 1990). Furthermore, while alcoholics show impairments in recognizing faces, this ability remains well preserved among the elderly (Amoretti & Ratti, 1990). The latter finding supports the right hemisphere hypothesis. A corresponding question concerning the possibility of rehabilitation after the termination of alcohol abuse is whether the impairment in recognizing faces is permanent or whether this cognitive function may be restored to some degree.

A selection of the tasks of our battery, very similar to the short form we presented earlier, was given to 91 alcoholics, 54 males and 37 females, who were between 40- to 59-years-old (mean age 48.2 years ± 5.6 years). Participants were included in the study if they had not been primary type alcoholics for at least 5 years, had not experienced previous acute episodes induced by alcohol abuse, and showed no other drug dependence, or indication of cirrhosis of the liver.

To test for spontaneous retrieval of cognitive functioning efficacy, a longitudinal subsample of 23 alcoholics (13 males and 10 females, mean age 49 years ± 5.9 years) was retested after having abstained for at least 1 year from alcohol consumption.

Table 6
Alcoholics Samples
Cross-sectional Sample

Level of Education Age	Primary	Junior	High/University	Total
40-49 years	31	16	11	58
50-59 years	20	6	7	33
Total	51	22	18	91

Longitudinal Sample

Level of Education Age	Primary	Junior	High/University	Total
40-49 years	7	3	3	13
50-59 years	5	3	2	10
Total	12	6	5	23

The results of the retest point to a general impairment except for visuo-spatial tasks. The alcoholics' scores, corrected for the effects of sex, age, and level of education, were much lower than those observed in the oldest group

Figure 1
Cognitive Impairment in Alcoholics

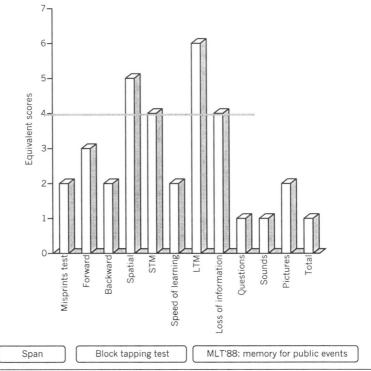

| Span | Block tapping test | MLT'88: memory for public events |

Notes: Span is the name for the measure of Short-term Memory.
Block tapping test is the name of a visuo-spatial test developed by Corsi.
MLT'88 is the name of a memory test for public events developed by Guido Amoretti and colleagues.
Equivalent score=4 represents the mean performance in the normative population on all tasks.

of the normative sample of aged persons (Amoretti, 1994). In addition, selective attention, memory span, and memory for public events appeared to be impaired in alcoholics as well (Figure 1).

We did not find a general improvement in the longitudinal sample of alcoholics who had abstained from alcohol for at least 1 year. Their selective attention, memory span, and visuo-spatial memory were substantially unchanged and their speed of learning decreased. In contrast, their memory for public events (sounds and pictures) showed a slight improvement.

These data suggest that there is damage in selective attention and memory for public events functions due to alcohol abuse, and they also support the hypothesis that a quick aging process occurs in alcoholics. Indeed, the alcoholics showed lower performance ability than the 72- to 77-year-old participants who lacked organic pathologies. The alcoholics' good performance on the visuo-spatial tasks also supports the quick aging hypothesis as opposed to the right hemisphere hypothesis. There was no evidence of a spontaneous retrieval of cognitive functions once they had been impaired by alcohol abuse.

Our results underline the importance of cognitive rehabilitation so that through being trained in metacognitive techniques and through various cognitive activities patients can activate alternative mechanism in order to reduce the aforementioned impairments. Such types of intervention have already been successfully employed by incorporating an emphasis on metamemory knowledge together with cognitive activities (Amoretti & Ratti, 1992), and by employing mnemonic techniques (De Beni, Pavan, & Saimandi, 1992).

BIBLIOGRAPHY

Albert, M.S., Butters, N., & Levin J. (1979). Temporal gradients in the retrograde amnesia of patients with alcoholic Korsakoff's disease. *Archives of Neurology, 36*, 211-216.

Amoretti, G. (1994). Batteria per lo studio delle funzioni cognitive nella terza età. *Bollettino di Psicologia Applicata, 209*, 39-46.

Amoretti, G., & Ratti, M.T. (1990). Ricordo di materiale visivo: effetti dell'età e dell'istruzione sul declino mnestico. *Ricerche di Psicologia, 2*, 77-120.

Amoretti, G., & Ratti, M.T. (1992). Si può migliorare la memoria? Un'esperienza con gli anziani dell'Università della Terza Età. *Psicologia e Società, XVII (XXXIX)*, 1-2, 178-189.

Andreani, O., Amoretti, G., & Baldi, P.L. (1990). Il test di memoria di eventi storici MLT '88. Costruzione e standardizzazione. *Bollettino di Psicologia Applicata, 196*, 3-17.

Andreani Dentici, O., Amoretti, G., & Ratti, M.T. (1992). La memoria nell'invecchiamento fisiologico: stabilità o declino? *Psicologia e Società, numero monotematico su "Memoria e invecchiamento" a cura di O. Andreani Dentici e G. Amoretti, XVII (XXXIX)*, 1-2, 15-42.

Brazzelli, M., Capitani, E., Della Sala, S., Spinnler, H., & Zuffi, M. (1994). *MODA—Milan Overall Dementia Assessment*. Florence: Organizzazioni Speciali.

De Beni, R., Pavan, G., & Saimandi, C. (1992). Programmi di insegnamento mnemonico e metacognizione nella terza età. *Psicologia e Società, XVII (XXXIX)*, 1-2, 178-189.

Elias, M.F., & Kinsbourne, M. (1974). Age and sex differences in the processing of verbal and nonverbal stimuli. *Journal of Gerontology, 29*, 162-171.

Florenzano, F. (1989). Il Rapido Esame dello Stato Mentale (R.E.S.M.) per lo screening dei disturbi demenziali. Validità e attendibilità. *Alzheimer, Longevità e Geriatria, 9/10*, 25-39.

Folstein, M.F., Folstein, S.E., & McHugh, P.R. (1975). Mini Mental State: A practical method for grading the cognitive state of patients. *Journal of Psychiatrics Research, 12* (3), 189-198.

Kaplan, E. (1980). Change in cognitive style with aging. In L.K. Obler & M.L. Albert (Eds.), *Language and communication in the elderly* (pp. 121-132). Lexington, KY: Lexington Books.

Lindsay, J., Jagger, C., Mlynik-Szmid, A., Sinorwala, A., Peet, S., & Moledina, F. (1997). The Mini-Mental State Examination (MMSE) in an elderly immigrant Gujarati population in the United Kingdom. *International Journal of Geriatric Psychiatry, 12* (12), 1155-1167.

Magni, E., Binetti, G., Bianchetti, A., & Rozzini, R. (1996). Mini mental state examination: A normative study in an Italian elderly population. *European Journal of Neurology, 3* (3), 198-202.

Medical Research Council (MRC), London (UK). (1998). Cognitive function and dementia in six areas of England and Wales: The distribution of MMSE and prevalence of GMS organicity level in the MRC CFA study. *Psychological Medicine, 28* (2), 319-335.

Ryan, C. (1982). Alcoholism and premature aging: A neuropsychological perspective. *Alcoholism: Clinical and Experimental Research, 6*, 79-96.

Spinnler, H., & Tognoni, G. (a cura di). (1987). Standardizzazione e taratura italiana di test neuropsicologici. *The Italian Journal of Neurological Sciences*, Supplement, *8* (6).

A CROSS-CULTURAL INVESTIGATION
COMPARING ATTITUDES TOWARD LIVING AND DYING

Leonore Loeb Adler, S. Patricia Clark, Molloy College, USA
Florence L. Denmark, Pace University, USA
Ramadan A. Ahmed, Menoufia University, Egypt
TaeLyon Kim, Ewha Women's University, South Korea
Suneetha S. de Silva, Ilinois University at Edwardsville, U.S.A.
Steven Salbod, Pace University, U.S.A.

"Doctor, doctor, shall I die?
Yes my child, and so shall I."
Anonymous, in Parkes, Laungani,
& Young (1997, p. 7)

The modern medical sciences, in recent years, have raised the hope of longevity and greater life expectancies. Population figures show that the life expectancy in many countries has reached a level that was unheard of in earlier times. While the quality of life and longevity have been increased, the fact remains that dying and death are inevitable realities.

Previously, Rosenblatt (1997) had pointed out that many communities and societies in developed or developing countries have created their own patterns to deal with death and dying. How people have accepted the inevitable and unavoidable circumstances of eventual death has been discussed by Tony Walter (1997). His presentation compares humanism and secularization, two ideologies that are concerned more with living and life than with the process of dying and with death.

The emotional expression and the attitudes toward living and dying were the focus of the present study. Attitudes in general, but especially attitudes toward living and dying, may change over the years. Lemme (1995) reported that "Americans now deal with death the way the Victorians dealt with sex. We simply do not like to acknowledge that it goes on" (p. 435). However, there are changes that may occur during different stages of the life span. Kastenbaum (1992) found that most people did not seem to face death, but showed only a low to moderate concern about death and dying in their daily routines. This could mean that the general population harbored only a low degree of death anxiety. Dividing the data for analysis according to gender, the results of death anxiety tests showed that the women's scores were higher that those of men (Lonetto & Templer, 1966). These findings are open to speculative interpretations, which could mean, for example, that because of women's greater involvement in providing care and help to people in need, they may be more aware of the possibilities leading to death (Lemme, 1995).

During the last few decades the topic of death and dying has become more prominent. An interesting, but also obvious fact was found with regard to age. As expected the evidence showed that there exists an increase in discussions and thoughts about death with increasing years throughout the life span.

While reports, such as those mentioned so far, involved only research in the United States of America, one study focused on the multicultural background of the participants. Kalish and Reynolds (1977) studied four populations living in Los Angeles, California. These included African-Americans, Anglo-Americans, Japanese-Americans, and Mexican-Americans. While their socioeconomic background may have affected their approaches toward death-related issues, the authors found many differences in their death-related attitudes. The authors reported that the Anglo-American population perceived the Mexican-American group as very emotional with regard to their attitudes toward death-related issues. On the other hand, the Mexican-American participants thought that the attitudes of the Anglo-American population were cold in response to death-related topics.

It is obvious that cultural values, norms, and beliefs influence the attitudes and behaviors of people, who are enculturated in different cultural environments. Therefore, it is important to test populations who are living in different ecologies, with specific cross-cultural research. Comparing a variety of cultural groups will give the answers about differences and similarities cross-culturally. "For example, the present scientific literature is much more likely to report differences rather than similarities between nations or cultures studied. On the other hand, cross-cultural research recognizes that while the discoveries of differences may be significant, the findings of similarities may provide even more meaningful information. Because of the ever-increasing spread of Western culture special emphasis should be placed on such aspects" (Adler, 1977, p. 1).

For many years, the basis for cross-cultural research depended on comparing people's behavior, when they lived in different cultural environments. However, with such attitudes many of the variables were either ignored or overlooked. Much more intensive research on cross-cultural issues is needed. In this context, an anecdote can describe cross-cultural differences in attitudes more succinctly. In one discussion of the topic of death and dying, a young Asian Indian woman, who had been listening, responded spontaneously: "I do not know why there is such a fuss about death and dying; when you die you are reincarnated." A typical Western response to this concept might be: "I never thought of it in such terms."

Due to the variations in upbringing and varieties in cultural backgrounds, people's thoughts and attitudes go in different directions. Therefore, it is necessary to include many more actions and interactions that shape people's orientations when pursuing cross-cultural research, focusing on influences in their behavior and lifestyles.

THE STUDY

Participants and their Countries

Instead of being a multicultural study, the present research was a cross-cultural investigation. Four countries with different cultural backgrounds were selected. These included Kuwait (tested during prewar times) ($n=160$), South Korea ($n=539$), Sri Lanka ($n=454$), and the United States of America ($n=563$). In each of these countries the participants included males and females.

Age Groups

The groups of participants were divided into three age *categories. Young adult* (18 to 33 years), *middle age* (34 to 59 years), and *old age* (60 to 85 plus years). However, the distribution of the participants in some of the countries that contributed data did not yield enough n's for three age groups to allow for statistical analyses. The only country with three large age groups was the U.S.A. Since this study was originally projected to test only the elderly, the data for "young adult" and "middle age" groups were missing in the Kuwaiti sample, since Kuwait was the first country to participate. Korea was missing data for the "middle age" group, and Sri Lanka did not reach a large enough n in the "old age" group. However, working with percentages the data could be evaluated and compared.

Questionnaire Method

In order to investigate attitudes toward living and dying in a cross-cultural investigation, the present study was conducted. Some years ago, TaeLyon Kim (1992) published the results of her research on "Attitudes toward living and dying" with Korean American senior citizens. The present investigation was based and modified on Kim's study. Both experiments used a questionnaire to assess the attitudes of the participants. Of the 27 questions/statements of the present test-booklets only a few items will be reported at the present time. The first page of the questionnaire contained the information on the demographic background. Fifteen questions gave multiple choices of "yes," "sometimes"/"rarely," or "no."

Ten questions offered five pertinent answers as a choice. In addition, there were two open-ended questions, which needed to be analyzed separately. The beginning included "non-threatening" items and the last few questions ended on a pleasant tone. To respond to the entire questionnaire required about 10 to 15 minutes.

RESULTS

The data were computer analyzed for specific questions and statements. As may be seen in Table 1, to the question "*Are you lonely?*," the choices of the responses were: "yes," "sometimes," and "no." In the U.S.A., Sri Lanka, and in Kuwait the strongest responses were "no" in all three age groups when men's and women's answers were combined. In Korea, however, the largest number of responses was given to "Sometimes."

Table 1
Responses to "Are you lonely?"

	Country			
Responses	USA ($n=557$)	Sri Lanka ($n=444$)	Kuwait ($n=160$)	Korea ($n=535$)
Yes	3.2%	7.2%	15.6%	20.2%
Sometimes	43.4%	27.0%	23.8%	55.0%
No	53.3%	65.8%	60.6%	24.9%

χ^2 (6, 1,696)=237.97, $p<.001$
Note: Figures given are in percentages. $N=1,696$. The difference between this size and the total sample size is attributed to omitting responses from persons who gave multiple responses.

Table 2 depicts responses to the question, "*If you feel like talking is there somebody, either in person or by telephone?*" Again the choices of the responses were: "yes," "sometimes," and "no." As with the previous question the answers by men and women in all age groups were combined. The results for the U.S.A., Sri Lanka, and Kuwait were mostly an impressive "yes." However, the responses in Korea were mostly split between "yes" and "sometimes."

Table 2
Responses to "If you feel like talking is there somebody there?"

Country

Responses	USA (n=555)	Sri Lanka (n=443)	Kuwait (n=160)	Korea (n=536)
Yes	89.0%	64.6%	60.0%	48.1%
Sometimes	8.1%	29.1%	31.9%	47.2%
No	2.9%	6.3%	8.1%	4.7%

χ^2 (6, 1,694)=229.10, $p<.001$.
Note: Figures given are in percentages. N=1,694. The difference between this size and the total sample size is attributed to omitting responses from persons who gave multiple responses.

The next item was a very timely and penetrating question, which asked: "*Do you worry about getting a terminal illness?*" The choices of answers were: "yes," "rarely," and "no." As may be seen in Table 3, this time all the responses that included both genders and all three age groups from Korea were a strong "no."

In Sri Lanka the answers were similar to those from Korea. However, the responses were about evenly distributed between the three choices both in Kuwait and in the U.S.A.

For the next question the choices of the answers were more specific. One of these queries explored a very personal attitude, namely: "*What would you do if you found out that you had an incurable illness?*" There were five answers to choose from: a) continue medical treatment; b) pray and hope to die quickly; c) stop medical treatment; d) do nothing—continue present routine; e) enjoy as much of life as possible, while I can. As may be seen in Table 4, both the men's and women's responses were combined, but the age groups were analyzed separately. The results obtained within the U.S.A. sample were reminiscent of Kastenbaum's (1992) findings. The majority of the participants were interested in enjoying themselves as long as they could; though with the two older groups replies increased in number to continue medical treatment. The Sri Lankan participants gave similar responses, i.e., the younger group wanted to enjoy life when it was still possible, while the older participants chose to continue medical

Table 3
Responses to "Do you worry about getting a terminal illness?"

Country

Responses	USA (n=556)	Sri Lanka (n=442)	Kuwait (n=160)	Korea (n=533)
Yes	31.7%	16.1%	32.5%	9.0%
Sometimes	34.4%	24.4%	36.9%	31.5%
No	34.0%	59.5%	30.6%	59.5%

χ^2 (6, 1,691)=152.53, $p < .001$.
Note: Figures given are in percentages. N=1,691. The difference between this size and the total sample size is attributed to omitting responses from persons who gave multiple responses.

treatment. This pattern of responses seemed to prevail also in Korea; while the younger age group in Kuwait was missing, only the older group's responses were recorded.

Another interesting question inquired: "*To whom can you confide your problems*?" The responses were selected from the following choices: a) spouse; b) children; c) friends and/or relatives; d) clergy; and e) nobody. The results, as depicted in Table 5, showed that men and women did not exhibit the same attitudes nor similar patterns of behavior. While the Young Adult male participants in the U.S.A., Sri Lanka, and in Korea (Kuwait had this age group missing) chose to confide mainly in c) friends and/or relatives, the Middle Age and Old Age groups confided overwhelmingly in their spouses. However, this pattern varied for female participants.

As may be seen in Table 6 and Figure 1, young women chose c) friends and/or relatives when confiding their problems. Yet elderly women turned frequently to their children or relatives, rather than to their spouses, in all four countries.

Table 4
Combined Responses for Males and Females to
"What would you do if you found out that you had an incurable illness?"

		Country		
Responses	USA	Sri Lanka	Kuwait	Korea
YOUNG ADULT	(n=159)	(n=207)	-	(n=296)
Continue medical treatment	3.1%	28.5%	-	19.9%
Pray and hope to die quickly	4.4%	18.4%	-	4.1%
Stop medical treatment	0.6%	1.9%	-	2.7%
Do nothing—continue present routine	3.1%	16.4%	-	27.7%
Enjoy as much of life as possible, while I can	88.7%	34.8%	-	45.6%
$\chi^2(8, 662)=156.48, p<.001$				
MIDDLE AGE	(n=118)	(n=173)	(n=18)	-
Continue medical treatment	15.3%	43.9%	61.1%	-
Pray and hope to die quickly	4.2%	10.4%	11.1%	-
Stop medical treatment	1.7%	1.2%	0.0%	-
Do nothing—continue present routine	7.6%	18.5%	11.1%	-
Enjoy as much of life as possible, while I can	71.2%	26.0%	16.7%	-
$\chi^2(8, 309)=67.65, p<.001$				
OLD AGE	(n=87)	(n=31)	(n=137)	(n=224)
Continue medical treatment	27.6%	51.6%	54.0%	31.7%
Pray and hope to die quickly	12.6%	3.2%	20.4%	19.6%
Stop medical treatment	0.0%	0.0%	2.2%	5.8%
Do nothing—continue present routine	9.2%	16.1%	19.0%	26.3%
Enjoy as much of life as possible, while I can	50.6%	29.0%	4.4%	16.5%
$\chi^2(12, 479)=99.36, p<.001$				

Note: Figures given are in percentages. $N=1,450$. The difference between this size and the total sample size is attributed to omitting responses from persons who gave multiple responses. When age groups are combined: $\chi^2(12, 1,450)=330.76, p<.001$.

Table 5
Male Responses to "To whom can you confide your problems?"

Country

Responses	USA	Sri Lanka	Kuwait	Korea
YOUNG ADULT	($n=59$)	($n=88$)	-	($n=131$)
Spouse	10.2%	4.5%	-	5.3%
Children	0.0%	1.1%	-	0.8%
Friend and/or relative	86.4%	74.0%	-	81.6%
Clergy	0.0%	1.1%	-	0.8%
Nobody	3.4%	19.3%	-	11.5%
$\chi^2(8, 278)=11.56,$ $p=.172$				
MIDDLE AGE	($n=55$)	($n=82$)	($n=15$)	-
Spouse	47.3%	51.1%	46.6%	-
Children	3.6%	3.7%	26.7%	-
Friend and/or relative	36.4%	24.4%	26.7%	-
Clergy	0.0%	3.7%	0.0%	-
Nobody	12.7%	17.1%	0.0%	-
$\chi^2(8, 152)=19.20,$ $p=.014$				
OLD AGE	($n=32$)	($n=9$)	($n=72$)	($n=106$)
Spouse	59.4%	66.7%	44.5%	40.6%
Children	28.1%	33.3%	33.3%	16.0%
Friend and/or relative	3.1%	0.0%	22.2%	30.2%
Clergy	3.1%	0.0%	0.0%	2.8%
Nobody	6.3%	0.0%	0.0%	10.4%
$\chi^2(12, 219)=29.63,$ $p=.003$				

Note: Figures given are in percentages. $N=649$. The difference between this size and the total sample size is attributed to omitting responses from persons who gave multiple responses. When age groups are combined: $\chi^2(12, 649)=104.33, p<.001$.

Table 6
Female Responses to "To whom can you confide your problems?"

Country

Responses	USA	Sri Lanka	Kuwait	Korea
YOUNG ADULT	($n=139$)	($n=126$)	-	($n=156$)
Spouse	8.6%	7.1%	-	2.6%
Children	0.0%	0.8%	-	0.0%
Friend and/or relative	90.7%	66.7%	-	90.3%
Clergy	0.0%	2.4%	-	1.3%
Nobody	0.7%	23.0%	-	5.8%
$\chi^2(8, 421)=55.27$, $p<.001$				
MIDDLE AGE	($n=59$)	($n=86$)	($n=3$)	-
Spouse	37.3%	40.7%	0.0%	-
Children	6.8%	10.5%	100.0%	-
Friend and/or relative	44.0%	26.7%	0.0%	-
Clergy	1.7%	5.8%	0.0%	-
Nobody	10.2%	16.3%	0.0%	-
$\chi^2(4, 145)=6.12$, $p=.190^a$				
OLD AGE	($n=45$)	($n=17$)	($n=68$)	($n=110$)
Spouse	26.7%	5.9%	17.6%	13.6%
Children	31.1%	70.6%	45.6%	36.4%
Friend and/or relative	31.1%	17.6%	35.3%	37.3%
Clergy	0.0%	0.0%	1.5%	3.6%
Nobody	11.1%	5.9%	0.0%	9.1%
$\chi^2(12, 240)=21.58$, $p=.043$				

Note: Figures given are in percentages. $N=809$. The difference between this size and the total sample size is attributed to omitting responses from persons who gave multiple responses. When age groups are combined, $\chi^2(12, 809)=104.33$, $p<.001$. [a]Kuwait was excluded from the analysis.

Figure 1
Percentage of Responses to "Spouse" Choice for Question:
"To whom can you confide your problems?"

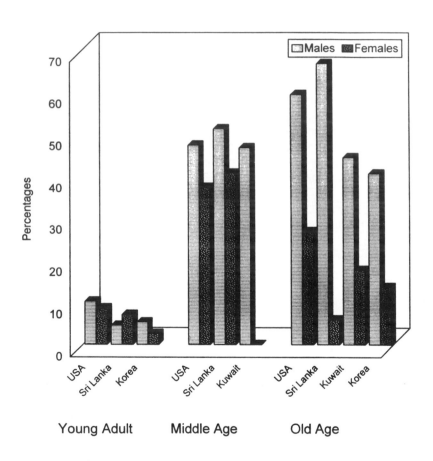

SUMMARY AND DISCUSSION

The present study investigated areas of the human experience that included some important and challenging aspects of living and dying. Therefore, some searching questions were asked. The answers, which were reported here, were insightful and revealing. The countries, Kuwait (prewar), S. Korea, Sri Lanka, and the U.S.A., that contributed participants to this research, were located far apart geographically around the globe. The cultural background of these four countries was quite diversified. Even though there were differences among the life-styles and the cultural backgrounds, many similarities in attitudes and behavior existed among the participants. For instance, the choices of the responses by men and women were similar, so that the data could be pooled. Generally, differences occurred between the various age groups. Concerns about health problems increased with the Old Age groups. In contrast, the Younger Adults tended to bypass the seriousness of an incurable illness and chose to enjoy life as long as possible. In addition, when asked to whom one could or would confide one's problems, men in the Middle Age and Old Age groups preferred to confide their problems to their spouses (See Figure 1).

Women, especially elderly females, confided frequently in their children. Considering that traditionally women were usually dependent on their husbands for their physical and intellectual well-being, these cross-cultural responses were certainly unexpected and surprising. Further studies may reveal some information for these attitudes. The Young Adults in this study felt probably comfortable to seek out friends and/or relatives. Yet it was pointed out to the investigators that one choice of the answers was missing, namely "parents," or more specifically "mother," since young women probably prefer to confide in their mothers. In addition, the question occurred: Do young men prefer to confide in their fathers? In future research these aspects will be investigated. However, as an explanation one could report that this study started out to investigate the attitudes and behavior of elderly people, and the Young Adult group was only added later.

It also could be that answers like "yes"-"no" are very direct. Such answers could be qualified with "sometimes." A case in point is the question about *loneliness*. The majority of men answered with "no." Also many women responded with "no" as the first choice; but the "sometimes" response followed closely behind. Perhaps this could be explained by the participants' life-styles. Women, who were at home taking care of the family members and the household, might not be able to interact with other individuals like the men, who work away from home and have more opportunities to contact other people.

This report of the present cross-cultural study found several pertinent and relevant results among the topics that were investigated. Among these was the fact that many of the responses to the questions were similar across cultures, which meant that the pattern of answers were similar, not only across cultures but also for the different age groups cross-culturally. Yet in closing it is well to point out the remarkable and important findings of the *similarities of the responses in different cultures* to these practically universal questions.

BIBLIOGRAPHY

Adler, L.L. (1977). A plea for interdisciplinary cross-cultural research: Some introductory remarks. In L.L. Adler (Ed.), *Issues in cross-cultural research* (p. 1). New York: Annals of The New York Academy of Sciences, Vol. *285*.

Kalish, R.A., & Reynolds, D. (1977). *Death and ethnicity: A psychocultural study*. Los Angeles, CA: University of Southern California Press.

Kim, T. (1992). Korean American senior citizen's perspectives on living and dying. *The Journal of the Korean Cultural Research Institute, 60,* 99-111.

Kastenbaum, R. (1992). *The psycholoay of death* (2nd ed.). New York: Springer.

Lemme, B.H. (1995). *Development in adulthood*. Needham Heights, MA: Allyn & Bacon.

Lonetto, R.I., & Templer, D. (1966). *Death anxiety*. New York: Hemisphere.

Parkes, C.M., Laungani, P., & Young, B. (Eds). (1997). *Death and bereavement across cultures*. London, UK: Routledge.

Rosenblatt, P.C. (1997). Grief in small-scale societies. In C.M. Parkes, P. Laungani, & B.Young (Eds.), *Death and bereavement across cultures* (pp. 27-51). London, UK: Routledge.

Walter, T. (1997). Secularization. In C.M. Parkes, P. Laungani, & B. Young (Eds.), *Death and bereavement across cultures* (pp. 166-187). London, UK: Routledge.

AUTHORS' NOTE

The authors want to express their appreciation to Mr. Gerald Knobelauch for processing the data for this research; to Ms. Patricia Shin for translating the Korean data; and to Mrs. Sheila Perera for translating the Sri Lankan data. The authors also acknowledge with thanks that the present cross-cultural research was supported in part by an award from Molloy College's Committee for Faculty Scholarship and Academic Advancement.

DEATH: THE FINAL END OR A NEW BEGINNING?
CROSS-CULTURAL EVALUATIONS

Pittu Laungani,
South Bank University, England

DYING AND DEATH

At a common sense level, we know what death is. Our emotional feelings notwithstanding, we know that the person we loved, or the stranger we met only casually, has died. At some point, the person was alive, and now, the person has died. In that sense death arouses no ambiguities in our minds. Thus, we tend to visualize life and death in terms of an "either-or." We know that a person cannot be alive and dead at the same time. It has to be one or the other. We also know that the body of the dead person, if left unattended for long, will rot, smell, and decompose. We are all able to equate death with a dead body.

But the problem is not as straightforward as it seems. When we move away from a common sense formulation to a scientific consideration of the problem, we run into a series of difficulties. From the point of view of medical science, it is not always clear how death shall be defined. Even the notion of death and life being an either-or has in recent years come to be questioned (Aries, 1981; Kastenbaum, 2000; Lofland, 1978; Moller, 1990, 1996). Such debates have gained some credence and legitimacy as a result of advancing medical research in this area. Serious questions concerning when it is legitimate to define death have been raised. For instance, should one look upon a patient on a life-support machine in a state of protracted coma as being alive or dead? Is one declared dead only when one is brain-dead? Should one live in the hope that one day perhaps, one's loved one, as a result of scientific advances, will recover, or should one accept the finality of death and request that the life-support machines be turned off? No clear-cut answers to these questions have been offered. The problem is compounded by the fact that serious moral and ethical debates surround this issue. Is it right to turn off the life-support machine? Who decides? On what moral grounds are such vital decisions to be taken? Do the doctors, in consultation with the family members and the relatives of the person on the life-support machine, arrive at a workable joint decision? By turning off the life-support machine, is one playing "God"? And by not turning off the machine, is one imposing a serious and needless financial and emotional hardship upon the relatives who anxiously await the miraculous revival of the patient? The questions, the dilemmas, the confusions are endless, and it is obvious that no satisfactory answers at least for the present are available.

The moral arguments become even more complex when one takes the factor of cost into serious consideration. To keep a person on a life-support machine for an indefinite period of time requires the expenditure of vast funds, which are by no means within the easy reach of persons of moderate means. (Even the nationalized health services in Britain would find their resources overstrained in such situations.) Given the uncertainty of outcome, is such expenditure justified? The relatives concerned may chafe at such an idea arguing that since they have the means, they should be allowed to pursue their private wishes. However, that does not necessarily resolve the moral dilemma. At a more general level, such a course of action creates a two-tier system in society: one for the rich and the other for the poor. Secondly, and more importantly, the occupancy of a bed in an intensive care unit remains tied to the person on the life-support machine for as long as the person continues to breathe, or when the funds get depleted and the life-support machine is reluctantly turned off. Is it right to keep the bed occupied, when it might have been made available to other patients? Again, no easy answers can be offered to these moral, social, economic, and medical dilemmas.

The moral dilemmas mentioned above are a recent phenomenon. They have arisen largely because of the spectacular advances in medical and scientific research in Western countries. As a result, death is seen not in terms of an "either-or," but as extending along the points on a continuum. As Moller points out, "saving life at all costs" has become the guiding philosophy of western medical science. This philosophy, in turn, has brought about a different set of expectation many of which are as unrealistic as they are unrealizable. Since life is to be saved at all costs and death is to be conquered, the sick, or the relatives of the sick, often insist on forms of treatment that are as expensive as their outcomes are uncertain. Demands for expensive forms of treatment, including the "keeping-alive-at-all-costs" phenomenon come to be seen as a matter of right. Such demands are often couched in convoluted secularist moral arguments (Fletcher, 1960).

In this context it is worth pointing out that in the third world countries, where medical resources are grossly overstrained, one would consider oneself lucky were one to receive even some cursory medical care. In India, for instance, the guiding philosophy concerning life and death is the belief that as one gets older one will become weak and infirm, and eventually, as one's time approaches one will die. Death is seen as the legitimate but by no means the final end to one's present life. To die in one's old age, *without undue pain and suffering,* after one has discharged honorably one's duties towards one's family members, one's community, and toward society, is construed as a "good death."

It is not uncommon for the old and the infirm in India to express a wish to die in one of the holy cities such as Varanasi or Hardwar. Ancient Hindu beliefs and customs guide such wishes. To die in a holy city, to be cremated along the banks of the holy river Ganges, to have one's ashes immersed in the river after all the appropriate prayers and rites have been performed, ensures the swift and peaceful repose of one's soul. Such sentiments are not construed as a form of mental aberration—as, in all probability, they would be in the West (Justice, 1997). They are often given serious consideration. Few attempts are made to dissuade the person from wishing to embark on this final journey. The relatives of the aged parent may, in fact, abide by those wishes and arrange for the aged parent to be taken to Varanasi, or wherever the person has expressed a wish to die. The person concerned is then placed in an *ashram* (a holy sanctuary). The aged parent shuns all forms of medication. The relatives, including the local physician who may have been summoned to examine the "dying" person, may do little to persuade the person to do otherwise. Justice (1997), who carried out a fascinating and enlightening field study in Varanasi, points out that the aged person at this stage often stops eating, and within a few days, nature, as it were, takes its own course, and the person dies. It is clear from this brief account, that death in nonwestern cultures—particularly in India—is seen as a fitting end to one's life. Attempts to keep death at bay, to conquer death, to keeping alive at all costs are ideas as alien, if not unethical, to the Hindus, as the above Hindu beliefs and practices would seem to most people in the West (Lynn & Childress, 1986).

For the purposes of this chapter, we shall accept the biological conceptualization of death, viz., looking upon life and death in dichotomous terms. Such a formulation has another distinct advantage. It allows us to conceptualize death as being irreversible. From a clinical point of view, the organism, upon death, ceases to function. This means that the person who has died has lost the capacity to breathe and to sustain a spontaneous heartbeat. Death, as Lamb (1985) points out, marks the cessation of integrative action between all organ systems of the body. The established medico-legal system demands that one's death be documented in terms of time, place, and cause.

The dead do not and cannot be resurrected

AWARENESS OF DEATH?

Let us now turn to the question that we raised at the start of the chapter. Can we have an awareness of death? Can we experience our own death? Does life end at death? Do we have any understanding of what happens after death, or what follows death? Are we ever likely to?

A moment's reflection is enough to make us ask the question: How can one be aware of one's own death? Sadly, one never acquires an awareness of one's death. One dies. With death all awareness ceases. To experience one's own death seems a contradiction in terms. How can one be dead and alive at the same time? Persons reporting what are referred to as near-death and even after-death experiences have made several absurd and fantastic claims (Moody, 1975, 1978). In spite of such claims, one does not really know what dying entails. Reports of after-death experiences contain all the ingredients of high drama. They often tend to get sensationalized. Different versions of the story begin to circulate each clamoring for attention, each asserting its own version of truth. This tends to make an objective assessment of the event even more difficult, if not impossible. Let me describe an event that I witnessed many years ago, and it had a powerful effect upon me.

A NEAR-DEATH EXPERIENCE OR A RETURN FROM THE DEAD?

This happened several years ago. I was about eight years old. We had come for our holidays to Tando Adam, a small, sleepy town not far from Hyderabad, in Sind, Pakistan. It wasn't Pakistan then. It was part of India. My father had inherited some ancestral property in Tando Adam. We came there every year, from Bombay, which is where we lived. It was nice coming to Tando Adam where I met my cousins, many of whom lived there.

Around four o'clock every afternoon, the familiar and welcome face of Kalia would pass by our house. Kalia was not his real name, but since he was pitch black in complexion, we all called him Kalia, which means black. Although Kalia might seem a derogatory term, it is also a term affectionately used when referring to the Hindu God Krishna. He didn't seem to mind that everyone called him Kalia. Kalia was a hawker who sold hot and spicy Indian savory snacks, made from potatoes, chickpeas, flour, and onions fried in batter; they were garnished with chutney made with mint, tamarind, chilies, lime, and fresh coriander. No sooner did we hear his familiar cries, when my cousins and I rushed out of the house to buy the snacks. Each of us clamored for attention, wanting to be served first. By the time Kalia reached the end of our street, our snacks had disappeared and we had started to lick our fingers while bitterly regretting the fact that we did not have any more money on us.

As usual, we waited for Kalia to arrive the next afternoon. But the following morning, we all heard that Kalia had died. We were heartbroken. Not for him, though, but for the snacks that we would never eat again. My cousin, who was the oldest of the kids at home, suggested that we should all attend Kalia's funeral as a mark of respect for the hawker who had given us such untold joy. My father was pleased and surprised that we all wanted to attend Kalia's funeral. Within our family and our community, no one had any qualms about taking young children to the crematorium. It seemed perfectly natural.

Since Kalia was a well-known and well-liked hawker in our area, virtually every one in the neighborhood (Muslims and Hindus) turned out for his funeral. By six o' clock in the evening, the crematorium was crowded with mourners. Kalia lay in his bier, which was placed on the floor, for all to see. His face was left uncovered, his body wrapped in a white shroud, bedecked with flowers. I had a glimpse of Kalia and was surprised and frightened to see how stiff and waxen he seemed. Like the others, I too bent down before the body to offer my final prayers. I almost jumped out of my skin when I thought I saw his nostrils twitch. But they were merely flies buzzing around his face. The Brahmin priest in charge of the funeral ceremony recited the sacred texts in Sanskrit, and asked for the body to be lifted on to the pile of logs that had been assembled for the funeral pyre.

Kalia's eldest son, his head shaven, dressed in a white *dhoti* and *kurta*, who could not have been much older than me, was expected to perform the final funeral rites. This of course was in keeping with the ancient Hindu traditions, which decree that it is the sacred duty of the eldest son to perform all the funeral rites of his deceased father—for this ensures the peaceful repose of the father's soul. A flame was lit. It was handed to Kalia's son. He was instructed to hold the flame near the logs. The logs took. Smoke began to rise from the logs.

And then, suddenly, to everyone's total astonishment, there was a piercing cry from the logs. Before the people could even gather their wits about them, the Brahmin priest rushed toward the pile of logs, and with his hands and feet started to dislodge the logs which had been piled on top of Kalia. Others joined in. Within a few seconds, the logs were removed and Kalia was lifted from the funeral pyre. They placed him on the floor. His chest heaved. He coughed. He choked. He sputtered. It was clear that he was breathing. He was alive!

"A miracle! A miracle!" people shouted.

Messengers were sent rushing to Kalia's house to inform his grieving wife, his two daughters, his mother, and all the other female relatives, who custom forbade to come to the crematorium. The women had parted from their departed loved one at the threshold of Kalia's house.

While Kalia was being revived, rumors wilder than the funeral pyre spread through the crematorium. People looked at the dazed Kalia, shook their heads and laughed. Everyone knew—it was common knowledge in their area—that Kalia and his wife did not get on well with each other. In fact, they hated each other. However, divorce was a taboo word, unheard of among Hindus. (It still is.) Kalia's death had seemed a God-sent deliverance for his wife. They all knew that she would go through the motions of crying and mourning. And now he would be returning home once again. The taunts, the torments, the quarrels, and the fights would continue.

When Kalia had recovered sufficiently and was able to stand and walk, someone suggested that Kalia should once again be placed on the bier and brought home. But the bier had got burnt. A huge procession of laughing, joking, cheerful "mourners" carried Kalia on their shoulders and brought him home. As children, we were able to enter the house and slip into the quarters where the women, until a few moments ago, had been wailing and mourning.

Kalia's wife, upon seeing Kalia, burst into genuine tears. She cried, she wailed, she beat her breast, and finally turned to her husband with fury, "You *shaitaan!* You tormented me while you were alive, and now as a black, evil *shaitaan*, you have returned to torment me after your death." Her screams rang through the house. They were greeted with laughter by all the people had gathered round the house.

At home, we debated whether Kalia had really died and had returned from the dead. Can people come back from the dead we asked? The only doctor—Dr. Gurudas—who lived in our neighborhood and could have examined Kalia, had gone to Hyderabad for a few days. It is possible that Kalia may have taken ill and slipped into a coma. Being unable to revive him, his family members and his neighbors may have concluded that he had died. We'd never know. Our neighborhood, however, buzzed with all kinds of fantastic speculations.

We wondered if Kalia would ever return to selling his savory snacks. A week later, Kalia's familiar cries had us all rushing out of the house to buy the snacks we all craved.   But by now we had imbued him with supernatural powers and were not a little frightened of him. We stopped calling him Kalia—as did indeed the rest of the people in our neighborhood—and referred to him by his real name, Satyavan. Different versions of Kalia's supernatural powers began to circulate and gain currency. Some saw Kalia as a person of immense saintly powers who had seen God and had returned from the dead. Others saw him in more malevolent terms, as though he had been in league with the *shaitaan*, the Devil. Gradually, however, people began to avoid him. Kalia, a poor, humble, uneducated peasant could not cope with the fear and anger he aroused among the people in the neighborhood.

A year later he threw himself into the well outside their house. His bloated body was fished out a few days later by his neighbors.

Hardly anyone—with the exception of his family members—attended his second funeral.

The above event raises several important questions: those related to Kalia's "death" and "resurrection" and those related to the attitudes and values of the people who lived in the area and were personally acquainted with Kalia, or were aware of the story of his "death." Did Kalia actually die? If so, how did he return from the dead? While he remained "dead," so to speak, did he have any experiences? If so, what kind of experiences? Was he actually aware that he had died? Would he have recovered had his "lifeless" body been brought out into the courtyard and left to warm in the afternoon sun? Would he have recovered had the funeral been delayed by a day? Was Kalia incorrectly diagnosed by his family members and pronounced dead? Why did the very same people who initially had imbued him with divine saintly powers shun Kalia? How did the "saint" turn into "Satan"? What brought about the cruel metamorphosis? Did he jump or was he pushed into committing suicide?

From an objective, scientific point of view, it is clear that these questions are difficult to answer. One might attempt a rational reconstruction of the event that transpired. But a post hoc analysis of such a dramatic event is beset with all kinds of methodological difficulties. For a start, it does not permit a clear, unambiguous testing of any specific hypotheses. No causal or even correlational connections can be made.

Although popular literature is replete with similar stories, one does not really know what dying entails. Nor does one truly know what follows death. Reports of after-death experiences, to re-echo the famous words of Mark Twain, may be grossly exaggerated. All one can do is speculate on this issue.

DEATH AND AFTERLIFE

Let us now examine the second question. Does life end at death? It is here that the field becomes murky. No clear-cut answers can be formulated.

In the past, religion acted as glue, which united societies and brought communities and its people together. Religion enshrined custom, guided behavior, promoted ritual, perpetuated tradition, and assailed doubts—thus, creating a certain degree of stability in society. Influenced by the teachings of religion, many people remained unperturbed by the questions that torment them today. They were as certain of heaven and hell as one is of one's hands held in front of one's eyes. But with the gradual rise of science that began to question the truthfulness of divine revelations, doubts with wily stealth began to creep into the European psyche. Copernicus, as it were, "cast the first stone." And Galileo, more brash, more arrogant, threw down the gauntlet. The Church was not amused. Any doubts concerning the truthfulness of religious teachings and revelations were seen as wicked attempts to undermine divine truth. Established religion had no room in it for doubters, skeptics, and atheists. Such acts were seen as heretical. A dismal fate awaited many heretics. Depending on the perceived gravity of the heresy, a disbeliever could be burnt at the stake, tortured, imprisoned, made to recant (as Galileo was compelled to do), or excommunicated.

But in the last hundred years or so, religion—established religion, in particular—appears to have lost its hold over the minds, beliefs, and values of many people. Religion, in a word, has been *excommunicated by the scientific papacy*.

Western societies have witnessed a decline in the status of established religion. At a psychological level this has resulted in diminishing beliefs in an afterlife, rebirth, and heaven and hell. This, along with the gradual dissolution of the extended family and community networks, has meant that the beliefs and practices, as well as the institutional structures that would have supported the bereaved are now often unavailable or inadequate. In addition, the sociopolitical processes of humanization and secularization have shifted our attention away from the destiny of the deceased toward the fate of the bereft. Sadly, the individual is left on his/her own to cope and come to terms with this fundamental human problem.

The general decline in religious beliefs has, to a certain extent, given rise to several different philosophies concerning life after death. There are many that would willingly admit that life ends at death. And there is nothing that follows death. This appears to be the favored view more frequently among people in the West than in the rest of the world. Why should that be so? Suffice it to say for the moment that this view has found favor among many humanists, secularists, evolutionists, and atheists. They have all argued in fairly similar and forceful ways that there is no way by which a person can ever know what follows death. Since death means a total cessation of bodily and mental processes and functions, how can an individual "know" what lies beyond death?

According to Kurtz (1983), humanists and theists differ on a variety of fundamental philosophical and teleological issues, such as, is there is an ultimate (or divine) purpose in human existence? Does the soul survive the death of the physical body? How can the soul be separated from the body? Does the soul retain its personal identity? Is the soul non-corporeal? Is the soul immortal? To the humanists, the concept of the soul is ambiguous, if not untenable. Nor, according to them, is there any evidence to support claims of immortality. Walter (1994, 1997) argues that there is merit in the acceptance of a humanist philosophy. It prepares its adherents to face death without fear. He points out that death equals extinction and therefore is not to be feared. Because we can never know of any life beyond the grave there is no point in worrying about it now. Therefore one learns to accept the inevitable with a sense of equanimity. What matters is not one's death, for that is inevitable and unavoidable, nor what lies beyond death. What matters most is *how one lives one's life.* A humanist is more concerned about living and life than about dying and death.

The humanist view of death, although seemingly attractive, is mistaken. It portrays human beings as rational beings, capable of making the most profound decisions on rational, objective, and scientific grounds. When examined critically, such rationalist constructions, to say the least, are counterintuitive and not supported by any firm empirical evidence. People do not live by reason alone. A humanist view has no room in it for emotions, and the potential impact of emotions on human beliefs and behaviors. The role of emotions has been written out of the humanist manifesto. In denying the startling power of emotions–both constructive and destructive—which may (and often do) have far reaching consequences on people's lives—the humanists have created a sad caricature of human behavior. However hard one tries, it is not always possible to bring one's feelings and emotions under rational control. Nor indeed is it possible to tame and bring under subjugation the dynamic powers of the unconscious mind, which knows of no boundaries related to time and death.

It is therefore unlikely that a humanist view will come to prevail as the dominant view. The majority of the people, not just in Western societies but all over the world, are unlikely to acquire the immunity from all the primeval dreads and terrors associated with death and extinction.

In addition to the humanists and the secularists, there are the objective epistemologists who subscribe to an objective, scientific approach to a variety of fundamental questions, including those concerning life and death. Since the question of what follows death is by all accounts unanswerable with any degree to certainty, they are unwilling to get drawn into metaphysical and ontological arguments related to the nature of being, existence, appearance, and reality. When pressed for an answer, they may take refuge in uncertainty, saying, "they don't know, they can't be sure"—thus displaying a rational, objective, and scientific attitude to such philosophical questions. A healthy skepticism allows them, in a sense, to "hedge their bets," should future scientific discoveries lead to more conclusive answers on this vital problem.

But the question of what follows death still remains an immensely intriguing question. No doubt one can speculate, as many do. Given rich and rewarding imagination, one can visualize what might happen after one has died. One can experience the stark terrors of the different layers of hell, poignantly portrayed by Dante Alighieri in *The Divine Comedy,* one can soar into the timeless heavens, or one can suffer the torments of purgatory. One could, like Ivan Illich, the central character in Tolstoy's novel (1886/1960), *The Death of Ivan Illich*, visualize with startling clarity one's own death. But such flights of fancy are possible only when one is alive. They cease upon death.

Yet, we would all like to know what follows death. There is, within each of us, locked away in the concealed layers of our psyche, a primordial fear which makes us unwilling to accept that upon our death, we shall cease to be and vanish from the earth without trace. To be in the world and then suddenly cease to be part of the world makes no sense. It seems totally devoid of meaning and purpose. Unless one follows in the well-trodden footsteps of Camus and Sartre, and a few other atheistic existentialists, one finds it immensely difficult, if not impossible, to accept the *purposelessness of human existence*–other than what one might subjectively bring into one's own life. The human psyche rebels at this terrible existential outrage. Most of us, from time to time, speculated over this question, sought an answer within the silence of our heart, read about it, turned to religious texts, both past and present, consulted "gurus," discussed it with others, but have been unable to find a satisfactory answer to the most baffling question of all.

The inability to find a satisfying answer has led to two interrelated reactions among many people in the West. The first one is concerned with the "dread of death" and all its variants. The second reaction has been a shift in focus, from death and dying to life and living.

DREAD OF DEATH

Death of others, be they strangers, social acquaintances, friends, or loved ones, raises within oneself fears of one's own mortality. To Kübler-Ross (1969) the fear of death is a universal emotional experience. According to her, one can never ever prepare enough for one's death. Why one should be frightened of an event which, as was pointed out earlier, one will never experience, is in itself a mystery. Whence such primeval fears come from, one does not know. Speculations abound. Whether the dread of death, or something after death, is due to the *"undiscovered country from whose bourn no traveler returns, "* or whether it is due to other unexplained factors, which include ideas of hell and damnation, fears concerning the Day of Judgement, extinction and annihilation, permanent severance from one's loved ones and from the material world in which one has lived, one cannot say with any degree of certainty. Yet the fact remains that no society, no human group appears to be totally exempt from the dread of death.

The fear of death has often made Christians and Muslims wonder whether the dead, on the Day of Judgement shall rise from their graves, whether death, according to Hindu and Buddhist religious philosophy, marks the end of one life and the beginning of another, thus forming a part of a series of lives and deaths, births, and rebirths (Gielen, 1997; Laungani, 1997; Madan, 1987), or whether death, according to humanist philosophy, is the end of life with nothing beyond it (Walter, 1997). These are crucial existential questions for which people have been attempting to find answers over the centuries. Answers to those questions doubtlessly play an important part in understanding the manner in which people all over the world conceptualize death in the abstract, their own death, and the manner in which they come to terms (or not) with the death of their loved ones.

In its attempts to combat the fear of death, the human psyche has shown great ingenuity. Let us understand a few of the techniques used to keep death at a distance, so to speak.

DENIAL OF DEATH

Becker (1973), in his Pulitzer Prize winning book, *Denial of Death*, argues that the most common reaction to the fear of death is to deny it. This is best achieved through bringing into play the unconscious defense mechanism of *repression*. Becker believes that we all have a cognitive awareness of death— knowledge of death in the abstract, so to speak. But we find it impossible to transform the abstract idea into a reality which, one day, will affect us. And although we might actually see others die, including our parents, relatives, friends, and partners, we still cling to the belief or the hope that we shall live forever. Even in situations such as war, natural disasters and calamities, where death, a hypothetical possibility, is transformed into an imminent reality, one deludes oneself into believing: "No, this will not happen to me. Others may die. Not me." There is in Becker's thesis the total unwillingness of the human psyche to accept the ultimate finality of its existence.

Becker argues that belief in our immortality is the cruelest self-delusional joke that we perpetrate upon ourselves. However, for such self-delusional processes to work effectively, they need to be aided and abetted by other factors operating in society. To ensure that death is kept at bay, several strategies, ruses, and subterfuges come into play.

CRYONICISTS

In recent years, doubts concerning the finality of death have spurred several enterprising scientists, referred to as cryonicists, to plan for the future. They are convinced that in the not too distant future, scientific advances will make it possible to revive the dead, who will then live forever.

The lure of immortality has persuaded several persons of affluence to volunteer their bodies to the cryonicists. But for the extortionist costs involved, such an enterprise would probably attract more persons seeking immortality than is true at present. Upon the death of the volunteer, the cryonicists take possession of the corpse, drain it of all its blood in their laboratory, sever the head from the body, and freeze the cadaver in hermetically sealed concrete vats of liquid nitrogen at a temperature of minus 196°C. It is expected that the body will remain frozen for an indefinite period, or until such time it becomes scientifically possible to revive the dead. Whether the scientists who have arranged to freeze the bodies will, one day— *assuming of course that they themselves are alive to perform the specialized surgery*—be able to revive the bodies and offer the resurrected immortal life, remains a futuristic issue.

MEDICALISATION OF DEATH

Given the recent advancements in medical research and science, death, in effect, has been appropriated by the medical profession. It is seen almost exclusively as a medical phenomenon (Moller, 1996).

Nowadays, people in Western countries seldom die of old age and general infirmity, as they do in many other parts of the world. Nor do people die because their life runs out. In the West, a person dies because the medical profession, despite concerted attempts at prolonged intervention, fails to prevent death of the person in a hospital. In other words, people die in hospitals and people die of an illness or of a disease that the medical profession is as yet unable to cure. Death then is seen as a medical failure, a phrase that has turned into an uncomfortable and worrying cliché. As soon as one construes death from an exclusively medical perspective, all the other factors on which one depended in the past, and which gave meaning and comfort to the dying individual, the grieving relatives, and society, fall by the wayside. If the medical profession is unable to help the dying individual, what can society, or the relatives, or the clergy do? Nothing.

The fact that death is seen as a medical failure has led to differential attitudes among the medical profession with respect to terminal patients and to patients who are likely to recover. Physicians in general tend to adopt a stance of emotional neutrality toward terminal patients and may even withdraw from offering medical care (Garfield, 1978; Moller, 1990). Without being told, the astute patient learns of his or her terminal condition from the demeanor of the attending physician. (My own experience of having worked for a while in a hospice in England confirmed the above observations. I was surprised to note that hardly any of the physicians or the psychiatrists working in the hospice used the word "death" with reference to their patients' terminal condition. Even the palliative care nurses followed the example of the physicians and avoided using the word death. Death was a taboo word—made conspicuous by its very absence.) Such attitudes have become integral not only to the medical profession but appear to have made inroads among the public, which is beginning to accept the awesome power of the medical profession in terms of saving (or not saving) lives. As Moller (1990) points out, the reliance on technology has had the effect of shifting the values of society from a moral and social order to a technical order.

Since death is seen as an uncomfortable word—because of its associations with failure—it has been replaced by polite but trite euphemisms: the patient has "passed on," "passed away," the "late," "gone to his/her Maker," "is in heaven," and other equally meaningless phrases. Even in hospitals, death is kept closeted. It is hidden from other patients in the hospital, and the most ingenious techniques are used to remove the corpse as swiftly as possible from the hospital bed to the morgue. Such a swift, secretive, and surreptitious approach merely adds to the feeling of alienation and depersonalization of death in modern Western society. The hasty removal of the body to the morgue prevents the bereaved relatives from seeing the body and expressing their grief and sorrow openly on the ward, thereby causing undue distress to the patients on the ward. The living need to be protected from the dead.

SANITIZATION OF DEATH

From the moment of death until the funeral, the bereaved family members have no important role to play in dealing with their loved one. By common consent, the body is taken away by the undertakers and placed in their parlor or chapel. Although it would be within the rights of the family members to take the body home from where they could initiate all the funeral arrangements, very few do. This is largely because a) they may have had no prior experience with death and dealing with all that follows; b) they may feel totally intimidated and overawed by the idea of what might be expected of them under the circumstances; c) they may feel incompetent at having to deal with a wide variety of bureaucratic and other administrative problems, with which they would be expected to deal in order to transport the body home, and then make the necessary arrangements for the funeral. Ignorance, fear, sorrow, horror to get close to a corpse, unwillingness to trust their own judgment, lack of familial and social support, may all combine to make them feel impotent in this situation.

Enter the undertaker—to whom it is safer to entrust these painful but necessary details. Thus, even the rituals of death—from the washing and bathing and the laying out of the body, to its dressing, placement in the coffin, and eventual transportation to the cemetery or the crematorium, etc., which in the past was done by members of the deceased's family, is now left to paid outsiders. Death too—however close the deceased might be to the bereaved— is left outside. It does not enter one's house—at least not through the front door. One is thus able to dissociate oneself from death and one's daily life remains uninterrupted. (It is astonishing how the use of a credit card allows one to insulate oneself from the immediacy of death!)

The undertakers and the embalmers themselves spare no effort in the process of what is generally referred to as the "sanitization" of the body. The body is carefully washed, dried, and perfumed, all the gases and other foul and smelly remains are carefully removed from the body, any disfigurements that may have occurred prior to death are painstakingly smoothed over, the pale, bloodless face is painted and made up to look pink and rosy, the body is dressed up in fine clothes, and placed in an expensive mahogany casket with soft silk linings—the illusion is complete! The ugliness of death is almost transformed into the beauty of life!

TRIVIALISATION OF DEATH

Nowhere has the trivializing, the impersonality, and the alienation of death been brought out more poignantly than in the opening paragraph of Albert Camus' famous novel, *The Outsider*. Camus preempted what might now be considered to be the norm in Western society. Death in the West is seen as a personal, private affair in the life of an individual, of little concern to society, unless of course the deceased was a person of significant social importance, e.g., Princess Diana. It affects only the individual and a few other members of the family who may have been close to the deceased. Other distant relatives, neighbors, work colleagues of the deceased, and other members of society, tend on the whole to remain personally unaffected by the death. One might attend the funeral, if invited to do so; not otherwise. Flowers may be sent along with messages of condolences and then one's involvement with the deceased and the grieving family ends. The bereaved are left to themselves to mourn and eventually come to terms with their loss.

Friends and acquaintances may tend to remain uninvolved and may keep away from the bereaved. *The fear of intruding upon someone's grief* becomes the classic rationalization offered by persons unwilling to get involved with the bereaved. Any involvement with the bereaved—emotional, social, therapeutic, or whatever—serves as a constant reminder of death, even bringing to one's consciousness one's own fears of mortality. "People need time to come to terms with their loss," "they need 'space' in which to grow and make adjustments," "they need to be left alone," "one would not wish to suffocate them by intruding into their private sorrow," are the clichés with which others not only justify their lack of involvement with the bereaved, but at the same time succeed in asserting their sincere moral concerns.

Most people see death as a hiccup in the lives of others. There is, thus, an unwritten expectation that people will overcome the hiccup and return to a state of normality within a fairly short period of time. This is evidenced by the fact that there is an expectation that people will return to work within a week (or soon after) after the funeral. A week is seen as a sufficient period of time for the bereaved to make the necessary positive adjustments in their lives.

This raises another question. What if a person is unable to make the necessary positive adjustments and return to work when expected to do so? It is here that a vast army of professionals specially trained to deal with the problems of death and dying, death and bereavement, "coming to terms," swing into action. They are specially trained to help the dying and the bereaved to cope. These important social and communal activities, which in the past would have been undertaken by family members, friends, relatives, the clergy, and would have been dealt with in unique, if not, idiosyncratic ways, are now entrusted to professionals specially qualified for such undertakings.

COPING WITH DEATH

The acknowledged fear of death has led several commentators on the subject to speak more in terms of ways of coping with death and bereavement, and a great deal of energy is expended in an effort to help the dying person, the family, relatives, partners, and friends to cope and move beyond the emotional trauma that can engulf the bereaved for several months and, in some instances, for years. Life is seen as having a beginning, followed by growth and development, and it has an ending; the end state as we know it is called death.

This life-span perspective dates back to the 18th century. It was introduced by Johann Nicolaus Tetens (1736-1807), Friedrich August Carus (1770-1808), and Adolphe Quetelet (1796-1874). They offered it as an initial step forward in the attempt to help the dying and the bereaved understand what is going on. The ideas of Tetens, Carus, and Quetelet suggest that development be treated as a continuous process from birth to death.

Briefly, the life-span theory of growth and development suggests that human development involves simultaneous growth and decline throughout life, that is from conception to death. Changes in different aspects of biological, psychological, and social function may have different starting points, end points, and developmental trajectories. Change is constant and the death of various parts of the organism is constantly occurring throughout life. Thus, when the entire organism ceases to function that change is called death—that is, the cessation of function or integrated function in all component systems of the organism as a whole.

It is clear that Western society has displayed great ingenuity in "avoiding" death. Several factors within society, as we saw, have engendered these beliefs. The focus has shifted from a concern with death to life and living.

LIFE AND LIVING

The second reaction to the fear of death has resulted in a shift in focus. The question of life after death has been skillfully turned on its head. It would appear that the present concerns of the West have shifted from questions of dying, death, and grieving, and questions related to an afterlife, to concerns of living. Life and living—and with it, the old Socratic question concerning the manner in which we ought to live our lives—have become the current central focus in Western lives. The emphasis in recent years has been on living, on remaining young, strong, virile, and healthy, on conquering and eradicating illnesses and disease, including the ones which old age is heir to. "Keeping alive at any cost" has become the leitmotif of Western life. Although death has not been excised, it has been banished into the unconscious layers of the human psyche, where it remains at a murky, shadowy distance, temporarily beyond reach. But the immunity from death is as real as a counterfeit note. Every day, every hour, every minute, every second, this is true: Whether it is the Grim Reaper, or Hades, or Lord Yama, the Lord of Death among Hindus, he is out there, placing his cold and clammy hand upon his next victim.

We now turn to Hindu beliefs concerning death and its meaning.

HINDU BELIEFS CONCERNING DEATH

Death among Hindus is seen as a family and communal affair. The dead, whether they die at home or in the hospital, or elsewhere, remain in the family home. It is the family members who perform all the rites and rituals related to the handling of the corpse.

Unless there is a compelling reason—such as when a family member gets delayed in arriving from long distances, or from overseas, or the deluge of the monsoons makes it difficult to light the funeral pyres—the deceased is cremated in less than twenty-four hours following death. Apart from reasons of hygiene, it is considered to be spiritually important for funerals to take place within twenty-four hours. A speedy funeral ensures the repose of the departed soul (Laungani, 1996, 1997).

As the funeral arrangements get underway, the mourners—informed by a relay of messengers or by telephone—begin to arrive. The house soon gets crowded with mourners. Funerals are open events; anyone who is in any way associated with the deceased or the deceased's family may come to the funeral. In a village, the entire village might turn out for the funeral—although this may be related to the social standing of the family and the age and gender of the deceased. Family members jostle with members of the subcommunity, the *jati,* and the members of the close-knit family, the *baradari,* to get a holy glimpse, or *darshan,* of the deceased.

HINDU CUSTOMS SURROUNDING DEATH AND BEREAVEMENT

There are a variety of social customs surrounding death and bereavement. For instance, the relatives, including their children, who arrive from other cities or distant villages for the funeral, often stay with the bereaved for twelve to fifteen days, and it is incumbent upon the bereaved to make all the necessary living-in arrangements for their guests. In addition to the houseguests, there is a constant stream of well wishers who might visit the bereaved family at all hours during the ensuing days to offer their condolences. It is obvious therefore that mourning is a social and communal affair; it is by no means the private and seclusive concern of the bereaved family as is generally the case in Western society.

The bereaved are expected to express their grief and sorrow in public. Not only must one grieve but one *must also be seen and heard to grieve*. During the twelve days of mourning, grieving and mourning occurs with unfailing regularity. Female mourners—relatives, neighbors, well-wishers, and the ones already staying with the family—visit the female members of the bereaved family every day at a fixed hour in the afternoon and persuade the bereaved family members to cry and openly mourn for the departed soul. As the days progress, the crying and wailing becomes less and less intense, and by the eleventh, twelfth, or thirteenth day, the crying is reduced to sniffs and whimpers.

This is an ancient custom, hallowed by tradition. To an outsider, such practices might seem primitive. However, as concerned psychologists, counselors, therapists, and health professionals, we might ask ourselves the question: What functions, if any do such practices serve? At a social level, its functional value lies in the fact that they provide a source of intense security and comfort for the bereaved persons. One knows—and one is made aware—that one is not alone with death. One is saved from the experience of having to come to terms with the death of a loved one, of having to make positive readjustments in one's altered way of life—*all on one's own, without support*—a legacy which the bereaved in the West inherit with a feeling of awesome dread. The members of the extended family and indeed of the entire community usually stand by the bereaved persons and are prepared to offer whatever help and support might be needed during the crisis.

At a psychological level, the daily communal crying, the weeping, the wailing, and in some instances, breast-beating, serves as a necessary catharsis for the entire family. As a result, it speeds up the process of recovery from the traumatic experience and enables the family to make positive adjustments to their loss.

HINDU BELIEFS CONCERNING AN AFTERLIFE

When we turn to the non-Western world, we notice that death signals the beginning of a new birth. The Hindus, the Buddhists, the Jains, and several other religious groups all over the world proclaim that life does not end with death. It is the human body that perishes. The spirit, described variously as the *atman,* the *brahman,* or the soul, is imperishable. It is indestructible.

The philosophy underlying the appropriateness of human action is expounded in the *Bhagavad Gita,* the Hindu religious text. The central theme of the *Gita* consists of the sermon which Lord Krishna preaches to Arjuna, when he sees how dismayed he is at the prospect of having to wage a war against his cousins, his uncles, and all his kith and kin, all of whom are lined up in front of him on the battlefield (Prabhupada, 1989; Radhakrishnan, 1948/1989).

"How can I?" cries Arjuna to Krishna, who is his charioteer, "fight against my own kith and kin? How can I use my weapons against them"? It would be better for him, says Arjuna, to live in this world by begging than to take arms against his uncles, who are his teachers and his superiors. How could he justify taking their lives? Saying this, Arjuna throws away his weapons, jumps off his chariot, and refuses to fight. It is at this point that Krishna preaches his sermon.

The *Bhagavad Gita* emphasizes several points (Parrinder, 1974; Prabhupada, 1989; Radhakrishnan, 1948/1989; Zimmer, 1951/1989). First, one needs to distinguish between the body and the *atman* (soul). The body is like the garbs one wears. When the garbs are worn out, one changes them. As a person puts on new garments, giving up old ones, the soul accepts new material bodies, giving up the old and useless ones. But the soul is imperishable and indestructible. The soul cannot die because it was never born. That which is not born cannot die. The soul is unborn, undying, eternal. The soul is not slain when the body is slain. Therefore, Arjuna need not worry about killing his kith and kin. To mourn for the body is not worthy of grief. Wisdom lies in lamenting neither for the living nor the dead. Krishna encourages Arjuna to perform his prescribed duty, *dharma,* without seeking any entitlement to the fruits of his action. Duty therefore needs to be performed for its own sake, with calm dispassion.

Although the *Gita* deals with a variety of other philosophical issues, our concern here is with those that throw light on Hindu beliefs and attitudes towards death and an afterlife. It is clear from the foregoing that the *Gita* posits a *deterministic* model of human life and action. The principle of *determinism* plays a crucial role in Indian thinking. This is in sharp contrast to the principle of *free will,* which serves as the major guiding philosophy to human action for many in the West.

The *Law of Karma,* which involves determinism and fatalism has shaped the Indian view of life over the centuries (Herman, 1976; O'Flaherty, 1976; 1980; Reichenbach, 1990; Sinari, 1984; Weber, 1963). In its simplest form, the *Law of Karma* states that happiness and sorrow are the predetermined effects of actions committed by individuals, either in their present life or in one of their numerous past lives. Things do not happen because we make them happen. Things happen because they were destined to happen. If one's present life is determined by one's actions in one's previous life, it follows that, for instance, the untimely death of a child in a family was destined to happen. "God willed it," is the most commonly accepted form of rationalization among Indians.

It should be stressed that the doctrine of *karma* is concerned largely with the moral sphere (Reichenbach, 1990). *Karma* is not concerned with the general relations between actions and their consequences. It applies mainly to the moral quality of one's actions and their consequences. The doctrine of *karma* is extremely significant because it offers explanations not only for pain, suffering and misfortune, but also for pleasure, happiness, and good fortune. From this it is clear that each of us receives the results of our own actions and not another's. Thus, the sins of our fathers are not visited upon us.

A Westerner, at this point, might be tempted to ask an important question. If human existence, according to Hindu philosophy, consists of an unending cosmic cycle of birth and rebirth, is there any purpose to human existence? The answer is simple. In Indian philosophy, the external world is seen as being illusory. It is *Maya* (Zimmer, 1951/1989). It is not, as many Westerners believe, composed of matter. (What constitutes matter is in itself a hotly debated issue among physicists in the West.) Because the world of the senses, the empirical world, is constantly changing, it is seen as an inconstant, illusory world.

The ultimate purpose of human existence is to transcend one's illusory physical existence, renounce the world of material aspirations, attain a heightened state of spiritual awareness, and finally liberate oneself from the bondage of the cycle of birth and rebirth. One's soul or *atman* then "merges" with the ultimate *Brahman.* Any activity that is likely to promote such a state is to be encouraged.

But how is such transcendence—inward-seeking consciousness—to be achieved, which will lead to *Moksha? Moksha* (or *Nirvana*) cannot be achieved overnight. It can only be achieved through continuous effort, which may involve a series of lives and deaths.

A belief in the virtually unending cycle of birth and rebirth, a belief that one's life does not end at death but leads to a new beginning, and that one's moral actions in one's present life or past lives will lead to consequences in one's future life, may create in the Hindu psyche a set of psychologically protective mechanisms in the face of death. These include:

1. A belief in an afterlife creates conditions that help to reduce the terror of death and the fear of extinction. (Those Westerners subscribing to humanist, secularist, atheistic, or scientific doctrines forfeit the protective mechanisms open to Indians.)

2. It may also take away the sting from suffering, since suffering is explained by one's individual actions in *karmic* terms; one's actions in one's past life have consequences for the individual in his or her present life. Consequently, no blame or guilt is attached to us for any sudden, unforeseen illnesses, calamities or disasters, which may befall us. (Westerners on the other hand, in choosing to adopt the doctrine of *free will,* become accountable for all their actions, leaving them with no choice but to accept blame for their failures and credit for their successes and personal achievements.)

3. It engenders in the Indian psyche a spirit of passive, if not resigned, acceptance of the vicissitudes of life. Such a belief may prevent a person, at least temporarily, from plunging into an abyss of despair. (Westerners, because of their fundamental belief in the doctrine of free will, cannot be so protected.)

4. It may lead to a state of existential, and in certain instances, moral resignation, compounded by a profound sense of inertia. One takes no proactive measures; one merely accepts the vicissitudes of life without qualm. (A Westerner, on the other hand, is more likely to take proactive measures to cope with expected or predicted crises.)

5. The acceptance of the doctrine of *karma* instills in one the idea that in the final analysis, no-one but we ourselves are ultimately responsible for the consequences of our own actions. *This brings the notion of individualism to its highest level.*

6. The unshakeable belief that upon death, one's indestructible spirit (*atman*) will survive the body and at some point during the individual's *karmic* cycle of birth and rebirth find abode in another (hopefully more pious and august) body makes the acceptance of death less painful. (Since such beliefs are unlikely to be shared by most Westerners, they may be seen as being irrelevant, if not meaningless to their own individualistic doctrines.)

CONCLUSION

We have traveled a long way. It is now time to pause and take stock. We have seen that death arouses fears, if not terrors, in the hearts and minds of people all over the world. No group or groups of people appear to be *totally* exempt from such unexplainable fears. People in the Western countries have tried to ignore, deny, and avoid death by resorting to a variety of self-deluding subterfuges. They would rather death died a permanent death! They could then live forever. The humanists on the other hand have asserted that such fears are meaningless because none of us knows what lies beyond the grave. This universal ignorance ought to insulate us from these unfounded terrors and make us look upon our own impending death and of that of our loved ones with a certain sense of equanimity. However, the mistake which humanistic thinking makes is to assume that human beings, having arrived at such conclusions, can rationally will themselves to overcome all the primeval fears that have been part of the human psyche since time immemorial.

For behaviors to become functionally autonomous, which is what the humanists appear to be proposing, they need to be reinforced at regular intervals. Adopting a cognitive-behavioral model, one might suggest a careful programming of reinforcement contingencies. To train people to accept the fears and terrors of death, one would need to offer "reinforcements" that, over time, would assist in bringing about the desired changes in attitudes and behaviors.

It is here that Indian philosophical thinking scores a victory.

Let us briefly return to *The Bhagavad-Gita*, whose origins date back to around 1500 BC. The *Gita* adopts a dualistic approach to body and spirit. The body dies and corrupts; the spirit is immortal and therefore indestructible. The spirit survives the body and after a while resides in another body. The process continues until such time the person who has passed through a series of such stages of birth and death, through effort, dedication, and the scrupulous performance of his/her duties, evolves to ever higher states of transcendence, eventually succeeding in attaining release from the bondage of the cycle of birth and rebirth, and merging his great soul, *maha-atma*, with the imperishable *Brahman*.

Examining this from a psychological perspective, one can see the glittering array of reinforcements on offer:

1. It is a relief to know that we do not die, because our spirit or soul survives our death.

2. It is only the body, or the casing that encloses the spirit, that corrupts

and is consigned to the flames.

3. It is gratifying to know that soon after our death we shall once again return to earth.

4. We shall return in a younger, newer, and healthier body.

5. The kind of body we inhabit and the kind of family we are born into is directly related to the kind of life we have chosen to live in our present life.

6. We are the architects of our own future lives.

7. It is within our means to reach an elevated state of transcendence.

8. We are each capable of attaining *moksha*.

In the light of these glittering reinforcements, what has the secular West to offer to its people, which would help them to come to terms, if not actually overcome, the terrors associated with dying, death, and the quest for an afterlife?

Clearly no culture, no society has all the answers concerning the ideal way of recovering speedily and positively from the death of one's loved ones. It is only when cultures meet—on equal terms and as equal partners—and display a genuine willingness to share and learn from each other, that one might find tentative answers to the questions which concern us all. But for the West to assume that there is little or nothing which they might profitably learn from Eastern cultures, many of which have sustained and perpetuated themselves for over four thousand years, is precisely the kind of attitude which is inimical to the creation of a genuine multicultural society and world.

BIBLIOGRAPHY

Ariès, P. (1981). *The hour of our death*. New York: Alfred Knopf.

Eysenck, H.J. (1985). *Decline and fall of the Freudian empire*. Aylesbury, England: Viking.

Festinger, L. (1957). *A theory of cognitive dissonance*. Evanston, IL: Row, Peterson.

Fletcher, J. (1960). *Morals and medicine*. Boston: Beacon Press.

Forster, E.M. (1927/1985). *Aspects of the novel*. Harmondsworth, England: Penguin.

Garfield, C. (1978). *Psychosocial care of the dying patient*. New York: McGraw-Hill.

Gielen, U.P. (1997). A death on the roof of the world. In C.M. Parkes, P. Laungani, & B. Young (Eds.), *Death and bereavement across cultures* (pp. 73-97). London: Routledge.

Herman, A.L. (1976). *The problem of evil and Indian thought*. Delhi: Motilal

Banarsidass.

Justice, C. (1997). *Dying the good death: The pilgrimage to die in India's holy city*. New York: State University of New York Press.

Kastenbaum, R. (2000). *The psychology of death* (3rd ed.). London: Free Association Books.

Kurtz, P. (1983). *In defense of secular humanism*. New York: Prometheus Books.

Lakatos. I. (1971). Falsification and the methodology of scientific programmes. In I. Lakatos & A. Musgrave (Eds.), *Criticism and the growth of knowledge*. London: Cambridge University Press.

Lamb, D. (1985). *Death, brain-death and ethics*. London: Croome Helm.

Laungani, P. (1996). Death and bereavement in India and England: A comparative analysis. *Mortality, 1*(2), 191-211.

Laungani, P. (1997). Why have a funeral? Hindu funerals in England: Past, present, and future. In J. Morgan (Ed.), *Dynamic responses to grief*. New York: Baywood.

Laungani, P. (1999). Danger! Psychotherapists at work. *Psychology Counselling Quarterly, 12*(2), 117-131.

Laungani, P. (2000). Cultural construction of schizophrenia: A proposed paradigm shift. *Dynamic Psychiatry, 176/179*, 267-292.

Lofland, L. (1978). *The craft of dying*. Beverly Hills, CA: Sage.

Lynn, J., & Childress, J.F. (1986). Must patients always be given food and water? In R. F. Weir (Ed.), *Ethical issues in death and dying*. New York: Columbia University Press.

Madan, T.N. (1987). *Non-renunciation: Themes and interpretation of Hindu culture*. Delhi: Oxford University Press.

Moller, S.W. (1990). *On death without dignity*. New York: Baywood.

Moller, S.W. (1996). *Confronting death: Values, institutions & human mortality*. New York: Oxford University Press.

Moody, R.A. Jr. (1975). *Life after life*. St. Simons Island, GA: Mockingbird Books.

Moody, R.A. Jr. (1977). *Reflections on life after life*. St. Simons Island, GA: Mockingbird Books.

O'Flaherty, W.D. (1976). *The origins of evil in Hindu mythology*. Berkeley, CA: University of California Press.

O'Flaherty, W.D. (1980). *Karma and rebirth in classical Indian traditions*. Berkeley, CA: University of California Press.

Parrinder, G. (1974). *The Bhagavad Gita: A verse translation*. Oxford: One World Publications.

Prabhupada, A.C.B. (1989). *Bhagavad-Gita.* Bombay: The Bhaktivedanta Book Trust.

Rank, O. (1931/1961). *Psychology and the soul.* New York: Perpetus.

Radhakrishnan, S. (1948/1989). *The Bhagavadgita.* London: George Allen & Unwin.

Reichenbach, B.R. (1990). *The Law of Karma: A philosophical study.* Honolulu: University of Hawaii Press.

Sinari, R.A. (1984). *The structure of Indian thought.* Delhi: Oxford University Press.

Sloane, R., Staples, E., Cristol, A., Yorkston, N., & Whipple, K. (1975). *Psychotherapy versus behavior therapy.* Cambridge, MA: Harvard University Press.

Walter, T. (1994). *The revival of death.* London: Routledge.

Walter, T. (1997). Secularization. In C. M. Parkes, P. Laungani, & B. Young (Eds.), *Death and bereavement across cultures* (pp. 166-187). London: Routledge.

Weber, M. (1963). *The sociology of religion* (4th ed.). London: Allen & Unwin.

William, J., & Spitzer, R. (Eds.). (1984*). Psychotherapy research: Where are we and where should we go?* New York: Guilford.

Zimmer, H (1951/1989) *Philosophies of India.* Bollingen Series XXVI. Princeton, NJ: Princeton University Press.

EPILOGUE

Marshall H. Segall
Syracuse University, USA

The Regional Conference of the International Council of Psychologists, held in Padua, Italy, in July, 1997, was the source of the more than thirty contributions that constitute this review of international perspectives on human development. The review's editors, Anna Laura Comunian and Uwe P. Gielen, also organized the Padua Conference, which I happily attended. The purpose of the conference, and of this volume derived from it, was to encourage the application of diverse cultural perspectives on human development. The contributions contained in this volume reflect diversity in a variety of ways, including topics covered, theoretical approaches employed, and in the home bases of the contributors. That the editors of this volume needed some nine sections in which to classify these contributions testifies to the range of topics, theoretical approaches, and home cultures represented.

I trust that all readers who have reached this point in the volume (its "epilogue") will have read all of the preceding contributions. If not, please return to any that you might have missed, for nothing should be skipped. And if, after reaching this point, you have forgotten any of the import of the first contribution—Gustav Jahoda's eminently readable and informative account of the prehistory of cross-cultural developmental research—you should go back and re-read it, immediately! It demonstrates the astonishingly great distance we have come, and throws an illumination upon the rest of this book that should allow us all to recognize that there has been progress in the manner in which we conceptualize human development. This progress reflects to a significant extent the internationalization (dare I say de-Westernization?) of developmental psychology.

The progress, however, leaves many avenues still to be explored. Comparing what our colleagues have done lately, as shown by the contributions to this volume, with where we were not so long ago, as shown in Jahoda's historical account, suggests also that the intellectual millennium has not yet arrived.

As an epilogue to this volume, I offer some thoughts about how a cross-cultural approach to psychology in general, including developmental psychology, might contribute to enhanced development for all human beings, throughout their life-spans, from now on, wherever in this diverse world they develop. The ideas contained in this epilogue reflect comments I was prompted to make during the Padua conference. In those comments, I exhorted us to consider taking a policy-relevant stance on real-world problems. In what follows, I expand this exhortation to psychologists to be less reluctant to share what they believe to be the case about human behavior and to assist policy makers to apply that knowledge to the search for a better world.

A number of social issues have become more salient in many parts of the world. These include: How people in all cultures relate to each other across gender and ethnic boundaries, how ongoing social and economic change in various parts of the world require careful attention to ecological concerns, and how behaviors that bear on matters of health, both physical and mental, may have to be monitored, if not controlled, by governmental agencies, both national and international.

To the extent that cross-cultural psychology is descended from modern, scientific, general psychology, it is part of an intellectual tradition, rooted in Europe but developed mainly in America, that was a reaction to an earlier European tradition of political and social philosophy. Rejecting this as "soft," the late 19th century founders of psychology followed the Wundtian laboratory tradition and adopted the controlled experiment as the *sine qua non* of scientific research. During the first half of the present century, and with great spurts of research funding, training grants, and hordes of graduate students, university departments with attached labs for animal and human subjects, proliferated in North America. The dominant ethos of the discipline became "pure science," and prestige and acclaim, as well as money, flowed mainly to those who shunned the real world in favor of the rarefied atmosphere of the laboratory. Generations of academic psychologists were taught that their discipline should endeavor to be "value-free," a "disinterested inquiry," a "pursuit of knowledge for its own sake."

As a result, many psychologists developed an allegiance not only to science, but also to what I call "scientism," or a worship of science. Many of these academics see themselves as Scientists, and bend over backward to avoid doing anything that might be seen as applicable to a real-world problem; they fear the contamination of the real world, just as the laboratory scientist in other sciences insulate their labs (sometimes with lead-shield doors) from extraneous influences.

Laypersons have other reasons for wishing psychologists not to meddle in the real world. One is that they believe either that psychologists know only what everybody else and his grandmother already knows, or that what psychologists do know is arcane, opaque, and irrelevant, things like sublimated urges, Oedipus complexes, and inferiority complexes. So they doubt that psychologists know anything worth applying.

Or, they are so impressed with the complexity of human behavior that they doubt anyone can ever make sense out of it, including academic psychologists. They see how difficult it is for psychologists to agree with each other, they see pages of competing theories, they see theories come and go like fashions, and so they doubt that psychology can ever succeed as a science. And, they conclude, if it is not science, it cannot be depended on as a source of technology.

Thus, both psychologists and laypersons have reasons for holding psychology at bay when it threatens to be used to illuminate public policy debates. For a long while this was true of developmental psychologists in Europe and in the United States and in other places influenced by the Euro-American ethos of science. In contrast, an "applied" approach has always had appeal for cross-cultural psychologists.

Cross-cultural psychology, although partly derived from general psychology, has diverse influences on it, including some that originate in such social-science disciplines as anthropology, sociology, history, political science, among others. For the most part non-laboratory disciplines, these disciplines have long labored in the field, out there among real people in real places and at real times. Less prone to search for universal, timeless truths, so-called "principles of human behavior," most cross-cultural psychologists believe such truths to be elusive, if not unattainable. Willing to settle for truth in context, both historical and cultural context, cross-cultural psychologists, more than general psychologists, take the world as it is and the people in it, as they are. Used to confronting, rather than hiding from, the real world, we come to know it. Knowing it means to discover its beauties and its blemishes. And since we are not Panglossian (we do not, like Voltaire's Dr. Pangloss in the classic novel *Candide*, shrug at man's inhumanity to fellow man and sigh, "this is the best of all possible worlds"), we are often tempted to apply what we know to make the world better than we found it.

Cross-cultural developmental psychology is an inherently international discipline. Its practitioners include many whose origins and present home bases are beyond the Euro-American world and their everyday surroundings call for useful work. Especially, but not only, in third-world settings, wherever human problems are severe, we know that the best of all possible worlds is a goal not yet attained, but our research ought to lend itself to pursuit of that goal.

In a recent review of cross-cultural psychology (Segall, Lonner, & Berry, 1998) examples were given of psychological research topics that have obvious potential applications. What we know about cognitive development and the influence of culture thereon has applications in educational policy, including what to teach, how to teach, and how to assess educatability and educational attainment. What we are learning about the spread of "free market" ideology, acculturational forces more generally, and resultant changes in values, has important implications for ethnotheories of childrearing. Accumulating findings regarding various facets of intergroup relations have obvious implications for the social environments within which children shall develop—in peace or as victims of warfare and genocide. Finally, given what we are now beginning to understand about the cultural construction of both gender and "race," we need now to study how popular misconceptions of both these constructs shape the way children, classified along both those dimensions, are socialized. We need to understand the conventional "wisdom" concerning how men ought to behave toward women, and how so-called white people ought to behave toward so-called people of color, and how these fundamental misconceptions have too long supported programs and practices that severely constrained the development of the vast majority of human beings the world over.

It is particularly important for developmental psychologists henceforth to keep in mind, and to spread the word, that "race" has no foundation in human genetics. Genetically, all humans are different, and all humans are part of the same family. That this is beyond dispute needs to be better known and understood.

The foregoing thoughts were generated for the Padua conference and reinforced by my reading of the contributions to this volume. With this call for an "applied" orientation to international, cross-cultural, developmental psychology, I close this "epilogue" and thank the contributors for their inspiration.

BIBLIOGRAPHY

Segall, M.H., Lonner, W.J., & Berry, J.W. (1998). Cross-cultural psychology as a scholarly discipline: On the flowering of culture in behavioral research. *American Psychologist, 53* (10), 1101-1110.